Elements of Effective Communication

4th Edition

Randal S. Chase
Wayne Shamo

Elements of Effective Communication
{4th Edition}

Send inquiries to:
Plain and Precious Publishing
3378 E. Sweetwater Springs Drive
Washington, Utah 84780

Send e-mail:
info@plainandpreciouspublishing.com

For more copies visit:
www.plainandpreciouspublishing.com

For a listing of all Plain and Precious Publishing products visit:
www.plainandpreciouspublishing.com or call 435-251-8520

Printed in the United States of America

978-1-937901-50-9

Cover design by Michelle C. Rowan

Table of Contents

Course Introduction

LEARNING OBJECTIVES

1. Experience career success and personal happiness by being a better communicator.
2. Know the most essential competencies required in the workplace.
3. Utilize the instruction and skills taught in this course.
4. Be capable of performing the activities and interpreting the results of activities presented in this course to obtain both success and happiness.

CHAPTER 1: Overview

1. Studying communication improves a basic life behavior, producing success and happiness to the successful student.
2. Improving communication skills permits better career development.
3. By improving communication skills, an ethical code is required to maintain a safe, successful, and happy society.
4. By improving skills, successful students prepare themselves for a more diverse, or multicultural society.

Everyone communicates. This includes the stone cold corpse, the angry teenager, the frustrated parent, or even Sleeping Beauty. But all of us can communicate better, by constantly monitoring our progress, absorbing principles, finding new data, expanding our vocabulary, refining our vocal production, etc.

This course is designed to provide a living laboratory to expand your skills and ability in communication. You can make significant progress by learning time honored concepts and applying them in practice situations under the direction of a skilled instructor. Benefits include developing the ability to improve your current life experiences in a more successful manner approved by your peers, your employer, your family, and your culture. Put simply, effective communication is critical to living successfully and happily in today's society. There is a direct correlation between how well you communicate and how satisfied you are with life.

Career Development Means Better Communication.

An employment counselor at the Workforce Services reported that sixty percent of all jobs listed require specific communication competency. Worker satisfaction also directly correlates with the atmosphere in the workplace. When communication correlates with aggression defined as bullying or other hostile activity, workers leave[1]. Job satisfaction, closely tied to communication among workers, accounts for almost one fourth of all people changing jobs. Bosses want workers at all levels who know how to speak, listen, and think. These skills translate into worker productivity, employer profits, higher salaries and benefits, and career development.

Personnel directors say: "Send me people who know how to speak, listen, and think, and I'll do the rest. I can train people in their specific job responsibilities, as long as they listen well, know how to think, and can express themselves well."

These conclusions also relate to families. In a nation where the divorce rate now exceeds 50 percent, communication plays a key role. Marital success is one of the top priorities of most people. But according to research, couples spend on average fewer than 4 minutes per day talking about issues that do not include schedules and children. The average divorce costs in excess of $20,000, and this does not account for the emotional impact upon lives of those involved[2].

This information strongly suggests that better communication creates successful, happy lives. We develop associations, occupations, and lifestyle around our ability to communicate. The average American has about fifteen people they can claim as friends. However, when asked to report only relationships that are active and intimate, the number drops dramatically to fewer than six[3].

Friends, partners, bosses, parents, and other people who impact our life require time communicating. Educators and psychologists teach that communication helps meet essential needs for all parts of society. Prisoners of war risk death for communication; people with severe health problems fair much better if they have positive relationships; health providers suggest communication is an essential ingredient of even new-born children. Psychologists maintain that great communicators list friendship, pleasure, affection, and inclusion as requirements of a satisfactory, attractive social life. It should be very obvious that there is a direct link between the quality of your communication and the quality of your life[4].

Communication and Ethical Behavior

It is essential that ethical standards help govern as communication creates the framework of our life. Unfortunately one needs only say the word: "Enron" and the world trembles. Because of the unethical business practices of a handful of people, the way American business is conducted has been changed. The entire structure and delivery of energy and power in the United States has changed because one company ignored ethical communication and rhetoric at the expense of the national economy.

People have been removed from political office, lost their jobs, committed suicide, been murdered, or been publicly chastised for violating ethical standards and codes. Many criminal acts are directly tied to unethical ways of using messages to convince people to invest in financial situations. Financiers have received prison terms for participating in "insider trading"–using illegally obtained information to make money on the stock market. Sharing such information constitutes an illegal act of communication.

Telling lies, whether done to hurt someone else, or to protect or enhance one's own position is also wrong. Though politicians spring to mind as typical offenders, other examples show that the problem is everywhere. A candidate for coaching a prestigious college football team lies on his job application, a popular war hero lies about why weapons were sold to foreign governments, national leaders lie about who is responsible for the mass murder of certain religious sects in third world countries, students "borrow" a term paper to pass a college course, and the list continues.

The ethical communicator speaks responsibly and gives credit to the sources that contribute to the message. An ethical communicator does not plagiarize or twist ideas to suit personal needs. Aristotle, writing over 300 years before Christ, said communication was most persuasive when the speaker spoke the truth[5]. Quintillion, another classic rhetorician stated it another way: the speaker must be a "good man speaking well."[6]

It should be noted that unethical communication may in fact constitute effective communication. Corporate executives Ken Lay and Jeff Skilling at Enron Corporation transformed a natural gas company into the world's largest trader of energy products. The unethical practices and misrepresentation of corporate profits escalated the wealth and holdings into an international scandal when such policies were revealed.[7]

If one person persuades another to do something morally wrong, the communication has been effective, but it is not virtuous. Unethical communication should never be condoned, even when it has appeared to succeed. A good deal of critical thinking is needed as we attempt to be effective *and* ethical communicators and as we evaluate others' communication to determine its ethical content. This should become a major criterion for the responsible communicator.

Communication and our Multicultural Society

Job transfers, changes in economic and political conditions, electronic media, and many other factors cause people to move from place to place, or create international communication nets that leave country of birth totally irrelevant when it comes to communication. U.S. society reflects an increase in this trend. When our order at Kentucky Fried Chicken or Burger Chef goes from the drive-up order mechanism to India or China, and then to the kitchen and desk of the business, we understand why at least one popular author has boldly announced the world is now flat![8]

What was once a population with a white majority with northern European roots is now a more diverse mosaic of peoples of different ethnic and cultural backgrounds. In this environment, we can all grow to appreciate the distinctions that make each culture unique as well as the interconnectedness shared by all, sometimes described as the "global village." But a great deal of knowledge, flexibility, and sensitivity are necessary if people of diverse cultural backgrounds are to communicate successfully and live well together.

Demographic trends in our country make it not an option, but a necessity to interact successfully with people of all racial, ethnic, cultural, and religious heritages. For example, in 1976, 24 percent of the total enrollment in U.S. schools was made up of nonwhite students. Projections were that 33 percent of students would be people of color.[9]

The 2000 Census figures—which indicate the largest growth ever in U.S. population, served this wakeup call: The Hispanic population exceeded all projections, becoming the largest minority group in the U.S., making up 13.5 percent of the population. Importantly, 52 percent of these Latino households have children, and approximately 25 percent of those children are 9 years old or younger.[10] Such projections imply a real potential for "whites" rapidly becoming the minority!

This reality dictates changes in approach, presentation, and perhaps even language from kindergarten to college. As backgrounds, language, and ethnic background change, so do strategies for communication, audience analysis, and even persuasive dialogue.

When you include the potential changes dictated by nonverbal messages, flexibility and adaptability of the communicator is impacted. Nonverbal communication behaviors such as physical stance, eye contact, style of speaking, dress, mannerisms, and a host of other communication messages are largely dictated by cultural background. Such influences require communicators to expand abilities to not only evaluate necessary communication skills, but also put them in practice quickly and efficiently. As changes occur, so must communication. Change can bring about enrichment, satisfaction, prosperity, and positive human interaction. Positive changes, however, are dependent upon society mastering these communication challenges.

Communication and Our Technological Society

The tremendous impact of cultural diversity upon communication is staggering. At the same time, electronic media has had significant impact on lifestyle, and specifically communication. The majority of people in our culture have almost instant contact with whomever they choose, merely by the use of cell phones. A recording device the size of a credit card can have on demand hundreds of messages or music selections. These devices also have the ability to record and store events of our life as equally well as sending messages.

The retail world has been forced to rethink even the way to do business or market a product because of electronic choices available to consumers.

A few short years ago, major colleges held as an academic standard the number of holdings at the library. Now the average college student carries in their pocket an instrument multiplying such options a thousand fold. If information and knowledge is power, then the average person is an intellectual giant, merely by having access to the electronic age.

A short time ago, we could read of historic incidents or happenings easily within a day's time. Now through the genius of electronic media, we can actually see the news happen! Technology has made the requirement of being an efficient receiver of information a necessity in today's world. If we are to merely survive in today's world, we must become an expert in both producing and consuming information. This is the goal of the communicator!

References

1. Lutgen-Sandvik, P., Tracy, S. J., & Alberts, J. K. (forthcoming). "Burned by bullying in the American workplace: Prevalence, perception, degree, and impact". *Journal of Management Studies.*
2. "How to Save Your Marriage," by Lee Bascomb
3. J. Reisman (1981) "Adult Friendships," S.W. Duck & R. Gilmore, *Personal Relationships: Developing Personal Relationships,* London: Academic Press.
4. John Steward,_*Bridges Not Walls,* Boston, McGraw Hill, p. 6, 7.
5. Aristotle, *The Rhetoric and the Poetics of Aristotle,* trans. W.R. Roberts and I. Bywater (New York: The Modern Library, 1954), 24-25.
6. Quintilian, *On the Early Education of the Citizen-Orator: Institution Oratoria,*
7. C. William Thomas, "The Rise and Fall of Enron," *Today's CPA,* March/April, 2002.
8. Thomas L. Friedman, *The World is Flat: A Brief History of the Twenty-first Century.* New York: Farrar, Straus and Giroux, 2005.
9. H.L. Hodgkinson, *All One System: Demographics of Education—Kindergarten Through Graduate School.* Washington, D.S.: Institute for Educational Leadership, 1985.
10. Arminda Figueroa, "Cross-cultural Relationships in a New American Landscape," *DSN Retailing Today, May 17, 2004.*

CHAPTER 2

Introduction to Human Communication

LEARNING OBJECTIVES

When students have completed this chapter and lesson, they should be able to:

1. Define communication and explain why it is difficult to achieve.
2. Identify the elements of the Feedback Model and explain how they function in the process of human communication .
3. Identify the major settings in which communication occurs and explain the differences between and among them.

CHAPTER 2: Overview

Effective communication requires a solid understanding of the process by which humans attempt to communicate. Communication models help us to visualize the process. Effective communication skills are valuable in all walks of life: at home, on the job and in the community. Intrapersonal communication, interpersonal communication and public speaking each offer the potential for personal and professional growth, leading to increased levels of self-confidence, sensitivity to others, and self-satisfaction.

This chapter discusses the importance of human communication, followed by an analysis of what communication is and how it occurs. Communication models are used to explain how human communication occurs, with particular emphasis on the Feedback Model and its individual elements. The chapter finishes by summarizing the types of human communication, beginning with intrapersonal (within the self) communication, and continuing on through interpersonal, small group, organizational, public, mass, and intercultural settings.

The Importance of Human Communication

This text is titled Elements of Effective Communication. The purpose of the text and the course it supports is to provide and enhance basic communication skills for use in interpersonal, group, and organizational settings. The course is required for many non-communication majors because it emphasizes successful communication strategies in workplace and interpersonal environments that we encounter every day.

The personal reasons for studying communication include our use of it to satisfy personal needs as well as the needs of others. Communication is essential to this process. Our relationships depend upon it, and ultimately our happiness and connectedness do as well.

Professional reasons include the fact that communication is the source of our productivity at work. The effectiveness of our communication largely determines our leadership opportunities, our knowledge and understanding, and our ability to persuade others.

There are also public reasons to study communication. In this course we learn how to do effective critical thinking, analysis, problem solving, and conflict resolution. Communication is essential to an informed citizenry in a democratic republic like ours. Those who communicate well can enhance the public discourse and have considerable influence on our society. Communication has been identified by the U.S. Department of Labor[1], the U.S. Department of Education[2], the National Communication Association[3], and by business and labor leaders as a core competency needed by graduating students.

After consultation with industry and government entities, the National Communication Association developed the following list of core communication competencies needed by college graduates:

—Listening and Media Competencies
- Speaking Skills
- Components of the speaking process in various contexts
- Effective strategies for speaking in various contexts
- Language clarity, persuasiveness and effectiveness
- Management of anxiety

—Listening Skills
- Components of the listening process in various contexts
- Identifying and managing barriers to listening
- Adaption of listening skills to the setting and purpose
- Ability to receive, interpret and respond to messages

—Media Literacy
- Understanding media effects (including new media)
- Competent use of media technology

All of these areas of human communication are addressed in this text, with the goal of helping you become a competent communicator.

Defining Communication

The first thing to understand about competent communication is that it is not automatic. Because we do so much of it, we tend to take it for granted—like breathing. We assume we are understood if we say it clearly enough. But unfortunately, this is not true. Communication is much more complicated and requires much more effort than that.

So we might begin by asking, "What is communication? How can we know that we've achieved it when we interact with others?" Let us begin by simply looking at the word itself:

Commun...ication

The first part of this word—*commun*—suggests something in common. The latter part of this word— *ication*—suggests understanding. So, taken together, the etymology of the word provides a suggested meaning, that communication has occurred if we achieve a *common understanding* of something. There are many more complex definitions of communication. Seiler and Beall (1999), for example, define communication as *the simultaneous sharing and creating of meaning through human symbolic interaction.*[4] We will adopt this more complete definition later in this chapter. But our simple one will suffice for the moment.

The question initially is, "Is a common meaning possible?" Can two people understand something entirely the same way? The short answer is "no." It is simply not possible. And even if it were possible, it would be impossible to know whether we had achieved it. All we can know for sure is what we ourselves understand something to mean. We simply assume that others understand it the same way.

So, should we cancel this course, close the book, and all go home? What's the point of trying to communicate if, in the end, it is not possible? The answer should be obvious. Our lives would be miserable if we had no interactions with others. We are social beings, and success in every aspect of our lives—personal, professional, academic, social, religious, etc.—depends upon our ability to interact effectively. While our communication may not be perfect, we can come close enough to be effective.

To illustrate this point, we can consider our relationships with others. What is a relationship? How do we conduct such a thing? We do it through communication. Indeed, we may say that our communication *is* our relationship. Please understand. This is not saying that we make our relationships better through communication. This is saying that our relationships *are* our communication. Communication is precisely the process by which we conduct relationships. And if our communication is poor, it follows that our relationships are poor. They are one and the same thing.

Let's return, now, to our more lengthy and complex definition of communication, which was introduced earlier. Communication is *the simultaneous sharing and creating of meaning through human symbolic interaction.*[5] This definition adds a number of important aspects, including:

- The simultaneous sharing of meaning.
- The simultaneous creating of meaning.
- The achievement of these things through symbolic interaction.

From this we can deduce that communication is a *process*—it is ongoing, never-ending, and simultaneous. To use a common figure of speech, communication is a journey, not a destination.

From this we can also deduce that communication is *reflexive*—it happens in the moment, created simultaneously with others in a back-and-forth manner. You influence me at the very moment I am influencing you. We change each other's understandings simultaneously and uniquely to the specific nature and context of our interaction. If we were in another place or if we were using other words, we might create an entirely different meaning.

Communication Models

Effective communication requires a solid understanding of the process by which humans attempt to communicate. Communication models help us to visualize the process.

References

1. U.S. Department of Labor (1991). *Scans Guidelines: Secretary's Commission on Achieving Necessary Skills.*
2. Jones, Elizabeth A., U.S. Department of Education (1994). *Essential Speaking & Listening Skills for College Graduates.*
3. Speech Communication Association (1992). *SCA Guidelines: Speaking, Listening and Media Competencies.*
4. Seiler, W.J. and Beall, M.L. (1999). *Communication: Making Connections* (4th Edition). Needham Heights, MA: Allyn & Bacon.
5. Seiler, W.J. and Beall, M.L. (1999).

CHAPTER 3

Meaning, Language, and Context

LEARNING OBJECTIVES

When students have completed this chapter and lesson, they should be able to:

1. Use the Meaning Model to explain how meanings are formed by each individual.
2. Understand and explain why meaning is unique to each individual.
3. Explain the parts of context and how they affect the meanings of our experiences.
4. Explain the difference between high and low context situations and cultures.
5. Describe how physical context can affect interpersonal communication and offer specific examples of proxemics, arrangement, and distances.
6. Describe how social context affects interpersonal communication and how kinships, friendships, work partnerships, social contracts, and acquaintances differ.

CHAPTER 3: Overview

Since people's experiences are unique, their meanings (understandings of those experiences) will also be unique. This means that communication requires more effort than simply "saying" something. It requires a substantial effort to understand how others are receiving and interpreting our messages. Communication and meaning models help us to visualize the process.

This chapter begins by discussing whether meanings are in fact shared, and how we come to form our individual meanings. The chapter then discusses context and how it affects our meanings. Hall's parts of context are explained, followed by high and low context, and then physical and social context. In all of these settings the effect of context on meaning is explored.

Meaning

We begin this chapter with the idea of *meaning*. When we communicate with others, do we transfer our meanings or just our symbols (words)? And if we share an experience with others, does that mean that we will have the same meaning for the experience? The third aspect of this definition of communication introduces an important concept—that meaning is accomplished through *symbolic interaction*. To understand this concept, we need a model that illustrates the process.

People sometimes erroneously assume that if they say something, or write it, or do it, then other people will automatically understand. "You just don't get it," is a commonly used criticism when they don't. The sad truth is, if others don't "get it," it's probably your fault. You have to do more than say it. You have to say it in a way that the other *can* understand your meaning.

Meaning is not automatic. It is more than just *saying* or *doing* something. The traditional view of communication assumes that if I tell you, then the meaning simply flows from my mind into yours, as illustrated by Figure 3.1.

Traditional View of Meaning

Figure 3.1

It is not that easy. It takes effort. We have to make an attempt to understand the other's world and life experience, and select words whose meanings for them will be at least approximately like the ones we intended. We have to respect differences of belief, values, culture, and experiences, and seek to communicate in a way that the other has at least a chance of understanding. We cannot be lazy or self-righteous in our approach. We have to do the hard work of understanding how others will understand what we say.

How Meanings Are Formed

Ogden and Richards' Symbol-Referent Model[1] provides a more useful and accurate illustration of meaning formation, as shown in Figure 3.2. For simplicity's sake, we will refer to this model as the "Meaning Triangle."

There are three corners of the triangle, each representing a key component in the formation of meaning. They are:

- The symbol (word)
- The referent (object)
- The reference (idea)

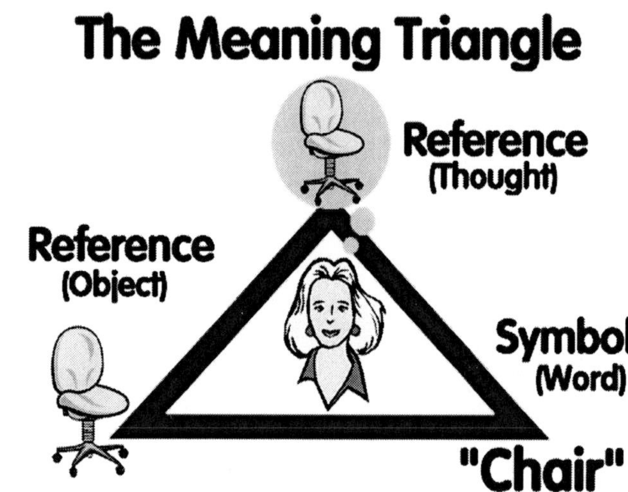

Figure 3.2 The Meaning Triangle

The *symbol* is the word or nonverbal sign that we use to represent our experiences and ideas. To illustrate, we may use the word "chair" as shown in Figure 3.2. The word "chair" is just a word; it is not an actual chair. We could choose any word we want to represent this object. Of course, in other cultures other words are used. But the assigning of a word to an object or experience is simply arbitrary. We use it for convenience in interacting and sharing ideas.

The *referent* is the actual object or experience that the symbol (word) represents. So, in this case, it is the physical object—the chair—for which the symbol stands. Over time, as our experience base grows and our vocabulary expands, we are able to communicate about thousands of objects or experiences with others, presuming they have had similar experiences and they share a common language (symbol set) with us.

The *reference* is the idea, thought, or memory of something. This resides in our brain, and is built up over time. We store both the memory of the object or experience and the symbol that represents it. And through association of the symbols and referents of our lives, we come to understand our world.

Think, for example, of a young child who is only just beginning to acquire words and experiences. He toddles into the kitchen and his mother says to him, "Hop up in the chair, please" as she taps the kitchen chair. The child has never heard this word before. What does he think "chair" means at that moment? He thinks it means *that specific object*—that one chair. He has no idea that chair can mean a whole host of other things as well.

Then, the following week, while visiting his grandmother, she invites him to "sit in the chair" in her living room, in this case a large recliner. The child looks around the room with a puzzled face. He does not see the object his mother identified as "chair" last week. Grandmother insists, patting the stuffy chair, and says, "Here, hop up in this chair." The child has now learned an important thing. "Chair" does not represent a single object but a class of objects— things upon which we sit. He adjusts his *reference base* (stored meanings) accordingly.

He may later learn the concept of the *hortatory negative*—discussing what things are not. For example, if he sits on his grandmother's coffee table, she might say something like, "Don't sit on that table. It's not a chair." There are a million more things that every object or experience is *not*, than there are that it *is*. And we often speak in such terms when trying to convey an idea to others. A young couple may agree (or disagree) that their relationship is *not* serious, for example.

Either way, whether discussing what things are or what they are not, it all gets stored in our reference and becomes part of our understanding of the world.

Implications of the Meaning Triangle

There are a number of implications if we accept the Meaning Triangle as being accurate in explaining how meanings are formed.

- We cannot *understand* something for which we have no symbol.
- We cannot *understand* something that we have not personally experienced.
- We cannot *understand* that which we cannot remember or cannot effectively store and associate in our minds.
- Meaning is personal, and wholly dependent on our individual experience.

We may experience something and not understand it. But if we want to understand it, we will need all three elements of the Meaning Triangle. To illustrate this principle, we might think of the inspiring story of Helen Keller and her teacher. Helen Keller was deaf and blind from birth. For all intents and purposes, she was a living organism with no understanding of her world and little prospect of ever attaining it.

Her teacher attacked this problem by continuously exposing her to both a *symbol* (the sign for water made into her hand) and an *experience* (thrusting her hand into the running water of a tap). This she did repetitively, tirelessly, day after day, until it finally clicked. Helen starting associating the sign in her hand with the experience of running water. She would excitedly sign "water" anytime she experienced it or whenever she wanted it. She had come to understand the relationship between the sign and its referent. She went on to become an accomplished Ph.D. and an inspiration to all who knew her.

Consider carefully what this illustrates. Helen could experience something (and did) without understanding it. But she came to understand it only when there was both a symbol and a referent and those two had been associated in her reference base. That is how humans come to understand their world.

We get around the problem of missing referents—not understanding something we have not personally experienced by using similes, metaphors, and allegories. A teacher might compare a concept to something that you already understand in order to help you understand the new object or experience. I might say, for example, that "taking final exams is like having your tooth pulled." Or you might tell a friend, "this class is over my head" (using the analogy of drowning). Or we might excitedly report that a new friend is our "soul mate." We use comparisons to help others understand something they have not experienced by comparing it to something that they have experienced.

Types of Meaning

When you say something to another, who decides what you mean? How does the other interpret what you say? Do they use your experiences or their own to understand your words? The simple answer is that *meaning is uniquely personal.* Nobody else understands something precisely as you do, because nobody else has lived your life and had your experiences. And when we communicate descriptions of our experiences, we are not sharing those actual experiences but only the words that represent them. The other person then takes those words and decodes them—using their own experience and reference base to do so. Thus, when we communicate, the meaning of what we say resides in the other. *They* are deciding (for themselves) what *we* mean.

There are thus three different kinds of meanings, as identified by Fisher and Adams (1994):[2]

- Intended meaning—the meaning that we wanted to communicate.
- Psychological meaning—the meaning that our words tend to carry (e.g., loaded words).
- Social meaning—the resulting meaning that is negotiated with the other.

When we communicate, we are doing so on the basis of *social meaning.* What we intended to mean is not what the other understands. Our success in communicating depends wholly upon the received meaning and is ultimately decided by the other who interprets our message according to his or her experience. This is why we concluded at the beginning of this chapter that we can never truly and fully communicate. No two people can or will have the exact same meaning for either a symbol (word) or a referent (experience). But we might come close with substantial effort. And so we try.

Language

With the background of the meaning triangle explained above (Figure 3.2), we can begin to understand the concepts of human language development and use. The meaning triangle illustrates the relationship between the symbol (what we call something), the referent (the actual object or experience), and the reference (the memory and meaning of both the symbol and referent). If necessary, refresh your understanding of these concepts before proceeding with the reading for this chapter.

The Universalist View of Language

We call those with an objective view of language "universalists." We call them this because they believe in a universal process by which human's acquire language. They also believe that lived experience controls our understanding, and that language is something we merely invent to represent those experiences and understandings.

Our Experiences =====> Understanding =====> Language

If we look at the meaning triangle in Figure 3.2, we can say that universalists believe that the referent (experience) controls our reference (understanding). The symbol is arbitrary—we can call our experience anything we want to so long as we agree on what to call it.

Language Acquisition. Language acquisition is the process by which the capability to use language develops in human beings. Universalists have disagreed over the years as to whether this results mostly from nature or nurture. But they agree that, either way, it comes from something outside of the individual. Hence, it is an objective view of language.

Language Acquisition Device (LAD). Chomsky believed that we are all born with a cognitive filter called a "language acquisition device," which receives, encodes, and decodes sounds, by comparing them with present and previous experience. This process begins even before birth as the baby hears and responds to the sounds of the mother's heartbeat and voice. It accelerates greatly after birth as every new experience is compared with the sounds that accompany it. Figure 3.3 shows a rough illustration of how this works.

Figure 3.3

Surface Structure:		Encoded &		**Deep Structure:**
	<===>	Decoded	<===>	
Sounds and Words;		by LAD		Meaning associated
Actual Experiences				with sounds & words

Thus, if a newborn baby experiences the secure feeling of being held closely and nursed by its mother, tasting the milk, feeling her warmth, and hearing her heartbeat, the child remembers that experience as being pleasing and comforting. Then, if every time the child has this experience, someone is saying the words (sounds) "mama," the child will eventually associate that sound with the experience of being held and fed. And when the child gets old enough to perform the sound, the child learns that it can summon the experience by making the sound. Thus, language as been acquired as a means to represent the actual lived experience and take control over it. A baby learns to cry (its first sounds) for the very same reason.

The Development of Language. Universalists believe that the human brain evolved over time into an organ that was complex enough to have thoughts, even without words (e.g., the taste, smell and sight of a guava fruit could create a certain impression even before it had a name). Humans invented words to represent experiences that were common to the group and to allow them to communicate about those experiences. But the experience always comes first. Language is invented to represent experiences, and is completely arbitrary—the word has no intrinsic meaning in and of itself. We just agree to call something by that name.

Universality of Language Development. Noam Chomski[3], a linguist with roots in psychology, believed that the ability to develop and use language is universal to all humans. He also observed that newborn babies make the same sounds no matter what the culture. They merely combine them differently as they program their LAD's according to their surrounding culture. Thus, the roots of all languages are the universal and instinctive phonetic sounds of babies.

The Relativist View of Language

We call those with an subjective view of language "relativists." We call them this because they believe that we create the order we perceive in our world, it does not exist independent of us. And they believe that the primary means by which we impose order on our experiences is through language. For the relativist, language controls our understanding of our experiences. Thus, language is crucial to a productive and happy interpretation of life.

Language =====> Understanding =====> Our Experiences

If we look at the meaning triangle in Figure 3.2, we can say that relativists believe that the symbols (words) we use control our reference (understanding). The experience is only understood in the context of the words used to describe it. Thus, what we call something is very, very important, and language relativists are therefore very big proponents of politically correct speech (PCS).

From the relativist perspective, language is a tool that is used to control our world, including our experiences, our understandings, and our relationships. With language we can accomplish all of the following, and more.

Cooperation. Humans need and want to be able to work together. Language makes it possible to coordinate actions and to cooperate for survival. Other life forms like bees and dogs and porpoises use language in a similar way for the same purposes. So in this aspect of language, humans are not unique.

Cohesion. Language also binds people together as they agree upon symbols (words) for things. It also motivates them to work together and gives them a common way of viewing the world. This involves the invention of personal meanings for things, which a group of people can share as a way of binding themselves together. Other life forms tend to lack context—they have only one way to communicate an idea —and therefore their language cannot fully achieve this aspect of language.

Narrative. Human language has the ability to create imagery, to tell stories, and through this process to bring people into a common view of reality. Thus, human language is more than a way to pass information. It is a way of building cohesion through common representations of the human experience.

Culture. Language can also be used to describe and support the beliefs and values of the group. For example, a "cow" is an entirely different concept in India than in the United States because of the language used to describe it and the narrative used to explain its role in our lives. In this and many other ways, language reflects culture. The English language reflects a linear (word=>sentence=>paragraph) view of the universe. Words are formed by sequential letters, which have no context outside the words they form. Asian languages reflect a holistic (concept=>picture) view of the universe. Entire ideas (not individual words and sentences) are represented by high-context pictures.

In summary, for the relativist our language produces our reality. How we talk influences how we think. How we think influences the meaning we give things. And the meanings we give things determine our understanding of the world.

Whatever their paradigm for the source and influence of language, linguists ascribe to the importance of language in the overall scheme of human understanding. Both objectivists and relativists subscribe to the ideas represented in the meaning triangle. They just differ as to which parts of the triangle they believe are most influential in producing and controlling human meaning.

Context

Context can be defined as the *rules* that tell us how to *interpret* our sensations and thoughts based on the *situation*. Context can either add to or subtract from our thoughts and perceptions.

Context adds by:

- Providing rules for interpreting the situation.
- Reflexively adding to meanings as we experience them.

Context subtracts by:

- Distracting you from things you would otherwise attend to.
- Limiting the range of behaviors (meanings) to choose from.

Edward T. Hall, in his research into context and meaning[4], identified five parts of context that we use to understand the meaning of our experiences and of the messages we receive.

- Subject: The topic of interest or discussion or the thing that is on your mind.
- Situation: The physical situation and the rules which control it.
- Status: Your position relative to the situation.
- Experience: Your personal background or experiences.

- Culture: A set of rules which define how we should react to or understand any of the above parts of context.

For example, if you are hanging out with a friend in your dorm room and discussing the math class that you both are taking, then the *subject* would be the math class and probably also math in general. The *situation* is your dorm room, where the rules of conversation are fairly open with few restrictions. Your *status* within that situation is that of a friend, where power is evenly shared, except for the fact that you're in your dorm room, which gives you certain privileges that your friend does not have in that space. Your *experience* with these kinds of situations and with this particular friend tell you that you can be blunt if you want to with few consequences, if any, for doing so. So you hold few things back in your evaluation. And finally, the *culture* within which you live has few, if any, rules about such interchanges except for your need to take turns in conversation (don't dominate the dialogue) and to be *reciprocal* (roughly equal) in tone to your friend's concerns and comments.

You learned these rules over your lifetime through experience and through being *socialized* by your parents, teachers, friends, the media, and other sources of information on what is appropriate or not appropriate in these circumstances. If you were in a different culture, or if you came from a different family, or if you tend to engage different media than your friend, it might mean that you would alter your behavior and your understandings of what was said and how.

In that regard, Edward T. Hall introduced the idea of *high context* and *low context*[5].

- High Context: A situation where most of the rules for interpreting meaning are built in.
- Low Context: A situation where few rules for interpreting meaning are built into us.

High and low context can be used to understand a variety of contexts, from individual relationships to situations like the one described above to entire cultures. For example, if you have been with another person for a long time, your relationship will likely have become very high context. A simple look or glance, or a very few words, can mean a great deal to a dyad that has a significant history behind it. On the other hand, when you first meet someone, the context is very low and very few things can be understood without "spelling it out" in detail.

Similarly, Edward T. Hall observed that entire cultures can be either high or low context. In a high context culture, very little need be said to carry significant meaning. This is the case is Middle Eastern cultures and Asian cultures, where certain gestures and behaviors carry immense meaning. On the other hand, a low context culture has few meanings built in, and things must be precisely and carefully defined (e.g., spelled out in writing) before the meaning is considered clear. This is the case in United States culture and Western culture in general.

Context can also be divided into two separate types: physical and social. Physical context is the objects and settings that exist where the interaction is taking place, such as the room, the time of day, the arrangement of chairs, and the like. Social context is the people and relationships that exist in the situation, such as the difference between talking to your friend and talking to your boss.

Physical Context

Physical context includes the physical objects and settings within which interact. The study of how we use space is called proxemics. Within that topic, we may discuss a number of important concepts.

1. **Territoriality:** We tend to take ownership of the space we inhabit. This may seem obvious in our homes or apartments. But we also take temporary ownership of public spaces. Note how people mark off their territory in the cafeteria

with their books, book bags, and coats. Note also how people tend to sit in the same place every day in class and seem disoriented if somebody else is found sitting there on a particular day.

2. **Arrangement:** The placement of people and objects in a space is also important because it affects accessibility, which Fisher and Adams identify as the most important consideration in interpreting physical contexts. These features of these arrangements may be divided into two types: (1) *design features,* which are the elements that are "built into" the setting, and (2) *decoration features,* which are elements that can be easily manipulated or changed. The placement of furniture at an interview is one example of arrangement. The seating of people around a conference table is another.
3. **Physical Distance:** Edward T. Hall[6] divided the spacing between ourselves and others into four categories.

- Intimate Distance 0 to 1.5 feet
- Personal Distance 1.5 to 4 feet
- Social Distance 4 to 12 feet
- Public Distance More than 12 ft

Based on our expectations in a given setting, we may interpret physical distance differently. For example, we normally don't like people in our intimate space with whom we are not intimate. If our boss steps into that space, it feels like a threat. On the other hand, if we are standing back-to-chest with someone in a crowded elevator we may not assign any significance to it at all. Personal distance is generally reserved for our friends. Social distance is comfortable with just about anyone. Public distance (e.g., when giving a speech) may be the most nerve-wracking of all even though it is the most distant.

Seiler and Beall[7] identify four things that influence our use of space:

- Status: People of differing social status tend to stand further apart.
- Gender: Men and women tend to use space differently. This tends to hinge on whether we are interacting with someone of the same or opposite sex.
- Culture: Hall's distances apply only to traditional American culture. In Asian or Latin cultures the rules would be different.
- Context: People in line at a teller machine tend to stand back, while those in line at a ticket booth stand closer together.

Social Context

There are numerous social contexts present in any relationship. Fisher and Adams[8] note that the strongest influence comes from the most immediate social context and they distinguish between two types:

n Socializing Context, which influences what we learn from belonging to it

n Relational Context, which focuses on the nature of interpersonal bonds

For this chapter, we will focus on relational context, the nature of our relationships or with others. Fisher and Adams categorize them as follows.

1. **Kinship:** Our kin are our blood relatives, including adoptive relationships. We do not choose our kin. This is a matter that is decided for us. Our kin remain our kin no matter what we may wish or what we may say (e.g., "I disown you").
2. **Friends:** Friendship is based on an assumption of equality between participants. They are voluntary, collaborative, balanced, and conducive to affection. Unlike kin, we definitely choose our friends, and friendships tend to be the most volatile of all relational contexts as we move into and out of friendships on a regular basis.

3. **Workmates:** Relationships at work tend to be a matter of coincidence. Choice is limited. We may choose where we work, but generally not who we work with at the worksite. Work relationships also involve a certain amount of hierarchy—some have more power than others while working.
4. **Social Contracts:** Social contracts feature specific obligations on the part of participants, usually with legal implications. Very often, they also involve others besides the immediate dyad. An example would be marriage or even cohabitation; there are many legal requirements and rights that arise, and others (e.g., children) are involved. Another example would be the student/teacher relationship at school.
5. **Acquaintances:** This may be thought of as the "all others" category. If a relationship is not one of the above types, then it is an acquaintance. These are people like the bank teller and most of our classmates. Interaction with them tends to be superficial.

All of us have some of each of these relationships in our lives, sometimes more than one with the very same person. The challenge comes from knowing which one we are in at a particular time and acting accordingly.

For example, can we be friends with our kin? The obvious answer is "yes," but it's not as easy as it may seem. We do not choose our kin but we do choose our friends and must act in an equal and collaborative fashion with them. That is not automatically the case with kin. If we want to be friends with our kin, we must treat them like friends.

Another challenge arises when we try to be friends with our bosses at work. With friends, there is an assumption of equality. At work, there is hierarchy and differing amounts of power. It may be possible to be friends with our boss, but normally not while performing our official work tasks. We may be friends at lunch, but when we return to work we must assume a different relationship for awhile. Some people have a difficult time doing this. An even more challenging situation arises when we are engaged in a family business, where we are trying to balance kinship, friendship, and work relationships all at the same time.

Conclusions

An effective communicator understands that communication is not easy, nor is it automatic. It requires significant effort to help others to understand our messages. Recognizing that the meaning of our messages resides in the other person—that they will decide what we mean—we must make the effort to understand "where they are coming from" as they use their experience and language to interpret our messages.

Communication is also not one-way. It is interactive, reflexive, and simultaneous in an ongoing process that never ends. It is also unique to the participants of each interaction because the meanings will be drawn from *those participants'* reference bases. The same conversation with another person will result in a different set of meanings.

Context provides rules for behavior, and we discussed the five parts of context and the difference between high and low context situations. We have also explored two types of context: social and physical. Social context includes the people and relationships that surround us. We discussed in detail our relational contexts—kinship, friendship, work relationships, social contracts, and acquaintances. Physical context includes the objects and arrangements that are present. Manifestations of physical context include proxemics—territoriality, arrangement, and physical distances.

Because of the complexity of the communication process, it requires significant effort to be effective. But the skills necessary can be learned. And that is one of the primary purposes of this text and the courses that use it.

Chapter 3: Analysis and Application Exercises

1. It is highly unlikely that any two people will ever understand anything in precisely the same way. Does this mean that we cannot communicate? Explain.
2. Education "broadens" our minds. Use the meaning model to explain how this process works, just as Dr. Chase used the model to explain how a little boy's understanding of "chair" might broaden over time.
3. Think about a particular context in which you interacted with someone in a particularly effective or ineffective way. How might the parts of context, high or low context, and physical and social context explain what happened and what might have made it better?
4. How do you manage your personal space at home or at work? Does it differ from others around you? How? Do you think ownership and control of personal space is important? Why or why not?
5. What challenges would arise in a family business, where kinship, friendship, and work relationships are all present at the same time? Can this work? Explain how.

References

1. Adapted from Ogden, C.K. and Richards, I. A. (1946). *The Meaning of Meaning: A Study of the Influence of Language upon Thought and of the Science of Symbolism*, 8th ed.; (New York: Harcourt, Brace &World, 11.
2. Fisher, B.A. & Adams, K.L. (1994). *Interpersonal Communication: Pragmatics of Human Relationships* (2nd Edition). New York: McGraw-Hill Companies, Inc.
3. Chomsky, N. (1975). *Reflections on Language.* New York: Pantheon Books.
4. Hall, Edward T. (1977). "Context and Meaning," Chapter 4 in *Beyond Culture,* Anchor Books, New York, N.Y.
5. Hall, Edward T. (1977). "Context, High and Low," Chapter 5 in *Beyond Culture,* Anchor Books, New York, N.Y.
6. Hall, Edward T. (1966). *The Hidden Dimension*, Doubleday, Garden City, N.Y., p. 1.
7. Seiler, W.J. and Beall, M.L. (1999). *Communication: Making Connections* (4th Edition). Needham Heights, MA: Allyn & Bacon.
8. Fisher, B.A. & Adams, K.L. (1994).

CHAPTER 4

Perception

LEARNING OBJECTIVES

Communication is the transfer of meaning.

Meaning is derived from carefully selected items of information that motivate us to action. These items of information are a collection of identifying statements we have classified as important to our feelings and behavior. When we learn, or store in our memory cells information, we do so based upon our perceived truths of what is important in our life and how it affects others. The following objectives guide us to choose information. To better assist us in understanding the process, we must:

1. Recognize what we consider important statements of information that excite, entertain, interest, or satisfy our thoughts. In other words, explain what and why we learn.
2. Be prepared to describe how we select, or abstract this key information.
3. Describe how one recognizes key information, then categorizes and labels it for future reference. Information storage differs from subject to subject. For example, we "remember" people differently than we do topics.
4. Recognize how this information provides motivational triggers influencing our accep-tance of additional communication.
5. Explain the interaction between selectively perceiving information, and stereotyping events, people, ideas, or activities.
6. Describe organizational concepts such as closure, proximity, pre-conditioning, similarity, and projection as they influence acceptance of new information.
7. Describe how successful communicators motivate their audience to replicate their perceptions. Success means communication; differences produce miscommunication.

CHAPTER 4: Overview

The chapter begins with examples of events containing perceptual errors. The perception process of selection, organization, and interpretation is explained. Successfully organizing perceived material requires a plan of collection using closure, proximity, and similarity of experiences. Interpreting the value of stored information is based upon personal experience and opinions of others. Errors of information storage result in a "quicksand" method of making faulty communication messages based upon stereotyping, conditioning, frozen evaluations, cultural learning, and media impact.

Lawn Chair Larry

Larry Walters of Los Angeles had a boyhood dream of flying. But fates conspired to deny Larry his dreams. He joined the Air Force, but because of poor eyesight, was disqualified from flight duty.

After he was discharged from the military, Larry worked as a truck driver. He never married, but did continue his desires to fly. He hatched his weather balloon scheme while sitting in his comfortable Sears lawn chair. He purchased 45 weather balloons from an army-navy surplus store, tied them to his tethered lawn chair he called "Inspiration" and filled the four foot diameter balloons with helium. Then he strapped himself into his flight chair with some sandwiches, Miller Lite, and a pellet gun.

Larry's plan was to sever the anchor and lazily float up to a height of about 30 feet above his back yard, where he would enjoy a few hours of flight before coming back down. But realities and plans did not match.

When the cord was cut anchoring his chair to his Jeep, he streaked into the Los Angeles sky as if shot from a cannon. Pulled by the lift of 42 helium balloons filled with 33 cubic feet of helium each, he quickly rose to a record height of 16,000 feet.

At that height he felt he could little risk shooting any of the balloons lest he unbalance the load and really find himself in trouble. So he stayed there, drifting cold and frightened with his beer and sandwiches for more than 14 hours. He crossed the primary approach corridor of Los Angeles airport, where Trans World Airlines and Delta Airlines pilots radioed in reports of the strange sight.

Eventually he gathered the nerve to shoot a few balloons, and slowly descended. The hanging tethers tangled and caught in a power line, blackening out a Long Beach neighborhood for 20 minutes. Larry climbed to safety, where he was arrested by waiting police. As he was led away in handcuffs, a reporter dispatched to cover the daring rescue asked him why he had done it. He replied, "A man can't just sit around."

The FAA was not amused. A safety inspector said, "We know he broke some part of the Federal Aviation Act, and as soon as we decide which part, a charge will be filed."

Larry's adventure cost him a $1500 fine, a prize from the Bonehead Club of Dallas, the altitude record for gas-filled clustered balloons, and a Darwin Award.[1]

The Kiss and the Slap

Riding in a railroad compartment during World War II was a French grandmother with her young and attractive granddaughter, a Romanian officer, and a Nazi officer—the only occupants. The train was passing through a dark tunnel, and all that was heard was a loud kiss and a vigorous slap. After the train emerged from the tunnel, nobody spoke, but the grandmother was saying to herself, "What a fine girl I have raised. She will take care of herself. I am proud of her."

The granddaughter was saying to herself, "Well, grandmother is old enough not to mind a little kiss. Besides, the fellows are nice, but I am surprised what a hard wallop grandmother has."

The Nazi officer was meditating, "How clever those Romanians are! They steal a kiss and have the other fellow slapped."

The Romanian officer was chuckling to himself, "How smart I am! I kissed my own hand and slapped the Nazi."[2]

Perception is the process of selecting, organizing, and interpreting information considered valuable enough to give importance and meaning to information one receives. We observe people, objects, events and circumstances. We isolate specific characteristics we deem important, assign them some type of label, and store that information in our memory banks. We have just "perceived" communication. If we choose to pass such information to another, we utilize the labels assigned, which are usually words, and send them on to someone else, fully expecting similar mental images, or another's "perceptions" to be created for them. We have just communicated.

The above scenarios suggest a host of potential hazards for misunderstanding. In the case of Lawn Chair Larry, imagery was easily achieved. Each of us can picture in our mind Larry gracefully floating among the jetliners. Even though clear communication may have been achieved, intelligent behavior is brought to question. A more serious observation might suggest that Larry himself, should have taken greater care in selecting his information about how flight can be initiated, controlled, and even how to end the flight. One might say Larry experienced selective perception: Choosing to fly, but not considering effects of the process, or the termination of the flight.

In the case of the kiss and the slap, each of the participants certainly perceived a different message. A difference between two perceptions does not necessarily make the perception of one person more correct or accurate than that of the other. It does mean that communication between individuals who see things differently may require more understanding, negotiation, persuasion, and tolerance. Perception, like communication, is a complex phenomenon.

In both incidents, perception has been an integral activity necessary for message preparation, but significantly filled with hazards providing inaccurate and even dangerous messages resulting in unexpected or surprising consequences.

The Perception Process

The amount of information available in any situation is unlimited. Far too much information exists for the brain to absorb all at once, so the brain ignores much of it. What is accepted is perceived as being meaningful, important, and vital to our anticipated results. This sorting and storing process might be considered selective perception. The brain identifies an important signal that triggers a memory bite to be created. This identification is based upon criteria formed by our previous experiences that have proven to supply safety, satisfaction, or another powerful but comforting feeling. Three types of behavior result during this selection process: selective exposure, selective attention, and selective retention.

Selective Exposure. This process explains choices we make to experience or avoid consequences. For example, Larry desired the exhilaration of flight, but avoided reviewing unexpected consequences of flying too high too rapidly or the inability to control where he was going. The passengers in the railroad car never checked their conclusions about the kiss and slap sounds, and most never understood what happened.

Choices we make include not only avoiding circumstances, but also people we purposefully avoid, or subjects in school we do not want to experience. Our choices of selective perception directly or indirectly govern not only our communication, but also our lives.

Selective Attention. This process focuses attention specifically upon some information while ignoring or downplaying other critical information. You concentrate on the data you wish to remember, in order to eliminate or reduce the effects and burden of all extraneous information. This simplifies our life. We not only reduce information to the overly simplified, but try to take the easy way out, avoiding as much strain and discomfort as possible. Larry may have considered how to stop his flight, but that was not his objective. The girl on the railroad car never considered the conflict of political persuasion between the two officers; she was interested in romance. The two officers' concern was insulting each other. The grandmother's focus was only on protection of her granddaughter. As a result, most of them missed the actual event.

To make sense out of the multitude of stimuli that surround us, we learn to focus our senses on a few stimuli at a time. This often magnifies the number of contradictory conclusions, and the end is miscommunication.

Selective Retention. Because we cannot possibly remember all the facts we encounter, we only retain the information we interpret as important or satisfactory to us. Selective retention occurs when we process, store, and retrieve information that has been already selected, organized, and interpreted. We remember information that agrees with our views and selectively forget information that does not. New information must fit existing information to make sense out of life. That explains why flying in a lawn chair is humorous to most of us, if not Larry. Lawn chairs have little chance of becoming a standard for flight.

Organization

We must organize new information, stimuli, and events in our environment to give us access to them. Organizing data is critical not only in how we perceive and create new communication, but how we expand our knowledge of people, events, and objects to make our life more pleasant and rewarding. In short, we must learn to be happy. Consider the following elements necessary for organizing information.

Have a plan. A story is told of a small boy beginning a great summer project. Through his resourcefulness, he had collected a pile of lumber trimmings from a local construction site. Finding a hammer and nails, he proceeded to join his find into a large collection of randomly placed bits and pieces. Questioned about what he was building, his response was: "I do not know. It is not finished yet!"

Without a vision, or plan, few of us have a chance to succeed, or communicate. The most logical way is to create a framework to store our newly acquired information. Without a plan, this becomes a difficult task. Look at **Figure 4:1.** Instructions to the puzzle require the participant to arrange the four pieces of the puzzle to form a block "T". Since the pieces contain many angles not anticipated by the general "plan" of writing, it becomes very difficult. Successful accomplishment requires the participant to change the perception of angles.

The example of the "T" illustrates how our perceptions place blinders on how we limit information into our system. Definite limits are given to our perceptions. For example, a student who was unhappy about a grade on an assignment asked how to earn a higher grade. The professor began to discuss ways for the student to improve work on the next assignment. The student, however, didn't really want to talk about improvement, but simply wanted a higher grade on the assignment at hand. For the student, the grade was to just have a block "T." The confusion of square angles, and the sharp edges were not part of the plan. The student was not even interested in additional instruction—just immediate results. For the instructor, improvement on the next assignment was to learn the task of fitting all the angles together before a "T" was formed. The communication message was influenced by how each person could fit the pattern to the perceived plan, or expectations. The communication was influenced by how each person organized thoughts regarding the importance of improving the grade.

Figure 4.1 The above indicates puzzle pieces, then the proper arrangement of pieces to solve the problem.

Figure 4.2 The picture is either a man wearing glasses, or a liar, depending upon your closure.

Closure. We tend to fill in missing pieces and to extend lines in order to finish or complete figures. This completion process is called closure. The behavior involved prepares information to be fitted to the plan, or stored in our memory banks to assist in communication. In **Figure 4.2** what do you see?

We see either a silhouette or writing, depending upon the "closure" or completion of the image by the observer. This occurs because we are always trying to make meaningless material meaningful.

Filling in the blank spaces or missing information helps categorize, label and make sense of things we see and hear. We sometimes do the same thing as we try to understand people. When meeting a stranger, we tend to fill in unknown information about backgrounds, actions or any number of unknown items of information in order to make sense of the person. Unfortunately, what we fill in may be based on bias or ignorance. This type of reaction can be the roots of racial prejudice, misunderstandings or incorrect opinions. When supplying missing information, we must remain aware of what we are doing and remember there is a vast difference between a man with glasses and a liar, as noted above. Otherwise we increase our chances of forming a wrong or at least inaccurate perception of who the person really is. Our inaccurate perceptions about others can adversely affect communication, and that can be costly.

Proximity and Similarity. Two additional concepts involved in organizing information are proximity and similarity. Proximity is the grouping of two or more things that are close to one another, based on the assumption that because objects or people appear together, they are basically the same. The political arena is rampant with such perceptions, often used to predict beliefs, actions, and even financial influence. If you are working in a union shop, you are assumed to be pro-labor, generally liberal in politics, and even a supporter of professional baseball. If you are a corporate executive, you favor the conservative politician, like opera, and drive luxury cars. The process of grouping people into categories we commonly refer to as stereotyping is often generated by both proximity and similarity.

Information structuring based on similarity involves grouping people or activities resembling one another in size, shape, color, or other traits. For example, Shelly, who likes baseball, might believe that others who enjoy baseball resemble her in other ways as well. Thus, if Shelly likes both baseball and opera, she might assume that others who like baseball will also like opera. Of course, this may be wishful thinking on her part. Just because two people are similar in one attribute doesn't automatically mean they will be similar in another.

When decisions are based on these perceptions, major sources of miscommunication can result. One need only mention the use of racial profiling as a method of pursuing illegal aliens or drug traffickers and problems become apparent. To associate religious or political preference with where one lives and how one relates to society is a vivid example of such organizational patterns. Political campaigns, sales promotions, and even movie releases depend heavily upon demographics to predict human behavior. Such widespread action based on inferences created by proximity and similarity play a major role in political activity, marketing research, and even newspaper reporting.

Interpretation

Organizing information and storing it into categories is the first step in the communication process. Interpretation of what has been stored is an integral part of how our communication and even our behavior develop. Interpretation is the assigning of meaning to our stored information. We use our experiences, both past and present, as well as the opinions of others to aid us in interpreting meaning and creating new messages to be sent to others.

Past experience. The more information we possess about a person or place, the more we can predict behavior, interpret actions, and feel comfortable around them. For example, when you first arrived on campus, you probably either had help or consulted with others about directions, buildings, or even policy. Your perception of campus layout was unclear. Experience reduced your uncertainty and discomfort. Soon you had no problems finding where you wanted to go, and learned what was expected of you when you arrived. In similar ways, all our experiences provide contexts that help us make sense of the world around us.

Figure 4.3 demonstrates the influence of past experience and memories of the past to interpret the data presented. Do you see a person? How old and what gender do you see? Is there an age attached to the image? Could this be a picture of two people? What items in the picture caused you to make your answers? Why did those items produce your conclusion? Look at the picture until you see both the young and the old women.

This picture has been published many times and in many ways, each demonstrating an illusion. Its main purpose is to demonstrate how easy it is for us to misinterpret what we see and to assume we see the full picture. We must be careful

Figure 4.3 This illustration illustrates influence of previous experience on interpretation. Perhaps it is the clothes, or a neck band we have seen, or wrinkles around the eyes of our grandmother. Maybe it is the old fashioned dress, but past experiences guide our interpretation: A grandmother type or a pretty lady!

to not let our selective perceptions dictate our interpretations at the expense of missing vital information. Use care in making conclusions on as much information as you can acquire.

If you are like most people, you come to a conclusion by your experience with either a young girl or an old woman you once knew. A most interesting result is that once you are set on an image, it is difficult to see the other view. This has to do with closure mentioned earlier.

New Situations. Good communicators know that most every issue has many sides. Misunderstandings can result if an issue is not examined from as many angles as possible before attempting to convey the message. Forming conclusions before understanding all the facts can be a useless exercise.

Although past experiences become the basis for our interpretations of information, we must be careful not to let these experiences keep us from finding fresh meanings in new situations or events. Without thinking outside the box, we can never assemble the "T" puzzle. Sometimes past experiences can act as blinders and thus produce inaccurate perceptions.

Opinions of others. Our perceptions are often altered or influenced by how and what others communicate to us. Much of what we learn comes from the Internet, newspapers, books, magazines, or television. Electronic media has created reality by influencing our perceptions. The world we know is shaped and created for us by the perceptions others have formed, then passed on to us.

A few years ago Washington, D.C. had several major snowstorms. One day the headlines in two different newspapers read "Blizzard Paralyzes Capital" and "Snow Gives 300,000 Day Off in D.C." Both headlines were factually correct, but they gave quite different interpretations of the same event. The first headline told of a storm; the second told of a day of pleasure. This example points out the perceptions of others can shape our understanding in different ways.

Perceptual Quicksand

The process of perception has been discussed as a strategy for obtaining, labeling, and storing information. Sometimes difficulties develop in establishing valid inferences or sufficient strategies for reaching sound conclusions. The thought process is analogous to the hiker suddenly trapped in quicksand.

Quicksand is a unique soil and water combination that is a deceptive pitfall for the traveler. When undisturbed, quicksand often appears to be solid, but a minor change in the stress on the quicksand will cause a sudden decrease in its stability. A person attempting to walk on it can cause the water and sand to separate and dense regions of sand sediment form, entrapping the victim. In effect, the traveler sinks into a liquefied state that quickly compacts into a dense sand encrustation. To move, the person must apply sufficient pressure on the compacted sand to reintroduce enough water to liquefy it. To remove one's foot from the quicksand at one centimeter per second would require the same amount of force as that needed to lift a medium-sized car.

The inference presented early in the chapter implies this process is a major factor in learning. By utilizing our senses, we gather information and store it for future reference. In doing so, we place interpretations on the information that govern our behavior, habits, likes, dislikes, and even directs our activities to provide pleasure and satisfaction. By word of caution, it should be stated that problems can occur when we use improper perceptual processes. By analogy, we can imply that perceptual quicksand can entrap us in areas of miscommunication

Selective perception, if not carefully monitored, can be quicksand for our success as a communicator. The following are classic examples of perceptual quicksand:

Figure 4.4 Stereotyping these women may lead to simplification, generalization, or exaggeration of traits and qualities. Stereotyping is not fertile ground for smooth or truthful communication.

Stereotyping. When one stereotypes a person, place, or a thing, information is categorized and stored without regard to unique individual characteristics and qualities. We assume the category describes the person, and that all people in the category have the same characteristics. As a result, all athletes are poor students, all illegal aliens are uneducated opportunists living on public assistance, all blacks belong to street gangs, and the false inferences continue. Through stereotyping we pigeonhole people. This tendency forces us to overlook individual characteristics. This oversimplification and generalization exaggerates traits or qualities based on half-truths, distortions, and false premises.

If you have these fixed impressions, you will, upon meeting a member of a particular group, often see that person primarily as a member of the group and apply to them only those characteristics fitting your label of that category. This includes characteristics that may not even relate to that individual, but since you are into quicksand labels, all characteristics given to that group apply, good or bad. Included in this faulty logic is the ability to add to or remove such description even though individual variations may be apparent. We are locked into a "quicksand label."

Conditioning or expectations. Another difficulty in obtaining unbiased information centers on our expectations. We receive a communication message, but because we have determined before hand what the message says, we never receive the facts.

Quickly read the statements inside the triangles in **Figure 4.5**. Look again. Did you notice two a's and two the words inside the triangles the first time you read them? If you did not, you are not alone. Most people fail to notice these extra words for several reasons: (1) the statements are familiar and common, (2) most of us have learned to read groups of words rather than each individual word, (3) the words are placed in an unusual setting and in an unusual arrangement, and (4) we

Figure 4.5 Many times we see only what we want to see. Familiarity tells us what is there, even though we do not read it, even if it differs from our expectations. How does this figure reveal how expectations affect us?

have been conditioned to ignore small filler words to achieve speed and efficiency in processing information.

Another example of conditioning or expectations influencing perception is illustrated in the following example.

> Count the number of "f's" in this statement: Finished files are the results of years of scientific study combined with the experience of years.

If you are a typical reader, you will count 4. If you are not conditioned to skip the small words, you might be fortunate to count as many as 6 "f's." Count again! Are you sure there are not 7 or even 8? Again the problem is the quicksand of conditioning or expectation. We "know" the truth before we actually examine the territory and fail to receive the message properly.

Perceptual conditioning, like stereotyping, does not always limit or hinder us. Sometimes it helps us make decisions more efficiently. We could not make sense of the world around us without perceptual patterns. They provide us with expectations of how things, events, or people should be. They enable us to compare our expectations with the reality of the moment and to respond accordingly. But sometimes we make decisions that provide incorrect information. Did we make the error of not counting "f's" in the direction statement as well? Individual differences and a more complete list of actual facts help us avoid the dangerous quicksand promise of a quick fix.

Time binding, or frozen evaluations. Closely aligned with stereotyping and conditioning is the category of freezing time and making decisions as if historical changes do not influence the environment. A quick acknowledgment of how information is stored in a library should illustrate the point well. A few years ago universities prided themselves on how many books they possessed in a library. Now the average college student has access to many times that number through the laptop computer they possess.

Not only has technology changed the world; technology has changed our perceptions. We must not base our conclusions on outdated or rigid information. A quicksand technique many of us make is to draw conclusions about our experiences, and fail to note the changes.

A classic example is the author's personal experience of his freshman year of college. He "knew" what it was like to be a college freshman. He lived through an entire year of it. It mattered little that the freshman class met with the local high school, and that fewer than 200 students, met in a few ancient buildings that do not now exist. Requirements were different, and even student activities differed, but that does not influence the assumption that "freshmen are freshmen" regardless of the time and season.

The errors are these: we form conclusions about events based upon past experience, and ignore the fact that times change.

Cultural Background. Cultural background can also affect the way in which people perceive other people, events, and things. There are many definitions of culture, including racial, national origin, or even religious belief. Perhaps it is the language we speak, or even the weather conditions we live in. Chapters 12 and 13 will treat this subject in more depth, but please note two things: First, culture is a learned condition created by the process of perception as has been discussed. We have not inherited our biases, prejudices, likes and dislikes. Our skin color, or our accent, or even our national origin do not dictate our cultural differences. Those unique characteristics have been learned from parents, teachers, friends, and personal experience.

Second, we formulate our communication based on the culture we accept. As a result, those we parent, teach, or befriend tend to accept our communication. Thus our culture, and unfortunately, many of our quicksand perceptions of prejudice and hatred of others tend to produce miscommunication. People no longer are individuals with unique talents, skills, and attributes. When making these quicksand perceptions, we often attach labels to intensify the negative, derogatory feeling, and the miscommunication continues.

Reprinted by permission of Jerry Marcus

Figure 4.6 illustrates well the concept of frozen evaluation. The age and physical height differences between the son and father clearly affect their perception of the snow depth. The father has not taken life changes into consideration as he communicates with a son who must be imagining what it would be like to be standing in snow up to his father's chin

Culture is an integral part of each of us and determines many of our individual characteristics. Culture identifies us as members of a particular group, shaping our values, biases, even dress and work ethic. Cultural influence occurs without our realizing it; typically we are not conscious of the fact that much of our behavior is conditioned by our culture. The way we greet others, the way we use language, our opinions about what and when to eat, and even personal preferences of athletic events and recreation are all culturally conditioned.[3]

The impact of culture on interpersonal communication is crucial to understanding actions of others. Just as they behave in a certain way, people also perceive and organize their thoughts, observations, and values according to the dictates of their culture. For example, in a purely scientific sense, the moon is a rocky sphere; yet when they look at the moon, many Americans see the "man in the moon." Some Native Americans view this same image as a rabbit; the Chinese interpret it as a lady fleeing her husband, and Samoans see in it the shape of a woman weaving.[4] These particular differences may not seem significant, but they point to the way people of different cultures view the same phenomenon quite differently.

Those who cannot appreciate the fact that perception and interpretation of information varies across cultures hit another path filled with quicksand. Those who automatically assume their own view and interpretation is superior to that of any other culture are considered ethnocentric. Quicksand has entrapped their thoughts and actions. Ethnocentric persons go beyond pride in their heritage or background to the conviction that they know more and are better than those of different cultures. Those who lack interaction or contact with other cultures and their practices may believe they are not as acceptable as our own. Even if we know of weaknesses in our own culture (too competitive, too materialistic, too informal) we are unlikely to criticize our culture when comparing it to others. We are frozen in our own quicksand of belief.

Gender Stereotyping. How men and women communicate in their personal relationships has been a hot topic in both academic and popular literature. It is commonplace to refer to a best selling book declaring that men and women actually develop different cultures that are as diverse as planets: men are from Mars and women are from Venus.[5]

The difference in communication between males and females implies a belief that two different cultures have developed because of cultural demands upon gender roles. Certainly the early assumption that men were the bread winners of the family while women raised the family to adulthood implied significant roles demanding different values, attitudes, skills, and consequently, different communication.

One claim is that women tend to be communal and men tend to be instrumental. Women are emotional while men are more logical. Frustrated at the stereotyped sensational differences between genders motivated one set of educators to conclude that if men are from Mars and women are from Venus, then it follows that Earth provides no home for either sex![6]

Research suggests that under controlled situations selecting people of common beliefs, similar roles, and similar backgrounds, gender becomes almost irrelevant and similarities in communication style are 99 percent consistent. However, one of the reasons the "Mars-Venus" hypothesis is so popular is that it resonates with many people's experiences. Perhaps the theory has created the reality, and the quicksand has become the problem![7]

We are still told there is a gender gap, and that men and women do not understand one another. Men are often confused when women want to continue to talk about something they think has been settled; women often find themselves frustrated when men do not listen or respond to what they say. The perceptions men and women have of each other and of themselves are not always clear, especially in this time of transition as the roles of men and women are changing. The most obvious conclusion is that it becomes easy to blame gender when in actuality the difference is a misunderstanding between people!

Hollywood effect. Many question whether we are still individuals as we become almost dominated by people who want to influence our perception plan. Advertisers, government leaders, political advocates, religious leaders, and even close associates attempt to shape our perception plan. We are not considered normal unless we vote with the majority, support the front running candidate, and eat the proper fast foods. Without accepting the overwhelming barrage of popular media messages, we are considered maladjusted.

Politicians are obsessed with media influence. They spend millions of dollars creating a positive image that supports what they infer is the majority opinion and therefore the appropriate answer to everything. Their quicksand stereotyping implies what should be our opinion about everything from stem cell research to popular health diets.

What about shows we watch on television? Do they create or alter our perceptions? Family sitcoms present lifestyles that are generally atypical yet they still influence our image of families. Network news shows select events from all the reports they receive and present them in a half-hour broadcast, which amounts to approximately 20 minutes of actual news. This condensed information is not only limited, but also selected and edited for our consumption, based upon someone else's perception of the world.

Conclusions

Perception has been presented as a critical behavior each person must utilize to learn information, which in turn influences our communication, and ultimately our behavior. The wise person will carefully construct a plan, or method of receiving, interpreting, evaluating, and storing information. Such a procedure determines our psychological state of being either happy or unhappy. The strong implication is that we dictate our own outcome.

There are hazards to such implications. Many scholars in communication believe that the greatest single problem with human communication is the assumption that our perceptions are always correct.[8] The good communicator continually monitors his perception plan, compares the results with his personal satisfaction, and makes mid-course corrections. The only error worse than not having a plan in place to perceive information is the error of complacency, being satisfied with the here and now.

Chapter 4: Analysis and Application Exercises

1. Develop a set of regulations governing how one perceives and stores information used for developing a communication message. Write 5 rules for accepting (things to do) information that governs our behavior and 5 rules for rejecting information (things to avoid).
2. Observe an evening news show. Note how many "quicksand" perceptions are reported as facts by the news reporter.

References

1. Ed Greany, Douglas Walker, Walter Hecht, "Lawn Chair Larry," www.darwinAwards.com, 1993 Honorable Mention, 1998.
2. Alfred Korsybski, "The Role of Language in the Perceptual Process," *Perception: An Approach to Personality*, ed. Robert R. Blake and Glenn V. Ramsey. The Ronald Press, Co., 1951.
3. N.E. Gage and D.C. Berliner, *Educational Psychology*, 6th ed. (Boston: Houghton Mifflin, 1998), 152-153.
4. N. Dresser, *Multicultural Manners* (New York: Wiley, 1996), 89-90.
5. J. Gray, *Men are from Mars, Women are from Venus*, New York: Harper-Collins, 1992.
6. J. Stewart, "Communicating with Intimate Partners," *Bridges Not Walls*, McGraw-Hill, 2006, P. 365
7. Ibid, p. 366.
8. C. Stewart and W. Cash, *Interviewing: Principles and Practices*, 8th ed. (Dubuque, Iowa: Brown, 1997) p. 13.

CHAPTER 5

Self-Awareness and Concept

LEARNING OBJECTIVES

When students have completed this chapter and lesson, they should be able to:

1. Know the difference between objective and subjective thinking and be able to correctly identify claims of each type.
2. Know and understand Aubrey Fisher's categories of the study of human behavior, be able to identify examples of each, and know how they relate to self- and other-awareness and concepts.
3. Understand the difference between personal traits, social attributes, and social roles, and how these relate to self- and other-concepts.
4. Understand how self-fulfilling prophecy, self as a process, and self as constructed through interaction are related to self-concept and how they affect our behavior.

CHAPTER 5: Overview

This chapter explores paradigms as a way of understanding human behavior and concepts. Objective and subjective ways of thinking are defined. These are further divided into the four main paradigms of human study identified by Aubrey Fisher—mechanistic, psychologistic, social action, and pragmatic. With this heuristic framework as a guide, the chapter then discusses the ways in which our concepts of self and of others are formed. The chapter introduces the ideas of personal traits, social attributes, and social roles, and it discusses how these can determine our self-concept and self-esteem. Finally, the chapter discusses the concepts of self-fulfilling prophecy, self as a process, and self as constructed through interaction. The chapter concludes by summarizing how our self-concept is constructed by our values and actions, and how a subjective and constructive approach to self-concept empowers those who use it.

Paradigms

Everyone knows umpires decide whether a baseball pitcher has thrown a ball or a strike. The question is, how do they decide? We can imaging three different explanations of the task of calling balls and strikes.

The first ref might say: "I call them as they are."
The second might say: "I call them as I see them."
The third might say: "They're nothing till I call them."

Ask yourself, "With which of the positions do I agree?" Your answer will reveal your *paradigm*—the way you see and understand the world, including yourself. And there is more than one way to understand both people and things, so we will not attempt in this chapter to tell you what the "truth" is, but rather how people choose to define themselves and those around them. Then, perhaps, armed with an understanding of paradigms, you'll be able to choose the one that is most comfortable for you and also understand the paradigms of others.

There are generally two views of what is "true" and "real." The Greek philosophers may have been the first to define and debate them, and we will explore their views in Chapter 18. But for now, as we answer the question of who and what you are—your self-concept—we will categorize these two paradigms as follows.

Two General Views of Reality

Different theorists use different words to define the two main views of the world. For example, Em Griffin (2006) calls them *objective* and *interpretive* and when talking about human behavior *determinism* and *free will.*[1] Liska and Cronkhite (1995) call them *mechanistic* and *human interaction.*[2] And West and Turner (2007) call them *covering law* and a *rules approach*[3] Other commonly-used terms for these paradigms include *reductionist* and *relativist, cause-and-effect* and *descriptive,* and *classical* and *modern.* Certainly, this is a confusing list of terms that all apply to the very same paradigms. But what we call them is not so important as understanding how the two world views differ. For our purposes, we will call these two views *objective* and *subjective,* and this is how they relate to other terms that have been used to define them.

Objective:		**Subjective:**	
	Quantitative		Qualitative
	Objective		Interpretive
	Determinism		Free Will
	Mechanistic		Human Interaction
	Covering Law		Rules Approach
	Reductionist		Relativist
	Cause-and-Effect		Descriptive
	Classical		Modern

There are actually more than just two world views, and all of them are studied in some depth by those who major in communication. But for our purposes, these two will do. We will, however, have to redefine the words *objective* and *subjective* from the way they are generally defined in everyday conversation. Western civilization is primarily objective in its thinking, so *objective* has come to be a positive term, meaning unbiased, truthful, and accurate, while *subjective* has come to mean personal opinion, un-factual, and unreliable. We will have to jettison these definitions for purposes of our discussion here.

Objective means that we see truth and reality as *objects*—facts or laws that are outside of ourselves and that act upon us in ways that are outside of our control. An example of this would be the law of gravity, which acts on all things in the universe according to fixed and known rules of physics.

Subjective means that we see truth and reality as *subjects*—things that come from our own experience rather than things that act upon, and they may be different for each individual. Also, using our free will we are responsible for our choices and for the results of those choices. Examples of this would be our relationships with others. The subjectivist would say we "create" those relationships through our choices and behaviors and the success or failure of a relationship does not *happen to us*—we *construct* it and are responsible for the results.

Because we've been taught subjective means "unscientific" or "biased," we are prone to think any personal opinion is "subjective." That is not so. A person may have an opinion that is objective in nature—for example, that there is a god in heaven who is in control of all things in our lives (an external force that "acts upon" us). Or a person may have an opinion that is subjective in nature—for example, we are responsible for the conditions we live in and can change them by changing our behavior. Still others may have views that are a combination of these. But it is the *nature of the claim* that determines its objectivity or subjectivity, not the location of the claim—who said it or how much "proof" they have. Figures 5.1 and 5.2 illustrate what makes a claim objective or subjective in nature.

Figure 5.1

OBJECTIVE THINKING

Truth and Reality are:

1. Outside the observer (it is independent of us)
2. To be discovered (we learn what is already true)
3. Determined or fixed (it is already pre-determined)
4. Stable over time (synchrony—it doesn't change)
5. Linear (cause-and-effect)
6. Summative (whole is the sum of the parts)
7. Progressive (we know more today than we did in the past)

Examples of its Use:

- Mathematics, chemistry, and traditional physics
- Traditional medicine and psychology
- Traditional bureaucratic management methods in organizations
- Passive viewer theory: television content "causes" reactions in people (e.g., violence)

Figure 5.2

SUBJECTIVE THINKING

Truth and Reality are:

1. Inside the observer (different for each person)
2. Created or constructed we create our own truths)
3. Indeterminate (it is not pre-determined)
4. Changing over time (diachrony—it changes)
5. Non-linear interactive & reflexive systems)
6. Non-summative (more than the sum of parts)
7. Not necessarily progressive (we may or may not know more than in the past)

Examples of its Use:

- Quantum physics
- Self-help groups and visualization techniques (you are what you think you are)
- Non-traditional management methods which emphasize employee individuality and creativity
- Active viewer theory: viewers choose what to do with TV content (e.g., violence).

STEINBECK'S FISH

John Steinbeck, the novelist, was a subjective thinker. He valued human experience as the basis for interpreting things. He was also an avid fisherman. He believed the most important things we can know about fish are not learned in a laboratory, where we bring in a dead fish, cut it open, count its scales and fins, and look at it as a mechanical object. These, to him, were objective *facts we cannot change*—the number and type of the fish's fins, etc. He believed to truly know and understand a fish you had to go fishing—to experience how the fish fought when you snagged it, how it looked, smelled, and tasted. These, to him, were subjective *facts of experience*, which give life its color and meaning, and he believed they are the only truths that really matter.

We might put Steinbeck's view to the test in our own lives and relationships. If you are in a significant relationship what are the "truths" that mean the most to you? Is your relationship based on the facts you cannot change about the other—height, weight, eye color, etc.—or is it based on your interactions and experiences each day? Most likely, the most valuable things to you are the experiential ones. And that was precisely Steinbeck's point.

Four Paradigms of Communication Study

Aubrey Fisher identified four major paradigms of communication study.[4] Figure 5.3 illustrates how these paradigms relate to the objective and subjective views outlined above and how they relate to each other. The two paradigms on the left are primarily objective paradigms, and the two on the right are primarily subjective paradigms.

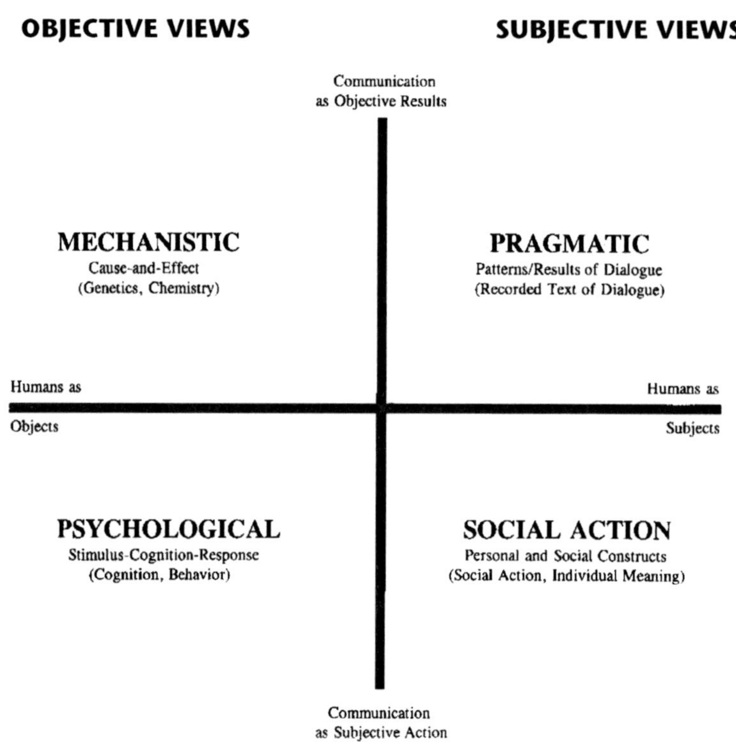

Figure 5.3 The Four-Way Model of Communication Paradigms

Mechanists believe the world is cause-and-effect. All things are part of a larger whole. We pay attention to how things fit together, and seek to understand the whole by understanding each of the parts. This view of human behavior is the oldest one. It emerged during the dawn of science, when researchers discovered many useful truths about the physical world. Social scientists used the same logic to study human behavior and produced such fields of study as genetics and chemistry, which they believed were the direct cause of all human behavior. Most doctors and nurses today have a mechanistic view of human behavior and health, and this is an objective view of human behavior and conditions.

Psychologists focus on responses to cognitive stimuli. Recognizing that identical twins with entirely the same genetics and environment will nevertheless behave differently, the field of psychology sought to explain those differences. The traditional formula is S-O-R, meaning stimulus-organism-response. So if, for example, one is subjected to abuse (the stimulus), how does the organism (the cognitive processes in the brain) affect the response (behavior). Within the field of psychology, *cognitivists* concentrate on the organism—the *cognitive filters* in our brain through which we process meaning—in order to predict and understand behavior. *Behav-*

iorists concentrate on the response—human action—believing that it is the only reliable manifestation of human thinking. One cannot see a cognitive filter, but one can directly observe manifested human behavior. By observing behavior they believe we can develop patterns of action which allow prediction or prevention.

Social Actionists focus on constructed meanings that are developed through interaction with others. The key word here is *constructed*, which suggests that people create their own meanings by acts of choice. The social actionist, rather than de-constructing behavior in a search for its cause (as behavioral psychologists do), focuses on how and why people construct or build their behaviors and understandings. They believe that rational adults are free to choose how they interpret meanings, and make deliberate choices which have definite consequences. Also, by changing choices they can change the outcomes. This is a subjective point of view that places control of one's meanings and reality squarely in the hands of the person, not on forces that are outside the person's control. The other key word in this view is *interaction*, which suggests that we cannot build these meanings alone. It requires social interaction with another person. We will re-visit this concept later in this chapter.

Pragmatics focus on patterns of interaction and the results thereof. They pay attention only to repeated patterns of interaction (not isolated incidents) as manifested in the content of the interaction (e.g., the content of a transcript of tape recorded conversation). Patterns are carefully monitored and graphed to reveal the "pragmatic" performance of interactions. Pragmatists are not interested in "why" people do what they do, but only "what" they do and "how" they do it. This is because they believe that the actual performance has consequences, not the intent or reason behind it. So, for example, whether I meant to hurt you or not, the pragmatic result may be that my behavior did hurt you. People may not even be aware of what they are doing until the pattern is revealed to them. Only by revealing and concentrating on performed behavior (and changing it) can any meaningful change occur. This is also a subjective view because it assumes that the power to change resides in rational human beings.

There are other types of communication research besides those listed in the Fisher model. A category called *Criticism*, which includes Marxism, Feminism, etc. are all forms of textual criticism, which also concerns itself with texts, but in a different way from pragmatists. The question is constantly asked: "What is the effect of saying (presenting) information in this way?" This has lead to a whole range of things such as "politically correct" speech and the questioning of established institutions and methods of communicating. We will not be discussing this category of research in our present chapter, but it is important to know that other ways of thinking exist.

Self-Concept

Generally speaking, when theorists discuss self-concept they do so from the psychological perspective. This makes sense since our concept of ourselves resides in our minds and involves some intrapersonal communication concerning who and what we are. However, this is not the only way to study and understand self-concept. Communication theorists often view this topic from a more subjective point of view—the social action perspective.

Social Action and Self-Concept

In the field of communication, the predominant way of thinking is social action, which means that it is subjective and constructive. For example, communicologists generally believe that:

Your relationships <u>are</u> your communication—not just that communication is important to relationships or that it can improve them, but *they are one and the same thing.*

We conduct relationships through our communication. Therefore, if our communication is bad, so are our relationships. And if our relationships are bad, so too is our communication. They are one and the same thing.

Other frequently stated tenets of communication study are the following, all of which are related to the social-action approach.

- *You cannot not communicate.* Whether a message is intended or not, it can and usually will be interpreted by other people as a message. Perhaps I could choose to stand in front of you and say nothing, intending not to communicate. What would happen? You would interpret my silence in order to make sense of it. I cannot control the meanings you apply to my words or behaviors. Either way, intended or not, a meaning will be communicated. How much better, then, for me to attempt to construct and communicate my meanings rather than leaving it all up to others.
- *Content and relationship.* Every communication has a content and a relationship. A message (e.g., "You're bad!") from a parent has a totally different meaning than the same message from a friend. I have to consider the relationship and other contextual factors in order to properly understand a message.
- *Differing patterns of interpersonal interaction.* In some ways and with some people, we prefer our interactions to be symmetrical. In others, we prefer complimentary interactions. In general, which do you prefer?

Symmetrical: Between parties who are equal or identical ("birds of a feather").

Complimentary: Between parties who compliment or offset each other ("opposites attract").

Constructs

Humans impose order on their world—their understandings of themselves, of other people, and of their experiences—by using constructs. Constructs provide a scheme for constructing meaning, which in turn provides a basis for acting and understanding. Let us look at this statement more closely in order to understand.

- *Humans order their world.* We often make order out of things even when no order actually exists. We are more comfortable with an ordered universe than with chaos. We try to make sense of things. And in doing so, we impose certain constructs on what we experience.
- *Using constructs.* Constructs are theories about the categories we encounter in our world. They may or may not be literally "true." For example, we may believe that "intelligent people are attractive." As a subjective concept, this belief may have great impact on a person's interpretation of the value of self and of others. Whether or not this statement is literally and objectively "true" is not the question. How it is used to understand people (and the results thereof) is the question that social actionists will ask.
- *As a basis for acting and understanding.* Once formed, constructs give us a basis for acting in each circumstance. They are heavily impacted by the cultures and groups to which we belong.

Meade on Constructs

George Herbert Meade[5] researched extensively into the idea of social constructs. Among other concepts, he made the following observations:

- *Cooperation.* We cooperate with each other to create our constructs and our meanings. We decide what all kinds of things will mean.

— Circumstances	"That means we can go now, right?"
— Language	Slang, secret words, or even technical terms with meaning only to those who "belong."
— Terms of endearment	Pet names for people we love.
— Significant symbols	Rings, clothing, flags, etc., that have a common meaning we have agreed upon.

- *Co-Orientation.* In an effort to understand our world, those around us, and ourselves, we engage in behaviors that are designed to check how our perceptions compare to those of others. For example, we may engage in *sparring*—making statements in an effort to test whether our concepts match those of others. A negative example would be saying, "Oh, I'm so stupid!" when we make a mistake, hoping that others will disagree by saying, "No, you're not. We all make mistakes." If they agreed with our statement we would then know they think we're stupid. If they disagree, then we're reassured others don't see us that way.
- *Self-concept is derived through social interaction with others.* Another way of putting this is, "You are what people say you are." If my parents tell me I am stupid all of my life, then I will conclude I am stupid. If I think I'm good-looking, it is likely because others have said so or I have compared myself in the mirror to others I have seen. In either case, it required interaction with others for me to know "who I am" or "what I am."
- Other-concepts are of two basic kinds:

  — *Generalized others*: A composite of the people, morals, and rules of your life.

  — *Specific others*: Specific other people you have encountered.

  For example, if I meet a woman for the first time, I will categorize her into a general category of "women," based on the generalized concept I have for the women I have known. That allows me to interact with her until I get to know her better. When I do, then I will categorize her as her unique self, though she may retain in my mind many characteristics of my generalized "women" category.
- *Constructs change.* Over time, through interaction with others, our constructs change. Because they are constructed through our experience, they cannot and do not remain stagnant. For example, even the most significant relationship will change over time, and the participants must adjust accordingly. To insist that people or circumstances remain the same over time is to insist on the impossible. Change will come. The nature of the change(s) may be:

  — Each person moderates and becomes more like the other(s).

  — One person changing to match the other(s).

  — Persons becoming even more different.

Personal Traits, Social Attributes, and Social Roles

Fisher and Adams[6] defined self-concept as "that part of your self which you conceive of as a set of relatively stable self-characterizations." So, for example, if I were to hand you a sheet of paper and say, "Write down who and what you are," the things you list on that paper would be concepts of your self you consider to be consistently true. The nature of the things you list were categorized by Kuhn and McPartland[7] into three categories: personal traits, social attributes, and social roles. We can define them as follows.

— Personal traits:	Characteristics that are physical or innate (e.g., "tall" or "intelligent').
— Social attributes:	Social characteristics in interaction with others (e.g., "friendly").
— Social roles:	Roles assumed in relation to others (e.g., "teacher" or "police officer").

These categories impact our self-concept primarily by what they assume about the characteristic involved. So, for example, if I am overweight then I would have the choice of characterizing it as:

— A personal trait: "I am large because I descend from a family of large Danes.

— A social attribute: "I am large because I'm a party-goer who enjoys eating and drinking.

— A social role: "I am large because I'm a chef who must constantly taste his wares.

The question is not, "Which of these statements is true?" The question is "Which of these statements is the one I use to explain myself?" The one that I select reveals how I view my largeness—as a personal trait that I cannot control, or as a social attribute or social role that I can change if I so choose. That, in turn, will reflect on how I feel about it (positive or negative) and will result in my "self-esteem." Figure 5.4 shows the relationship between all of these.

A CONSTRUCTIVE MODEL OF SELF-ESTEEM

How I interpret my characteristics	How I feel about them	The net result
Personal trait ("I can't help it; I'm a victim")	My "valence":	My
Social attribute ("I choose it by my action	+ positive (" I like it")	Self-Esteem
Social role ("It's part of my social duties")	– negative ("I don't like it")	

Figure 5.4

From this model we can see that I have two options for improving my self-esteem. I can either change the way I interpret my characteristics, or I can change my valence for them. So, for example, if I have assumed I am large as a result of a personal trait I can either (1) redefine it as a social attribute or social role and thereby give myself permission to change it, or (2) I can decide to be happy about it. Either way, my self-esteem will improve. And either way, my self-esteem is not something that happens to me, it is something that I can control by the assumptions and choices I make. That is a subjective and constructive approach to self-esteem.

Some Other Implications of a Constructed Self-Concept

If we assume that we can control "who we are" by the choices we make, a number of other concepts come into play.

Self-fulfilling prophecy is the idea that we become what we think we are. If I say, "I'm no good at math," then I will likely not be good at math—not because I'm incapable naturally but because I won't really try. I rise only to the level of my lowered expectations. On the more positive side, I can decide that I have the capability to learn the piano, and because I'll put the necessary effort into it, I will likely achieve my goal.

Self as a process. Rather than seeing oneself as a set of fixed characteristics, this approach to self-concept sees the "self" as a process that is reflexive, social, and always evolving.[8] The term reflexive means that it is simultaneously multi-directional—me affecting you at the same moment that you are affecting me in a simultaneous and dynamic interaction. To say that the self-concept is social means that it is achieved during interaction with others, not alone by myself. And to say that self-concept is always evolving means that it is constantly changing over time, not static and fixed.

Self as constructed through interaction. We come to know "who we are" through our daily interactions with others. As Jurgen Ruesch[9] said, "It is well to remember that all the information a person possesses about himself is derived from others. His impression of the impact he had upon others is what makes up the picture of himself." This is what Meade[10] called the "social self," and what Cooley[11] called the "looking-glass self." We decide, through the reactions of others toward us, what we think we are. If I tell a joke and you do not laugh, then I will not conclude that I'm funny. If you compliment me on my hair today, I will assume that I look good. And so it goes. "You see reflected back to you, in the behaviors of your fellow interactants, an image of your own self."[12]

Who Are You?

In summary, let us return to the list of things you might write down about yourself—your self-concept. If you were to list ten things, would those be all there is to say about you? Are you those ten things and nothing more? Of course not. You are a wonderfully complex and varied person who is capable of many things. So what about the list? What does it represent? It represents what you *value*—what you want others to think about you or what you want to believe about yourself. So if I say that I am "friendly" I am not really claiming that it is "who I am" but rather that it is "who I want to be, and what I want you to think of me." I will attempt to behave in ways that support the notion that I am "friendly," and thus will likely be perceived as such by others. But it happens because I make it happen, not because it is a natural trait.

There are, admittedly, some things about ourselves that are natural traits—the color of our eyes, our gender, etc.—but the majority of things you might put on your list are subjective and constructed. And that means you have much more to say about who you "are" than perhaps you might have thought. In the end, you are who you want to be and who you are willing to work to become. That is the empowering principle behind subjective and constructive approaches to self-concept.

Chapter 5: Analysis and Application Exercises

1. Many contemporary social issues are debated within a framework of objective vs. subjective thinking. Using the framework outlined at the beginning of this chapter, listen to the claims of people who are advocating for a social issue and determine whether their approach is fundamentally objective or subjective in nature.
2. Aubrey Fisher identified four major paradigms of communication study, but emphasized that they were all equally valuable. They simply differ in their assumptions and approach to the human condition. As an example, let's assume that I am depressed. How would a mechanist respond to this problem (e.g., what solution would they offer)? How would a psychologist respond? How would a social actionist respond? How would a pragmatist respond? Be prepared to defend your answers by referring to what each of these paradigms focuses on in explaining the human condition.
3. How do constructs work, and with what effect, in understanding oneself, others, and the relationships within which we live?
4. What difference does it make whether I consider some aspect of myself to be a personal trait, a social attribute, or a social role? How does all of this relate to my self-esteem, and what options do I have for improving it?
5. How does the social action approach to self-concept differ from the psychologistic one? What advantages are there (if any) to a more subjective and constructive approach?

References

1. Griffin, Em (2006). *A First Look at Communication Theory,* 6th ed. New York: McGraw-Hill Companies, Inc., 6–13.
2. Liska, J. & Cronkhite, G. (1995). *An Ecological Perspective on Human Communication Theory.* Fort Worth, TX: Harcourt Brace College Publishers, 94–95.
3. West, R. & Turner, L.H. (2007). *Introducing Communication Theory: Analysis and Application,* 3rd ed. New York: McGraw-Hill Companies, Inc., 56–60.
4. Adapted from Fischer, B.A. (1978). *Perspectives on Human Communication.* New York: Macmillan.
5. Meade, G.H. (1934). *Mind, Self and Society: From the Standpoint of a Social Behaviorist.* Chicago: University of Chicago Press.
6. Fisher, B.A. & Adams, K.L. (1994). "Awareness of self" and "The self-concept," in *Interpersonal Communication: Pragmatics of human relationships,* 2nd ed. New York: McGraw-Hill Companies Inc., 62–65.
7. Kuhn, M. & McPartland, T.S. (1954). An Empirical Investigation of Self-attitudes. *American Sociological Review,* 19, 58–76.
8. Fisher, B.A. & Adams, K.L. (1994). "Awareness of self" and "The self-concept," in *Interpersonal Communication: Pragmatics of Human Relationships,* 2nd ed. New York: McGraw-Hill Companies Inc., 63.
9. Ruesch, Jurgen, as cited in Wilmot, W.W. (1980). *Dyadic Communication,* 2nd ed. Reading, MA: Addison-Wesley, 44.
10. Meade, G.H. (1913). The Social Self. *Journal of Philosophy, Psychology and Scientific Methods,* 10, 374–380.
11. Cooley, C.H. (1922). *Human Nature and the Social Order,* rev. ed. New York: Scribners.
12. Fisher, B.A. & Adams, K.L. (1994). "Awareness of self" and "The Self-concept," in *Interpersonal Communication: Pragmatics of Human Relationships,* 2nd ed. New York: McGraw-Hill Companies Inc., 63.

CHAPTER 6

Nonverbal Communication

LEARNING OBJECTIVES

After reading this chapter, you should be able to:

1. Recognize and explain the importance of utilizing nonverbal codes for communication
2. Define nonverbal codes by listing and illustrating categories of non-verbal behavior.
3. Identify and explain three problems people have interpreting the nonverbal codes they receive.
4. Know and identify benefits the successful communicator has achieved by understanding nonverbal codes.

CHAPTER 6: Overview

Chapter 6 begins with a short description of an event where no verbal communication takes place, but an event is graphically described. Characteristics of nonverbal communication are explained. Successful nonverbal communication considers the context of the event, and becomes more dependable than the verbal communication. Most communication events begin and utilize many types of nonverbal activities. The effective interpretation of nonverbal cues is often developed and taught within the culture. Without knowing cultural expectations, and not understanding proper perception, nonverbal cues can be vague, misunderstood, or missed completely. Specific types of nonverbal communication including facial expression, body movements, touch, and paralanguage techniques are reviewed. Then a communication event of a love relationship was developed tracing nonverbal events.

To Build a Fire

Jack London

He was safe. Toes and nose and cheeks would be only touched by the frost, for the fire was beginning to burn with strength. He was feeding it with twigs the size of his finger, in another minute he would be able to feed it with branches the size of his wrist, and then he could remove his wet footgear, and, while it dried, he could keep his naked feet warm by the fire, rubbing them at first, of course, with snow. The fire was a success. He was safe. . . He started to untie his moccasins. They were coated with ice; the thick German socks were like sheaths of iron halfway to the knees; and the moccasin strings were like rods of steel all twisted and knotted. He tugged with his numb fingers, and then drew his sheath knife. But before he could cut the strings, it happened. It was his own fault. He should not have built the fire under the spruce tree. He should have built it in the open. But it had been easier to pull the twigs from the brush and drop them directly on the fire. Now the tree under which he had done this carried the weight of snow on its boughs. High up in the tree one bough capsized its load of snow. This fell on the boughs beneath, capsizing them. The process continued . . . It grew like an avalanche, and it descended upon the man and the fire, and the fire was blotted out! . . . It was as though he had just heard his own sentence of death.

Nonverbal communication refers to any information or behavior that is expressed but does not involve spoken words. The above story of tragedy and death carries no vocal communication, but is easily visualized.

We are surrounded by a world that communicates, though language is absent. One can go into the yard and see the message from the parched vegetation that water is needed for their survival. The fruit shouts loudly that it is ready for harvest with its bright coloration. Birds and small animals show you the harvest is desirable by their chatter and activity eating it.

Nature is not the only place we recognize the importance of nonverbal communication. The restaurant owner is well aware that the smell of roast chicken brings customers into his business. The marketers of shampoo know that to have an advantage over a hundred other competitors they must have the right fragrance and color before sales occur. Automobile dealers know orange and bright green are not the best display items for the show floor.

Color as a communicated message can be startling. The hollering hand-cuffed man kicked arresting officers as they led him to the pink room. They tossed him in and waited with knowing smiles for his screams to subside. Within minutes, the prisoner's rage turned to calm. He'd been pinked![1]

Trained communicators, however, utilize nonverbal codes they can control, and that assist in developing visual images within the mind of listeners as the message is formulated. Nonverbal cues include tone of voice, facial expression, posture, gesture, appearance, and any other nonverbal tool that can assist in influencing the listener.

The study of nonverbal communication is relatively recent. We tend to take nonverbal communication for granted because it is so basic, but its importance is unmistakable and its connection to communication is undeniable. Research indicates that we spend more time communicating nonverbally than verbally and our nonverbal messages carry more meaning than our verbal messages. Several studies have estimated that the average person speaks for only ten to eleven minutes per day and that the average spoken sentence spans about 2.5 seconds. In a normal two-person conversation, 60 to 90 percent of communicative meaning is transmitted through nonverbal behaviors.[2]

People do indeed reveal much about their current modes, preferences, and emotions through nonverbal communication; however, the process of reading and deciphering such information is far more complex and subtle than it appears on the surface.[3]

Nonverbal communication is very much a personal thing, and to state absolutes becomes risky. Some people depend more heavily on verbal messages, and others seem to rely on nonverbal messages.[4] One study found that nonverbal behaviors were twelve to thirteen times more powerful in impact compared to the accompanying verbal message.[5]

Without our realizing it, nonverbal communication becomes the basis for many decisions. Regardless of how you ask questions, request favors, or give instruction, you approach each event based upon how you perceive the recipient's nonverbal acceptance of the communication. If the listener is smiling, friendly, and open, your approach will be significantly different than if that person frowns, ignores you or angles away from you with the shrug of a shoulder.

Characteristics of Nonverbal Communication

If something is observed, nonverbal communication occurs. If we are visible, others receive some kind of message about us. To initiate nonverbal communication is not a problem. However, interpretation can be difficult. Consider the following example.

Jack is always perfectly groomed and smells of expensive aftershave lotion. George has shoulder-length hair and always wears sweatshirts and jeans. By looking at them, we cannot tell what the two men intend to communicate. Jack may be neat and use aftershave lotion because it feels good, or he may want to communicate that designer clothes and expensive aftershave lotion are his trademark.

George may simply like to dress comfortably, or he may be attempting to communicate that he disdains society's seeming obsession with outward appearances. He may even be leaving a dirty cleaning job he detests. Ultimately, it's not so much what Jack and George intend to communicate as what others perceive. The communicated message is always in the mind of the listener. Both George and Jack, intentionally or unintentionally, are communicating something about themselves through their appearance.

Nonverbal Communication Depends on Context

The context in which nonverbal communication occurs plays a crucial role in its interpretation. Pounding on a table to make a point during a speech means something entirely different from pounding on the table in response to someone calling you a liar. Direct eye contact with a stranger can mean something entirely different from direct eye contact with a close friend.

A good example of nonverbal communication impacting an event is to review nonverbal events influencing a screening interview for employment. The time you arrive at the interview is your first nonverbal signal. If you are too early, you send the message that you are too eager for acceptance. However, that message is significantly better than being late. Job applicants who show up five minutes late have less than a twenty percent chance of getting a job offer.

Some hiring managers claim they can spot a possible candidate for a job within 30 seconds or less, and while a lot of that has to do with the way you look, it's also in your body language. Do not enter while pulling up your pantyhose or readjusting your tie; pull yourself together before you stand up to greet the interviewer. Avoid a "dead fish" handshake and confidently grasp your interviewer's hand and make eye contact while saying hello[6].

Interviewers stress how critical the nonverbal cues of posture, dress, and subtle movements are in forming a positive impression of potential employees. Albert Mehrabian of UCLA found that 55 percent of communication is received from body language[7].

When you communicate, nonverbal and verbal cues usually supplement and support each other. Your appearance, tone of voice, eye contact, and posture reveal much about you. Without understanding the context in which communication occurs, it is almost impossible to tell what a specific nonverbal behavior may mean. In fact, misunderstandings can occur even when the context is fully understood. That is why we must think twice about our interpretation of others' nonverbal behavior and their possible interpretations of ours.

Nonverbal Communication is More Believable Than Verbal Communication

People tend to believe nonverbal communication, even when it contradicts the accompanying verbal message. Police interrogation constantly refines the art of lie detection in questioning suspects. Some people lie well verbally, but expose themselves as being deceitful by the way they move.

Nonverbal indicators of deception are much easier to recognize than the verbal messages. Parents learn to assess such behavior as they raise children. Bosses learn about deceiving employees. People just "know" when deception begins. Much of this recognition is a perception of nonverbal cues. Police interrogation usually gives preference to nonverbal reactions of a suspect over their verbal response when evaluating guilt or innocence.

Physical reactions of someone who is consciously trying to hide information from the police follow behavior born and breed in the human specie. The process begins with the fight or flight scenario, and your body prepares to wage war or run from the scene. The blood and adrenalin start pumping, changing the body chemistry. Adrenalin quickens the heart rate, increasing respiration and accelerating digestion. Your glands start secreting lubricant to keep other mammals from grabbing you. The complexion lightens, the stomach growls, the mouth will go dry, making conversation difficult. Body odor even changes. Hand movements change, along with foot and tongue movement.[8]

The old adage that "actions speak louder than words" is never more evident than reading nonverbal communication of deception.

Nonverbal Communication Is a Primary Means of Expression

We can often detect other people's feelings of frustration, anger, sadness, resentment, or anxiety without their actually saying anything. We can detect others' emotions because nonverbal communication is so powerful. As young children we express how we feel by our body movement, our emotional responses, even our health and response to pain, fever, or tears. Biologically we communicate nonverbally. We often reserve verbal communication for the intellectual messages.

Nonverbal Communication is Related to Culture

Culture contributes significantly to differences in nonverbal behavior. Norms and rules that govern the management of behavior differ from culture to culture (For more in depth analysis, see Chapter 12). Yet because human beings around the world share common biological and social functions, it should not be too surprising to also find areas of similarity in nonverbal communication. For example, studies comparing facial expressions have found that certain universal expressions, such as those indicating sadness and fear, are easily understood across varying cultures.[9] Although much outward behavior is innate such as smiling, eye contact, and touching, we are not born knowing what meanings such nonverbal messages communicate. Most scholars would agree that cultures formulate display rules that dictate when, how, and with what consequence nonverbal expressions are exhibited. For instance, we are all born with the capacity to cry, yet what makes us cry and who is allowed to see us cry is learned within our cultural boundaries.

Nonverbal Communication is Ambiguous

Because nonverbal messages are always present, and because it is impossible to isolate the verbal and nonverbal parts, the instruction on nonverbal communication becomes difficult. Like any communication, the interpretation becomes a private interpretation because each listener is different. The message is abstracted from the real world and absorbed by selective perception discussed in chapter 4. What this all means is that nonverbal messages can be ambiguous, abstract, and arbitrary. We cannot assume a given message has a rigid meaning universal to all receivers. For example, does crying always signify grief or sadness, or could it also express joy, or pain, or surprise? Interpreting nonverbal behavior requires knowing the context and circumstances of the event and the cultural norms governing it. Even when a person understands the dynamics of nonverbal cues, successful communication is based on education, background, or personal experience. Interpreting the impact of the message includes a wide spectrum of potential response.

For example, does the yawn of a fellow student signal boredom, or fatigue, or stress? Does a speaker tremble because he is nervous or excited, or perhaps even chilly? Most nonverbal behaviors have a multitude of possible meanings, and to automatically assume only one possible meaning could lead to a serious misunderstanding.

Types of Nonverbal Communication

When you dress in a suit for a meeting, smile at someone, sit in a specific seat in class, use your hands while talking, play with a pen or pencil while listening, dim the lights to create a romantic atmosphere, play music loudly, look someone directly in the eyes, or burn incense to create a pleasant odor, you are communicating nonverbally. Every day we perform a wide range of nonverbal behaviors without even thinking about them, yet such behaviors can convey definite messages to others. Because nonverbal communication is so diverse, complex, common, and informative, we need to be more sensitive to its many manifestations. The nonverbal messages attributed to human communication have been grouped into three basic classifications.

Facial Expression and Body Movements

One of the first messages we receive from a person is how they are walking, and the look they have on their face. We use these features to create an infinite number of messages. **Kinesics**, sometimes referred to as "body language," is any movement of the face or body that communicates a message. Two particularly significant categories of kinesics are eye behavior and facial expressions. **Eye Behavior** is a subcategory of facial expressions that includes any movement or behavior of the eyes and is also referred to as **oculesics**. The eyes have the primary function of establishing relationships, or breaking contact, depending upon their use. **Facial expressions** include configurations of the face that can reflect augment, contradict, set a mood, or appear unrelated to a speaker's verbal message.

Eye Behavior or Oculesics. Eye behavior is the first and primary characteristic noticed by people. When approaching a person, direct eye contact is required before conversation. Duration of contact is also a factor. If the contact is prolonged, the recipient interprets the behavior as offensive, and breaks away. Without some contact, the interpretation is that no communication is desired. To look someone in the eye, then roll our eyes up and away is a definite message of rejection. However, if we look down, then back up and smile, that is a definite signal to begin speaking.

Research found that during interaction people spend about 45 percent of the time looking at each other's eyes.[10] Eye contact establishes relationships, sends messages of acceptance or rejection, and even conveys various types of emotion. Eye behavior can serve one of six important communicative functions: (1) influence attitude change and persuasion; (2) indicate degree of attentiveness, interest, and arousal; (3) express emotions; (4) regulate interaction; (5) indicate power and status; and (6) form impressions in others.[11]

Notice how difficult it is to talk to someone wearing dark glasses. The reason: we judge the success of our communication by watching eye response. Ancient poets described the eyes as "windows to the soul." Through these "windows" we judge other's feelings, emotions, and the success of our conversation. We associate a high level of gaze or direct eye contact from another as a sign of liking or friendliness.[12]

If others avoid making eye contact with us, we conclude that they are unfriendly, dislike us, or are shy.[13] Although a high level of eye contact is positive, there are some exceptions. If a person continuously stares at us, this generally is an unpleasant experience, producing nervousness or distrust in the other person.[14] When confronted with unwanted staring, most of us withdraw from the situation.[15] Unwanted stares are interpreted as a sign of hostility or anger.[16]

Eyes become a major tool in nonverbal communication. How they are used, and the duration of exposure should be carefully employed by the skillful communicator. By mastering use of the eyes, communication can be significantly enhanced. Misuse can terminate communication, perhaps permanently, .

Facial Expression. Facial expressions typically display emotions, but because of their complexity they can be difficult to interpret. Take for example the smile. The first response to a smile is acceptance, but that signal can also be a disguise, masking embarrassment, fear, sarcasm, or uncertainty. The human face is said to produce over a thousand different expressions.[17] Most of these expressions are easily identified with different emotions.

The face is one of the most important sources of emotional information. Most observers can identify the specific emotional content of the expression with high accuracy; the meanings associated with other facial expressions can differ from culture to culture. For example, expressions of happiness or sadness can be interpreted quite accurately as to intensity and meaning, but other facial expressions such as confusion or misunderstanding are more difficult to interpret.[18] Interpretation of emotions is learned and usually conforms to specific cultural expectations.

Body language sends messages which reflect agreement, contradict or are unrelated to what is happening. This player's immobilised posture suggests either that the game has been lost, he did not play well, he is exhausted, or perhaps something else we do not know about.

Body Movements. To make sense of thousands of different body movements, Ekman and Friesen have devised a classification system based upon the origins, functions, and coding of nonverbal behavior.[19] Their system divides body motions into five categories: emblems, illustrators, regulators, affect displays, and adaptors (See Table 6.1).Because there are so many body motions, many of which are interdependent, it is important to understand that the categories are not mutually exclusive. Some body motions may be classified under more than one category.

Body and facial movements that can be directly translated into words or phrases are called **emblems**. These include hand signs for most sporting events indicating game violations, activities, or significant recognition like scoring. Such signs of "OK," "I want a Ride" with the thumb, "peace," "power" and many other signs that we use for specific words carry great meaning. These signs carry a specific meaning as well as other implied meanings, such as the famous Bronx Cheer. Its use can precipitate significant emotion and even a hostile action.

The meanings of emblems are like the meanings of words because they are arbitrary, subject to change with time, learned, and culturally determined. An example of such an emblem is the "peace" sign, covering changes from the wartime "V for victory" initiated by Winston Churchill during World War II to the trademark of the flower children of the '60's and their message of peace.

Table 6.1

Categories of Body Movements and Facial Expressions

CATEGORY	CHARACTERISTICS	EXAMPLES
Emblems	Translate directly into words	Extended thumb of a hitchhiker
Illustrators	Accent, reinforce, or emphasize a verbal message	A child holding up his hands to indicate how tall he is while saying, "I'm a big boy"
Regulators	Control, monitor, or maintain interaction	Eye contact, shift in posture, nod of head
Affect displays	Express emotion and feelings	Sad face, slouching, jumping up and down
Adaptors	Help one feel at ease in communication situations	Scratching, playing with coins, moving toward someone

Body motions that accent, reinforce, or emphasize an accompanying verbal message are called **illustrators**. An instructor who underlines a word on the chalkboard to emphasize it, a child who indicates how tall he is by holding his hand up, a softball player who swings her arms while describing a hit, children who use their thumbs and fingers as if they were guns—all these people are using illustrators. The process becomes so critical to some people that they would become almost mute without the ability to "speak with their hands."

Body motions that control, monitor, or maintain the exchange between speaker and listener are **regulators**. Regulators include eye contact, shifts in posture, nodding the head, and looking at a clock or wristwatch. These cues tell us when to stop, continue, repeat, hurry, elaborate, make things more interesting, or let someone else speak.

Body movements that express emotions and feelings are **affect displays**. The face is the primary means of displaying emotions, but the body is also used. The slouch conveys laziness or sadness, the slam of a fist conveys anger, jumping up and down conveys excitement or joy. Affect displays communicate messages that may repeat, contradict, supplement, replace, or not even relate to verbal messages.

Our body motions can also help us adapt to a situation. They are the most difficult nonverbal signals to interpret because interpretation requires speculation. Scratching, playing with a pencil, sitting straight in a chair, crossing arms and legs, grooming motions, and smoking are examples of **adaptors**. Interpretation requires the listener to speculate whether crossed arms really implies rejection and blocking someone out, or whether it is a relaxation movement. People are especially likely to use adaptors in stressful or highly emotional situations where interpretation of the cues are vague or unclear. When someone is trying to control strong emotions or exhibit a strong favorable impression, the person will try to adapt to his perception of most acceptable behavior. The most common is to laugh at a remark, even though the humor is in question. A person will try to control a tear to adapt to a less stressful condition by implying a dust particle in the eye.

Touch

Touching is referred to as tactile or haptics communication. Touching is a basic, biological communication event almost essential to life itself. Studies at the University of Miami's School of Medicine have shown that premature babies grow faster and gain more weight when massaged.[20] Many researchers have reported the importance of touching in the maintenance of personal assurance. "Reach out and touch someone" is a slogan once used by a national phone company. The idea behind the advertisement is that touch is a personal and powerful means of communication. Touching is a primitive way of relating to others. It gives encouragement, expresses tenderness, and shows emotional support. Often the pat on the shoulder from a friend can be one of the most comforting communication messages one can receive. Categories that describe variations in touch have been listed as functional-professional, social-polite, friendship-warmth, love-intimacy, and sexual arousal.[21]

Functional-professional touch is an unsympathetic, impersonal, cold, or businesslike touch. This is a doctor's touch during a physical examination or an athletic trainer's touch of an injured athlete. It is purely medical. A tailor who takes customers' measurements is also professional touching. The person being touched is usually treated as an object or nonperson in order to prevent implying any other message.

Social-polite touch acknowledges another person according to the norms or rules of a society. In our society, the handshake is the most predominate form of touching—used as a greeting and recognition of another. In many European countries, a kiss is used in the place of the handshake to acknowledge another.

Friendship-warmth touch expresses an appreciation of the special attributes of others. Friendship-warmth touch is also the most misinterpreted type of touching behavior because it can be mixed or confused with touching related to sex. For example, you see two men meet in an airport, hug, and walk off with their arms around each other. Are they relatives, partners, close friends, or perhaps lovers? Similar touching includes a pat on the head, gripping both hands, or a hand on the shoulder.

Love-intimacy touch usually occurs in romantic relationships between lovers and spouses. It includes caressing, hugging, embracing, kissing, and many other forms of intimate touch. It is highly communicative. Usually this form of touch requires consent between both parties, although one person can initiate love-intimacy touch and the other person being touched may not always reciprocate.

Intimate touch conveys strong caring, devoted, enamored, and loving interpersonal messages. It also complements and validates verbal messages such as "I love you" or "You are someone special in my life." Intimate touch does not necessarily imply sexual involvement. Sometimes confusion between intimate and sexual touch leads to dissatisfaction in some special relationships.

Sexual-arousal touch is the most intimate level of personal contact with another. Sexual touch behavior having mutual consent is extremely pleasurable for most people, but without consent it can also produce fear, insecurity, and anxiety.

The meaning of touch communication depends on the type of touch, the situation, who is doing the touching, and the cultural background of those involved. Some cultures are more prone to touching behavior than others. Research has found that people in the United States are less touch-oriented when compared to other cultures. For example, a study examining touching behavior during a one-hour period in a coffee shop found that people in San Juan, Puerto Rico, touched 180 times in an hour; those in Paris, France, touched 110 times; and those in Gainesville, Florida, touched only 2 times.[22]

Gender differences in touching behavior are also interesting. Men tend to touch more than women do; women tend to be touched more often than men. Women seem to value touch more than men do. Gender differences in touching behavior may be partially attributed to men's sexual aggressiveness in our culture and their expression of power and dominance. According to Nancy Henley, men have access to women's bodies, but women do not have the same access to men's bodies. According to one researcher, our way of exerting power by touch represents an invasion of another's personal space.[23]

Paralanguage

Paralanguage is the study of all cues, sounds or silence, other than the content of words themselves used in communication. Paralanguage cues include not only speech sound, such as groans, yawns, coughs, laughter, crying, and yelping but also speech rate, accent, articulation, pronunciation, and silence. These cues are nonsymbolic but can communicate very specific messages. Expressions such as "ugh," "uh-huh" "ya know," "like" and "OK" are referred to as vocal fillers and are considered paralanguage. Vocal fillers are often interspersed in conversations without forethought or a set order. They may reflect nervousness, speech patterns of a particular subculture, or personal habits. In any case, the use of vocal fillers can influence our image positively or it can damage and degrade others and us.

Paralanguage conveys meaning just as definitely as do words themselves. In some instances, vocal emphasis or volume can convey more meaning. Certainly the message "Stop!" can carry a much different meaning when whispered softly than if it is screamed at full volume.

We rely more often on paralanguage than on the words when interpreting another's message. Note the meaning of a sentence may vary according to the word emphasized:

1. ***Jane's*** taking Tom out for pizza tonight. (not Hilary or Dana)
2. Jane's taking ***Tom*** out for pizza tonight. (not Bill or Dave)
3. Jane's taking Tom ***out*** for pizza tonight. (not staying home)
4. Jane's taking Tom out for ***pizza*** tonight. (not seafood or hamburgers)
5. Jane's taking Tom out for pizza ***tonight.*** (not tomorrow or next weekend)[24]

Even though the words are identical, the meaning changes with a change in voice emphasis.

Paralanguage includes pitch (how high or low the voice is), vocal force (intensity or loudness) rate (speed of pronunciation) quality (overall impression of the voice), and pauses or silence. The way we vary our voices convey different meanings to receivers. Just as vocal emphasis changed the meanings of the sentence above, a change in rate of delivery can accomplish much the same thing. Even when the words are the same, if the range, force, pitch, and quality differ, the receiver's interpretations will differ. Research finds that 38 percent of the meaning of oral communication is affected by our use of voice, by the **way** we say something rather than **what** is said.[25]

Silence or vocal pauses are very communicative also. Vocal pauses or hesitation are usually short in duration, whereas silence generally refers to extended periods of time. Vocal pauses can be used to emphasize a word or thought or to make a point. Hesitations are usually the result of gathering thought or nervousness. Silence is expected in certain contexts, for example, during a funeral or while listening to a speech presentation, or it can be self-imposed as a way of thinking or doing nothing at all. Silence has many possible meanings. The next time a good friend says "Hi," pause for five to ten seconds before reacting. You will quickly learn the affect silence can have as a message.

Love Signals[26]

A good summation of nonverbal communication can be illustrated by developing a scenario of a communication event from start to finish illustrating not only the critical role of nonverbal signals in the communication process, but to also show the progression or development and complexity of the system as the entire process develops. The scenario involves the beginning, development and culmination of the love relationship. The object is to review the love signals as the courtship develops.

Stage I, the attention phase: The setting is obvious: the presence of males and females. The object is to get the two together. Each carries on a ritual of getting acquainted, much like crickets chirp, peacocks display, and lions nuzzle, humans shout their presence nonverbally. The male first establishes his territory in a public place, marking it well with cell phones, brief cases, newspapers. He is usually joined by other male friends. The female dons bright colors, floral prints, bold lines, and geometric shapes. There is bright jewelry and perfume to also announce her availability. She moves through the territory, even brushing lightly against the male, sweeping her eyes from side to side, smiling brightly, and nonverbally announcing "Here I am!" There is an exaggeration of sexual identity through makeup, hair cues as well as dress. Much attention is given to spacing: too close too fast is a no-no. But timing must be provided for introductory casual conversation.

Stage 2: The Courtship. An appointment is made to establish common ground. The site of preference is a dinner engagement. Eating is an activity that welcomes acceptance. During this stage, eye contact is vital. The rule of thumb is that if the pupils dilate, there is interest; if pupils constrict, there is threat or dislike. Legend reports that 18th century Europe recommended women take eye drops of belladonna, using them to dilate eyes if the occasion favored a positive reaction. Looking into one's eyes rarely lasts much beyond a few seconds, but as romance blossoms, duration can be extended, followed by facial flushing (a sexual attraction response), followed by gazing downward, implying submissiveness and smiling, meaning acceptance.

If the process is rejection, the negative cues are just as obvious: gaze aversion or angling the upper body away, generally referred to as the cut-off, or cold shoulder. Arms are crossed, the stare is blank, there is no facial reaction, and boredom is implied. The "Unavailable" sign has just been given.

Stage 3: Friendship stage. Conversation becomes important, but the critical cues indicate acceptance of the conversation topics. Men rate women attractive and desirable if they are highly agreeable. This implies much laughter, the nonverbal message of acceptance. Women rate men more physically and sexually attractive if they solicit opinion, show sensitivity, and display warmth and agreeableness with much humor.

If the process is rejection at this stage, the negative cues include gazing too long with a blank stare, turning aside, and in-rolling the lips into a thin line.

Stage 4: Bonding or Intimacy Stage. Entering this stage implies that both parties have nonverbally agreed to elevate the relationship to a more personal level. The implication is that through acceptance and tolerance at this stage, a formal signification of permanent relationship is desired. For these reasons, behavior is less ambiguous and more behaviorally oriented. Without a clear understanding of intent, and without mutual agreement, such activity could be abusive.

The central focus of bonding behavior is touchin, a progressive activity, beginning with the hand to a neutral location—shoulder, arm, or a hand. Throughout this activity, visual monitoring becomes critical. The immediate reaction is either acceptance or rejection. Even the slightest startle sends a signal. The eyes suddenly widening, or a flinch or freezing response sends a "hands off" signal and the event is over. Negative reactions include tenseness, hesitation, angling away, or a "dead man" no response at all.

Positive responses to the touch are lifting shoulders, head tilt, perhaps a slight swaying motion, and returning the touch, which is always a positive sign.

A more advanced stage of touching is the kiss. When used at an introduction, this is a preliminary action, but if a progression of events as implied above occur, the kiss is a strong positive, joint reaction. Note this romantic description: "Locked in an embrace, ever so slowly the couple's heads may loom closer and closer, like a docking spacecraft. Three inches away and closing, their faces roll several degrees right or left, in synchrony, so the noses will clear, and the lips begin a cautious link-up. The pair seals the fourth stage of courtship with a **kiss**!"[27]

Stage 5: Love making. From signals obtained in the touching phase couples progress to the final stage: sexual intercourse. This is usually a slow negotiation through mutual consent based upon both verbal and nonverbal messages. This becomes standard procedure throughout this stage.

After physically bonding in love, there is less need to negotiate closeness achieved in earlier stages. Couples thus tend to emit fewer and fewer love signals. Without such positive reinforcement, the satisfaction of this stage can loose its impact, and since they take the distance between them comfortably for granted, they give off fewer "come hither" signals, and the romance can begin to dim. Care needs to be taken to insure earlier stages of the love relationship are not completely forgotten at the expense of this final stage.

The above description of a series of events related to a communication agreement implies that various stages of communication occur, with a progression and change of nonverbal activity an integral part. Reflection can teach us that many such events: purchasing a car or home, changing religions, joining a club or social group, gaining an education, or even taking a college course will produce a series of communication events requiring a progression of activity. Obviously some events will be longer, more intense, and more complex. The point to be observed, is the necessary interaction between the verbal and the nonverbal messages being carefully integrated and interpreted to achieve communication satisfaction.

Interpreting Nonverbal Communication

Three critical conclusions can be made about nonverbal communication:

1. *Nonverbal cues have multiple meanings.* By clearly understanding the context, being carefully observant of human behavior, and by improving personal perception, the communication has a better chance of success.
2. *Nonverbal cues are interdependent.* Remember that meaning is a conclusion developed by accumulating as much information, both verbally and nonverbally, as possible. It must be remembered that as conditions change, so do technique, verbiage, and even motivation. Be alert to developmental changes as they impact the final conclusions.
3. *Nonverbal cues are subtle.* Constantly monitor feedback from all people involved in the communication event to understand how receivers of the message interpret the overwhelming number of possible interpretations presented. This can have a big impact on how continuing messages are formulated, presented, and accepted to clarify misinterpretations, and present new information.

Chapter 6: Analysis and Application Exercises

1. The meaning of nonverbal codes can vary among cultures and co-cultures. Think of two nonverbal codes (gestures, clothing, etc.) you commonly use in a group to which you belong (club, sports team, organization, etc). Would outsiders to the group accurately interpret what these nonverbal codes mean? Why or Why not?
2. Select an activity that requires stages of development, similar to the "love Stages" example above. (eg: Building a home, purchasing an automobile, selecting a major, etc.) List at least three different stages of communication with unique nonverbal events required for successful completion of the event.
3. Prepare a presentation for the class. The presentation must be done completely nonverbally. No written or spoken language can be given. The presentation would

include having the class perform some type of activity or event. The presentation must last at least 10 minutes. Success will depend upon how successfully the class accepts the communication. Did they learn the task, or perform the activity desired?

References

1. *Police find Pink Pacifies Prisoners.* Associated Press, RKCI Publishing Group, Inc., 1997
2. M.L. Hickson III and D.W. Stacks, *Nonverbal Communication: Studies and Applications,*3rd ed. (Dubuque, Iowa: Brown and Benchmark, 1993), 4; A. Mehrabian, *Silent Messages: Impact Communication of Emotions and Attitudes,* 2nd ed. (Belmont, Calif.: Wadsworth, 1981), 77; R.L. Birdwhistell, *Kinesics and Context: Essays on Body Motion* (Philadelphia: University of Pennsylvania Press, 1970) 158; R. L. Birdwhistell, "Background to Kinesics," ETC 13 (1955): 10-18; A Mehrabian and S. R. Ferris, "Inference of Attitudes from Nonverbal Communication in Two Channels," *Journal of Consulting Psychology* 31 (1967): 24-252.
3. B.M. De Paulo, J.L. Stone, and G.D. Lassiter, "Deceiving and Detecting Deceit," *The Self and Social Life,* ed. B.R. Schlenker (New York: McGraw-Hill, 1985), 323-70.
4. M.;L. Knapp and J. Hall, *Nonverbal Communication Human Interaction,* 4th ed. (New York: Harcourt Brace, 1997), 24.
5. M. Argyle, F. Alkema, and R. Gilmour, "The Communication of Friendly and Hostile Attitudes by Verbal and Nonverbal Signals," *European Journal of Social Psychology* 1 (1971): 385-402.
6. C. Corner, "The Interview: Body Language Do's and Don'ts," *CareerBuilder. Com.*2007 Microsoft.
7. K. Lorenz, "Ace that First Impression," *Careerbuilder.com,* 2007, Microsoft.
8. C. Whitcomb, *Cold Zero: Inside the FBI Hostage Rescue Team.* (Boston: Little, Brown & Co, 2001), 368.
9. J. Stewart and C. Logan, "Making Contact Verbally and Nonverbally," *Bridges, Not Walls,* 9th ed, ed. J. Stewart (Boston: McGraw Hill, 2006), 129-130.
10. S.W. Janik, A.R. Wellens, J.L. Goldberg, and L.F. Dell'osso, "Eyes as the Center of Focus in the Visual Examination of Human Faces," *Perceptual and Motor Skills* 4 (1978): 857-58.
11. D. Leathers, *Successful Nonverbal Communication: Principles and Applications* (New York: Macmillan, 1986).
12. C.L. Kleinke, "Gaze and Eye Contact: A Research Review," *Psychological Review* 100 (1986): 78-100.
13. P.G. Zimbardo, *Shyness: What Is It and What You Can Do About It* (Reading, Mass: Addison-Wesley, 1977.
14. J.C. Strom and R.W. Buck, "Staring and Participants' Sex: Physiological and Subjective Reactions," *Personality and Social Psychology Bulletin* 5 (1979); 114-17.
15. P. Greenbaum and H.W. Rosenfield, "Patterns of Avoidance in Responses to Interpersonal Staring and Proximity: Effects of Bystanders on Drivers at a Traffic Intersection," *Journal of Personality and Social Psychology* 36 (1978): 575-87.
16. P.C. Ellsworth and J.M. Carlsmith, "Eye Contact and Gaze aversion in Aggressive Encounter," *Journal of Personality and Social Psychology* 33 (1973): 117-22.
17. P. Ekman, W. Friesen, and R. Ellsworth, *Emotion in the Human Face: Guidelines for Research and an Integration of Findings* (New York: Pergamon, 1972).
18. P. Ekman and H. Oster, "Review and Prospect," in *Emotion in the Human Face,* 2nd ed., Edited by P. Ekman (Cambridge: Cambridge University Press, 1982), 148.
19. P. Ekman and W.V. Fiesen, "The Repertoire of Nonverbal Behavior: Categories, Origins, Usage, and Coding," *Semiotica* 1 (1969): 49-98.20. T. Adler,

"Congressional Staffers Witness Miracle of Touch," APA Monitor (February, 1993), 12-13.

20. T.Adler, "Congressional Staffers Witness Miracle of Touch," APA Monitor (February, 1993), 12-13.21.R. Heslin and T. Alper, "Touch: A bonding Gesture," in Nonverbal Interaction, ed. J.M. Wiemann and R.P Harrison (Beverly Hills, Calif.: Sage, 1983), 47-75.
22. S.M. Jourard, *Disclosing Man to Himself* (Princeton, J.J.: Van Nostrand, 1968).
23. N. Henley, "Power, Sex, and Nonverbal Communication," *Berkeley Journal of Sociology* 18 (1973-1974):10-11.
24. B.E. Gronbeck, R.E. McKerrow, D. Ehringer, and A.H. Monroe, *Principles and Types of Speech Communication*, 11th ed. (Glenview, Ill.: Scott Foresman, 1990), 325.
25. M.L. Knapp, *Essentials of Nonverbal Communication* (New York: Holt, Rinehart and Winston,1980), 7; M.L. Knapp and J. Hall, *Nonverbal Communication in Human Interaction*, 4th ed. (New York: Harcourt Brace, 1997), 10-11.
26. Ideas came from a publication D.B. Givens, *Love Signals: A Practical Guide to the Body Language of Courtship* (New York: Saint Martin's Press, 2005). See also *The Nonverbal Dictionary of Gestures, Signs and Body Language*, http://members.aol.com/nonverbal2/diction1.htm
27. Ibid.

CHAPTER 7

Interpersonal Communication: Pragmatics

LEARNING OBJECTIVES

When Students have completed this chapter and lesson, they should be able to:

1. Identify the five principles of pragmatics used in understanding dyadal relationships.
2. Distinguish between spoken and unspoken contracts and explain their effects.

CHAPTER 7: Overview

The traditional approach to interpersonal relationships focuses on whether two people are "compatible." This trait-like approach can be contrasted to the pragmatic approach, which focuses on what people "construct" between them through ongoing patterns of interaction. Using the latter approach, communicants take full responsibility for their behavior and the meanings they co-create for those behaviors.

This chapter begins with the five basic principles of pragmatics as they relate to interpersonal communication. The author then discusses some elements of physical context—proxemics, arrangement, and distance—followed by the expectations that arise in various social contexts—kin, friends, workmates, social contracts, and acquaintances. The chapter ends with a discussion of spoken and unspoken contracts in interpersonal relationships.

Pragmatics

To the average person, the word "pragmatic" means "practical" or "applied." In that spirit, the pragmatic approach to human relationships focuses on how people jointly construct relationships through ongoing patterns of interaction and choices. The pragmatist cares most about results, not endless discussions of "why." The pragmatic question is not "What do people mean?" It is "How do people mean?"—what do they do, how do they act, and how do those actions function to construct or de-construct the relationship they share?

Using this approach, communicants manage both physical and social contexts and take full responsibility for their behavior, meanings, and relationships. In theory, any two persons (or more) who wish to can create and maintain a relationship. The outcome is in their hands; it is not predetermined.

One of the best explanations of pragmatics is found in Fisher and Adams' (1994) book *Interpersonal Communication: Pragmatics of Human Relationships.*[1] Their text was a standard for years in many communication-based relationship classes, and provides the theoretical framework for this chapter. Some of their most important ideas are summarized here.

Relationships as Social Systems

The pragmatist assumes that all relationships are *social systems*. Social means that relationships are constructed through social interaction with others. System means that relationships are not linear.

Communication is Social: Figure 7.1 illustrates the way communication settings are "nested." At the most basic or inner level is intrapersonal communication. This operates inside of individuals who are also engaged in interpersonal communication with others.

Interpersonal communication, in turn, operates within and among small groups. Those groups are normally parts of larger organizations, which in turn operate within a larger societal system such as a culture. These settings influence each other and also the nature of communication that occurs within them.

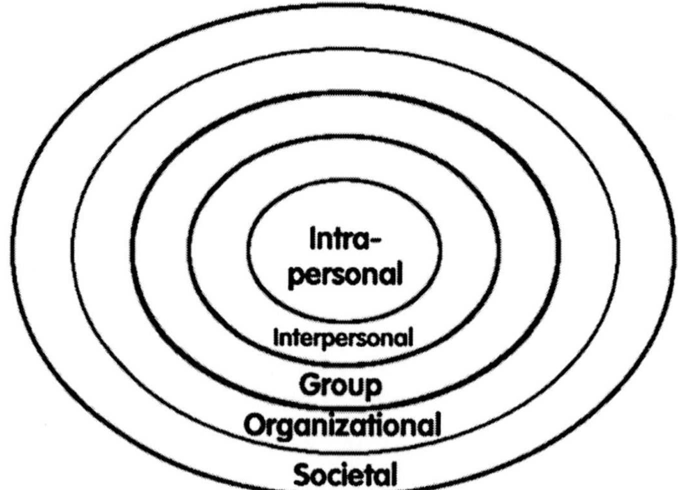

Figure 7.1

Relationships are Systems: The pragmatic approach is based on system theory. Simply put, system theory assumes that interactions between and among parts of the system are not linear (cause and effect). Instead, they simultaneously influence each other in multiple and multidirectional fashion. Figure 7.2 illustrates a system as being like a "soup" of vegetables marinating each other in a cup. Each part of this soup influences all the other parts while, at the same time, being influenced by them. It is messy to map, but it is an excellent metaphor for how relationships work.

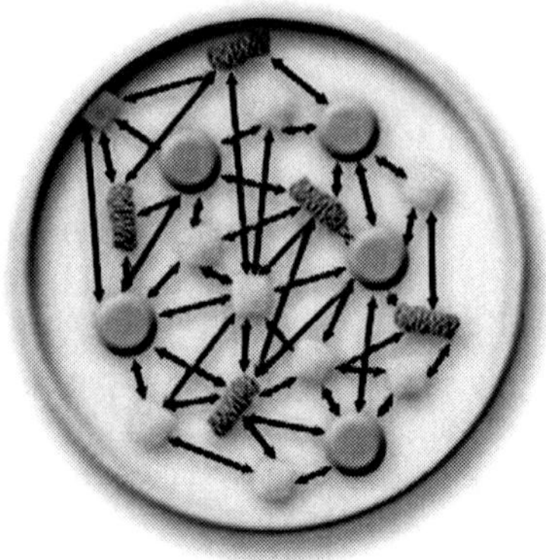

Figure 7.2

Communication and Relationships: The traditional idea of relationships is based on a psychological model. Human behavior is assumed to be the result of internal psychological processes. It assumes people can have shared understandings about things they have experienced in common and that the intersection of that shared experience is what we call "relationship" (see Figure 7.3).

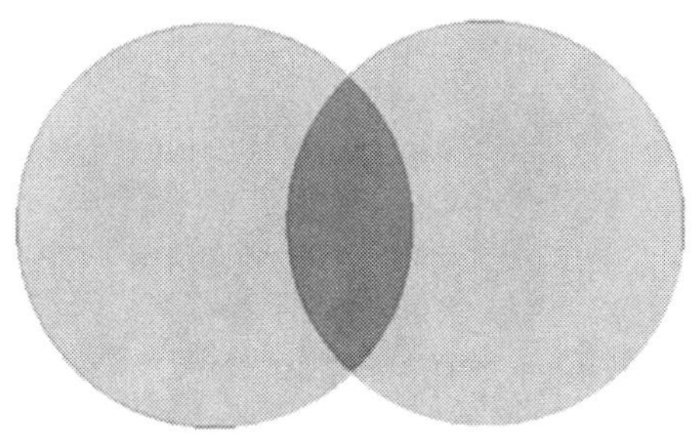

Figure 7.3

Pragmatists believe relationships *are* communication. That is not saying that communication "affects" (e.g., improves) relationships. It is saying relationships you have with others *are* your communication with them. Relationships and communication are the same thing.

Dyads: For purposes of this chapter's discussion, interpersonal communication is defined as communication in *dyads*—exactly two people, no more, no less. Pragmatics can be applied to any communicative setting, but here we are interested in a pragmatic approach to dyads.

Others: There are two kinds of "others" that we deal with in our dyads :

- Specific Others — Specific individuals with whom we interact.
- Generalized Others — A composite of all the experiences we've had with "that kind" of person (e.g., "men" or "women").

Pragmatic Principles

Fisher and Adams[2] identify five basic principles of the pragmatic approach to relationships, which are summarized below. These principles set pragmatics apart from other more traditional approaches to interpersonal communication.

1. Focus on Behavior: Behavior (what people do) should be the focus of our interest, not what they think or intend. We can observe behavior, but not intent. We can only infer (guess) intent. Furthermore, all behaviors can and will be interpreted by others. This leads to the idea that "you cannot not communicate"—every action (or lack of action) will be interpreted by the other.
2. Interpret Patterns of Behavior: Relationships are really "patterns of behavior," not isolated incidents. Messages (content) and interaction are correctly understood only in the context of a specific relationship's patterns. An example would be the difference between your classmate giving you a high-five in the hallway while saying, "You're bad!" and the same message from your mother when you've done something wrong.
3. Make Sense Retrospectively: We decide what something means after it happens, not while it is happening. As we do so, we "punctuate" certain elements of messages or events—giving more emphasis to one aspect than another. Also, different people will punctuate the same experience differently.
4. Consider the Context: The meaning of any message or event is context-bound. It must be interpreted in light of both the social context (people, relationships, and expectations) and the physical context (physical objects, arrangements and environments). More detailed information on context is provided below.
5. Ask "How" not "Why": Asking "why" people do things often leads to a discussion of personal or cognitive traits that are predetermined and cannot be controlled or changed ("That's just the way I am.") Pragmatists do not ask "why;" they ask "how." The implication of this difference is that pragmatists pay attention to the constructs people make about things (e.g., "Students hate homework") rather

than traits. A construct may be correct or incorrect, but either way it serves as a basis for action. More detailed information on constructs is provided at the end of this chapter.

Constructs

Constructs are assumptions about people and events. They are also meanings that we assign to them. We use constructs to reduce uncertainty and help us know how to act in a given circumstance or with a given person. Some principles related to constructs are:

- **Cooperation:** We cooperate with others in building constructs. They are co-created through social interaction.
- **Self-Concept:** We cooperate with others in building our self-concept, such as who and what we think we are ("smart," "ugly," etc.)
- **Significant Symbols:** These are objects or actions that we agree will have symbolic meaning (words, names, clothing, rings, traditions, etc.)
- **Sparring:** This is when we make statements to test how the other sees it (e.g., saying, "Oh, I'm so stupid!").
- **Contracts:** We make agreements about what things will mean or what we will or will not do.

Elements of Contracts: Contracts may be spoken or unspoken, but either way they involve obligations and their results. Concepts related to contracts include:

—Rules: Very important contracts with serious consequences.

—Expectations: Less important contracts with less serious results

—Rewards: Benefits for keeping a contract.

—Sanctions: Punishments for breaking a contract.

Whenever we have a social contract with someone, there are rules and expectations involved. When we keep these rules, we receive benefits. When we break them, we receive sanctions. The magnitude of the benefits or sanctions reveals how serious the contract is to the relationship. We can think of this as being on a magnitude scale where expectations are at one end and rules at the other. They are really the same thing, but of a different degree of seriousness.

Expectations	Rules
(low intensity)	(high intensity)

Every contract would fit somewhere along this scale, as revealed by the rewards or sanctions involved. For example, I have made a habit of calling my wife every day when I leave work to come home. Over time, it has become an expectation, and if I forget to do it, the sanctions will be very low in intensity—perhaps a simple "Oh, you're home. You didn't call me," or perhaps no reaction at all. On the other hand, if I were to choose to spend the night with another woman, I would be violating a rule, and the sanctions for doing so would be very severe—perhaps the end of our relationship. Obviously, rules are much more serious that expectations.

Unspoken Contracts: It is not too difficult to keep a social contract when we know the rules and expectations through open discussion. Unspoken contracts are less fair and may even be damaging to the relationship. With unspoken contracts, the other often doesn't know what is expected until the contract is broken, and in the case of rules the results can be quite serious. If we value our relationships with others, the safest policy is to clearly speak our expectations, and to avoid unspoken contracts.

Summary

In this chapter we have explored the pragmatic approach to interpersonal communication and relationships. Using this approach, we have learned that communication is your relationship—they are the same thing. We have also learned to focus on patterns—not isolated incidents—when interpreting events.

We have learned that relationships are constructed. It's not traits ("are we compatible?") but choices (actions) that make the difference. People can construct whatever relationships they want to through social interaction.

Finally, we discussed social contracts—our rules and expectations—and the superiority of spoken contracts over unspoken ones. It is best to speak them rather than waiting for someone to break them and then punish them for something they didn't even know was an expectation or a rule.

Chapter 7: Analysis and Application Exercises

1. If your communication is your relationship (if they are one and the same) then what does that suggest about the solution to dysfunctional relationships? Are relationships a matter of compatibility of fixed traits or of controllable behaviors? Explain.
2. Think about patterns of behavior that you or your other has—things that you repeatedly do that affect your relationship. Are these traits, habits, or controllable behaviors? What difference would your answer to this question make in terms of solutions? How does the pragmatic approach to relationships empower the participants?
3. Have you ever been the victim of an unspoken contract—an expectation or rule that somebody had for you that you were not even aware of until you broke it and were punished for doing so? Why is this unfair and unproductive from a pragmatic perspective? What is the solution to this problem?

References

1. Fisher, B.A. & Adams, K.L. (1994). *Interpersonal Communication: Pragmatics of Human Relationships* (2nd Edition). New York: McGraw-Hill Companies, Inc.
2. Fisher, B.A. & Adams, K.L. (1994).

CHAPTER 8

Interpersonal Communication: Part 2 Relationships

LEARNING OBJECTIVES

When students have completed this chapter and lesson, they should be able to:

1. Give three characteristics that distinguish an interpersonal relationship from an acquaintance.
2. Define self-disclosure, and give three reasons for its importance in interpersonal relationships.
3. List and describe the stages in the development of interpersonal relationships.
4. List and describe the stages in the decline of interpersonal relationships.
5. Identify two kinds of supportive communication behaviors and two kinds of defensive communication behaviors, providing an example of each.

Susan

Susan was always the first student to class every day. She never missed. Susan was a very attractive, well dressed girl, and her schoolwork suggested she was very intelligent. When the teacher arrived she would be sitting next to the wall in the back of class, quietly reading a book or working on an assignment.

Susan seldom took part in classroom discussions, although when given a group assignment she always completed her work well, but was generally quiet and shy. During the course, she never formed any bonding relationships, or seemed close to any of the students.

One of the class assignments was to meet someone during the course of the semester. The assignment required spending at least fifteen minutes with this person in a direct conversation four different times. A final paper was then to be written describing the new-found associate, and whether a friendship was developed during the semester.

When Susan's paper came in, it read something like this:

I did not meet anyone this semester. In fact, the only friends I have are those I find in books I read. I can only remember having one friend during my school years. Her name was Mary, and she was my friend for 6 months during the fifth grade. When her parents moved away, my only friend left and I have never had a friend since.

I tried to find someone this semester, but I could never get the courage to start a conversation with anyone, including the students in our class. I live alone and never talk to anyone. I am very lonely and want a friend more that anything else, but I do not know how or where to get one.

Susan illustrates a major problem encountered by many. As social animals, we sometimes resist a fundamental need of human development: forming interpersonal relationships to create a pleasant, healthy, fulfilling association with other people. An understanding of interpersonal communication can make a major difference in solving this problem for most people.

Interpersonal Communication

In Chapter 3, **interpersonal communication** was defined as the informal exchange of information between two people. Intrapersonal communication occurs within us; interpersonal communication involves outward expression that allows us to establish relationships with others. A **relationship** is an association between at least two people and is described as intimacy or kinship with an acquaintance, girlfriend, boyfriend, lover, or relative. Sometimes relationships are based on roles—roommates, partners, neighbors, boss and employee, teacher and student, doctor and patient, minister and church members. Relationships may be based upon activities: "We played on the same ball team;" "We go to the same church;" "We work together;" "We are in the same dorm."[1] We establish relationships and build friendships because human nature requires companionship of some kind for satisfaction and pleasure. Being with others satisfies our basic human drive for companionship and communication. Even religious text teaches that it is not good for humans to be alone.

The Motivation to Communicate and Form Relationships

By interacting with others we learn more about ourselves. Humans who have been raised in isolation become the subject of books, make national news, and are identified as rare individuals. We are motivated to get involved with others; to establish relationships with people who like the same activities, experiences, and conversations as we like. The interpersonal phenomenon of wanting to know more about others can be explained by uncertainty theory.[2] **Uncertainty theory** suggests that when we initially meet someone who attracts us, our need to know about them tends to make us draw inferences about them from the physical data we observe. An urge or need to reduce our uncertainty about them motivates our desire for further communication.

Everyone has many different physical and emotional needs to satisfy. We all need to feel safe in our environment. We want protection from hunger and protection from the elements. We want to feel accepted by others. These needs can be filled by communicating with others about activities or materials that will assure us the physiological and psychological demands have been met for providing a satisfying life-style. The more we understand about our personal needs, and the resources others have to help us with our desires, the more competent we can become at interpersonal communication.

Maslow's Hierarchy of Individual Needs

The physical and psychological needs of people remain constant across all groups and periods in time. Abraham Maslow developed a theory of individual needs that is old, but very useful because it shows why and how individuals' needs and motivations vary. Human needs can be classified into seven categories: psychological, safety, social, self-esteem, self-actualization, knowing and understanding, and aesthetics. The categories can be ranked in order of priority.[3] According to Maslow, our lower-order needs take precedent over higher order needs. To fulfill higher order needs, lower order needs must be satisfied first. Maslow uses a pyramid, shown in Figure 8.1 to demonstrate how the categories relate.

Physiological needs. The first need we all have is to merely exist. The most basic biological requirements include food and water, sleep, shelter and sex for procreation. Preservation of the species is our first priority.

Safety needs. Once we have satisfied our own preservation, we immediately begin improving our position. We want to believe that our achievements will be protect-

FIGURE 8.1

Maslow's Hierarchy of Individual Needs

This hierarchy illustrates how needs build upon each other. The lower needs in the hierarchy begin with physical needs and then move to higher, more abstract needs, which depend more heavily upon our interaction with others.

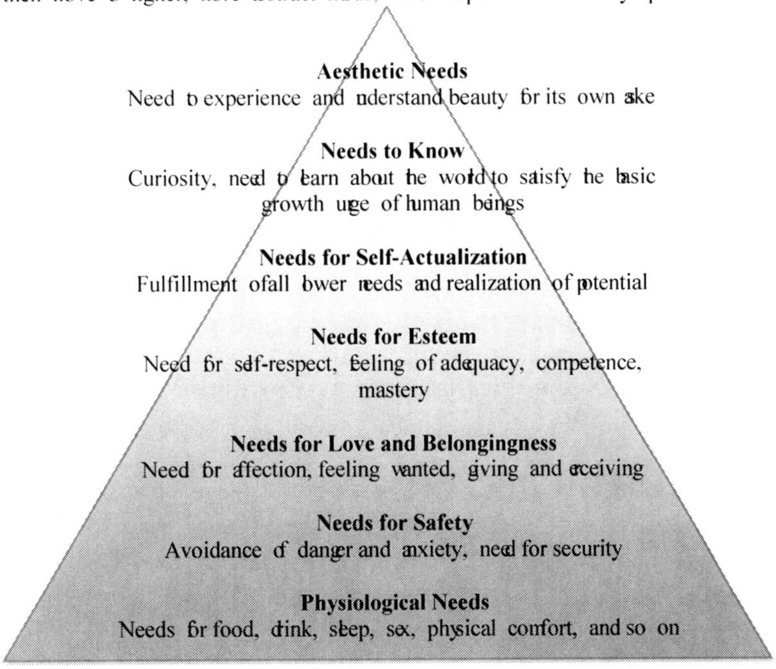

Aesthetic Needs
Need to experience and understand beauty for its own sake

Needs to Know
Curiosity, need to learn about the world to satisfy the basic growth urge of human beings

Needs for Self-Actualization
Fulfillment of all lower needs and realization of potential

Needs for Esteem
Need for self-respect, feeling of adequacy, competence, mastery

Needs for Love and Belongingness
Need for affection, feeling wanted, giving and receiving

Needs for Safety
Avoidance of danger and anxiety, need for security

Physiological Needs
Needs for food, drink, sleep, sex, physical comfort, and so on

ed. We now look for stability, order, freedom from health problems, and protection against intruders. We want to believe we are **safe** to continue our existence. Once these two basic needs are met, we can then consider moving to higher orders.

The need for love and friendship. Acceptance by others, and the giving and receiving of affection are prerequisites for character and career development, or even self-satisfaction. This level starts to set the human race apart from other species because it becomes a process by which our own efforts make a major difference. The high priority we place on belonging and love is the basis for interpersonal communication that creates bonding relationships. The need to belong and to be loved is such a strong motivator that some actually give up their need for safety to meet this need. This occurs in abusive relationships.

The need for self-esteem. Self esteem is a personality trait we develop based on what others express they feel toward us. From others' actions, we judge ourselves by how we believe others see us. We label these characteristics adequacy, competence, skill, talent, and acceptance by others. Our need to be judged well by others motivates us to seek out and associate with people who give us positive reinforcement. We attract such people by giving the same type of responses to them.

The need for self-Actualization. This is an action step we perform to achieve our full potential in the goals, talents, skills, and relationships we have created. This is a self-fulfillment, or internal motivation to do the very best we can to achieve our life goals. To have skills and never utilize them causes us to fail self-actualization, which in turn, causes us to lose our self-esteem, leading to lost relationships. Interpersonal communication and positive relationships preserve the self-actualization level.

The Need for Knowing and Understanding. We are extremely curious beings. Our need for knowing and understanding (uncertainty theory) is one reason we enter relationships. To satisfy our need for knowledge and to reduce uncertainty about people and events that interact with our lives, we must communicate. The more competent we are as communicators, the more likely we are to gain accurate and complete information about who we are, who others are, and the world around us.

Aesthetic Needs. The highest-level need is the need to experience and understand beauty. Our need to observe and absorb the world around us becomes the source for such fulfillment. We do not need to judge our surroundings, but merely accept them for what they are and how they connect to us. We have the luxury of including in our lives those elements that please us, and reject those that do not. The fulfillment of this need requires a deep understanding of intrapersonal communication and high self-esteem.

According to Maslow, we all attempt to achieve these needs. The ultimate goal is satisfaction, joy, and happiness. But until we can complete them to our own satisfaction, we consider ourselves failures. It should be obvious that the key element to success becomes the fuel that drives the system: communication. Successful interpersonal communication endows us with the power to accomplish the needs for a successful life.

Relationships: Getting to Know Others

Most are in agreement that fulfilling needs and forming relationships are critical to our plan of happiness. But occasionally we find a "Susan" who has not accomplished the skill of meeting people. As critical as the need for friends is, many of us are not all that competent in forming friendships. American research shows that people claim to have about fifteen "friends." But when asked to focus only on the number of relationships that provide the type of reinforcement suggested by Maslow, the number drops dramatically to around 6. This is an average, and many will admit to having only one or two close friends.[4]

It is estimated that there are between five and six billion people that all require friendships in the world. We will have access to only a small part of that population, but since everyone is looking to fulfill the basic needs outlined above, there are hundreds of potential contacts and friends to be made. Many books have been written about forming relationships, suggesting that the average person must follow a simple procedure for building friendships: First, we must make the effort to speak up. Find someone who has a moment, and start a conversation.

To make an acquaintance, first learn their name, then say it enough times in the first conversation to remember who they are when you meet again. Eye contact is vital. When you look someone in the eye, it controls their attention, but an overdose can become a stare, driving them away. Use eye contact in small doses, but maintain it throughout the conversation.

Use your nonverbal skills. A genuine smile is important. Lean forward a bit; nod the head casually, but in a positive, relaxed way. A little humor in good taste is always welcome.

People like to talk about themselves, but they also want to know the basics about you. However, personal disclosure, your problems, gripes, and negative attitudes are not welcome.

The most critical part of forming friendships is to find the time for communication. Find a relaxed time for three or four occasions to have a light, casual, but positive and fun discussion. As events progress, move from acquaintanceship to exploring mutual interests, then provide opportunities to build on these interests to form mutual experience of enjoyed events.

Above all, this is not a taskmaster requirement of forcing our attentions on an uncooperative, unlucky passerby. This is an opportunity to connect two willing persons for a potential positive experience. We all want friends.

Davis and Todd[5] found we regularly *expect* that being a friend demands someone who is honest, open, shows affection, tells their secrets and problems, gives us needed help, trusts us and is trustworthy themselves, shares time and activities with us, treats us with respect, and obviously values our friendship.

However, the basic *rules* of good friendship are: a good friend holds a good conversation, does not disclose confidences to others, refrains from public criticism, repays debts, and swaps favors. High quality friendship also includes support, trust, and confiding personal information.[6]

It should be noted that friendships require an *exchange* of such communication. A critical factor is that each person in the friendship should have a part in contributing to decisions, attitudes, and opinions. Openness and honesty provide opportunities for depth and strengthening of the friendship bond.

A true friendship is *voluntary* for both parties. The strength of the bond increases over time and contact. The longer the relationship, the more trusting, committed, and valuable the relationship. A long relationship provides an alliance, offering emotional stability, problem solving capacity, and the ability to relieve stress and develop companionship.

Relationships—Self Disclosure

Relationships are built on interactions. The more sincere, honest, and open the interactions, the stronger and more lasting the relationship. Much of our "getting acquainted" communication, however, is small talk-about the weather, sports, class assignments, movies, work, television, and so on. Light conversation usually does not provide a means for us to learn who we are, fulfill our interpersonal needs, or allow for growth in our relationships. This requires a disclosure of information we reserve for "special" people we define as friends.

In order to fulfill the rules of a strong friendship, each of us must participate in a process known as **self disclosure,** the voluntary sharing of information about ourselves that another person is not likely to know. It can be as simple and unthreatening as telling our name or as complex and threatening as revealing deep feelings.

To be an effective communicator who discloses information to build a bond of friendship, we must explore our self-concept—what we believe and value in our own life. This fits the category Maslow referred to as our self-esteem, or our self concept.

Chapter 3 discussed our process of perceiving information about our surroundings, culture, and lifestyle. Our perceptions are stored in our memory banks, but that storage includes a value placed on our interpretation of our personal culture. As individuals we create a set of "bylaws" about our society and surroundings. These laws create for us a set of rules on how we *believe we should act.* These laws not only attempt to direct our actions, but also help direct us to people we consider similar. We then develop friendships with them, want to be with them, and begin to act like they act.

As we determine the kind of person we wish to be, we place a value on these "bylaws." They govern everything from what we eat or drink to how long we sleep, the activities we will do or avoid, what we will study, places we visit, and even the thoughts we should entertain. Each regulation is given a value, and its importance often directs how well we fit our own code of ethics.

We then "measure" ourselves by comparing our own behavior against our bylaws. Our self-evaluation is given a score for success to determine how well we are actually becoming the person we wish to be. As we establish a value of ourselves based upon our self-imposed standard, we come up with a score of self worth, or self-concept.

By following this strategy, we build up or tear down our image of self-worth by creating value statements about ourselves. Some are degrading, others uplifting. We seek outside criticism to reinforce these statements. We then seek out people who function within our own "satisfactory" self. We accept values of what we "wish" or "want" our actions and behavior to be. These friends are considered "successful" and help us maintain our self-worth. Their association becomes highly valued.

Some danger signs involving friendship should be reviewed. Sometimes the error of stereotyping enters the scene, and we evaluate friendships based upon family surname, or school attended, or church membership and not upon performance and behavior. We fail by ignoring individual character talents and behavior. Sometimes we create bonds based on what we *wish* were traits we desire, and imagine vicarious experiences we desire. We associate with football players, not because we can ever be one, but so we can pretend. We marry a partner we perceive is weaker than we are because we imagine the pleasure of control or misdirected power, and again fail the friendship goal.

As we practice building and disclosing our self concept, the better we know ourselves, and the easier it is to make friends. The more of self we disclose, the more we strengthen the friendship bonds. However, a warning is necessary: *The more of self we disclose, the more we risk destroying the bond.* We share our weaknesses and shortcomings with others, counting on the assumption they will not pass on such damaging information to others. We perform the communication, hoping those we confide in will not destroy us with others, but help us with our problems. We trust our friend not to share personal information, but use it to help us. Our friend extends the same trust. *Trust is the glue that cements the friendship.*

Friendships then become a part of building our self concept. Philosopher Eric Hoffer stated that "we are what other people say we are. We know ourselves chiefly by hearsay." Educators Aaron Bleiberg and Harry Leubling stated it well: "I am not what I think I am. I am not what you think I am. I am what I think you think I am!"

If we find ourselves with only one or two friends, we can draw some inferences about our level of interpersonal communication:

1. We disclose very little of ourselves. Our communication is limited to small talk, and we do not receive, nor do we share Maslow's fulfilled need to build friendships, love, self esteem, or self actualization.
2. We disclose other's behavior too harshly—we impose our "bylaws" on them and give them no choice to be themselves.
3. We disclose too many negative characteristics. No one wants to be a friend to someone who has nothing good to say about himself.
4. We disclose too many conflicts with the existing culture. This gives the view we think we are better than everyone else.
5. Our acceptance of the friend's personal "bylaws" is too limited. We do not give them a chance to be themselves.
6. Our success or failure of our friendship bonding is often reflected in our attitude: We validate self-fulfilling prophecy. We get what we say we will get.

Rhetorical Sensitivity

According to communication scholars Roderick Heart and Don Burks, **rhetorical sensitivity** is a form of communication that can be applied to situations in which too much self-disclosure can be damaging. It represents a cautious approach to exchanging information while developing relationships.[7] Rhetorically sensitive people balance their self-interest with the interests of others. They adjust their communication to take into account the beliefs, values, and mood of the other person. This does not mean changing your own view or position to their beliefs, but it does mean finding an effective way to communicate your ideas without offending or hurting the other person. Honest self-disclosure can do harm if it is stated in a way that damages the relationship.

Rhetorically sensitive individuals generally display the following attributes:

1. They accept personal complexity; every person is made up of many selves: for example one could be a mother, daughter, Asian American, an abuse victim, a student a consumer.
2. They are flexible and avoid rigidity in communicating with others.
3. They do not change their own values, but they can communicate them in a variety of ways to avoid offending others.
4. They sense when it is appropriate to communicate something and when not to.[8]

Rhetorically sensitive people understand self-disclosure and know how to adapt their messages to a particular audience and situation.

General Conclusions about self-Disclosure

Research findings support these general conclusions about self-disclosure, whatever the interaction level obtained in a relationship:

1. Disclosure increases with increased relational intimacy.
2. Disclosure increases when rewarded—the reward outweighs the risk of disclosing.
3. Disclosure increases with the need to reduce uncertainty in a relationship.
4. Disclosure tends to be reciprocal—when one person in a relationship increases self-disclosure, the other person will typically follow suit.
5. Women tend to disclose personal information more often than men do.
6. Women seem to disclose more with those to whom they are close, whereas men seem to disclose more with those whom they trust.
7. Disclosure is culturally regulated by norms of appropriateness.

Guidelines for Appropriate Self-Disclosure:

1. Use reasoned self-disclosure. Although open and honest relationships are desirable, it is important to recognize situational constraints. Too often national news and justification for revealing truth exceeds wisdom and common sense. Self-disclosure should be limited to the immediate situation, and be used with caution, making sure the ultimate conclusion does not destroy the process at the expense of being brutally honest. Use wisdom in all things.
2. Make self-disclosure a two-way process. Relationships built on one-sided exchanges are not enduring, meaningful, or healthy. People are more likely to disclose information when they feel safe and when their open communication is positively received. It also needs to be voluntary and reciprocal. Each party will feel safer if both are involved in the process. Once a mutual give-and-take is established, disclosures increase, trust increases, and the bonds of friendship are strengthened.
3. *Match self-disclosure to the situation and to the person.* Personal disclosure provides the risk of rejection. We minimize this risk by carefully matching the disclosure to the person and the situation. Develop the disclosure slowly, carefully, using both verbal and non verbal cues. Disclosing too much too soon or disclosing to the wrong person can lead to embarrassment and pain—and sometimes to serious harm.
4. *Take Diversity into Account.* The appropriateness of and the level of self-disclosure varies by culture, group, and individual. The Japanese culture, for example, does not foster self-expression in the same way U.S. or Korean cultures do. Consider these differences as you decide how to disclose personal information.
5. *Avoid indiscriminate self-disclosure.* Once you disclose something, you cannot take it back, though you may try to qualify what you have said.

6. *Be positive.* Avoid negative disclosures about people and issues, particularly in newly formed relationships. Negative disclosure can be a real turnoff as well as a tremendous drag on any relationship.

Chapter 8: Analysis and Application Exercises

1. Engage the same stranger in conversation on at least four separate occasions for the duration of at least fifteen minutes each time. The conversation should be limited and private. The conversation can be about anything; the critical factor is number of occasions and the duration of time. Upon completion, define the results in terms of establishing a bonding relationship. What progress was made in becoming friends? How did the concepts of disclosure and trust play into the conversation? Will there be other contacts with this individual? How did your perceptions of this person change over the course of conversations? How did the conversation change from one meeting to another?
2. Describe an interpersonal relationship you currently have. Explain how you are interdependent; list a few of your consistent patterns of interaction, and describe how the relationship has developed over time.
3. Write a short paper based upon your current "best" friend. How does your communication with that person differ from how you talk to a teacher, a stranger, a parent, and a clerk at a store?
4. Which members of your family are you more likely to self-disclose more information to and why? How does trust influence self-disclosure? Do you agree that self-disclosure should be reciprocal? Why or why not?

References

1. M.L. Knapp and A.L. Vangelisti, *Interpersonal Communication and Human Relationships*, 3rd Ed. (Boston: Allyn and Bacon, 1996), 31.
2. C.R. Berger and R.J. Calabrese, "Some Explorations in Initial Interactions and Beyond: Toward a Developmental Theory of Interpersonal Communication," *Human Communication Research* 1 (1975): 98-112; C.R. Berger, "Response—Uncertain Outcome Values in Predicted Relationships: Uncertainty Reduction Theory Then and Now," *Human Communication Research 13* ((1986): 34-38.
3. A.H. Maslow, *Motivation and Personality*, 2nd ed. (New York: Harper & Row, 1970), 35-150.
4. S. Duck, "Our Friends, Ourselves," *Bridges, Not Walls*, 6th ed. (Boston: McGraw-Hill, 2006), 327-338.
5. K.E. Davis and M. Todd, "Assessing Friendship: Prototypes, Paradigm Cases, and Relationship Description," in S.W. Duck and D. Perlman (eds) *Understanding Personal Relationships*. (London: Sage, 1985).
6. Duck, Ibid., p. 330.
7. R.P. Hart and D.M. Burks, "Rhetorical Sensitivity and Social Interaction," *Speech Monographs*, 39 (1972): 75-91.
8. S.W. Littlejohn, *Theories of Human Communication*, 4th ed. (Belmont, Calif.: Wadsworth, 1992), 112.

CHAPTER 9

Small Group Decision Making

LEARNING OBJECTIVES

1. Give three reasons people participate in the small group process of decision making.
2. List the basic steps of the reflective thinking process, and explain how each step is used in solving a problem.
3. A problem solving group develops in stages. List and explain the five stages of personal development experienced in participating in the small group decision making process.
4. Identify and explain participant roles during the problem solving process.
5. Identify and explain the differences among leadership styles as used in the small group process.
6. Explain various approaches to leadership.
7. Identify the impact of roles, information, and power upon the success of the group in solving problems.

CHAPTER 9: Overview

The chapter defines groups and discusses why people join groups. The chapter provides a detailed discussion of how groups are formed, the roles of participants, and the requirements of successful decision making. The process of problem solving, including methods of analyzing a problem, stating the question for discussion, and reviewing the reflective process is reviewed. The concept of leadership and leadership style, along with its implications of successful group process, is explained.

Space Shuttle Challenger

The **Space Shuttle *Challenger* disaster** occurred over theAtlantic Ocean, off the coast of central Florida, at 11:39 a.m. on January 28, 1986. The Space Shuttle disintegrated seconds into its flight after an O-ring seal in its right solid rocket booster failed. The seal failure caused a flame leak from the solid rocket booster, which impinged upon the adjacent external booster fuel tank and everything suddenly exploded.

A decision had been made by the small group who gave the instruction to launch. The initial launch was scheduled six days earlier, but had been postponed because of potential problems. But NASA was reluctant to cancel the flight again because public support was failing for their project, and a successful event was needed quickly. Engineers had known since 1977 that the O-ring construction had a fatal flaw. However, based on the fact that the Challenger had flown nine successful flights, concerns from engineers warning about the dangers of the flight were ignored. The Challenger, with all 7 crew members, disintegrated 73 seconds into the flight.

The "Rogers Commission," another group investigating the disaster, gave nine recommendations NASA had to fulfill before another flight was authorized some six years later.[1]

Figure 9.1 The iconic image of Space Shuttle Challenger's smoke plume after its breakup 73 seconds after launch. The accident caused the death of all seven crew members of the STS-51-L mission.

Why Study Small Group Process?

Modern organizations are undergoing major transformations to better use human potential through small group processes. The concept that "two heads are better than one," and the idea that the pooling of resources, knowledge, and ideas produces better, more reliable, and more creative results have dictated the decision making process for new products, and even work satisfaction. The Gallup organization reported over 1 million workers and 80,000 managers of all types of organizations, both profit and non-profit, desire work that includes team problem-solving and group involvement.[2]

Small groups provide solutions to problems, invent new ideas, or build major projects. These are rarely done by one person. Space flight itself could not happen from the mind of one individual. Being part of the human race requires we work with others to make decisions and accomplish great feats.

Current research has found that most groups are better at making decisions than are individuals. In one study, groups outperformed even their best individual members 97% of the time.[3] Each member of a group brings a unique set of experience, knowledge, and viewpoint that interacts with another person's background, producing a collage of developing ideas, results, and solved problems.

By properly understanding intelligent problem solving, anyone can develop better solutions than did the Challenger group. There are many potential disadvantages to group decision making. Groups are generally slower making decisions. Sometimes decisions are made for the wrong reasons, ignoring and even denying careful examination of alternatives for personal reasons or in fear, of insulting a superior's chosen idea. This is referred to as "groupthink," (See Chapter 10) a term made famous by the ill-fated invasion of Cuba when U.S. Military. Secretary of Defense Robert McNamara pushed through the invasion of the Bay of Pigs in Cuba. The defense department made the decision without the proper use of group process.[4] A collection of people making wrong decisions is not a proper definition of group problem solving.

What Is A Group?

A group is not just a number of people gathered in the same place. To qualify as a group, a collection of people must be related in six ways:

1. *Perceptions:* Do the members make an impression on one another?
2. *Motivation:* Are there rewards for being together?
3. *Goals:* Do the persons have a common purpose?
4. *Organization:* Does each person have some role or task?
5. *Interdependence:* Must each person depend on the others for his or her efforts to be successful?

6. *Interaction:* Is the number of persons small enough so that each person can communicate with every other person?[5]

This could describe a football team, a taskforce, a sales group working in a fast food restaurant, or a collection of students given a classroom assignment. People standing at a corner waiting for a bus, for example, meet some of the criteria of a group. They have a common purpose of looking for a ride; they may interact; they may make an impression on one on another; they may even get some satisfaction from the fact that they do not have to stand alone. But they are not interdependent and they do not take on roles or tasks assigned by the group. They do share a certain basic goal such as getting to a given destination safely. But they do not expect to interact in the future and usually do not perceive themselves as a part of a group. However, if the bus suddenly ran over one of the group, their status would change radically, with the objective of administering service and protection to others.

A group exists as something apart from the individuals who belong to it. Just as twelve lines, when put in the proper relationship, form a cube, several individuals forming a relationship to work on a problem become a group. Just as lines disappear when arranged in the shape of a cube, individuals disappear into a group when confronting a task.

Group Formation: Why Do People Join Groups?

Think about the groups you have joined: student organizations, clubs, teams, religious groups, social groups, work groups, groups of friends. Why did you join them in the first place? Research suggests that at least five reasons explain why people join groups:

1. Groups form to fill the need to have companionship, attention, and a feeling of acceptance by others. Project yourself into the situation of Susan, discussed in chapter 8. The thing most frightening to Susan was to force herself to join others. She was totally alone; a prospect not appealing to anyone.
2. Groups provide the manpower, motivation and ideas that make things happen. Groups do things that individuals cannot do. Groups perform tasks, develop policy, solve problems, make complex decisions, and the list goes on. There are power, resources, ideas, finances, and synergy not available to individuals.
3. Groups can provide multiple sources for resources, information, knowledge, even personnel not available to one individual.
4. Groups provide a safety net to protect our work, ideas, and activity. The old saying that there is safety in numbers is a fact of life. Groups are formed specifically for that purpose: neighborhood watch groups, civil air patrol, search and rescue and many other agencies are examples.
5. Groups help build our personal image or self concept (see Chapter 5). The status of the group varies, and as we join more specialized groups, our self image changes. We build our career, personality, and even our pleasures by the groups we select.[6]

Groups form for many reasons. Obviously, the procedure for a group giving therapy for psychological problems will require different skills, atmosphere, instruction, and behavioral structuring than will a group trying to decide whether to attack Cuba at the Bay of Pigs, or initiate stem cell research. The one obvious point is that when a group forms, the cohesive factor motivating them and keeping them together is a **common goal.**

But a common goal is not the only requirement. A group gathered together to watch the leader do all the work is not a problem solving group. Yet this is the most frequent complaint from students regarding groups: they are a waste of time—students feel they can do more on their own. The reason: they have not formed a truly constructive group. To achieve the success and effectiveness of a group process, including satisfaction with the work and conclusions of a group, we must return to the definitions of a true problem solving group.

A successful group must become Interdependent.

The life of a group is much like a living organism: each participant must receive satisfaction for belonging. There is almost a sequence of how this process is achieved.

1. First, there must be recognition and immediate gratification for belonging to the group. No one remains where they feel unwanted. Each person engages others to satisfy his own need: harm-avoidance, acceptance, a feeling of belonging, and a way of becoming self-fulfilled.
2. The second need is to convince the individual there is personal growth in the group. Without a commitment for all persons to maintain the group, insecurity is generated limiting personal growth. There must be a strengthening commitment to group goals and objectives.
3. There must be evidence that progress is being made in solving the problem. Nothing is so frustrating as developing the agenda and defining the terms at every meeting. True messages of progress must be achieved.
4. As the solution progresses, each participant must be able to claim ownership for part of the solution. Each person must be able to set personal goals pursuant to finalizing the final objective. Everyone must be able to define their portion of ownership in the final project.
5. By feeling satisfied with a successful conclusion, the group as a unit becomes both source and recipient of new capabilities and more complex tasks. It is a consensus, or group concept of excellence achieved.[7]

A successful group participant must become committed.

Each participant must be involved and uniformly trusted. The group process is much like personality development. We first must define our personal role, be accepted by others, accept them, then sacrifice all for a term referred to as consensus, and build team unity and purpose.

A good example of how critical group commitment becomes is to view the reverse. Notice how a successful football team acts as a single unit. No one focuses upon the skills of just one individual. But when failure occurs, we look to blame another team member. We try to define who is more important: the blocker or the ball carrier. Which is the best offense: a pass or a run? Who can lift the most weight? The conclusion is obvious: as we define the unit as a whole, we make progress, but when we tend to fragment tasks to determine success and excellence of outstanding individual performance, we have sacrificed the group objective.

A successful group must be cohesive.

This category is an an extension of commitment. Cohesiveness refers to the attraction group members feel for each other. Cohesive groups stick together, not just for the goal objective, but also in activities beyond the group objective. Cohesiveness is a form of loyalty or commitment.

Care must be taken to not extend cohesiveness beyond excellence in group performance. Incidents mentioned at the beginning of the chapter like the Space Shuttle Challenger Disaster, the Bay of Pigs debacle, and other examples where **groupthink** bypassed good decision making procedure can be self destructive. (See Chapter 10)

A successful group is a small group.

Although there is no perfect number of members for a group, groups of certain sizes seem appropriate for certain kinds of tasks. It is generally agreed that groups should have an odd number of members: 3,5,7, etc. This tends to facilitate overcoming problems of polarization and facilitates consensus. If the group gets too large, individual participation, thus individual worth, is significantly reduced. More success and progress is achieved if groups are kept to small numbers. Large groups should be split into small groups to work on the problem independently.

The larger a group is, the greater the variety of skills and information that will be presented. But as more opinions are presented, the longer the discussion, the greater the conflict, and the larger the amount of frustration and dissatisfaction is experienced. When deciding the size of a group, remember:

1. Large groups reduce the time and amount of individual interaction.
2. Large groups provide a greater opportunity for aggressive members to assert their dominance. As a result, less assertive members may feel isolated and may with draw from the group.
3. Large groups make it difficult to follow a set agenda. It is easy for someone in a large group to switch topics or introduce subjects that are not related to the original topic.

Problem Solving and Decision Making

To solve problems and make decisions, a group must consider alternatives and arrive at a joint conclusion. The most effective approach requires members to organize information that applies to the problem, determine the exact nature of its causes and effects, and consider many aspects and potential solutions. The easiest way to approach this task is to formulate the problem into a written question. The type of question and the way it is stated can assist in narrowing possibilities and suggest answers. Consider the following ways to state a problem:

1. **A question of fact** asks whether something is true or false. Its answer can be verified. How many items of a product have sold? What age is the person buying their first automobile? These types of questions require fact finding and research tasks.
2. **A question of interpretation** asks for the meaning or explanation of something. How does the economy of the state affect tuition? How can athletics contribute to a better education? These types of questions require an opinion after facts have been collected. Often information is sought by authorities who have experienced the effects of factual answers to such questions.
3. **A question of value** asks whether something is good or bad, desirable or undesirable. Which college offers the best education for its students? Do coeducational dormitories provide satisfactory living conditions? Answers usually require a judgment call by the participants after facts have been reviewed. Most often case studies and single events play a big role in the interpretation. Conflict and disagreement are common since judgmental values are often influenced by other factors such as government regulations, financial concerns, or even religious values. The value judgments included in interpretation make consensus difficult because of the emotional involvement in conclusions.
4. **A question of policy** asks for action to be taken. What restrictions should be placed on alcohol consumption on campus? What role should students have in evaluating instructors on campus? How much voice should students have on tuition increases? The degree of discussion is contingent on how policy impacts the participants.

Regardless of what type question is asked, for best results consider the following guidelines about wording any question:

a. The wording should reflect the discussion purpose or task at hand.
b. The wording should focus attention on the real problem.
c. The wording should specify whose behavior is subject to change.
d. The wording should not suggest possible solutions.
e. The wording should avoid emotional language.[8]

Whenever discussion problems center around interpretation and decision making that impacts the lives of participants, group interaction takes on significant implications. People take the discussion more seriously because it means their lives are being impacted. This produces more direct involvement, and more impact on participants after a conclusion has been made.

Most decision making groups desire high acceptance and high quality conclusions. Because this is the case, problem solving groups rather than isolated individuals are recommended to determine solutions and set policy. Groups become critical since acceptance of the solution is much more likely to be accepted when people are involved in formulating a solution. We have already seen that groups tend to produce better-quality solutions than do individuals.

Participant decision making not only can result in high quality decisions and increased acceptance of the solutions, but also may result in increased levels of satisfaction, commitment, and loyalty to the solution and to the group.[9] The process itself becomes part of the solution.

Discussing the Problem

There are many approaches to problem solving, but the basic standard revolves around the following five specific steps developed by the philosopher John Dewey: definition of the problem, analysis of the problem, suggestions of possible solutions, selection of the best solution, and putting the best solution into operation.[10] Here is an outline of a typical problem-solving discussion:

I. Definition of the problem
    A. *Symptoms.* How does the problem show itself, or what are the difficulties?
    B. *Size.* How large is the problem? Is it increasing or decreasing? What results can be expected if the problem is not solved?
    C. *Goal.* What general state of affairs is desired (in contrast to the present unsatisfactory one)?
II. Analysis of the problem
    A. *Causes of the problem.* What causes or conditions underlie the difficulties:
    B. *Present efforts to solve the problem.* What is being done now to deal with the problem? In what ways are these efforts unsuccessful? What hints do they provide for further attacks on the problem?
    C. *Requirements of a solution*
        1. *Direction.* Where shall we attack the problem?
            a. Would an attack on some outstanding symptom be the most fruitful approach?
            b. Is there a cause that would be worthwhile to attack? It would need these two essential characteristics:
                (1) Would its removal substantially eliminate or greatly modify the problem?
                (2) Could its removal be accomplished with facilities—personnel, equipment, finances—that are (or can be made) available?
        2. *Boundaries.* What other values—social customs, laws, and institutions—must not be harmed in attempting to solve this problem?

III. Suggestions of possible solutions:
  A. One possible solution
    1. *Nature.* What, specifically, is the plan?
    2. *Strengths.* In what ways would this plan effectively fulfill the requirements or criteria of a solution? Can notable progress be made,yet stay satisfactorily within the boundaries of a solution?
    3. *Weaknesses.* In what ways would this plan fall short of effectively fulfilling these requirements or criteria?
  B. *Another possible solution*
  C. *Another possible solution*
  D. *Another possible solution*

IV. Selection of the best solution
  A. *Best solution (or solution with modifications).* How does this solution excel the others?
  B. *Part of problem unsolved.* If the solution leaves any part unsolved, why is it still considered the best?

V. Putting the best solution into operation
  A. Major difficulties to be faced
  B. Possible ways of overcoming difficulties
  C. Best way to overcome difficulties

Variations on the Discussion Process:

The analytical process of Dewey is the basis for any problem solving process, for it supplies the logical thought process of discovering the cause of the problem. Then with the proper logical criteria, the best potential solution is chosen to remove the problem. However, variations on the approach can produce a wider diversity of solutions. Here are some examples.

Brainstorming. Brainstorming is a term used to explain a lateral thinking process. Lateral thinking processes encourage the thinker to think outside of his or her regular framework to gain new perspective. The basic idea is to reverse the analytical process, and recommend as many solutions as possible without regard to criteria or logical factors for acceptance. The emphasis is to develop new, creative ideas. The following suggestions should govern a brainstorming discussion:

1. *Put judgment and evaluation aside temporarily.* No criticism is allowed. All ideas are recorded within a "try anything" attitude.
2. *Turn imagination loose, and begin offering results.* The wilder the idea, the better. Quantity is preferred over quality with the assumption that this is the only way to discover the truly creative solution.
3. *Think of as many ideas as you can.* Quantity breeds quality. This incourages multiple approaches and truly divergent thinking.
4. *Seek combination and improvement.* This encourages improving upon someone else's idea, or combining suggestions.
5. *Evaluate all ideas in a more reflective thinking atmosphere.*[11]

Six Thinking Hats. DeBono recommended a method for decision making in groups by assigning a "role-playing" concept to force divergent thinking. Each role or type of thinking is represented by a different colored hat. Those wearing the white hat were asked to be emotionally neutral on the topic. The red hat represented emotions, gut instincts, intuition and feelings. These were the "love" or "hate" people. The black hat represents in-depth analytical thinking, emphasizing the limitations or cons of an idea. The yellow hat represents sunny, optimistic, positive thinking.

These are the movers and shakers, hoping for positive outcomes. The green hat represents creativity, new ideas, alternatives, and possibilities, recommending change and nontraditional approaches. The blue hat represents coordination, control, and the discipline to know when to use which hat. The group leader often comes from this group.[12]

Other problem-solving programs are provided by many different authors, each recommending techniques of creative problem solving. To generalize, scholars agree that gathering concerned people together to work on a problem is the best way to improve life.

Virtual Small Groups. Electronic technology has emerged to facilitate group communication across the globe. These include online meetings, user groups, videoconferencing, teleconferencing, webinars, or any number of combinations. The use of virtual meeting technologies has exploded. It is now commonplace in today's workplace, and includes satellite work stations, eliminating the need for a central location for employees. An extension of this idea to small groups is now the norm rather than an exception.

Virtual meetings require a new type of communication and etiquette. Some of the challenges of this new communication include loss of many non-verbal messages, and concentrated emphasis on visual aids such as graphs and photos. By combining teleconferencing with e-mails, faxed documents, and video recording, even legal business can be conducted. It requires more concentration on preparation of materials and staying on track. But its availability provides opportunities for interaction world wide. With thoughtful preparation, virtual groups have the potential to be as effective as face-to-face groups with the advantage of linking people world wide into a single group. The potential seems limitless.

Group Participation: Task, Maintenance, Leadership

To be a productive member of any group, the participant must get involved in the process. There are three general categories of productive participation. If we were to compare humanity to a beehive, we could see the divisions clearly. The majority of bees are workers. Their assigned role is to provide food and protection for the colony. However, there are occupants of the colony called drones. This element could be considered the glue that keeps everything together. They supply the recreation, entertainment, and well-being of the colony. The critical participant is the queen, or leader. These three elements are the essential requirements of a successful small group.

Task Participants. These are people whose major emphasis is to get the job done. These workers are always present, on time, and have completed their assignment. These are the worker bees. Group participants filling this role are people who supply the facts and figures. Their presence provides a supportive climate where movement toward a solution is progress. As participants, they supply material that is descriptive rather than evaluative. They indicate problems associated with things rather than with people. Their focus of attention is on the objective and not on the bad guys. Their emphasis is on setting goals, and working to see goals are met. Their main motivating force is to get the job done.

One problem is that highly motivated people often sacrifice incompetent participants for the good of the cause. They have little tolerance for people who fail to complete their assignment. Task people attempt to use all available means to get the job done, including their use of power, influence, and effort. Their tolerance for those not working as they do is limited and can cause stress within the group.

Maintenance Participants. These are the people who grease the skids. They make life tolerable and the job more fun. Their objective is togetherness and group bonding. If conflicts arise, they are the chief engineers of conflict resolution and compromise. They supply the comic relief, enjoyment, and satisfaction for the group. They emphasize cooperation as the group's first objective. Maintenance needs pertain to intangibles such as atmosphere, structure, role responsibility, praise, and social-emotional control. The key role is that of gatekeeper. As the gatekeeper, the maintenance participant ensures everyone an opportunity to speak and be heard. Some people try to dominate the discussion. When this happens, the gatekeeper helps create more balanced participation by asking questions and directing attention to those offended or reticent to speak.

Maintenance participants are quick to acknowledge others' participation and reinforce their ideas. The maintenance person could also be an encourager and harmonizer. This generally requires good listening behavior—hearing what others say. The good maintenance person is also sensitive to potential tension and stress in the group. The maintenance person tries to mediate conflict, avoid polarization of opinions, and generally keeps peace in the family.

The maintenance participant is the key to building a trust relationship within the group. Much like trust in an interpersonal relationship, without each group participant having trust in the other members, goal accomplishment and satisfaction can never be achieved. Even if the problem is solved, the group will have little satisfaction in the results.

Care must be taken to limit maintenance from completely dominating the group. If all the time is spent making people feel comfortable in the group and enjoying the event, little progress is made toward solving the original problem. Comments like, "we never got to a solution, but we had lots of fun getting there" indicate the purpose of the group was not achieved. A proper balance between task and maintenance is essential for good group process. The achievement of such balance is the role of group leader.

Leadership. A leader is the person at the center of a group's attention, or the person to whom the group members address their messages. For example, in business meetings, the boss is usually the leader, and the employees will center their attention on the boss.

Another way to identify a leader is by the behaviors displayed in guiding a group to its specific goal. When a direction is shown and the group follows that direction toward the goal, a leader has emerged. Implied in the definition of leadership is the concept that the leader has the ability to inspire, motivate, direct, and challenge other group participants. Harvey Robbins and Michael Finley offer the following advice on how to be an effective leader:

1. Project energy.
2. Be involved and involve others.
3. Assist evaluation and change for the group.
4. Persuade and persevere.
5. Look beyond the obvious.
6. Maintain perspective.
7. Utilize pyramid learning (teach others).
8. Target energy on success opportunities.
9. Foster task linkage with others (outside the group).
10. Influence cooperative action.
11. Support Creativity.
12. Take the initiative.
13. Eschew the negative.
14. Never be satisfied (seek continuous improvement.)[13]

Leadership style includes utilizing power and control over group participants. Without going into great detail, power can be basically described as influence and support of people. The more support a person has, the greater that person's power base. There are three basic ways a person achieves enough power to become a successful group leader. Researchers have identified the three primary styles of leadership as autocratic, democratic, and laissez-faire styles.[14] Each style has a distinctive approach to the communication occurring in the group. (see Table 9:2)

Table 9.2

Leadership Styles: A Comparison

AUTOCRATIC	DEMOCRATIC	LAISSEZ-FAIRE
Keeps complete control	Shares control	Gives up cotrol
Sets policy and makes al decisions for the group	Involves members in setting policy and making decisions' does not make any decisions without group members	Gives total freedom to group members make polcies and decisions; gets involved only when called upon
Defines tasks and assigns them to members	May guide task assignment to be sure work is accomplished, but allows members to divide work	Completely avoids participation

Autocratic Leaders are micro-managers. The effect of such a leader is often very rapid, direct, and with little reflective thinking utilized in the decision process. This type of leader is needed in crisis situations for rapid action, aggressiveness and control. Under stressful and confusing events, this is a "take charge" person dispensing confidence as well as advice. Immediate results are expected. Power is usually achieved by appointment, and held together by fear and threat rather than by willing support.

If autocratic leadership bypasses in-depth examination and reflective thinking; low satisfaction levels are expected from participants. Elements of fear and anxiety are expected from group participants because questioning of leadership decisions is usually followed by some type of retribution: removal from the group, reprisal, or reprimand. The end-product can be groupthink decisions or temporary stopgap measures. As the group continues, conflict, contesting for group leadership, and competition can be expected. Because of the unrest within the group structure, autocratic groups tend to be unstable.

If an autocratic leader governs a group that discusses issues not immediately perceived as critical for participants, many participants will be slow to action, or even withdraw from participation, depending upon the leader to do all the work. If the leader assigns the work, only minimum effort will be expended by participants, with little chance of "taking the risk" of a creative proposal.

Democratic Leaders are usually elected. As a result, an actual vote number translates into power strength of the leader. The major emphasis of this style provides each person in the group an equal share of influence. The group leader posses influence over the group by mutual consent: the members of the group have relinquished their influence to their chosen leader. The most obvious result is that decisions can be prolonged because much discussion is required before decisions are given. Because everyone has a part of the solution, the decision is deemed more creative, sound, and valuable.

Since all participants have ownership in decisions, satisfaction in the solution is much greater, thus support by all concerned is much greater. In a business community, productivity and improvement is often expected, even with lower quality decisions because the group supports the conclusion more completely.

Not only is satisfaction greater in a democratic group, individual participation in the discussion is greater. Tasks are more readily accepted by all, and a "group commitment," even proselytism, might be observed. The drawbacks of democratic processes include long time delays, getting off the subject, and failing to address the immediate problem because of fear of upsetting someone.

Laissez-faire Leader. Everyone in the group has equal power. No one steps forward to claim ownership of the group. There is total freedom for all participants, and as a result most participation is avoided. No change is anticipated. This includes energy levels, productivity and creativity. This type of leadership is used when group members do not want or need a rigid structure to accomplish their goal, if one is even set. If such a group needs a leader, they would probably nominate one by acclamation, not anticipating any discussion, change, or renovation. The leader would merely be a contact person serving as a gatekeeper to pass information, policy, and data on to all members of the group. In most cases the group does not desire or require any assistance, and so it remains leaderless, with little change in productivity, output, or policy.

Evaluating Small Group Performance

To ensure success, every group must periodically evaluate its effectiveness. The evaluation can take place at any time or at the end of one task and before another begins. Evaluation is also important in classroom exercises. As students learn about group communication, they need their instructor's feedback and should also evaluate themselves. Such a self-evaluation should take into account the following questions:

1. Are we using our time efficiently? If not, why not?
2. Does everyone have an opportunity to participate?
3. Are some people dominating the discussion?
4. Are people listening to what others are saying?
5. Is each person bringing adequate information and research to the discussion?
6. Is the atmosphere free from personal conflict?
7. Does the group communication stay within the agenda?
8. Are the members happy about what is taking place in the discussion? If not, why not?
9. Do we set realistic goals for our meetings?
10. Do we get things accomplished? If not, why not?

For an evaluation to produce results, its findings must be made known to the group. A crucial requirement for such sharing is a non-threatening atmosphere. The leader and members must examine all issues without becoming defensive. The group's success is related to everyone's cooperation. If the group is not getting its job done, or if members are unhappy, corrective steps must be taken. Otherwise people will lose interest, and the group disintegrates or becomes unproductive and dysfunctional.

Chapter 9: Analysis and Application Exercises

1. Observe a group on three separate occasions for a period of time. Determine :
   A. What major objectives or tasks the group is reviewing.
   B. What kind of leadership style is being used?
   C. What "roles" did group members play in their participation?
   D. What problems in group process were observed? How could they have been corrected?

2. If you were the CEO of a company selling health insurance, or new cars, or even a grocery store manager, what major considerations would you consider as you put together your collection of workers? How would you organize them?
3. What was the most productive work or community group you were ever a part of? What made it so? Try to identify the factors that contributed to its productivity.
4. How does leadership emerge in a group that has no history? Give examples from groups you have been part of or observed. Can you think of situations where leadership did not follow the norms presented in this chapter?

References

1. "Space Shuttle Challenger Disaster," Wikipedia//http.
2. M. Buckingham & C. Coffman, *First Break all the Rules,* New York: Simon & Schuster, 1999.
3. L.K. Michaelson, W.E. Watson, and R.H. Black, "A Realistic Test of Individual Versus Group Consensus Decision Making," *Journal of Applied Psychology,*74 (1989) 834-839.
4. I. Janis, *Victims of Groupthink,2nd ed.* (Boston: Houghton Mifflin, 1982). I.L. Janis & L. Mann, *Decision Making: A Psychological Analysis of Conflict, Choice, and Commitment.* (New York: Free Press), 1977.
5. M.E. Shaw, *Group Dynamics: The Psychology of Small Group Behavior, 2nd Ed.* (New York: McGraw Hill, 1976), 6-10.
6. P.B. Paulus, ed., *Psychology of Group Influence, 2nd ed.*(Hillsdale, N.J.:Erlbaum, 1989).
7. T.M. Mills, "A Paradigm for Groups," *The Sociology of Small Groups* (Englewood Cliffs, N.J: Prentice-Hall, Inc. 1967) 101-118.
8. R.V. Harnack, T.B. Fest, and B.S. Jones, *Group Discussion: Theory and Technique,* 2nd ed (kEnglewood Cliffs, J.J.: Prentice Hall, 1977), 153-54.
9. S.L. Tubbs, *A Systems Approach to Small Group Interaction, 9th ed.* (New York: McGraw Hill, 2007) 348-349.
10. J. Dewey, *How We Think* (Lexington, Mass: Heath, 1933).
11. Tubbs, Ibid, p. 283.
12. Ibid, p. 287.
13. H. Robbins & M. Finley, *Why Teams Don't Work.* (Princeton, NJ Peterson's/ Pacesetter Books, 1995) 94-100.
14. R.K. White and R. Lippitt, *Autocracy and Democracy: An Experimental Inquiry* (New York: Harper & Row,1960), 26-27.

CHAPTER 10 Avoiding Groupthink

LEARNING OBJECTIVES

When Students have completed this chapter and lesson, they should be able to:

1. Know the dimensions of group processing–social and task–and how they relate to the development of groupthink.
2. Understand how groupthink develops and be able to identify it when they see it in small group interactions.
3. Be able to arrest groupthink when it happens through the tactful use of conflict.

CHAPTER 10: Overview

This chapter explores how small groups sometimes make faulty decisions due to a phenomenon called groupthink, which was originally identified and explored by a Yale social psychologist named Irvin Janis.[1] Groupthink is a destructive force that usually results in bad decisions and often results in disastrous ones. Since much of what we do in our personal and professional lives is done in group settings, the topic is important for us to understand.

In this chapter, groupthink is defined and explored in some detail. This includes the circumstances under which it occurs, why it occurs, how it occurs, and the results it produces. We also explore how and when to take steps to prevent it. Janis' theory of groupthink provides an excellent heuristic for both understanding groupthink and preventing it.

Defining Groupthink

When the space shuttle Challenger exploded in midair during its launch from Kennedy Space Center in Florida on January 28, 1986, it shocked our nation. Not only did seven brave astronauts die, but also the reputation of NASA as a zero-tolerance-for-error organization. How could this happen? President Ronald Reagan launched an immediate investigation. After four months of testimony, the findings (stated in highly-technical terms) blamed the leak of hot gases through faulty O-rings. But how were such faulty rings allowed to be used in the first place? The presidential commission blamed that on a highly-defective decision making process.

Irving Janis, who had previously written a book on groupthink, suggested that this was a classic case of it. He was well-known for his use of this theory to explain a number of national scandals: "Roosevelt's complacency before Pearl Harbor, Truman's invasion of North Korea, Kennedy's Bay of Pigs fiasco, Johnson's escalation of the Vietnam War, Nixon's Watergate break-in, and Reagan's Iran-Contra scandal."[2] We could add others to this list since that time: Clinton's failure to arrest Osama Bin Ladin prior to the 911 tragedy and Bush's invasion of Iraq. In all of these cases, groups of people were involved in the decision making process, and somehow they ended up making unproductive (and some even disastrous) decisions. All of them, it seems, had engaged in groupthink.

Groupthink is the feeling of invulnerability, naive optimism, and moral potency which may arise in a group. The term applies only to negative group thinking, and occurs under identifiable conditions.

To fully understand how groupthink occurs, one must first understand how small groups work, which was the subject of our previous chapter. In particular, we need to understand the dimensions of group processes that were identified by Aubrey Fisher3 (see Figure 10.1).

Dimensions of Small Groups

Figure 10.1

The Social Dimension	**The Task Dimension**
Output: Cohesion	Output: Productivity

All groups have both a social and a task dimension. The output (result) of the social dimension is *cohesion*—the ability of the group to stick together and work together. The output of the task dimension is *productivity*—the ability of the group to finish their assigned task or accomplish the purpose for which they came together. Both of these dimensions are important. If the group has no cohesion it is doubtful they will ever fully achieve their task. If a group is focused only on the social dimension it is doubtful they will be productive. Indeed, when this happens, they are engaging in groupthink.

Groupthink, then, can also be defined as "cohesion gone bad"—when a group becomes so focused on getting along, on agreeing with each other, on maintaining their social status with each other, that they give insufficient (or no) attention to the task. It becomes secondary to their "groupness." As Janis said:

"The more amiability and esprit de corps among members of a policy-making in-group, the greater is the danger that independent critical thinking will be replaced by groupthink. . . . The social constraint consists of the members' strong wish to preserve the harmony of the group, which inclines them to avoid creating any discordant arguments or schisms."[4]

Common Symptoms of Groupthink

When groupthink occurs, some common elements are often manifest. The following list is a general summary of a much longer list originally identified by Janis.

- *A feeling of moral potency.* Because of their assumed cohesion and unanimity of thought, group members assume that whatever they do together will be right.
- *A feeling of invulnerability.* The feeling that nothing can go wrong so long as we stick together.
- *Dehumanization of the opposition.* Research shows that the best way to engender unity is to define a common enemy. In the case of groupthink, the enemy is anybody who might disagree with the group's decisions or actions. One manifestation of this is name-calling—referring to the opposition with stereotypes and dehumanizing names: geeks, pigs, fools, idiots, etc..
- *Group censorship.* Gatekeepers within the group withhold information from the group, coming from the outside world, with which they do not agree.
- *Personal censorship.* Not wishing to upset the group's cohesion, or out of fear, group members who disagree stay silent.
- *An illusion of unanimity.* Because those who disagree remain silent, there is an assumed unanimity of thought. Silence is interpreted as agreement.

Conditions Under Which Groupthink Often Occurs

Groupthink can occur in any group at any time. But there are some conditions under which it is likely to occur and under which group members must be especially careful to avoid it.

Highly cohesive groups. When the people in a group were already highly cohesive before the group was formed, it is much more likely that they will engage in groupthink. Think of those situations where you have been placed in a group at school with someone who is your good friend. What was more important to you—your cohesion with your friend or the quality of the group's decision? It's highly likely (and maybe even appropriate) that your cohesion mattered more. But it will definitely increase the chances that you will do groupthink rather than good, solid decision making in the group. This is why your instructors may take measures when forming groups to make sure you and your friends are separated.

Highly insulated groups. Groups that are cut off from external sources engage in groupthink more easily and with fewer chances that it will be identified and mitigated. Unfortunately, in some cases (even for good reasons) groups must operate in this way due to issues of privacy or potential bias, such as in a courtroom jury. Where possible, groups should not cut themselves off from those outside the group, nor seek to keep their work exclusively within the group. This can easily lead to groupthink. And if groupthink arises in a group that must be isolated, members should take care to keep it from continuing.

When a vocal member initially pushes for a specific solution. Especially if the person is a well-liked or feared opinion leader, the group may feel some pressure to go along in order to get along. Also, sadly, group members sometimes just want to get the task over with and aren't really concerned with the quality of the decisions. Going along in those circumstances just seems more efficient and less trouble.

Crisis situations. When high stakes are involved, the pressure on decision makers increases greatly. Sometimes this can lead to a reluctance for a group member to question an idea or decision. "If everybody else agrees on something, who am I to disagree?" Also, "People are counting on us to decide what to do. We need to make a decision and get on with it." Another crisis circumstance arises when the group finds itself under a time deadline and just wants to make a decision—any decision—so they can finish the task on time. This happens all too often in school groups who waste some of their initial group time and then find themselves facing an imminent due date for the assignment.

To illustrate how these conditions affect decision making, and how they sometimes are combined to create an even greater chance that groupthink will occur, consider the following story.

On one occasion, a jury retired to deliberate on a sexual assault case. There had been some evidence that the man was involved in such an activity. There had also been some evidence that his accuser disliked this neighbor very much and made a number of attempts for a variety of reasons to get him out of the neighborhood. The jury was charged with looking at the evidence and deciding his fate. As the jury walked into the jury room, one member said very forcefully, "He's guilty as hell. Let's get this over with and go home. I don't want to miss any more episodes of NYPD Blue." Several other jury members, for their own reasons, said, "Yes, let's not string this thing out. We've got things to do." The jury foreperson, who is charged with making sure the jury follows the instructions of the judge and makes a sound decision, had to intervene by saying, "I really don't care how many episodes of NYPD Blue you miss. This man's liberty is at stake, as is the safety of our community. We're going to stay here until we've considered all the evidence and rendered a reasonable judgment." And they did.

In this circumstance, the group was isolated, had a strong opinion stated early on by a vocal member, and was in a crisis situation where a man's freedom and the city's safety were at stake. Had the jury foreman not put an end to it immediately, groupthink most assuredly would have occurred.

Stages of Groupthink

Consider the following illustration of how groupthink begins and progresses.

The stages are numbered in a commonly occurring sequence. While groupthink is not necessarily linear, and not all of these stages will always occur, this is a typical situation for the development of groupthink.

Let us take an example that actually occurred in a mid-sized American city a few years ago. A group of bus drivers became aware of serious problems with bus maintenance and ended up participating in groupthink rather than properly resolving the issue.

1. **Decision Problems:** Problems are not always easy. Difficulties often arise when making a decision, especially when they have:
   (a) *Moral vs. practical considerations:* The bus drivers knew that they should report the bad brakes on the buses (moral) but they were all part-time drivers and they knew that if the buses were shut down they would be out of work for awhile (practical).
   (b) *The possibility of financial or social backlashes:* Both were clearly present in this situation. If the buses were shut down they would lose money. If anything happened to the children as a result of the bad brakes they would face condemnation and possibly lawsuits.
   (c) *The irony* of this stage of groupthink is that in fear of these consequences, groups sometimes take actions they think will avoid the consequences, but which ultimately are the direct cause of those same consequences.

   And as a result. . . .
2. **Anxiety Is Created:** It feels terrible to be stuck in such a dilemma. These circumstances create very high levels of anxiety in the members with some predictable results.
   (a) *Fear of the perception of incompetence:* Anxiety naturally leads to the fear that others will consider you weak and incompetent. These bus drivers didn't want to look weak in the eyes of their colleagues who were also depending on this income and would also be hurt.
   (b) *The irony* of this stage of groupthink is that in fear of these consequences, group members eventually were perceived as both weak and incompetent—the very perceptions they were trying to avoid.

   Which leads to. . . .
3. **Loss of Self Esteem:** When people feel powerless to resolve an issue they lose self-esteem and the moral conviction that they might otherwise maintain. These bus drivers needed the money to support their families, but could only resolve the problem by doing something that would cut off their income. They felt helpless in this circumstance, and later said so.

   Which leads to. . . .
4. **Concurrence Seeking:** Ultimately, this is why groupthink happens. Feeling anxious and with low self-esteem, group members seek a number of things.
   (a) *Confidence in unity:* Though the bus drivers felt individually powerless, they were renewed in their confidence by the fact that they were not the only ones keeping the secret—"everybody is doing it."
   (b) *Righteousness in unity:* Their confidence was also bolstered by a feeling of moral potency—"everybody can't be wrong," so our decision must be right.
   (c) *Collective rationalization:* Of course, the bus drivers conversed among themselves about the problem and shared their powerless views. "This isn't our fault. Why should we have to lose work because others aren't doing their jobs?" Every new and plausible rationalization is welcomed as a way to relieve the powerlessness they would otherwise feel.
   (d) *Responsibility sharing:* If things turn out badly, we will have the defense that "we" made this decision." No one person will be at fault and it will seem like the logical thing to have done because so many came to that conclusion.

Which leads to. . . .

5.Dehumanization of Enemies: The best way to maintain group unity is dehumanize those who might disagree with us. It relieves us of having to do the harder work of maintaining cohesion through positive activities and means, and it does a number of other things that make us feel better.

(a) *Leads to name calling and stereotypes:* In this case, we will call the administration "incompetent" for not tracking this problem ("it's their job, not mine"), and we will call the mechanics "lazy" and "stupid" for not keeping all of us out of this dilemma ("what's wrong with them, anyway?").

(a) *Releases us from the moral dilemma:* Since those who don't agree with us are less intelligent, less informed, or even stupid, we are not bad people for making the "reasonable" decisions we have made together.

(b) *Alleviates group tension:* It displaces recriminations from the group members to the "enemy"—"it's not our fault, it's theirs, so why should we feel bad?"

And also. . . .

6. Censorship: Groupthink would be dispelled by allowing those who don't agree with the group's decision to have any power in the matter. Therefore, groups engaging in groupthink tend to carefully control what information gets into and out of the group.

(a) *Self-censorship:* Largely because of the perceived need for concurrence with group members, individuals self-censor their doubts or alternative suggestions. This silence, then is often perceived as agreement by the other group members. In this case, the bus drivers each admitted knowing they should inform the administration, but none dared suggest it.

(b) *Group censorship:* The entire conspiracy could be exposed if any one group member started talking to outsiders. So groups engaged in groupthink will often seek reassurances from each other that "nobody's going to talk" to others. Also, little or no information to the contrary will be allowed into their discussions. In the bus drivers' case, there was a feeling that "nobody else could possibly understand" their dilemma, so why even ask?

Which both lead to. . . .

7. Distorted and Inaccurate Perceptions: This is what groupthink really is:

(a) *Only positive information is included:* Censorship leads to the exclusion of any information which does not support the group's conclusion. They did not inquire as to whether the administration would provide other buses or whether they might still be compensated for other activities, out of fear that if the problem were known the would lose their jobs for awhile.

(b) *Possible outcomes are limited to a few alternatives:* Because limited information has been permitted to enter or exit the process, the possible outcomes are limited to a few—perhaps to just one. In the case of these bus drivers, they considered only one alternative: to remain silent.

(c) *Immediate rejection of alternatives:* If any member of the group raises an alternative, they are silenced. The group cannot maintain its concurrence without absolute acceptance by all members of the decision they've already made. Don't confuse them with the facts. That is certainly what happened with these bus drivers, because they all admitted to being afraid to suggest anything else.

And. . .

8.Bad Decisions: Since the information is limited and perhaps even bad, and since their perceptions are flawed as a result, groups who move through each of the steps outlined above will most certainly make a bad (perhaps even a disastrous) decision. While that is not always the case, it is all-too-often the outcome.

(a) *Groups who do groupthink fail to do critical analysis.*
(b) *Groups who do groupthink usually have few or no contingency plans:* We're right, so why bother.

The result in the bus driver case was predictable. Eventually, the brakes on one of the buses failed on a slippery icy road and struck a telephone poll. Several children were hurt. And the very thing that the bus drivers thought they were avoiding–being unemployed–became permanent rather than temporary, as it would have been had they acted properly in the beginning. Worse, lawsuits followed which held not only the administration and mechanics liable for faulty maintenance, but also the bus drivers who engaged in groupthink in an effort to hide the problem.

Conflict: The Solution to Groupthink

Since groupthink generally happens when the social dimension of groups has gone bad, it would follow that the solution to groupthink involves taking the social dimension down a notch. This can best be accomplished through the introduction of conflict. *Conflict*, in communication studies, does not mean fighting; it means disagreeing on actions or conclusions, thus forcing the members to critically think about what they are doing and saying. An example of this is the jury foreman described earlier who put jurors on notice that they were not going to jump to a conclusion but would carefully consider all the evidence. That put an immediate end to any possibility of groupthink in that jury.

We might accomplish the same thing in groups we belong to by questioning things. Sometimes we should do this even if we agree with the conclusion, thus causing the group to consider a little bit more whether they have made a good decision. We might say things like, "I'm not sure I'm completely comfortable with what we've decided" or "Have we considered all the alternatives carefully enough?" Good critical thinking and groupthink do not occur at the same time in groups. If you introduce some tactful conflict you can put an end to any tendency to engage in groupthink.

Chapter 10: Analysis and Application Exercises

1. It is said that a group cannot be productive unless they are cohesive. This suggests that the task dimension of a group cannot be achieved without the social dimension. What about the reverse? Can a group focus on the social dimension and never achieve their task? Why or why not?

2. Think about a group you've participated in where groupthink occurred. How many of the above stages of groupthink did the group pass through? How do you feel about the decisions that were made? When and how, could you have put an end to groupthink in that situation? Explain.

References

1. Janis, Irving (1982). *Groupthink*, 2d ed., Boston: Houghton Mifflin.
2. Griffin, Em (1991), Groupthink of Irving Janis, in *A First Look at Communication Theory*, 3d ed., New York: McGraw-Hill Companies, Inc., 235.
3. Fisher, B. Aubrey (1974). *Small Group Decision-making: Communication and the Group Process*. New York: McGraw-Hill Book Co.
4 Janis, Irving (1972). *Victims of Groupthink*, Boston: Houghton-Mifflin, 198, and Janis, Irving (1979). *Crucial Decisions: Leadership in Policymaking and Crisis Management*, New York: Free Press, 56. Griffin (1991) puts these two statements together to show the consistency of Janis' thinking over the years: *A First Look at Communication Theory*, 237, 509.

CHAPTER 11

Presenting Small Group Communication

LEARNING OBJECTIVES

When students have completed this chapter and lesson, they should be able to:

1. Define small group results and know how to present them to an audience.
2. Explain the importance of roles in group presentations and reasons why people assume them.
3. Describe the behaviors that reduce group productivity.
4. Describe factors affecting group climate.
5. Describe and demonstrate ethical behavior in information presentation.

CHAPTER 11: Overview

This chapter reviews the existence of groups in action: How they are formed, how business is conducted, and the rules of engagement. Guidelines are discussed about group control, and ethics of both conduct and procedure. The use of technology is also discussed, including use of electronic technology as well as PowerPoint® presentation of material.

Definition of Democracy

In the backwash of a terrible war, fear and resentment take the place of courage and hope in many minds. Ideals once firmly established, words once proudly and affectionately used, fall under grave suspicion. At such a time, a bold gesture of affirmation, a clean-cut definition, comes like a gust of fresh air to a fetid room. Seldom does one find this in a bitter congressional investigation, but that was precisely what happened when David Lilienthal answered Senator McKellar of Tennessee during a congressional investigation of the Atomic Energy Commission. After a barrage of emotionally loaded questions about qualifications, impacts, and control of the Commission, Senator McKellar, then seventy seven years old, asking one loaded question after another, finally said: "Well, what are your convictions on communist doctrine?"

The implications were clear: Are you a communist sympathizer? Are you creating impossible barriers for democracy? How dare we trust atomic energy to be placed in the hands of someone so young and inexperienced as you? The witness, who had shown no signs of emotion or anger under McKellar's harangue, suddenly wheeled in his chair to face his antagonist in a voice which was low, but electric with fervor: "I believe—and conceive the Constitution of the United States to rest upon, as does religion—the fundamental proposition of the integrity of the individual; and that all government and all private institutions must be designed to promote and protect and defend the integrity and the dignity of the individual; that that is the essential meaning of the Constitution and the Bill of Rights, as it is essentially the meaning of religion. . . . (anyone who) places arbitrary power over men as a fundamental tenet of government, are contrary to that conception, and therefore, I am deeply opposed to them."

There was complete silence when Lilienthal finished. Then Senator McMahon, the farseeing statesman of atomic energy, said: "I congratulate you on that statement. In my opinion it is the creed of a very real American." The remarks filled newspapers throughout the land. It was recommended for anthologies and for required reading in schools, and was compared with the noblest declarations in all human history.[1]

Reporting results of small group process is one of the major factors determining whether the group experience was satisfying and fulfilling, or whether it was a waste of time. Problem solving procedures, perceptions, nonverbal and verbal communication, forming interpersonal trust, and many other communication principles affect a group's success. A successful problem solving group requires members to respect one another, speak clearly, provide credible information, support and help others, foster a positive climate, listen effectively, intellectually analyze a problem, and hold high ethical standards.

Small group process is an integral part of our lives. Most of our waking hours are spent with some type of group: family clusters, fellow employees, professional organizations, social clubs, civic clubs, political party associations, school groups, and activist organizations help to socially, academically, and culturally involve us with associates who vary in age, education, beliefs, and actions. Groups play a significant role in our every day lives, and the more we know about the dynamics of group communication, the more effective and successful we will be. Their results can change the direction of history, as did David Lilienthal.

Small group communication involves the exchange of information among relatively small number of persons, usually three to twenty, who share a common purpose, such as doing a job, solving a problem, making a decision, or sharing information. How to successfully communicate such information becomes the object of this chapter.

Conducting a Meeting

When a meeting is called to order, the group members begin by introducing themselves and briefly tell their reasons for joining the group or what they hope to accomplish as members. Following introductions, organizing the group is the next step. A secretary is selected to keep a written account of the discussion, important business, and items of business to be discussed later.

To ensure efficiency, procedures must be established, and meetings must be conducted according to a well-organized plan. The best way to accomplish this is by producing an **agenda,** a list of all topics to be discussed during a meeting. The leader usually determines the agenda, either alone or in consultation with the group's members before meeting. Sometimes, at the end of one meeting, the agenda for the next meeting is established.

A typical meeting agenda might look like this:

1. Call to Order.
2. Introduction of new members.
3. Reading, correction, and approval of minutes from previous meeting.
4. Unfinished business.
5. New Business.
6. Announcements.
7. Adjournment.

Not all meetings operate in exactly the same way, but having an agenda should make any meeting run smoother. Classroom groups may not follow a formal structure, but in general, they need a sense of organization and an informal agenda.

GUIDELINES

Planning and Managing a Meeting

1. Identify a purpose, plan an agenda, and disseminate the agenda in advance.
2. Invite only people who need to be there (*not* everyone who might have an opinion on the topic).
3. Establish start, break, and stop times, and stick to them.
4. Have a moderator (leader) keep the discussion on track.
5. Decide what follow-up actions are needed after the meeting, and set deadlines for their completion.
6. Avoid holding unnecessary meetings.
7. Do not let people drone on, dominate, or avoid participation during discussions.
8. Do not allow conversations to wander off the subject.
9. Follow up to make sure that members act on decisions made at the meeting.[2]

Member Participation

A successful group involves all members in the presenttion. The first and most critical member of the group is the leader. The leader's role is to facilitate presentation of materials, while making sure all group members are recognized, heard, and assisted in such a way that each participant feels a part, but does not dominate or misdirect the objectives of the group. (See Chapter 9 for a more detailed analysis of group leadership).

Group participants need to study the meeting's agenda in advance so they will be prepared to contribute. Where more in-depth information or perhaps a more complete presentation of information is necessary, a more formal presentation is recommended. An excellent approach is to present a PowerPoint® directed presentation. (Note below). One of the greatest weaknesses of beginning group participants is their tendency to arrive at meetings unprepared. The group must then either spend time helping them catch up or do without their contributions. Either way, valuable time, effort, and input are lost.

PowerPoint® Presentations.

An excellent way of avoiding many of the pitfalls mentioned above is to have assigned presentations facilitated by PowerPoint® presentations. Such a procedure accomplishes several objectives.

1. Time constraints are more easily managed. The presenter can easily determine how much time the presentation will take.
2. Structure and organization are more easily assured with a well prepared presentation. A logical, well planned presentation is a requirement for successfully presenting a message that is convincing and interesting.
3. Validation, accuracy, and ethical information are more easily controlled by such presentations.
4. Interest levels are generally higher with visual presentations. Technology has made possible better visual aids, which even can include audio and video clips, giving the presentations more appeal.
5. These presentations have become almost a standard requirement because of their efficiency in the business community. They are now accepted as professional presentations.

PowerPoint® presentations themselves, however, can provide many pitfalls and distractions. Key to success is to remember that the group is meeting to solve problems, carry on business, and become enlightened. Sometimes the presenter focuses on the visual aids and not the topic at hand. Some speakers become so enamored generating graphics or creating a jazzy multimedia program that they forget their primary mission: to communicate through the spoken word and through their physical being. Other presenters hide behind their electronic paraphernalia, merely reading the slides to the audience. The primary word of caution is to keep the objective of the message in mind, knowing what you want to communicate, and clearly describing to the audience the purpose of the presentation. Always remember that the PowerPoint® presentation is a visual aid supporting your message. It is not the message!

Many computer programs provide an easy, tutorial approach to creating your presentation: PowerPoint®, Corel®, AppleWorks®, and others. Carefully following their instruction can successfully guide you through the preparation of the presentation. Some helpful guidelines can improve your product:

Tips for Using PowerPoint®:

1. Use mixed media (audio and clip art) to add interest.
2. Achieve a common look by repeating colors, fonts, shapes, and lines.
3. Maintain continuity by repeating icons on slides that pertain to the same idea cluster.
4. Limit the amount of clip art on any slide.
5. Use contrasting colors.
6. Avoid backgrounds with patterns or excessive detail.
7. Avoid distracting noises—clanging and banging of shutters.
8. Use *sans serif* typefaces; avoid highly ornate fonts.
9. Keep font size between 18 and 36 points.
10. Each slide should support a single idea.
11. Limit the material to 5 or 6 lines on a slide.
12. Do not exceed 40 characters on a line.
13. Do not mix sentences and phrases on the same slide.
14. Use parallel grammatical structures.
15. Allow sufficient white space on slides.
16. Use bullets to designate different points.
17. When presenting, stand to the side of the screen; stay open to audience.
18. Refer to the screen but maintain eye contact with your audience.
19. Use a remote to change the slides.
20. Use the shutter device to hide an image and talk about the ideas.[3]

Always remember that your presentation is a public speech, and criteria for good public speaking should be considered. This includes audience adaptation, and inviting audience participation, questions, and discussion. Remember: the PowerPoint® presentation is a visual aid, not the message. As public-speaking author Ron Hoff notes, "It's OK to be partially electronic—everybody can use a bit of glitz—but when all votes are counted and all scores are in, the presenter who is most alive will carry the day." [4]

Group Attitudes and Behavior. Attitude and atmosphere of a group will directly influence acceptance or rejection of discussion material. Group outcomes depend on group-centered attitudes and behaviors, which enhance participation and member satisfaction. They include open-mindedness, a positive attitude, ability to listen, willingness to contribute, and preparation.

Self-centered attitudes and behaviors hinder or disrupt participation and lead to group member dissatisfaction. They include closed-mindedness, a negative attitude, inattentiveness, lack of preparation, poor meeting attendance, and barriers to communication.

Favorable, or group-centered attitudes are observed with the following characteristics:

1. Respect and open-mindedness toward others.
2. A flexible, permissive interaction with a willingness to contribute.
3. Sensitivity to communication barriers and a desire to overcome them.
4. An understanding of how the group process works.
5. The ability to speak clearly and to the point.
6. Attentive listening.
7. The ability to think logically and analytically.
8. The desire to resolve conflict through compromise and cooperation to achieve group goals.[5]

Unfavorable, destructive attitudes and self-centered, behavior-blocking unsuccessful group processes include:

1. Aggressiveness: People who belligerently confront another's feelings when they perceive themselves to be powerful, do not value the other person, lack emotional control, and make others feel defensive.
2. Blocking progress: People whose behavior or position on an issue opposes the group making a final decision. They create barriers to completing work, casting a vote, or making a decision.
3. Seeking recognition: People whose major objective is obtaining recognition or credit for work others complete. They want the honor.
4. Self-confession: People whose interest is centering all attention upon themselves by claiming the major problem or lack of talent and skill. This also draws attention they strongly desire. They become the group problem.
5. Acting the buffoon. People who seek attention by pulling pranks or make fun of others in an attempt to focus attention upon themselves.
6. Dominating: People obsessed with the need for power. They are not satisfied unless they control the decisions of the group. They like action, as long as they control the action.
7. Seeking help: People who want all attention focused upon them. They wish to be the center of the problem, not one of the problem solvers.
8. Withdrawing: People who remove themselves from the group, either because they loose interest, or because the group does not focus on them. They often utilize excuses of failure, depression, or lack of resources as a reason for withdrawal.

Being able to recognize and handle counterproductive contributions is the responsibility not only of the leader, but also of each group member. Sometimes the best approach to these situations is to discuss them openly: "John, you sure have been quiet about this problem. What do you think?" "Sally, your jokes seem to indicate you do not see the issues as very serious. Why?" Sometimes the conflict injected by self-centered people needs to be resolved with a vote by the group. This lets individuals know what the position of the majority is, so that discussion can move along.

Norms

Every group has expectations of behavior. These can be formal rules, such as *Robert's Rules of Order* that give rigid guidelines for conducting social, business, and governmental meetings. Other "norms" may be religious dogma, educational qualifications, or dress standards such as black trench coats or leather jackets and jeans.

For a group to function effectively, its members must agree on how things are to be done. Therefore, no matter what their size or task, groups establish norms. This is done for a variety of reasons, but the strongest one is that shared ways of behaving enable members to attain group goals and to satisfy interpersonal needs. Without guidelines for behavior, most groups would be ineffective and disorganized.

Norms also help give structure to a group. If members know what is expected of them, they are more likely to act accordingly and function more efficiently. Norms can be as simple as getting the task done or as involved as participating in complex rituals and ceremonies that must be respected if a member is to remain in the group. Adherence to such requirements builds commitment, loyalty, and support for the group.

The stronger an individual bonds with the group, the more complex the norm requirements become. Formal rules specify the roles members play, how they behave, how meetings are to be conducted, and how topics for discussion are to be introduced, discussed, and accepted or rejected by the group members. The group will often determine a "leader" or interpreter of group norms, possessing power from the group to expel participants should they fail to achieve the "norm."

The brief description of the Atomic Energy Commission hearing vividly illustrates the importance and impact of both climate, and establishment of norms or descriptions of what the group wishes to set as standards as they begin their task.

As can be seen, establishing the rules or "norms" of the group becomes critical for group success in focusing on both behavior and subject content. This translates into success or failure for the group. Setting norms, following the procedures, and bonding within the group become a self-perpetuating process. Without guidelines, the group has no direction, and thus no capability for reward in accomplishing group goals. Without reward, participants become disenchanted, and the group fails.

Group Culture

Just like societies, organizations, and other large groups, small groups develop unique cultures. **Group culture**, according to communication experts Brilhart and Galanes, includes "the pattern of values, beliefs, norms, and behaviors that are shared by group members and that shape a group's individual personality."[6] As this bonding develops, the group can accomplish something together that they cannot do alone. The group objective creates energy individuals cannot generate on their own.

As this energy develops, a group climate or system develops, taking on a personality of its own. A group has a "boundary" of membership created by the norms adopted by the group. A variety of consequences follow for a person, depending on whether he is located "inside" or "outside" a particular group. The group has a dynamic character—forces may operate on individuals to bring them toward or take them away from the group. These forces effectively stimulate creativity, interest, and task performance. How effective the constellation of such forces are for any given group determines its bonding structure, and consequently, its group effectiveness in task solutions, creativity, and problem—solving capacity. The power of a group to influence its members is related to this cohesive quality.[7]

The group's culture underlies all of its actions and behaviors. The culture of a group is not static—it is constantly changing and developing as it adapts to each new situation or event it confronts and to the needs of the group and its members. A group's culture is expressed in behaviors such as how its members organize it, who begins the interactions, how much interaction is allowed by any one member, who interacts with whom, how formally or informally people behave, how much or how little conflict is allowed, how much or how little socializing takes place, how much or how little tolerance the group allows for ambiguity, and even the depth and latitude of information presented. These factors weave together to create each group's unique culture.

Ethical Behavior

As a civilized society, we are expected to follow laws, rules, standards, or agreed-upon norms of a general culture. These same expectations apply to behavior within groups. As the influence and power of groups increase, there are special ethical concerns that should be considered, since their influence becomes increasingly significant on our culture.

The first ethical principle is that all group members should have the right to state an opinion or a unique perspective. No barriers should exist to limit open expression, even if those ideas are unpopular. Of course, group members must also be sensitive and responsible in making sure their statements are honest, well conceived statements that do not violate others' civil rights or freedom of expression. Similarly, it is inappropriate to ridicule or belittle members of the group in private or public because they disagree with a certain point of view. There is nothing wrong with disagreeing with another's ideas; it is wrong, however, to attack the person instead of the ideas.

The second ethical principle is that all group members conduct themselves with honesty and integrity. Members of a group should not deliberately deceive or present information that is false or untruthful. Persuasion by falsehood is propaganda, and not acceptable. Incomplete information and distorted facts have no place in problem-solving. Missing data cause errors, and errors lead to wrong solutions. Group members should be willing to place the good of the group ahead of their own individual goals. The bottom line is that group members should ultimately do everything they can to benefit the group's goals.

A third principle is that confidential information shared in the group should remain confidential. It is extremely unethical to share information outside of the group that has been given to the group in confidence.

A final principle is that group members must use information ethically. They should give credit to the source of the information, should not falsify or change data, and should present all relevant information and all points of view to prevent bias. Ethical use of information helps produce effective, sound results, whatever the task.

Technology

Today's technologies also influence the nature of group behavior and communication. Comment has already been made about the use of PowerPoint® presentations. It should also be mentioned that additional technology vastly impacts communication efficiency, speed, and accuracy, providing for better problem-solving ability. The use of teleconferencing, cell phones, text mail, video conferencing, voice mail, electronic bulletin boards, e-mail, and interactive computer conferencing is becoming more and more prevalent. Ultimately, the success of any technology for group sharing depends on access and availability.

If the technologies are to be useful, participants must establish rules of usage, and the technology must be available to everyone. If an individual fails to check messages regularly, comes poorly prepared to teleconference, or is not included in the exchanges by the other group members, success will be limited. Clearly, training and experience, along with quality of technology can dictate success or failure of the group task.

Chapter 11: Analysis and Application Exercises

Identify a group to which you currently belong: family, a team, club, organization.

a. Identify the type of group
b. Outline briefly the "norms" of the group.
c. How are the rules or "norms" of the group enforced?
d. How cohesive is the group? What factors influence the group cohesiveness? (Give examples)

References

1. H. Peterson, "David E. Lilienthal offers a Definition of Democracy," *A Treasury of the World's Great Speeches,"* (New York: Simon and Schuster, 1954)806-809.
2. Harrison Conference Services, Business Schools at University of Georgia and Georgia State University.
3. S.D. Ferguson, *Public Speaking: Building Competency in Stages (*New York: Oxford University Press, 2008), 220.
4. R. Hoff, *I Can See You Naked,* rev. ed. (Kansas City, Mo.; Andrews McMeel, 1992), 143.
5. M.H. Farwell, "An Explanation of a Televised Method of Teaching Group Process." (Unpublished Master's Thesis, The Pennsylvania State University, University Park, 1964).
6. J.K. Brilhart & G.J. Galanes, *Effective Group Discussion,* 7th Ed., 124.
7. D. Cartwright & A. Sander, *Group Dynamics Research and Theory,* 3rd ed. (New York: Harper & kRow, Pub., 1968) 69.

CHAPTER 12

International Communication and Diversity

LEARNING OBJECTIVES

1. Recognize the importance of cultural diversity in many contexts: work, government, schools, communities, and in most personal relationships.
2. Recognize dominate cultural and co-cultural dimensions of society.
3. Describe the impact of cultural differences on international business relationships.
4. Distinguish between characteristics of high and low context cultures, individual and collective cultures, masculine and feminine cultures, and differing levels of power distances between the leader and the followers of a group.
5. Understand the stress created when two cultures conflict and determine how to resolve this conflict among different cultures.
6. Explain why cultures are created and maintained.
7. Understand strategies for improving communication among cultures.

CHAPTER 12: Overview

This chapter first defines culture, then discusses typical characteristics of a communication message that crosses cultural lines. Advice is given for adapting to a new culture and for becoming a more open communicator in diverse culture environments.

You look around the classroom you are about to enter. This is your first day of course work at a new school. There are several people present: some males and some females. This group can be classified in many ways. You notice some are racially labeled by skin color: black, white, yellow, and native American. Their hairstyle immediately places some in one group and some in another. You listen to fragments of conversation and discover that some are football players, others soccer players or baseball players. You notice religious markings on some by jewelry or dress. As you observe the group, you notice that some are wearing expensive clothing and jewelry, others are more cheaply dressed. By observing the clothing and hairstyle, you make judgement about the kind of music, or entertainment they prefer. Other signs separate the group into smaller groupings (tattoos, computers, and perhaps even cell phones). As you listen to conversations you recognize accents that designate where they have lived: accents that suggest foreign languages, or even areas of the country like New York or the Deep South. Perhaps you start to form opinions: There are more Spanish speakers now than in earlier years. Your training and experience influence where you will sit. Cross cultural communication dictates your behavior, and perhaps even your thoughts.

As American society becomes increasingly diverse, the ability to communicate with members of other cultures becomes a necessity. Diversity includes nationality, physical ability, language, ethnicity, even likes and dislikes on recreational activities and music. Diversity manifests itself in a great variety of norms and cultural values, such as high or low context, individual versus collective groupings, power distance, and degree of uncertainty avoidance. Viewing these differences as opportunities for enriched experience and learning, allows diversity to become an exciting challenge. Treating people from different backgrounds with respect is essential. Being willing to acknowledge and discuss cultural differences helps us understand and appreciate one another.

But cultural diversity is learned, then shared through communication. For communication to work, people must have some common ground: an agreement on likes and dislikes, a value on what is important and unimportant, and even how satisfaction is achieved. By understanding others' moods and meanings, we know what topics to avoid, and we can sometimes even complete another's thoughts. Uncertainty and stress are minimized; communication is spontaneous, open, and comfortable.

Communicating with strangers is more difficult. By knowing another's cultural beliefs, we can at least base our messages on shared attitudes, beliefs, and life experiences. Without knowing another's culture, we are at a loss to know how to relate to and bond with them. Without knowing their culture, uncertainty of communication outcome is increased. Even the communication function may be strange to us.

Imagine that you are working in Morocco. A colleague has invited you to his family home for dinner, but is a little vague about when dinner will be served. You have to ask several times before fixing the date. When you enter your host's home, his wife is nowhere to be seen, and when you ask when she'll be joining you, the host looks flustered and says that she's busy in the kitchen. When his little boy enters, you remark how cute and clever the child is, but rather than being pleased, your Moroccan colleague looks upset. Before dinner is served, you politely ask to go to the washroom to wash up. During the meal you do your best to hold up your end of the conversation, but it's hard going. Finally, after tea and pastry, you thank the host and politely leave. You have a feeling the dinner party was not a success, but you do not know what went wrong.

According to Craig Storti, almost everything you did was inappropriate[1]. In Morocco an invitation to dinner is actually an invitation to come and spend time. At some point food will be served, but what is important is being together. Discussing the specific time for your arrival for dinner is like asking your host how long he wants you around, and it also implies that your major concern is to be fed. Your questions about his wife and your compliments to his son were similarly inappropriate. It is not customary for a Moroccan wife to eat with guests or even be introduced, and praising a child is considered unlucky because it may alert evil spirits to the child's presence. Washing up in the washroom was also impolite. If you would have waited, your host would have arranged for water to be brought in to you in an expensive decorative basin that would have shown his good taste as well as his concern for your comfort. Finally, it was rude to carry on a conversation during dinner. Talking interferes with the enjoyment of the meal and can be interpreted as a slight against the food.

People who spend time in other cultures may encounter many misunderstandings, which over time can take their toll. If cultural differences can get in the way of a friendly meal, imagine how they might seriously affect complicated business or diplomatic relations. Because cross-cultural contexts add an additional layer of complexity to normal interactions, some grounding in inter-cultural communication is essential for anyone who travels abroad or interacts with strangers anywhere.

Although many difficulties occur, cross-cultural communication is not doomed to failure. As Harry Hoijer has remarked, "No culture is wholly isolated, self-contained, and unique. There are important resemblances between all known cultures. . . Intercultural communication, however wide the differences between cultures may be, is not impossible. It is simply more or less difficult[2].

Intercultural communication is possible because people are not "helplessly suspended in their cultures."[3] By developing an openness to new ideas and a willingness to listen and to observe, we can surmount the difficulties inherent in intercultural interactions.

What is Culture?

According to anthropologist Ruth Benedict, we spend our lives following the patterns and standards learned from birth:

> From the moment of birth the customs into which an individual is born shape his experience and behavior. By the time he can talk, he is a little creature of this culture, and by the time he is grown and able to take part in its activities, its habits are his habits, its beliefs his beliefs, its impossibilities his impossibilities.[4]

As Benedict points out, in a critical sense, we are formed and become the product of our culture, learned from parents, associates, and the location of our early teaching.

Donald Klopf gives a very simple definition of culture: It is "that part of the environment made by humans.[5]" Culture includes all the material objects and possessions a social group invents or acquires. It also includes the group's less tangible creations: the shared customs and values that bind its members together and give them a sense of commonality. Culture includes a group's collective answer to the fundamental questions: " Who are we?" " What is our place in the world?" "How are we to live our lives?"[6]

Characteristics of Cultures

Cultures are learned. Americans act like other Americans, not because we are predisposed to do so, but because we learned to do so. Much of our early training is an attempt to make us fit cultural patterns. If we do not learn the lessons of our culture, we pay "through a loss of comfort, status, peace of mind, safety, or some other value. . ."[7] We may even be imprisoned or labeled insane for acting in ways that would be perfectly acceptable in other cultures.

We seldom think we are programmed by our parents, teachers, and associates. Our cultural norms satisfy us, and we follow them without even considering them "false." Yet had we been brought up in Korea by Korean parents, an entirely different set of norms would appear just as natural. We would be culturally Korean. We would speak Korean, follow Korean norms and customs, and see the world in typically Asian ways. If we were raised from birth in Iran, we would think and act as Iranians do. Although this point seems obvious, it is one we often forget. When we observe another culture, we consider it strange, and our first impulse is to label them unfavorably and blame them for our disagreement with their actions. We seldom stop to realize that had we been brought up in that person's culture, we would likely express ourselves just as they do!

Cultures are shared. This means we act as members of a group and not as individuals. Cultures are group understandings rather than individual ones, and belonging to a culture means acting according to norms set up by the group. Fitting into a group and following their norms means acceptance and fellowship. Individuals with different life goals from the group defines us as an outcast or deviant from society and we become rejected both physically and mentally. Fitting into a cultural group is very important because it provides us with feelings of security, fellowship and love. We equate being alike with being right and being different with being wrong. Regardless of the reason, we learn very early to separate the world into "us" and "them," and we work very hard to make sure others recognize which of the two we are. Little boys are mortified if they are mistaken for little girls; they will spend a good part of the rest of their lives living up to the masculine ideal. The wealthy do not wish to be thought poor; thus, they act in ways that signal their status. Mistakes that mix "us" with "them" undermine our sense of self.

Because we share this feeling with others, and it becomes a group belief, we are not entirely free to act as we wish. We spend time proving who we are and that we live up to the expectations of the group. As long as we conform to the group norms, we are happy. We seldom consider the effects of national racial, class, or gender rules on our beliefs and behaviors. Only when we step outside our circle of friends and experience other cultures are we likely to see the extent to which our culture affects us[8].

People who frequently move between cultures are often more sensitive to the fact that culture is shared. Wieder and Pratt give an interesting example of the importance of shared cultural identity and the difficulties it presents for minority group members. In their article "On Being a Recognizable Indian Among Indians," they discuss ways in which Native Americans of the Osage people let one another know they are "real Indians" rather than "White Indians." Wieder and Pratt's research not only illustrates the universal need to demonstrate cultural identity, but also shows how central communication style is to that demonstration.[9]

One of the primary differences between the communication styles of European Americans and Native Americans is the value the latter places on being silent. "When real Indians who are strangers to one another pass each other in a public place, wait in line, occupy adjoining seats, and so forth, they take it that it is proper to remain silent and to not initiate conversation.[10]" Once Native Americans do engage in conversation with each other, they take on substantial obligations, among them the necessity of interacting whenever their paths cross. For students and businesspeople, this obligation may be problematic, for it takes precedence over attending class or keeping appointments.

Talking like a "real Indian" also means being modest and not showing oneself to be more knowledgeable than other Native Americans. Being asked by a European American teacher to volunteer information in a group discussion where other Native Americans are present puts a well-informed Native-American student in a difficult bind. To avoid appearing arrogant, a refusal to participate often occurs.

The desire to avoid arrogance occurs in public speaking situations as well, where speaking is reserved for tribal elders. Only certain individuals are entitled to speak, and they often speak for someone else rather than for themselves. It is customary to begin a speech with a disclaimer such as "I really don't feel that I am qualified to express the opinions of others, but I am going to do the best I can, so please bear with me."[11] Compare this custom to the rule taught by most European-American communication teachers that a speaker should build his or her credibility at the beginning of a speech, and you will see how communication styles across cultures can conflict.

To use the cultural rules of the Native American in front of other listeners of the same culture often means the "real Indian" is misunderstood by an outside culture such as European-American. Pratt, who collected the primary data, and who is a participating member of the Osage people, reported instances where his identity as a graduate student conflicted with his identity as a Native American. Pratt and Wieder conclude:

> Being a real Indian is not a material thing that can be possessed and displayed. It consists of those patterns of appropriate conduct that are articulated in such a way that they are visible and recognizable to other Indians as specific Indian ways of conducting oneself. In the performance of these visible patterns, being a real Indian is realized.[12]

The point made is that when cross cultural communication takes place, each member of a culture must prove himself to other members by acting in ways that are culturally approved. One must "talk in the language" of the listener for acceptance.

Cultures are Multifaceted. As we communicate, we are surrounded by cultural norms. At minimum, culture directly affects language, religion, basic world view, education, social organization, technology, politics and law, all interacting with one another.[13] If you touch a culture in one place, everything else is affected.[14]

The classic example of interaction directly effecting all levels of society is to look at "politics" on an international level. Terms such as "freedom" and "rights" must be operationally defined by which country and government is being discussed. Such rights include everything from hairstyle to religious rituals to sexual restrictions. Freedom is a classic example. A group of foreign students visiting the United States were taken to visit a local city council meeting. Even though many of the students were from a democratically-governed country, they could not comprehend local residents interacting directly with city officials in a meeting. That level of interaction was very different from their understanding of democracy. Terms such as democracy and freedom are common to people who live together in social groups and are thus examples of **cultural universals,** yet the enactment of these activities varies dramatically from culture to culture. In every culture, for example, people adorn their bodies, eat, educate their children, recognize family groupings, keep track of time, and the list goes on. How people in a particular culture do these things, however, is unique. Although all people eat, what they consider edible and how they prepare food varies widely. The idea of eating dog, a food offered in many of the best hotels in South China, is considered revolting by most Americans. The idea of eating a ham and cheese sandwich, a perfectly acceptable meal for many Americans, is offensive to Arabs and Orthodox Jews. Thus, what is common practice in one culture may be taboo in another. To be functioning members of a culture, we must internalize rules governing a huge variety of activities; and to communicate with people from other cultures, we must recognize and learn to respect their customs.

Cultures are dynamic. The culture of Iraq in 1990 under the leadership of Saddam Hussein certainly has been changed in many ways to become the Iraq of 2008. Yet in many ways the culture remains the same. With a change in the government comes changes in the economy, technologies, and living conditions. Even in the United States, just the activity of boarding an airplane has radically changed over the past few years. Cultures are constantly changing. As economic conditions change, as new technologies are developed, and as cultural contact increases, old ways of doing things change and people must learn new behaviors. Just as you understand a culture, you may find the rule is obsolete. The technology of cell phones has changed the concepts of interpersonal communication and instant information dramatically in the past few years. Access to information and ability to speak to people at large distances immediately has changed relationships occurring in families, governments, and even religion. Rather than learn set rules of interaction dealing with differences, prepare for intercultural contact to become more sensitive to the differences occurring between cultures and develop the ability to learn by observing and by immediate and direct contact with others. Since both visual and oral contact with other cultures are available at a moment's notice, develop the ability to learn by observing and listening as you make contact.

Cultural Identities are Overlapping. As we have discovered through the discussion of the complex issues of cultural interaction, we all have the same basic problems of life. We just choose to solve them in different ways. As we interact with people, we find that we belong to multiple overlapping cultures, some of which work together and some of which conflict. At a minimum we all belong to national, regional, class, ethnic, professional, age, and gender cultures. As we grow and develop, our perspective of each category changes with our experience, age, and understanding of both people and issues. At various times, one or more of these identities becomes critical while others take a back seat for a time. Where the overlapping cultures create significant differences, conflicts arise.

For example, the woman who believes in equal rights, yet belongs to a traditional culture in which women are subservient to men feels pressure from each identity. Messages received from the conflicting parties places the woman in a state of cognitive dissonance. To rationalize her sanity and be able to explain rational behavior, the conflict must be resolved, either by compromising her group memberships and sacrificing one, or breaking tradition and changing her interpretation of the messages received. Multiple memberships inevitably cause stress that must be resolved in some way.

If we are lucky, our overlapping identities fit together into a coherent whole. By converging our beliefs and actions, we arrive at a satisfied state of agreement with the cultural groups where differences develop our levels of communication. Where multiple cultural memberships can be evaluated and compromised, they become a source of strength, allowing us to be unique individuals rather than cultural clones. Seldom are any two people members of exactly the same cultures, and none of us manage to follow all of the rules of the culture where we claim membership.

As Marshall Singer points out, "that is precisely what makes each of us humans unique. And while that makes for a more rich, varied, and interesting world, it also makes generalizing about people that much more hazardous and difficult."[15] The task that confronts each of us is to find a unique sense of self in the face of our conflicting cultural identities that satisfies our desire for acceptance, rationalizes our behavior, and makes us acceptable to the groups we wish to join. We aid this conclusion by recognizing when we speak to others their cultural identities are also complex and overlapping, and they also must resolve a satisfying compromise as they accept our culture.

Why Communicate Cross-Culturally?

Everyone understanding communication becomes more difficult when people do not share the same attitudes and values. Why, then, should we bother to communicate cross-culturally? Answer: We cannot afford to ignore people from other cultures. When our financial network is so intertwined with other cultures that our purchase of a hamburger is ordered at our local Wendy's® by a radio transmission that goes through India or China, we have no choice but to communicate with them. Isolation from other cultures is not an option in the global village. There may have been a time when learning how to communicate across cultural boundaries was a luxury rather than a necessity. Nowadays it is impossible to remain isolated from others, and international, thus intercultural communication is a necessity.

Living in the Global Village. Intercultural communication has significantly expanded over the past two decades. The impact of the Internet and telecommunication has placed the world in an immediate communication mode.

The term *Global Village* was made popular by the writer Herbert Marshall McLuhan in "The Gutenberg Galaxy: The Making of the Typographic Man," in 1962. The basic theme of the book was that the Gutenberg press restructured the world with published material, and technology has revitalized the information explosion by creating a global village with instant communication.[16] The idea was furthered by a book entitled "The World is Flat," by Thomas Friedman. Worldwide coverage by electronic media has leveled the playing field of economics, communication, and even culture, providing almost instant communication and even business management and control without regard to political boundaries or even limitations of cultural business practices. In effect, products, communication, exchange of ideas and information, even work services are available at the touch of a button.

While international travel is open to more people, international communication is available to anyone who can push a button on a computer. We are surrounded by ideas, practices, and influences of the world as if each neighbor in our community came from a foreign land. Figuratively, we all live in a community made up of every culture, race, and religion in the world.

Even if you do not travel outside the United States, you still find yourself interacting with people from other cultures. Not only have foreign born people moved to the United States, access to them via computer has further removed barriers to immediate contact.

Familiarity with the problems that arise when people communicate interculturally can ease the adaptation that both immigrants and host nationals must make. Adjusting to the global village is by no means easy. As Porter and Samovar express it, "The difficulty with being thrust into a global village is that we do not yet know how to live like villagers; there are too many of 'us' who do not want to live with 'them'."[17]

Coming to terms with Diversity. America has been known as the "melting pot" of the world. This refers to the fact that people from cultures worldwide have moved to become our neighbors. The ethnic shift is already being felt. Where European immigrants were once the majority, the majority of immigrants are now from Latin and African origins. We are a country of many coexisting cultures. Groups that were outside the mainstream several years ago are now demanding recognition and respect from majority cultures. Even when we speak the same language, we find overcoming cultural difference difficult. Yet if we are to live in harmony with our neighbors, overcoming differences is a requirement.

Intercultural Communication and Personal Growth. Intercultural understandings serve not only to make contacts more comfortable but also to enrich us on a personal level. Communicating with people from other cultures allows us access to the experiences of other human beings. Intercultural contact shows us that there are other ways to act in the world than those we have been taught; it widens our field of choices and stimulates our imagination. People involved with this development talk about intercultural identity, a sense of belonging to an original and a new culture at the same time. People who achieve this identity are more open to change and are willing to transcend their own cultural biases. Young Yun Kim expresses it this way:

> Not all strangers may evolve this far in their adaptation process. Yet those who do will be able to enjoy a special kind of freedom, making deliberate choices for actions in specific situations rather than simply being bound by the culturally normative courses of action.[18]

Adapting to New Cultures

Despite all the difficulties, people do manage to adapt to one another. All individuals who move to another country and immerse themselves in a strange new land experience stress. Some adapt better than others, finding ways to feel at home with people who are quite different. Research has identified a number of factors associated with successful adaptation. These include the nature of the host culture, the personal attitudes and predispositions of the newcomer, and most important, the kind of communicative bonds the newcomer makes. Just as one maintains contact with one's own culture through communication, one's ability to enter a new culture successfully is also determined by communicative behavior.

The Nature of Common Cultural Differences[19]

Cultural traits often dictate everything from personal behavior to acceptance into the culture and what role the individual plays in the overall structure of the society. Four basic traits, leadership, work productivity, group allegiance, and task commitment, help define cultural differences.

Leadership. Every group requires certain commitments from participants for culture to form. One of the easiest ways of designating differences among groups is to review governance or leadership. Where the focus centers on leadership, the key characteristic is that of power or influence. Power is defined as the right to manipulate the outcome of health, welfare, and even critical decisions of protection. **High power** group leadership suggests the few in power formulate policy and activity of the many. Labels often accompany the leader: dictator, chief, patriarch, minister, judge. Even though examples are generally in terms of governed groups, high and low power differences can exist between husband and wife, minister and congregation, boss and employer, or even group leader and participant.

High power establishes priorities in authority, levels of respect, and demands upon followers. For example, when North Vietnam became a dictatorship, the sudden military control replaced medical doctors and educators as leaders and the educated were driven out. The same observations were discovered under the dictatorship in Iraq. Strong religious groups often put restrictions on political, educational, or social standards. Government tolerance for acceptable leaders indicate cultural pressures. But standards change with the emphasis on where power resides. For example, when John Kennedy ran for president, a big political issue focused on Kennedy being Catholic. However, when John Kerry ran a few years later, after Kennedy had broken down the cultural issue of religion, very few people even realized John Kerry was a Catholic also.

High power places large emphasis on such things as symbols, dress, titles, and personal possessions.

Work Productivity. The bipolar characteristics of this culture focus primarily upon production issues such as the work force or family organization. The characteristic primarily emphasized is referred to as "masculine" or "feminine." However, these labels do not refer to the gender but the descriptive behavior of group participants. Workers are rewarded for productivity. Characteristics describing a masculine culture include aggressive or assertive behavior, resulting in competitive success. The objective of such a culture focuses upon success in competition. "Winning" is rewarded with high honor.

Feminine culture focuses on modesty, quality of life, and tenderness. Workers are rewarded for work satisfaction, and salaries are determined, not on productivity, but on need.

In a masculine work environment, unions stand for high salaries, large output, and major impact. A feminine culture focuses on compatibility, unions supplying needed employees, with little emphasis on status.

Group allegiance. The key bipolar difference focuses on the impact of the individual, rather than commitment to the group. In the individual orientation, the individual has the ability to change the standards of the culture. Examples of individuals who have restructured the culture include Jesus Christ, Mohandas Gandhi, and Adolph Hitler. The persons need not be government leaders, but people who changed the culture as individuals: Bill Gates is a classic example. Sometimes it is not a person, but a group projecting an idea. Take for example "Compound Interest," as a concept which changed the world's economy.

Where emphasis is placed on the group, sacrificing everything for the supremacy of the group can change the culture. Note the impact of suicide terrorists upon society. Their arrival on the world stage changed governments, societies, even the way we travel and how we enforce security around major events such as sporting events or government meetings. Within this culture, the group decides what individuals will do. Depending on the group, an individual's choices about behavior, education, life work, and even marital status can be determined by the group.

Task commitment focuses upon elements controlling the group such as tradition and commitment to the group versus the individual. High context cultures resist change, and ask that participants make few changes. What was good enough for father and grandfather, is good enough for me. The major focus in a high context society is to protect the society from any change. Silence is an attribute, and slogans such as "If it ain't broke, don't fix it," or "Make do or do without!" are common.

Where the culture is low context, the welfare of the group is bypassed for the good of the cause. The goal is to get the job done. Silence is considered a sign of weakness leading to frustration, indecision and loss of productivity. The focus is on the "here" and "now." Change, growth, and innovation are positive attributes.

Communication among Cultures

Some cultures have more permeable boundaries than do others. Some make outsiders feel more at home than do others. One factor associated with successful adaptation is the host country's attitude toward foreigners. If citizens of a country consider outsiders barbarians and infidels, then adaptation will be difficult.

Cultural distance, or the extent to which two cultures differ, affects ease of communication.

Countries can be considered cultures, and agreements vary in difficulty as much as do individuals. Japan and United States, for example, are quite different in a number of important dimensions. The former is collectivist and the latter, individualist. Americans have what Hall and Hall call a monochromic sense of time; Americans tend to segment and sequence time and value speed. Although on the surface the Japanese may seem **monochromic,** below the surface they are **polychromic,** especially when it comes to interpersonal behavior. People in polychromic cultures change plans often and easily and consider schedules as objectives to be met, not as definite commitments. Thus, in polychromic cultures it may take a lot longer to do things than in monochromic cultures.[20]

Another difference between Japan and the United States is the language spoken. The distinction between them is much greater than the distinction between English and French or German. Aspects of material culture (housing, transportation, and so on), as well as artistic and literary conventions, are also quite distinct. Except for the fact that in both Japan and the United States technology is quite advanced, these two countries exhibit large differences.

Germany and the United States, however, may differ in some ways, but these countries share more similarities. Although their languages, educational systems, managerial styles, and problem-solving approaches exhibit some differences, people in these countries share common beliefs and impulses as well as mutually familiar material cultures.

Interactive variables focus conflicts on issues in such a way that large differences appear in one area of the world and not in others. Although Catholics and Protestants coexist quite peacefully in the United States, this is not the case in Northern Ireland. Sometimes the variable of national identity may have little influence on people, while issues like homosexuality and heterosexuality can provide major conflict. In general, the more aspects of a culture that differ, the more problematic interpersonal communication becomes.

Personal Predispositions

Having an open mind is clearly a prerequisite for adaptation. A second factor related to international interactions is personality. Included here are such factors as one's openness, resilience, and self-esteem. Some tolerate ambiguity and find being an outsider distressing. Others lack confidence and may displace their feelings of anxiety onto those around them. Still others have great difficulty handling tension. Since adapting necessities change and are always accompanied by stress, people with these predispositions will experience difficulty in adaptation.

Education and preentry training are also important. The more a newcomer knows about a culture ahead of time, the more prepared he or she is for contact. The traveler who reads about the host culture and makes contacts with host nationals prior to entry will be more comfortable in the new setting.

Communication Bonding

The third factor affecting communication is the way the newcomer interacts with the host. Openness and confidence can help, but must be implemented for complete success. Kim argues that newcomers' exposure to communication networks in the host culture and their relationships with members of the home culture are two important determinants of intercultural success.

Kim believes that visitors should expose themselves as much as possible to host social communication. They should make interpersonal contacts and become familiar with mass communication within the host culture. They should avoid depending too heavily on ethnic communication networks. The newcomer who interacts only with other foreigners, who refuses to make any attempt to learn the language, and who reads only books and newspapers from home needlessly isolates him or herself. Although others who share the same ethnic identity can form a support group and can teach a newcomer the ropes, they often inhibit real cross-cultural contact.

Developing an open communication style is a key variable in successful adaptation. This means being willing to plunge in and explore new cultures with enthusiasm. Basically, change is needed, often through trial and error. One must learn the behavioral competence to act in new ways more appropriate to the new situation.

Becoming a More open Communicator

Much emphasis has been placed on communication between people of different nationalities. Keep in mind differences in culture include many other variables that make us different. Go back and read the first paragraph of this chapter. Notice that just about every person you meet belongs to a different culture than you do in some way. Everyone deserves respect and decency, regardless of their culture. Consider the following guidelines to minimize cultural differences, regardless of their source.

- Make new contacts. Remember that prejudiced people hold distorted and erroneous beliefs and seldom have any direct experience with members of the groups they target. Although contact can reinforce negative perceptions, it can also dissolve misunderstandings and negative expectations. The best way to bridge cultural differences is through personal contact. Think of your own circle of friends. How many of them are from a different racial, ethnic, or religious background? If your answer is none or few, you might consider widening your field of experience.
- Learn about history and the experiences of people from diverse cultures. One of the major complaints of minority groups is that their history has not been told. Most people know very little about other co-cultural groups, and this ignorance is a barrier to understanding. By taking a course about, or by experiencing the cultural behavior of someone else, you can gain a deeper understanding and appreciation of another culture.
- Examine yourself for possible stereotypes. Prejudices and stereotypes are founded on lack of understanding about someone else. The first step in becoming fair-minded and open lies in admitting the possibility that some of one's judgments are unfair or untrue.
- Responsible and open communicators are willing and able to see the world from another's perspective. Project yourself into another's viewpoint. Actively try to understand how others make sense of their world and actively try to experience what they feel. Although complete empathy is impossible, getting a better sense of what others think and feel is possible.
- Finally, each of us should work on becoming more self-confident. The better we

feel about ourselves, the more likely we are to feel good about others and the more able we are to learn from them.

Chapter 12: Analysis and Application Exercises

1. List three co-cultures to which you belong. What specialized verbal or nonverbal codes do you use in each group? What functions do they serve?
2. Describe an experience that you have had interacting with someone from another culture or or co-culture. Did the interaction meet your expectations? Why or why not? What did you learn about the other person? What did you learn about yourself?

References

1. C. Sorti, *The Art of Crossing Cultures* (Yarmouth, ME: Intercultural Press, 1990), p. 25.
2. H. Hoijer, *Language in Culture* (Chicago: University of Chicago Press, 1954) p. 94
3. C. T. Patrick, "Understanding Others: Kellyian Theory, Methodology and Applications," *International Journal of Intercultural Relations* (1982), vol 6, p. 403.
4. R. Benedict, *Patterns of Culture* (New York: Penguin, 1946), p 2.
5. D. W. Klopf, *Intercultural Encounters: The Fundamentals of Intercultural Communication*, 2nd Ed. (Englewood, CO: Morton, 1991), p. 31.
6. S. Trenholm & A. Jensen, *Interpersonal Communication* (Belmont, CA: Wadsworth), p.368.
7. Klopf, 33.
8. M. Singer, *Intercultural Communication: A Perceptual Approach* (Englewood Cliffs, NJ: Prentice Hall, 1987), p. 53.
9. D.L. Wieder & S. Pratt, "On Being a Recognizable Indian Among Indians," *Cultural Communication and Intercultural Contact* (Hillsdale, NJ: Lawrence Erlbaum Associates, 1990), 450-64.
10. Ibid., 51.
11. Ibid., 61.
12. Ibid. 63.
13. L.A. Samovar & R. E. Porter, Communication between Cultures (Belmont, Ca: Wadsworth, 1991), p. 15
14. Ibid, 20.
15. Singer, 53.
16. "Global Village," Wikipedia, 2008.
17. R.E. Porter & L.A. Samovar, "Basic Principles of Intercultural Communication," *Intercultural Communication, A Reader*, 6th ed (Belmont, CA: Wadsworth, 1991), p. 6.
18. Y.Y. Kim, *Communication and Cross-Cultural Adaptation: An Integrative Theory*

CHAPTER 13 Intercultural Communication

LEARNING OBJECTIVES

When students have completed this chapter and lesson, they should be able to:

1. Define intercultural communication and discuss its relevance in their lives.
2. Compare and contrast the assimilation and accommodation perspectives on diversity.
3. Describe several co-cultures you as a student encounter.
4. Define the term "co-languages" and give some examples.
5. Define the term "coenetics" and discuss its importance in intercultural communication.
6. Describe three barriers to effective intercultural communication.
7. Describe three ways to help improve intercultural communication

CHAPTER 13: Overview

The chapter discusses barriers to intercultural communication including examples of culture and perception, language, rules, attitudes, stereotypes, prejudices, anxiety and withdrawal, and ethnocentrism.

Luis Marcos, a psychiatrist, describes the cross-cultural communication with friends in his health profession: "When we first went out for meals together, my impulse was to pay for both of us," he says of another doctor, a Black woman who taught him not to leave his own behavior unexamined. "It wasn't that I thought she couldn't afford to pay; we were equally able to pick up the check. It was just that the cultural habit of paying for a woman was ingrained in my personality. But she misconstrued it. She felt I was trying to take care of her and put her down as a Black, a professional, and a woman. In order for our friendship to survive, she had to explain how she experiences things that I don't even think about.[1]

Despite its importance, learning to communicate across cultures is extremely difficult. A variety of barriers keep culturally different people from understanding one another. In this incident, that most common error "did not think" led the way. As individuals, we never consider anyone else not thinking or arriving at the same conclusions we accept. That "allness" mistake we commonly make forces us to assume that, culture set aside, men should always buy for the woman regardless of what the situation.

In this chapter attitudes that impede our ability to communicate clearly will be reviewed–attitudes such as prejudice, ethnocentrism, and ignoring differences such as knowledge, traditions, and circumstances. First, let's review how culture impacts communication.

Cultural Impact upon Communication

Culture is multifaceted, affecting every aspect of mankind. Culture affects most of our actions: how we interpret reality, understanding, role relationships, goal setting, self concepts, and even the messages we communicate.

Perception was discussed in chapter 4, but the impact of *culture on perception* becomes an interactive interpretive process. Meaning is not "extracted from nature" but is projected by people constructing nature. People's behavior can be misunderstood only in terms of their own personal thoughts, and many of these constructs are products of the customs, traditions, beliefs, and actions we label as our "culture.[2] When we perceive events and people, we attach values to them, accept them, form judgments about them and act on them. Our values and actions are culture-specific, as the following example reported by Klopf shows.[3]

Nancy, a native Californian, moved with her husband, an executive with an oil company, to Iran. Because the climate was very hot and humid, Nancy often wore shorts and casual tops when she went to the local market to shop. As she walked alone to the market one day, an Iranian man grabbed her and made lewd suggestions. Upset, she shook herself free and called the police.

Nancy, working from an American point of view, saw the Iranian as a degenerate and his behavior as an attack. The Iranian, however, was astonished by her reaction. When he looked at Nancy, he saw a prostitute, for in Iran no other woman would ever appear in public in shorts or walk alone. From an Iranian point of view, Nancy was giving clear signals that she was sexually available. The way each saw the other was influenced by cultural values and beliefs.

Had Nancy known more about the culture in which she was a guest, the incident might have been avoided. In *Beyond the Veil,* F. Mernissi describes the cultural codes that govern relations between the sexes in many Muslim countries. In these nations, sexuality is territorial, and there are strict boundaries delineating the spaces belonging to each sex. Mernissi goes on to explain:

> Women in males' spaces are considered provocative and offensive. If [a woman] enters [the male sphere], she is upsetting the male's order and his peace of mind. She is actually committing an act of aggression against him merely by being present where she should not be.[4]

A similar problem confronted the United States military as they joined with Iran in confronting Iraq and Saddam Hussain during the 2003 invasion. An agreement had to be made between Iran and the U.S. Military that when a woman was in uniform, she was not considered anything but a soldier. However, when not in uniform, she was to be treated as any other female in Iran.

With these cultural values in mind, the Iranian male's response to Nancy or the U.S. female warrior is logical, given his interpretation of the female behavior as an example of aggressive sexuality and exhibitionism. Knowing the reasons behind the behavior of both parties does not necessarily lead to an acceptance, however, The Iranian may still feel that behavior such as Nancy's is immodest, and Nancy may still find his behavior sexist. The same attitude would be observed with the woman soldier, or the woman out of uniform. Nevertheless, cultural knowledge can place behavior in context and can reduce misunderstandings. Everyone in uniform is to be respected!

To communicate effectively, both the situation and people must be evaluated realistically. In an intercultural context, this means being aware of cultural conventions and familiarizing oneself with basic values and customs. Not knowing the values of another culture can result in momentary embarrassment, or can lead to the loss of millions of dollars and months of work, as the following story illustrates.[5]

An American engineering company spent months negotiating a huge contract with a Saudi Arabian firm. To signal the importance of the contract, the American executives bound their final proposal in costly leather. Unfortunately, they chose pigskin, unaware that Saudis consider the pig an unclean animal. Had the Americans wanted to insult their hosts, they could have found no better way. The proposal and binder were consequently burned, and the Saudi firm threw the American company out of the country. A cursory knowledge of religious custom could have averted this disaster. Unfortunately, however, no one had bothered to do basic research on the Saudi beliefs.

As we live our lives, we assume various roles. One minute we are a student, the next minute a child in your family. Perhaps you are a waiter in your job, or perhaps an athlete as you participate in athletics. Each role is different, each requiring a list of guidelines as to behavior, actions, and even thought processes. Our culture also dictates the *cultural role identity* we must assume, and what actions must accompany our role. In every culture, people are classified according to factors such as age, status, occupation, gender, even the type of clothing we are wearing. We do not expect the young and the old, princes and peasants, or men and women to act exactly the same way. Being a good communicator means recognizing role distinctions and adapting our communication accordingly.

The Ashanti of Ghana, for example, address all older men as "my grandfather," a title of respect.[6]

The Maasai of East Africa also afford great honor to their elders. Skow and Samovar explain that the Maasai equate age with wisdom and belief that those who are wise must be treated with special care. Young people, no matter how clever, cannot reach the truth until they pass through all of life's stages.[7] The Chinese hold a similar view.

Americans, on the other hand, value youth more than age. Rather than welcoming old age, Americans perceive time as creating diminished capacity. Americans believe age may induce psychological states of "oldness." Carmichael argues that "it is quite possible that many older people have aged prematurely by adopting the age-related characteristics they have come to believe must exist after a certain age.[8]

Gender roles are also culturally derived. In parts of the Arab world, women do not work or drive cars, whereas in Israel and China, women do the same jobs as men. In parts of India, women must wait to eat until after men have finished, and in traditional Vietnamese households, women must eat smaller portions of food than men.[9] In modern America these kinds of distinctions are seen as demeaning and offensive. Even the characteristics seen as basic to the sexes may differ from culture to culture. According to E. Hall, in Iran it is men who express their emotions freely, whereas women are considered to be coldly practical.[10]

Culture and personal goals are closely related. The culture dictates what goals we should pursue and how to pursue them. Americans have high achievement motivation. Americans are described as **effort-optimistic,** or believing that hard work will pay off. People in other countries may "expect to be rewarded on the basis of the social position of their family or clan" rather than on their own efforts, or perhaps not be rewarded at all.[11] American culture maintains people control their own fate as opposed to other countries. Sitaram and Cogdell explain this cultural difference with the following example:

> If you ask a Hindu why he got only ten bags of corn from his land while nearby farmers got much more, he would say it was the wish of God. An American farmer's answer to the same question would be, "Hell, I didn't work hard enough."[12]

Goal orientation of middle-class America is evident in popular slogans: "No pain, no gain! "Just do it!"Americans also experience high stress levels and burnout. Many people from other countries consider Americans overly ambitious. What Americans think of as a healthy work ethic is considered needless effort or even arrogance from our foreign associates.

Another critical factor influencing differences in cultures is *self concepts* held by cultures. How one feels about himself affects basic notions of human nature, including the extent to which individuals evaluate themselves and their personal influence. Beliefs about self are important because they are central to all other values and because they affect every aspect of behavior, including communication. Despite their importance, self concepts held by a culture are often ignored.

Samovar, Porter, and Jain argue that most Americans hold three basic beliefs about human nature: first, that human beings are rational, or at least attempt to be; second, that they are perfect, or can become such; and third, human nature is highly susceptible to social and cultural influence.[13] The **rationality** premise–the belief that most people are capable of discovering the truth through logical analysis–underlies many American institutions, including democracy, trial by jury, and free enterprise, all of which are based on the idea that the average person can be trusted to make good decisions. The **perfectibility premise** is based on the old Puritan idea that humans are born in sin but are capable of achieving goodness through effort and control. Finally, the **mutability premise** assumes human behavior is shaped by environmental factors and the way to improve humans is to improve their physical and psychological circumstances. A belief in the idea that every person deserves an education follows from this assumption. President George Bush's "no child left behind" is the latest in educational mottos resulting from this premise.

Another Americanized belief in the value and worth of an **individual** follows these assumptions.

The idea is that the individual acting in his or her own behalf is the most important social unit in society. American individualism is evident from the fact that Americans are encouraged "to make their own decisions, develop their own opinions, solve their own problems, have their own things, and, in general, learn to view the world from the point of view of the self."[14] Researcher Hofstede found the United States to be the most individualistic of the forty nations he studied. The countries highest in individualism were Western or European countries, while those lowest in individualism were Asian or South American.[15]

The opposite of individualism is **collectivism.** In collective cultures people believe it is right to subordinate personal goals for the good of others. For collectivists, shared identity is more important than personal identity. Triandis and his colleagues conclude that naming practices may reflect where a culture stands on the collectivist-individualist scale. In Bali, a person is referred to by the position he or she holds in the family (for example the "first son" of X family, or "mother of Y"). Similarly, in China, one's family surname comes first, followed by a personal name. In more individualist cultures, the personal name comes first.[16]

People in collectivist cultures are comfortable in **vertical relationships,** where some are given privileged status, whereas individualists feel most comfortable in **horizontal relationships,** where everyone is equal. Members of collectivist cultures rarely compete on a personal basis, although they will fight fiercely for the good of the group. The converse is true in individualist cultures. In a collectivist culture like Japan, workers feel strong loyalties to their work groups, and the qualities sought in a leader are patience and the ability to listen.[17] Leaders in individualist cultures are more likely to be prized for quick thinking and an ability to take the initiative.

Triandis, Briskin, and Hui list harmony, face-saving, duty to parents, modesty, moderation, thrift, equality in reward distribution, and the satisfaction of others as the most important collectivist values. The top values for individualists are freedom, honesty, social recognition, comfort, hedonism, and reward distribution based upon individual performance. Table 13.1 outlines their complete research findings.

Culture and language style by nature of misunderstandings and just communicating are a critical barrier to cross-cultural interaction. But the problem is not just misunderstandings; language differences create different thought processes. Our world is filtered through our language habits, and it therefore stands to reason people from different language communities perceive the world differently.

There is an assumption that if the concept can be expressed in one language, it can be said in another, implying direct translation. This is simply not the case. Anyone who speaks more than one language knows that direct translation conveying exact meaning is very difficult.

Table 13.1

Rules to Increase Cooperation between Collectivists and Individualists

RULES COLLECTIVISTS SHOULD FOLLOW WHEN INTERACTING WITH INDIVIDUALISTS	RULES INDIVIDUALISTS SHOULD FOLLOW WHEN INTERACTING WITH COLLECTIVISTS
1. Don't expect to be able to predict an individualist's attitudes and behavior on the basis of group affiliations. Although this works in your country, individualists have their own ideas.	1. Expect collectivists to abide by the norms, roles, and obligations of their groups. If group membership changes, expect members' values and personal styles to change as well.
2. Don't be put off when individualist take pride in personal achievement, and do not be too modest yourself.	2. Do not disclose personal information unless asked. Feel free, however, to disclose your age and salary.
3. Expect individualists to be less emotionally involved in group affiliations than is the norm for you. Do not interpret this as coldness or as a personality defect.	3. Do not criticize collectivists or openly refuse their requests. Expect them to be more sensitive to loss of face than you are.
4. Do not expect persuasive arguments that emphasize cooperation and conflict avoidance to be as effective as they are in your culture. Do not be offended by arguments that emphasize personal rewards and costs.	4. Persuasive arguments based on authority appeals or on the good of the group will be more effective than those based on personal rewards.
5. Do not interpret initial friendliness as a signal of intimacy or commitment. Expect relationships to be good-natured but superficial and fleeting according to your own standards.	5. Spend a great deal of time getting to know others. Be patient, expect delays, and do not adhere to a rigid timetable.
6. Pay attention to written contracts. They are considered binding.	6. Do not be surprised if plans are changed after everything was seemingly agreed upon. Do not be surprised if negotiations take a lot longer than you consider necessary.
7. Do not expect to be respected because of your position, age, sex, or status. Do not be surprised if individualists lack respect for authority figures.	7. Let others know your social position, job title, and rank. A collectivist has a strong need to place you in an appropriate niche in the social hierarchy.
8. Expect individualists to be upset by nepotism, bribery, and other behaviors that give in-group members an advantage over others.	8. Gift giving is important, but do not expect to be paid back immediately.
9. Do not expect to receive as much help as you would in your own country. After initial orientation, you may be left to do things on your own.	9. Remember that for collectivists, family and social relationships are extremely important. Expect collectivists to take time off from work for family matters.
10. Do not expect an individualist to work well in groups.	10. Do not expect to be afforded as much privacy as you may be used to.

For example, the Japanese concept of *amae* comes from the verb *amaeru*, "to look to others for support and affection." As Hall and Hall explain, *amae* has its roots in the psychological relationship between a child and the mother, but the child later transfers *amae* to teachers, bosses, and other authority figures. Although *amae* may be translated "dependence," it is more than that: it is a willingly assumed, reciprocal relationship that blurs the distinction between the world of work and the interpersonal realm.[18] Because English speakers have no exactly comparable term, we may have difficulty grasping the subtleties of the concept. Since we cannot translate the word exactly, we miss much of the meaning. One of the reasons that learning a foreign language is both frustrating and exhilarating is that it opens up new ways of perceiving the world.

Culture affects not only the semantic content, but also the pragmatic rules as well. It is important to keep in mind that language is a part of the culture; what we do with language, how we use it, is a product of shared understanding. Speech forms such as teasing, flattery, charm, effusiveness, implied meanings, or directness have different values in different cultures. Even lying (which Americans tend to class as one of the worst possible sins) may be valued in a culture in which maintaining harmonious relations is more important than being certain about the facts.

Americans value plain, direct, efficient language use. In many cultures, people are expected to circle around a point rather than attack it directly. In cultures that value ambiguity, plain speaking may be shockingly rude. Americans distrust anyone who "lays it on too thick;" while many other cultures believe in offering one another effusive or heavy praise.

Nonverbal communication compounds the issue significantly more. A single behavior may signify different meanings in different cultures. In some cultures, for example, looking away from or momentarily turning one's back and walking away from a speaker is a mark of respect and appreciation. It should not, therefore, be taken as an insult. As we saw in chapter 5, shared behavior is an important hidden language that can affect the success of any interaction.

Culture and business transactions produce a combination or interaction with many of the variables previously discussed. Good feelings and perceived understanding are critical and important. But when you add financial gain to the equation, even more barriers emerge. Salacuse describes six distinctive features of international business negotiations.[19] Problems begin with negotiators making two false assumptions about doing business in an international setting: First, many businessmen assume business deals will happen naturally if correct governmental policies and structures are in place, and second, they assume they can simply extend their successful domestic strategies to the international setting.

Salacuse identifies six elements common to all international business negotiations that differ with domestic negotiations: First, both parties must deal with laws, policies and political authorities that may not have the same interpretations as the domestic issues. The second factor is the presence of different currencies, creating problems of equality over time and the impact of unexpected losses or gains. The third factor is the participation of governmental authorities in the mix. Governmental bureaucracies are significantly more invasive than are those involved in American business. A fourth factor is that international ventures are vulnerable to sudden and drastic changes in circumstances. Political structures, economic structures, and even social structures are capable of swift and devastating changes. Finally, cultural differences are critical, including differences in value structures, perceptions, and philosophies. As a result, certain ideas may have very different connotations in different cultures.

International marketing history suggests a few catastrophic examples of where intercultural communication failed to consider some of the hazards mentioned above. For example, a General Motors auto ad with "Body by Fisher" became "Corpse by Fisher" in Flemish. A Colgate-Palmolive toothpaste named "Cue" was advertised in France before anyone realized that "Cue" happened to be the name of a widely circulated pornographic book about oral sex. Pepsi"s "Come Alive with Pepsi" campaign translated for the Taiwanese conveyed the unsettling news that "Pepsi brings your ancestors back from the grave!" One American airline operating in Brazil advertised that it had plush "rendezvous lounges" on its jets, unaware that in Portuguese (the language of Brazil) "rendezvous" implies a special room for having sex.

Because culture affects so may aspects of our lives, it can be a barrier to effective communication. This is especially likely if we hold negative attitudes about cultural differences. The following are some destructive beliefs that can guarantee intercultural misunderstandings.

Attitudes That Diminish Understandings

International contacts often frustrate rather than stimulate positive communication experiences. Too often intercultural encounters are approached with preconceived attitudes that insure misunderstanding. Among such attitudes are some old faithful communication wreckers for our own culture: holding and advocating stereotypes and prejudices, inferences that similarities in belief and behavior exist, a tendency to withdraw from novelty, and a deep belief in the superiority of one's own culture.

Stereotypes and Prejudices. The use of prejudice and stereotypes is the main barrier to intercultural understanding. People enter cross-cultural interaction with preconceived notions that make it impossible to find any common ground. Our attitudes and beliefs of stereotypes distort accurate perceptions. **Stereotypes,** which are "generalized 2nd-hand beliefs that provide conceptual biases from which we 'make sense' out of what goes on around us, whether they are accurate or fit the circumstances" are one kind of preconception.[20] Although stereotypes fill certain functions, such as reducing the anxiety that comes with uncertainty and making the world seem more predictable, they interfere with objective perception. It is easier to classify an entire group of people, or total culture with defining characteristics, usually with negative qualities, than to explain the complexities involved with the uniqueness of each situation and the individual differences inherent with each event. Once we have decided that Germans are obsessed with order, that Japanese are workaholic, or that Central Americans lack ambition, we stop thinking about people objectively. Stereotypes are loaded with negative, inclusive elements that declare the accuser a superior advocate, and the inferior opposition must automatically conform.

Prejudice is a special kind of stereotype, a "negative social attitude held by members of one group toward members of another group," an attitude that biases perception and provides a rationale for discrimination.[21] Prejudices are the products of in-group interaction; very rarely are they the result of direct contact with out-group members. People learn prejudices from secondary sources and seldom make any attempt to check their validity. By deciding that members of a target group are dangerous, unintelligent, or lazy, we develop prejudices, avoid contact, and ultimately ignore the truth.

The purpose of prejudices is not to enable us to understand the world accurately, but to "draw a line between in-group and out-group members, a line that divides those who are 'superior' from those who are 'inferior'. In drawing this line people often use distorted data and unwarranted assumptions."[22] Table 13.2 shows some of the cognitive biases people use to keep their prejudices intact, biases that allow them to see differences where none exist or to distort differences into negative characteristics that do exist.

Assumed Similarities. Almost as serious a stumbling block to intercultural understanding as prejudice is an unwarranted **assumption of similarity,** a refusal to see true differences where they exist. Assuming that everyone is "the same under

Table 13.2

Cognitive Biases Used to Maintain Prejudices

Negative Interpretation	Interpreting everything the target group does as negative *Example*: If we see "them" relaxing, we interpret their behavior as shiftless and irresponsible; when we relax, we are simply unwinding after a hard day.
Discounting	Dismissing information that doesn't fit a negative stereotype *Example*: If one of "them" succeeds, it must be due to favoritism or luck; their success is simply the exception that proves the rule.
Fundamental Attribution Bias	Interpreting another's negative behavior as internal rather than external *Example*: If one of "them" is rude, it's because they're that way by nature; if one of "us" is rude, it's because we're under stress.
Exaggeration	Making negative aspects of out-group behavior seem more extreme *Example*: a simple argument is seen as a violent confrontation; a demonstration is reported as a riot.
Polarization	Looking for differences and ignoring similarities *Example*: An immigrant who has assimilated in almost every respect is still seen as one of "them" and as fundamentally different from "us."

Adapted from *Communicating Racism: Ethnic Prejudice in Thought and Talk* by Teun ban Dijk, 1987. Newbury Park, CA: Sage.

the skin" may reduce uncomfortable feelings of strangeness, but it may also result in insensitivity. By assuming members of a different culture see the world the same way we do, we overlook real differences. When an American sees a foreign visitor smiling and nodding as the two interact, the American may assume the interaction is a success. It may be the case, however, "that the foreigner actually [understands] very little of the verbal and nonverbal content and is merely indicating polite interest or trying not to embarrass himself or herself."[23]

Smiling is a good example of an assumption of similarity for this "universal expression" takes on quite different meanings in different cultures. In some countries it is considered extremely impolite to smile at a stranger; a smile may be interpreted as a sexual invitation or as a sign of derision. Foreign travelers in the United States may be insulted or taken aback by the Americans' friendly smile, as is evidenced by this Japanese student's comment:

> On my way to and from school I have received a smile by non-acquaintance American girls several times. I have finally learned they have no interest for me; it means only a kind of greeting to a foreigner. If someone smiles at a stranger in Japan, especially a girl, she can assume he is either a sexual maniac or an impolite person.[24]

An American tourist, on the other hand, whose greetings are not returned may consider host nationals rude or standoffish. These misinterpretations are a direct result of failing to recognize cultural differences in nonverbal behavior.

An American woman working in Tunisia stops by the local newsstand to get a copy of the *International Herald Tribune*.[25] The vendor tells the American that he'll have the newspaper the next day, and instinctively adds the phrase "*N'sha 'llah*" (God willing.) The next day, when the American returns, there's no newspaper. The American is upset, because she interpreted the vendor's words as a promise. A

Tunisian would have heard something quite different. To a Tunisian, the vendor's statement would have clearly meant: "I don't know if there'll be a paper tomorrow; in fact I doubt it, but it's not for me to say what may or may not happen in the future. That is in God's hands." In short, when the vendor said, "yes, *N'sha'llah,*" he meant "no." We can only assume that, over time, this traveler will come to realize that in Tunisia, at least, "yes" does not always mean "yes."

Anxiety and Withdrawal. Other potential barriers to intercultural understanding are anxiety and tension. New situations almost always cause stress. Some tension and excitement can be energizing, but a large amount is very debilitating. If you have been faced with deciphering an unfamiliar language, you understand how exhausting it can be. When tensions get too high, **culture shock** takes over, and "the anxiety that results from losing all of our familiar signs and symbols of social intercourse" can be overwhelming.[26]

When we are in our own cultures we depend on familiar routines. We know what to expect from even strangers around us if we ask. But as Stori puts it, "if we were not instinctively sure that people would be civil unless provoked, stay on their side of the road and stop on red, that shopkeepers would give us goods in return for money–if we could not routinely depend on these things happening–the resulting uncertainty would immobilize us."[27]

The uncertainty of our new surroundings removes our predictability of what can happen, and we begin to feel isolated and adrift. It is ironic that the conditioning that makes it so easy for us to function at home is the very thing that makes it difficult for us to function abroad.

Severe culture shock produces feelings of helplessness and reduced self-esteem, a desire to return home, insomnia, depression, and even physical illness. The person becomes almost completely dysfunctional and attempts to withdraw from contact with the native culture. During severe culture shock, people are likely to distort perceptions and feel hostility toward members of the host culture.

Although severe culture shock can be devastating, mild periods of stress followed by withdrawal can be productive. In her **draw-back-to-leap** model, Young Yun Kim argues that brief periods of culture shock may be a "necessary precondition for adaptive change, as individuals strive to regain their inner balance by adapting to the demands and opportunities of their new life circumstances."[28]

As our foreign traveler experiences stress, often withdrawal (the draw-back phase), engages tension-reducing behaviors, and permits an opportunity to reorganize thoughts and feelings. Once cultural differences have been processed, the strength to continue to adapt (the leap-forward phrase) results. According to Kim, some degree of stress is to be expected. By taking it easy when stress occurs, the individual avoids complete withdrawal.

Ethnocentrism is the final barrier to intercultural understanding. This is the belief that one's own culture is superior to all others and the tendency is to judge all cultures by one's own criteria. Although it may be natural to believe that anything different is wrong, this is a negative attitude. Blaming people for not behaving the same way we do is irrational, especially when economic or physical factors can explain the difference. An ethnocentric American may be aghast to find out that people in another culture "waste" two hours of the middle of the day in resting. Our American may fail to consider that in that location the temperature often rises above ninety degrees and there is no air-conditioning. An ethnocentric individual may look down on the "natives" for using "primitive" farming methods without understanding they have no money to buy modern machinery. The way "they" do things makes sense based upon their circumstances.

Samovar and his colleagues say that it is naive to believe that our culture has all the answers. They pose the following questions:

> The Jew covers his head to pray, the Protestant does not–is one more correct than the other? In Saudi Arabia women cover their faces, in America they cover very little–is one

more correct than the other? The Occidental speaks to God, the Oriental has God speak to him–is one more correct than the other? The American Indian values and accepts nature, the average American seeks to alter nature–is one more correct than the other? A listing of these questions is never-ending. We must remember, however, that it is not the questions that are important, but rather the dogmatic way in which we answer them.[29]

When we admit differences do not always mean deficiencies, and when we concede our culture is not necessarily superior in all things, we begin to establish the trust and respect necessary to enable successful intercultural communication.

Chapter 13: Analysis and Application Exercises

1. Do you think America should be a "melting pot" where individuals from other cultures blend in with each other, a "salad bowl/stew" where individuals retain their own unique flavor, or something else? Should there be just "one American Culture" or should we be a group of many cultures? Why do you feel this way?
2. Some observers state that the "dominate culture" in America is white, male, and upper middle class. Do you agree? Will this change in the next 20 years? Why or why not?

References

1. L.C. Pogrebin, "The Same and Different: Crossing Boundries of Color, Culture, Sexual Preference, Disability, and Age," In J. Stewart, Bridges, *Not Walls*, 9th Ed (Boston:McGraw, Hill, 2006) 556-571.
2. G. Kelly, as cited in C.T. Diamond, "Understanding Others: Kellyian Theory, Methodology and Applications," *International Journal of Intercultural Relations*, 1982, pp 396-397.
3. D. W. Klopf, *Intercultural Encounters: The Fundamentals of Intercultural Communication*, 2nd Ed, 1991, p. 57.
4. F. Mernissi, *Beyond the Veil: Male-Female Dynamice in Modern Muslim Society*. 1975 (Cambridge, MA: Schenken) 81-86. For a discussion of a similar incident, see C. Storti, *The Art of Crossing Cultures*, 1990 (Yarmouth, ME: Intercultural Press), 66-67.
5. Klopf, 20.
6. C.H. Dodd, *Dynamics of Intercultural Communication*, 2nd Ed., 1987 (Dubuque, IA: Brown), 44.
7. L. Skow & L.A. Samovar, "Cultural Patterns of the Maasai," in L.A. Samovar, R.E. Porter & N.C. Jain, *Understanding Intercultural Communication*, 1991 (Belmont, CA:Wadsworth) 119.
8. C.W. Carmichael, "Intercultural Perspectives on aging," Samovar & Porter, *Intercultural Communication*, 130.
9. Samovar, Porter, & Jain, p.119; Dodd, 45.
10. E.T. Hall, "The Silent Language," (Garden City, NY: Doubleday, 1959) 67.
11. M.Argyle, "Intercultural Communication," in S. Bochner, *Cultures in Contact: Studies in Cross Cultural Interaction*, (Oxford, Eng.; Pergamon, 1991), 61-79.
12. K.S. Sitaram & R.T. Cogdell, "Foundations of Intercultural Communication," in Samovar, Porter,& Jain, p. 94.
13. Samovar, Porter, & Jain, 73-74
14. Samovar, Porter, & Jan, 76.
15. G. Hofstede, *Culture's Consequences*, 1982 (Newbury Park, CA: Sage), 1982.
16. H.C. Triandis, R. Briskin, & C. H. Hui, "Cross-Cultural Training across the Individualism-Collectivism Divide," *The International Journal of Intercultural Relations*, 1988, p. 12.

17. E.T. Hall & M.R. Hall, *Hidden Differences: Doing Business with the Japanese*, 1987 (Garden City, NY: Doubleday, anchor).
18. Hall & Hall, 54-56, 157.
19. J. Salacuse, "Making Deals in Strange Places: A Beginner's Guide to International Business Negotiations," in J. W. Breslin & J. Z. Rubin, Edts. *Negotiation Theory and Practice*, (Cambridge: The Program on Negotiation at Harvard Law School, 1991), 251-260.
20. L.M. Barna, "Stumbling Blocks in Intercultural Communication," In Samovar & Proctor, *Intercultural Communication*, 348
21. S. Trenholm & A. Jensen, *Interpersonal Communication* Belmont, CA: Wadsworth, 1992), 386.
22. Trenholm & Jensen, 388.
23. Barna, p. 346.
24. Barna, p. 345.
25. Storti, 26, 64-65.
26. K. Oberg, "Culture shock: Adjustment to New Cultural Environments," *Practicing Anthropology*, 7, 1985, 170-179.
27. Stori, 52.
28. Y.Y. Kim, *Communication and Cross-Cultural Adaptation: An integrative Theory* (Philadelphia: Multilingual Matters, 1988), 56-57.
29. Samovar, Porter, & Jain, 145-146.

CHAPTER 14

Negotiation and Conflict Resolution

LEARNING OBJECTIVES

When students have completed this chapter and lesson, they should be able to:

1. Describe the difference between destructive and productive conflict.
2. Describe the potential outcome of conflict in terms of bonding relationships.
3. Recognize the necessary attitudes and skills for the win-win negotiating style in communication.

CHAPTER 14: Overview

The chapter reviews conflict management styles, followed by conflict management skills. Specific suggestions are made for managing negotiations for a "Win-Win" cooperative negotiation. Special skills for anger management, and conflict negotiations are reviewed. Assertive and aggressive behaviors were reviewed to conclude that "I" ownership of our communication becomes central to cooperative conflict negotiation.

My Friend—My Foe
William Blake

I was angry with my friend.
I told my wrath, my wrath did end.

I was angry with my foe:
I told it not, my wrath did grow.
And I watered it in fears,
Night and morning with my tears;
And sunned it with smiles,
And with soft deceitful wiles.

And it grew both day and night,
Till it bore an apple bright;
And my foe beheld it shine,
And into my garden stole
When the night had veiled the pole.

In the morning glad I see
My foe outstretched beneath the tree.

Conflict is a fundamental characteristic of life itself. Whenever two life forms exist in the same environment, each carves out a position of comfort, most often overlapping the other life form. We refer to this as competition, sharing, existing within the same environment, or perhaps just communicating. The negotiation of conflict is inevitable. The goal should be to handle differences and disagreements constructively.

Conflict is the interaction or communication of independent people who perceive incompatible goals or disagree with others in attaining the same goal. Conflict is a communication event. It can result in overt communication, such as shouting, arguing, or reasoning. Some actively avoid communication and refuse to resolve the issues.

People also perceive incompatible goals and blame others as the major interference in attaining goals. This leads to misinterpretation, misunderstanding, or perhaps incomplete communication. Regardless of the cause, conflict becomes a progressive event—moving in cycles and always expanding or decreasing the impact of the communication.

It should be emphasized that communication problems are not the sole cause of conflict. The vast majority of conflicts would not exist without some real difference of interests. Even though these interests vary, there must be a goal or objective for both parties. In order for the goal to be achieved, interaction or communication must occur.

One thing is clear, however. Conflicts are always characterized by a mixture of incentives to cooperate and to compete.[1]

There are five ways to handle conflict: avoiding, accommodating, competing, collaborating, or compromising. Each of these approaches has both advantages and disadvantages, so situational factors will usually govern which one to use at a given time. Negotiations occur when two or more parties discuss specific proposals to find a mutually acceptable agreement. Negotiating skills are essential to conflict resolution and to productive cooperation among participants.

So how do we manage conflict: fight or flight? Do you tackle conflict head-on or seek ways to remove yourself from it? Most of us do not have a single way of dealing with differences, but we do have a tendency to manage conflict following patterns we have used before. The pattern we choose depends on several factors: our personality, the individuals with whom we are in conflict, the time and place of confrontation, and other situational factors.

Conflict Management Styles

Several researchers have attempted to identify the patterns or styles of conflict. One philosophy establishes two dimensions: (1) How concerned are you for others? (2) How concerned are you for yourself?[2] Recent literature[3] considers dimension either productive or unproductive styles. The unproductive conflict is considered unrealistic because it focuses on hurting people. It is an open expression of aggression designed to defeat or humiliate people. The communication has an inflexible "my way or the highway" approach. It is considered unrealistic because the role of communication is directive with only one solution possible. In the role of competition this procedure is considered "I Win—You Lose."

The end product is that the aggressor either wins or withdraws. No compromise is possible. Threats and bad feelings are a definite byproduct. Most communication events in any conflict can best be pictured as cyclical events that either expand the impact or reduce it. In the **confrontational style**, the cyclic event always diminishes because improvement in the problem is reduced. Since movement is only one-way, there is nothing to build on, and eventually the situation terminates without a solution.

Typical communication behavior includes name calling, blaming, accusations of fault, or seeking a scapegoat—someone else to accept blame of failure. Threats and warnings are common, always directed away from the aggressor.

Another unproductive behavior is avoidance, or **non-confrontational style**. Many people would rather experience an unresolved conflict than go through the pain of solving the problem. Typically, they seek approval and try to avoid threats to their self-worth. Virginia Satir, author of a book entitled *Peoplemaking*, describe these people as "syrupy, martyrish, and bootlicking."[4] It is easier to concede than face the conflict. They bring up new issues and change the subject. They remove themselves from the conflict. They leave the scene or drop out of the discussion. They are unproductive and also unrealistic. The conflict is not resolved but only complicated more by the avoidance. This is a "Lose-Lose" conclusion.

To be a productive manager of conflict, the participant must focus on solvable problems. The focus is on activity, events, and things. People become participants, and not the object of conflict. Attitudes are flexible, and compromise is a major tool. Those who take a cooperative style of conflict management view conflicts as a set of problems to be solved, rather than games in which one person wins and another loses. They use other-oriented strategies and foster a "Win-Win" climate, by using the following techniques:[5]

1. **Separate the people from the problem.** They leave personal grievances out of the discussion, describing problems without making judgmental or evaluative statements about personalities.
2. **Focus on shared interests.** They ask questions such as: What do we both want? What do we both value? Where are we already agreeing? There is a conscious attempt to emphasize common interests, values, and goals.
3. **Generate many options to solve the problem.** They use brainstorming and other techniques to generate alternative solutions. They consciously develop conflict management skills.
4. **Base decisions on objective criteria.** They try to establish standards for an acceptable solution to a problem—similar to criteria established when problem solving in group processes. Is it financially possible? How can the work be distributed? Where do we start?

Of the three styles of conflict management, the most obvious approach to productive conflict management focuses on the concept of cooperation. The byproduct of cooperation can provide the following benefits:

1. Cooperation can produce new and creative ideas.
2. Cooperation can release tension, thus strengthening relationships.
3. Cooperation can force reevaluation and goal clarification.
4. Cooperation can stimulate social change to eliminate inequalities and injustice.

It may be true that cooperation and compromise do not provide everything desired, but they can provide the most good for the most participants. They produce the "Win-Win" solution most desired.

If an unproductive or unrealistic conflict management style is in progress, degenerative spirals of criticism, negative comments, and blocking of suggestions halt any progress for conflict resolution. Changes should be initiated to break the cycle or pattern of communication to reduce the unproductive power struggle being produced by the uncooperative participants.

For instance, a relational conflict can arise over whether to spend money on the purchase of a new car. Perhaps Chris objects. Taylor withdraws emotionally. Chris expresses dissatisfaction to Taylor for not wanting to talk about the car and Taylor turns on the television at a high volume. Chris leaves, and goes out to visit a friend. The negative cycle is in full control.

William Wilmot, in his book *Relational Communication* suggests five concrete suggestions to alter degenerative cycles:[6]

1. **Do what comes unnaturally!** Spirals are created by actions of both parties in a relationship. Change is impossible if the same approach continues by both participants. At least one person has to do something "unnaturally." Someone must make a positive, reinforcing, **cooperative** suggestion.
2. **Use third parties.** These can be friends, counselors, clergy, or family. A new, nontoxic idea can often come from an informed but not intimately involved outsider.

3. **Reaffirm your relational goals.** It helps the couple reaffirm the commitment they have to the relationship. This refocuses the issue on the original relational goals, and places the conflict in a positive perspective.
4. **Try "metacommunication."** This just means the communication is about the communication. You talk about the relationship, the strategies, and reasons producing the conflict. This can expose misunderstandings, redefine objectives, and place more perspective on the conflict and less on actions of the people involved.
5. **Try changing the subject.** Spend less time with the person and consider changing the external situation. Changing the mix of the environment can also break troublesome patterns.

Conflict Management activities

Obviously the first two conflict management styles listed above do not solve problems effectively, nor do they foster healthy long-term relationships. Conflict management skills, mentioned in the discussion of cooperative styles can give significant reinforcement to help remedy the problem.[7]

Managing conflict, especially emotion-charged ego conflict, is not easy. Even with a fully developed set of skill, you should not expect to melt tensions and resolve disagreements instantaneously. The following skills can help you generate options that promote understanding and provide a framework for cooperation.

RECAP

Conflict Management Styles

Nonconfrontational Style	Avoids conflict by placating (agreeing), distracting, computing (becoming emotionally detached), or withdrawing from the conflict.
Confrontational Style	Wants to manipulate others by blaming and making threats' sets up win-lose framework.
Cooperative Style	Seeks mutually agreeable resolutions to manage differences. Works within an other-oriented, win-win framework: ▪ Separates people from the problem. ▪ Focuses on shared interests. ▪ Generates many options to solve problems.

Manage Your Emotions

If we are involved with others, it is given that conflict will develop. One of the most fascinating aspects of human behavior is that we do not always obey the laws of the physical world, at least with regard to what causes us to act. So when conflicts arise, there is a knee jerk reaction to immediately determine *who* is at fault, and delay any action until blame is assessed. If we spent half as much time changing the ways we respond in conflict situations as we do trying to figure out who is at fault, most of our troubles would soon vanish.

The laws of physics are based on a model of "linear causality." Human behavior is best described as being based on "circular causality." What this means is that unlike the physical world, where it may be determined that one thing *causes* another, which in turn *causes* something else, human interactions are both causes *and* effects of what transpired previously. Invariably conflict actions are interdependent, playing off of and reacting in response to each other's behavior. More often than not, circular causality is the most appropriate model for explaining what takes place during conflict situations.[8]

The best way to change this negative spiral is to take responsibility for your part of the conflict. Ask yourself four questions: "How are you disowning the problem? In what ways are you making excuses for yourself? What are your favorite scapegoats for diverting blame away from yourself? What might you do internally to feel more in control over what happens externally? If these questions can be discussed with the other person, and honest answers are given by both participants, you can quickly move into actually working on the problem, and not assigning guilt for failure to the people involved.

Another typical response, which again forces the attention away from the issue and forces individuals to concentrate on people, is anger. Often the first sign that we are in a conflict situation is a feeling of anger, frustration, fear, or sadness, which sweeps over us like an ocean wave. If we feel powerless to control our own fate, then we will have difficulty taking a logical or rational approach to managing the conflict. Expressing our feelings in an emotional outburst may make us feel better for the moment, but it may close the door to logical, rational negotiation.

When we are emotionally charged, we experience physical changes:

...our adrenalin flows faster and our strength increases by about 20 percent. The liver, pumping sugar into the bloodstream, demands more oxygen from the heart and lungs. The veins become enlarged and the cortical centers where thinking takes place do not perform nearly as well. . . . the blood supply to the problem-solving part of the brain is severely decreased because, under stress, a greater portion of blood is diverted to the body's extremities.[9]

Manage Anger

A common emotion described above is anger. Anger is unique to human behavior. It is a biological function producing increased activity in both energy and emotion. It can result in expressions of strong displeasure or develop into violent attacks. It may be either beneficial or harmful. Its drawbacks include action without thought and expressions we really do not mean but which help us vent. It pushes our behavior beyond control or logical action, but sometimes does provide a vent to reduce tension. But uncensored angry words can escalate the anger you feel and also increase others' anger. The best solution to convert anger into a beneficial emotion is to consider the following rules for anger management:

Rule 1: Recognize and acknowledge your anger. If you know you are going to face a situation that rapidly elevates your negative emotions, acknowledge the danger signs and prepare yourself. Assertively express your feelings but make yourself promise not to degenerate into a shouting match or physical retaliation.

Rule 2: Clarify the issues and the setting. This means the best argument has both parties on the same page. It is embarrassing to have a good fight, then find out you were discussing two separate ideas. One person should not be standing and the other sitting. Face each other eye-to-eye. Monitor the conversation closely to provide equal footing, equal stature, and level ideas.

Rule 3: Be silent, then accurate. If you are angry and afraid you might say something you will regret; listen before you speak. Expressing hostile words can cause you to lose friends and make enemies. Not expressing your feelings can cause your anger to grow, distracts you from the goal, and can sidetrack your intensions. Hidden anger never goes away. Listening first, then speaking, can temper your aggression, improve your logical thought, and permit the other person to release some tension before you begin.

Rule 4: Express your concern nonverbally. Perhaps you can find a friend who will serve as a sounding board to practice on. Exercise—take a walk, and even act out the motions you will use when confronting the conflict. Since much of the emotional message is communicated nonverbally, use your facial expression and eyes to let the other person know you care about him or her. Your communication partner will believe what you do more than what you say. Therefore, a good rehearsal can prepare your actions for everyone's benefit.

Rule 5: Express your anger directly, yet make an appropriate empathic statement. "I think I see why you are so upset!" "I have similar feelings so I know how you feel." These remarks describe both views of the issue objectively. Focus on the task and not the person. Be assertive, not aggressive.

Rule 6: After the event, let go of the anger. Remind yourself that no one can make you angry. This puts you back in control of your own emotions. Realize that no matter what others may do, your angry emotions are created within your own mind and body. Even though others may do and say things that can upset you, you are the only person who can control you and your response to others.

Rule 7: Recognize that angry emotional outbursts rarely change someone's mind. Exploding in an angry tirade may make you feel better for a moment by getting it "off your chest" but it usually does little to advance understanding and manage the issues at hand. Resolving issues is never achieved by attacking people!

Such actions influence our fight-flight responses. If we choose to stay, verbal or physical violence may erupt; if we flee from the conflict, we cannot resolve it. Until we tone down but not eliminate our emotions, we will find it difficult to participate in worthwhile communication.

Conflict Management Skills

So as conflict negotiations begin and progress, applying the following strategies can improve your conflict management success:[10]

Select an acceptable time and place for a calm discussion. Obviously the heat of battle does not provide the atmosphere for calm discussion. After a cooling off period, set a time where both of you can rationally discuss the issue. Do not procrastinate indefinitely, but provide enough time to gain control of your feelings and think the issue through. Sometimes issues need to be discussed on the spot and you may not have the luxury to wait. But whenever it is practical, make sure the other person is ready to receive you and your message. This also implies you will give the other person a fair opportunity to present the other side of the issue calmly.

Plan your message. Take the time to organize your message. In this world of confusion, organization is key! Identify your goal, including the anticipated conclusion. State clearly what you would like; do not barge in and pour out your emotions, either tears or violence.

It helps to discuss your plan with a friend first to see if they understand your proposal. If you do not talk with a friend, consider writing down the key ideas you want to express. Let your notes cool for a few hours and reread them. This gives you a chance to separate your emotions from your words. This can be an excellent way of framing the issues of disagreement in a less inflammatory rhetoric.

Monitor Nonverbal Messages. Keep in mind that your actions speak more loudly than your words. Your facial expressions, the fire in your eye, and the tone of your voice can convey anger, pity, sarcasm, or sincerity though the words never change. Speaking calmly, using direct eye contact, and maintaining a natural facial expression will signal you wish to discuss rather than control. Your nonverbal message should also support your verbal response. If you say you are listening to someone, but you continue to read the paper, work on a report, or talk on your cell phone, you are showing lack of interest in both the issue and the person involved.

Avoid Personal Attacks, Name-calling, and Emotional Overstatement. Using threats and derogatory names can turn a simple conflict into an ego conflict. Attack requires protection, and this means a refocus of strategy, goals, and even issues. Also try to avoid exaggerating your emotions. If you say you are irritated or annoyed rather than furious, you can still communicate your feelings, but you will take the sting out of your description.

Avoid the bad habit of gunny sacking. This occurs when you dredge up old problems and issues from the past, like pulling them out of an old bag or gunny sack, to use against your partner. Keep your focus on the issues at hand, not old hurts from the past. Gunny sacking usually succeeds only in increasing tension, escalating emotions, and reducing listening effectiveness. Keep your discussions productive rather than allow them to degenerate into emotional shouting matches.

Use Self-Talk. When Tom was chairing the committee meeting, Monique accused him of falsifying the attendance numbers at the last fine arts festival. Instead of lashing back at Monique, he paused, took a slow, deep, yet unnoticed breath, and thought, "I'm tired. If I snarl back, all we will do is escalate this issue out of proportion. I'll talk with Monique later after we have both cooled down." Perhaps you think that talking to yourself is an eccentricity. Nothing could be further from the truth. Thoughts are directly linked to feelings,[11]and messages we tell ourselves play a major role in how we feel and respond to others. Ask yourself whether an emotional tirade and an escalating conflict will produce the results you want. A critical effect of self talk is that it requires you to "think" about what is happening. Too many times we disengage our thoughts but keep our mouth running. Without rational thought, no conversation is worthwhile. In conflict it can breed violence, bad feelings, and destroyed relationships.

When Eleanor Roosevelt noted that "No one can make you feel inferior without your consent," she was acknowledging the power of self-talk in affecting our emotional response to what others say and do. It can make all the difference between success and failure in conflict resolution.

Manage Information

Because uncertainty, misinformation, and misunderstanding are often byproducts of conflict and disagreement, skills that promote mutual understanding are an important component of cooperative conflict management. The following specific suggestions can help you reduce uncertainty and enhance the quality of communication during conflict.

Clearly Describe the Conflict-Producing Events. Instead of just blurting out your complaints in random order, think of delivering a brief, well-organized message. Simply put, describe the situation, giving the essential facts. The events should be presented in chronological order. Offer your perspective on what created the conflict, sequencing the events like a well-organized story. Include definitions and parameters of the issues. Think of yourself as a journalist who is reporting on a news event. After the facts have been presented, conclude by presenting the problem as an either-or, question, or proposed policy, introducing at least two choices for points of discussion. When proposing potential solutions for discussion, always consider the perceived goal for both parties. Without mutual goal perception, the issue becomes a persuasive argument and not a conflict resolution.

"Own" Your Statements by Using Descriptive "I" Language. "I feel upset when you post the week's volunteer schedule without first consulting with me," reveals Katrina. Her statement describes her feelings as her own. If she had said, "You always prepare a schedule without telling anyone first. All of us who volunteer are mad about that," her statement would have had an accusatory sting. Beginning the statement with "you" sets the listener up for a defensive response. Also, notice that in the second statement, the speaker does not take responsibility for the problem; she suggests that it belongs to several unidentified people as well. If you narrow the issue down to a conflict between you and the other person, you put the conflict into a more manageable framework.

Use Effective Listening Skills. Managing information is a two-way process. Whether you are describing a conflict situation to someone, or that individual is bringing a conflict to your attention, good listening skills are invaluable.

Give your full attention to the speaker and make a conscious point of tuning out your internal messages. Sometimes the best thing to do after describing the conflict-producing events is simply to wait for a response. If you do not stop talking and give the other person a chance to respond, they will feel frustrated, the emotional pitch will go up a notch, and it will become more difficult to reach an understanding. The negative spiral effect mentioned earlier will expand the problem, multiply the misunderstandings, and increase the stress of the conflict.

Finally, focus not only on the facts or details, but also analyze them so you can understand the major point the speaker is making. Try to use your understanding of the details to interpret the speaker's major ideas. You might even repeat the key issues back to the speaker to be sure you are both on the same page. Remember to stay other-oriented and "seek to understand rather than to be understood."[12]

Check Your Understanding of What Others Say and Do. Respond clearly and appropriately. Your response and that of your conflict partner will confirm that you have understood each other. Checking perceptions is vital when emotions run high.

When Others Are Not Other-Oriented: Be Assertive.

Even if you master collaborative conflict management skills, others may be irrational, issuing inappropriate demands that create conflict and tension. In these instances, you will need to assert yourself, especially if someone has aggressively violated your rights.

To assert yourself is to let your communication partner know that their behavior or message is infringing on your rights. To maintain cooperative negotiation and produce a positive spiral of successful communication, you have the right to refuse a request someone makes of you, the right to express your feelings, and the right to have your personal needs met. However, your partner has the same privilege, and you are required to honor their rights and feelings also.

Aggressiveness means pursuing your interests by denying the rights of others. This creates hostilities, negative spirals, and unprofitable negotiations. Assertiveness is other-oriented; aggressiveness is exclusively self-oriented. Aggressive people are coercive. They blame, judge, and evaluate to get what they want. They use intimidating non-verbal cues such as steely stares, a bombastic voice, and flailing gestures. Assertive people can ask for what they want without judging or evaluating their partner.

Assertive communicators take ownership of their wishes and requests by using "I" messages to express their thoughts and feelings rather than "you" messages that push negative implications on others. "I" messages describe what you want by expressing your feelings and goals. "You" messages lead with an attack on the person. "You creep! You ate the last breakfast taco" is an aggressive "you" statement. "I asked you to save one taco for me; now I won't have anything to eat for breakfast" is an assertive statement that reaffirms your rights and describes the consequences of violating them.

BUILDING YOUR SKILLS

How to Assert Yourself

Working with a partner, describe a situation in which you could have been more assertive. Ask your partner to assume the role of the person toward whom you should have been more assertive. Now replay the situation, using the following skills:

1. **Describe**: Tell the other person that what he or she is doing bothers you. Describe rather than evaluate.
2. **Disclose**: Then tell he other person how you feel. For example, "I feel X when you do Y..."
3. **Identify Effects**: Tell the other person the effects of his or her behavior upon you or your group. Be as dear and descriptive as you can.
4. **Wait**: After you have described, disclosed, and identified the effects, wait for a response.
5. **Reflect**: Use eflective listening skills: question, paraphrase content, paraphrase feelings.

Observation of Assertiveness Skills

Ask your classmates toobserve your roleplay and provide feedback, using the following checklist.

When you have finished asserting your point of view, reverse roles.

Clearly describes what the problem was. __________

Effectively discloses how he or she felt. __________

Clearly describes he effects of the behavior. __________

Pauses or waits after describing the effects. __________

Uses effective questions to promote understanding. __________

Accurately paraphrases content. __________

Accurately paraphrases feelings. __________

Has good eye contact. __________

Leans forward while speaking. __________

Has an open body posture. __________

Has appropriate voice tone and quality. __________

Chapter 14: Analysis and Application Exercise

1. Interview two people who have been in conflict negotiation: one who succeeded and the other who failed. This can be a person who has been in a business partnership that succeeded and a person who has been in one that failed, or someone who has a successful marriage and one whose marriage has failed.
2. Determine the differences of the above in terms of conflict resolution skills, how one person succeeded and one failed. Determine this by interviewing each on the way they resolved conflicts when they arose.

References

1. J. Stewart, "Managing Conflict by Turning Walls into Bridges," *Bridges Not Walls*, 9th ed. (Boston: McGraw Hill, 2006) 478.
2. R. Kilmann & K. Thomas, "Interpersonal Conflict handling Behavior as Reflections of Jungian Personality Dimensions," *Psychological Reports* 37 (1975): 971-80.

3. Stewart, Ibid, P. 482-485.
4. V. Satir, *Peoplemaking* (Palo Alto: Science and Behavior Books, 1972).
5. R. Fisher & W. Ury, *Getting to Yes: Netgotiating Agreement Without Giving In* (Boston: Houghton Mifflin, 1988).
6. Wilmont, as quoted in Stewart, Ibid, p. 488.
7. Our discussion of conflict management skills is based on several excellent discussions of conflict management prescriptions. We acknowledge: Fisher and Ury, *Getting to Yes*; R. Boulton, *People Skills* (New York: Simon & Schuster, 1979); D. A. Romig & L.J. Romig, *Structured Teamwork Guide* (Austin TX: Performance Resources, 1990; O. Hargie, C. Saunders, and D. Dickson, *Social Skills in Interpersonal Communication* (London: Routledge, 1994); S. Deep & L. Sussman, *Smart Moves* (Reading, MA: Addison-Wesley, 1990); J. L Hocker & W.W. Wilmont, *Interpersonal Conflict,* Madison, WI: Brown & Benchmark, 1994); M.E. Davis, E.L. Eshelman, & M. McKay, *The Relaxation and Stress Reduction Workbook* (Oakland, CA: New Harbinger Publications, 1982). W.A. Donobue & R. Kolt, *Managing Interpersonal Conflict* (Newbury Park CA: Sage Publications, 1992); O. Hargie, ed., *The Handbook of Communication Skills* (London: Routledge, 1997; J. Stewart, "Managing Conflict by Turning Walls into Bridges," *Bridges Not Walls* 9th ed. (Boston: McGraw Hill, 2006) 473-540.
8. J. Kotter, "Taking Responsibility Without Blaming," *Bridges, Not Walls,* Ibid, 505-513.
9. Bolton, *People Skills,* 217.
10. A. Ellis, *A New Guide to Rational Living* (North Hollywood, CA: Wilshire books, 1977).
11. Ellis, *A New Guide to Rational Living.*
12. S.R. Covey, *The Seven Habits of Highly Effective People* (New York: Simon & Schuster, 1989), 235.

CHAPTER 15

Conflict Climate

LEARNING OBJECTIVES

When students have completed this chapter and lesson, they should be able to:

1. Explain the communication climate of conflict.
2. List and give examples of four causes of conflict.
3. Understand the role of communication in conflict.
4. Understand the advantages of creating supportive as opposed to defensive climates.
5. Understand the myths about conflict.

CHAPTER 15: Overview

This chapter describes the degree of stress and intensity of assertive behavior influencing the communication climate surrounding negation. Characteristics influencing the climate include egos, misunderstandings, goal objectives, gender and culture. Barriers to productive climates are reviewed. Ethics and myths about conflict negotiations are also reviewed.

The Garden Bottle

In my living room on display is an old fashioned five gallon wine bottle, except it does not contain wine. Permanently corking the narrow opening is a large rubber stopper. It successfully cuts off all contact with the real world. But the inquiring eye can see through the light green glass a perfect world without conflict. Green, lush foliage fills the interior. Living in a beautifully controlled climate, each plant constantly regenerates itself, never taking more than its share of space, moisture and nutrients. Each occupant gives back to the environment as much as it takes, and everything lives in perfect harmony. The plants are as vital as they were over thirty years ago when the garden was planted and the stopper put in place. The garden bottle has a conflict free environment. It is beautiful, but unchanging. It is attractive to the eye but nothing ever happens!

Conflict Climates

As we learned in Chapter 14, interpersonal conflict is a struggle that occurs when two people cannot agree on a way to meet their goals. When goals are incompatible, or when resources are limited, or when individuals opt to compete rather than cooperate to achieve their desires, then conflict occurs. In figure 15.1, Keltner developed his "struggle spectrum," describing conflicts that range from mild differences to violent fights.[1]

This illustration can best be understood if we consider this a view of the "communication climate" surrounding a discussion between two people. Both people are individuals with different goals, experiences, genders, cultures and even educational levels. Each participant brings a background filled with skills to be used in creating a consensus among all participants. Since each introduces a different perspective, the climate governing the discussion changes.

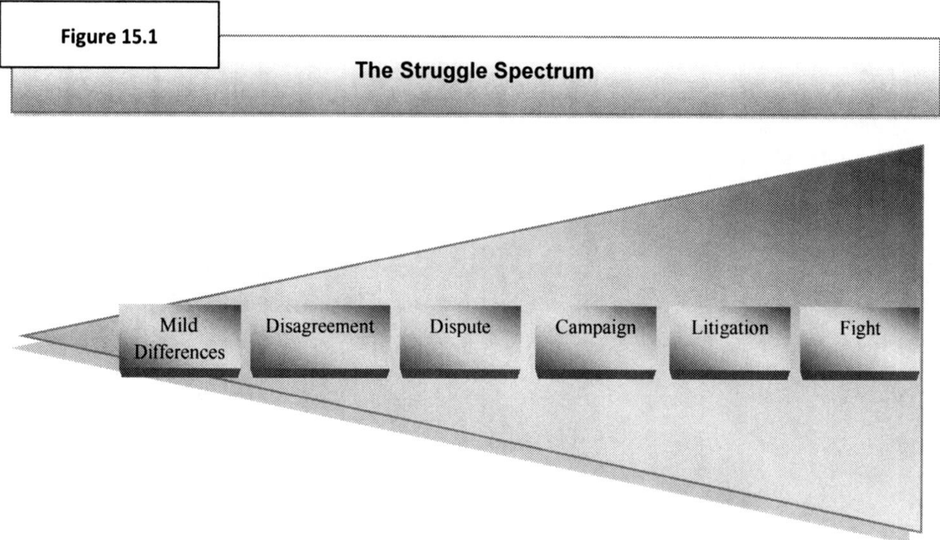

As can be seen, intensity and stress occurring in the communication can dictate the climate of the communication. To obtain a perfect balance in the climate, as observed in the garden bottle, five types of conflict illustrate the problem as well as suggest potential solutions.

Miller and Steinberg list three terms describing intangible variables contaminating the communication climate:[2]

1. Pseudo Conflict: This is miscommunication, misunderstanding, or incomplete information.

Bank Teller: Put your "John Henry" on the bottom line.

The customer begins writing ""John Hen—"

"No! No! I mean *your* name."

"That is my name: John Henry Hall!"

The meaning of the message was misunderstood. Additional information or clarification can protect against larger conflict.

2. Simple Conflict. Simple conflict stems from differences in ideas, definitions, perceptions or goals. You want to go to Disney World for your vacation; your spouse wants to go to Washington, D.C. Your spouse wants to fly; you want the train. You understand each other, but you disagree. The key to unraveling a simple conflict is to keep the climate focused on issues at hand and not focus upon personalities and individual personality traits.

3. Ego Conflict. Ego conflict occurs once differences are observed in the desired solution; the discussants leave the issues and start describing the inadequacies of the opposition party. A classic example can be observed in many political conflicts as people compete for elected office. Once the candidates are selected, too often the major communication becomes description of character traits, past histories, implied slander, or any number of remarks that change the climate from examining skills of each candidate as matched to job description, and deal in character assassination. Certainly the climate changes from inquiry to accusation, and cooperation changes to competition, with everyone losing.

4. Gender Conflict. Much controversy exists about differences in communication between males and females. Popular authors have capitalized on differences, proclaiming men are from Mars; women are from Venus.[3] Many have declared this communication conflict is a creation of the media, but certainly merchandisers believe men and women differ in their purchases. Almost anyone would agree the

Figure 15.2

Females	Males
Concerned with equity and caring; connect with and feel responsible to others.	Concerned with equality of rights and fairness; adhere to abstract principles, rules.
Interact toachieve closeness and interdependence.	Interact for instrumental purposes; seek autonomy and distance.
Attend to interpersonal dynamics toassess relationship's health.	Are less aware of interpersonal dynamics.
Encourage mutual involvement.	Protect self-interest.
Attribute crises toproblems in the relationship.	Attribute crises toproblems external to the relationship.
Are concerned with the impact of the relationship on personal identity.	Are neither self- nor relationship-centered.
Respond to conflict by often focusing mainly on the relationship.	Respond to conflict by often focusing on rules and being evasive until aunilateral decision is reached.

conversations of groups of each gender tend to be quite different. The most obvious differences in gender communication concluded by Olsen[4] are described in Figure 15.2:

Discussions of gender communication suggest that women are more likely to focus on relationship issues, and men review tasks. Women are interested in bonding and intimacy, but men are job oriented. Men are often more aggressive and assertive than women when pursuing a goal or conquest[5]. Even though it is difficult to assess differences in the communication skills and usage of different genders, in most cultures, gender directly affects the climate and intensity of communication. There is a tendency in such climates to infer the conclusion is influenced by a feminine or masculine attitude. Again the secret to success is to focus on issues and events—not men or women!

5. Culture Conflict. As stated in Chapter 13, cultural differences significantly impact understanding based on background, training, and location. Even though culture is a learned behavior, and "unlearning" for the good of the cause is possible, the influence of home and family provide significant influence on behavior. Even the determination of what is credible material can be influenced by such elements as religion or political influence, limiting the flexibility of accepting recommended decisions. The best approach to conflict resolution when cultural influence contaminates the communication climate is to focus on the issues relating to an accepted and previously agreed-upon goal. Successful negotiations may happen in a "micro climate" where we leave our hat and badge at the door, enter the negotiation as just an "I" person not representing our background and culture, and talk to another person who has also left behind their cultural ties until a solution is reached. In effect, we enter a "Garden Bottle" climate to solve our conflicts!

Barriers to Productive Conflict Climates

Individual egos, educational backgrounds, and even personality traits can create differences in an individual's ability to self disclose and relate to another's interpretation of the situation. Conflict, properly handled, often produces stronger and more durable relationships. Conflict in itself should not be considered negative or destructive, but a natural part of any relationship. However, when the atmosphere for communication involves persons defending opinions by engaging in attacks on others, there is no productive climate. Here are some potential barriers to a productive negotiation climate:

- One of the participants becomes a winner while someone loses.
- At least one of the negotiators holds so tightly to their opinions that they are willing to act aggressively. One withholds his feelings or withdraws in fear of losing, or both resort to name calling, emphasizing the other's inadequacies.
- At least one participant places a different importance on the goal, placing either too much or too little value on their personal objective.
- At least one participant feels inadequate or not equal to the other participants.
- One of the participants interprets the solution as being incompatible with their personal values. They feel they are forced to do things they do not want to do.

The end product of a negative negotiation climate is destructive, and deemed a failure to at least one participant. Communication systems break down, negotiation spirals out of control, feelings are hurt, and often relationships end.

The following statistics related to divorce in the United States illustrate that conflict can be destructive. Over 50 percent of marriages will end in divorce. The rate of divorce has increased by 700 percent since 1900. Most divorces occur between the second and sixth year of marriage. In *USA Today,* Karen Peterson reported the risk for divorce in second marriages is almost 70 percent. Finally, more than one third of the children in the United States have endured the painful experience of their parents' divorce.[6]

All conflict is not necessarily destructive. The two people resolving an issue provides a climate that stimulates activity. Personalities interpret such stimulation as either motivational or painful. Some people are moved to action. Other people flee the uncomfortable feeling convinced they are foolish, inadequate, or angry. The negotiation is destroyed.

For better success, practice **Self-regulation.** Control your emotions and avoid inflammatory talk. Avoid hurtful communication. **Self-expression** of descriptive rather than accusatory or defensive explanations makes the atmosphere more pleasant.

Practice the skill of **Negotiation.** This implies compromise, finding a "Win-Win" solution for all participants. Keep in mind the relationship is more important than the solution. "We are confirming the importance of the relationship when we give its survival a higher priority than winning the conflict." The bottom line is effective communication.[7]

Unfortunately, the American Way is often to "beat the other team at any cost," "stick to your guns," "my way or the highway." We are competitors and we love to win. But the desires to get along with others—yet beat them in competition—are contradictory. The idea that if one person wins, the other must lose, is implanted in the American mind early in life.

Supportive and Defensive Climates

As each of us participates in a meaningful discussion, an emotionally charged atmosphere significantly influences both the amount and quality of participation and information contributed to the discussion. Human nature requires a feeling by each participant that everyone is accepted, our ideas are considered, and we are supported by those we consider important associates. This is true of social groups, athletic teams, study groups, work groups, or any other number of people who surround us. Researchers have determined support in communication is behavior that is descriptive rather than evaluative and provisional rather than certain. Conflict negotiations have a strong tendency to polarize based on the acceptance level created by the atmosphere of the negotiation environment. Jack Gibb classified this bipolar climate as either supportive or defensive.[8] Gibb's classification listed six categories:

Defensive Climates	Supportive Climates
Evaluation: Causes defensiveness—limits our responses.	**Description:** Open and willing to share—we feel accepted
Control: Conveys feeling of discomfort and coercion—discourages suggestions. Wants conformation, not help.	**Problem Orientation:** Encourages suggestions and unique ideas. Participants have a vested interest.
Strategy: Implies hidden agendas and secrets not shared. Turns off thinking.	**Spontaneity:** Encourages input and new ideas. Free thinking rewarded.
Neutrality: Implies lack of concern—just mediates with no ownership in results.	**Empathy:** Someone cares about us. Others share our emotion—feels *with* us.
Superiority: On an ego trip—a *better than you* attitude, implying no compromise! Causes rejection and poor listening.	**Equality:** Open minded attitude—encourages opposing viewpoints. Implies together we are invincible.
Certainty: Implies no tolerance for different ideas. My way or the highway!	**Provisionally:** Open—minded attitude. Supports expression of all ideas.

Because supportive climates are descriptive rather than evaluative, and provisional rather than pre-determined, people are motivated to contribute creative ideas. Defensive climates force carefully guarded comments that might be misunderstood. Fewer risks are taken because of the fear of judgment. As a result, negotiations are limited, usually creating a defensive "Win-Lose" condition. The loser is rejected, and bonded relationships are stressed or broken. Future negotiations are rare, and the entire negotiation process terminates, usually along with any type of bonding relationship between parties.

Defensive climates create a psychological barrier, causing you to react by throwing up a barrier against that threat. This creates lack of trust and cooperation, resulting in limited communication, a reluctance to make commitments, and few suggestions towards a settlement.

If a supportive climate makes the participant feel secure, accepted, and trustworthy negotiations are more likely to produce positive results and stronger bonding relationships. A supportive negotiation climate produces better understanding of group members and issues, better involvement, increased motivation, better decisions, and greater group cohesiveness.[9] These benefits are more likely to occur when groups open themselves to collaboration and compromise.

One author referred to this communication atmosphere as "**principled negotiation.**"[10] This procedure is based on ethical principles that encourage respect and compassion. Information is exchanged by asking questions instead of making demands or taking a rigid position on differences. There is a compatible relationship among all participants regarding the outcome. Participants must take into account other participants' views and consider them in the way they would like their own views to be considered. To resolve conflict, participants must communicate in a climate that permits free discussion of all differences. All must avoid a competitive, defensive atmosphere where ideas are censored before being discussed. Two key words governing this climate are cooperation and respect.

Ethical Behavior and Conflict

Brilhart and Galanes suggest that using ethical behavior during a conflict situation creates a better understanding of the issues and increases cohesiveness. Using ethical behaviors minimizes destructive outcomes, such as hurt feelings and personal attacks. They recommend the following:

1. Express disagreements openly and honestly.
2. Stay on topic. Be direct and get to the point.
3. Criticize ideas, not people.
4. Base conclusions on solid evidence and good reasoning—avoid rumor, emotional outbursts, or undocumented information.
5. Receive all disagreements and avoid censorship. Keep an open mind and listen carefully.
6. Remain calm. Do not take criticism personally.
7. Look for ways to integrate ideas and to negotiate differences.

Myths about Conflict

Many people distrust the negotiation process and harbor feelings of concern and avoidance for the process. This is often because of misconceptions about the negotiation process. Judgmental, stressful, hostile, aggressive, negative situations or climates, and even family traditions might be called Conflict Myths:[11]

Myth 1: Conflict can always be avoided. "If you can't say anything nice, don't say anything at all." Tradition implies conflict is unnatural, harmful, and leads to stressful conversations and broken relationships. It is a myth to avoid negotiation.

Myth 2: Conflict always occurs because of misunderstanding. It is a common myth to blame everything on misunderstanding. Too often we use this approach as a platform to launch our own persuasive argument, implying that if you understood me, you would agree with me. The major problem is that we disagree about whose goal is most important. Conflicts do sometimes flare up because of a lack of understanding or empathy for the other person, but there are times when individuals simply have different needs or goals. It is a myth to blame conflict on misunderstanding.

Myth 3: Conflict is always a sign of a poor interpersonal relationship. It is an oversimplification to link all conflict to underlying relational problems. Constant bickering and sniping can be a "climate" for deeper problems, but disagreements do not signpost a broken relationship. Overly polite, stilted conversation is more likely to signal a problem than are periodic disagreements. Such exaggerations clearly signal an unfriendly climate or basic distrust. The free expression of honest disagreement is a hallmark of a healthy relationship. Conflicts imply interest in a strong relationship. It is a myth to blame a weak relationship on conflict.

Myth 4: Conflict can always be resolved. Consultants and corporate training experts teach elimination of conflict, almost commanding good will and harmony to prevail. Some people claim that with the application of a few skills and how-to techniques, conflicts can disappear, much like a stain from a shirt laundered with the right kind of detergent. This is not true. Not all differences can be resolved by compromising, listening more carefully, or paraphrasing your partner's message. Some disagreements and personal goals are so intense and the perceptions so fixed that individuals may have to agree to disagree and live with it. It is a myth to say every conflict can be completely resolved.

Myth 5: Conflict is always bad. It is a common fantasy to dream of eliminating all interpersonal conflict from our relationships. We think that if we extinguish all disagreement, hassle, haggling and tension life would be blissful. In fact, if a relationship is conflict-free, the individuals are probably not being honest with each other. They would be living in the garden bottle. Nothing ever happens—positively or negatively. By avoiding conflict, we eliminate the potential for significant positive change. It is a myth to say conflict is bad.

Chapter 15: Analysis and Application Exercises

1. Describe a recent conflict you have experienced. Analyze it according to the following:
   A. How did you feel during conflict? How about those with you? Describe the stress, bad feelings, motivation, or other measures of the climate.
   B. Describe how the resolution created either a supportive or defensive climate. What was the positive or negative result?
   C. Differentiate the difference between "skills" used in negotiation as apposed to "attitude" of the participants.
   D. Relate the impact of personal goals, skills, attitudes, and values on conflict resolution.

2. Choose a member of your immediate family. How do you handle conflicts with that person? Does one management style dominate? Describe with examples.

References

1. J.W. Keltner, *Mediation: Toward a Civilized System of Dispute Resolution* (Annandale VA: Speech Communication Association, 1987).
2. G. Miller & M. Steinberg, *Between People: A New Analysis of Interpersonal Communication* (Chicago: Science Research Associates, 1975), 264.
3. J. Gray, *Men are from Mars, Women are from Venus* (New York: Harper-Collins, 1992).
4. M. Olsen, *The Process of Social Organization* (New York: Holt Rinehart, & Winston, 1978).
5. J. Hocker & W. Wilmont, *Interpersonal Conflict* (Dubuque, IA: Brown and Benchmark, 1994).
6. K.M. Gavin & B.J. Brommel, *Family Communication: Cohesion and Change*, 3rd Ed (Glenview, Ill: Scott, Foresman, 1991), 7; L. Bumpass, "Children and Maritial Disruption: A Replication and Update," Demography 21 (1984): 71-82; H.S. Friedman, J.S. Tucker, J.E. Swartz, L.R. Martin, C. Tomlison-Kelsey, D.L. Wingard, and M.H. Criqui, "Childhood Conscientiousness and Longevity: Health Behavior and Cause of Death," *Journal of Personality and Social Psychology* 68 (1995); 696-703.
7. W.W. Wilmot, *Interpersonal Conflict*, 3rd ed. (New York: Random House, 1987) 230; Wilmot & Hocker, Interpersonal Conflict, 236.
8. J. Gibb, "Defensive Communication," *Journal of Communication*, ll, 141-148.
9. J. Brillhart & G. Galanes, *Effective Group Discussion*, 9th ed. (New York: McGraw-Hill, 1998), 274-277.
10. R. Fisher & W. Ury, Getting to Yes: *Negotiating Agreement Without Giving In* (Boston: Houghton Mifflin, 1981).
11. R.J. Doolittle, *Orientations of Communication and Conflict* (Chicago: Science Research Associates, 1976), 7-9.

CHAPTER 16

The Ethics of Communication

LEARNING OBJECTIVES

When students have completed this chapter and lesson, they should be able to:

1. Differentiate between morals and ethics.
2. List and describe the four essential ethics of our culture, including why they are needed.
3. Describe how to react when ethics and morals clash.
4. List and explain the ten ethics of communication.
5. Demonstrate an ability to make ethical decisions in communicative settings.

CHAPTER 16: Overview

Ethics and morals are codes of conduct by which we discipline our lives. While morals are personal codes, ethics are societal—codes that are nearly universal within a given culture. To be ethical, communicators must know what the ethics of our culture are, know how to apply them, and personally resolve to do so, particularly in communicative settings with other people.

This chapter begins with an overview of ethical approaches that have been identified and used in the past. The relationship between morals and ethics is discussed, along with the importance of ethics to our sense of community. Four general ethics of United States culture are identified and illustrated. The chapter ends with a list and discussion of ten ethics of communication.

INTRODUCTION

The current difficulties in our society and in our relationships illustrate the need for ethics. Without rules to guide our conduct, the potential to do harm is great and we can never know what to expect. The U.S. Departments of Education[1] and of Labor[2], plus many other associations and corporations[3], have noted a pressing need for college graduates who know how to work ethically with fellow citizens and workers.

The question arises, "Which ethics should apply?" Vivian[4] identifies dozens of ethical types and approaches, including but not limited to the following:

- Prescriptive ethics: Do this and don't do that
- Utilitarian ethics: Whatever tends to the greatest happiness
- Pragmatic ethics: Judging by the results
- Egalitarian ethics: Ignoring social position and other discriminating factors
- Social responsibility: Serving society responsibly
- Deontological ethics: A duty to follow good rules
- Teleological ethics: Concern for the consequences
- Situational ethics: Deciding based on the facts of the situation

This confusing array of ethical codes could make applying ethics difficult unless some universal set of them can be established for communication settings. Having reviewed these, and many others, the author of this chapter offers a set of four general ethics and ten that are related specifically to communication.

Ethics and Morals

A quick review of most college textbooks in the past would reveal one pervasive trend: ethics were simply not discussed. Why? The answer probably involves some confusion over the definition of an ethic and how it differs from a moral. Morals discussions are important and appropriate in church and personal settings. They are not appropriate—indeed, they are unethical—in a public school setting. So, what is the difference between a moral and an ethic?

Both morals and ethics are codes of conduct—standards or rules that people use to guide their behavior. Both are also culturally bound. Most of ours are based on Greek, Latin, and Judeo-Christian traditions. In a different cultural setting, different rules would apply. We can distinguish between morals and ethics as follows:

- Morals are personal codes of conduct—those that may differ from one person to the next and tend to be very personal. We all have morals (our own set of rules), but others are not obligated to agree with them and they should not be imposed on others against their will.
- Ethics are codes of conduct that are society-wide. These are rules on which a given society has come to agree.

Here is a useful definition of an ethic:

An ethic is a code of conduct that is so widespread in its acceptance within a particular culture or group that it is nearly universal.

For this definition to work we have to define "acceptance." Acceptance means it is *expected*, but not that people will always *do* it. People violate ethics all the time. When they do, we call them "unethical." If an ethic is violated, a penalty follows.

Why do we need ethics? Why aren't morals sufficient? Figure 16.1 illustrates the answer. Within a society, there will be many sets of morals—moral pockets that are subscribed to by one subgroup or another. The basis of a larger community is ethics—shared values that all participants acknowledge (know about), whether or not they choose to observe them. If there are no such shared values, there is no community. We are left with only our moral pockets from which we proceed to argue (sometimes make war) over each other's values.

Figure 16.1

An Ethical Boundary

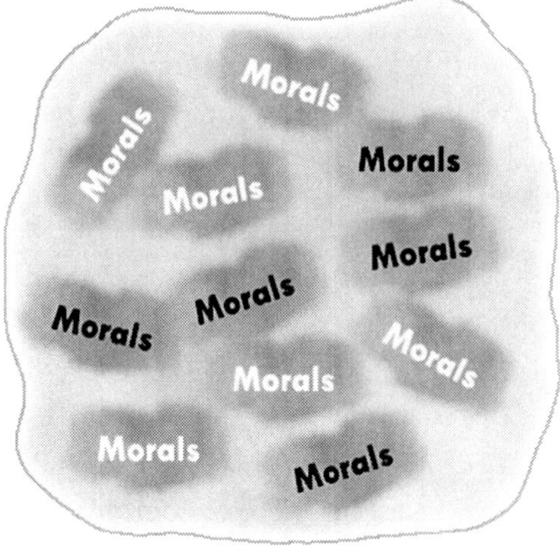

No Ethical Boundary

Examples of such moral pockets would include street gangs and militias. The moral codes by which these groups operate may be completely unacceptable to those outside them, and the groups themselves acknowledge only those values and rules that are their own. This is a formula for the destruction of society as we know it. Ethics are the glue that holds us together, the boundary that surrounds our various moral pockets and provides universal protection.

Four General Ethics

Returning to the definition of an ethic given earlier, the question may be asked, "What codes of conduct (if any) are so widespread in their acceptance within our culture as to be nearly universal? In the setting of the United States, there appear to be at least four.

1. Honesty: By definition, all ethics are nearly universal. This particular one is so widespread in its acceptance that we may choose to call it the *"universal ethic."* It is expected in all situations and circumstances—personal, educational, professional, etc. If it is violated and that violation is discovered, a penalty follows. Does this mean that all people are honest, or that any one of us is always honest? No, but honesty is always an expected behavior.

   Under what circumstances might dishonesty be the better choice? We can illustrate an example with what the author calls "the ugly baby test." Imagine a person entering a room carrying the most grotesquely ugly baby imaginable and saying, "Hey, everybody, this is my baby! Isn't he cute?" It is likely that those present will not be totally honest: "No, actually, he is the ugliest baby I've ever seen." Instead, they will most likely say, "Yes," or offer a qualified answer: "He certainly has dark hair." Why will they do this? Why will they not be completely honest? The answer reveals a second ethic.

2. Dignity of the Individual: In our culture, we generally assume that people's feelings are more important than the raw truth. This concern for individuals is certainly imbedded in our founding documents—the Declaration of Independence and the Constitution. Individual rights are held supreme in most instances, so we may choose to call this ethic the *"supreme ethic."* It takes precedence whenever it comes into conflict with any other ethic. In other words, it would be ethical to be dishonest about the ugly baby because of the higher ethic of individual dignity that is involved.

   Another example would be our courts of law. The Bill of Rights specifies that we are all entitled to a speedy, fair, and public trail in front of an unbiased jury of our peers. But it also provides for freedom of the press. In those instances where these two rights are in conflict—for example when press coverage might unalterably prevent a fair trial—the judge may deny the exercise of the larger societal right (free press) in favor of the individual right of the accused to a fair trial. In such a case, the press may be "gagged."

3. Obedience to Law: The Constitution establishes the rule of law in our society, and by definition, laws are ethics. They are universally acknowledged codes of conduct. If something is lawful, it is ethical, whether or not it accords with our personal morals. Laws provide the opportunity for a safe society, to avoid anarchy and tyranny. For this reason, we may choose to call the laws our "safety ethics," and if I break the law (even the speed limit) I am behaving unethically.

4. Accountability: There is no incentive to keep the law (or any other ethic) if there is no accountability for violations. For this reason, accountability might be considered the "essential ethic." Accountability is more than accepting responsibility; it is accepting the consequences.
   - Responsibility: "I did it"
   - Accountability: "I will repair it" or "I will pay the price"

   Unfortunately, our society seems to be trending to a "Don't Blame Me" philosophy. People are willing enough to take credit for good outcomes, but reluctant to take responsibility and accountability for bad ones. "It's not my fault" is an all-too-familiar claim today. Politicians have learned to take responsibility ("I'm accountable. The buck stops with me") but not accountability ("No, I will not resign").

A Review of the Four Primary Ethics:

• Honesty	Universal ethic
• Dignity of the Individual	Supreme ethic
• The Laws	Security ethic
• Accountability	Essential ethic

Imagine the difference that would result in our culture if people were willing to live by just these four general ethics. They are universally acknowledged as being important. They are not universally observed.

Communication Ethics

How do these ethics relate to communication? This interesting question was researched by Deirdre D. Johnston in her 1994 text *The Art and Science of Persuasion*[5]. She identified ten ethics that are important in persuasion. They are summarized below, with some modification for their application to all communicative settings.

1. Mutuality: We must pay attention to the needs of others, as well as our own.
2. Individual Dignity: Generally speaking, we should not cause another person embarrassment or a loss of dignity.
3. Accuracy: We should ensure that others have accurate information. This involves more than honesty; it means telling them everything they have a right and need to know, not just making sure that what you do tell them is true.
4. Access to Information: It is unethical to bolster the impact of our communications by preventing people from communicating with each other or by hindering access to the supporting information.
5. Accountability: We should take responsibility and accountability for the consequences of our relationships and communication.
6. Audience: The audience or receiver of the information also has ethical responsibilities. A good rule of thumb is the "200% rule." Both the communicator and the receiver have full (100%) responsibility to ensure that the message is understood and that ethics are followed. This is not a 50/50 rule. It is a 100/100 rule.
7. Relative Truth: Communicators should always remember that their own point of view may not be shared by others and that their conclusions are relative to their perspective. We must allow others to respectfully disagree or see it differently.
8. Ends vs. Means: While no rule can be applied without reservation to <u>any</u> situation (remember the ugly baby test), it can generally be said that the end goal of our communication and the means of getting to that end must <u>both</u> be ethical.
9. Use of Power: In some communication settings, we have more power than others present (e.g., a teacher with a student, a parent with a child). In those situations where we have more power we also have more responsibility for the outcome.

10. Rights vs. Responsibilities: We live in a wonderful society where our rights are protected by law. However, not everything that we have a right to do is ethical. We must balance our rights against our responsibilities.

Summary

In this chapter we have discussed the nature of ethics and morals and the importance of ethics to our maintenance of community. We have also stressed the need to be personally ethical and to require the same of those around us. Finally, we have identified four general ethics and ten communication ethics that can guide us maintaining ethical relationships.

Chapter 16: Analysis and Application Exercises

1. Have you ever told a "white lie" to someone because you thought it would be better than telling them the whole truth? When and why did you do it? Was your decision an ethical one? Why or why not? Justify your answer in terms of the four essential ethics of communication.
2. How does "honesty" relate to "accuracy" as discussed in this lesson? Can you be honest without being accurate? Why or why not?
3. How does "responsibility" relate to "accountability" as discussed in the lesson? Can you be responsible and yet not accountable? Why or why not?
4. In our culture, what should you do if you consider an ethic to be immoral? What are your alternatives if your morals are unethical?

References

1. Jones, Elizabeth A., U.S. Department of Education (1994). *Essential Speaking & Listening Skills for College Graduates.*
2. U.S. Department of Labor (1991). *Scans Guidelines: Secretary's Commission on Achieving Necessary Skills.*
3. Speech Communication Association (1992). *SCA Guidelines: Speaking, Listening and Media Competencies.*
4. Vivian, John (1999). *The Media of Mass Communication* (5th Edition). Needham Heights, MA: Allyn & Bacon, pp. 491-498.
5. Johnston, Deirdre D. (1994) *The Art and Science of Persuasion.* Dubuque, IA: Brown & Benchmark, a division of Wm. C. Brown Communications, Inc., Chapter 3.

CHAPTER 17
Critical Thinking Part 1 Arguments

LEARNING OBJECTIVES

After reading this chapter, students should be able to:

1. Develop intelligent criteria for critical thinking.
2. Describe the difference between a fact and an inference.
3. Demonstrate the ability to use facts and assertions in developing claims for an argument.
4. Demonstrate the ability to classify claims of fact, value, and policy.
5. Understand and demonstrate the use of Toulmin's model for analysis of an argument.
6. Demonstrate competencies for developing and supporting conclusions to a successful argument.
7. Demonstrate the ability to critically evaluate arguments presented in public, business, and personal decisions.

CHAPTER 17: Overview

I can win an argument on any topic, against any opponent. People know this, and steer clear of me at parties. Often, as a sign of their great respect, they don't even invite me.

—Dave Barry, Newspaper Columnist

Critical thinking is essential to accuracy and productivity. When making arguments, or listening to them, communicators must carefully analyze the arguments to make sure they are warranted and adequately supported by examples and evidence. Unfortunately, making unsupported and unwarranted claims is far too common in our culture. This lesson provides a model whereby arguments can be critically analyzed to insure accuracy and completeness.

Critical Thinking is Essential.

The media abounds with statements about the intelligent use of military action. News stories describe questionable activities, and publicize actions of popular entertainers. Decisions made by political figures and influential business people are brought into question. Simplistic answers to complex questions too often prevail as individuals get their news from the media or the neighbor who claims that a great catastrophe is being forced upon an unsuspecting public. Only the fears are given—the actual facts are missing! Recent news events illustrate the lack of critical thinking skills being employed in politics, media, education, even communication. Results would be humorous for us if they did not dictate our comfort, safety, or economic security. Critical thinking by decision-makers definitely needs improvement.

Critical thinking is a systematic way of making critical judgments about arguments that are all around us—messages we read, hear, write and speak. Critical thinkers do not advance or accept unsupported assertions, and critically thinking audiences refuse to accept unsupported claims.

There are many methods of making reasoned judgments about arguments. An ancient method, Aristotle's classical rhetoric, will be covered in Chapter 18. A more recent method, Stephen Toulmin's analysis of an argument, will be presented in this chapter. Eventually, in Chapter 21, both of these models will be applied to written and spoken communication.

Ingredients of Critical Thinking

The justification for critical thinking is that everyone wants a foundation, or grounded premise for a platform to anchor decision making. Decisions directly lead to life experiences that become satisfying, unnerving, or disastrous, depending on the success or failure of how our "life plan" is developed. Mentally, we evaluate basic "conclusions," or action statements we formulate to direct our lives. These evaluations are based on evidence we collect through observation, experience, or outside input from friends, media, or others. The stability or truthfulness of information becomes critical in establishing action statements. This is done in three steps:

1. Gather evidence. This consists of information, experience, or exposure to outside information through reading and listening about experiencing the topic area under consideration.
2. Develop statements of action, referred to as "claims" that are statements believed as "truth" about the idea under consideration. Evaluate these statements as to their importance, value, and impact on your life. Then accept them as beliefs about how you should react in a given situation.
3. After a sufficient number of "claims" have been developed, look for a common thread to the claims that recommends an action which will produce favorable results. Basically, this is your solution to the problem being considered.

As claims are being developed for our arguments, evaluation of evidence should be briefly discussed. Weight should be given to the term "Truth." We want to know what is true before we utilize the information to formulate a significant claim. Basing decisive action on falsehoods can bring disaster. But the formulation of truth is not always easy.

For a statement to be considered true, as opposed to an inference, or implied fact, it must meet the following criteria:[1]

Factual Statements:	**Inferential Statements**
Made only after observation	Made any time
Limited to what has been observed	Go beyond observation
Made only by the observer	Made by anyone
Made only about the past or present	Made about any time: past, present, future
Approach certainty	Truth is in degrees of probability
Are subject to verifiable standards	Not subject to verifiable standards

The strongest "claims" used in an argument should be based upon factual evidence. In valid argument, only new, more impressive facts can replace what has already been established. In other words, it is rare to see "truth" change, although it is not an unknown phenomenon.

However, it becomes difficult to find facts that establish values, actions, or even policies. For these reasons, the strongest claims for these arguments are based on the "truth" of an inference. This holds true for projecting future events, or creating cultural or society standards. Since these issues are critical in terms of our desired lifestyle, care should be given to their "degrees of probability." We attempt to increase our "chances" for success because it is "more probable;" our proposal is better than the proposal presented by the opposition.

Once sufficient evidence has been collected for logical claims to be established, statements of conclusion, known as solutions, can be presented. Vidlak and West list five principles that can be used to evaluate the strength of our claims and proposal:[2]

1. The critical thinker should explore issues and ideas.
2. The critical thinker is open-minded.
3. The critical thinker is skeptical.
4. The critical thinker is intellectually honest.
5. The critical thinker respects other viewpoints.

Please refer to Chapter 36, Critical Thinking, for further information.

Toulmin's Analysis of an Argument[3]

Stephen Toulmin is a British philosopher, author, and educator whose practical analysis of arguments is considered his most influential work, particularly in the field of rhetoric and communication. Toulman's model of an argument actually shows us what a successful argument "looks" like. The Toulman method can be used as a paper or speech plan and saves time often wasted by writing multiple drafts. It also uncovers fallacies in the reasoning process. Toulman presents three types of claims: factual claims, value claims, and policy claims:

1. **Factual claims:** Assert the observable existence of something. A recent economic summit gave statistics showing a strong correlation between the increased numbers of young adults significantly increasing their net worth, and the expense of residential real estate.
2. **Value Claims:** Assert the *quality* of something. An example of this type of claim is the argument that communication is a good choice for an academic major. A support for that claim is the assertion that future employers want good communicators. (See Figure 17.2)
3. **Policy Claims:** Assert that something should be done. Policy claims advance a need for a change from the present system. Claim: Juveniles should be tried and punished as adults. The warrants for such claims are (1) Juveniles commit adult crimes, (2) Punishment acts as a deterrent, and (3) adult punishment will protect society. (See Figure 17.3.)

Stephen Toulmin's model of the components of an argument show how all parts of the relationship interact. Any substantive claim must have all items listed on the model. (See figure 17.4)

1. **Claim:** A statement or inference that something is of a certain nature; that something has a certain value; or that something should be done. For example, Hillary Clinton defended President Clinton by claiming he was a victim of a "vast, right wing conspiracy" on NBC Today Show.
2. **Qualifier:** This important element qualifies the strengths and limitations of the claim. It helps the speaker avoid sweeping claims that leave arguments open for attack. Some useful qualifiers include the words: "necessary," possible," "probably," "impossible," "presumably," "in all probability," "very likely," "maybe," "apparently," among others. Our example: "President Clinton, in all probability, is a victim of a right wing conspiracy."
3. **Grounds:** The facts we use to establish the foundation for the claim. These are statements about persons, conditions, events, things that provide evidence for the claim. Hillary Clinton said data existed to prove her claim, but did not present any. Her statement became an unsubstantiated inference.
4. **Warrant:** A general statement that justifies using the data as basis for the claim. The warrant establishes the action link between the claim and the data. This becomes our solution to the problem. Given the evidence for your claim,

reasonable audience members would agree to this solution. Had evidence been given, the controversy around President Clinton would have been reduced.

5. **Backing for the Grounds:** Supporting evidence and credentials designed to certify the inferences expressed in the warrant. This includes more specific data and applies directly to the warrant. For example, the statement "President Clinton is a victim of right wing conspiracy " is a claim. Backing for such a claim was never presented, so the argument was never concluded.
6. **Backing for Warrant:** Statements recognizing the restrictions to which the claim may legitimately be applied. Rebuttals are used to question the validity of the warrant. For example: "President Clinton was elected for a second presidential term. History has never supplied data of a "right wing conspiracy." The warrant was never verified. (See Figure 17.1)

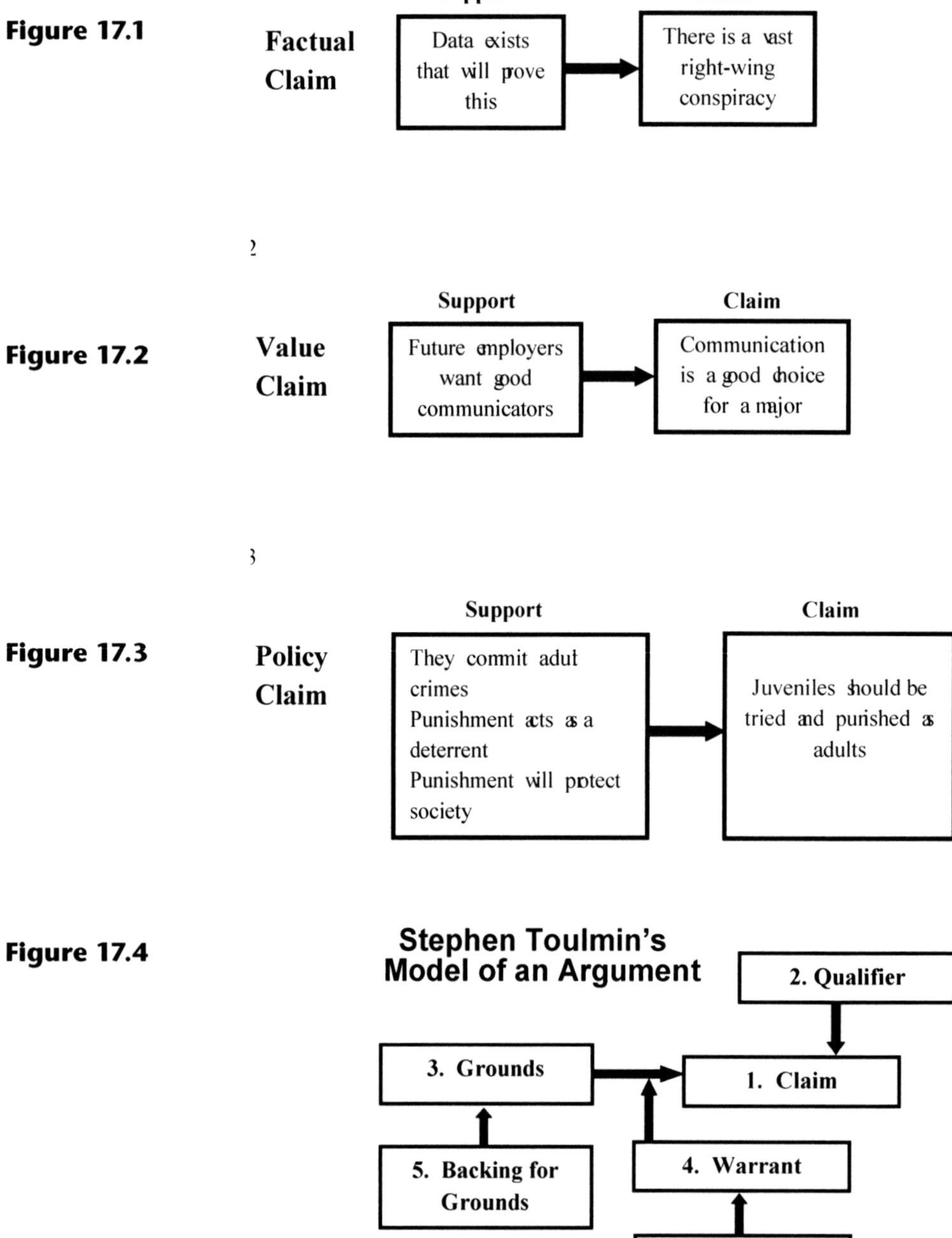

It is important to note that there is much more to Toulmin than is presented here. His model allows for highly complex arguments. His complexity can be discouraging to students. The key factor in labeling argumentative statements as data (facts and evidence given), claims (interpretation of data), and warrants (a solution statement to understanding and solving the issue claimed) assists the student in visualizing a logical thinking pattern to arriving at solution to the argument.

It also provides a more distinct pattern in arriving at a less emotional, reactionary policy. The end product is an attempt to solve difficult problems with a minimum of hurt feelings, misunderstandings, and unconvinced participants. It also provides opportunity for opposition to have any questions answered by rebuttal. It forces more "in depth" analysis, with less risk of missing critical evidence. It also excludes information not relevant to the issues under debate.

Examples

Examining all parts of the argument as they relate to the claim easily reveals any valid or fallacious nature of the claim. A simple argument examining the policy claim: "You should pick up my socks" may sound trite, but illustrates the claim, or inference that can be valid or invalid, based upon the support offered by the arguer. The first example is an INVALID claim. The second is a VALID one.

Example 1: Picture a husband and wife—Beth and Bob—relaxing in their living room on a Friday night. Both are relieved that the work week is over. The room is tidy except for Beth's socks in the middle of the floor. Beth says, "Bob, you should pick up my socks." This is a policy claim. "Why should I pick up your socks?" Bob asks. The data and grounds for support are clear: "Because my socks are red!"

Clearly this is an invalid argument. It is a fact that the socks are red. Why is this an invalid request? A Toulmin analysis tells us why. (See Figure 17.5.)

The claim is invalid for several reasons. First, the claim is not qualified in any way and second, the backing does not support the grounds. Third, the major flaw is that the claim is unwarranted. There is no link between red socks and the request to remove them. Unless Beth can offer evidence that she and Bob have an agreement that Bob will always pick up Beth's socks, or that the color red requires removal for a justifiable cause, the claim does not follow. The argument does not withstand scrutiny. Let's look at another example.

Figure 17.5

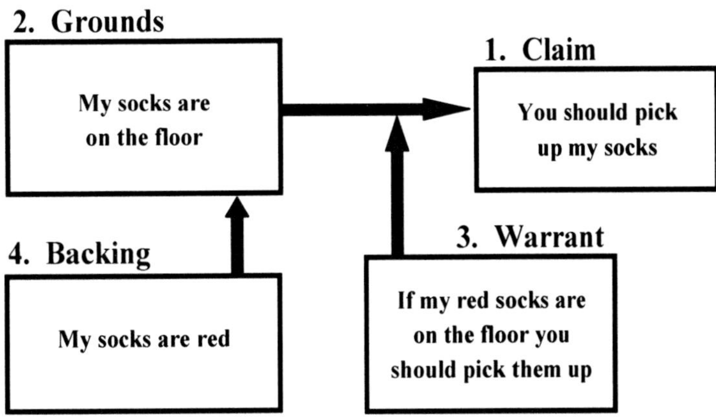

Example 2: Again, Beth and Bob are relaxing on Friday Evening. The telephone rings. Since Beth is closest to the phone, she answers it. Immediately upon hanging up, she says to Bob, "Bob, you should probably pick up my socks!" Bob answers, "Why should I pick up your socks?"

Beth says, "Because that was your mother on the phone and she is on her way over. We don't want her to see my red socks on the floor do we? We both know that the doctor said I should not bend over. I think it would be a good idea for you to pick up my socks!" (See Figure 17.6)

Unlike Example #1, the argument above is valid. The claim is qualified, offering some initial protection of the claim's validity. Secondly, the grounds are backed. "I clearly *cannot* pick them up on doctor's orders. YOUR mother is on her way, and neither of us wants the place to appear messy when she comes." Finally, it is a warranted claim. There is a clear link between the grounds and the claim, via the warrant, which validates the entire argument. Toulmin's diagram shows the relationships that make the reasoning clear.

Figure 17.6

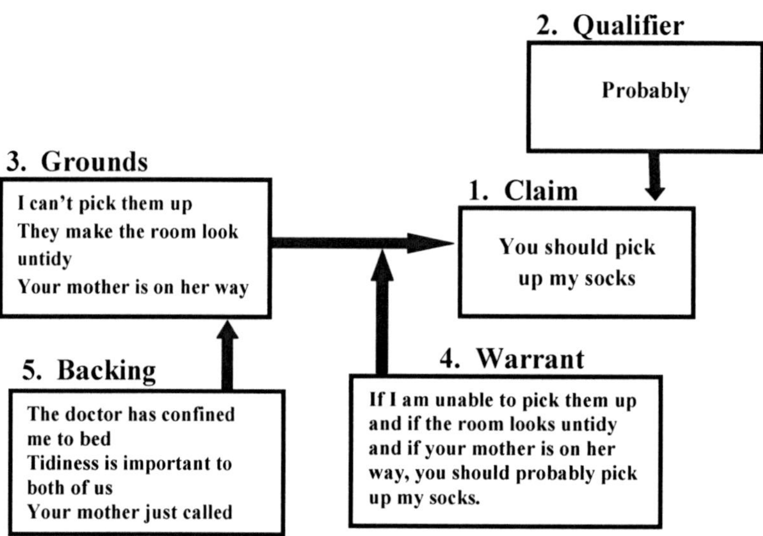

Summary

- Scholars should know what comprises critical thinking in order to be reason-based thinkers.
- "Argument" is a term whose definition is broader than we realize. Argument shares the same meaning as "thesis" or "claim."
- There are three types of claims: fact, value, and policy.
- Toulmin's model of what an argument looks like helps us analyze the validity of the argument.
- A complete argument contains: claim, grounds, warrant, qualifier, and data.
- Examples of valid and invalid claims clarify the appropriate relationships of all arguments related to the claim, allowing valid judgments.

Chapter 17: Analysis and Application Exercises

1. At the beginning of the football season, someone makes the statement: "We have a lousy football team at this school." Is this a warranted claim? Why or why not? What elements are present (or would need to be) to qualify it as a warranted claim?

2. Make a list of ten unsupported claims you have heard today. Were they personal, political, or social? What portions of Toulmin's model were not fully covered by the claims? How could they each be validated?

References

1. W.V. Haney, *Communication and Organizational Behavior* (Homewood, Ill: Richard D. Irwin, inc) 194-197.
2. R. West & L.M. Vidlak, *Student Study Guide for Speaking with Confidence Telecourse* (Madison, WI: McGraw-Hill Co, Inc., 1997).
3. Stephen Toulmin, Wikipedia Encyclopedia. Retrieved August 8, 2007. http://en.wikipedia.org/wilki/Stephen-Toulmin. S. Toulmin, R. Rieke, & A. Janik, An *Introduction to Reasoning*, 2nd Ed. (New York: Macmillian Pub. Co., 1984).

CHAPTER 18

Rhetoric

LEARNING OBJECTIVES

When students have completed this chapter and lesson, they should be able to:

1. Define the term "rhetoric" and explain how it relates to communication studies.

2. Identify and explain the views of the major Greek philosophers in the Idealist and Sophist traditions.

3. Know and understand Aristotle's five canons of rhetoric

4. Know and understand the elements of Toulmin's model of an argument.

CHAPTER 18: Overview

This chapter deals with the rhetorical form of arguments, in both spoken and written form. The chapter combines principles of classical rhetoric with more modern approaches to rhetoric and persuasion.

The previous chapter discussed argument in some detail, but it would be well to clearly define the term again here. In everyday language, the word *argument* is loaded with negative connotations of people disagreeing, perhaps even heatedly, on some subject. This is not the definition we use in communication studies. In communication, an *argument* is a claim and its supporting logic and evidence. For example, the subject matter or thesis of a paper is an argument, such as, "Textbooks are becoming more expensive and less used by students today."

In everyday use, *rhetoric* has been turned into a derogatory term. When advertisers, politicians, or charlatans attempt to deceive, we tend to call their deceptions "rhetoric." But in the field of communication studies it has a more scholarly definition. Rhetoric is the study of the nature and form of arguments. So when we are analyzing an argument or even framing one for ourselves, we are engaged in *rhetorical analysis*.

Classical Rhetoric

Citizens in ancient Greece and Rome studied and used rhetoric as a way of life. As Dr. Shirley Jones said, "Schools of rhetoric were common for freeborn sons of wealthy landowners anxious to retain and add to their means and access to influence. They needed to defend themselves in the courts (forensic speaking), create public policy in the legislature (deliberative speaking), and engage in ceremonial rhetoric (epideictic speaking), heaping praise or blame as was deemed appropriate by occasions and audiences."[1]

The Greek world was centered in Athens in about 500 B.C. and extended outward to much of the Mediterranean. The Greeks reveled in philosophy, and they are the primary source of Roman, European, and American thought to this day. They also believed in democracy—but only for free men (not women, children, or slaves).

For the Greeks, rhetoric—the use of words to change ideas—was common. At least initially, they were known for their *homogeneity*—holding a common view of the world and the purposes of society. This uniformity of values made rhetoric a valued and respectable skill. In our diverse society today, the same is not true. And as the Greeks began to diversify, so too did their view of rhetoric. There were at least two major schools of thought.

The Idealists

The idealists believed in the value of Truth (with a capital "T"). For these philosophers, truth was an objective, fixed, and external reality, not something that could change for each person or circumstance. Knowing the truth was the supreme goal of life and learning. This view is the one that has most profoundly influenced Western thought and culture to this day. You will probably recognize the names of its most famous proponents.

Socrates was an idealist, believing in and celebrating the discovery and learning of fixed truths. He was also a demanding tutor. He never wrote anything down because he believed that it would destroy memory. The only reason we have the ideas and arguments of Socrates is because Plato, his student, followed him around and wrote down everything he said.

Plato also believed in idealism (one reality). He was born at Athens' height, but by the time he was a young man, Athens was in decline. He blamed Sophistic rhetoric for this decline, and as a result he did not like Sophists; he called them "crooked lawyers." His lifelong goal was to return Greece to its original ideals: "health, beauty and honest wealth."

Plato identified four levels of reality:

- Perception: The things we see around us.
- Faith: Some truth and some opinion.
- Understanding: The beginning of real knowledge.
- Reason: The highest knowledge—comprehending the good and true.

Since Plato felt that reason was the highest form of knowledge, he identified some methods by which we achieve reason.

- *Knowing correct names for things:* This kind of knowledge is gained from a teacher, and organizes truth and reality into categories. Plato was one of the first people in the world to organize the plant and animal kingdoms into named categories.
- *Geometry:* This was the highest form of natural science at that time. A circle illustrated that something could be imperfect in life (nobody could create a perfect circle) but still be perfect in its concept. Plato believed understanding these concepts moves us closer to the one reality.
- *Dialectics:* Synthesizing what is and what is not into a new concept that incorporates both. Plato believed that ultimately, through this process, humans can reach the one true reality.

Allegory of the Cave: Plato illustrated the difference between fixed ("real") realities and those that we only think are real by giving us an allegory. He asks us to imagine several slaves chained to chairs in a cave, facing a wall, with a large fire behind them that gives both heat and light to the cave. These poor slaves have spent their entire life there, facing the wall. It is the only reality they know. Since they have known nothing else, they are content with their reality. As the fire blazes, it casts shadows on the wall for objects and people behind them. All they can see is the shadows of things—not the real things themselves. They give names to these shadows and recognize them when they see them again. But they have no idea that there is anything other than shadows to experience in their lives.

If we were to suddenly take one of these slaves and turn them around so they could see the three-dimensional objects and the bright red and yellow flames of the fire, they would be frightened by the new reality and would want to return as quickly as possible to what they had always known and understood—the shadows of things. But, if we can keep them there for awhile and let them see how exciting and satisfying this new knowledge is, they might then come to prefer their more "enlightened" condition.

Of course, the cave is the not the entire world. Plato would want the slaves not only to understand the realities behind them but also the external world outside the cave. He would take them outside and let them see the sun—which in this allegory represents the ultimate truth of all things. However, if we were to take a slave directly from his seat of shadows and drag him outside, the light of the sun and the vastness of the world would be so great that it might even frighten him to death. We have to move him slowly from shadows to firelight and then eventually to sunlight. This, he felt, is the duty of a teacher.

Plato believed that our daily lives are a lot like these slaves' lives—there is a larger reality we don't see. All we see are the shadows of reality—cast by the light of the fire. If we could escape the "caves" of our lives and observe the "light of the sun" (the absolute truth) we might at first be unable to look at it. But after having comprehended such light, neither the shadows on the walls nor the light of the fire would be satisfying to us anymore. Plato believed it is the light of absolute truth represented by the sun that we need to strive for.

The Sophists

The Sophists were originally from Sicily, but they went to Athens when they became successful. They were itinerant teachers (belonging to no university or school) who came to students and taught them for a fee. To follow them was to become "sophisticated"—meaning wise. The Sophists espoused *relativism*—the idea that truth is subjective, that there are many realities, not just one fixed one.

They taught their students how to do well by making use of verbal persuasion. Drama, semantics, and communicative style all started with the teachings of the Sophists, and much of what we do in communication studies originated with them. However, in a world dominated by the thinking of the Greek Idealists, you may not be as familiar with some of the most famous proponents of this view.

Protogoras focused on the idea of *social contracts*—the people join together to achieve greater power and order. As they do so, they make up rules which became their ethics and morals, their rules and laws. Language was created by humans to facilitate such order. Protogoras also believed that "man is the measure." We make up reality by saying what it is. There is no truth or falsity outside of humans. Meaning is internal, not external.

Gorgias agreed with Protogoras about reality. He said nothing exists outside of our awareness of it. If it did exist outside of our awareness, we couldn't know it. And even if we could somehow know it without being aware of it, we couldn't communicate it. He also noted that no matter how precise our descriptions, we cannot transmit our experiences; we transfer only our words, and our words are too inexact to pass what's inside of us to another person. This makes words very powerful because we act on the basis of these words we pass (what he calls "opinion"). They rule our actions. And when we change someone's opinion through words, we motivate them to action.

Hypias was particularly fascinated with the power of the human mind. He was known for his incredible memory skills. He could bring 500 people into a stadium and have them each introduce themselves by giving their name and telling where they came from. As they did so, he would instantaneously memorize their names and where they were from, and when the group had finished standing and introducing themselves, he would repeat back the information they had given him, in any order.

"The Gorgias" — A Classical Greek Philosophical Debate

The differences between these two schools of thought are perhaps best illustrated by the debate that took place between Socrates and Gorgias, as written down by Plato in his chapter called "The Gorgias" within the *Dialogues of Plato*.[2] One must read the entire debate to fully appreciate the intellect and humor of these two great Greek thinkers, but a quick summary will work for our purposes here.

Rhetoric: Gorgias defined rhetoric as the "art of persuasion." He considered it a creative art, worthy of our highest respect, and a primary tool of social action in the legislature, the courts, and in our everyday lives. Socrates defined rhetoric as an "artiface of persuasion." Rather than an art, he considered rhetoric to be skill which convinces people without requiring them to actually know anything.

Belief vs. Knowledge: Both agreed that rhetorical persuasion can lead us to either "belief" or "knowledge." They also agreed on the following premises:

- We can *believe* things that are true as well as things that are not true.
- We can *know* things that are true.
- We cannot *know* things that are not true.

We might think, then, that they fundamentally agree on what is true. But they don't. They are saying the same thing, but meaning quite different things. For Socrates, truth is a fixed and external reality, and while we can *believe* anything we want (even if it is not true), we can only come to *know* things that are already true, as we discover and learn them over time. Gorgias, on the other hand, believed that truth was an individual matter, and that whatever we have individually experienced is the only truth we will ever *know*. Everything else is simply *believed*. When we have experienced something for ourselves, we then know it, and it is true—for us.

As the debate pressed on, and Socrates realized that Gorgias did not share his view of truth or knowledge, in his frustration he denigrated rhetoric as an empty form of argument that might indeed convince people, but could leave them "ignorant" of the truth. And worse, he was disgusted that the Sophists themselves did not even need to know the truth in order to persuade people to do or to think something. This was unacceptable to him, and he characterized it as "the ignorant persuading the ignorant." He said sophistic rhetoric is to truth (1) as cookery is to medicine, (2) as gym clothing ("tiring") is to gymnastics, and (3) as flattery is to truth. For him "knowing the truth" was the thing of greatest value, and only true knowledge could persuade properly, not mere rhetoric.

Gorgias felt that persuading free men to take action was of the greatest value to society. He told the story of a family member who was sick and needed to take his medicine. The doctor (an Idealist) told him the facts but failed to persuade him. Gorgias stepped in, without knowing anything at all about medicine, and was able to persuade him to take his medicine. Gorgias then asked, "Who did the greatest good?" He went on to say that legislators, courts, and the masses are persuaded to action by sophisticated rhetoric, not by facts alone. When Socrates protested that rhetoricians don't have to know anything in order to persuade, Gorgias responded with a simple, "Yes, and isn't it wonderful?" Human agency, not external facts, move the world.

Aristotle

Aristotle was a student of Plato, who was a student of Socrates. This places Aristotle firmly in the Idealist tradition. But he had great respect for the power of Sophistic reasoning, and rather than condemning the Sophists he essentially adopted their methods for the purpose of bring people to the "Truth."

Aristotle systematized rhetorical principles, centering upon the necessary elements of: (1) the speaker, (2) the speech, (3) the audience, and (4) the occasion. He also identified the five *canons of rhetoric*: invention, arrangement, style, memory, and delivery (see Figure 18.1.) These proceed in a linear fashion, in keeping with the four elements listed above, as follows:

Invention: First, the speaker seeks to "invent" the argument (what he/she wants to say), keeping in mind their strengths and limitations as a speaker and the expectations of their audience.

Arrangement: Second, the speaker arranges the content of the speech, again taking into account the constraints of the rhetorical situation.

Style: Third, the speaker chooses the stylistic elements of the speech—the examples, metaphors, and stories that will be used, and when and how they can be most effective.

Memory: Fourth, the speaker would commit the material to memory, though this may also include memorizing the main points and sequence of things as opposed to the entire speech.

Delivery: Finally, after some practice, the speaker delivers the speech, and as with all of the previous canons of rhetoric listed above, matches the delivery to the speaker, the speech, the audience, and the occasion.

All of these are reviewed in more detail below, and will be used again later in our chapters on preparing and delivering a speech.

Dr. Shirley Jones summarized classical Greek rhetoric, as expounded by Aristotle, in Figure 18.1. Each of these principles are then summarized below.

Figure 18.1

Classical Greek Rhetoric in a Nut Shell

A. Three main elements within the context (rhetorical situation)
   1. Speaker
   2. Speech
   3. Audience
   4. Occasion

B. The five canons (criterion, principles, necessary elements)
   1. Invention:
      a. Inartistic Proofs (examples: force, coercion, torture–rejected by Aristotle)
      b. Artistic Proofs
         (1) Logos (Logic)
         (2) Ethos (Credibility)
         (3) Pathos (Emotion)
   2. Arrangement (organization)
   3. Style (determined by audience)
      a. Legislative
      b. Deliberative
      c. Epideictic
   4. Memory
   5. Delivery

Invention: As speakers "invent" topics they draw heavily from their personal life experience, usually selecting something they care and know about. They also select "proofs" to use in support of their topics. This process is *heuristic*—drawing on a variety of available experiences and proofs in support of the chosen topic. Aristotle preferred common and universally understood topics that could be applied to all subjects, such as: definition, comparison, relationship circumstances, and testimony.[3] The selected heuristic can provide a framework for selecting and organizing a topic, as when a journalist uses the five "W"s and an "H"—who, what, when, where, why, and how—to investigate and report a story.

Proofs: These can be thought of as the supporting material and rhetorical arguments that inform and persuade the audience. There are, of course, *inartistic proofs*—like coercion or torture—which persuade by force. Ethical speakers reject these, as Aristotle did. Instead, we turn to the *artistic proofs* that can support any type of claim: logos (logic), ethos (credibility), and pathos (emotion, or values).

These are the types of proofs that support any claim. And, we remember, critical thinkers do not accept unsupported assertions.

- Logos is defined by Aristotle as logical proofs or appeals to reason. Rational people respond well to logic because "rationality is man's essential characteristic."[4] Logical arguments can be organized inductively or deductively.

  Inductive Reasoning: Reasoning from a specific instance to a generalization (see Figure 18.2). An example would be to show a picture of a hungry and starving child (the specific instance) and then reason with grounds, warrants and backing to arrive at the general conclusion that child starvation (the general condition) is a serious problem that deserves our attention.

  Deductive Reasoning: Reasoning from the general condition to the specific instance (see Figure18.3). This is the more common form of argument and the one that is used frequently with logical claims. An example of this kind of logic is the famous *syllogism* concerning Socrates:

All men are mortal	The general condition
Socrates is a man	A qualifier that could be supported by grounds and warrants.
∴ Socrates is mortal	The specific condition

Figure 18.2

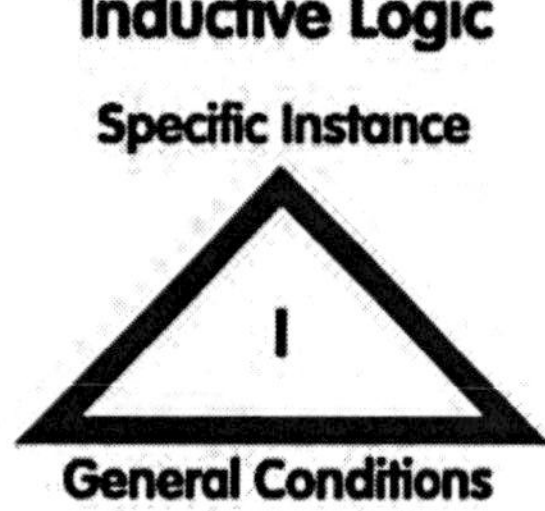

Figure 18.3

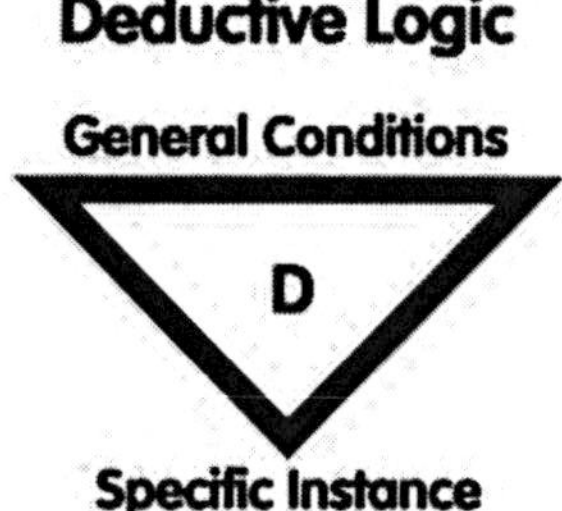

  A syllogism contains three statements: a major premise (the general condition), a minor premise (the qualifier and its support), and a conclusion ("therefore....). This can be shortened sometimes into an *enthymeme*—an incomplete syllogism—when the other parts are already known to the audience. For example, if I run into a theater and shout "The building is on fire!" I do not have to say after that, "People die in burning buildings, therefore get out" to complete the syllogism. The danger in doing this is that we might inappropriately leave out necessary or required parts of the syllogism we are offering. This happens, for example, when people state the general condition and then *jump to the conclusion* without necessary or adequate qualifiers and support for that particular argument.

- Ethos is defined by Aristotle as ethical proofs or credibility. He recognized the persuasive value of the speaker's character as well as the character of those whom the speaker might cite or quote. A person's *personna*—how he or she has come to be perceived by the audience—has been created over time. This personna may be the product of the speaker or source's efforts, or it may have been constructed by the audience, or both. A positive ethos would include such things as competence, integrity, and good will. A negative ethos in these or other matters is very difficult to overcome, so maintaining a positive ethos is important to every one of us.

- *Pathos* is defined by Aristotle as emotional proof or values. Emotion exerts a powerful force in our lives, and it can affect just about everything we think, do, or say. Using pathos to persuade can be very powerful, particularly with young audiences and others who are less prone to demand more logos and ethos. And it can be combined with logos and ethos to give additional power to an argument. A student giving a speech on organ donation might list all of the logical and ethical reasons why donating is important, but if she can then add that she herself is alive today only because someone donated a kidney to her, it would add a powerful pathos to the appeal. But one must be careful with pathos. Unjustified emotional appeals are logical fallacies.

Arrangement

Arrangement refers to organization of the argument or discourse. We are all familiar with the standard (1) Introduction, (2) Body, and (3) Conclusion arrangement of a typical college paper. But Cicero said the orator ". . . should arrange his matter, not only in a certain order, but according to the weight of the matter and the judgment of the speaker." [5]

Primacy and Recency. The order of presentation of ideas can affect the importance and memorability of each argument. So, for example, if you have three points to make about a particular topic, and we represent them as being 1 (most important), 2 (next most important), and 3 (least important), what would be the ideal order of presentation? The answer is provided by research and makes use of two important effects: the primacy effect and the recency effect.

The *primacy effect* says that people remember most readily and give more importance to whatever you spend most of your time or space arguing. The *recency effect* says that people remember most readily and give more importance to whatever you say most recently. Both of these being true, it would seem that we should place our most important argument last in our presentation and give it more time or space than any of the other arguments. And overall, the most powerful sequence would be 2–3–1.

Classical Organization is as follows: (1) the introduction; (2) the statement of circumstances or facts that are relevant to the subject; (3) the proof; (4) discrediting of opposing views; and (5) the conclusion.[6]

There are many questions to answer while deciding the arrangement of our argument or discourse. "When is an introduction necessary and when can it be omitted or abbreviated? . . . . Under what circumstances can we omit the statement of facts altogether?. . . When is it advisable to present our strongest arguments first and when is it best to begin with our weakest arguments and work up to our strongest?. . . Should we attempt to refute our opponents' arguments as a whole or deal with them in detail?. . .Should we reserve our emotional appeals for the conclusion or distribute them throughout the discourse? . . . What evidence or documents should we make use of and where in the discourse will this kind of argument be most effective?"[7]

Whatever arrangement is selected, the speaker or writer must give organizational guideposts to the audience so they know where they are within the argument's overall structure. Dr. Shirley Jones said, "Although organization is important to both, the speaker needs to provide more obvious organizational signals than does the writer. A reader can go back and review and locate organizational signals, where a listener cannot. Therefore, subtlety has place and can be a virtue in written discourse, but is seldom so in public speaking."[8]

Style

Aristotle liked the use of figures of speech, particularly metaphors, in persuasive discourse, which is an indication of his *style*. Corbett considers style to include diction—whether the presentation is general or specific, abstract or concrete, formal or informal. He also includes length and kind of sentences, along with variety of patterns, sentence euphony, articulation, and paragraphing.[9]

Both Em Griffin[10] and Shirley Jones consider Martin Luther King's "I Have a Dream" speech delivered on the steps of the Lincoln Memorial in Washington D.C. in August, 1963, as a speech that illustrates superb rhetorical style making use of all of the above listed elements of style. Many communication scholars consider King's speech as the best public speech of the 20th century.

Memory

Memory was more important in Aristotle's day than it is today. As noted earlier, Socrates was against writing things down, believing that it would destroy memory. Today, technology has made it possible to have written text with us instantaneously and continuously through a variety of digital devices. Yet still today, when giving a speech, simply reading a text is seldom effective. The more spontaneous the delivery, the more believable the message because of the ethos of competence that extemporaneous delivery exhibits.

Delivery

Delivery, the final Aristotelean canon, is perhaps the most essential of all of them. This is where the message meets the audience, and if your delivery is poor then none of the above canons can rescue you. The key to effective delivery is practice, and a speaker who fails to do so is likely to fail. On the other hand, to commit to memory all or part of a speech, and then deliver it in a persuasive and extemporaneous style, is without doubt the most powerful way to make a point (logos), appear confident and competent (ethos), and stir your audience's emotions (pathos).

Written arguments are no less demanding in terms of delivery. The written word becomes an object unto itself, separate from the writer. Your grade on a paper is not an evaluation of you personally, it is an evaluation of the paper you have created. And once committed to paper, it must stand on its own. There are official rules of written language (called *langue*) that apply to writing but not to speaking. If you speak on the street like you are required to write, you would sound strange to your peers. The rules of spoken language (called *parole*) are less formal than those for writing. Manuscript styles like APA (American Psychological Association) or MLA (Modern Language Association) must be strictly followed in associated academic disciplines, and your ability to follow them when writing adds credibility (ethos) to your writing.

Claims

When you make an argument, you construct a claim and offer support for that claim. The strength of your argument is determined by whether others accept your claim. For an argument to be effective, both the speaker and the listener must use solid critical thinking when constructing or hearing a claim.

There are several types of claims:

- **Factual claims**: To assert the existence in the material world of something that can be observed.
- **Value claims**: To assert the quality of something, someone, or an idea.
- **Policy claims**: To assert that something should be done.

Fallacies

Fallacies are errors in reasoning. When we put forward a claim, we are expected to use solid reasoning and evidence. Even if we have good solid evidence for something, if we fail to use good reasoning to make the claim, we may commit a *fallacy.* Effective communicators do not put forward or accept fallacies. They also do not put forward or accept assertions that are unsupported or that have inadequate support. The most common fallacies are as follows.

- *Post hoc:* If something follows another thing, it was caused by that thing.
- *Ad hominem:* A personal attack against someone rather than a reasoned argument.
- *Ad populum:* Suggesting something is valid because it is popular, or that it is invalid because it is unpopular. Often, this takes the form of using ridicule, humor, prejudice or stereotypes in an argument.
- *Undistributed middle:* If someone or something shares some attributes of another, then they share all attributes of that other. The most common form of this fallacy is *guilt by association.*
- *Straw man:* Setting up a weak argument so it can easily be refuted. This is usually done in summarizing an opponent's argument in a weak way.
- *Non sequitur:* A thought or conclusion that does not logically follow a preceding one.
- *False dilemma:* Suggesting that something is either one thing or another, when those are not the only two possibilities.
- *Partial facts:* Leaving out important facts, such as telling only one side of a story.
- *Distorted facts:* Falsely or incorrectly characterizing supporting facts.

Toulmin's Model

What, then, would a complete, well-reasoned, and supported argument look or sound like? For the answer, we can turn to Stephen Toulmin's model of an argument (Figure 18.4). Any valid claim must have all elements found in this model.

Figure 18.4

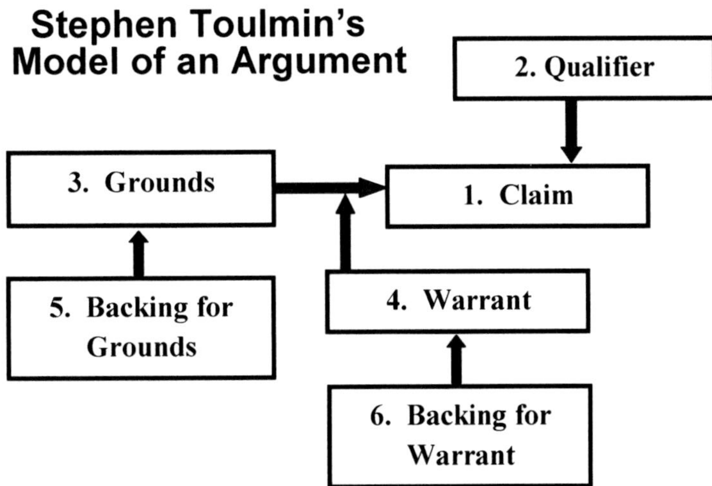

Claim: A statement (assertion) put forward to others to gain their acceptance (adherence). The nature of the adherence desired would depend on the nature of the claim.

- Factual claims would seek their adherence to nature or logic of the idea.
- Value claims would seek their adherence to the value of something.
- Policy claims would seek their adherence that something should be done

Qualifier: This part of the argument qualifies things—stating the strengths and limitations of the claim. Qualifiers might begin with words like necessarily, certainly, presumably, in all probability, very likely, maybe, or apparently. One of the most abused forms of qualifiers is to overstate a claim by saying things like "*everybody* knows that. . ." or "*all* of them were. . ." or "*nobody* cares about. . .", etc. If you say something like, "*Most* consumers have been affected by rising gas prices," be sure that your qualifier is not overstated.

Grounds: When somebody says that support is available to provide a reason for acceptance of the claim, then he or she has offered *grounds* for their argument. This might sound like, "There is good reason for most consumers to be upset about gas prices."

Backing for the Grounds: After someone has claimed grounds for an argument, they then must offer backing for those grounds. This can be any form of support that provides more specific data for the grounds—evidence, examples, data, etc. For example, "Gas prices have doubled in just the past fourteen months."

Warrant: Whenever backing is offered for an argument, the speaker or writer must also provide a statement that justifies the use of the grounds for a claim. This would link the grounds to the claim in some way, show why those grounds are connected and relevant to the claim. If the warrant is strong, then reasonable audience members will agree to this warrant. If the warrant is weak (seemingly irrelevant or disconnected to the claim) then the audience will reject both your claim and the grounds that are offered. For example, "These data come from the American Petroleum Institute, which tracks average gas prices all across the country, showing that the rise in the cost of fuel is a national problem, not just a local one."

Backing for the Warrant: Just as grounds for a claim need support, so too do warrants need support. Backing for your warrant supplies more specific data or reasoning that connects the warrant to the grounds and the claim. So for example, "This particular study was done just three weeks ago, and was compared to prices fourteen months ago at the same stations."

Summary

Rhetoric is not the negative thing that the word evokes in our culture, but an organized way to understand the nature and validity of arguments. And although they are ancient, the principles of rhetoric invented by the Greeks are still useful and relevant today. The Greek idealists valued fixed truths, while the sophists valued human agency and experience as the locus of truth. Aristotle combined the powerful and persuasive methods of the sophists with the idea of fixed truth. In doing so, he produced a variety of heuristic methods for categorizing and understanding rhetorical methods.

Aristotle's list of rhetorical elements includes the speaker, the speech, the audience, and the occasion. His five canons of rhetoric include invention, arrangement, style, memory, and delivery. Within these, there are choices concerning proofs (logos, ethos, pathos), logic (inductive or deductive), and organization. In more recent times, Toulmin has invented a model for making a sound argument and avoiding fallacies. Toulmin's model includes the claim, qualifiers, grounds, backing for the grounds, warrants, and backing for the warrants. All of these heuristic lists and models can help us to create and deliver powerful and effective arguments.

Chapter 18: Analysis and Application Exercises

1. In light of Plato's critique of the Sophists, how did his student Aristotle justify the use of rhetoric? Do you find his argument convincing? Why or why not?
2. Aristotle spoke of the importance of ethos when making an argument. How well does this compare with your own experience of "liking" or "trusting" a person who is attempting to persuade you? Is ethos important to logical or emotional arguments as well? Why or why not?
3. One benefit of using Toulmin's model for making an argument is that we can avoid some fallacies by doing so. What fallacies might be avoided by doing so? What fallacies might still be present even if someone follows Toulmin's model, and why?

References

1. Jones, Shirley. Critical Thinking Pt. 2—Rhetoric, in R.S. Chase and S.G. Jones, *Elements of Effective Communication*, 2nd ed., Boston, MA: Allyn and Bacon, 199.
2. "The Gorgias," in *The Dialogues of Plato*, translated into English by B. Jowett, 4 vols., Oxford: Clarendon Press, 1953, 2:501–628.
3. Corbett, Edward P.J. *Classical Rhetoric for the Modern Student*, 2nd Ed. New York: Oxford University Press, 1971., v.
4. Corbett, *Classical Rhetoric for the Modern Student*, 50.
5. Cicero. De Oratore, I, 31.
6. Corbett, *Classical Rhetoric for the Modern Student*, 298.
7. Corbett, *Classical Rhetoric for the Modern Student*, 302.
8. Jones, Shirley. Critical Thinking Pt. 2—Rhetoric, in R.S. Chase and S.G. Jones, *Elements of Effective Communication*, 2nd ed., Boston, MA: Allyn and Bacon, 202.
9. Corbett, *Classical Rhetoric for the Modern Student*, pp. 440-447.
10. Griffin, Em. *A First Look at Communication Theory*, 4th Ed. Boston: McGraw Hill, 2000, p. 282.

CHAPTER 19
Interviewing Principles

LEARNING OBJECTIVES

After completing this lesson, students should be able to:

1. Distinguish between an interview and a two person conversation.
2. Describe the structure of an interview.
3. Describe three interview characteristics: the opening, the body, and the closing.
4. Create three types of questions.

CHAPTER 19: Overview

One person interviewing another is a unique type of communication. In an interview, like in other communication, the interviewee needs to be successful. It must make the interviewee feel included in society and that their opinions are accepted. This sets the stage for either structured interviews, providing specific data that leads to inferential conclusions, or unstructured interviews providing diverse, broad interpretation and deep understanding. Interviews have three major objectives: information gathering, information giving, and persuasive direction. The direction dictates the type of questions often asked. Open questions seek understanding and broad interpretation. Closed questions seek closure and statistical inference. The interviewer asks questions, then based on answers, asks follow-up questions. Most often interviewers seek to be neutral, but the use of leading questions can also provide valuable insight. A successful interviewer will prepare a schedule of questions that best fits the objective. If chronological or biographic data is needed, the tunnel sequence is recommended. If analytical data is sought, a funnel sequence is recommended.

Mike Wallace, Interviewer

In 1968, CBS news initiated a program entitled 60 Minutes. The major player was a news reporter named Mike Wallace. Given the opportunity, Wallace designed a show to invite well-known people to the television audience by interviewing them. The objective was to broadcast to the world who these people were and what significant contribution they made. Wallace's reputation quickly grew, and he was described various ways:"More than a few of our prospective interviewees were wary of being grilled on network television by a guy who had been described by one captious critic as "Mike Malice" and by another as "The Terrible Torquemada of the TV Inquisition." At least two presidents —Franklin D. Roosevelt and Harry Truman — had publicly accused him of being a chronic liar."[1] His reputation as a hard interviewer has grown over the years, and his television broadcasts have etched biographies into history because of their insight and hard-hitting questioning. The following two chapters attempt to explore this method of communication.

Interviewing is a form of oral communication that involves two people sending and receiving messages. At least one of these people has a purpose or goal. This goal might be administering therapy, introducing a product sale, or engaging someone in employment. As in the case of Mike Wallace, the goal is to gather and record information as well as serve as a source of news, history and entertainment.

The interview context usually involves a face-to-face encounter. It is relational in character because there is personal interaction and an interpersonal connection between the two parties. As the encounter develops, the implication is that changes will occur in participants through the process. Someone gets a job, receives critical therapy, or gathers information distributed to a willing audience. In effect, much of the world's change results from people engaged in an interview.

Much like other types of communication events, the outcome is often subjected to perceptions, individual needs, and the creativity of participants. If the interviewer is successful in formulating proper questions, and if the interviewee is successful in supplying the desired verbal response, an effective interview can result.

Although everyone has some degree of understanding, experience, and expectation, significant differences in how we organize and present our answers to an interviewer, or how we frame our questions seeking information will dictate the results of the interview. Success or failure in interview communication rests almost entirely on the degree of sophistication in asking and answering questions.

The Introduction: Setting the climate

Three underlying dimensions affect human relationships.[2] The dimensions of **control, inclusion,** and **affection** have the potential to enhance or diminish the effectiveness of an interview.

Personal **control** of a situation relates to power. Power in an interview, as in all types of communication, implies the support of participants, or endorsement of people. *Status, prestige, and custom dictate who will exert the most influence in an interview.* Since an interview has an objective for at least one of the participants, dominant power is to be avoided. The intent is to keep the interaction progressing toward a productive end for both parties. Thus, a proper climate is produced when both parties share control and neither seeks a dominant role. The interviewer controls the structure of the interview and the questions asked, while the interviewee controls the content, or answers. As with the case of dominant power versus empowerment, or sharing of responsible control, participation by both parties greatly contributes to the success of the interview. In other words, some degree of control resides in how and what is said, regardless of who asks the questions.[3]

Inclusion refers to *how much each party wants to participate in an interview and how much each party wants to include others in the interview.*[4] One of the basic survival traits of humanity is to be included in the events providing the necessities of survival. This holds true, however, only as long as both interviewer and interviewee believe that a successful interview directly affects their existence. Then the event requires the development of mutual trust between interviewer and interviewee. This trust becomes the basis upon which communication thrives in an interview.

A final characteristic recommends an atmosphere of **affection.** Underlying the interview is a need to belong and be appreciated. Not only do we wish to be a part of the system, we have a strong desire to have our skills and knowledge appreciated. In the case of interviews where the interviewer is seeking information, or giving therapy, the interviewee may not be a friendly participant. Whenever the climate of the interview is "defensive" rather than "supportive" as reviewed in Chapter 15, the success of the interview may be less than desirable. Even though the level of affection is less than ideal, every attempt should be made to manage it.

Compatibility and willingness to include both parties should be constantly assessed, and efforts to establish common ground. This process evolves throughout the interview by both participants seeking areas of mutual interest, and understanding the anticipated benefits of the interview as it relates to the needs of both participants.

Interview Approaches

How an interview is approached depends on the objective of the interviewer, including the type and quantity of information desired. In a highly structured interview where a large quantity of quantifiable data is required, the interview is considered a **direct** or **structured** interview. This type of interview usually includes a prepared questionnaire with standardized, objective questions that have quantifiable answers. Examples include "How much. . . " "On a scale of one to ten . . ." Which person, product, or candidate would you select from the following list. . ."

Even though the interview can be conducted many ways, the information requested is predominantly the same. It can be quantified, compared, and inferences developed from a series of interviews. The **standardized** or **direct** interview may be used once on a number of respondents, or may be used on a series of occasions with a panel of respondents to determine the stability of attitudes, values, and practices.

Because the **structured** interview is designed to collect the same information from each respondent, the answers of all respondents must be comparable and classifiable. Data must deal with precisely the same subject matter, and differences or similarities between the responses must reflect actual differences or similarities between respondents, and not due to differences in the questions asked.[1]

The second form of interviewing is called **nonstandardized** or **indirect** interviewing. The unstructured approach is used to explore a broad problem or research question seeking such information as causes, social effects, or psychological consequences. The attempt is made to cover a wide range of opinion and purposes. In-depth information is sought, providing descriptive data covering a wide range of knowledge, exposure and influence. Even though questions asked may be quite standard, they seek widespread response for providing in-depth explanation of the topic under investigation. Conclusions from nonstandard interviews seek explanation and in-depth understanding, as opposed to generalization of narrow conclusions.

A combination approach is used when freedom of expression is called for but pertinent facts and consensus on conclusion from data are needed.

Types of interviews

Interviews can be classified into three general categories, depending on the interview objective: (1) information gathering, (2) information giving, and (3) persuasion.

Information gathering interviews cover a wide range of objectives, including everything from gathering evidence for a legal trial to determining the consumer preferences for type and consistency of laundry detergent. Much research is conducted by gathering data by interview. Surveys, political polls, and consumer satisfaction studies provide the public with information. News gathering and investigative journalism all begin with an interview. Regardless of the subject matter, the tool of choice to find information is to ask questions. Much of the remaining chapter will focus on methods of information gathering through the interview process.

One of the largest uses of interview involves the employment process. Chapter 20 will focus specifically upon the survey, the health provider interview and the employment interview as examples of information gathering.

Information giving covers an equally broad spectrum of communication. Areas of training, counseling, evaluation, and orientation are types of interviews. The interviewer has a body of information to convey most effectively in a one-on-

one approach. Teaching, coaching, instructing, and appraisal all use interviewing as a tool for distributing information.

Persuasion is a general, broad category of interacting one-on-one using the interview process. Interviews are used to recruit employees, military personnel, or even club members. Most sales calls are interpersonal encounters including a type of interview. Fundraising, soliciting support for a cause, or building membership in the local civic club starts with the interview process.

Interview Structure

The Opening

Most interviews begin with two individuals making contact. The interviewer has an objective: to successfully complete the intent of the interview. To succeed, a communication climate must be created very quickly, with the interviewee confident that his/her integrity will not be compromised. This simply means that the interviewer must provide an image, complete with proper clothing, demeanor, and rhetorical attitude to at least demand the attention of the interviewee. Within seconds a trust must be established, showing that the information gathered will not cause later harm to the interviewee. Interviewers should introduce themselves properly, establish some rapport with the respondent, and provide an orientation to the interview. This process is not only necessary, but it generally helps reduce what is known as relational uncertainty,[2] *a state of suspicion or doubt.* If respondents know what to expect during an interview, they will be more trusting and will be more apt to relax and concentrate on the process of answering questions. The interviewer also should establish the purpose of the interview at the outset. For example:

> Hello. I'm John Doe, representing the fact-finding committee for the City Planning Commission. I would like ten minutes of your time to get your opinion on the proposed new airport facility scheduled for construction one mile south of our city. Could I ask you a few questions about your opinion on that subject?

What you state as the purpose for the interview should include an appeal to the respondent that his/her responses will be important and valued. There must be some indication that responses given will be reviewed, honored, and play a vital role in any proposed action. Otherwise, cooperation may not occur.

The respondent must be made to feel their responses are of importance, and can make a difference in their life. They must also not feel that a negative response could bring punitive action or negative impact. The first questions should be "icebreakers," gracefully introducing the topic but not placing the respondent in a position of voicing an opinion or embarrassing them for lack of knowledge. Remember that small talk is a nice introduction, but people are busy and do not want to spend much time on the weather.

Give a brief orientation of the topic, including the issues to be presented, then move into the subject in a neutral way.

The Body

As with any public communication, organization is key! An organized message is always more respected, effective, and credible. It saves time, explanation, and rapidly creates its own credibility. The best method for organizing the body of an interview is to *develop an outline of topics and subtopics to be covered.* This outline guides the interview. You will want to arrange your major ideas or points in a logical fashion covering all critical areas. There are five general topic approaches to outlining the sequence of interview questions.[3]

Topic sequence of questions permits the interviewer to choose a natural division of analysis based on critical issues making up the categories of subject areas about the topic. For example, an interview during a search for a graduate school might include admission criteria, areas of study, degree requirements, faculty, funding sources, and school reputation. The traditional journalist's guide recommends six key words of a topic analysis: who, what, when, where, how, and why.

A time or chronological sequence treats the analysis of a topic as it could happen. The purpose is to describe a series of developments in time or a set of actions occurring sequentially. For instance, an interviewer explaining a tour of Yellowstone Park might begin with travel to Wyoming, then proceed to find a place to lodge, either in a local community, or within the park itself. The next consideration may be finding a suitable method of moving from location to location, either by tour bus, or private auto. A decision must also be made about which venues to visit, based upon duration of your stay. Will you want to visit just geyser areas, or will the trip also include backpacking, fishing, or animal spotting? The first day may be at Old Faithful Lodge, the Second day, the Grand Canyon of the Yellowstone, and the third day, fishing on Yellowstone Lake.

A space sequence attempts to focus the interview based on the physical arrangement of a place, scene, event, or object. This includes right to left, top to bottom, north to south, or neighborhood to neighborhood. It might list a group of commercial grocery stores to review, or a list of theatres to visit.

A cause to effect sequence reviews a list of problems and attempts to relate reasons why these problems exist. What caused a specific change in college enrollment? Was it due to the sudden popularity of the basketball team? Did the college suddenly offer several new advanced degrees? Are there commercial businesses that recruit graduates from the college? The interviewer might begin with a cause or causes, and then proceed to effect, or discuss an apparent effect and then move to possible causes.

A problem-solution sequence examines the nature and significance of a problem and examines the justification for a proposed solution. Why are knee injuries the major health problem of football teams? How might such injuries be avoided?

An interview guide is usually sufficient for your pre-interview preparations. However, when you want to be more prepared and confident, you should develop the outline into a more elaborate document: an **interview schedule**. *This contains lists of major questions and follow-up questions; it is a useful tool in keeping the interview focused on the topic or issue of concern.* This schedule can also be developed into a manuscript that allows the interviewer to write arguments or instructions to be used in the interview. Each interviewer needs to decide what format is necessary and sufficient for each interview.

The Closing

The closing of an interview has three primary functions.[4]

First, the closing signals the termination of an interview, but not a relationship. It is entirely possible that the interviewee may be contacted for a follow-up interview. There may be continued professional, social, or casual bonding created. Future interaction may be needed. In interviews such as screenings or annual evaluations, closings can even contain agreement on a future meeting. For these reasons, the message must be sent that a bonding has resulted, and future interviews are permissible.

Second, the closing should express supportiveness to enhance the relationship and bring the interview to a positive close. Implied is that one or both parties may express appreciation, pleasure and intention of future contacts.

Third, the closing may summarize the interview to verify important data obtained. Even when there is no systematic summary, either party may use the closing to bring the interview to an orderly ending. Be sure the summary is accurate and addresses major areas of information, analysis or agreement.

Do not rush the closing. This can make the participant feel their information is not what was desired, or that the interviewer is in disagreement with the information received. Research suggests that people recall the last thing said or done during an interview, so being rushed or dismissed with an ill-chosen statement may jeopardize the interview's effects, your relationship, and future contacts with the interviewer.

Both verbal and nonverbal cues signal the end to the interview. The interviewer might stand when making concluding remarks such as thanking the interviewee for the information, and a statement of what will be done with the information gained are both clear termination cues. A hand shake, expressing appreciation, and an indication of future meetings are recommended.[5] In an ideal interview closing, both parties understand the signals and respond appropriately.

Types of Interview Questions

One definition of an interview is that one person asks another person questions. Asking and answering questions is essentially all that happens in an interview. Questions are the instruments that drive the interview process. They govern the flow of information exchange, and even dictate the amount and kind of information received. The efficiency of the process depends on the types of questions used in the interview.

Questions are usually grouped into three major classifications: (1) open or closed questions; (2) primary or secondary questions; and (3) neutral or leading questions. The type of questions dictate whether the interview will be structured or unstructured, and even control the amount and type of information one anticipates.

Open and Closed questions

Open questions are used in the unstructured interview. The purpose is to obtain a broad understanding of the topic, exploring the material in depth. As more information is obtained, the questions change to incorporate more in-depth examination on the subject area that may not have been considered at the beginning of the interview.

Open questions *permit freedom in terms of the length and nature of the response.* Analysis of data uses content analysis, expanding the subject area to include all subcategories of information to obtain a complete understanding of the issue under consideration. Open questions motivate and encourage interviewees to communicate, particularly in the first minutes of probing interviews.

Wording of open questions is generally more abstract, encouraging a broad interpretation and explanation of answers. They encourage *divergent thinking,* with more creative and expansive answers. The objective of the interviewer is to obtain as much new and creative information as possible. Open questions encourage discussion and free thinking.

Closed questions are restrictive, limiting data to quantifiable answers. They request specific information or supply answer options from which the respondent chooses. The objective is to force consensus. Often the most closed questions are bipolar, restricting the respondent to two choices.

The objective of the interviewer is to develop information that can be statistically analyzed, resulting in definitive answers. The data produced by closed questions are usually repeatable, reliable, and statistically compatible. The object of the research is to supply answers that reflect percentages, averages, and measurable differences. The results are then used for projections and inferences. Typically, such interviewing attempts predictions like who will win the election, or whether the bond levy will pass the popular vote.

Interviewers utilizing closed questions ask every respondent the same questions, providing as little divergence in interpretation as possible. Good data include characteristics of reliability, repeatability, and validity of final conclusions.

Primary and Secondary questions

Primary questions are usually open questions designed to gather wide divergence of interpretation with creative answers. They are used to introduce areas of inquiry and are coherent in themselves. They attempt to broaden the topic of discussion and increase potentially new areas of inquiry.

Primary questions are usually followed by secondary questions. One of the most widely used secondary question is the fundamental tool of the interviewer: the single word "Why!" This nudging question tells the respondents that additional information is needed, permitting them to supply not only new information, but more often the justification for their answer on the primary question.

If the interview focuses on alcohol sales, the primary question might be:

"How do you feel about lowering the legal drinking age to 18 years?"

The respondent then renders a decision, usually opinionated by an emotional view. Justification with examples and verifiable data can be obtained by asking "Why?" after the answer is received.

The value of the secondary question lies in the fact that, by using follow-up questions, the interviewer is less likely to form false conclusions about a topic and is more apt to find useful, accurate information. The types of secondary questions that assist an interviewer are questions that produce all pertinent information about their general answer: What do you mean when you state that? Can you add any additional insight? The nudging questions like Why? questions that add additional information are critical, because they ask for data or evidence to back up an unsupported statement made as a primary statement. If the primary answer is vague, or unsupported, the interviewer can ask for clarification, or additional information. The total objective for primary and secondary questions is to expand information in its more complete form. This can save the embarrassment of unverified conclusions or illogical reasoning.

Neutral and Leading questions

Neutral questions permit respondents to provide an answer consistent with their position on an issue, their beliefs, their attitudes and values, or the facts as they know them. This implies that any one of a series of interviewers will obtain the same answer from each interviewee. Results are reliable and repeatable. The intent is to determine the unbiased understanding of beliefs, actions, or choices of those interviewed. When leading questions are asked, the desired answer is telegraphed to the respondent, and the results of interview questions are more apt to reflect the attitude of the interviewer than the interviewee.

Leading questions have their place in the interview process also. These questions often are used when the interviewer seeks to elicit a particular response. The wording of a question usually suggests the direction of the answer. Obviously, a leading question can be intentional or unintentional, but interviewers and respondents should know that the content of the question has the potential for bias. This can become the point of persuasion in a sales interview. Every successful salesperson understands that the proper question requesting a commitment is essential for closing the sale. "You do understand that the purchase of this automobile is your best logical action don't you?" "How much money can you put down on your purchase?"

Cannell and Kahn[6] caution that questions be phrased without containing a suggestion as to what the most appropriate response might be, as respondents often affirm the answer to a leading question as their final answer.

However, when sensitive or potentially embarrassing information is sought, leading questions may be the only way to obtain a response. Alfred Kinsey discovered as he tried to explore the sexual behavior of human males that to ask a neutral question was too easily answered "no" if patients were simply asked whether they had engaged in a particular activity. Consequently, males were always asked when they *first engaged* in such an activity, and since it becomes apparent from the form of the question that no one would be surprised if he had had such experience, there seemed to be less reason for denying it. Kinsey interviewers said there was no indication that false admissions of such activity were ever encountered.[7]

Table 19.1

Neutral vs Leading Questions

Neutral Questions	Leading Questions
What do you think about the new federal budget?	Don't you think senior citizens will be harmed by the new federal budget?
What is your attitude toward the situation in Iran?	Don't you think the situation in Iran is. . .?
How does this product compare with what you normally purchase?	Surely you would agree that this product is superior to any other wouldn't you?

When you develop your interview schedule of questions, you must consider not only which type of questions to use but how you want to arrange the questions systematically.[8] A question sequence links questions into a series to assist the interviewer in reaching the objective of the interview. Questions are like signposts that lead the person through a self-guided tour. There are opening questions that begin the sequence, and as one nears the end of the path, other types of questions announce the closing.

The Tunnel Sequence

Consider the interview a pathway through a mountain. A traveler who does not wish to scale the heights, elects to follow the signs through a tunnel. The Tunnel sequence, sometimes called a string of beads, is a series of questions. Each question may cover a different topic, asking for a specific bit of information, attitude, or feeling. Such questions might be arranged in a chronological or cause effect pattern, asking the respondent to tell the entire sequence. Using the tunnel sequence requires the interviewer to plan the questions in such a way so as to complete the story from start to finish. This strategy not only helps the interviewer as he writes the report, but also assists the interviewee in recalling information more easily.

The Funnel Sequence

Just as it sounds, a funnel sequence proceeds from open questions to gradually more closed questions. This sequence is used when the interviewer wants to elicit open responses to questions and when the respondent is familiar with the topic. This type of interview becomes useful when conducting diagnostic interviews, or interviews trying to determine the cause of political disruptions. Any problem of a diagnostic nature that requires a general examination, narrowing to a specific cause, starts with broad questions, and ends with very specific, closed questions.

Open, broad questions also are easier to answer, pose less threat to a respondent, and start people talking. This can be of great help if establishing credibility is necessary for sensitive interviewing.

The funnel sequence also avoids possible conditioning or biasing of later responses. With emotionally loaded topics such as gay marriage, beginning with broad, open questions does not force the respondent to take a polarized position. Open questions produce more information and less qualified positions.

The Inverted Funnel Sequence

The inverted funnel sequence begins with closed questions and gradually moves to open questions. This sequence is especially useful when the interviewer needs to motivate a respondent to participate, or to break down emotional barriers that may result. If the interviewee is highly emotional, or feels inferior, specific questions easily answered can be a great icebreaker. A respondent's memory or thought processes may need assistance, and closed questions can serve as great warm-ups.

To begin an interview following a tragic event may be overwhelming to someone deeply involved. Without knowing where to start, they may feel overwhelmed and incompetent. By asking specific, easily answered questions, the interview can open doors to more in-depth questions.

The Quintamensional Design Sequence

George Gallop, the famous poll designer, developed the quintamensional design sequence to assess the intensity of opinions and attitudes.[9] This five-step process develops specific questions to address the interviewee's awareness and reasons for specific attitudes. This helps explain the intensity of beliefs and leads to making inferences about trends in decision making and potential policy as influenced by public opinion. Responses to this type of interview can attempt to predict trends in policy change, or even voting results. For example:

1. *Awareness:* Tell me what you know about the college becoming affiliated with the University?
2. *Uninfluenced attitude:* How do you think it will affect the city?
3. *Specific attitude:* Do you approve or disapprove of the proposed change in the college name?
4. *Reason:* Why do you feel that way?
5. *Intensity of attitude:* How strongly do you feel about this—strongly, very strongly, or no room for change in attitude?

In the next section, you will apply your understanding of the components of the interview, question types, and question sequences to conduct information-seeking interviews.

Chapter 19: Analysis and Application Exercises

1. Watch an interview conducted on television by a newsperson or talk show host. Use the principles outlined in the video for this lesson to answer the following questions: Did the interviewer appear to be prepared for the interview with some kind of agenda? How could you tell? What kinds of questions were asked? What kinds of sequences? Where the questions and sequences appropriate and effective? Why or why not? What changes would you have made?
2. In the same interview, what there an identifiable opening? How long did it last? Was it effective? Why or why not? Was there an identifiable closing to this interview? Was it effective? Why or Why not?
3. Write out a ten question interview schedule using two different sequences. Describe what differences in results you would expect, based on the different sequences used.

References

1. Exerpt from a book: Terry Gross, Mike Wallice, *Interviewer: You and Me*. Hyperion, 2005.
2. William C. Schutz, *The Interpersonal Underworld* (Palo Alto, kCA: Science and Behavior Books, 1976).
3. Charles J. Stewart & William B Cash Jr., *Interviewing Principles and Practice*, 12th edition (New York: McGraw-Hill, 2008), 6.
4. Stewert and Cash, 7.
5. S.A. Richardson, B.S. Dohrenwend & D. Klein, "Interviewing: Its Forms and Functions," (New York: Basic Books, 1965) 34.
6. M. Knapp, *Social Intercourse: From Greeting to Goodbye* (Boston: Allyn & Bacon, 1978).
7. Stewart & Cash, 85. D. O'Hair, R, Stewart, H. Rubenstein, *A Speaker's Guidebook Text and Reference*, 3rd Ed. (Bedford: St. Martin's, 2007) 185.
8. Stewart and Cash, 93-94.
9. M.L. Knapp, R.P. Hart, G. Friedrich, and G. M. Schulman, "The Rhetoric of Goodbyes: Verbal and Nonverbal Correlates of Human Leave-Taking," *Speech Monographs*, 40 (1973): 182-98.
10. C.F. Cannell & R.L. Kahn, "The Collection of Data by Interviewing," In L. Festinger & D. Katz, *Research Methods in the Behavioral Sciences*. (New York: Dryden Press, 1953) 327-380.
11. A.C. Kinsey et al., "Interviewing," *Sexual Behavior in the Human Male* (Philadelphia: W.B.Saunders Co., 1948).
12. For additional information on question sequences see Stewart and Cash, p.86-93. See also S.L. Payne, *The Art of Asking Questions* (Princeton, NJ: Princeton University Press, 1951).
13. G. Gallop, "The Quintamensional Plan for Question Design," *Public Opinion Quarterly*, 11 (1947), p. 385.

CHAPTER 20

Interviewing Types: Surveys, Health Exams & Employment Interviews.

LEARNING OBJECTIVES

When students have completed this chapter and lesson, they should be able to:

1. Review in-depth information gathering interviews specifically designed for surveys, employment, and health examinations.
2. Successfully develop questions designed for surveying, using reliability and validity as criteria for successful information gathering interviews.
3. Develop a health care interview focusing on creating a collaborative relationship of trust to insure the best information available for creating life preserving information.
4. Define the interview for finding a successful worker, and for finding the correct working condition.
5. Develop successful rules describing information gathering interviews.

CHAPTER 20: Overview

Three types of interviews are discussed: The survey interview, the health care interview, and the employment interview. In each case, a description of what can be anticipated for each situation, including the procedure, questions asked, and the overall process of the interview, will be offered.

The survey interview considers who should be interviewed, and how many interviews should take place. Characteristics of the interviewer are reviewed, along with the type of questions asked (open or closed), and what the finished project would report.

The health care interview must mitigate problems that create communication barriers between the health care provider and the patient. Types of questions and demeanor of both participants are considered. Getting complete information, yet avoiding embarrassing, misunderstood, or frightening questions becomes a challenge. The conclusion, often vital to the patient must be clearly presented to, understood by, and accepted by the patient.

The employment interview affects most people several times in their life. Because the world changes so rapidly, so does the employment process. Care is taken to discuss questions and information that can legally be requested in the interview. The employment process entails a screening or introductory interview that selects the top candidates for a given job. This is generally followed by the determinate interview. Questions and techniques associated with both interviews are discussed.

The Fox News Channel executives thought they had found an asset when they hired the gruff, barrel-chested former military man as a consultant to help in the network's coverage of the fighting in Afghanistan. He claimed to have won the Silver Star for bravery, served in Vietnam and was part of the secret, failed mission to rescue hostages in Iran in 1980. But records indicate that Joseph A. Cafasso's total military experience was 44 days of boot camp at Fort Dix, N.J., in May and June 1976, and his honorable discharge as a Private, First Class.

Dateline Los Angeles, Aug 16, 2001. A judge who falsely claimed he had once worked for the CIA in Laos and fought in Vietnam was ordered removed from the bench Wednesday.

The state Commission on Judicial Performance found Los Angeles Superior Court Judge Patrick Couwenberg guilty of willful misconduct in office, conduct prejudicial to the administration of justice and improper action under the state constitution.

``He lied to become a judge, elaborated on his misrepresentations for his enrobing ceremony and subsequently lied to the commission in an apparent attempt to frustrate its investigation," the commission said in an order signed by Chairman Michael A. Kahn.

Couwenberg's attorney admits his client is a compulsive liar but says it is because of a curable mental condition called ``pseudologia fantastica," said Couwenberg.

SOUTH BEND, Ind. (AP)—George O'Leary resigned as Notre Dame Football coach five days after being hired, admitting he lied about his academic and athletic background.

O'Leary claimed to have a master's degree in education and to have played college football for three years, but checks into his background showed it wasn't true. O'Leary never earned a letter playing football at New Hampshire even though his biography says he earned three. In fact, the school said he never played in a game.

These three job applicants were not the only job searchers tempted to embellish their résumés. A review of 2.6 million job applications in 2002 revealed 44% contained some lies. These errors were not carelessness. These people misrepresented their work histories, falsified reports of their education, and even falsified credentials or licenses.[1]

Over thirty million interviews are conducted in the United States every year by some 2,000 research firms, federal and state governments, companies, universities, medical centers, political candidates, and others too numerous to mention. Thousands of patients are interviewed by their doctor, nurse, or medical examiner. Most of us participate in some type of interview almost daily.[2]

The information gathering interview is by far the most common form of communication practicedin our culture. The world of work and the constantly growing demand for more skilled workers have placed the employment interview in the critical role of being a pivotal event in most of our lives. The above news items suggest how vital the employment interview has become as applicants are so concerned they falsify their information to do well in such an interview.

This chapter reviews three major types of interviews: the survey, employment interview, and health care interviews. These categories were selected because of their characteristic of being generalized to many other types of interviews, and because few people ever escape being directly involved with all three types of communication.

The Survey

As discussed in the previous chapter, both open and closed question surveys are conducted. Each type has its unique method and purpose, based on the intent of the interviewer. If the intent is to describe in-depth the situation, place, or event, the surveyor needs to focus upon three considerations: 1. People interviewed, 2. the type of questions asked, 3. the finished report, or conclusion of the interview process.

The most critical element of the survey is determining who should be the interviewees. Those questioned should represent a sample of the population covered by the survey questionnaire. Selected methods of sampling need to include elements that make up critical factors of the group being surveyed. Typical widespread characteristics like economic influence, age, and type of culture need to be considered.

By carefully choosing who is surveyed, the interviewer can almost predict the answers received. So if the intent of the survey is to describe a population, people sampled randomly for interviewing usually represent the entire population best. the type and number of interviews become a factor in valid results. Questions like "How many people need to be questioned before we have a true representation of the population?" are critical. The answer is that if more people were added to the sample and the results did not change, you have sufficient numbers. Obviously, if opinions are evenly split, the entire population should be reviewed before an inference could be made.

If a complete description of the interview topic, with in-depth answers reviewing all possible avenues of understanding is needed, open questions are preferred. If the concern is to focus on narrow, bipolar responses asking for specific conclusions, closed questions are preferred. The ideal is that each interviewee is asked the exact same questions. Should the same person be asked the same questions by several interviewers, the results would be the same. In summary, survey interviews require questions that produce both reliable and repeatable answers.

The obvious intent of such interviews is to determine differences in populations, products, or activities. Receiving such answers, automobile manufacturers might have predicted the striking difference in consumer response to the Ford Edsel and the Ford Mustang. The assumption, however, is that unbiased questions asked by a reliable interview staff would have produced valid answers. Correct surveys of an unbiased population would have created a different automobile than engineers created by guessing what the consumer wanted. As a result, the Edsel Ford was not the "car the people built" as it was advertised. The greatest mistake in automobile design could have been avoided, and perhaps "the car that people bought," the Ford Mustang, one of the most accepted car design models in automobile design history would have been built earlier.

It is easy to make statements about unbiased questions, or emotionally loaded words. However, it is not always easy to formulate them. How do you respond to the following question pairs?

1. Is it OK to smoke while praying?
   Is it OK to pray while smoking?
2. Do you think it is OK to allow public speeches against democracy?
   Do you think we should forbid public speeches against democracy?
3. Do you agree with this statement: My work is meaningful.
   Do you disagree with this statement: My work is not meaningful?
4. How do you feel about the new government imposed restrictions on taking liquids aboard airplanes?
   How do you feel about restrictions against taking liquids aboard airplanes?
   Are you for, against, or have no feeling about restrictions against taking liquids aboard airplanes?

The above shows that wording can have a direct result on answers received. Interviewers should carefully consider phrasing of questions, and develop strategies allowing the most objective answers available. Survey interviewers have developed question strategies to assess knowledge level, honesty, consistency, bias, order effect, and many fallacies of developing good questions. Strategies include asking the same question more than one way, eliminating the <u>don't know</u>, or <u>undecided</u> answer, and favoring questions that force choices. Limit the choices to a manageable number, and do not ask too many questions so that fatigue becomes a factor. Sometimes a ranking of choices is best. Perhaps offering a second or third choice is helpful.

Several sample surveys trying different questions could be helpful in clarifying conclusions or generalizations. Even then, be careful you do not generalize beyond the questions asked.[3]

A careful description of the population being tested, the number interviewed, and how they were selected become critical factors in how strongly you can accept your conclusions. The generally unworkable conclusion is that everyone in the population be surveyed. When this is neither practical nor possible, results are usually reported in probability of error. The standard for most scholars is either a one percent or five percent error. Statistical formulas can estimate such values.

Many problems have been examined with survey interviews, and even the crudest approach is more valuable than making an unsupported guess. Our culture has been conditioned to accept numbers as a credible factor in controlling and suggesting conclusions to difficult questions.

The Health Care Interview

Modern society has developed a system of health care providers with what at first view, seems to be an impossible situation of information exchange. One person, usually a medical expert, armed with the status of being in control of the interviewee's health, asks a patient a series of questions, armed with a vocabulary that most patients have little chance of understanding. Questions may include terms unfamiliar, intimate, or embarrassing to the patient. The situation can involve everything from getting an immunization shot, to reviewing upcoming coronary bypass surgery.

Communication barriers can be caused by gender, levels of understanding and vocabulary, conditions of illness and health, and even the provider dressed in a uniform and the patient partially nude. Placed in an environment of possible life-threatening consequences, the interview structure has many built-in communication barriers. Patients often face such interviews openly admitting that their health problems are out of control and they are forced to turn to others for help. Life itself often appears out of control, and patients feel vulnerable because they are without the security of home, job, routines, and normal relationships. They find themselves in a threatening environment, deprived of their dignity, autonomy, authority, and freedom.

The interviewer is faced with limited time, and high expectations from often emotionally-charged patients. Conditions require typical interviews to establish strong results with little time to create a proper atmosphere. Trust is a critical factor because they deal with intimate and sensitive personal information requiring maximum self-disclosure. Trust must be established at a high level very quickly for both parties. Confidentiality is a fundamental right of patients, and breaches may lead to discrimination, economic devastation, or social stigma. Health care providers must enhance trust through supportive talk that increases patient participation in the interviews, and by giving full disclosure of information, clarification, and by reinforcing social and psychological factors for the benefit of the patient. Because of the differences in vocabulary between the provider and patient, and because of fear of bad news, miscommunication can be high.

The provider should create an atmosphere where the patient feels free to express opinions, feelings, and attitudes. This climate must be conducive to the patient giving complete, detailed cooperation. Counsel must be clearly understood, and cooperation between parties essential. The setting for the interview must be comfortable, attractive, quiet, nonthreatening, and free of interruptions. The atmosphere must insure confidentiality. Type of room and privacy can go far in creating such a feeling.

The provider must be aware that the patient is filled with apprehension, particularly discussing sensitive and embarrassing topics. Apprehension can be moderated by carefully explaining procedures, being attentive and relaxed, yet being concerned for the best treatment of the patient. Try to have the patient dressed in street clothes rather than a backless hospital gown or seminude.

The greeting should be pleasant, and should quickly establish the credibility of the provider. Try to minimize the superior-to-subordinate relationship, yet develop a confidence in the patient for the provider. Take care to avoid baby talk. Words like "Hi, sweetie!" or "What's up, big guy!" are not appropriate. Such language can induce depression, reduced self-esteem, and cause the patient to withdraw.

Establishing rapport through small talk can build the relationship and help both parties relax, but dragging out the interview should be avoided. Be pleasant, but get directly to the issues at hand. Nothing can be more frustrating to the patient than being asked long lists of questions that have little relationship to the issues. Both parties are looking to get directly to the point after a brief, pleasant orientation. An introduction must explore the complete reason for the patient's visit.

As the provider questions the patient, it cannot be assumed that patients will provide accurate information. Many patients try to minimize, or maximize their illnesses. Depth of self-disclosure becomes a critical factor in the interview. Information will remain shallow if the patient does not trust the provider. A patient may give short answers in hopes of ending an uncomfortable situation. Others tend to give answers they think providers want to hear or attempt to please them to avoid bad news. For this reason, relevant, pointed questions should be asked as soon as possible. However, a series of short, rapid-fire closed questions can clearly imply the provider is in a hurry and not really interested in the patient. Remember that providers control the climate of the interview with the kind of questions asked and the general way of asking them. Avoid jargon, acronyms, or large medical words that can confuse or frighten the patient. Most patients either do not understand, or can be frightened with such terms as abscesses, sutures, tumors, cervix, edema or triglyceride.

Ambiguous questions pose equally serious problems. What does *regular* mean? How much is *too tired?* Who does not have *shortness of breath,* especially in a strange place with threatening sounds and unfamiliar surroundings? Try to ask focused, explicit questions.

As the provider structures the interview, it is recommended that the funnel or inverted funnel approach be used to narrow the options, or attempt to explain the exact problem. The funnel sequence gives the patient the feeling of being able to guide the provider to the exact problem. The inverted funnel helps the patient understand the implications of a specific pain or concern. If possible, give the patient time prior to the interview to write down questions they want answered.

As the interview draws to a close, be sure to give the patient written vital items of instruction, explanation, and definition. The patient, often placed at a difficult disadvantage of listening, will often forget vital information without written reminders. Instruction should include specific directions on what to do or avoid, medications to be given, and cautions that could increase problems. Future appointments should also be written. These written instructions should be given to someone accompanying the patient if possible. Instructions should be short and clearly written. Too often information overload can create more problems.[4]

Both providers and patients need to understand that communication skills do not come naturally in the high stress environment often accompanying a health care interview. Each party must learn to listen as well as ask questions, understand as well as inform, and commit as well as seek resolutions to problems. Both parties need to work at arriving at understanding and agreements for successful conclusions.

The Employment Interview

The world of work is a communication system that in many ways is a structured process, and in other ways a complex and confusing amalgamation of people. Because we live in a modern age of information and technology, requirements of the workforce are uniquely changing. A recent report from a workforce service organization pointed out that by the year 2012, the baby boomers who impacted the workforce dramatically in the fifties and sixties will be retiring. There will be 70 million workers over the age of 65. Almost half the workforce will be eligible for retirement. Many of them will not possess the skills necessary to replace themselves—computer literacy, academic knowledge, and even skills associated with work demands.

Cultural changes are also making an impact on the workforce. Hispanic workers are rapidly increasing in percentages of the total workforce. The same is true for African-Americans and Asian-Americans. The one consistency in the workforce is a demand for more education and more refined skills.

Choosing a career is a challenging task in an age where new career paths are being created and old ones are disappearing at an increasing rate. The new employee is vastly different from those of the previous generation in many aspects. Demographics, new technology, kind and amount of education, the economy, leisure and recreational opportunities, and even the diversity of the market place, converge to make our global economy.

The successful, happy person of the future will have prepared carefully and wisely in creating a career that will be both challenging and equitable. A careful self analysis of marketable skills includes not only personality and physical fitness, but also a strong background in communication skills, a good education, and a strong value structure. As the person prepares for a career, they must have created and kept a credible description of successful experiences to successfully compete in the new world economy. This is referred to as a resume.

Those entering the workforce with a strong background will have a decided advantage over those who failed to build such credentials. Economists fear the end product will be almost a feudal separation of "haves" and "have nots," creating even more intense social and political divisions in the culture.

Because of the technical nature of many jobs, coupled with high salaries and a shortage of applicants in critical fields such as information technology, medicine, and engineering, applicants may only go through a Screening Interview with reference checks, transcripts, drug test, and an assessment score from a standardized test such as the Myers-Briggs, ACT, or other IQ tests at the first level. The second level, in-depth, or Determinate Interview concludes the employment process.

If security and safety are requirements, other standardized tests can be given to determine honesty, morality, and ethics. Others may require physical fitness, and skill tests such as driving, or computer skills.

Armed with this résumé that uniquely but professionally describes your preparation for the workforce (See Chapter 22), you are now ready for entering the job market and participating in the employment interview process.

Legally, employers must approach the employment process with much preparation also. Based on federal legislation, beginning with the Civil Rights Act of 1964, and including the Age Discrimination in Employment Act of 1967, the Americans with Disabilities Act of 1990, the Uniformed Services Employment Reemployment Rights Act of 1994, and ending with the Immigration Reform and Control Act, the interviewer must be well schooled in knowing what kinds of information can be asked of the perspective employee before judging suitability for employment.

Basically, these acts forbid a company to discriminate against prospective employees on the basis of sex, age, race, national origin, religion, physical disability, or veteran status. These characteristics are called protected classes and questions about any aspect of these topics during an interview are illegal. The interviewer must avoid all questions that could seem legally questionable, such as those about height, weight, age, marital status, religious or political beliefs, dependents, birth control, birthplace, race, and national origin. If the interviewer has a question about legality of a question, it is a good rule to measure a question's status by the role it plays in determining the candidate's ability to perform a job. If the question does not relate to the workforce skill required for satisfactory work, the question is deemed illegal.

The screening Interview is the first level of obtaining employment. This can occur in many locations. Placement centers; recruiting visits to community centers, college and university locations; or job fairs held at special occasions start the process. The screening interview is an initial contact between the applicant and the company representative. It is used to reduce the pool of applicants in the employment selection process. It combines with the prescreening written information provided to employers to create a sense of who the applicants are and what they can bring to the organization. Organizations hire because they have a need or problem, and they are looking for solutions in job applicants.

Attitude in the initial interview is critical. Psychologists report that the screening interview produces the highest anxiety of any communication event. If the applicant is well prepared, has successfully gathered information about the company, and sincerely desires the job, anxiety is reduced. A positive attitude, or *self-fulfilling prophecy* that a successful event is about to take place, also increases success rates. One study revealed that good first impressions lead interviewers to show positive regard toward applicants, give important job information, sell the organization to them, and spend less time gathering information.[5]

The applicant should be no earlier than 15 minutes to the interview, or the first impression will be one of being too interested. Fewer than 5 percent of applicants coming late receive an invitation for a return visit. If you cannot be on time for the interview, can you make it on time for work?

Even if the company boasts casual dress at work, the applicant should be well dressed for the interview. Dress and appearance are critical elements in favorable first impressions. In a survey of college recruiters, 95 percent cited professional image as important.[6] No objections can be made for being well dressed. Being sloppy or too casual implies you do not have as high regard for the company as you should.

Greet the employer pleasantly and dynamically. Do not use the interviewer's first name unless invited to do so. Sit when asked to do so and never sit before the interviewer does. Be an active participant during the opening, avoiding a string of yes and no answers. Respond openly to the icebreaking questions as you would in any normal conversation, but do not try to dominate or be too reserved. How you handle yourself during the first few minutes tells the interviewer a great deal about your interpersonal skills. It is estimated over 50 percent of interviewers make a decision to whether or not to invite the applicant to a second interview within the first five minutes of the screening interview.

Successful applicants listen carefully to the whole question without interrupting or trying to second-guess the interviewer. They think before replying, and then give answers that are succinct, specific, and to the point of the question.[7] All successful applicants are prepared to handle frequently asked questions such as:

1. Tell me about yourself.
2. What do you know about our company?
3. Why should we hire you?
4. How does this job fit into your overall career objectives?
5. What are the five most significant accomplishments in your life?
6. What are your strong points?
7. What are your weak points?
8. Describe what skills and qualifications you think are essential for success in this job?
9. What are your career goals?
10. Do you have any questions for me?[8]

The closing part of the interview is usually brief. Take an active part in the closing by expressing your interest in the position and ask what will happen next.

Find out if you need to contact them, or will they report to you. Find out who you should contact if another appointment is necessary. As you depart, remember that the interview is not over until you leave the company and all people connected with it, even if they take you to lunch, or some other spot for entertainment. That could be part of the interview also.

The Determinate Interview

Once that employers decide that certain applicants meet their criteria for further consideration, applicants are invited to a **determinate interview**. This second part of the employment process determines whether the applicant is hired, interviewed further, or dropped from consideration. In such interviews, several scenarios are possible. Some companies employ stress tactics, a deliberate attempt to create anxiety for the applicant and then observe and assess their ability to handle difficult situations. Tactics include insults or affronts, long periods of staring, a change from cordial to a hostile attitude, unexplained silences or inattention, or trick questions to provoke contradictory answers.

Another common technique for in-depth analysis is to present brainteasers or logic questions to determine a candidate's intelligence, creativity, and analytical skills. For these types of questions, the best approach is to remain organized, and approach each problem in a logical series of tasks. For instance, if the challenge was to determine China's market potential for disposable diapers, the steps might be:

1. Estimate the population of China.
2. Select a percentage of child-bearing-age mothers.
3. Estimate the number who would have children.

Keep in mind such vital information as knowing that Chinese families usually have just one child, and assume what percentage would be below age three. Use round numbers. Your answers may not be accurate, but the idea is to show your problem solving skills and logical thought process.

During such interviews, the applicant should keep in mind that an attitude of positive self-fulfilling prophecy is a great help. Self confidence and belief in one's ability is a critical factor in most employment interviews. Optimism and a positive attitude go far in impressing employers. To control stress, remember that ultimately you will determine whether to accept the position or not.

As with the screening interview, the close of the interview should be on a positive note. The applicant should know what comes next. Thanks should be given to the company for the interview. A thank you note written to the company is in good taste.

Chapter 20: Analysis and Application Exercises

1. Visit your local employment center and see what jobs are available. Find out what the requirements are for applying and request instructions for interviewing and preparing for an interview.
2. Role play a job application interview with another student.

References

1. http//the cheating culture.com(2002).
2. P. Rosenfeld, J.E. Edwards, and M.D. Thomas, "Improving Organizational Surveys," *American Behavioral Scientist*, 36 (1993), 414.
3. For a more complete analysis of question development, see C.J. Stewart & W.B. Cash, *Interviewing: Principles and Practices*, 12th ed. (Boston: McGraw Hill, 2008) p.145-154.

4. For a more complete analysis of health care interviews, see C.J. Stewart and W.B. Cash, "The Health Care Interview," *Interviewing: Principles and Practice*, 12th Ed (Boston: McGraw Hill, 2008) 379-406.
5. T.W. Dougherty, D.B. Turban, & J.C. Callender, "Confirming First Impressions in the Employment Interview: A Field Study of Interviewer Behavior," *Journal of Applied Psychology* 79 (1994), 659-665.
6. K.A.D. Johansen & M. Steele, "Keeping Up Appearances," *Journal of Career Planning and Employment*, Summer, 1999, 45-50.
7. Stewart & Cash, p. 245.
8. Http://Therese Droste, "Interview Tricks are No Treat," editorial.careers.msn.com, 11/3/2003.

CHAPTER 21

Effective Written Communication

LEARNING OBJECTIVES

When students have completed this chapter and lesson, they should be able to:

1. Understand the elements of the APOSSE model and how they may be used to plan and write a well-organized, well-supported, and well-reasoned paper.
2. Understand the elements of the Toulmin model and how they may be used to plan and write a well-organized, well-supported, and well-reasoned paper.
3. Understand how these two models relate to each other and how they may be combined for maximum effectiveness in writing a well-organized, well-supported, and well-reasoned paper.

CHAPTER 21: Overview

Many have successfully applied classical rhetorical theory to spoken communication, and we will discuss that application later in our text when we learn about public speaking. But the principles of rhetoric can also be applied to written communication. This chapter applies the principles of classical and modern rhetoric to written communication through the use of the APOSSE and Toulmin models.

This chapter also discusses the challenge of deciding upon a specific subject for a paper and how to apply the principles of both rhetoric and argument to the planning, organizing and presentation of an academic paper.

The APOSSE Model

Dr. Shirley Jones introduced the use of the APOSSE model for effective written communication in the previous edition of this text.[1] The acronym APOSSE stands for audience, purpose, organization, subject, style, and evidence. It fits well into the classical rhetorical models we discussed previously in chapter 18 of this text. Some of those principles have particular application to the APOSSE model, and are bolded below for emphasis.

The four main elements within the context (rhetorical situation):

1. Speaker
2. Speech
3. Audience . . . . **Audience**
4. Occasion

Aristotle's five canons (necessary elements of rhetorical persuasion)

- 1. Invention: . . . . **Subject**
  - a. Inartistic Proofs (avoid)
  - b. Artistic Proofs . . . . **Evidence**
    - (1) Logos (Logic)
    - (2) Ethos (Credibility)
    - (3) Pathos (Emotion)

2. Arrangement . . . .**Organization**
3. Style . . . . **Style**
4. Memor
5. Delivery

Audience

Any message, written or spoken, must consider who will read or hear the communication. Things like their history, their culture, their level of education, and their expectations must be considered. You must clearly understand the issues that are important to them, and you must address those issues. Remember that the success or failure of your writing will largely revolve around whether you have addressed what your audience thinks is important and have done so in a way that is pleasing to them. Otherwise, your message will be rejected and ineffective.

Purpose

Ask yourself, "Why am I writing this?" One general question might be, "Am I writing to inform my audience, or am I writing to persuade them?" To answer this question you must clearly know what your audience needs or expects from you and what you want them to do as a result of your communication. Do you want them to do something or just to agree with you? Is this a course paper that you are writing for a grade? Is it an application for a job? Is it a personal message in which you want to be clearly understood? Whether it is any of these or many other possibilities, you must clearly know your purpose before you begin and then remain true to that purpose throughout your communication. Any deviation from that purpose will only confuse your audience and obscure what you really wanted to say or write.

Organization

Especially in written communication, there are many conventions (expectations) that you must follow to appear competent and therefore informed and persuasive. First, there are the specific requirements of your particular audience. If your audience is your professor, you must write your paper in precisely the form required by the assignment. Also, there are the discipline-specific guidelines that may apply. For example, if you are writing a paper for a communication class you must follow APA (American Psychological Association) style in your citations and references. If you are writing for an English class you must use MLA style, and if you are writing for a journalism class you must use Associated Press style. Then there are the cultural expectations that may apply. In the United States, using gender-specific words when it is not necessary is now considered insensitive. Know the rules of your audience and follow them precisely.

Another issue of organization is how to organize your thoughts within the message. You should always organize your written communication in the easiest-to-follow and remember way possible. This might include the use of *signposts*—clues within the text that organize things for the reader or listener (e.g., "First, I'm going to.., Second, we can turn to...", etc.) Then there is also the consideration of what order to put things in to maximize the effectiveness of your message. In chapter 18 we discussed both the primacy effect and the recency effect, and these are important considerations for your message's organization. Another effect sequence is the "problem–solution" sequence where you first present the problem and then suggest the solution or solutions that will be responsive to it. We will discuss more of these organizational issues as they relate to speaking when we get to that part of our course and text.

Subject

Selecting a topic can be a challenge. In doing so, you essentially "discover" what to write about, and then "invent" what you want to say. Of course, your topic or subject must be clear to you and to your audience. We sometimes refer to your point, your subject, or your topic as your *thesis*. If you do not know what your point is, or if your audience can't understand it, your cause is lost and your communication is in vain.

Generally, you should write about subjects that interest you and that you already know something about. When possible, select a subject about which you feel strongly. And remember that you must also meet the expectations of the audience in this matter, and make the point that they want you to make. Overall, your subject should be interesting to both you and your audience.

Your topic is closely connected to the purpose of your communication, and you must ensure that you do not wander from this subject. Stay appropriately focused, and do not allow yourself to be either too broad or too narrow in your treatment. One way to test whether your topic is appropriately focused is to answer this question: "In one complete sentence, can you tell me the purpose of your communication?" If you can, you are probably appropriately focused; if you cannot, then you may need to trim your expectations or your purpose.

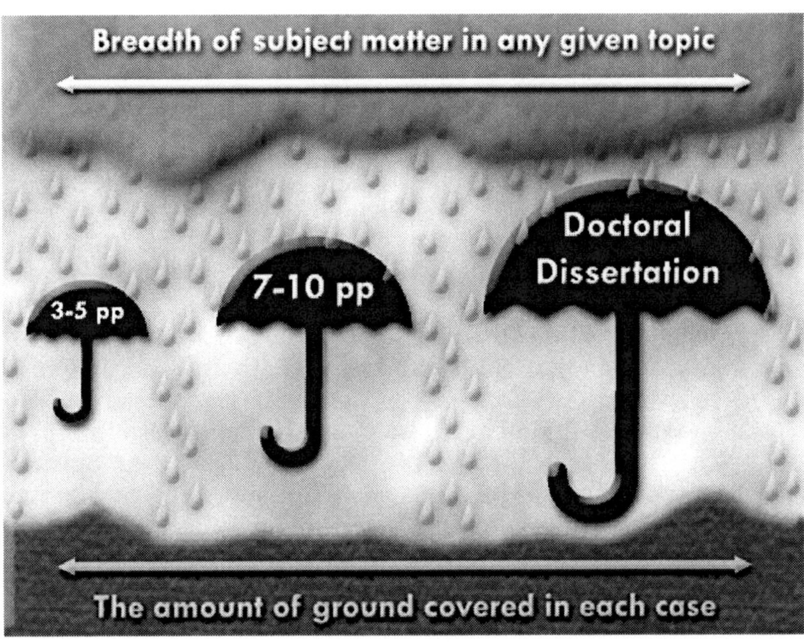

Figure 21.1

Once you have selected your general topic, you must limit it to the size and nature of the assignment. One danger arises from making our topics so broad that we cannot adequately cover them. Dr. Shirley Jones encourages students to think of their subject as an umbrella. "The umbrella should be of such a size that your paper should cover *everything* that falls under that umbrella. If assignment asks for a 2-3 page paper, then your umbrella should be quite small. On the other hand, if your assignment calls for a 7-10 research paper, then your umbrella can be considerably larger."[2] (See Figure 21.1.) The material in this chapter can be helpful in properly focusing your subject.

Using Dr. Jones' metaphor, no detail, no matter how interesting, can be presented in your paper unless it falls under your topic umbrella. "If that detail is so interesting to you (and you think it might be for your audience), consider moving your umbrella. If you decide that there are no interesting details as you research a subject, you probably would be better off finding yourself another rainstorm!"[3]

Figure 21.2 illustrates how a given topic might be treated with varying degrees of breadth. Your decision is made based on what portion of the subject you wish (or are required) to cover.

EXAMPLES OF TOPIC BREADTH

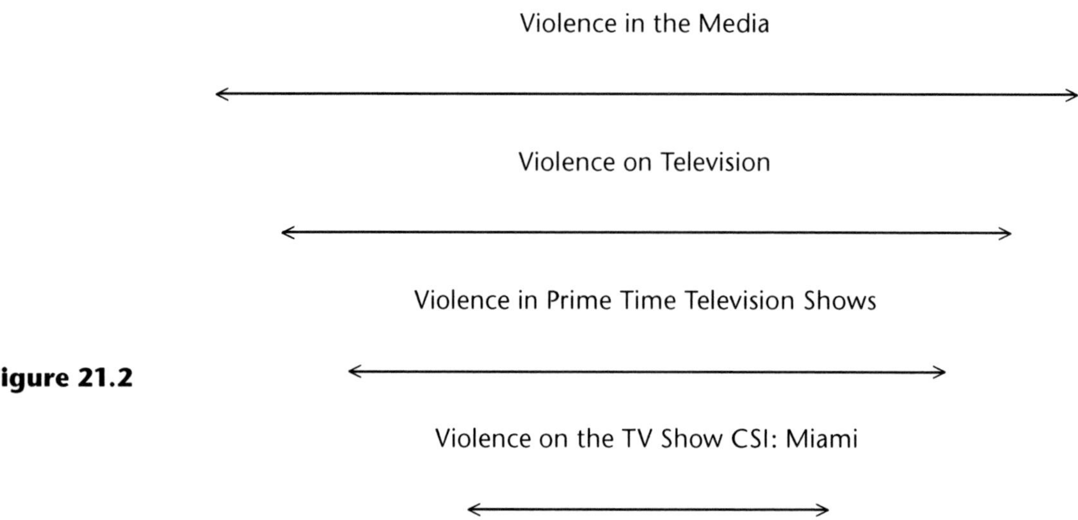

Figure 21.2

Style

Aristotle liked the use of figures of speech, particularly metaphors, in persuasive discourse. When a speaker or writer chooses the examples, metaphors, and stories that will be used, and when and how they can be most effective, this is part of the overall style of the communication. Corbet says other stylistic choices include whether the treatment of the topic is general or specific, abstract or concrete, formal or informal. He also includes length and kind of sentences, along with variety of patterns, sentence euphony, articulation, and paragraphing.[4]

Written arguments must also conform to certain official stylistic rules of written language (called *langue*) that apply to writing but not to speaking. The rules of spoken language (called *parole*) are much less formal than those for writing. For example, any kind of formal writing must be grammatically correct to be taken seriously in our culture. Also, manuscript styles like APA, MLA, or AP must be strictly followed in associated academic disciplines, and they will affect not only the style of your writing but also its organization (see "Organization" above).

Evidence

Your evidence is your proof, appropriate to the type of message you are conveying to your audience. If you are using a logical (logos) approach, then data and evidence will be particularly important. If you are relying heavily on ethos, then you must present evidence as to why people should trust what you (or the people you are quoting) say. If you are using pathos, then you need an emotionally powerful example that will move your audience to action. The communicator must be concerned not only with the type of evidence offered (appropriate to the method) but also the amount of evidence. Have you given enough? Is it too much? Your choice and use of evidence will be the most important thing you do after you have evaluated your audience. Choose it carefully.

Figure 21.3 shows how an interview assignment used in one Communication 1010 class might use the APOSSE model as a guide to writing the paper.

Assignment: Prepare an Interview Analysis paper that considers the suitability of a particular career path for you.

Instructions: Interview someone currently holding a responsible position in a career that interests you. Write a 2-3 page paper reflecting on the interview process that analyzes what you learned about the appropriateness of this field as a career choice for you.

Figure 21.3

Rhetorical Concerns:

(a) Audience: Your audience is an academic one; specifically, your instructor and classmates.

(b) Purpose: Your purpose is analysis—examining your expectations against what you learned in the interview process so you can make important future career choices.

(c) Organization: Academic papers are usually deductively organized, with your thesis or claim early in your paper. Suggestions for organization:
Introduction: Find an interesting way to begin your paper. Your paper's thesis and organization (for example, topical, chronological, compare/contrast) should be clear to your audience at least by the end of your second paragraph.
Body: This part of your paper will develop your thesis with relevant and specific detail. Lead your reader through your paper with transitions and organizational signals.
Conclusion: Summarize and restate your thesis without being redundant. Be certain that you provide a concluding sentence that fulfills reader expectations.

(d) Subject: You will want to focus your subject to enable you to use an abundance of evidence. Choose a subject that is most useful to you. Some possible thesis statements follow:

1. Through the interview process I found my preliminary career choice suits (or does not suit) my career goals.
2. My interview did (or did not) fulfill my goals for the interview.
3. From my interview, I found there are advantages (strengths) and disadvantages (weaknesses) for me in choosing this career path.

(e) Style: Formal, academic language style—no slang or colloquialisms. Formal stylistic rules include APA style for citations. Paper should be typewritten or word processed, double spaced, and on one side only of 8 1/2 x 11 inch white paper. Maintain one inch margins left, right, top and bottom. On the first page of your paper, single spaced in the upper right or left-hand corner, place your name, the instructor's name, class and section number, and the assignment title. All pages (except the first) should be numbered.

(f) Evidence: Remember that academic audiences do not accept unsupported assertions. Also, for an academic audience a logical (logos) approach would be most appropriate, though you may include some ethos and pathos as well. This would suggest a deductive organization of your evidence, which will include (1) specific examples, (2) answers to your questions, and (3) your personal assessment, all in support of your conclusions.

The Toulmin Model [5]

Steven Toulmin's model for constructing a rhetorical argument was introduced in Chapter 17. Just like the APOSSE model, this model can also be used effectively to plan for writing a paper. If we look at the interview analysis paper assignment contained in Figure 21.3, we can use the Toulmin model to ensure that we have adequately covered our topic with appropriate support for our arguments.

The example that follows (Figure 21.4) is a specific instance of a paper that a student might write in response to the interview assignment. The student could fill in the boxes of this model as he or she "discovers" or "invents" the subject. Then, as the student continued to find information about the topic, he or she could change the contents of these boxes appropriately until the paper was fully researched and ready for writing. This 52-year-old bank teller wants to be an accountant. She researched what was required in order to fulfill her goal, and then decided if the result was going to be worth the effort. In doing so, she not only wrote a paper for an assignment but also answered important life-changing questions about her goal.

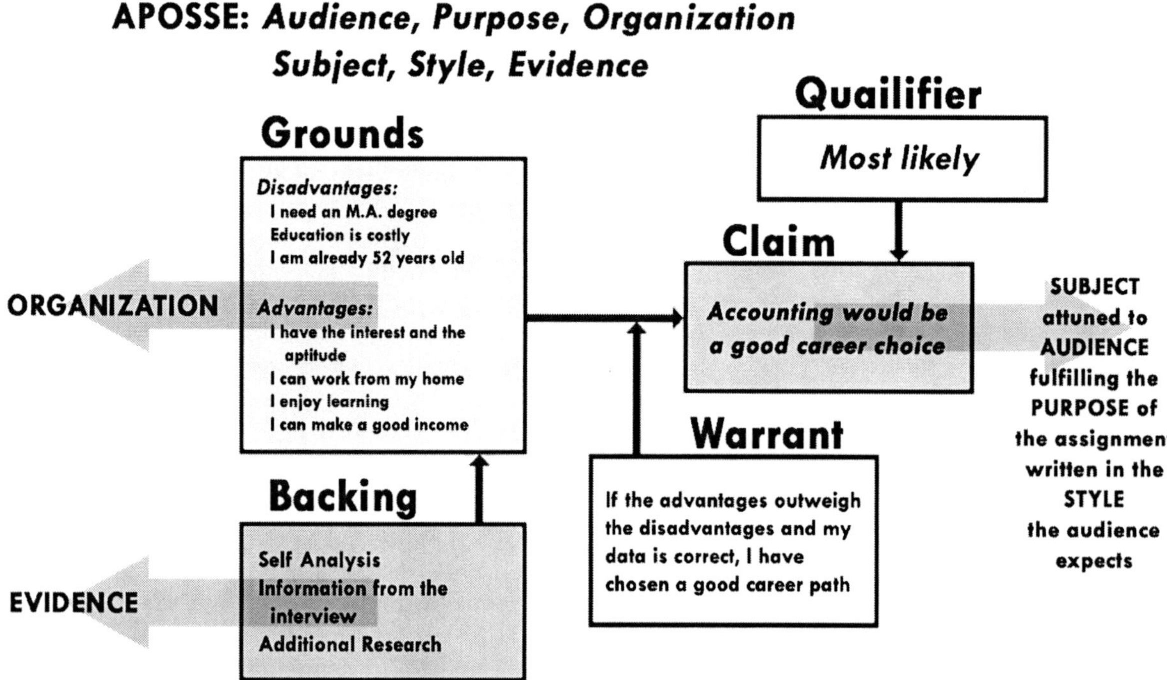

Figure 21.4 A sample paper plan using the Toulmin and APOSSE models

The Toulmin model helped this woman choose ("invent") her specific subject and provided the organization for the paper. Along the way, she also fulfilled the requirements of the APOSSE model as she filled in the various boxes of the Toulmin model. These two models fit nicely together to provide heuristic guidance for satisfying the rhetorical and critical thinking requirements of a well-written paper. But doing it well is not quick nor easy. It requires good research and the writing of a well-reasoned paper.

Summary

The principles of rhetorical persuasion apply to written communication as well as to speeches. To be effective, claims, and arguments must be appropriately focused—limited to the specific subject and breadth that you have chosen. The APOSSE and Toulmin models, used together, can provide a strong heuristic strategy for planning and writing your papers. If each of the elements of these models are considered and properly addressed, the result will be a properly-focused, well-reasoned, well-supported argument that will have persuasive power with your audience.

Chapter 21: Analysis and Application Exercises

1. Some of the elements in the APOSSE model and the Toulmin model are identical. What are they, and why would they be so universally important?

2. Figure 21.3 illustrates how an interview assignment and paper might make use of the APOSSE model. If you are presently writing a paper for any of your courses, try using this model to outline how you will approach your topic. Does it work well? Why or why not?
3. In academic writing, a logical (logos) approach is generally preferred. Nevertheless, adding some elements of ethos and pathos can add greater strength and interest to your arguments. If you were writing a paper like the one shown in Figure 21.3, how and where could you use ethos to strengthen your claims and conclusions? How and where could you use pathos?

References

1. Jones, Shirley. Written Communication, in R.S. Chase and S.G. Jones, *Elements of Effective Communication*. 2nd ed. Boston, MA: Allyn and Bacon.
2. Jones, Shirley. Written Communication, in R.S. Chase and S.G. Jones, *Elements of Effective Communication*. 2nd ed. Boston, MA: Allyn and Bacon, 233.
3. Jones, Shirley. Written Communication, in R.S. Chase and S.G. Jones, *Elements of Effective Communication*. 2nd ed. Boston, MA: Allyn and Bacon., 233.
4. Corbett, Edward P. J. *Classical Rhetoric for the Modern Student*. 2nd Ed. New York: Oxford University Press, 1971, 440–447.
5. Toulmin, Steven, Rieke, Richard and Janik, Allan, *An Introduction to Reasoning*. 2nd ed. New York: MacMillan Publishing Co., 1984.

CHAPTER 22 Writing for Professionals

LEARNING OBJECTIVES

When students have completed this chapter and lesson, they should be able to:

1. Know and be able to properly use the conventions for résumés.
2. Know and be able to properly use the conventions for business letters.
3. Know and be able to properly use the conventions for memos.
4. Know and properly avoid the problems that emailed memos can present.

CHAPTER 22: Overview

In this chapter, we will first consider the general concerns for written work in a business environment. We will then review the formatting rules for résumés, letters, and memos. At the end, we will discuss the importance of proper spelling and grammar.

Colleges and universities constantly seek guidance from business and industry to insure their academic programs are relevant to the needs of those who will hire their students. And whenever such conversations ensue, two requests are consistently included.

- Please send us people who know how to think critically and solve problems.
- Please send us people who know how to write.

This chapter deals with the second of these two requests—writing in a work environment. Nearly every job requires writing skills. Yet, far too many college graduates do not meet the professional standards expected in a business environment. Spelling and grammar errors persist. And many documents are not formatted properly. The net result is that the worker looks incompetent, as does the business itself. Here are some general concerns.

General Business Writing Concerns

Typing. Today, the ability to type with more than two fingers is essential to your success. Both business writing and general computer competency require that your keyboarding skills be up to par. No attempt will be made in this chapter to address keyboarding issues except to say that unless you can type with accuracy up to a minimum standard of 80 words per minute you probably need to take a keyboarding class and sharpen up your skills.

Paper and Organization. In business environments, 20 pound white paper is the standard. Businesses sometimes use light gray or beige papers, but never brightly colored pastels or neons that call attention to the paper rather than the message. As a general rule, content is on one side only of the paper (except in manuals or other instruction booklets, which may be two-sided). Margins should be at least one inch all the way around. Text should be single spaced within a paragraph, but double spaced between paragraphs. Each paragraph should also be indented on the first line to make reading easier. Normally, each page except the first page should have a header that identifies the document. And each page should be numbered, either at the bottom or as part of the header.

Formatting Rules for Résumés

Elements of a Résumé

The following are the common elements of a résumé. All of these should appear on any résumé that you may prepare.

- Name, current address, and current phone number
- Job or career objective
- Education
- Experience
- Special interests and aptitudes
- Certification
- References

The following are things you should not include in a résumé because they reveal information on protected classes and will make your résumé legally impossible to consider.

- a photograph
- your age
- your gender
- your race
- your ethnic background
- your religious preference
- your sexual preference

Organization of Résumés

The sequence shown above for the elements of a résumé is fairly typical. They should appear in this order unless there is a compelling reason for a different order.

- Your name, address, and telephone number should always come first.
- All information—major headings, minor headings, lists, etc.—should be listed in "parallel" fashion (formatted and worded like other similar headings).
- Use major headings ("Education," "Experience," etc.) for each element in parallel fashion.
- Use sub-headings if needed under major headings—in parallel fashion.
- Within each segment of your résumé, organize the information in a way that makes it easy to follow. Bulleted ("•") ("—") or numbered ("1.") lists usually help.
- Spacing is also important. Use wide margins and leave plenty of "white space" on the page, rather than cramming too much information into a limited area.
- Do not use the word "I" in your résumé. It diminishes the professional feel of it.
- Absolutely no spelling, grammar, or mechanical errors are permissible. Your résumé must be perfect in this regard.
- Chronologically organized résumés are the norm. Place items under a major heading in order of date—with the most recent item first.
- Functional résumés are useful when targeting a specific skill set that the employer needs and which is represented on your résumé. In this case, place items into groups by type, with the most relevant first.

General Considerations for Résumés

Strong résumés always focus on the employer's needs. Do some research before you begin to find out precisely what they are looking for and what they value most. This will help you in both the content and organization of your résumé.

Strong résumés are concise. Long sentences and paragraphs discourage reading and make you look rambling and imprecise. That is why bulleted lists are generally more likely to get read than those organized into paragraphs of information.

Strong résumés are honest. Never mislead your reader in any way. If you falsify your information or you mislead in any other way, that will be certain grounds for termination when it is discovered. Also, if you tend to over-emphasize some aspects of your résumé it will likely be noticed by skilled business people who have read many such documents. Bombastic claims are a red flag that suggests that you are not being totally honest and they will probably not seriously consider you as a result.

Traditional Résumé

As summarized by George Searles (1999),[1] traditional résumés can be organized in accordance with any one of three basic styles: chronological, functional, or a combination of both.

"A chronological résumé is the most common, and the easiest to prepare. Schooling and work experience are presented in reverse-chronological order, with schools' and employers' names and addresses indicated, along with the dates of the applicant's attendance or employment. Descriptions of the applicant's specific job responsibilities or courses of study are provided as part of the Experience or Education categories. This style is most appropriate for persons whose education and past experience are fairly consistent with their future career plans, or for those seeking to advance within their own workplace.

"A functional résumé, on the other hand, highlights what the applicant has done, rather than where or when it has been done. The functional résumé is skills-based, summarizing in general terms the applicant's experience and potential for adapting to new work challenges. Specific chronological details of the person's background are included, but are not the main focus of such a résumé. This style is most appropriate for applicants wishing to emphasize their actual proficiencies rather than their work history.

"As the term suggests, the combination résumé is a blend of the chronological and functional approaches, featuring a relatively brief "skills" section at the outset, followed by a chronological detailing of the applicant's background. The combination approach is most appropriate for applicants whose experience is relatively diversified, and whose skills span a range of functional areas."

Scannable Résumés

Given the rapid advancement of computer and Internet technology, many companies now use electronic scanners to load letters and résumés into databases. This allows them to quickly evaluate all applications received and to search for and pinpoint applicants' credentials on the computer. The problem with this approach is that many scanners do not retain the original formatting of the résumé, creating a rather bland and jumbled result on the screen. For this reason, you should greatly simplify your résumé if it's going to be scanned, by using a no-frills, flush-left format. There is a hidden benefit in this. The simpler format permits more information to be included and eliminates unnecessary frills.

Also, it is now possible to explore the Internet for job postings and other such information using tools like Google and other search engines, and even to post your own credentials to on-line résumé banks. These are three examples:

Career Mosaic < http://www.careermosaic.com >
NationJob < http://www.nationjob.com >
Net Temps < http://www.net-temps.com >

And of course, Internet services like Facebook also provide opportunities to post résumés and other information in an easy-to-find and universally-recognized place on the Net.

Example of a Résumé

Look at the example of a résumé submitted by a student seeking a job as an ESL aid in elementary schools, which appears on the following page as Figure 22.1. How would you rate this résumé, using the following checklist of the principles explained above?

Contents:

- name, address, phone number
- job or career objective
- education
- experience
- special interests/aptitudes
- certification
- references

General Considerations:

- focused on employer needs
- contents are concise
- contents are honest

Formatting:

- name, address, phone first
- all lists in parallel fashion
- major headings for sections
- sub-headings (if needed)
- bulleted or numbered lists
- adequate margins
- adequate white space
- no use of the word "I"
- no spelling, grammar errors
- chronological in reverse order or functional in order of importance

Figure 22.1

What is strong or weak about this sample résumé?

STEVEN W. HANSEN

résumé

PRESENT ADDRESS:
5120 South 2100 East, Salt Lake City, Utah 84117
Phone: (801) 272-3210

OBJECTIVE: Seeking an entry-level position as an aid for ESL students in elementary and secondary schools.

EDUCATION:
Currently Attending Salt Lake Community College
Associate Degree, Gen.Education, Salt Lake Community College,
Expected May 1997

Major: Gen.Ed. with emphasis in Spanish, English, and Communication

Graduate, Olympus High School, SLC, Utah, June 1992
Member, Olympus Track Team and School Band
Graduated one year early due to aggressive completion of requirements

WORK EXPERIENCE:
Teacher's Aid, Granite School District, Redwood Elementary

Nov 96-Present
Assisting teachers by translating Spanish for ESL students & parents
Church volunteer among the people of Guayaquil, Ecuador

Oct 94-Sep 96
Living among and teaching the people of Ecuador, where I became fluent in Spanish and familiar with the Latin culture.
Cassette Loader/Duplicator, Videomatic USA

Jan 91-Sep 94
Worked in high-tech videotape manufacturing and duplication
Field Worker and Student, Youth Developmental Ent., Maui, Hawaii

Jan 90-Dec 90
Participated in work/study program in Hawaii, working full time while continuing high school and learning about Polynesian culture.

SPECIAL INTERESTS AND SKILLS:
Fluent in Spanish and English, and currently learning French
Experienced a variety of cultures first-hand over a three-year period
Teaching and leadership skills training native Ecuadorians in missionary work
Music - played percussion in high school band
Writing - special interest/abilities in writing, both personally and academically

HONORS AND CERTIFICATES:
Eagle Scout, awarded June 1993

PERSONAL: References and recommendations available upon request

Formatting Rules for Letters

Elements of a Letter

The following are the common elements of a business letter. All of these should appear on any letter for business that you may prepare.

- Heading: Letterhead block with company name, address, phone.
- Date: Date the letter was written.
- Inside address: Company name, address, city, state, and zip of addressee with company name, address, and city/state/zip each on a separate line.
- Salutation: "Dear Mr. Campbell:", "Dear Wal-Mart:", etc. (use a colon (:) unless you are personally familiar with the addressee.
- Body: The paragraphs containing your message.
- Complimentary close "Sincerely," is most common. "With thanks," or something else appropriate to the tone and message of the letter.
- Signature block: Skip a few lines to make room for a signature, then type the name, title, and company (if no letterhead is used), usually with each item on a separate line.

Additional Elements of a Letter

The following are additional elements that may appear in your business letter, if they are appropriate to the circumstances.

- Addressee line: Specific person's name may appear above the company name.
- Attention line: Or, in between the inside address and the salutation, you may insert an "Attn:" or "Attention:" followed by the person's name.
- Subject line: You may include a "Subject:" line above the salutation.
- Postscript: A "P.S." line may appear after the signature block, if appropriate, for additional comments or information.

The following additional elements may appear at the end of your business letter, usually at the bottom left or right of the last page.

- Reference initials: The initials of the person typing the letter.
- Enclosure line: "Encl:" following by a description of enclosed materials.
- Copy line: "cc:" following by those to whom a copy of the letter was sent.
- Mailing line: The date on which the letter was mailed.
- Second page head: If the letter is more than one page, every page should have a brief header which identifies the letter (e.g., "Letter to Richard Rogers"). Normally these pages are not put on letterhead.
- Page numbers: If the letter is more than one page, every page except the first one should be numbered. The number may appear in the head or it may appear elsewhere, but be consistent.

Additional Requirements of a Business Letter

Along with the above-listed standard components, nearly all business letters follow the same three-part pattern of organization described by George Searles (1999):[2]

1. A brief introductory paragraph establishing the context (by referring to previous correspondence, perhaps, or by orienting the reader in some other way) and stating the letter's purpose concisely;
2. A middle section (as many paragraphs as needed) conveying the content of the message by providing all necessary details, presented in the most logical sequence;

3. A brief concluding paragraph politely requesting action, thanking the reader, or providing any additional information pertinent to the situation.

A fairly recent development is the "open punctuation" system in which the colon after the salutation and the comma after the complimentary close are omitted. This variation is gaining widespread acceptance.

Tone

Every form of communication, including letters, must convey an appropriate tone. Letters are more formal than memos because they are assumed to be more public. The tone of the letter should reflect and uphold the image of the sender's company or organization—usually meaning a high degree of professionalism. Letters should also be more polished than memos because they take more time to compose. Still, they must be readable, so this should not be overdone by sounding too pompous or "official." Today's business letters feature a nice, friendly but professional approach with easy-to-understand language, careful construction of the message, and *no* grammar errors.

Cover Letters

Cover letters are always required when you send a résumé to someone, or when you are sending any other kind of document (e.g., a contract) that stands on its own. This provides you with an opportunity to communicate with the intended recipient about the purpose or nature of your enclosure. There are certain conventions of business letters that should be followed.

- Contact established in the first and final paragraphs (e.g., "My name is Jodie Williams, and...", etc., at the beginning and "Please feel free to contact me at....", etc. at the end).
- Somewhere in your letter you should reference your enclosure. (e.g., "I have enclosed my résumé with this letter...").
- Middle paragraphs contain a quick summary of the contents of the enclosure. For example, when sending a résumé you should stress your educational and work experiences ("As you will see on the résumé, I have experience in...").
- Generally one page only. Do not become too wordy or attempt to list everything that's on your résumé or in the enclosed document. This is your chance to emphasize, not to re-state.
- Somewhere toward the end of your letter you should add some kind of closure ("Thank you for considering my résumé...", etc.)
- Your visual presentation should be pleasing, with appropriate margins and white space, and an un-crowded look to the page.
- Your letter should have an appropriate tone. Do not be overly personal or overly cold. Adopt a friendly but professional tone for most cover letters.
- There can be absolutely no spelling, grammar, or mechanical errors in any business letter, including a cover letter. You will not be taken seriously if you don't care about being professional and correct in your wording.

Contents:

- heading (letterhead or typed)
- date of letter
- addressee (optional) or...
- attention: (optional)
- subject:(optional)
- complimentary close
- signature block
- postscript (optional, if needed)

Conventions:

- establish contact in 1st/last paragraphs
- appropriate tone throughout
- enclosure contents summarized only
- appropriate closure toward the end
- no spelling, grammar errors

Formatting:

- full block paragraphs, no indents
- paragraphs aligned on left margin
- paragraphs not indented
- paragraphs double-spaced
- adequate margins
- adequate white space
- page headers on subsequent pages
- pages numbered except first page
- initials, date, cc:, encl:, mail date at bottom (optional)

Figure 22.2

What is strong or weak about this sample letter?

Steven W. Hansen

5120 South 2100 East
Salt Lake City, Utah 84117
(801) 272-3210

December 2, 2007

Dr. Thomas Peebles
Superintendent
Granite School District
4550 South 700 East
Salt Lake City, Utah 84117

Dear Dr. Peebles:

I am writing today because I am both qualified and enthusiastic about ESL education. ESL is one of the fastest growing and most demanding needs in education today. Finding qualified people who are enthusiastic about this work is challenging, to say the least.

I am now working as a teacher's aid at Redwood Elementary where I assist both teachers and students by translating Spanish for ESL students. I love this work and would like to expand my opportunities.

My qualifications are more than linguistic. I am fluent in Spanish. But equally important, I am familiar with Latin culture, having lived among Latinos in Ecuador for nearly two years as a volunteer. In addition, I lived among and came to understand the Polynesian culture in Hawaii for nearly one year while I was in high school. My experience is, therefore, first hand and extensive:

- Fluency in Spanish and English
- Two years experience among Latin culture in Ecuador
- One year experience among Polynesian culture in Hawaii

If you are interested in someone who has these skills and experience, I would be delighted to have an opportunity to meet with you at your earliest convenience. I look forward to hearing from you.

Sincerely,

Steven W. Hansen

SWH
12/02/07
Encl: résumé

Formatting Rules for Memos

Memos (including e-mail) are one of the most common forms of communication in the workplace. The use of memos has greatly expanded with the invention of email, creating literally hundreds of messages per day on some business manager's computers. Some of them are essential to fundamental business transactions and procedure. Others fall into the "junk mail" category, which has become a huge problem because of the ease of sending messages.

Traditionally, memos have been used as a vehicle for internal communication (within an organization). But with the invention of email, they have greatly expanded in use to include all kinds of messaging between and among individuals and companies.

In many (if not most) internal communication situations, however, the writer and reader(s) are well acquainted. The contents of the memo (email) might even be known in advance because it has been discussed previously and someone is waiting for the message and perhaps attachments. Often, the purpose of memos is to establish a written and dated record of communication and/or to verify a previously communicated message that happened in person, over the telephone, or through the grapevine.

Therefore, memos are usually quite direct in their approach. They are not letters, so you need to come to the point quickly and not ramble or confuse the reader with irrelevant details. A good memo is sharply focused on what the reader needs to know. Depending on the subject, three or four short paragraphs should suffice, and one is often enough.

Elements of a Memo

The word "memo" is short for memorandum. Memos are not intended to be letters—neither in length nor in form. They are quick communications within a group or organization and sometimes between individuals. As a result, the requirements for a memo are much simpler than for a letter.

The format for memos is fairly standard, though a few variations do exist. In general, all memos—including e-mails—share the following standard features:

- Heading: The word "Memo" or "Memorandum," or some equivalent term, at the top of the page. On printed memos, a letterhead, memo head, or typed header is used. See requirements for letters with regards to headers.
- To: Addressee. In printed memos, use the full name, title, and department of the person to whom you are writing. This makes sure that your memo will be targeted to the correct and intended person. In emails, this line contains the email address of the intended recipient (e.g., John Taylor <taylor@funsites.com>)
- From: Sender. In printed memos, use your full name, title, and department. In emails, this line contains your email address.

  TO and FROM lines on memos eliminate the need for a salutation ("Dear Mr. Taylor") and a complimentary close ("Sincerely"); although sometimes these are included anyway to make the memo more personal. But they are not required and are usually omitted.
- Cc: Who received a copy besides the addressee (optional). In emails, this is the email address of the person(s) who received a copy of the memo.
- Date: Date the memo is sent, not the date(s) on which it was created. On emails, this is automatically provided, along with the exact time of day.
- Subject: Quick title of the communication. This identifies the topic in a very few words. This usually summarizes what is to follow. Try to keep subjects under three words when possible. In emails, when you are responding to somebody else's email, this line it automatically filled in with the subject that appeared on the original email with a "re:" in front of it. (e.g., "re: time of appointment").
- Attachments: Attached materials (if any). A brief description of any attached documents. In emails, this is where attachments are actually attached to the message, and the name of the file(s) attached appears here.

The actual message or content of the memo follows the header. Usually, three or four paragraphs is the maximum for a memo. But use as few as necessary. Some emailed memos are as short as one paragraph or even one sentence. Get to the point quickly. Communicate all that is necessary, but not much more. Figure 22.3 illustrates a properly formatted memo from a professor to his students. This is not an emailed memo, so email addresses are not used.

Figure 22.3

Example of an emailed memo

To: Comm 1010 students
From: Prof. Phillip Tucker, University of South Florida
Date: Feb. 6, 2008
Subject: Evaluation of your Group Project

Please complete and submit to me a detailed memo regarding your documentary film production assignment experience. It is due on Friday, February 24.

First describe your group experience to me. Use the criteria in the text as a guide to your evaluation. How was your experience as compared to the ideal that is represented in the text? What did you like best about your group experience? What did you like least? What functional roles did individual members of your group fill? Did you think the work was evenly divided between group members?

In the end, were you happy with your group's film production? Why or why not? If your group's production had been ordered by a local firm, do you think they would be pleased with the final product? How did your group processing affect the quality of your work, and why?

Remember, this memo is for my eyes only; I would appreciate your honest appraisal.

E-mail

Companies today almost universally depend on computerized communications systems that enable workers to use e-mail. As a result, and because of the ease and speed of emailed communication, it has become the most used (perhaps overused) form of business communication. Email is considerably faster and more efficient than conventional business correspondence. But it also has its drawbacks.

Overuse. The same ease with which e-mail can be generated encourages overuse. A lot of needless correspondence is produced. Also, whereas memos in the past tended to be more complete—waiting until all the facts were known—emails often dole out information in bits and pieces, thus making it hard to gather together all the information on a given topic.

Compulsive use. Also because of the ease of use, emails on sensitive issues are often sent off without sufficient reflection and careful wording. The instantaneous feel of an emailed message creates a sense of urgency to respond that, in the past, was not present. This sense of urgency all but eliminates any time for second thoughts.

Keyboarding and grammar errors. Because emails are hastily constructed, many typing errors and grammar errors, omissions, and other fundamental writing problems occur. These are often corrected in subsequent emails, creating the phenomenon of"e-mail about e-mail." Also, since emails are often written by the sender and not by a secretary, the filter for correction that once existed is gone. The resulting errors can result in a serious loss of credibility unless the sender takes the time to correct all such errors.

Excessively personal messages. The workplace is not an appropriate place for personal messages or an overly-conversational style. Those can be accommodated on bulletin boards (actual as well as electronic) or otherwise. A professional business tone should be maintained, avoiding the temptation to turn every communication, on any subject, into a personal note.

Flaming. Emails have become notorious for openly hostile or abusive comments, aimed at either the reader or a third party. There is a sense of false privacy when one is emailing, sitting as we do at a desk with nothing in front of us but the computer monitor. We feel more free to say things that we would not dare to say in a face-to-face situation. This is both dangerous and inappropriate. We must be careful not to violate the basic principles of workplace courtesy.

- Netiquette is the term used to describe the rules for proper electronic messaging. We will not attempt to list or review those rules here, but those whose work relies heavily on emailed communication should probably familiarize themselves with these rules.
- Screaming is one such rule. On the Internet, typing a word in all CAPITAL LETTERS is considered screaming. If you wish to emphasize a word, it is best not to capitalize it, nor to underline it (since this usually indicates a link of some kind). The proper way to emphasize a word is to place an asterisk *before and after the word* which on most systems will then also bold it.

Spamming. It's very easy to send a copy of your email to large groups of people at the same time. This gets magnified when answering a memo that has been sent to a large list of people. If you "reply to all" you will fill up everybody's mailbox with your reply. Unless you have good reason to reply to everyone, reply only to the sender. These practices fill email boxes with literally hundreds or thousands of unwanted messages, through which the person must wade in order to find the truly essential messages. These kinds of unwanted messages are called *spam*. It is annoying and unprofessional. You can solve the problem by not sending an email to everyone unless it really applies to everyone.

Spelling and Grammar

This chapter is not a style guide, so it will not present comprehensive information on how to check your business correspondence for proper spelling and grammar usage. Many such style guides exist, such as *Elements of Style* by Strunk and White (2000)[3], which is intended for traditional English-language college and business usage, and the *AP Stylebook*,[4] which is intended for print and electronic media journalists. Many of these are now available for free on the Internet as well.

Common Writing Problems

We will only briefly list the most common writing errors that business and college writers commit. Then, you may consult your favorite style guide to obtain details of the problem(s) and the solution(s).

1. Sentence fragments—incomplete sentences.
2. Punctuation problems.
3. Spelling problems.
4. Passive voice.
5. Lack of parallel structure on sentences.
6. Lack of proofreading before sending or submitting messages.
7. Use of clichés, redundancies, and verbal "fluff."
8. Overstatement—unnecessary emphasis or generalizing.

The following clever list created by well-known writer William Safire[5] illustrates these and other writing problems with examples of the problem used to describe the rule.

1. No sentence fragments.
2. Avoid run on sentences they are hard to read.
3. A writer must not shift your point of view.
4. Do not put statements in the negative form.
5. Make an all out effort to hyphenate when necessary but not when un-necessary.
6. Don't use Capital letters without good REASON.
7. It behooves us to avoid archaisms.
8. Reserve the apostrophe for it's proper use and omit it when its not needed.
9. Write all adverbial forms correct.
10. In writing, everyone should make sure that their pronouns agree with its antecedent.
11. Use the semicolon properly, use it between complete but related thoughts; and not between an independent clause and a mere phrase.
12. Don't use no double negatives.
13. Also, avoid awkward or affected alliteration.
14. When a dependent clause precedes an independent clause put a comma after the dependent clause.
15. If I've told you once, I've told you a thousand times: Resist hyperbole.
16. If any word is improper at the end of a sentence, a linking verb is.
17. Avoid commas, that are not necessary.
18. Verbs has to agree with their subjects.
19. Avoid trendy locutions that sound flaky.
20. And don't start a sentence with a conjunction.
21. The passive voice should never be used.
22. Writing carefully, dangling participles should be avoided.
23. Unless you are quoting other people, kill all exclamation points!!!
24. Never use a long word when a diminutive one will do.
25. The rigid rule of "i before e except after c" raises spelling to a sceince.
26. Proofread carefully to see if you any words out.
27. Use parallel structure when you write and in speaking.
28. Boycott eponyms.
29. Ixnay on colloquial stuff.
30. Of all the rules about indefinite pronouns, none is useful.
31. Zap onomatopoeia.
32. Resist new verb forms that have snuck into the language.
33. Better to walk through the valley of the shadow of death than to string prepositional phrases.
34. You should just avoid confusing readers with misplaced modifiers.
35. One will not have needed the future perfect tense in one's entire life.
36. Place pronouns as close as possible, especially in long sentences—such as those of ten or more words—to their antecedents.
37. Eschew dialect, irregardless.
38. Remember to never split an infinitive.
39. Take the bull by the hand and don't mix metaphors.

40. Don't verb nouns.
41. De-accession euphemisms.
42. Always pick on the correct idiom.
43. If this were subjunctive, I'm in the wrong mood.
44. Never, ever use repetitive redundancies.
45. "Avoid overuse of 'quotation "marks."'"
46. Never use prepositions to end sentences with.
47. Last but not least, avoid cliches like the plague.

Overstatement

Writers often overstate things, thinking dramatic words add emphasis and color to their writing. In fact, overstating things has the same effect as putting an exclamation point (!) at the end of every sentence. Be careful not to overstate things, especially when describing emotions or reactions to things.

The following Table 22.1 is just one example of words which mean essentially the same thing, with their relative intensity values. The emotion or reaction being described appears at the top of each column.

Table 22.1 **Expressions Used to Describe Anger**

Strong	Moderate	Mild
furious	resentful	uptight
enraged	irritated	disgusted
seething	hostile	bugged
outraged	annoyed	turned off
infuriated	upset with	put out
burned up	agitated	miffed
fighting mad	mad	irked
nauseated	aggravated	perturbed
violent	offended	ticked off
indignant	antagonistic	teed off
hatred	exasperated	chagrined
bitter	belligerent	cross
galled	mean	dismayed
vengeful	vexed	impatient
hateful	spiteful	displeased

The general rule is to always use the mildest form of expression possible to accurately represent what you're trying to say. This is especially important in emailed messages, where words have a tendency to be "amplified" in their intensity just because they are electronically created, sent, and received.

Summary

Writing for business is one of those fundamental skills that just about every employee must have. At some level, formally or informally, we are all expected to communicate to others via printed documents or email. The mastering of these skills is one of the two greatest needs for college graduates, according to industry representatives. Unfortunately, this skill is largely ignored by many who think it is unimportant. They pay the price in lost opportunities. It is not just what your write about, but how you write it, that reveals your intelligence and reliability.

Chapter 22: Analysis and Application Exercises

1. The author of this chapter claims that there is a "zero error tolerance" in business communication such as résumés, cover letters, and memos. 'Why does he say this?

Do you agree? Why or why not? Given this situation, have your English composition classes given appropriate emphasis to such things as spelling and grammar'? Why or why not?

2. Résumés should generally be prepared according to the type of organization to which you are applying. When would you use a chronological résumé and why? When would you use a functional résumé, and why? Which have you most commonly used in the past?

References

1. Searles, G.J. (1999). *Workplace Communications: The Basics*. New York: Allyn and Bacon. In Chase, R.S. and Jones, S.G., Elements of effective communication, 2nd ed., Boston, MA: Pearson Custom Publishing, 256.
2. Searles, G.J. (1999). *Workplace Communications: The Basics*. New York: Allyn and Bacon. In Chase, R.S. and Jones, S.G., Elements of effective communication, 2nd ed., Boston, MA: Pearson Custom Publishing, 246–248.
3. Strunk and White, (2000). *Elements of Style*, 4th edition. Neeham Heights, MA: Allyn & Bacon, a Pearson Education Company.
4. *The Associate Press Stylebook* (2008). Christian, D., Jacobsen, S., and Minthorn, D., eds. New York: Associated Press.
5. Saffire, William (1990). "A Few Writing Rules," in *Fumblerules*. New York: Doubleday.

CHAPTER 23

Public Speaking Principles

LEARNING OBJECTIVES

When students have completed this chapter and lesson, they should be able to:

1. Identify the differences between informative, persuasive, and special occasion speeches.
2. List and explain the four general purposes and requirements of an informative speech
3. List the three general purposes and the three methods of a persuasive speech.
4. List and explain the two forms of logic.
5. List and explain the five primary means of motivating people.
6. Explain the requirements for special occasion speeches.

CHAPTER 23: Overview

An attempt is made to define differences in both goals and techniques for presenting informative, persuasive, and special occasion speeches. Emphasis is placed upon speaker application of subject material to audience expectations and needs. In a situation requiring transfer of knowledge, techniques for informing an audience successfully are examined. Where the occasion focuses on the speaker influencing the attitude, belief, or action to be taken by the audience, strategies of persuasion are examined. Focus is placed on the strategies most applicable to attitude change, with emphasis given to ethical procedures. Importance is given to matching strategies to the needs, type, and cultural style of the audience. When considering special occasion speaking, concern is given to audience expectations dictated by the purpose of the meeting. Audience analysis and consideration given to the reason for the speech play vital roles in such occasions.

Informative Presentations

More is required of informative speeches than just transfer of information. A popular cartoon showed a large auditorium in apparently a college environment. At the front was a projection screen showing a speaker giving a political science lecture. At each desk was a blackberry carefully recording the message. Information transfer was occurring: between electronic machines! Preferably information transfer will occur among humans.

Information transfer occurs many ways. An office manager instructs employs on the new voice mail system. A human resources specialist explains federal and state laws governing nondiscrimination in hiring to a committee who will interview new job candidates. The foreman of a construction job gives the client a report on the progress of the project. Corporate recruiters speak to an audience of college students on the opportunities in their company.

These examples give a variety of information transfer methods. The messages may be general and brief, giving a basic overview. Others may be to large groups receiving intensive training on a new strategy. Management may be explaining how the new acquisition of the company by a large corporation will affect their jobs. It may be a three day workshop on new accounting procedures.

Whatever the reason for the meeting, delivering informative material in an effective way makes business work. Information messages make society happen. The business of commerce, politics, and even recreation could not happen without transfer of information. Recent college graduates recognize this fact: when a group of alumni were asked to rate the importance of a wide array of speaking skills, informative speaking wound up at the top of the list. But just because such communication is important does not mean it is effective. Almost half of the vice-presidents surveyed at the nation's top 1,000 corporations reported they found the majority of business presentations "boring," and 40 percent admitted they had dozed off at least once during a presentation.

Successful and effective informative speaking will help keep your audience awake, alert, and informed. We will explore informative speaking more clearly in Chapters 41 and 42. Most informative presentations fall into these categories: reports, briefings, explanations, and training.

The purpose of **reports** is to describe the state of an operation. Some reports are frequent and informal such as the report of daily sales. Others are more formal such as financial reports given by managers to stock-holders, or the final report of a new project given by a project manager to the CEO. In between is a range of reports such as a progress report on a new product, an update of business progress during a manager's absence, or a plant supervisor's report on workers' reaction to a new machine.

The world of informative speaking plays a role in every aspect of life, from religion to entertainment, and can include everything from how to grow a tomato plant to booking a cruise for a honeymoon. The topics, audiences, and purposes are very diverse, but all include transfer of information. The successful communicator can accomplish the task more rapidly and more effectively than the inept informer.

Group Presentations

Group presentations are common in our culture. Much information is transferred by a committee or group presenting to a given audience. Group members know that several presenters can be more effective than a single speaker. The division of work increases the intensity of preparation. The increase in the number of people presenting an idea can increase its credibility.

A project team gives a status report to management. A computer support staff introduces a new software package. Union representatives brief members on the negotiation progress. Sales teams make pitches to potential customers. Public officials explain their actions to their constituents. Representatives from health-care providers explain insurance benefits to employees. School officials inform parents about curriculum changes.

Group presentations provide variety and novelty to information transfer. Not only does a group build interest and add skill and novelty to the presentation, but also gives a feeling of completeness and credibility. Often presentation teams are balanced for gender, ethnicity, age, income level, and a variety of other factors aimed to enhance audience appeal.

Delivering a Group Presentation

Group presentations bring special problems that a single speaker does not experience. The potential for mix-ups, mistakes, or omissions because of lack of coordination is great. Group efforts require rehearsal and review prior to presentation. Issues like speaker arrangement, topic organization, and coordination of who will answer questions or present specialized material should be decided in advance. How will the presentation take place? A series of speakers? Everyone sitting in a semi-circle? Will presenters sit in the audience? Order and structure should be planned in advance.

Items to remember

1. Speakers coming from the audience take time and sometimes break continuity.
2. Speakers sitting around a table may have problems being seen or heard without proper staging.
3. A series of speakers takes planning. Presentation by spontaneity means some speakers might dominate, and others not speak at all. Order of speaking must be considered.
4. All members of the presentation group should watch whoever is speaking. This helps the audience focus.
5. Always consider how the group will look to the audience, even when they are not speaking.

Special Occasion Speeches

Special occasion speaking is explored in more depth in chapter 45, so we'll provide just a quick introduction here. One should be alert to the fact that at work, at church, at parties, or almost any social setting, you may be called on to voice an opinion, accept an award, welcome guests, etc. Perhaps the boss is retiring, and you are asked to give a tribute; perhaps the new boss has arrived and you are asked to offer a welcome.

The secret to success in these occasions is to keep the remarks short, simple, and to the subject. Keep in mind that every context is unique; you will want to adjust to the physical, social, chronological, and cultural context of each occasion. Review chapter 45 for guidelines that will help you feel confident and achieve your goals when speaking at a special occasion.

Types of Persuasive Presentations

A formal speech attempting to change opinion, attitude, or behavior will be given more extensive treatment in Chapters 43 and 44. However, in the world of business, four categories of persuasive messages will be introduced:

Sales Presentations

Advertising is a billion dollar business. The average person is exposed to over 1,000 advertisements every day. Salespeople make presentations about such diverse goods and services as real estate, insurance, merchandise packing, telephone systems, advertising space, banking and credit cards, car rentals, and restaurant meals. Critical factors for these people are to grab attention quickly and within seconds develop a reason for their service, explain options, and make a sale closing.

Proposals

In an organization, the goal of most proposals is to persuade higher management. Many proposals involve plans for a new program such as a new product line or an advertising campaign. Some involve requests for resources, additional staff, larger budgets, or new equipment. Still others involve changes in policy or procedures: a new compensation plan or a change in the way a job is handled. Still others are personal requests for change: a raise, involvement in a particular project, or a promotion. A developer seeking a zoning variation from the local planning committee, an account executive presenting a new campaign to a customer, and an executive proposing contract revisions to a union leader are examples of proposals common to the workplace. Critical factors governing success of these proposals include: evidence of improving job conditions or income revenue, better customer appeal or satisfaction, or increase in business. This reward must provide management a justifiable and appealing reason for making a change.

Motivational Speeches

At their worst, motivational speeches can combine the most oppressive elements of a bad sermon and a high school pep rally. On the other hand, when delivered effectively and at the proper time, such presentations can produce good results. A manager trying to persuade subordinates to fill out a lengthy, time-consuming financial report by telling them it is essential for the good of the company will arouse only resentment if everyone knows that management reads only two lines on the reports (the gross margin and the pretax profit). The manager will probably be more successful at the same task by agreeing that the form is largely useless but saying, "Look, you know how those financial guys are. They don't know anything about the market—they only know whether your numbers add up. We'll get a lot less interference from above if we give them the numbers they need to look good."

The key to success in motivation messages is knowing and using information that is vital to the person being persuaded. Always keep in mind the ***need*** to change must exist for the receiver of the message. The message must offer some measure of satisfaction to the receiver, and the motivator must present the change clearly, pointing out the benefits of the change.

Goodwill Speeches

A corporate recruiter addressing graduating seniors and a bank economist explaining economic forecasts are making speeches of goodwill. So is the utility company's representative addressing the press after an accident in a nuclear power plant. Representatives of organizations frequently speak to audiences to promote interest or support for their organizations.

These goodwill speeches may seem informative, but they also try to change the attitudes or behavior of their listeners. The corporate recruiter is trying to encourage some students to apply for jobs with his company; the economist is trying to build the image of her institution as a leading business bank; and the utility-company representative is trying to soften negative reactions to price increases.

In all of the above presentations, it is necessary that the communicator supply a message to the listener. The message must be prepared in such a way to fulfill a need in the recipient. A successful message produces the desired change in the listener, whether that change is a willingness to receive new information, or changing an attitude or behavior. Communication puts dynamics in society.

Chapter 23: Analysis and Application Exercises

1. According to the text, as well as your own experience, how can a speaker simplify a complex idea and present it in a more appealing way to help the audience accept the new idea? Offer an example to illustrate your answer.

2. Give an experience of when someone has attempted to:
   a. Persuade you.
   b. Coerce you.
   c. Manipulate you.

   What is the difference in strategy and technique?

   Was the difference in the strategy of the speaker, or your perception of what was said? Explain.

CHAPTER 24

Introduction to Public Speaking

LEARNING OBJECTIVES

When students have completed this chapter and lesson, they should be able to:

1. Identify and explain the difference between interpersonal communication and public speaking.
2. List and explain the elements of the public speaking process.
3. Describe the transactional model of communication.
4. Explain first impressions and their influence on the audience hearing a public speech.

CHAPTER 24: Overview

The role of public speaking in a free society is reviewed. Specific advice is given for learning the skills and techniques of public speaking as opposed to other elements of communication. The relationship between public speaking and interpersonal communication is explained. The rhetorical situation is analyzed, including the critical role of public speaking in society. Critical skills and techniques are reviewed, and the importance of understanding the occasion, requirements of the speaker, and techniques constructing the speech itself are reviewed.

A basic goal for the speaker is to be comfortable in the speech environment by being more forceful and less nervous. Organization is crucial as you prepare a speech. You must think more clearly and more critically. This course helps students prepare to be effective public speakers.

Ethos, your character as perceived by the audience, is influenced by first impressions. A self-assured, confident stance is the best possible beginning toward establishing positive ethos.

Barack Obama

During a time when electronic media heavily influences communication in society, a public speech has little opportunity to change the world. However, a young law professor from Illinois did not believe that inference. Having lost his only bid for a federal office (the House of Representatives) in 2000, Professor Obama was relatively unknown. However, winning the primary for the office of Senator from Illinois landed him a spot as keynote speaker at the Democratic National Convention in 2004. Within 4 years he was the Democratic nominee for President of the United States. Most political analysts, both friend and foe, indicated Obama's public speaking changed politics, offered new solutions, and launched a career. A self-assured, confident candidate, perhaps lacking in political battle experience, but a poised speaker, was candidate for President of the United States and spokesman for the Democratic Party in 2008! This example illustrates public speaking is just as vital and influential as it was in the days of Patrick Henry or Daniel Webster.

Apply What You Learn

As you study creative and critical thinking, sensitivity to audiences, and effective speech presentation, the skills you learn will

- Help you critically evaluate messages and appeals of all kinds.
- Make you more sensitive to people and situations.
- Increase your self-confidence and your willingness to engage in serious dialogue with others[1].

Outside the classroom, these attributes will enhance your value as an employee and as a citizen. Employers and career counselors often put "good communication skills" at the top of the list of qualities they seek in people.[2] The reason is simple: Each year our economy becomes more dependent on information and the ability to communicate it.

Your study of public speaking will also help make you a more competent, more active citizen. The skills listed above will make you better able to understand public issues and social controversies, to decide what you think about them, and to participate effectively in resolving them—whether on your campus, in your neighborhood, or in the larger public forum. It may not place you in a position to run for president of the United States, but it has happened in the past!

Develop Specific Communication Skills

The communication skill of Critical Thinking is the ability to form and defend your own judgments rather than blindly accepting or instantly rejecting what you hear or read. The following habits will be learned:

- How to listen carefully and critically in order to understand and evaluate what others say.
- How to select motivating speech topics and select proper supporting material; to validate the topic.
- How to find the material for a speech: examine your own experience, consult with others, and use valuable information sources such as the library and the Internet.
- How to think critically about what you read and observe so you will reason soundly when addressing an audience.
- How to organize a speech: make it clear, coherent, sensible, and effective.
- How to use language skillfully to convey both meaning and mood.
- How to use your voice and your body to present yourself and your message in an effective, compelling way.
- How to adapt general principles to your particular speaking situation, with emphasis on the dimensions of informing, persuading, and entertaining.
- How to understand and benefit from reactions to your speeches so the audience's response helps you improve your skills.

This set of skills has been studied and taught for about 2,500 years (in different ways over the years, of course), so you are taking part in a very old and valuable academic tradition.

Focus on Critical Thinking and Strategic Planning

Public Speaking is in large measure an exercise in critical thinking. Public Speakers should develop the ability to form and defend personal value judgments rather than blindly accepting or instantly rejecting what they hear or read. Critical thinkers can analyze and understand various points of view, and they can quickly recognize the difference between fact and opinion.

Facts, as we will see in detail later, are statements that—at least in theory—can be verified by someone else. The source of facts is observation or personal experience. If a speaker says that the world's population has doubled every 25 years, the statement can be observed by checking population statistics. In contrast, opinions are subjective judgments that presumably are based on another's experience or expertise. If a speaker asserts that the world's population is growing too fast, that opinion cannot be verified externally; it stands or falls depending on the insight and judgment of the person who offers it.

Critical thinking is the basis of those "good communication skills" that employers seek and democracies need. As a listener, critical thinking will help you recognize a speaker's unstated assumptions. As a speaker, it will help you form precise statements that embody your thoughts. Overall, critical thinking will place ideas into a broader context, showing how they relate to other things that you already know or believe. The critical thinker goes beyond observation and experience by accumulating a collection of inferences. By carefully analyzing inferences that reach the same conclusion, the critical thinker can improve the probability of a truthful inference. This happens when increasing numbers of similar results reduce the chance of change through consistency. However, if a probable fact is accepted, it is done on the assumption that truth is conditional until additional information proves it differently. A strong inference can often be treated as a fact.

Strategic Planning A speaker operates in a world of choices: whether to speak, when to speak, what to say, how to phrase a particular point, how to explain or defend it, how to organize the message, what tone to give it, and exactly how to relate it to the audience. Even all these options do not exhaust the possibilities! Some speakers make these choices unconsciously, without real thought (and relying on luck). But effective speakers make their choices strategically through careful planning and in-depth research. They identify their goals and determine how best to achieve them.

Public Speaking and Communication

Strategic planning is the process of identifying your goals and then determining how best to achieve them. Communication Interaction builds connections between people and these goals, helping speaker and listener understand each other and recognize common interests. Opinions disrupt strategic planning. Opinions are subjective judgments based on experience or expertise, not capable of being verified by someone else.

When you give a speech, you and your listeners are involved in communication, meaning that you interact in order to build some sort of connection whereby you can understand each other and recognize common interests. How does this happen? And how does public speaking differ from other forms of communication such as personal conversation and written essays?

Early theories of communication viewed public speaking as a series of one-way messages sent from speaker to audience. In fact, however, the audience participates with the speaker in creating shared meaning and understanding. The speaker's ideas and values are tested and refined through interaction with the audience, and listeners' knowledge and understanding are modified through interaction with the speaker. Thus, public speaking is a continuous communication process in which messages and signals circulate back and forth between speaker and listeners. This is illustrated as we observed the speaker and listener validating facts.

From the audience's point of view, each listener comes to the speech with a framework of prior knowledge, beliefs, and values, and each listener "decodes," or interprets, the speaker's message within this personal framework. To a particular listener some ideas will be more important, or salient, than other ideas. If the speech is about vegetarian diets, for example, some listeners will approach it with special interest in health and nutrition, others will be concerned about the welfare of animals, and still others will view vegetarianism as a fad for eccentrics. The speech may support, challenge, or modify any of these frameworks, but each listener's framework will shape how he or she interprets and understands the speech. Audience members work actively to assess what the speaker says against what they already know or believe, constantly make judgments about the message, and convey them back to the speaker through facial responses and other nonverbal clues. Unfortunately for the speaker, meaning and interpretation always rests with the listener. That is why feedback is so critical to the successful speaker. Feedback can validate the speaker's successful message, or report it was not delivered successfully.

From the speaker's point of view, knowing about the audience is crucial in preparing and delivering a speech. A speech about campus social life, for example, would be different for an audience of prospective students than for an audience of alumni. Even if the basic points of the speech were the same, the nature of the audience would affect how they are developed and explained and what tone or attitude the speaker projects. In preparing the speech, the speaker would analyze the audience and try to match listeners' expectations appropriately. Moreover, as listeners respond during the speech (by frowning, nodding approval, looking puzzled, etc.), the speaker would constantly modify how key points are organized and phrased, trying to acknowledge or respond to the audience's concerns. The successful speaker monitors feedback, then restructures messages until satisfied the feedback reports success.

Figure 24.1 depicts this interplay between speaker and audience. Suppose you plan to speak about the benefits of a vegetarian diet. In preparing the speech you'll remember some listeners think vegetarianism is healthful, others think it is a passing fad, and still others associate it with eccentrics who don't really understand nutrition. As you speak, you'll be watching for responses from the audience that signal how they are reacting to what you say. Most responses will be nonverbal, such as frowns or nods of approval. Feedback might prompt you to acknowledge some people doubt the merits of vegetarian diets; you might even admit you had doubts yourself but now are a committed vegetarian. Throughout the speech—beginning with its preparation and lasting through its presentation—you will be sensitive to

FIGURE 24.1

how well your ideas match your audience, and you'll use feedback to improve the fit as you speak.

Remember that audience members will not be passive. Each will assess everything you say against what he or she already believes. You may convince some to change their beliefs; others may interpret your message in ways consistent with their beliefs; and if the discrepancy between their beliefs and your message is too great, some listeners will reject your message. In any case, the audience will be actively involved as you speak, interpreting and testing what you say against their own beliefs and values and letting you know their reactions.

The Rhetorical Situation

As we have seen, the speaker and listeners simultaneously participate in creating the message. Another unique characteristic of public speaking is that it occurs in response to a specific situation. Unlike great dramatic or literary works, which "speak to the ages," the principal test of a good speech is whether it responds to the needs of the situation and audience to which it is presented.[3]

The situation is the particular context in which a speech is given. Compared with poems and stories that are timeless, most speeches have a short life span. For example, student Mohammed Ghouse's first speech to his classmates concerned an important and timely issue:

> We read about a people getting killed every day in Sarajevo—infants who are shot in their Mothers' arms, children who dodge sniper fire to attend school in the bombed-out shell of a schoolhouse, young men who have lost limbs to this horrifying ethnic war. We must do whatever we can to stop the bloodshed—as individuals and as a nation.

Although Mohammed's speech probably could be appreciated long after the war in Bosnia ended, it was created in response to a particular event and was designed primarily to be heard by a particular audience.

The study of how messages affect people has long been called rhetoric. This ancient discipline is concerned with the role that messages play in:

- Shaping, reaffirming, and modifying people's values
- Binding people closer together or moving them farther apart
- Celebrating significant events
- Creating a sense of identity among people
- Conveying information and helping people to learn
- Nurturing, strengthening, or changing people's beliefs
- Leading people to take (or not to take) action

A rhetorical situation, then, is a situation in which people's understanding can be changed through messages.[4]

The following example shows how student Adam Paul Vales responded to a rhetorical situation by urging classmates not to park their cars on streets surrounding the campus:

> When you park on the streets, you make life miserable for the people who live in the apartments there. Sometimes, residents of those streets have to carry groceries four blocks through the snow because they are unable to find parking near their homes! When you go home, do you have to drive that far to find parking, or do you park on your own street? Is it fair to take that convenience away from our neighbors?

> I know you park on these streets because you have no place to park on campus. But the only reason the university is not building more parking lots is that they know the easier solution is just to force you to park on the street. This solution may be easy for the uni-

versity, but it is very hard on the community. By refusing to park on the street and by demanding new parking lots, you will force the university to live up to its responsibilities to its students and to the local community.

Adam's message addressed a particular audience and asked its members to consider a specific problem and solution. The speech was timely and the message affected how listeners understood the situation. A well-conceived, well-presented speech can help resolve a problem that causes a particular situation, or it can help listeners to see the situation in a new light. An ineffective speech will leave the situation unchanged or may even make matters worse.

Determinants of the Rhetorical Situation

Figure 24.2 shows the four basic factors that determine the success of any rhetorical situation: the audience, the occasion, the speaker, and the speech itself.

The Audience. Whereas a poem or a novel is addressed to all potential readers over time, a speech is usually presented to a specific audience. Most speakers, most of the time, want to present their ideas in a way that achieves identification with the audience about a specific issue; that is, they try to find common ground between what they know about the audience and what they want to say. A speaker sometimes might want to avoid common ground and even antagonize listeners to get their attention or motivate them to participate.

Ultimately, of course, the audience determines whether the speech was successful—whether a "speech to entertain" really was entertaining, whether a speech about a problem really did provide new information and insights, whether listeners actually will take the action that the speaker advocates.

The Occasion (and Purpose). The occasion is the specific setting for the speech, the circumstances in which it occurs. The date, time, place, and purpose all influence the rhetorical situation. "A commencement speech about school reform, delivered at Western State University in June of 1998" is an example of an occasion; "growing unease about the quality of public education" is the rhetorical situation to which this speech was a response.

FIGURE 24.2

Determinants of the Rhetorical Situation

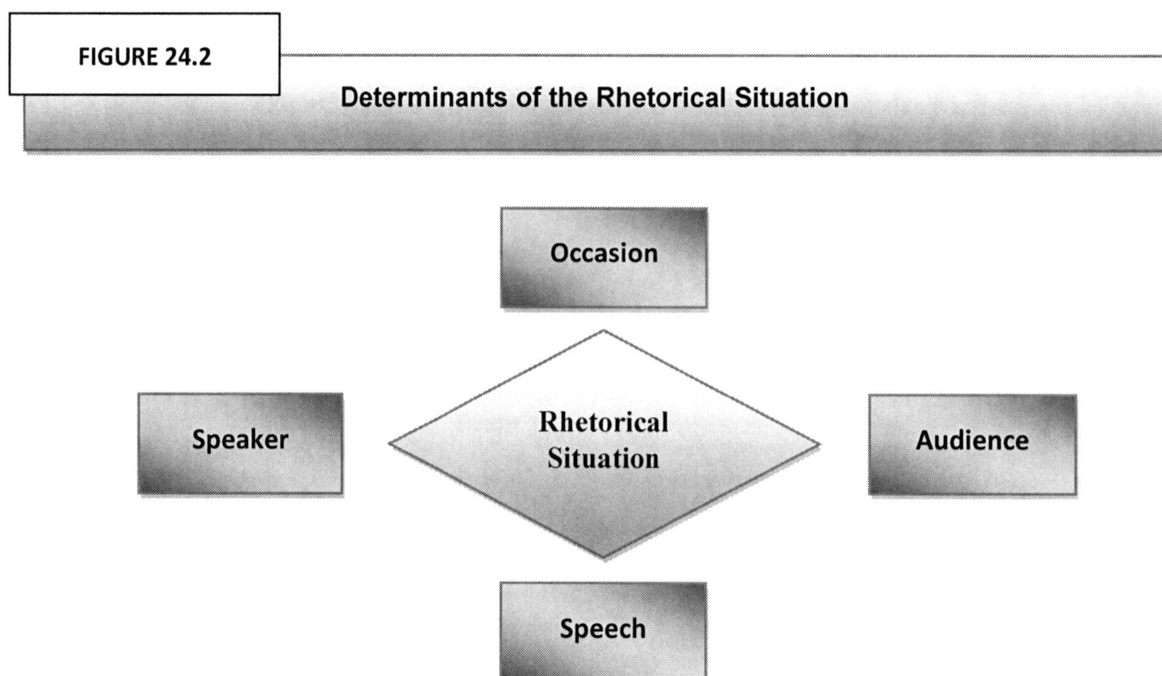

People speak on all kinds of occasions and for many reasons. Some speeches commemorate an important event or enact a ritual, such as presenting or accepting an award, delivering a eulogy, introducing or toasting someone, or entertaining an audience. Other speeches involve problem solving and decision making, such as giving an oral report or a sales presentation, advocating a policy, or refuting an argument. Still other occasions arise in which the speaker wants to lead the audience in deciding what is true, or in passing judgment on actions, or in applying some rule or social convention.

Whatever the occasion, the audience arrives with ideas about what is and what is not appropriate behavior. Such expectations have developed over time, and they limit what a speaker can do in responding to the rhetorical situation. For example, listeners expect a eulogy to offer a favorable view of the deceased, and they normally would think it inappropriate for a speaker to dwell on the person's failings. On the other hand, an after-dinner speech is usually expected to be lighthearted; a speaker who instead presents a highly technical lecture would not be responding appropriately to the occasion.

Simultaneous events further define the occasion. For example, the fact that a presidential campaign is underway helps to define the occasion for a speech about health reform. The retirement of a popular athlete helps to set the stage for a speech about retirement trends in industry. And if listeners only last week were urged to give up tobacco, that may affect their judgments about a speech urging them to give up red meat.

The purpose of the speech also defines the occasion, and we will look closely at three basic purposes: informing, persuading, and entertaining. Most speeches will be deliberative, meaning that the purpose is to share information and to influence listeners' beliefs and actions. We also will examine other reasons for speaking, such as celebrating and entertaining, and how they affect the rhetorical situation.

The Speaker. The same speech delivered by different speakers will produce different reactions and effects in an audience. The concept of ethos, which we will examine in more detail later, refers to the speaker's character as the audience perceives it. Developing and maintaining positive ethos will contribute immeasurably to the success of a speech. If you appear interested in your topic, the audience will be more likely to be interested also. If you appear to know what you are talking about, listeners will be more likely to trust your judgment. Fortunately, you can learn the skills that enable a speaker to contribute positively to a rhetorical situation, and so throughout this book, we focus on how to develop and maintain positive ethos.

The Speech. Although the situation has been stressed as something the speech develops, the message itself also works to shape the situation. Before Adam Paul Vales spoke about parking on campus, his audience thought of the side streets as a convenient parking lot; but during the speech they began to see those streets as symbols of campus politics and community responsibility. The message had redefined the situation.

In most cases, an audience's understanding of a situation can be improved by a speech that is organized effectively, that includes interesting examples and memorable phrases, and that is presented enthusiastically. Although many factors determine whether or not a speech responds successfully to a rhetorical situation, by understanding the basic factors involved you can better shape your message as a speaker and can participate more fully as a listener.

Chapter 24: Analysis and Application Exercises

1. Throughout the video, several students talk about the benefits they received from taking a public speaking course. Which of the benefits was the most appealing to you? Why? Can you think of any other benefits that you might get from this course? Explain.
2. What do you think about the statements concerning communication apprehension in the textbook? Do you believe that they are accurate? What communication situations make you anxious? What do you do to help reduce your anxiety?

References

1. B. Rubin & E.E. Graham, "Communication Correlates of College Success: An Exploratory Investigation," *Communication Education*, 3 (January, 1988), pp. 14-27.
2. Business employers have named oral communication skills the number one priority for college graduates seeking employment and the number 2 priority for successful performance once they have a job. D.B. Curtis, J. I. Winsor, & R. D, Stephens, "National Preferences in Business and Communication Education," *Communication Education*, 38 (January, 1989), 6-14.
3. For a discussion of this difference between literature and oratory, see H.A. Wichelns, "The Literary and Criticism of Oratory," first published in 1925, reprinted in *Methods of Rhetorical Criticism: A Twentieth Century Perspective*, ed. R. L. Scott & B. L. Brock (New York: Harper & Row, 1972).
4. L. Bitzer, "The Rhetorical Situation," *Philosophy and Rhetoric*, 1, (Winter, 1968), 1-14.

CHAPTER 25

The Ethics of Public Speaking

LEARNING OBJECTIVES

When students have completed this chapter and lesson, they should be able to:

1. List and explain Deirdre Johnston's ten ethics of persuasive communication.
2. List and explain David Zarefsky's four ethics of public speaking.
3. Know and explain how these two lists correspond to the other.
4. Demonstrate an ability to make ethical decisions in public communicative settings.

CHAPTER 25: Overview

Public speakers exert tremendous power in our culture, and those who do it well can achieve tremendous power. But with that power comes tremendous responsibility to use it ethically and for more than self-serving purposes. By definition, public speakers usually seek to inform and/or persuade others. In doing so, they selectively gather and disseminate facts. They also seek to shape the audience's perspective and understanding of the topic. There is ample opportunity to deceive and mislead when doing this, and some kind of ethical standard should guide what speakers do and how they do it. We discussed the subject of ethics and morals in chapter 16, but in this chapter we will focus on how ethics can and should be made manifest in our public speaking.

The rules that apply to the speaker also apply to the listener. Listeners have an ethical responsibility to listen and critically think about what is being said. Seeking to silence someone with whom you disagree is not ethical in a society where we believe in free speech, and rejecting an idea outright because it differs from your own view shows a lack of intellectual depth. Listeners should listen. They should think about what is being said. And then, and only then, they should respond with reason to the message received. We will discuss all of these things in this chapter.

Communication Ethics

In chapter 16 we identified four primary ethics by which we should live in our culture:

Honesty	The universal ethic
Dignity of the Individual	The supreme ethic
The Laws	The security ethic
Accountability	The essential ethic

Imagine the difference that would result in our culture if people were willing to live by just these four general ethics. They are universally acknowledged as being important. They are not universally observed.

The general behavioral ethics also apply to communication. Deirdre D. Johnston in her 1994 text *The Art and Science of Persuasion*[1] identified ten ethics that are important in persuasive discourse. These are summarized below, with some modification for their application to all communicative settings.

1. **Mutuality:** We must pay attention to the needs and views of others, as well as our own.

2. **Individual Dignity:** Generally speaking, we should not cause another person embarrassment or a loss of dignity.
3. **Accuracy:** We should ensure that others have accurate information. This involves more than honesty; it means telling them everything they have a right and need to know, not just making sure that what you do tell them is true.
4. **Access to Information:** It is unethical to bolster the impact of our communications by preventing people from communicating with each other or by hindering access to the supporting information.
5. **Accountability:** We should take responsibility and accountability for the consequences of our relationships and communication.
6. **Speaker / Audience Responsibility:** The audience or receiver of the information also has ethical responsibilities. A good rule of thumb is the "200% rule." Both the communicator and the receiver have full (100%) responsibility to ensure the message is understood and ethics are followed. This is not a 50/50 rule. It is a 100/100 rule.
7. **Relative Truth:** Communicators should always remember their point of view may not be shared by others and their conclusions are relative to their perspective. We must allow others to respectfully disagree or see it differently.
8. **Ends vs. Means:** While no rule can be applied without reservation to *every* situation (remember the ugly baby test), it can generally be said that the end goal of our communication and the means of getting to that end must *both* be ethical.
9. **Use of Power:** In some communication settings, we have more power than others present (e.g., a teacher with a student, a parent with a child). In those situations where we have more power we also have more responsibility for the outcome.
10. **Rights vs. Responsibilities:** We live in a wonderful society where our rights are protected by law. However, not everything that we have a *right* to do is ethical. We must give balance our rights against our responsibilities.

Public Speaking Ethics

Narrowing the topic down even further, David Zarefsky[2] (1999) identified four important ethical standards for speakers that are related to these general ethics:

- Respect for your listeners
- Respect for your topic
- Responsibility for your statements
- Concern for the consequences of your speech

We will use Zarefsky's list as a general guide to our discussion of public speaking ethics in this chapter. We will use Johnston's list to show how her ethical standards relate the four that Zarefsky identified.

Respect for Your Listeners

Mutuality: We must pay attention to the needs and views of others, as well as our own. When public speaking we seek to establish a common bond with our listeners. To accomplish this, the audience members must feel both that we can relate to them and that we care about them—the old adage is "I don't care what you know unless I know that you care." If we achieve this common bond, the the audience members will feel more actively involved in the subject of our speech. Also, to achieve mutuality the speaker must be sensitive to listeners' perspectives. This requires some homework—careful analysis of the audience and the selection of materials and strategies that are appropriate and effective for that particular audience. Zarefsky suggests the following as an important ethic of respect for an audience.

Make sure your message merits the audience's time. The audience has chosen to spend their time listening to the speech. In return, they expect speakers to be well prepared, to be on time, and to have something valuable and original to say. Recognize that you are receiving a gift of their time, and prepare a speech that deserves their gift. For example, don't devote the entire speech to what listeners already know or believe, making them wonder why they took the time to hear you.

Relative Truth: Communicators should always remember their point of view may not be shared by others and their conclusions are relative to their perspective. We must allow others to respectfully disagree or see it differently. Zarefsky suggested the following:

> **Respect the cultural diversity of your audience.** Not all listeners will share your perspective. Your audience may include people with diverse cultural and family backgrounds, and these will certainly affect their attitudes and opinions. Do not engage in ethnocentrism, to assume that your views are typical of everyone else's. Not only is this demeaning to listeners who have different cultural backgrounds but it also reduces the likelihood of your success in informing or persuading them through your speech. The ethic of mutuality suggests that you need to take the time to inform yourself concerning your audience's experiences, perspectives and cultures.
>
> **Individual Dignity:** Generally speaking, we should not cause another person public embarrassment or a loss of dignity. Zarefsky had a couple of suggestions.
>
> **Meet listeners where they are.** Rather than ignoring listeners' views, incorporate them into your speech, showing respect by meeting listeners on their own ground. Acknowledge the audience's current position and make it your point of departure—even if you disagree with it. You can say something like, "I know that you generally favor a woman's choice in abortion because you consider it to be a personal matter for the woman who is carrying the baby and you don't want government intrusion into such personal things." Then, rather than tell them they are wrong or that their view is without merit, show how your position might be consistent with theirs in important ways. Or, if that is not possible, ask them to consider another perspective that is equally important. But never, ever humiliate or denigrate an audience (or any member of it) in public. The ethic regarding the dignity of the individual would not permit this.
>
> **Don't insult listeners' intelligence or judgment.** This means that you must do more than simply acknowledge an audience's differing views; you must also examine them and give due consideration to them before attempting to refute them. Your tone is also important. Never "talk down to" the audience. Also avoid suggesting that anyone who does not agree with you is somehow unintelligent or ill-informed. Always treat your audience's differing views with complete respect, even if you don't agree with them.

Use of Power: In some communication settings, the speaker has more power than others present (e.g., a teacher with a student, a parent with a child). In those situations where we have more power we also have more responsibility for the outcome. We have to make judgments about "what is best" for our audience with a genuine concern for their well-being and happiness. To abuse such power is to become a tyrant.

Respect for Your Topic

Zarefsky points out that "you will be speaking about a topic that matters to you, and you will have something important to say. When you speak, you are putting yourself on the record; your words will outlast the actual speaking situation. You are also asking listeners to accept you as a credible source of ideas about the topic. To justify their confidence in you, and to meet your own high standards, you need to know what you are talking about in enough detail that you can present it clearly and fairly. You must demonstrate that you care enough about the topic to study it thoroughly. Otherwise, why should the audience take your ideas about the topic seriously?"[3]

Speaker and Audience Responsibility for Understanding: A good rule of thumb is the "200% rule." Both the communicator and the receiver have full (100%) responsibility to ensure that the message is understood and that ethics are followed. This is not a 50/50 rule. It is a 100/100 rule. This would mean that you should assume full responsibility to be understood by your audience as you speak. Prepare yourself well enough to answer all of their key questions and objections. Respond to audience questions and give clarification whenever necessary. In short, make sure they understand.

The audience or receiver of the information also has an ethical responsibility to listen respectfully and to consider critically whatever is being said. Speeches are not public shouting matches, where two sides come together to intimidate each other. Sadly, many speeches on college campuses have devolved into that kind of brutish behavior. Patrick Henry said, "I may not agree with what you say, but I will defend to the death your right to say it." This should be our own motto as an audience member. At some point, you will be the speaker and you will hope that your audience gives you the same attentive ear.

Responsibility for Your Statements

Accuracy: We should ensure that others have accurate information. This involves more than honesty; it means telling them everything they have a right and need to know, not just making sure that what you do tell them is true.

> **Respect listeners' ability to assess your message.** You want your audience to understand your message and to voluntarily agree with you. Zarefsky said, "You should never mislead listeners about your purpose or conceal what you want them to believe, feel, think, or do. If you are urging them to make a choice among alternatives, do not try to manipulate them by hiding options or by casting any particular option in unduly favorable or unfavorable light. If it is your goal to advocate one option over another, you will best defend your position by explaining how it is superior to the alternatives, not by distorting or ignoring the options that you dislike."[4]

Access to Information: It is unethical to bolster the impact of our communications by preventing people from communicating with each other or by hindering access to the supporting information. In speaking situations, where listeners cannot see the printed word, you must carefully distinguish between fact and opinion, clearly identifying to which of these two categories your claim belongs. A common tactic is to "make up facts" or "overstate facts" in an effort to sound convincing. Another is to use only a part of somebody's quote in order to make it appear that they are saying something they are not. For example, if a book critic calls a book "a stunning failure," it would be unethical to quote him or her as calling the book "stunning." An ethical speaker will provide adequate citations for any quote, paraphrase or fact that is used in a speech, never seeking to block audience access to the sources of the information.

Plagiarism—using another person's words as if they were your own—deserves special mention. As with writing, using somebody's else's ideas in a speech as if they are your own is unethical. Your audience has a right to know where you got your ideas and where they might go to check on your representation of things. Zarefksy lists the following as essential to avoiding plagiarism:

1. Never present someone else's unique ideas or words without acknowledging them.
2. Specify who developed the ideas or said the words that you present ("As discovered by Professor Smith," "Socrates said," and so forth).
3. Paraphrase statements in your own words rather than quoting them directly, unless the exact wording of a statement is crucial to your speech.
4. Draw on several sources rather than relying on a single source.

It is also plagiarism to give someone else's speech as if it were your own. Every speech you present should be your own original work.

Concern for the Consequences of Your Speech

Accountability: Speakers must assume both responsibility and accountability for the consequences of our relationships and communication. Remember that in chapter 16 we defined responsibility as acknowledging that you did something; whereas, accountability is being willing to accept and deal with the consequences of your act. This applies to speaking in a number of ways. One would be to say something and then later deny that you said it. Another would be to say something that creates an unwanted outcome and then be unwilling to accept accountability for the effect of your speech.

Ends vs. Means: While no rule can be applied without reservation to *any* situation (remember the ugly baby test), it can generally be said that the end goal of our communication and the means of getting to that end must *both* be ethical. Thus, it would not be ethical to lie to somebody in order to get them to do the right thing. Your ethos—your credibility as an honest and informed and accountable person—will be damaged by your lie no matter how well intentioned it may have been. Find an ethical means to whatever end you seek. Ethical communicators will do no less.

Rights vs. Responsibilities: We live in a wonderful society where our rights are protected by law. However, not everything that we have a *right* to do is ethical. We must give balance our rights against our responsibilities. I have a full constitutional *right* to say whatever I want in a public speech, even if what I say is not true. But that would not be the *responsible* thing to do. And yes, you have recourse to sue me for damages if I defame you, but that does not remove the stain or pain you might have been caused by my false allegations. Ethical communicators will be responsible in their use of their rights.

Chapter 25: Analysis and Application Exercises

1. Record an advertisement from the television or radio. Identify the purpose of the ad, the target audience, and the statements, stories, phrases, or other supporting materials that are used to advocate the goals of the ad. Finally, evaluate the ethics of the ad. Should advertisers be held to the same ethical requirements as public speakers? Why or why not?
2. Observe a conversation between two people and note their verbal and nonverbal behaviors. Are the participants being ethical speakers and listeners? Why or why not?

References

1. Johnston, Deirdre D. (1994) *The Art and Science of Persuasion*. Dubuque, IA: Brown & Benchmark, a division of Wm. C. Brown Communications, Inc., Chapter 3.
2. Zarefsky, David (1999). *Public Speaking: Strategies for Success*, 2nd ed., Boston, MA: Allyn & Bacon.
3. Zarefsky, *Public Speaking: Strategies for Success*, 2nd ed., quoted in Chase, R.S., and Jones, S.G., *Elements of Effective Communication*, 2nd ed., Boston, MA: Allyn & Bacon, 1999, p. 283.
4. Zarefsky, *Public Speaking: Strategies for Success*, 2nd ed., quoted in Chase, R.S., and Jones, S.G., *Elements of Effective Communication*, 2nd ed., Boston, MA: Allyn & Bacon, 1999, p. 283.

CHAPTER 26

Student Speeches

LEARNING OBJECTIVES

When students have completed this lesson, they should be able to:

1. Identify and describe several verbal and nonverbal elements which make a public speech effective.
2. Distinguish between a speech of self introduction, a demonstration speech, an informative speech (speech of description), and a persuasive speech.
3. Offer their own opinions concerning the strengths and weaknesses of a speech through constructive criticism.

CHAPTER 26: Overview

Both novice and experienced speakers can learn valuable lessons by analyzing the speeches of others. Each presentation teaches techniques we should model or avoid in our own preparation and delivery, ultimately improving our performance as public speakers.

There is no chapter to accompany this lesson.

Chapter 26: Analysis And Application Exercises

1. Is it important that the speaker's purpose is clear? Why or why not? Is it important that the speaker's main points are clear? Why or why not?
2. Roger's self introduction speech used an example of an embarrassing moment that had taught him some lessons. Do you think the use of a story about an embarrassing moment is a good way to tell an audience more about yourself? Why or why not? What does it tell you about Roger? How comfortable are you disclosing personal information about yourself? What would you want an audience to know about you? What personal story might help you convey that information?
3. What is the difference between an informative speech like Marcie's, and Deb's persuasive speech about volunteering? What kinds of supporting evidence did Deb use to support her assertion that people should volunteer? Did you believe she was asking you to make a personal commitment? Why or why not? How might she have strengthened her appeal? What presentational aids might she have used?

CHAPTER 27

The First Speech

LEARNING OBJECTIVES

On successful performance of the first speech, speakers should be able to:

1. Describe three methods of establishing speaker ethos with an audience.
2. List in detail three primary purposes for delivering the speech.
3. Identify and define three major divisions in a speech.
4. Define and relate the terms "credibility," and "ethos" as they apply to delivering a speech.
5. Explain how the terms ""credibility" and "ethos" can be developed in a speech by the speaker.

CHAPTER 27: Overview

I Have a Dream

USA *Today* identified the speech given by Martin Luther King, Jr., August 28, 1963 at the Lincoln Memorial in Washington D.C. as the most credible speech of the 20th century. An excerpt from the speech demonstrated the power of convincing the audience with the best example possible of fulfilling the roman philosopher Quintillion's challenge of a good man speaking well. The following paragraph illustrates what is truly meant by developing credibility and ethos as one speaks:

Let freedom ring from the prodigious hilltops of New Hampshire. Let freedom ring from the mighty mountains of New York. Let freedom ring from the heightening Alleghenies of Pennsylvania! Let freedom ring from the snowcapped Rockies of Colorado! Let freedom ring from the curvaceous peeks of California! But not only that; let freedom ring from Stone Mountain of Georgia! Let freedom ring from Lookout Mountain of Tennessee! Let freedom ring from every hill and molehill of Mississippi. From every mountainside, let freedom ring.

The atmosphere and feeling created by King's remarks have etched his name, along with the freedoms he so strongly desired for people of color into history forever. The key to the success of this great speech was the fact that the speaker established his credibility through the power of the language and the convincing delivery of a sincere speaker.

For the beginning speaker attempting a first public speech, the process requires a few simple, fundamental concepts necessary for success: A single, simple but clear message; an established, positive image as a speaker; and a well-organized, simple structure. Upon completion of a successful first speech, the speaker can easily move on to become a polished, professional speaker.

Establish a Clear Message

The first speech should have a single, well defined topic that can be expressed in a simple thesis statement. This thesis statement should be a sentence that expresses your main idea and reason for speaking. It should be expressed in an idea that summarizes exactly what you want your audience to accept and remember.

To be successful in forming your thesis sentence, you must know exactly what you want to accomplish. Do you want your audience to remember important information you will present? Do you want them to understand how important freedom is for every person, as did Martin Luther King? The successful beginning speaker will know what they want their audience to remember. Know what you want to accomplish.

To begin clarifying the message, the beginning speaker should write out the **purpose**. Following the title, write: "My purpose is to . . ." This fragment should be followed by a speech objective such as *inform*, or *persuade,* or *entertain*. These descriptive words guide the speaker into not only *what* to say, but even give guidance on *how* the speech should proceed.

The purpose statement is not usually given to the audience in the speech, but is written as a guideline for how the speech should continue and develop. By stating a purpose as an introductory sentence, the speaker may create a barrier to the audience by challenging them to *not* be informed, or to *not* be persuaded. The Introduction, however, should give the audience clear direction of what to expect by presenting a **thesis statement**. This is a statement that clearly expresses your main idea, and what you wish the audience to remember after you have concluded.

The thesis statement should be given in language that quickly gains the attention of the audience, motivating them to not only listen, but to also give careful consideration to the message you wish to convey. Again, King's thesis can be quoted decades later because of its simplicity, impact, and profound message: "I have a dream that my four little children will one day live in a nation where they will not be judged by the color of their skin but by the content of their character."

After your speech is over, listeners should have little doubt about what you actually said or what you mean. If you find it difficult to state your main idea in a sentence or two, you may be trying to cover too much. Even complex technical claims should be reducible to simple, basic thesis statements.

If the effort to state your thesis results in a statement like: "I'm going to speak on segregation" or "computers" or "vacations," you have not focused sharply enough on your subject; you have only identified a general area. No imagery, motivation, or excitement has been generated. The audience immediately concludes that another general, boring presentation is about to begin, and they refocuse their attention on something more interesting.

The key to generating interest is to address the impact your subject can have in the lives of the listeners through the ideas and examples you are presenting to them. Their listening to your speech will provide them with ideas, events, and experiences specifically directing them to a more interesting life. By stating the topic and focusing on a main, central idea that relates to audience interest, as well as something that has been of great interest to you the speaker, a successful event can occur.

Establish Positive Ethos

The second goal for your beginning speech is to establish a good reputation as a speaker. 2500 years ago, Greek teachers of public speaking referred to this as **ethos,** a strong, positive character.[1] But ethos does not refer to innate character traits, those at the core of a person's identity. Rather, **ethos** refers to the character that is *attributed* to a speaker by listeners on the basis of what the speaker says and does in the speech. This judgment is based on the climate or atmosphere created by the speech.

Ethos as a speech characteristic is a judgment by the audience as to how reliable, sincere, and honest the speaker is as he or she attempts to convey ideas, opinions and actions. Overall, the feelings and atmosphere present in the room during a speech can be classified as ethos.

It is much easier to talk about creating credibility than it is to achieve it. Ferguson suggested that credibility is made up of the following characteristics: audience-perceived composure, dynamism, trustworthiness, sociability, status, competence, and objectivity. He then concludes that all training is of no value unless the speaker has *sincerity!*[2]

Research does attribute much credibility to speaker skill in using proper delivery techniques. It is also true that the speaker must utilize information that is both entertaining and interesting. If the speaker can hold the attention of the audience, that can produce acceptable credibility. But as a novice speaker, keep in mind the following additional tenants of creating audience response:

1. An audience's judgments about a speaker's character can be quite detailed. As the speaker approaches the podium, you determine speaker confidence by their eye contact with the audience; by the apparent confidence in preparation. What does speaker delivery tell you? Does the speaker read everything?

Within a few seconds, audiences judge a speaker's intellectual level based on vocabulary. Conviction, sincerity, and honesty are judged by the way the introduction is delivered. It becomes quickly apparent how much thought and work went into preparation, and audiences want to feel the speaker has made an effort to reach them intellectually and emotionally.

Judgments are made based on speaker confidence, fluency of delivery, and the intellectual value of subject matter. Even topic selection plays a role in judgment of speaker credibility. Subjects like "How to Use a Toilet Plunger," "How to Change a Baby's Diaper," or "Six Ways to Use a Beer Can Opener," do not inspire credibility. Audiences have a sense of the person's intellect, emotions, judgment, relationships with others, power, confidence, and sense of self. Each characteristic is an important dimension of a person's character, and listeners make many such judgments about the speaker.

2. Judgments about a speaker's character are made quickly. The first speech lasts only a few minutes, and yet it gives many insights into the person's apparent character. Assessments of ethos often reflect superficial first impressions. Whether the speaker walked confidently to the front of the room, looked at the audience, and then began to speak, or whether the speaker was unsure, looked at the floor, and spoke before reaching the front of the room gives many clues. The audience judges speaker comfort, speaker values, and speaker confidence as the speech begins. Such judgments may be wrong, but they are based on information received with quick exposure and first impressions.

3. Assessments of ethos are durable. First impressions not only shape how audiences judge the speaker, but also how they think about the speech and interpret what comes later. Once the speaker learns of these assessments, they almost function like a self fulfilling prophecy: the speaker may begin the next speech believing the feedback. Negative traits can be intensified, or audiences might accept only previously perceived conclusions.

The first speech is an icebreaker, an opportunity to learn about your classmates and to share things about yourself. Because an audience's assessments of a speaker are detailed, are formed quickly, and are durable, the goal of developing positive ethos in your first speech is just as important as having a clear statement of your purpose and a meaningful thesis statement.

Strategies for Organizing Your Speech

Critics maintain that award winning forensic competitive speaking uses as the highest criteria the ability to organize. The previous sections talked about gaining the attention of an audience, and obtaining a positive response from listeners. An audience wants a speaker to appear logical and organized. Retention and understanding are improved with a well organized speech.

Basically every speech has three parts: a beginning, a middle, and an end. Communication people label these divisions the *introduction,* the *body,* and the *conclusion.* Each category contains certain elements and performs certain functions. The audience anticipates and expects these functions to be met, or the speech looses credibility, respect, and audience support.

The Introduction

The introduction should be designed to accomplish three distinct tasks:

1. *Get the attention of the audience.* Included in this requirement is to start the topic. A common misunderstanding is that a good joke is necessary in an introduction, even if the story has no relationship or relevance to the topic. This is a false conclusion, because people believe you are tricking or deceiving them. A humorous story that introduces the topic can be effective, but subject area must agree. Some teachers suggest that the most interesting, startling, or humorous bit of information on your topic should be commissioned for use as an introduction. Remember that your first statement is the first impression of the speech, and the listener decides to continue listening based on that first impression.

2. *State your thesis.* This introduces your topic. This should also lead the audience to understand what the topic will be and provide possible hints as to how the subject will be approached. This could even give a preliminary sketch of what will be presented in the body of the speech. For example, the speaker could introduce the main subject, state how he or she would cover this topic in two or three major divisions, then move to the main body of the speech. This prepares the audience to anticipate and know what to watch for as material is presented.

3. *The introduction identifies the speaker.* Through the use of a skillfully worded thesis statement and an interesting beginning, the subject is introduced, the interest level of the audience is piqued, and the ethos of the speaker is established. In summary, the introduction presents a topic, introduces the speaker, and develops an interest in the listener.

The Body

The body is the largest portion of the speech; it gives information about the thesis statement through *forms of support* (see chapter 34) organized into categories that lead to logical conclusions and acceptance of the major idea presented in the thesis statement.

It is recommended for a first speech that the body consist of one major idea, or one key thought supported well by evidence including stories, statistics, and perhaps even a visual aid. This simplifies the task of integrating the three divisions of the speech, limits the amount of time necessary to maintain audience attention, and helps the organization structure. If the speaker does not have to worry about integrating three ideas into a logical sequence, but states a point, supports it with evidence such as personal experience, statistical data, and even a picture of what is being described, the task becomes easier, and chances of success are enhanced. This greatly helps prepare the speaker for more advanced, complex speeches.

After an appropriate introduction, the speaker presents the thesis. The thesis statement is the central idea of the speech, stated in a simple, declarative sentence. This statement concisely expresses what the speaker wishes to say. This serves as a guideline for the remainder of the speech, and prepares the listener for supporting evidence to validate the statement.

Supporting materials are all forms of evidence the speaker wishes to present, validating the truthfulness of the thesis statement. Evidence explains or clarifies what the speaker believes. Colorful experiences, narratives, or stories, or even statistical data can provide evidence that the thesis is indeed true.

This material is for the purpose of establishing the truthfulness and validity of the thesis sentence. It also provides interesting narrative to maintain audience attention and provide a pleasant, satisfying experience for the listener.

Stories and personal experiences have been found to be the most effective material in maintaining audience interest and acceptance, with statistical data being considered the least interesting. Stories and personal experiences have been found to be effective in maintaining audience interest and acceptance; statistical data builds credibility by being impressive, but is not considered as interesting as personal examples. A brief example or story can illustrate a point more dramatically than a long statement of statistics. People love listening to stories, and they appreciate research that stimulates curiosity. By combining a balance of facts with stories and examples, a definite climate of positive experience and acceptance can be created. By experiencing a positive first speech, the novice has started a learning experience that leads to excellence.

You can use *narratives*, or stories, for supporting material; people often explain, and understand, situations in terms of a story. For example, in a speech about child abuse, student Stacey Gerbman illustrated the impact of the problem by telling the story of five-year-old Joey, who was abused by his father:

Joey was afraid of his father. He hadn't meant to drop the milk jug, but it was so heavy. As he cringed in the corner of the kitchen, his father was screaming at him. Maybe he was a scrawny wimp, as his father said. Only a coward would whimper at the prospect of a beating. When the blows actually came, Joey couldn't stop crying. The next day, he had bruises on both body and soul.

Stacy ended the speech—and concluded the story—by telling how Joey later became a violent man himself:

When Joey grew up and raised his own family, he too beat his children and showered them with verbal taunts. Sadly, he had learned that behavior all too well from his own father.

The logical approach for the body of the speech is to first present the thesis sentence. The speaker then carefully explains through appropriate wording exactly what he or she means to explain. They verify the truth and build the credibility of the statement using supporting material. Stories and narratives build interest and understanding. Statistics and numbers supply data to explain the amount or degree of importance with the statement.

Organizing the evidence. Whenever you offer more than one piece of supporting material, you must decide in what order to arrange your evidence. Obviously, the more support, the stronger the argument. Suppose, for example, that you want to use facts, narratives, and opinions to support the claim. Which type of material should you present first?

Sometimes the decision is just a matter of preference—which seems to naturally follow. The speaker can give a statement, the definition, followed with a story about the event. Statistics can illustrate quantity of the problem. Finally, quotations from people actually involved can verify your topic's importance.

Other times, supporting material may suggest an organizational arrangement. There may be a series of events that dictate an order. Cause and effect impact on changing events can suggest conclusions. A time order of events can clarify understanding of how policies occur. A space order is most logical. When going on a vacation, location can be critical in the explanation. In each case, a logical sequence helps the listener flow with the speech.

Other common organization patterns are cause-effect; problem-solution; and topical structure. Strategies for using different organizational patterns will be explored in later chapters.

The Conclusion

The final part of the speech is the **conclusion,** which has two basic tasks. First, it should draw together the ideas in the speech so they can be remembered. Obviously, the key to the first speech is to remember the idea presented in the thesis statement. This is sometimes done by a brief summary of the argument. Sometimes it is a restatement of the thesis sentence. Sometimes it is a stated conclusion of what should be remembered. Regardless of which method is used, it should be short, concise, and to the point.

The second task is to give a strong note of finality to the speech. It is frustrating to have the speaker announce several times "In Conclusion. . ." Once should be sufficient. A conclusion might restate the idea in the introduction to suggest a completed circle. It might challenge the audience with an interesting question. Or it might draw on the claims in the speech to appeal for a specific action on the part of the listeners. Regardless of the strategy, it should give a definite feeling of ending!

Chapter 27: Analysis and Application Exercises

1. Prepare a five minute speech consisting of an introduction, body and conclusion. The introduction contains a thesis statement, the body contains a single point illustrated by a statement, a story, an interpretation and a statistic. The conclusion ends the speech with a restatement of the thesis statement.

References

1. Ethos is discussed extensively in Aristotle, *The Rhetoric,* translated by W. Rhys Roberts, New York: The Modern Library, 1954. See especially Book II.
2. S.D. Ferguson, "Building Credibility through Delivery," *Public Speaking,*(New York: Oxford University Press, 2008) 1264-184.

CHAPTER 28
Anxiety

LEARNING OBJECTIVES

Speakers in control of their feelings and emotions should be able to:

1. Identify and describe communication apprehension, or speech anxiety.
2. Explain why such emotional feelings are common, and how they can become beneficial.
3. List and describe the causes of speech anxiety.
4. Identify the emotional and physical feelings of speech anxiety.
5. Understand and control such feelings, permitting them to produce an acceptable speech performance.

CHAPTER 28: Overview

Great Speakers were nervous also

History is filled with great orators whose rhetoric helped build and create a nation. The great patriot Patrick Henry led the cause for liberty by declaring "Give me liberty or give me death!" Yet he readily admitted that fear and rejection were his companions. On one occasion he rose to his feet, hesitating for a few moments while he struggled to find words that would not come. Spectators felt sorry for the young barrister who was overcome with fear. Ralph Waldo Emerson, a writer, minister and great lecturer reported that stage fright was so real a bogeyman for him that in 1859, in his lecture on "Courage," he linked the bravery of advancing into the cannon's mouth with the bravery of standing before an audience to deliver a speech. Edward Everett, orator and statesman reported that prior to his first speech in Congress, he could not sleep the preceding night, and arose that morning with a splitting headache. He commenced his speech by saying, "I rise to address the committee in a state of indisposition, under which I ought in prudence to be at home rather than on this floor." Angelina Grimke, an early abolitionist and orator, reported, "I was so near fainting under the tremendous pressure of feeling, my heart almost died within me. . . I well nigh despaired, but stood up and spoke for nearly two hours." Communication anxiety is a real experience, which can have a detrimental effect on public speakers, even the most experienced ones[1].

Managing Speech Anxiety

All public speakers experience some sort of speech anxiety. These feelings have been labeled stage fright, speech fear, communication anxiety, and even interpersonal anxiety. The secret is not to label such feelings or even avoid them. The secret is to learn how to manage them so they do not get in the way of preparing and delivering a meaningful oral message. By thinking of anxiety as energy, the speaker is taking the first step toward enhancing a presentation, rather than allowing anxiety to sabotage a good speech.

Depending on the situation and the intensity of your fear of giving a speech, you can experience many specific, uncomfortable feelings. Your heart rate will begin to increase as the time to give the speech approaches. When you know it is your turn to speak, as you walk before the audience, your pulse might climb as high as 170 beats per minute.

You may feel as though you are temporarily insane because catecholamine is released into your body and brain. You hear your pulse pounding in your head from a major artery passing near your ears. Your body is demanding lots of oxygen to service your "runaway" thoughts. Even though you crave oxygen, you might struggle to take a deep breath because the intercostals muscles between your ribs are under stress. You get light headed. Your "fighting muscles" used in hand-to-hand combat can become tense, making it hard to move your upper back, neck, and arms. Your field of vision narrows. You may feel slightly nauseated from the adrenalin flowing in your blood. This chemical reaction causes the "butterflies" in your stomach. But your mental messages demand the body overrule such physical change, and you attempt to appear poised and cool, and deliver a smooth presentation![2]

Definitions of Speech Anxiety

Anxiety is defined as fear of possible harm. This speech anxiety translates into the communication world as communication apprehension. It is also identified as shyness, Social Anxiety Disorder, or Social Phobia.[3] Communication apprehension has been defined as an "individual level of fear or anxiety associated with either real or anticipated communication with another person or persons."[4] This anxiety is a significant problem at the elementary school level. Research reveals that at least 11 percent of elementary students experience severe anxiety, and an additional 20 percent may experience enough anxiety to warrant some sort of intervention. But the problem may not end here. It can continue through life.[5]

One interesting principle about the discomfort related to speech and communication apprehension is that the response appears to be learned by some, and inherited by others. In societies where the need to conform is great, there is a higher degree of communication apprehension. For example, residents of China, Korea, and Japan exhibit a significantly higher degree of anxiety about speaking out in public than do members of individualistic cultures such as the United States and Australia.[6]

Every year increasing numbers of international students and Americans whose first language is not English enter higher education in the United States. In spite of their differences, most of these students do not ask to be treated any differently than any one else. But because of the language and cultural differences, these students have bad experiences. They deserve understanding and patience as they communicate with people who are native to our culture. Ester Yook and Bill Siler found that most Asian students were anxious about presenting a speech. They were concerned about whether or not they would be understood because of their accent, tone, and pronunciation.[7] They were also concerned that if they were unable to "think in English," they might not be able to find the right word or expression needed on the spot, resulting in a humiliating experience.

Another source of anxiety for foreign students occurs because they can have difficulty understanding the speech assignments. Potential for misunderstanding the assignment and lack of English fluency lead many foreign students to memorize the speech. The memorization prevents them from being conversational in style and adds to their perceived ineffectiveness and anxiety as communicators. Speaking in front of others creates some anxiety for most of us, but being from a different culture and speaking English as a second language creates more stress.

Native Americans often have more anxiety when speaking because of cultural differences. In the Native American culture, eye contact is limited. In speaking situations in the dominant culture, eye contact is expected. Our Native American students explain that they feel even more uncomfortable when they are asked to make more eye contact.

Communication apprehension may also be inherited. Research suggests that 10 to 15 percent of all babies are born apprehensive, and continue with such tendencies as shyness, rapid pulse, widening pupils, and vocal cord tenseness into school.[8]

If you have had to speak before a group, you probably know a little about speaker anxiety, one fear that many Americans identify as high on their list of fears, which include snakes, darkness, and death.[9]

Communication apprehension in its worst form can be seen in individuals who, either consciously or subconsciously, have decided to remain silent. They perceive their silence offers them greater advantages over speaking out, or that the disadvantages of communicating outweigh any potential gains they might receive. Communication-apprehensive individuals fear speaking in all contexts, including one-on-one communication and discussion in small groups. Among the fears of those with communication apprehension is the fear of speaking before a group. However, everyone who fears speaking before a group does not necessarily suffer from communication apprehension. That term refers to the much deeper problem of virtually cutting oneself off from most, if not all communication with others.

Symptoms of Speech Anxiety

Speech anxiety refers more specifically to the fear of speaking before a group. Anxiety is a condition during which our bodies secrete hormones and adrenalin that eventually overload our physical and emotional responses. These chemical reactions are the same as those you might experience when you are threatened by a vicious dog about to attack, or an angry mobster in a dark alley. Human nature immediately switches into a fight or flight condition, preparing the body to chose which physical action is considered most safe. Your heart begins to beat faster, and your blood pressure begins to rise. More sugar is pumped into your system, and your stomach may begin to churn. The palms of your hands and bottoms of your feet begin to perspire. Your respiratory system begins to increase, raising the oxygen level in the blood. Your breath comes more rapidly, and your energy peaks.

When you experience these reactions, you may feel as if your body is operating in high gear and that little or nothing can be done about it. You have to realize that some of these feelings are perfectly normal and, for most of us, will not interfere with our speech performance.

Speakers who experience speech anxiety often display the visible signs listed in Table 28.1. These behaviors can occur separately or in any combination, depending on the degree of anxiety the speaker is experiencing. They may expand the problem by making telling statements or apologies such as "I'm not any good at this anyway," "I didn't really prepare for this because I didn't have enough time," or "I never was able to say this correctly." These comments compound the problem by drawing more attention to the nervousness, magnifying the problem.

Speech anxiety causes the speaker to overestimate how much the audience notices about their behavior. The audience, on the other hand, tends to underestimate the stress being experienced by the speaker. They do not feel the butterflies, or see the rapid heart rate, unless it affects the delivery of the speech.

Causes of Speech Anxiety

Just as a physician can better treat an illness by knowing the cause, so people can better reduce and control speech anxiety if they can determine the underlying problem. Many people with speech anxiety treat only the symptoms and tend to ignore the causes, but trying to remove the symptoms without understanding the causes is usually ineffective.

A major cause of speech anxiety begins at an early age as a result of learning from negative feedback in the home. Children who are not encouraged to communicate or are punished for doing so learn that communicating is undesirable and silence is beneficial. Thus communication apprehension becomes a conditioned or learned response.

A person engages in communication encounters expecting them to be rewarding or fulfilling. If, instead, the experiences are unrewarding, embarrassing, or pu-

Table 28.1

Physical Signs Associated with Speech Anxiety

Voice	Quivering Too Soft Monotonous, nonemphatic Too fast
Fluency	Stammering, halting Awkward pauses Hunting for words, speech blocks
Mouth and Throat	Swallowing repeatedly Clearing throat repeatedly Breathing heavily
Facial Expressions	No eye contact, rolling eyes Tense facial muscles, grimaces, twitches
Arms and Hands	Rigid and tense Fidgeting, waving hands about
Body Movement	Swaying Pacing Shuffling feet
Nonvisible Symptoms	Sweating Blushing Having too much saliva Dry mouth or "cotton mouth" "Butterflies" in the stomach

nitive, the person's expectations are violated. If the violation occurs often enough or is of great intensity, the person is conditioned to expect punishment as a result of communication encounters.[10] The punishment can be physical, although it is usually of a psychological nature such as ridicule.

The novice speaker understands quite clearly the potential for such negative conditioning. A survey of the basic speech classroom indicates that anxiety levels of the beginning speaker is significantly higher when the speech is delivered before peers than if delivered before a group of strangers.

The novice speaker then reviews the situation and realizes the speech could create a negative reaction from a group of peers the speaker wishes to impress. Motivated with a strong desire to communicate effectively, anxiety can be elevated dramatically. To add to the frustration, the speaker anticipates an evaluation from the instructor, who can readily observe the building anxiety and grade accordingly.

People may also develop speech anxiety if they constantly hear that speaking in front of others can be a terrible experience. Being told immediately before giving a speech, "Don't worry about it—you'll do fine," reinforces the notion that something can go wrong. If speakers believe something can go wrong and they might make fools of themselves, they lose confidence and anxiety rises.

Winning, and being "number one" are too often considered measures of success. When we do not achieve "number one," we identify ourselves as failures. No one likes to fail. Thus, we conclude that success means reward and failure brings punishment. Winners are praised and losers are ridiculed. As a result, we place tremendous pressure on ourselves to be successful. Anything less than total success produces anxiety.

In most types of competition, we perceive winners as being very few, and failure becomes only temporary. No one likes to lose, but playing your best and losing is often acceptable. When someone makes a mistake in a speech, however, we may be more critical. Rather than acknowledge that the person is making an honest effort, we perceive them as inadequate or unskilled. Consequently, the stress created by fear of making mistakes in front of others may be so great that it produces anxiety and sometimes complete avoidance of speaking.

Among the other most common causes of speech anxiety are the following:

- Fear of physical unattractiveness
- Fear of social inadequacy
- Fear of criticism
- Fear of the unknown
- Conflicting emotions
- Excitement from anticipation
- Fear of peer rejection[11]

We learn to respond in specific ways when facing something that creates anxiety because we have become conditioned to do so. Each of these common reactions to a speech-making situation is **learned.** Because speech anxiety is a learned behavior, the only solution for its sufferers is to examine the reasons for creating the anxiety and learn how to manage events in the speech experience to reduce the discomfort.

Treating Speech Anxiety

Although speaking before a group may produce stress and anxiety, few people allow their nervousness to prevent them from trying and succeeding.[12] As noted in the beginning, even famous well-known speakers feel nervousness before the speech, but they learned to *control* it. The key to successful control of anxiety is the desire to control it. To cope with speech anxiety, we must realize the potential for failure always exists, but we cannot let it stop us from trying. Possibility for failure exists with most of what we do. To give up without trying, and not believing we can overcome will limit us from accomplishing anything. A child beginning to walk is a prime example of how most of our learning occurs. At first, the child wobbles, takes a small step, and falls. But when the child falls, someone usually is there to offer help, support, and encouragement to continue. In addition, the child usually is determined to walk regardless of the falls. Speech making, like learning to walk, involves the same process. Help, support, and encouragement are important, but the essential ingredient is self-fulfilling prophecy: believing that we will succeed on the next attempt.

Successful people will tell you that success was preceded by failure and embarrassment. But their drive and self-confidence forced them to try again. In the typical classroom most first speeches are not very good, and the speakers are all quite nervous about speaking before classmates. However, it does not take long to realize even the best speakers feel the same anxiety as much as the next person. The only difference between success and failure is the willingness to risk failure and the possibility of making a mistake.

Many new speakers are too hard on themselves. After giving a speech, most novice speakers will admit they were extremely nervous, but the audience never detected any sign of nervousness at all. To the audience the speaker appeared relaxed and in control.

There are no cures for speech anxiety—only ways to reduce, manage, or control it so that it does not interfere with the presentation. Experience shows that after a successful presentation, the anxiety levels are less on the next speech, and eventually deteriorate to a tolerable level after giving several speeches. It should be noted that the right amount of anxiety can be a good thing. It makes you feel alive and sharpens your performance. If you do not care about your listeners, if you have insufficient passion for your message, your communication will be flat and passionless also.[13]

Experts have suggested several guidelines for helping the novice attain a comfortable anxiety level when speaking:

1. **Select a topic you enjoy, have information about, and know.** The more you know about a subject, the easier it will be for you to talk about it. According to one research study, people who are highly anxious tend to be more negative in their assessments of themselves and more concerned with what others think of them. In addition, they tend to choose unfamiliar speech topics, which compounds their problem.[14] Sometimes it is not possible to choose your own topic. In business settings, for example, speakers are often required to report information for specific situations selected by circumstances. In this case, the speaker must work harder to have adequate information and to focus on accomplishing what is necessary for the situation. Anxiety should be focused as a source of energy for finding and preparing quality supporting materials.
2. **Be prepared!** People suffering speech fright are more negative in their self-assessments. They tend to believe they will fail no matter what they do. As a result they spend less time preparing, convinced that additional preparation will have little effect on success. Thus, they set themselves up for failure, which perpetuates and intensifies the cycle of anxiety and failure. Preparation and the self fulfilling prophecy of believing that they can produce a great speech can break the cycle. Know your audience and become familiar with the physical surroundings where you are going to speak, including the room, the lighting, placement of microphone, and audiovisual equipment. Be familiar with any visual aids or equipment to be used in the speech. Confidence in location and facilities reduces the unknown and predicts success.
3. **Be confident.** Confidence plays a key role in controlling anxiety. Self-fulfilling prophecy works both directions. If one believes success cannot be achieved, the prophecy is fulfilled. But belief that success can be achieved, and preparation of materials that are exciting and interesting reinforce the confidence and reduce anxiety.
4. **Think positively.** Visualize giving a successful speech. Experience has shown that those who think positively and visualize themselves doing well often surpass even their own expectations. The power of positive thinking has long been considered a major motivator and predictor of success. Experience shows the public speaking stage is even more sensitive to positive thinking. It should be emphasized, however, that a belief in failure and thinking you will do poorly is a sure path to failure.
5. **Practice.** The better you review the content of your speech and practice your delivery, the more comfortable you will feel about your presentation. Few skills are ever achieved without a combination of practice and preparation. The quar-

terback who throws the touchdown pass, the gymnast who scores a 10 on floor exercise, the actor who presents a flawless performance, the artist who paints the masterpiece, the person who passes the road test for a driver's license, and the person who gives a polished and interesting speech have spent hours—and sometimes years—in practice. Even masters do not accomplish their goals on the first attempt. Much training, practice, and even failures have prepared them for their accomplishments.

Controlling Speech Anxiety

1. You are not alone! Everyone has some speech anxiety.
2. Speak on a topic familiar and exciting to you! It's your choice!
3. Know about the audience and location of the speech.
4. Use the power of positive thinking. Prepare and believe. You will succeed!
5. Practice! Practice! Practice!
6. Ask for help from your instructor.
7. Never give up!
8. Understand that your audience wants you to succeed also!

If none of the guidelines and suggestions in this chapter have helped reduce your anxiety, you should seek professional help. People who suffer from abnormal levels of speech anxiety should know that the negative feelings associated with communicating in front of others have developed over a long period of time. These negative feelings do not disappear easily. But speech anxiety is a problem that can be helped. Most university settings have trained professionals prepared to help reduce the fear of speaking in public. There may also be special classes for beginning communication courses for those who are anxious about speaking in front of others.

If your school does not offer help in reducing anxiety[15] there is another alternative called systematic desensitization. **Systematic desensitization** is a technique in which relaxation is associated with an anxiety-producing situation. For example, a student who suffers from public speaking anxiety might be asked to visualize speaking in front of a class and then immediately associate the frightening experience with thoughts of relaxation. The theory behind systematic desensitization is that a mental rehearsal will associate relaxation with situations that create tension. Repetition of the association may help those suffering from anxiety learn that relaxation can replace tension and thus reduce their fear of speaking in public.

Overcoming anxiety in public speaking situations is not easy, but remember: anxiety can be helpful and a normal reaction to speaking in public. When students were asked how they dealt with their personal fear of speaking, the following suggestions were made:

1. **Practice.** Have your main points and conclusion clearly in your head. Once the speaker knows these three key speech divisions, it is a lot easier to remember details.
2. **Walk confidently to the speaking area.** This helps to create the power of positive thinking. If you are confident, you will feel more relaxed. Positive attitudes produce positive results.
3. **Do not begin until you are ready.** Students believe that having everything under control before one begins makes it easier to relax and concentrate on the speech. Personal feelings can be set aside.
4. **Look at the audience and focus on friendly faces.** Students believe that concentrating on those who give positive feedback helps reinforce positive feelings and produces successful results.

The successful speaker will build on the suggestions presented above. Continue giving speeches whenever the opportunity is provided. Take more classes that will provide opportunities to speak under the supervision of a trained instructor. Your fear of speaking can be controlled and your skills can be improved, but they need constant practice to maintain the progress you make.

Chapter 28: Analysis and Application Exercises

1. Take five deep breaths breathing from the diaphragm instead of moving your shoulders. Inhale to the count of three, exhale on the count of seven. What do you notice after doing this exercise? Do you think this technique will help you calm down and perform better?
2. Identify and describe the types of anxiety and fears you think you might experience when you present your speech. Try to be as honest as possible, perhaps discussing any past speaking opportunities in which you were fearful.

References

1. R. T. Oliver, *History of Public Speaking in America,* Boston (Allyn & Bacon, Inc, 1965), pp 57, 125, 225, 440.
2. Corey Goldstein, M.D. "Managing Communication Anxiety: Action Steps You Can Take." P. 83.
3. Joannie M. Schrof and Stacy Schultz, "Social Anxiety;," *U.S. News and World Report* (July 21, 1999), p. 50.
4. J.C. McCroskey, "The Communication Apprehension Prospective." In *Avoiding Communication: Shyness, Reticence, and Communication Apprehension.* J.A. Daly and J.C. McCroskey, eds. Beverly Hills: Sage Publications, 1984)
5. K.R. Harris "The Sustained Effects of Cognitive Modification and Informed Teachers on Children's Communication Apprehension," *Communication Quarterly* 28 (1980), 47-56. L.R. Wheeless, "Communication Apprehension in the Elementary School." *Speech Teacher* 10 (1971), 297-99. Beth Azar, "Shy People have Inaccurate Self-Concepts," *American Psycholog8ical Association Monitor* (November, 1995), 24.
6. D. Klopf, "Cross-cultural Apprehension Research: A Summary of Pacific Basin Studies." In J. Daly & J. McCroskey, Eds. *Avoiding Communication: Shyness, Reticence, and Communication Apprehension* (Beverly Hills, CA: Sage, 1984), 157-169.
7. E. Yook & W. J. Siler, "An Investigation into the Communication Needs and Concerns of Asian Students in Speech Communication Performance Classes," *Basic Communication Course Annual* 2 (November, 1990), 470-75.
8. "Is Shyness Inherited?" *Healthy Decisions* (Georgetown University Medical Center) (Winter, 1997), p.2.
9. J.C. McCroskey, "Classroom Consequences of Communication Anxiety," *Communication Education,* 26(1977) 27-33.
10. M.J. Beatty & P.J. Beatty, "Interpersonal Communications Anxiety," *Interpersonal Relations and Education,* Vol 15, No 5, pp368-372.
11. E.C. Buehler and W. Linkugel, *Speech: A First Course* (New York: HarperCollins, 1962).
12. D.W. Staacks and J.D. Stone, "An Examination of the Effect of Basic Speech Courses, Self-Concept, and Self-Disclosure on Communication Apprehension", *Communication Education* 33 (1984), 317-32; R.S. Littlefield and T.L. Sellnow, "The Use of Self Disclosure as a Means for Reducing Stage Fright in Beginning Speakers," *Communication Education* 36 (1987), 62-64.
13. Goldstein, p. 84.
14. J.A. Daly, A.L. Vangelisti, H.L. Neel, and P.D. Cavanaugh, "Pre-Performance Concerns Associat4d with Public Speaking Anxiety," *Communication Quarterly* 37 (1989), 39-53.

CHAPTER 29 Listening

LEARNING OBJECTIVES

We learn by listening more than from any other process. When we listen, we receive, attend to, and assign meaning to incoming stimuli. How effective we are as listeners depends on our interests, our priorities, and our attitude. No matter how efficient we are as listeners, our competence as a communicator will be based on our competence as a listener. Our competence can be improved by mastering these objectives:

1. Explain why listening is important.
2. Describe how the trained listener processes and stores information.
3. Describe the barriers to effective listening.
4. Know the thirteen rules for good listening.
5. Distinguish between informative and evaluative listening, and demonstrate both.

CHAPTER 29: Overview

The chapter begins with discussing the importance of effective listening and the current recommendations to accomplishing this skill. Included are the stages of effective listening and the functions of each. Barriers to effective listening are identified. The chapter ends with thirteen rules for better listening.

Listening is the act of hearing intently. This definition suggests what semanticists would call reflective thinking. For example, it means that a rose is a rose. This is overly simplistic. Listening is an event that is a thought process requiring our attention to incoming information received by our senses and compared with our existing understanding of the universe so we can be consistent with our knowledge, past experience, current attitude, and even our secret desires.

Look at Figure 29.1. Even though it is a visual message, it illustrates the transmission of a message that a group of "listeners" would receive from a simple message we might label "The Swing." The message was sent, and nine listeners got a message. The complexity of the process is illustrated by what each "listener" received.

In the listening process, selected audio sounds are produced and associations are formed with symbols we call words attached to reality. Obviously the meaning of the words in this illustration were different for the project leader than they were for the customer, each of whose collection of symbols attached reality to different pictures. The same process happened with the system analyst, the programmer, the business consultant, the person who wrote up the description, the construction team, the billing department, the public who heard about it, and even the original customer who started this confusion in the first place.

Listening requires effort and concentration, and it is difficult to know when someone is listening and when they are not. Each person in the scenario appear to be listening, but their background, training and education get in the way of correct understanding.

Haney[1] reported a very similar phenomenon described in a popular magazine a number of years ago. The following description was given to three artists who were instructed to sketch what they had read:

Figure 29.1

The body is stout, with arched back; the limbs are short and stout, armed with strong, blunt claws; the ears long; and the tail thick at the base and tapering gradually. The elongated head is set on a short, thick neck, and at the extremity of the snout is a disc In which the nostrils open. The mouth is small and tubular, furnished with a long extensive tongue. A large individual measured 6 ft. 8 in. In color it is pale sandy or yellow, the hair being scanty and allowing the skin to show.

The rendition of the artists are quite different from the actual picture of this "Aardvark or Anteater,"as illustrated in Figure 29-2. These examples vividly demonstrate that transmitting actual messages can be difficult. It is amazing that we understand each other as well as we do. As bizarre and diverse as these drawings appear, note one extremely significant point: Each is a legitimate interpretation of what was read. Who can deny that the back is "arched," the ears "long," and the tail is "thick at the base and tapered gradually?" Differences were a result of transmitting verbal symbols that were interpreted by training and experience of the "listener."

As important as listening skills are to all levels of society, it is startling to note that few have ever received formal training on listening skills. A survey of Fortune 500 executives indicated that graduates need more work on communication skills; listening being high on the list of those required skills.[2] Wolvin and Coakly conducted a survey to determine the status of listening training in Fortune 500 corporations. They learned that more than 50 percent, including Boeing Aircraft and U.S. West Communications, consider listening so essential that they provide special listening training for their employees.[3] Ineffective listening spawns wasted time, poor customer relations, and the need to redo many tasks. Poor listening is an expensive habit.

The Importance of Effective Listening

It is amazing that poor listening is so widespread, given that we spend more time listening than any other activity except sleeping. A study by Barker and his colleagues found that college students spend nearly half of their communication time listening, almost one third if it speaking, and less than one third of it reading and writing.[4]

From the time we get up in the morning to the time we end the day, we are constantly listening to something. Yet most of us give little thought to the role that listening plays in our lives. Recently a commercial was aired on television showing two friends together. One of the young men is busily eating, while the other is distraught and thanks his friend for always "being there" and for listening to him as he talks about how his girlfriend dumped him. When the first young man finishes eating, he says to his friend, "So, how's that girlfriend of yours?" Do your friends listen similarly?

A survey of graduates majoring in business and professional occupations at a major university recently reported they wished they had more training in listening because it was the communication skill contributing most to job success.[5] The Academy of Certified Administrative Managers found that listening ranked as the number one "supercritical" competence required of a successful manager.[6] From personal experience, most of us know how critical listening is for everyone.

Stages of Effective Listening

Current communication texts endorse listening as a critical skill, however agreement is not clear on how the job might be done. A current communication text by Osborne, Osborne, and Osborne places the responsibility of good listening on a successful, well-trained speaker[7]. They recommend four critical tasks the speaker must accomplish to produce good listeners:

1. The speaker must adapt the topic to the audience.
2. The speaker must support the ideas very well, using strong supporting material, including facts, figures, and stories.
3. The speaker must strongly support persuasive claims with logical and well-reasoned conclusions.
4. The speaker must establish strong, credible credentials to motivate listeners to accept the ideas.

Canary, Cody and Manusov maintain good listening requires a good bonding relationship between the speaker and listener.[8] The speaker must have the ability to fit what is heard into creating a bonding relationship. Rather than evaluation of the message, it is the application of the message that produces this communication bond.

The context of the communication becomes a critical variable. Marriage is used as an example of communication event. Listening well helps each partner develops the ability to take the other's perspective. Operationally defined, this could be referred to as empathetic listening. Lack of perspective suggests concentrating on negative results based on discrepancies and differences. How we listen or accept information is then governed by the relationship, not the message, as suggested by Osborne.

Canary, Cody, and Manusov review listening in the workplace on the same basis. Listening is evaluated by emphases placed on organizational skills, non-verbal cues, and manners. Again, success focuses on relationships, not messages sent. Behaviors observed were attentiveness, perception, and responsiveness. Medical contexts stressed the degree of trust established among participants, and not upon messages. Stress was given to "interpersonal competence." Issues focus on attention, attitude, and behavior as perceived by "concerned" people defined good listening. Educational context listening skills depended on "attitude" of success in general academic aptitude.

Devito[9] and Wood[10] concentrate on a more intellectual activity where the participant consistently makes conscious judgments. The speaker is "mindful," or chooses to participate. Listening becomes a process of receiving the message almost mechanically. Involved is a selective process of only accepting a portion of information transmitted, then placing a value on what was perceived before storing it for future reference. The process inevitably includes both evaluation of the message and interpreting the bonding relationship supplying the message.

Berko, Wolvin and Wolvin[11] base listening on an interaction of meaning and its impact on information storage almost inherent within the system. The emphasis is on evaluation of the message and how it relates to our inherited sensitivity to the meaning of the message. For example we may have left brain or right brain characteristics dictating information preference. Do we like written or oral messages best? Do we like maps, or oral directions? Do we like multiple choice or essay exams? Because our cultural preferences interact with communication expectancies, we listen not only selectively, but with prejudice.

The Stages of Effective Listening

Based on the review of literature suggesting listening training, it is not surprising listening training has fallen short of desired results. The difficulties arise in that each listener receives a multilayered signal containing many interpretations. We receive messages based upon background, interest, and motivation.

Hearing

Our receiver becomes sensitive to sounds, and chooses those sound waves that are most meaningful. Subconsciously we may filter out the sound of voices, the air conditioner, the car passing, but hears our iPod®, or perhaps one person in the crowd. All other sounds are interpreted as background noise and filtered out of the system.

Selecting

Since we function in a supersaturated environment of messages, we are forced to choose which stimuli we will listen to and which we will ignore. So a value is placed on the signals, and only those messages that are deemed important are selected. For example, if you are talking to a friend during a party where loud music, much laughter and confusion surround the two of you, your friend's voice would take precedence, and all other sounds and stimuli would be filtered out. Stop reading for a moment, and listen to the sounds around you. Notice you never heard the traffic noise, the ticking clock, the refrigerator motor, the distant sound of music. Selecting what you will hear does not necessarily mean you are not fully listening. It does engage you in the second stage of the listening process.

Attending

Attending is the mental process of focusing on specific stimuli while ignoring or downplaying other competing stimuli. Your attention span is normally limited to a short period of time. The more things you notice around you, the less able you will be to concentrate on one single thing and listen to it effectively. Therefore it becomes critical to prioritize sounds you hear. Many elements contribute to this selection process, including your mental alertness, interests, values, priorities, and perhaps even your physical being. Stress, depression, elation, or curiosity can all directly influence your selective perception.

Understanding

Once you have heard, selected, and attended to sounds, you assign meaning to them. Although there is no commonly accepted explanation of how understanding develops, it is known that past experiences play a vital part. You subconsciously relate and compare the new sounds to those you have heard in the past. To learn calculus, for example, you must learn algebra. If you hear calculus before hearing algebra, you may hear the message, but since you are unable to interpret and place in perspective the new message, you will not "listen" to what is said. Understanding is one measurement of listening effectiveness.

Evaluating

Another critical factor of listening is evaluating. If you do not understand, or if you judge the sounds heard as not of value or importance, the information will be removed from the system, and nothing is received. It will be filtered out much like the background stimuli were. A critical factor about evaluation is that it becomes a stop sign for information flow. Once the judgment has been made that the information being heard is of no value, the system shuts down, and no "listening" takes place. We no longer hear and attend to other incoming messages.

Remembering

The last stage in the complete listening process is being able to recall what was said. We may say we pay attention, and hear something, but we never truly listen unless we can recall the information at a later date. Our memory then becomes the final key in defining not only learning and listening, but also placing a value on its importance in our life. Table 29.1 compares the stages of listening with the International Literary Association definition of listening.

Unfortunately, many of us do not remember information for long. Why we remember some things and not others is not completely clear. Some evidence sug-

Table 29.1

A Comparison of the Stages of Listening with the ILA Definition of Listening

STAGES OF EFFECTIVE LISTENING	ILA DEFINITION OF LISTENING
Hearing means that we are aware of sound or that we receive stimuli.	The *process of receiving* indicates that we *hear*.
Selecting indicates that we choose to respond to some sounds and not toothers. This is part d the conscious choices lsteners make when sifting through the various stimuli with which they are bombarded.	In the International Listening Association (ILA) definition, the stages d selecting, attending, understanding, evaluating and remembering may be seen as part d the *constructing meaning from* portion of the ILA definition because all fou of those stages are set in motion when a listener tries tomal sense of communication events.
Attending suggests that people focus on some things but not on others as hey try to make sense of communication messages.	Listeners have to *do something* with those messages; hey must hink through, weigh, and try to internalize and personalize the information gained. Listeners, according tc the ILA, first hear and then process messages sothat they c follow through on them.
Understanding is a direct tie-in to the ILA definition because listeners must asign meaning to the communication behaviors they experience.	
Evaluating is a part d thinking, analyzing, and drawing conclusions about messages.	The ILA goes one step further in defining the process of listening with the phrase *responding to spoken or nonverba messages*. The implication here is that listeners do more th think about communication events; hey also remember anc actively respond to other's messages, both verbal and nonverbal, and it dso suggests, according to some, that we *listen to* and respond to messages n all communication events including internet messages, face-to-face communication, observed behaviors, and mediated events.
Remembering suggests that listeners place the information into short-term or long-term memory in order to be able to use it a some time in the future.	

gests that we remember approximately half of newly heard, meaningful information immediately after we hear it, but after a month we forget more than half of what we remembered in the first place.[12] Just as our understanding depends on the selecting and attending stages, so does our memory. Research suggests that 25 percent of what most people listen to can be recalled. Of that 25 percent, 80 percent is distorted or not received accurately; this leaves only 5 percent of the total message accurately received.[13] Factors such as our priority of importance, change of mind as to importance, and even contradictory information received at a later date can influence how stable our memory can be.

Responding: Sending Feedback

The listener either verbally or non-verbally verifies the reception of the message. Total silence suggests the message was either rejected or ignored. A smile or frown can confirm acceptance, hostility, or rejection. Head movement can suggest either acceptance or rejection. A request for clarification can communicate effectiveness.

Feedback to the source of the message is critical to the effectiveness of the event. Feedback insures understanding, defines the degree of success, and even signals for either more or less additional signal. Feedback reassures the sender how the message was received, and acknowledges or disavows success of the message. It prepares both the sender and receiver for what is anticipated in the future.

The Functions of Listening

From the first sound heard in the morning to the last sound at night, everyone experiences a wide range of listening events. We apply the mechanics of listening to each event based on our judgment as to its effect on us. How well we receive these messages can protect our life, improve our relationships, deliver satisfaction and comfort, create boredom and frustration, or stimulate us to action. Below are listed some general "listening styles" we often employ based on our evaluation of the message and its importance to our lifestyle.

Listening for Information.

Students listen for information on how to improve their lives. We learn how to become better, more satisfied, even more wealthy people from what we hear. We mold our lives around information we gain from listening.

Listening to Evaluate

We place judgments on information we hear. We listen to our car operating to detect performance. We listen to salespeople as they tell us about their product. Someone has suggested we are bombarded with over 2000 advertisements every day. We must evaluate the ones that are important.

Listening with Empathy

Empathy is a special kind of listening we do as we try to understand personal relationships and emotional events in people's lives. As we either hear or reveal our problems, successes, or failures, we generate strong feelings that result in bonding relationships, assistance, and life improvements. Listening emphatically can be a healing, soothing, even learning process. Empathic listening indicates we are aware of, appreciate, and understand another person's feelings. By being an empathic listener, we put ourselves in the other's place and try to feel what they are feeling during times of trial, misfortune, or even great blessings. This process builds strong bonds of love, friendship, loyalty, even patriotism. Such listening is sometimes difficult because of strong feelings developed. But it should be remembered that if we fail to empathize with others, we also fail to understand them.

Listening for Enjoyment

Sometimes we listen purely for pleasure, satisfaction and appreciation. We hear music, humor, inspiration, or enthusiasm because they make us feel good. Such an experience has both a physical and psychological impact on our inner feelings. It should be noted that even when we listen for pleasure and enjoyment, we are busy selecting, attending, understanding, evaluating, and remembering.

Barriers to Good Listening

Since listening often requires little physical input, laziness and failure to pay attention can create bad listening habits, resulting in poor listening. Listed are several barriers that create poor listening habits.

We Do Nothing!

During an exposure to messages, too often we take an extended journey to a more pleasant experience. A quick judgment has suggested the messages being received are of no interest and we mentally go fishing, take a trip to Europe, or visit an exciting ball game. We may even have disconnected thoughts, drowsiness, or day dream. But we do not listen!

Empathetic Sidetrack.

We listen with our emotion, then substitute or include emotional experiences from our past. We feel sorrow, joy, pain, or even exuberance with the source, but in so doing we focus more on our own past than what the speaker is saying, and we get lost in our own memories and feelings.

This barrier in listening can also make us susceptible to persuasion and acceptance.

Disagreement or Antagonism

As the person sends us a message we find disagreeable, we create ideas, incidents, or statistics that counter what is being said. Our reception is negative, which encourages rejection. This often causes us to think more about our rebuttal than what is actually said. If the disagreement is strong, hostility and anger can result in irrational thinking. We end up criticizing the person rather than the message.

Focus on Detail Rather than Concepts and Ideas

It is a human tendency to focus on dates, statistics, names, and detail rather than on concepts and ideas. This requires too much effort in categorizing the information and disjointed ideas that never relate to concepts. Analyze a situation to determine what kind of information is required to understand the topic. If facts are important, listen for them. If ideas are the key, remember them. This will make facts easier to remember.

Avoid Difficult Listening Situations

Difficult situations include being exposed to technical information that is unfamiliar, or being in a setting where competing stimuli such as music or noise compete with the message. Technical jargon, but overwhelming amounts of information, too rapid a delivery, or even acoustic problems, all are great distractions.

Improving Listening Competence

Listening competence can be improved by just becoming aware that it is a skill like reading or writing, and can be improved by conscious effort. Focusing attention on the source of the message, and a desire to listen are great steps in making improvement. We should actively participate by expanding what we hear and making it apply to our personal needs. We accept the ideas presented, then positively build on them. We apply the new concepts to our own body of information on the subject. We ask questions and actively get involved in the communication. We maintain eye contact with the source of information. This helps focus our attention and stimulate our conscious thoughts to embrace the new information.

As new ideas form and combine with our existing information, we build on our personal knowledge, experience and feeling. Learning theorists refer to this as "deep listening."

Thirteen Articles for Better Communication

The following recommendations have assisted many in improving listening skills. The list incorporates both physical and mental activity which help improve concentration on the message.

1. **Become a compulsive note taker.** Even the most learned man is not too proud to take notes. This means having your own paper and pencil, not borrowing from your neighbor. Any good note-taker not only writes, but also reads the notes after writing them!
2. **Make sure the notes written are of value.** This means you can read them; they say what is important; they are brief.
3. **Select the right word for the right message.** This is true in both receiving the message, taking notes, or formulating your own ideas. Precision is as critical in communication as it is in science or engineering.
4. **Be organized.** This means plan ahead and listen. Review the topic. Follow the schedule. No one has the time or tolerance to afford the luxury and frustration of disorganization.
5. **Do not omit information.** If there is something you do not understand, ask questions, but do not ignore what you miss or do not understand. What may not be important to you maay be the key of success to someone else.
6. **Distinguish between what is said and what you think was or should have been said.** Remember: the bore at every party is the guy who supplies his own punch line to everyone else's joke. Do not guess the end of the story; listen and find out for sure.
7. **Do not try to be a record setter when you want someone to listen to you.** At every competitive event, whether it is the Indianapolis 500, the Kentucky Derby, or the Olympics, competitors try to break the record. When you talk, do not try to break the record. The best communicator is not the one who talks the longest. Just send one idea at a time and be sure it gets across. In the end you will be the winner.
8. **When sending or receiving a message, use more than one method of communication.** If you want your message received, speak it as well as send a written message. Do not forget non-verbal cues. When you speak or listen, let your body say the same thing your words say. If you use several channels, you have a greater chance of finding one of them open.
9. **Determine what is important.** Do not be the victim of selective perception. Choose the key idea and try to remember it.
10. **Preview and review.** In sending the message, tell 'em what you're gonna tell 'em. Tell 'em. Tell 'em what you told 'em. Then they will listen. In taking notes, write 'em. Read 'em. Review 'em. You will remember and be a better listener.
11. **Be sure your listener understands.** Ask questions on what you have just said. If you are the listener and do not understand, ask questions.
12. **Do not trust your own memory.** Every lost person I have ever met was in the process of trying to remember something he knew he would never forget.
13. **Work at it!** All good speakers and listeners do!

References

1. William V. Haney, *Communication and Organizational Behavior,* Richard D. Irwin, Inc,: 1967, pp. 223-225.
2. American Council on Education, *Spanning the Chasm: Corporate and Academic Cooperation to Improve Work-Force Preparation,* Washington, D.C.: American Council on Education, 1997).
3. A.D. Wolvin and C.G. Coakley, "A Survey of the Status of Listening Training in Some Fortune 500 Corporations," *Communication Education*, 40 (1991), 152-64.
4. L. Barker, R. Edwards, C. Gains, et al. "An Investigation of Proportional Time Spent on Various Communication Activities by College Students," *Journal of Communication Research*, 8 (1980), pp. 101-109.
5. V. Di Salvo, "A Summary of Current Research Identifying Communication Skills in Various Organizational Contexts," *Communication Education*, 29 (July, 1980), pp. 283-90.
6. H.T. Smith, "The 20% Activities That Bring 80% Payoff," *Training Today* (1978), p.6.
7. M. Osborne, S. Osborne, and kR. Osborne, *Public Speaking*, 8th ed. (Pearson Education, Inc, 2009) pp 74-93.
8. D.J. Canary, M. J. Cody, V. Manusov, *Interpersonal Communication, A Goals-based Approach*, 4th Ed (New York: Bedford/St. Martin's, 2008) pp. 93-122.
9. J.A. Devito, Human Communication, The Basic Course, 11th Ed. (Boston: Allyn and Bacon, 2009), pp.81-99.
10. J. T. Wood, *Communication in Our Lives*, 5th Ed (Boston: Wadsworth Cengage Learning, 2009), pp. 77-102.
11. R.M. Berko, A.D. Wolvin, and D. R. Wolvin, *Communicating: A Soicial and Career Focus*, 10th Ed. (Boston: Houghton Mifflin Co., 2007) pp. 84-112.
12. A..G. Dietze and G.E. Jones, "Factual Memory of Secondary School Pupils for a Short Article Which They Read a Single Time," *Journal of Educational Psychology*, 22 (1931), pp. 586-98, 667-767.
13. S.S. Benoit and J.W. Lee, "Listening: It Can Be Taught," *Journal of Education for Business*, 63(1986), 229-32.

CHAPTER 30
The Audience

LEARNING OBJECTIVES

When students have completed this chapter and lesson they should be able to:

1. Define audience analysis and explain why it is essential in public speaking.
2. Define demographic and psychographic characteristics. What are their implications for public speaking. Give Examples.
3. List and explain four methods of audience analysis.
4. Describe the situational factors that affect a public speech.

CHAPTER 30: Overview

A general discussion of audience characteristics and their importance is discussed. Suggestions are given for checking audience demographics and respecting audience culture, self-interest, personal interests, beliefs, and values. A general discussion of audience psychology is discussed. Both formal and informal strategies of audience analysis are presented.

Two students were presenting speeches to their classmates about the dangers of smoking. Both spent a great deal of time preparing, but they had strongly different attitudes about how to develop their speeches. The night before speaking, they met to compare their preparations. The first student said:

> I had no idea there was so much research information about this topic. I had to cut short my explanations in order to fit everything in. If I talk faster than usual, I just might make it within the time limit. I want everyone to know that I prepared thoroughly and that I take the topic very seriously.

His classmate took a different approach:

> Well, you may be right, but I don't think people want to hear about all the research. They need to know that the studies exist, but they really need to hear about how smoking has hurt someone they know. I want to tell a story that listeners can relate to, so that they'll be interested in my message.

The first student viewed the assignment only from his own perspective as speaker, worrying about how to include all the research and how to ensure a good grade. The second student considered the audience's perspective. She was determined to make the message interesting to classmates, and she carefully reviewed each bit of information from the viewpoint of someone hearing it in a short speech. Both speakers had the same general topic and goal, but to the audience the first speech was abstract, complicated, and dull, whereas the second was stimulating and full of common sense.

It may seem surprising that even your attitude toward preparing a speech can create such a difference in the audience's reaction, but it's natural for listeners to give appreciation, attention, and support to a speaker who considers their comfort, interests, and beliefs. Even though an audience can thus be a constraint on a speaker's freedom, you can work with that constraint by careful audience analysis on three different levels:

- By checking *audience demographics*, you consider how your speech should respond to certain characteristics of the audience as a whole—such as its size, age range, and educational level.
- By respecting *audience culture*, you become aware of how listeners approach your speech in terms of their interests, beliefs and values, prior understanding, and common knowledge.
- By understanding *audience psychology*, you realize that listeners are selective about what they attend to and perceive.

The relationships among audience demographics, culture, and psychology are illustrated in Figure 30.1.

Checking Audience Demographics

Size

How large will your audience be? The more listeners there are, the greater your sense of distance from them, and consequently the more formal your presentation is likely to be. Someone speaking to a dozen people in a small room clearly faces a different situation than someone addressing a large lecture hall or a mass-media audience.

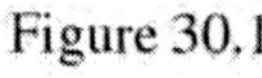

Figure 30.1

Levels of influence on audiences

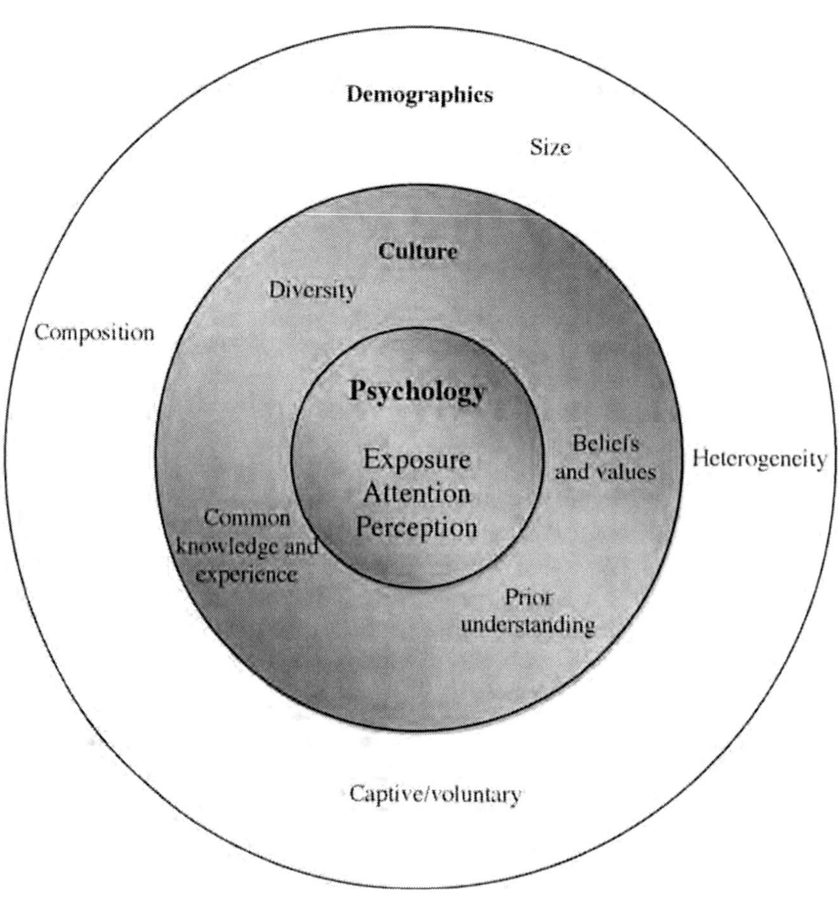

Classroom speakers probably have an audience of about 20 to 25 listeners, an audience size that is typical of many speeches to service clubs, neighborhood groups, and work-related organizations. This size lets you address a public without losing sight of individuals, and the setting is a middle ground between highly formal and extremely informal.

Heterogeneous Audiences

Variety or diversity among audience members: dissimilarity (Heterogeneity) refers to the variety or diversity of audience members—the degree of dissimilarity among them. The smaller the audience, the more likely that its members will have similar assumptions, values, and ways of thinking. Small audiences may show marked differences in these criteria, but a large audience virtually ensures that members will have different values and assumptions as well as learning styles; the audience is usually assumed to be heterogeneous. Exceptions result from specialized groups at conventions, or work-related gatherings.

The more heterogeneous your audience, the more you need to find examples and appeals that will be meaningful to all kinds of listeners; or you might combine appeals that are relevant to different segments of the audience. Avoid materials that are significant to some listeners but beside the point to others. The goal is to appeal meaningfully to a diverse audience without resorting to vague generalizations and platitudes. One way to avoid some "special interest" groups is to avoid use of buzzwords, slogans, or phrases that contain limited information, but identify the speaker with certain populations within the audience. Such groupings include age groups, interest groups, or special clubs or gangs.

An audience can be heterogeneous even if its members share the same cultural background, but a culturally diverse audience is particularly likely to be heterogeneous. Diversity also insures the presence of opinionated groups strongly opposed to your topic. The audience for the speeches against smoking might include a student or two from countries where smoking is unrestricted, and they may not share their classmates' concerns about the health risks of smoking. Heterogeneous makeup anticipates a spectrum of opinion on your topic, and you as a speaker must anticipate this problem to succeed.

Voluntary Versus Captive Audience

Under what circumstances has the audience assembled? In general, people who have chosen to hear a speech are more likely to be interested and receptive than are people who have been coerced into attending. A captive audience may resent having to hear the speech, which may undercut the speaker's ethos and message.

Students who are required to attend an assembly, employees whose jobs depend on participation in a seminar, and churchgoers who find themselves listening to a political message when they expected a sermon are examples of captive audiences. Speakers cannot assume captive listeners have any interest in them or their subject, and they must work particularly hard to motivate them.

Some of your classmates may be captive listeners, especially if the course is required or if individuals don't recognize the value of effective listening. With luck, you can turn them into voluntary listeners as they become interested in what you have to say and as they begin to improve their own speeches by listening carefully to yours.

If you assume your audience is voluntarily and you make no effort to motivate them, you could be setting yourself up for disaster. If you are wrong in your assessment and your listeners do see themselves as captive, their feelings of boredom or hostility are likely to overwhelm any message you present. For this reason, when you don't know the status of the audience, it is best to assume that listeners are captive and that you need to motivate them.

Composition

Speakers should also analyze audiences in terms of such categories as age, gender, religion, ethnicity, educational level, or socioeconomic status. A young audience would be less interested in a speech about retirement planning than an older audience would be. Teenage boys would be more interested in joining athletic leagues than would the "retirement plan" group. Likewise, you might assume that listeners with a high level of formal education can think in figurative as well as literal terms and can deal with complex issues. If an audience is made up mostly of a particular religious or ethnic group, you well may tailor your presentation to take advantage of their commonality.

Warning should be given, however, that a common error in audience analysis is stereotyping.

Stereotyping assumes that all members of a demographic category are all alike in all respects. Individual differences, desires and motivations are consequently ignored, and solutions to problems become over-generalized. Stereotyping becomes a tempting substitute for audience analysis, setting up neat, well-ordered, and oversimplified categories into which we can slip our evaluations of people, situations, or happenings.

For example, it is less true today than in the past that women and men differ in the likelihood of their being persuaded by a speaker. Nor do all people from rural areas think alike; and not everyone from a particular region has the same set of beliefs and values.[1] In short, demographic categories can provide important hints about an audience, but do not assume that the hints apply to everyone.

Respecting Audience Culture

Imagine you are scheduled to speak about the joys of ham radio operation to a troop of Girl Scouts. Now imagine that your topic is the same but that your audience is a high school computer club or a convention of retired people. In what ways might you adapt your presentation to fit these different audiences?

No matter what your topic and purpose, to plan an effective message you must focus on the particular culture of your audience. Audience culture refers to subjective factors that characterize a particular audience and make its situation distinct: interests, beliefs and values, common knowledge and experience, roles and reference groups. Thinking critically while carefully considering all of the audience attributes will enable you to strategically plan a speech that fits your audience. By matching audience demographics with known audience attributes, the speaker increases the chance of success significantly. Consider the following critical attributes:

Self-interest

Listeners have self-interests; they stand to gain or lose personally, depending on what is done. For example, a proposal to raise students' tuition and fees would not be in the self-interest of those who are working their way through college, whereas a proposal to increase funds for financial aid would appeal to the self-interest of those same students. Self-interest goes beyond economic matters, however. A speech that advocates limits on listeners' freedom or power or that casts them in an unflattering role also will be at odds with the audience's self-interest.

Most listeners resist messages that clearly challenge their self-interest. If you must challenge the audience's self-interest, consider whether you can develop your message in a nonthreatening way while still being true to your beliefs. Perhaps you can plan the speech with a strong combination of appeals so that listeners will look beyond their self-interest to consider some broader concept of what is good.

For example, one common strategy for challenging listeners' self-interest is to suggest that their short-term sacrifices will bring long-term benefits (and so their self-interest will be satisfied in the long run). One student took this approach in arguing that course work should be more difficult. She began by admitting outright that her speech would challenge the audience's self-interest:

> Talk to any student at this college, and you'll hear about how busy they are, how much work they have to do, how much time their classes take. I'm sure it's true, because many of us have never really been challenged to work hard before this. The last thing most students want is to hear someone say that classes should be made even harder. But if we can improve the academic reputation of this college, not only will it attract better students, but in the long run our own degrees will be more highly valued.

This student attempted the most rational way of overcoming self-interest by substituting immediate results with more rewarding, more fulfilling long-range goals.

Personal Interests

Listeners also have personal interests, and so you need to assess how likely it is that your topic will interest others. Even though you may be an avid student of military history, you cannot assume that others will be captivated by a speech about battle planning. And although you may be thrilled by the details of auto mechanics, realize that many listeners only want to know how to turn the ignition key to start the car.

If you think that listeners will be strongly interested in your topic, a straightforward presentation maybe fine. But if interest may be low, deliberately plan the speech to capture the audience's attention and hold their interest. Avoid technical language, jargon, and abstractions unless you know that the audience is familiar with and interested in the topic. Startling statements, rhetorical questions, personal anecdotes, and narratives are especially good ways to involve listeners in your topic and enhance their interest. The objective is to quickly provide materials that make the topic a critical one for listeners. Often lack of knowledge is the largest barrier to the acceptance of new ideas.

Sometimes listeners do have a casual interest in your topic but do not regard it as particularly important or of high priority. Then your task is less one of arousing initial interest and more a matter of impressing the audience with the urgency of the situation and the significance of your message. In any case, by analyzing the audience's level of interest in your topic, you are better able to determine how to select more captivating material for the speech.

Beliefs and Values

Beliefs are statements that listeners regard as true; values are positive or negative judgments that listeners make. For example, a listener might believe that homelessness is a serious problem (belief) and might also regard government aid for the homeless as a good thing (giving it a positive value). Another listener might agree that homelessness is a serious problem (belief) yet might object to government aid (giving it a negative value). Still another listener might not believe that homelessness is a serious problem and might think that its scope has been exaggerated. For the last listener, government aid is not an issue because no problem has been acknowledged.

As these examples show, an audience's beliefs and values are the starting point for crafting the strategy of your speech. You want to uphold your own beliefs and values, but you can do that and advance your purpose without alienating your audience if you emphasize the connections between listeners' beliefs and values and your own. Sometimes the best approach is to specifically point out agreements and differences. This establishes a common ground to present a dialog. Strategies of compromise, give and take, or upgrading are options. The critical factor is that a dialog has been created, and options are provided. Success of the communication will then result on how successfully the speaker utilizes strategies discussed in other chapters, including logical reasoning, persuasion, supplying information, or even compromise. This becomes the platform for communication.

Prior Understanding

How much do your listeners already know about your topic? Have they heard about any of your points before? Do they have enough background information to follow your reasoning? Answers to these questions can help you design a powerful speech without boring or confusing your audience.

Speakers sometimes mistake intelligence for knowledge, thus overestimating what the audience knows. Fearful of condescending to listeners—of talking down to them and assuming they can't think for themselves—some speakers present complex material too quickly, omit important steps in an explanation, or relate events out of sequence. Sometimes we avoid conflicting issues or ideas of change because we are fearful of the clash, anticipating anger, loss of friendship, or rejection.

Another danger of poor audience analysis is speaking to listeners but giving them no new information. If the listeners believe a speaker is wasting their time and saying nothing new, they are less likely to pay attention. Worse, they may become angry or resent the speaker as a person. You can avoid all these dangers by analyzing what the audience already knows.

Sometimes listeners know a good deal about the topic and have strong feelings about it. To be successful, speakers must respond to what the audience already knows about the topic or situation. Opportunities for success include considering compromise, upgrading the present condition, and expanding the issue to include greater good. But the secret is knowing what your audience knows, and what they are thinking. Proper audience analysis can give you that information. Critical analysis can help you form the compromise, or the redirection.

President Ronald Reagan was dubbed "The Great Communicator" in part because he could render complex subjects in simple, understandable terms. In a 1983 speech seeking support for his Strategic Defense Initiative, he used simple terms to describe sophisticated military and strategic concepts, and he also overcame complex arguments about defense spending:

> But first, let me say what the defense debate is not about. It is not about spending arithmetic. I know that in the last few weeks you've been bombarded with numbers and percentages. . . .The trouble with all these numbers is that they tell us little about the kind of defense program America needs or the benefits and security and freedom that our defense effort buys for us.

In simple language President Reagan then explained the importance of a defensive missile system: "I've become more and more convinced that the human spirit must be capable of rising above dealing with other nations and human beings by threatening their existence;" and "Wouldn't it be better to save lives than avenge them?" He admitted but downplayed the difficulties of developing this new system and called on the scientific community, "those who gave us nuclear weapons, to turn their great talents now to the cause of mankind and world peace, to give us the means of rendering these nuclear weapons impotent and obsolete." If President Reagan had focused only on technical and scientific issues in the belief that "everyone understood" the difference between offensive and defensive systems, his speech would have been far less effective. His secret to being the "great communicator" was understanding what his audience knew, and what they desired. He then capitalized on this knowledge to win support for his proposal.

Common Knowledge and Experience

What cultural facts in your listeners' general store of knowledge will be relevant to your speech? Surveys frequently report that embarrassing percentages of Americans cannot name their senator or representative, do not know when the Civil War was fought, or cannot locate a particular country on the globe. Such evidence does not argue that people are stupid or that a speaker must spell out everything for an audience. Rather, in recent years educators have been less concerned with teaching facts than with teaching students how to find information.[2] Thus, for a general audience, you may need to identify or explain cultural facts important to your argument. But if your audience is specialized—say a group of Civil War buffs—you can assume listeners are familiar with basic information about your topic.

Speakers often make **allusions**, or brief references to things they assume listeners know and understand. But if listeners don't "get" the allusion, they also will miss the point of the comparison. So you need to have a good sense of which allusions your audience will recognize. Well into the twentieth century, speakers could assume most listeners were familiar with the Bible and with classic literature. Late in the century, however, popular culture—especially television—became the source of many allusions. For example, supporters of President John F. Kennedy fondly remembered his administration by referring to the popular musical Camelot. During the 1984 presidential campaign, Democratic candidate Walter Mondale dismissed the argument of a primary opponent by asking, "Where's the beef?"—quoting a popular television commercial for a chain of hamburger franchises.

When a message is unfamiliar, listeners tend to perceive it in their own familiar context. Current speakers should realize remarks about energy and fuel may well be heard in the context of the listeners' personal experience in coping with high gasoline prices.

Similarly, in a classroom speech about nuclear power, Steve Cortez alluded to the animated television program "The Simpsons":

> What comes to your mind when you hear the words "nuclear power"? If you're like most Americans, you probably conjure up images of Three-Mile Island and Chernobyl. Or if you're a fan of "The Simpsons," you might think of the nuclear-waste-induced three-eyed fish found near the plant in a recent episode. Maybe you think of Homer Simpson eating doughnuts and sleeping while he's supposed to be monitoring the plant's safety equipment, or of Mr. Burns, the diabolical plant owner. Whatever your immediate impression of nuclear power, it's probably negative, and it shouldn't be.

By analyzing and understanding his audience's shared cultural experiences, Cortez was able to allude to "The Simpsons" characters to build a strong introduction that captured interest and prepared listeners for his main point. Note as he did so, he inferred that nuclear plant safety was not the national calamity everyone thought, and comparing it to a cartoon reduced the seriousness of its impact. As the energy crisis increased to double digit inflation of gasoline and electric power costs, cries about the danger have faded into history. Current experience has greater impact than a forgotten crisis that never personally impacted many U.S. citizens in the first place.

Roles and Reference Groups

Each listener occupies a variety of roles, or socially assigned positions, and these are an important part of an audience's culture. An earlier example was given about a group of Girl Scouts. A listener who is a Girl Scout is also a young woman, a student, and a daughter; and she maybe a member of a church, the Honor Society, and the dance club. Depending on which role is dominant for her at any given time, different topics and appeals are likely to be effective. If, while listening to a speech, she thinks of herself mainly as a Girl Scout, she may be more interested in physical adventure or social service than she would be if she thought of herself mainly as a dancer. In analyzing your audience, therefore, you need to decide which roles are most important to listeners while you speak.

Listeners also identify with many reference groups, whether or not they actually belong to them. Because reference groups serve as guides or models for behavior, they can influence listeners' beliefs, values, and actions. For example, a student may model his taste in clothes or hairstyle on the members of a popular band; he isn't a member of this band, but he likes people to think of him as sharing its characteristics. Another student may take cues about the importance of good study habits from older friends in her residence hall; they are a reference group for her because she likes to be thought of in reference to them. In other situations, each of these students will model different reference groups—family, friends, peers, public figures, and ethnic groups. By knowing which reference groups and values are important to your listeners, you can strategically plan effective appeals and supporting materials that will be most influential.

Cultural Diversity

We have been discussing culture as though audience members all share a common culture. In some respects they probably do, but a speaker who assumes that an audience has a single set of beliefs, values, or experiences is inviting disaster. The result resembles problems discussed in stereotyping. Rarely does an audience possess a single set of such complicated attributes.

The United States has increasingly become a multicultural society, and today's audience members represent a diversity of cultures and backgrounds. This is true of public speaking classes particularly, because schools, colleges, and universities have sought to attract international students and students from various racial and ethnic groups. It is also true of society at large, as racial and ethnic minority groups make up a growing proportion of the population. Everyone, whether speaker or listener, must acknowledge and relate to people who have characteristics developed from a multicultural background. The importance of understanding the impact of cultural diversity is vividly demonstrated by the history of racial discrimination, illegal immigration, illegal aliens, and foreign language learning.

Speaking to a multicultural audience challenges you to become aware of your own cultural assumptions and predispositions. It is common for people to regard as universal the values of their specific culture. But reflection and careful self-analysis can help you avoid seeing your own values as universal and thus seeming insensitive to cultural differences.[3]

Many beliefs about other cultures are based on negative, unflattering stereotypes, and should be avoided when addressing a multicultural audience. Consciously resist bipolar contrasts or stereotypes such as implying one culture is hard-working and another is lazy, or that one is educated and another is ignorant, or that one is compulsive and another is relaxed. These bipolar value judgments are invalid, based on prejudice or inaccurate information. The reality is far more complex, and simple-minded attitudes will rightly both insult and antagonize an audience.

Speakers adapt to a culturally diverse audience in two basic ways. One approach is to derive examples from many cultures so that all listeners feel that they are being addressed within the framework of their own culture. Even if some cultures are not mentioned specifically, the speaker's acknowledgment of diversity may make everyone feel more included![5] This approach requires the speaker to know which cultures are represented by audience members.

The other approach is to resist culture-specific references altogether; search instead for appeals that transcend cultures. An appeal based on preserving the planet for the next generation, an appeal to the common interest in peace, or an appeal based on the beauty and wonder of nature may well transcend the limits of any particular culture.[6] In a speech in 1963, President Kennedy illustrated this approach. After speaking about the need to recognize diversity among nations and cultures, he noted that all people hold certain values in common:

> For in the final analysis, our most basic common link is that we all inhabit this small planet. We all breathe the same air. We all cherish our children's future. And we are all mortal.

Understanding Audience Psychology

A term commonly used in audience psychology is ***selective exposure.*** Selective exposure is a tendency to expose oneself to messages that are important personally and that are consistent with what one already believes. This automatically implies that messages that are judged as not important are either rejected or never acknowledged. They are omitted from the communication message.

Selective attention is a conscious or unconscious choice the listener makes to either focus or ignore, or misinterpret messages that have been judged as inconsistent with personal beliefs. The listener judges whether or not to focus intently on a speech, absorb and process its contents, and take it seriously.

Selective Exposure and Selective Attention

Each day an infinite number of potential communication stimuli are available to us. We can converse with anyone we meet and can overhear the conversations of others; we can call or write to each other; we can read newspapers, magazines, and books; we can listen to the radio or watch television; we can see films or videos; we can attend speeches, listen to lectures on tape, hear sermons, or join group discussions. And while we're busy doing all this, our computers can log on to the Internet to exchange mail and collect any information we specify.

Even if we did nothing except engage in communication, there is clearly too much for any of us to do. How do we choose which speeches to hear, which magazines to read, which television programs to watch, and which Websites to visit? In short, how do we select the communications to which we will expose ourselves?

We selectively expose ourselves to our communication. Our choices are not random; we select messages that are important to us and that are consistent with our beliefs. We ignore and bypass messages we judge as not being useful or pertinent to us. We do not listen to speeches other than entertainment speeches merely for pleasure. Few of us relish an attack on what we believe. Instead, we read magazines, listen to speakers, and make friends whose views are similar to *our* own.

Although selective exposure governs messages we hear, sometimes audience members are not given a choice. Your classmates, for instance, are captive listeners who do not have the option of not hearing you, even if you disagree with them. But both captive and voluntary audiences can exercise a second level of control over potential communications. They are selective about whether or not to focus intently on a message, to follow it, absorb it, or take it seriously. These choices, sometimes made unconsciously, are called selective attention. Hearing a message does not guarantee we listen to it.

It takes effort and energy to listen carefully and critically to a speech. Listeners' minds tend to wander—to events of the day, people they want to see, things they need to do, problems they hope to solve. Making the effort to listen requires motivation, and the speaker can help supply that for the audience.

Student speaker Scott Poggi overlooked this opportunity when he decided to develop a speech based on his own special interests. On weekends Scott worked as a stagehand for a production company, and his speech demonstrated his expertise in the subject. He told his classmates all about the backstage area, introducing them to the light designer, the head light technician, and the light crew; mentioning the "FOH" (footlights and overheads), the electrics, and the cyclorama; telling them about the necessity of "testing and gelling the lights;" introducing them to the sound crew and their equipment; and finally describing the stage manager's many duties. By the time Scott finished, many in the audience were half asleep. Not only did he provide too much technical information without explaining it (classmates still had to ask, "What is an FOH, and how do you 'gel' a light?"); but he also never gave the audience any reason for wanting to know this information in the first place. Better audience analysis might have shown Scott that he would have to convert hearers to listeners.

The speaker can motivate the audience in at least three ways:

- Make the message personally important to listeners.
- Make the message stand out.
- Make the message easy to follow.

Perception

An audience is changed from hearers to listeners when they carefully interpret the speech as the speaker intends. **Perception** is the particular interpretation or understanding that a listener gets from a speech. When listeners decide what a speech "means," they are perceiving it in a particular way. Unfortunately, a speaker cannot ensure that the audience perceives the meaning of the speech in the same way that the speaker does. Individual ideas may be interpreted differently by speaker and audience.

Any message is open to different interpretations and can result in different perceptions. Clearly, speakers need to understand how most listeners perceive things. Review again material presented in Chapter 4, reviewing perception in depth.

Recall that perception, like attention, is selective; we interpret messages in ways that render them simple, stable, and consistent with our expectations. Complex or conflicting messages are simplified; qualifying statements and subtle distinctions may be lost. The following examples of how people perceive messages selectively are based on research, and they can help you plan your speech.

1. People tend to view their experiences as structured, stable, and meaningful rather than random, chaotic, or pointless. Seeking order, listeners are predisposed to accept any pattern the speaker can offer to explain seemingly unconnected facts.
2. People tend to view events not as accidental but as having causes; they also tend to simplify the web of causal connections and sometimes even seek a single cause to explain complex effects. Given that the brevity of a speech also leads to simplification, speakers must be careful to not allow listeners to oversimplify the relationships among events.
3. People tend to view individuals as being responsible for their own actions and to assume that actions reflect a person's intentions.
4. People tend to view others as being basically like themselves. When a speaker discusses personal experiences, listeners often assume the speaker thought and acted just as they would have in the same circumstances. If the audience is heterogeneous, the speaker can anticipate a spectrum of interpretations on issues that are not clearly presented.
5. People tend to interpret things in the way their reference groups do. The desire to fit in and to be accepted by important peers may cause some people to accept the group's perception as their own—without even being aware they are doing it.
6. People tend to perceive messages within the framework of familiar categories, even at the risk of distorting the message. For example, if someone believes Democrats generally favor government intervention in the economy and Republicans do not, the person is likely to perceive any pro-Democratic message as calling for government involvement in the economy.

Although the tendency of listeners to perceive selectively can distort the speaker's message, knowing about selective perception can help the speaker plan the speech so that it will be interpreted as desired. Selective exposure, attention, and perception are characteristic of almost all listeners. Whenever you plan a speech, design strategies to overcome these tendencies.

Strategies for Analyzing the Audience

Knowing that audience analysis is so important to your success as a speaker; how do you go about it? Various methods are available, ranging from the highly formal to the frankly speculative.

Formal Methods

Companies developing a new product typically engage in market research. They conduct surveys to learn the needs and desires of consumers (their "audience"); they ask the target group to select adjectives to describe a concept or product; they may convene small discussion groups (focus groups) to probe people's feelings about a product. In principle, methods like these are available to speakers, too, and such formal analysis often is used in large-scale efforts such as political campaigns. But for most speeches this approach is impractical. You will have neither the time nor the resources to conduct formal surveys or in-depth interviews of classmates in preparation for a speech. Instead, a general audience survey like the one in Figure 30.2 can be invaluable. Your instructor might ask the class to complete such a survey and then might make the results available to everyone.

Figure 30.2

Audience Survey

Age __________ Gender ______________ Year of Graduation __________

Home town ____

High School Attended: Public Private

Parents' occupation(s) ____

Taking course as: Requirement Elective

Politically, I would describe myself as:

strongly conservative	moderately conservative	middle of the road	moderately liberal	strongly liberal

In general, where do you fall along the following scale:

____

Prefer the familiar — Prefer the new

What three adjectives most accurately describe you?

____

What three adjectives would you most like to describe you?

____

I regard college primarily as a time for

____

What are the three most pressing problems confronting you in the next five years?

____

What are the three most pressing problems confronting the country or the world in the next five years?

____

[NOTE: The survey might well contain addtional questions.]

Table 30.1

How to Do Audience Analysis

1. FORMAL METHODS	3. SIMPLIFYING DEVICES
• Surveys	• Focus on the general public
• Focus Groups	• Focus on specific audience roles or topic fields
2. INFORMAL METHODS	**4. CRITICAL APPRAISAL**
• Prior knowledge of audience members	• What do you know? How reliable is the information?
• Interviewing The host or moderator People similar to the audience members Others who have spoken to similar audiences	• What gaps remain? How important is it to fill them?
• Reading materials that the audience probably reads	• Are you relying on stereotypes or jumping to conclusions?
• Library research about the audience	• Would the speech satisfy a universal audience?
• Direct observation of audience members	

Informal Methods

Even if you can't conduct a formal audience survey, you still can learn quite a bit about your listeners. Here are some ideas:

1. Think back to what classmates said about themselves in their introductory speeches. They may have given you clues about their interests, their political leanings, their attitudes toward higher education, their family backgrounds, and other key aspects of audience culture.
2. In preparing to speak to an unfamiliar audience, ask the host or moderator some questions ahead of time. You may be able to find out which topics most interest audience members, how previous speakers were accepted, how successful they were, and what topics were discussed. How attentive is the audience, and what are their motives for coming together to hear you?
3. If you know the demographic composition of your audience—its size, its average age, and the occupation of most members, interview people who represent this mix of variables. Although talking with just a few people is not a scientific sample, you may still get clues about the interests, beliefs, and values of the people who will be in your audience.
4. If you know other speakers who have addressed an audience like the one you

will face, talk with them ahead of time to learn what they encountered and what they think your audience will be like.

5. If you know which newspapers or magazines your listeners are likely to read, examine some recent copies before you speak. Besides getting a sense of what interests your listeners, you may locate allusions that will be especially meaningful to them.
6. Sometimes library research can help you analyze an audience. In Chapter 32 you will learn how to investigate your topic, and the same methods can help you investigate your audience. For example, you can find recent periodicals with surveys about the political attitudes of college students, or polls showing how older Americans feel about health care, or articles about how gender differences influence how people think or feel.
7. Don't overlook the most obvious method of audience analysis: direct observation. As your listeners assemble, size them up. About how many people are there? Are they all about the same age? What is the ratio of men to women? How are they dressed? Are they interacting or sitting apart? Do they seem enthusiastic? Such questions cannot give you perfect information about the audience, because they are superficial first impressions, but they often provide valuable insights that allow you to adapt your message appropriately and effectively.

Chapter 30: Analysis and Application Exercises

1. What is the difference between conducting audience analysis and engaging in stereotypes? Can you effectively construct a speech based upon audience demographics and psycho-graphics and not stereotype? Provide examples to support your view.
2. Is it possible to shift your original assessment of an audience? What cues might make you do that? Can it be done during your speech? If so, how? If not, why not?

References

1. Joshua Meyrowitz makes the argument that traditional social differences between gender and age groups have been eroded in postmodern culture by the backstage information provided through television. See *No Sense of Place: The Impact of Electronic Media on Social Behavior*, (Oxford England: Oxford University Press, 1985).
2. See E. D. Hirsch, Jr., *Cultural Literacy* (Boston: Houghton Mifflin, 1987) p 5.
3. Cultural differences may even influence expectations about the form and purpose of a speech. See Alessandro Duranti, "Oratory," *International Encyclopedia of Communications*, New York: Oxford Univ. Press, 1989, vol. 3, pp. 234-36.
4. To gather examples that include the concerns of different cultural groups, you might want to examine some speeches created by and directed toward those different cultural groups. One compilation of culturally diverse speeches is *American Public Discourse: A Multicultural Perspective*, ed. Ronald K. Burke, Lanham, Md.: University Press of America, 1992.
5. Michael Osborn has written about how language is often used to appeal to universal themes. See "The Evolution of the Archetypal Sea in Rhetoric and Poetic," *Quarterly Journal of Speech*, 63 (December 1977) 347-63.

CHAPTER 31 The Speaker

LEARNING OBJECTIVES

When students have completed this chapter and lesson they should be able to:

1. Understand the relationship between audience and speaker.
2. Define source credibility and explain its importance in public speaking.
3. Understand the importance of self confidence in public speaking.
4. List and describe the four dimensions of source credibility.
5. Introduce another speaker and enhance the speaker's credibility.

CHAPTER 31: Overview

Qualities of an effective speaker are reviewed. Emphasis is given to the speaker's credibility, knowledge, preparation, self-confidence, and appearance (both before and during the speech). Considerations are focused on grooming, posture, gestures, facial expression, and eye contact.

Winston Churchill

History will record that one man: Winston Churchill, was a major factor in preserving world democracy and unifying a free world from the terrors of Nazi Germany. History will long record him as one of the great leaders of the free world. But it was not so at the beginning. Always politically active, Churchill filled many governmental roles, but in 1924 was voted out of office. For ten years his voice and words were heard only as a writer and speaker. It was said of Churchill that if only one horse were in a race, Churchill could not pick the winner. Yet in the early days of 1940, with the Nazi threat of total domination of Europe progressing at an alarming rate, Churchill stepped forward to guide a nation and stand as a great voice for freedom. When asked to form a new government for King George VI of England, he quickly calmed a nation and seized the reigns of leadership. Burned in history are his famous words: "I have nothing to offer but blood, toil, tears, and sweat." He recorded in his journal that as he accepted this great role, he knew in his heart he would not fail.

Analyzing Your Own Ethos

As you begin preparation to become a public speaker, care and thought should be given to your "ethos" or reputation and attitude about approaching your audience. Elements such as age, education, and understanding of the speech environment should be considered. Are you older or younger than most of your listeners? Is your ethnic, cultural, or economic background different? Are your personal interests similar to theirs? Do you have different general orientations toward change? If listeners judge you to be very different from themselves, they maybe less likely to respond positively to your message. To establish a reputation with your audience is critical. Without the almost desperate faith the people of England had in Churchill, his effectiveness could have been compromised. His effective public speaking would not have had such dramatic results. Perhaps the world as we now know it may not have been the same.

Knowing what you do about yourself and having thought about the similarities and differences between you and your listeners, consider how audience members are likely to perceive you. Will they see you as knowledgable and competent or as arrogant and condescending? In the first case, you can expect listeners to welcome your efforts to share information and ideas; in the second case, expect them to resent your seeming to tell them what to do.

Critical self-assessment should point you to modifications that might improve your ethos. Sometimes minor changes will do the trick. Something as slight as different wording—"We all need to remind ourselves" rather than "I want to remind you," for instance—may help build a sense of community between you and your listeners rather than emphasizing your superiority and their dependence. Attention to this aspect of ethos is especially important when your audience is culturally diverse. What seems like a straightforward presentation to listeners from a single cultural background may be seen as patronizing to listeners whose backgrounds are different.

You also should think critically about your own beliefs and values. It is tempting to assume that your ideas are self-evidently correct and hence should be accepted by everyone. But that assumption may be wrong; if audience members question or reject your values, they may also question or reject your message. Although you may believe that everyone should appreciate the economic opportunities that our society provides, listeners who have recently lost their jobs, are struggling to make ends meet, or are victims of discrimination will probably see things very differently. If you take your personal values for granted in this situation, your speech will fail. The audience will judge you to be naive, if not misguided, and you will think them ungrateful or unmotivated.

Similarly, you may find that you and your audience have different role models, different common knowledge, and different life-shaping experiences. On each of these dimensions it is important to think critically about yourself and about how the audience is likely to perceive you. Then you can determine whether you want to make any adjustments in how you present yourself. As always, the goal is to remain true to yourself while taking the audience's characteristics into consideration.

Adjustments in these areas are not difficult to make, because the speaker controls much how an audience assesses ethos. After all, you can choose whether or not to establish eye contact, whether to smile or frown, whether to pause at the podium before returning to your seat, and so on. You decide which supporting materials to use, how to organize them, and matters such as word choice and gestures. All these aspects of presentation are under your control, and you can use them to influence how the audience judges you.

You want listeners' assessments of your ethos to be positive because you like to have others think well of you. Your concern goes back to the belief, first articulated by Aristotle, that a speaker's apparent character may well be the most important resource to use in persuasion. How listeners perceive your ethos will affect what they think about your speech.

Qualities of Effective Speakers

Audience interpretation of your ethos is based on their belief about three basic characteristics: 1. Are you an ethical or trustworthy person? 2. Are you knowledgeable and prepared about your topic? 3. Do you communicate self-confidence?

Ethics

Ethics, an individual's system of moral principles, plays a key role in communication. As speakers, we are responsible for what we tell others. We should always hold the highest ethical standards. We must communicate with honesty, sincerity, and integrity. In addition, a responsible, ethical speaker presents worthwhile and accurate information in a fair manner. David Zarefsky (1996) suggests that the ethical speaker respects the audience, topic, and occasion and takes responsibility for his or her statements.[1]

Ethical speakers do not distort or falsify evidence to misrepresent information, do not make unsupported attacks on opponents in order to discredit them, do not deceive an audience about their intention or objective in an attempt to persuade or take advantage, do not use irrelevant emotional appeals to sensationalize the message and divert attention from the facts, and do not pose as an authority when they are not.[2]

Ethical speakers always cite the sources of their information. Any time you use information and ideas that are not your own, you are obligated to cite the originator or source. The use of another person's information, language, or ideas without citing the originator or author, thus making it appear you are the originator, is referred to as **plagiarism**. For example, it is unethical to use statistical data, direct quotations, or any information that you did not originate without giving credit to the originator. Most speeches, unless otherwise specified, require that you as the speaker be the originator of the speech's content. Of course, it is perfectly legitimate to use a reasonable amount of information and ideas from others, as long as you give them credit and cite your sources.

Similarly, listeners also need to be responsible for determining the truth. As listeners we must be willing to verify the information we receive to ensure it is accurate and valid. Zarefsky states listeners should not refuse to consider the message nor reject the message because it differs from their own beliefs; neither should they blindly accept what the speaker says.[3]

Knowledge

Knowledge is a speaker's greatest asset. Knowing your subject is essential to "reach" your listeners. To enhance your understanding of events, people, and values, you must read and observe things around you. Speakers are to exhibit the role of "educated person" on their topic. Many colleges, universities, and businesses have identified the characteristics of an "educated person." As an educated person, you should not only know about past international, national, regional, and local events, but also keep abreast of current events. You should read all kinds of books, at least one trade (professional) magazine, and one daily newspaper, in addition to listening to news broadcasts and documentaries.

In Chapter 33, we provide suggestions for completing the research part of your speech preparation. It is important that you understand that knowledge is gained from research and analysis. Too often speakers believe they can "get away with" superficial information in their presentations. This is not the case! Any public speech presentation is an important project. If you want to establish your credibility as a knowledgeable person, you will gather far more information than you think is necessary to present in your speeches. What does that accomplish? More information provides you with a sound foundation for the presentation. Also, if your listeners ask questions, your solid knowledge base will allow you to answer most questions and thus come across as a credible speaker.

Preparation

People rarely make speeches without at least some preparation, and the most successful speakers are very well prepared. Imagine what went through the mind of Winston Churchill when he was asked to take over England's government. His personal journal reported confidence and not fear. Imagine Secretary of State Madeleine Albright and Defense Secretary William Cohen when they were delivering their "town hall speeches" in February 1998 on the need for U S military action against Iraq. At Ohio State University, the site of the event, Albright and Cohen were faced with hecklers who tried to disrupt the speeches. Each speaker, however, was able to maintain poise and confidence in the face of difficult circumstances. Why? Because they were carefully briefed on potential disruptions, were prepared for almost every eventuality, and had practiced carefully so they were very familiar with the content of the message.

A successful speech is somewhat like a successful business meeting or athletic event—all require planning, preparation, and work. Preparation means more than practicing the speech ahead of time. Preparation also means speakers will think through the situation and correct possible snags or problems.

For the beginner as well as the experienced speaker, preparation, practice, and knowledge of the fundamentals are important. Remember, however, you don't want to practice so much that your speech sounds memorized or "canned." Effective speakers should sound conversational, not mechanical. Too much practice can make you lose the spark of spontaneity and will reduce your effectiveness.

Self-confidence

Self-confidence, or the belief in oneself, is essential to becoming an effective speaker. Imagine Churchill forecasting his success as he wrote "I *knew* I would not fail!" Much of this book's content is aimed at helping you create this belief in yourself. You may wish to look back at the information in Chapter 3 to make the connections between self-image, self-concept, self-confidence, and a variety of communication situations. Because self-confidence is so strongly influenced by anxiety, we discussed this problem in detail in Chapter 28.

A good speech depends on good delivery and good delivery almost always depends on practice. After organizing and writing a speech, present the speech out loud in an informal setting to a friend, making changes, if necessary, to make the speech more effective.

Physical Appearance

Even before you begin to speak, audience members are forming impressions about the sort of person you are. This happens quickly and on the basis of superficial judgments, but those judgments are durable. Consequently, you want to avoid doing anything that will make you seem unprepared, incompetent, or unreliable.

***Before you speak* consider the physical arrangement of the speaking space.** Decide such things as how to approach the podium and what to wear. Is the setting large and impersonal or small and intimate? How formal or informal is the setting (and occasion)? Will you be able to establish eye contact with listeners, or will you be far away from them, speaking with a microphone? Will there be problem areas where people cannot hear or see? Are there distraction areas where other events will distract either you or the audience?

Your appearance to an audience at an outdoor rally will be far different from how you appear to the same audience in a cathedral. Similarly, the settings for a retirement banquet, a business meeting, a commencement address, and a medical lecture are all different and can influence how the audience perceives you. Whenever possible, you should examine the speaking space and practice in it before presenting your speech.

Approaching the Podium. Your physical appearance begins to create impressions as you walk to the podium. If you start speaking while you walk, before facing the audience, you may seem in a hurry to finish and so unsure of yourself that you won't look the audience in the eye. Likewise, if you shuffle uncertainly toward the podium, the audience may think you lack confidence and don't know what you are talking about. Such assumptions may be wrong, but they affect your ethos and create a "credibility deficit" that you'll have to overcome.

No matter how you feel about speaking, create the best first-impression you can. Walk firmly and purposefully to the podium, pause to collect your thoughts, look directly at the audience, and then begin with confidence. Your body acts as a visual aid for the speech—the audience will be looking at you. Try to make your body's message match and reinforce the message of your words.

Clothes and Grooming. What you wear and your personal appearance—everything from hairstyle to footwear—are the stuff of first impressions and will affect your ethos. A badly dressed, unkempt speaker easily becomes the focus of attention and distracts the audience from the message. If you constantly push hair out of your face, wear a baseball cap that makes eye contact impossible, or fiddle with keys or jewelry, you practically beg the audience to focus on distractions rather than the speech.

Typically, speakers dress more formally than audience members do.[4] The general public may attend a speech in sports attire, but the speaker is a major figure and is expected to look the part. In recent years this unwritten "dress code" has relaxed considerably. President Jimmy Carter made a point of appearing in shirtsleeves without a tie, and President Bill Clinton's jeans and running clothes became part of his image. Yet both men were well advised to wear suits and ties when addressing the public—when they wanted to project a serious image. Spiro Agnew, vice president to Richard Nixon, was so concerned about the clothing he wore in public that he made a point of never crossing his legs when he sat because it might wrinkle the crease in his pants. The famous slogan "Clothes make the Man" holds true for all speakers, including women!

Movement

How and where you position your body while speaking can also enhance or distract from the message. When student speaker Rachel Samuels stood behind the large, heavy podium in her classroom, only her head was visible. Recognizing the problem, Rachel stepped away from the podium to present her speech.

Even if the height of the podium does not hide your appearance, it's a good idea to step away from it occasionally. Many beginning speakers grip the podium as though tensely steering a car that is out of control. This may give a sense of security, or hide shaking knees, but it also puts a barrier between you and the audience. Instead, if you loosen your grip and step away from the podium at points in the speech, your body language will provide visual cues. For example, you can signal transitions in the speech by moving a step or two forward or to the side. By moving toward the audience, you can show your trust and break down any imaginary walls between you and listeners.

The 1992 presidential debates between Bill Clinton, George Bush, and Ross Perot included one format that resembled a town meeting in which citizens in the audience asked questions. At one point, when Bill Clinton was asked how the federal budget deficit had affected him personally, he did not respond right away. First he took a few steps toward the questioner and established eye contact. Although he was actually speaking to a television audience of millions, Mr. Clinton seemed to be responding to this citizen one on one. The unstated message was that speaker and audience had a common bond. Because Mr. Clinton had to face the cameras to answer his questioner, television viewers felt he was responding directly to them—and had a bond with them.

Although purposeful, planned movement will benefit your presentation, constant or aimless movement will be a great distraction. A speaker who moves all around the room for no apparent reason puts a burden on listeners; it's up to them to follow the movements and maintain eye contact. Many will simply stop trying—and stop listening as well. Speakers also should avoid shifting their weight from side to side. Like vocalized pauses, this nervous response calls negative attention to itself.

Just as you should not begin speaking until you have reached the podium and sized up the audience, so should you not gather up notes and start returning to your seat while you are still speaking. The audience will not have a chance to absorb your final thoughts, and your conclusion will be weakened. You also will give the impression that speaking to them was painful and that you want to finish as soon as possible. Take your time, and take control over the situation. When you do return to your seat, walk confidently without calling attention to yourself.

Gesture

The term "gesture" refers to the movement of hands and arms during the speech as a means of emphasis. Many speakers are especially self-conscious about their hands and what to do with them while they speak. Some put their hands into their pockets—not to create an informal, conversational tone but just to get them out of the way. These speakers usually seem tense, as though they are tightly clenching something buried deep in their pocket. Other untrained speakers fidget, moving their hands and arms aimlessly as a nervous reaction. Since such movements are not coordinated with the speech, they call attention to themselves and detract from the message.

Some speakers use gesture as a crutch. Perhaps it is a pencil gripped in your hand, or an up-lifted finger of emphasis raised, but some speakers cannot speak without such gestures. These "starting" mechanisms become habits, and can distract from both speaker and message. One student in a speech class memorized his speech and imagined it was written on a piece of paper taped to the back wall. As he stood before the class and spoke, he read his speech above everyone's head. Some audience members even attempted to catch his attention without success. Laughter erupted and obviously the message was lost.

In contrast, a well-timed, purposeful gesture heightens the power of both your text and your voice. But what is such a gesture like? Centuries ago, theorists of public speaking believed that certain gestures went naturally with particular words or ideas. They wrote manuals illustrating hundreds of gestures and their matching words. Speakers learned the gestures by rote and performed them automatically when reciting the matching text.[5] Today this approach is considered nonsense; such a presentation is so artificial and contrived it becomes a comedy performance.

Not all speakers are naturally expressive with their hands. Whether you use many or few gestures does not matter; what matters is that your gestures support your message, not draw attention away from it. If you videotaped yourself in informal conversation, you probably would discover gestures you are unaware of—they simply come out naturally when you talk. A few possible uses of gestures are to emphasize the importance of a point, to suggest balance or opposition ("on the one hand," "on the other hand"), and to position ideas in space and time.[6]

Above all, gestures used in presentation should appear natural. Achieving this is less a matter of memorizing gestures than of becoming familiar with the general rhythm of gesture. It begins with an anticipation step, which simply means that you bring your hands to a position from which a gesture can easily be made. If you are gripping the podium or handling several pages of notes, gesturing will be difficult and awkward. First you need to be in a position that lets you execute a gesture naturally.

Being ready to gesture, you next move to the implementation step—the few seconds in which you execute the movement as you intended. Typically, a speaker's gestures occur somewhere between the waist and shoulders, an area that eases natural movement and is also visible to audience members. Untrained speakers often make a half-gesture, raising a hand partway without completing the movement. Such a gesture has little purpose or effect, suggesting instead that the speaker is nervous.

Having implemented the gesture, during the relaxation step you return your hands to their normal position, whether at your side, in front of you, or resting on the podium. Without this step you risk being trapped in continuous gesture. Since your hands are in the visual space where gestures take place, and you haven't returned them to rest, you may find yourself gesturing repeatedly and in the same way for every word or idea. That, of course, dilutes the power of the gesture when you really do want to emphasize something. It can again take on the characteristics of a comedy routine, and distracts from the message entirely.

Finally, don't worry too much about gestures. Although "what to do with my hands" is a concern for many speakers, the issue is relatively unimportant. Gestures tend to take care of themselves as long as you avoid distracting mannerisms, practice the three steps of gesture, and concentrate on your message.

Facial Expression

The speaker's facial expressions are another powerful element of nonverbal communication that heightens or detracts from the speech. Obviously, a smiling speaker communicates something much different from a frowning one. But someone who smiles and grins throughout the presentation will seem out of place and hence not believable, as will a speaker who delivers a lighthearted message but shows no facial expression at all. Again, it is valuable either to videotape your speech or to have someone observe you practicing it. Discover whether your facial expressions are consistent with and support the message in your text.

Eye Contact. Eye contact deserves special attention. Speakers who do not look the audience in the eye may lose credibility. In mainstream American culture, not looking at someone is widely thought to mean the person is lying or has something to hide. In fact, speakers from cultures with different norms about eye contact may be misunderstood and misjudged by an American audience.

Another important point is that eye contact lets you see how the audience is responding to the speech; it provides feedback. Listeners' facial expressions often indicate whether the message is clear or needs explanation, whether claims seem persuasive or not, and so on. Feedback helps you adjust your presentation to fit the audience while you speak. But if you stare at your notes or gaze at the back wall, you cannot make eye contact and take advantage of feedback.

Chapter 31: Analysis and Application Exercises

1. Which one of the first three speakers in the video lesson was most credible to you? Why? What verbal or non-verbal aspects of their speaking affected their credibility?
2. Choose a topic and list three things you could do to signal your competence on that topic. Be as specific as possible.

References

1. D. Zarefsky, *Public Speaking Strategies for Success Boston*: Allyn & Bacon, 1996), 25.
2. J. Wenburg & W.W. Wilmot, *The Personal Communication Process* (New York: Wiley, 1973); R.L. Johannesen, *Ethics in Human Communication*, 2nd ed. (Prospects Heights, Ill.: Waveland Press, 1983).
3. Zarefsky, op. cit.
4. Studies have shown that a speaker's attractiveness has an influence on the persuasiveness of the message. Attractiveness can be achieved at least partly through clothing and grooming. See Shelly Chaiken, "Physical Appearance and

Social Influence," *Physical Appearance, Stigma, and Social Behavior: The Ontario Symposium*, Vol. 3, ed. C. Peter Herman, Mark P. Zanna, and E. Tory Higgins (Hillsdale, NJ.: Lawrence Erlbaum, 1986), pp. 143-177.

5. For examples of this, see John Bulwer, Chirologia: Or the *Natural Language of the Hand*; and *Chironomia: Or the Art of Manual Rhetoric*, first published 1644, ed. James W. Cleary (Carbondale: Southern Illinois Univ. Press, 1974); and Gilbert Austin, Chironomia: Or, *A Treatise on Rhetorical Delivery*, first published 1806, ed. Mary Margaret Robb and Lester Thonssen (Carbondale: Southern Illinois Univ. Press, 1966).
6. For more discussion of gestures in informal conversation and in speeches, see P. E. Bull, *Posture and Gesture* (New York: Pergamon Press, 1987), especially Chapter 10: "The Use of Hand Gesture in Political Speeches: Some Case Studies."

CHAPTER 32

Selecting a Speech Topic

LEARNING OBJECTIVES

When students have completed this chapter and lesson, they should be able to:

1. Select a topic from their personal interests.
2. Identify, describe, and be able to use the five methods of topic discovery.
3. Describe and utilize the characteristics of a good topic.
4. Discuss and utilize the standards of appropriateness in topic selection.
5. Define and be able to develop a thesis statement for a speech.

CHAPTER 32: Overview

A detailed discussion of the rhetorical situation can help novice speakers select a topic appropriate to their personal interests; make that topic acceptable to the given audience for the proper occasion; and develop a framework for an appropriate speech.

The speaker rose from his seat and proceeded to the podium. There was a long pause, then a few mumbling sounds that suggested the ignition of a 1950 Ford pickup. Ten seconds of silence was then followed with another attempt at saying something intelligent, concluded by the bold statement that could be the introduction of most beginning speakers: "I do not have a thing to say!"

From the novice to the seasoned speaker, discovering a topic is often the most difficult step in speech preparation. Not only are you as a speaker asked to select something that would appeal to many individuals grouped together as an audience, you have to select something that interests you, the speaker. But interest is not enough. You must also satisfy your critics, which could easily be someone like a teacher who will judge your attempts and give you a grade. This all leads to your success, not only as a speaker, but also as a person in a world that demands speakers with exciting and influential speeches.

Sometimes the *occasion* can assist in selecting your topic. If the audience is gathered to celebrate a given holiday, themes are generally required. If you are accepting an award, the award and what it represents dictate the topic. If the speech is a eulogy, the life and character of the deceased will dictate the topic. If you are roasting a coworker who is about to retire, your material will be humorous. Perhaps the occasion is a religious setting, again giving a limited number of topic choices, and perhaps even dictating subject matter.

Sometimes the classroom speaking assignment will dictate the topic. More typically, the topic choice will be left up to you, with the understanding that you will address your classmates. In this situation, your best choice is selecting something that draws your interest. In the classroom it is particularly important you assess the situation and then stand up for what you believe and can share with others. In the real world, when you are asked to speak without having an assigned topic, the answer is the same: the audience is interested in *you, your achievements, and your ideas*. That is why you are asked to speak.

This immediately means your first step in topic selection is to consider your personal interests. What are you interested in? What kinds of programs do you watch on television? What do you learn from the Internet? When you have nothing to do, what do you do? If you walk into a library, not knowing what book you want, where do you start? What magazines do you select from the bookshelf? When you are waiting in an office for an appointment, what do you select from the reading material before you?

If you find yourself with an entire evening with nothing to do, what would you do? Where would you go? What kinds of activities would you choose for yourself? If you could go on a vacation to anyplace in the world, where would you go? If you had your choice of recreation, what would you select?

The above questions are part of a process called *brainstorming*. The process taxes your limits on what interests and motivates you. Begin thinking of questions and write the answers. Make a list of everything, even items you think would be nonsensical. When asked what he likes best to do, one student laughingly remarked: "Sleep!" Upon examining that area a bit, the student realized many people cannot sleep for many reasons. Loss of sleep produces many psychological and physical problems. Insomnia is one of the greatest causes of depression, and perhaps even suicide. Suddenly many topics fruitful for a good speech were discovered.

To expand on the concept of brainstorming, write down subjects as they come to you. Then go back and write down five topics that are associated with each idea. Very quickly you will generate many potential avenues of interest that can be developed.

Classical rhetoricians discovered that the mind followed certain habits productive to creative thinking. Using categories that contained topics with similar traits, and contrasting them with other descriptive labels, students could generate more creative ideas, and discover new approaches to common ideas. These paths were called *topoi*. Osborne, Osborne and Osborne describe the process as it leads to developing speech topics. By using such pathways to discovering topics for exploration, we increase our ability to link objects with activity. This leads the creative mind to relate such concepts of value with time spent, or events with such things as entertainment or even physical fitness. The end product can appear in the form of questions that guide the mind–directly leading to speech topics or even theme statements[1]:

1. What *places* are interesting?
2. What *people* do you find fascinating?
3. What *activities* do you enjoy?
4. What *things* do you find to do?
5. What *events* do you visit?
6. Which *ideas* intrigue you?
7. What *values* are important to you?
8. What *problems* concern you most?
9. What *local concerns* do you have?
10. What *political issues* move you to action?

Once you have discovered categories that stimulate you, list specific items, events, or places that fit such a category. Once the categories have referents, you then attach feelings, events, descriptions, statistics or even stories about the category. Read about what others have written. Soon you will have more material than can be covered in a single speech. From this point your task becomes one of defining, refining, and placing in proper language ideas that motivate not only you but others.

Understanding the Rhetorical Situation

Whether your topic is determined by the occasion, assigned by your host, or selected by you, topic selection is influenced by the speech event. Each event becomes a new experience. No two speeches are exactly the same, because speaking situations are not identical. As a consequence, you as a speaker adapt to even insignificant changes in the situation to present a remarkably unique product. As elements in the situation change, you as a speaker adapt your message to the audience by devising a strategy, or plan of action that will respond to the constraints and desires of the audience.

For example, when the Space Shuttle *Challenger* exploded in 1986, the world watched the tragedy unfold. Children watched a beloved school teacher who wanted to explore space suddenly killed before their eyes. Taxpayers wondered whether the space program was worth their tax dollars. Others were concerned whether space science was worth the risk. Still others believed that the vaunted American technology had failed. The nation suddenly needed reassurance, and that was provided in a speech by President Ronald Reagan.

Certainly the event dictated the rhetorical situation. Americans needed consolation. The occasion was one of collective grief, uncertainty, and doubt. The speaker was the President known as "The Great Communicator."

As it happened, the night of the tragedy President Reagan had scheduled his annual State of the Union Address. Instead he chose to deliver a eulogy prepared by White House speech writer Peggy Noonan. The events clearly dictated that honoring the *Challenger* crew was more important than the state of the union: "They, the *Challenger* seven, were aware of the dangers–and overcame them, and did their jobs brilliantly. We mourn seven heros." At the same time the speech was designed to turn the audience away from sorrow and toward a new commitment to the space program: "The Challenger crew was pulling us into the future–and we'll continue to follow them." By comparing the astronauts to Sir Francis Drake, an early explorer of the North American continent, the speech transformed the senseless tragedy into a heroic action to open a new frontier. The speech succeeded in redirecting the audience's emotions; it provided a transformation from mourning to renewed dedication. Careful evaluation of the situation allowed President Reagan and Ms. Noonan to plan an effective strategy.

In preparing a speech, the rhetorical situation is influenced by audience values and emotions. These are constraints directing your task. At the same time, you have the opportunity to modify listener's beliefs and values by what you say. By understanding the constraints and opportunities in a rhetorical situation, the speaker's desires can be achieved and audience expectations can be fulfilled. The key elements are the audience, the occasion, the speaker, and the speech itself.

The Audience

A public speech is a unique event combining the skills of the speaker with the listening skills of the audience. This is why audience analysis, discussed previously, is so important. The audience provides the rhetorical environment suggesting what materials should be presented, what level of knowledge to assume, how to organize the materials, and what the specific purpose of the speaker should be.

The successful speaker attempts to identify with the audience by trying to find common ground between what they know about the audience and what they want to say.[2] Without distorting the message, the speaker attempts to emphasize ideas that are most likely to strike a responsive chord with the listeners. A classic example is Martin Luther King's "I have A Dream," speech that attempted to influence both white and black listeners with a common American dream of judging acceptance on integrity instead of skin color.

It seems rather obvious, but the make-up of the audience is critical in selecting topic area. How successful do you think a speaker would be presenting the vital statistics of milk production of a Holstein cow to a group of New York Life Insurance Executives? How about a speech persuading a group of transient farm workers on the advantages of owning a Rolls Royce automobile?

The speaker must show relevance of the topic to the listeners, or as discovered in the discussion on listening, no one will pay attention to the subject. Relevance must include not only topic area, it must prove worthy of the listener's time. If the topic is frivolous or trivial, they may feel they have wasted their time. Unless there is something unique about the approach, a topic such as "How to Open a Beer Can," or "How to Change a Disposable Diaper on the Baby," has little to offer. Light-hearted humor or new insights on familiar subjects can work well in a speech, but the the audience must believe their time is not wasted.

The Occasion

Some speech occasions are ceremonies, such as presenting or receiving awards, or introducing a guest speaker. The occasion could be a funeral requiring a eulogy, or the dedication of a historical location. Here the topic selection and even the potential supporting material are limited. The match between the event and the presentation can be critical in evaluating the successful speech.

The classic example a successful **ceremonial speech** was given by Abraham Lincoln at the dedication of the national cemetery at Gettysburg. The famous orator Edward Everett delivered a two hour discourse to over fifteen thousand people gathered for the occasion. Almost as an afterthought, President Lincoln was asked to give a few remarks. In two minutes his remarks about the sacrifices of the Civil War for a new birth of freedom became a major statement of American democracy[3]

Deliberative speeches describe company policy, financial circumstances, or proposed company changes that are soon to come. These become planning masterpieces, providing the speaker with the opportunity of providing motivation, dedication, and commitment to the cause. The occasion is also ceremonial because the manager's presence demonstrates a personal interest in workers' well-being and because the speech provides reassurance and motivates workers to do their best. Audience motivation is a critical.

A third category of speech occasion, traditionally known as **forensic speeches** is concerned with rendering judgments about events or policy. Although this is the dominant form of speaking in legal situations or debate forums, it is generally not considered public speaking. The rhetoric includes the major elements of communication, including forms of support, evidence, and even significant oral delivery. Again, the topics and facilitation for exchange of information are determined by the occasion.

The occasion has a specific impact on topic selection, preparation, and presentation. Each different occasion raises certain expectations about what subject matter is appropriate, and can even suggest subject matter and type of delivery.

The Speaker

As noted at the beginning of this chapter, the speaker becomes the first source and the major factor in determining the topic of the speech. Without complete dedication and interest in the subject, even the best speaker will be found wanting. The same speech delivered by different speakers can produce quite different reactions and effects. The speaker's interest in the subject—as made evident through voice, delivery, and the vividness of imagery—helps determine audience reaction. Speaker commitment affects listener comprehension by developing a positive ethos and an impact upon audience reaction.

As the speaker presents the material, he or she also develops skills, gains experience, and receives audience feedback. This directly impacts comfort level of both speaker and audience, resulting in more success and satisfaction of both speaker and listener. Such learning directly impacts selection of speech topics for future events.

The Speech

Although we tend to think of the rhetorical situation as predating the speech, the message itself works to shape the situation. If the topic is frivolous or trivial, it becomes extremely difficult to please an audience. Unless there is something unique about the approach, a topic such as "How to Open a Beer Can," or "How to Change the Baby's Disposable Diaper,"or "How to Use a Toilet Plunger," leaves something to be desired. This does not mean the topic must be profound or deadly serious; light hearted humor or new insights on familiar subjects can work very well in a speech. The question to keep in mind is whether the audience will believe what you have to say is worth their time.

A speaker can go to the opposite extreme also. The topic must not only please the audience, but should develop ideas to an appropriate degree within the time available. Even though U.S. Foreign Policy may be an excellent topic area, the depth and explanation of materials are unattainable in five minutes. Likewise, no matter how bright the student, or expressive the verbiage, one cannot do justice to the events leading up to the Civil War in five minutes.

Selecting an appropriate speech topic is like pouring sand through a funnel. What goes into the large end is too much to manage, but what comes out the small end can be focused effectively.

References

1. M. Osborne, S. Osborne, and R. Osborne: *Public Speaking*, 8th Ed.(New York: Allyn & Bacon) 2009, ppp. 125.
2. C.R. Smith and P. Prince, "Language Choice Expectation and the Roman Notion of Style." *Communication Education*, 39(January, 1990), 63-74.
3. H. Peterson, *A Treasury of the World's Great Speeches* (New York: Simon & Schuster,1954), 519-522.

CHAPTER 33

Finding Information

LEARNING OBJECTIVES

When students have completed this chapter and lesson they should be able to:

1. Explain the role of personal experience in providing information for a speech.
2. List the reasons why a library should be consicered a primary source for information.
3. Identify five types of resources not available electronically.
4. Define, explain, and demonstrate the appropriate use of oral footnotes.

CHAPTER 33: Overview

Supporting material will be classified into categories of experience, common knowledge, observation, examples, documents, and statistics. Advice is given for utilizing supporting materials from published works. Advice will be given about utilizing electronic information sources from the Internet.

Chapter 32 introduced the novice speaker to the idea that selecting a topic was a dramatic adventure that could lead to an infinite number of interesting subjects with a multitude of potential conclusions. When looking for materials to support the topic, the job becomes almost overwhelming. A quick check of the Internet suggested 83.4 million references to the word "terrorism" alone. The electronic age has literally exploded the concept of the term "Knowledge is Power!"

The process of finding supporting material for your speech requires a combination of **research** and **analysis**. Obviously, the supply of materials is limitless, and without some direction, your investigation would be frustrating. Take for example the use of Internet sources. If your topic is "water," there are only 764 million references to that topic. It helps little to suggest "water polution." Your sources are now reduced to a meer 36,000!

Whether your research precedes or follows your analysis, you will want to accomplish three basic goals:

- To develop or strengthen your personal knowledge on the topic.
- To find information supporting your ideas.
- To help formulate ideas that are clear, understandable, and pertinent to your listeners.

These objectives may demand several kinds of information before you feel comfortable expressing your ideas to others. This suggests using what is referred to as supporting material discussing your topic.

To research materials for your speech, you first must decide which types of supporting material you need. The following seven types illustrate the array of possibilities:

Types of Supporting Material

- Personal experience
- Common knowledge
- Direct observation

- Examples
- Documents
- Statistics
- Testimony

Personal Experience

The first and original source of information is your own experience. If something you wish to discuss has happened to you, you are the best person to talk about it. The concern you must have is that your experiences must directly relate to your subject material. Be sure the details, wording and numbers you relate are accurate and descriptive. Include enough specific detail to clearly report your emotions, feelings, and memories graphically. Attempt to have the audience relive the actual experience with you in a way they can share in the experience.

For example, one speaker described his experience of having a heart attack. Notice how the selection of words and detail almost project the experience to the listeners:

The first indication I had was a question: If I had a heart attack, would I feel any different than I do now? Would I feel light headed? I seemed to be looking down a white, blurry tunnel. Pain seemed like an invisible cloud that totally surrounded and strangled me, but for some reason did not hurt. My arms and legs would not work properly any more. I did not remember laying down, but suddenly I was looking up at the sky and it felt like someone was standing on my chest. People were crowding around me, breathing up all the air and I could not get any. Everyone was talking and trying to get my attention, but they were addressing my body, which seemed to be laying on the ground a short distance away from me. The dizziness made my head hurt so I decided to go away. It was like a fade out on the TV, and suddenly everything was dark.

With the use of proper language and tied to personal experience, the description establishes a credibility of its own.

Common Knowledge

An often-overlooked type of supporting material is **common knowledge,** the understandings, beliefs, and values that members of society or culture generally share, sometimes referred to as "common sense." Others refer to it as "social knowledge," assuming that we know these things to be true on the basis of broad social consensus.[1]

Common knowledge is often expressed in the form of *maxims,* like "Work expands to fill the time available for its completion," "You can't trust the people who made the mess to clean it up," "Nature abhors a vacuum," or "If you want something done right, do it yourself." These are *generally held beliefs* that are generally accepted by society. Common knowledge also is expressed in *value judgments,* such as the importance of protecting the environment, having the right to privacy, and a preference for practical solutions over ideological disputes.

Common knowledge is not always correct, of course; people certainly can believe things that "ain't so." But common knowledge has the status of **presumption**–we are correct until we are proven wrong. Because this knowledge is "common" and widely believed, it can be useful as supporting material.

Direct Observation

Direct observation and personal experience are very valuable in gathering supporting material. Philosophers for centuries have held to the belief that personal observation and experience are the only valid tests for what we each consider truth. Simple, direct observation is the heart and base of the scientific method. If you wish to know how college students spend their evening hours, watch where they go. If you want to know how skilled the football team is, watch their games. If you want to know how careful and law-abiding auto drivers are, stand at a busy intersection for an hour and observe. Nothing can make you an authority any faster than to be an eye-witness.

Examples

When you use an example, you make a general statement more meaningful by illustrating a specific instance of it. Examples are samples of reality. This kind of support for a claim strengthens the statement you are communicating by providing a slice of reality where it actually happened. Here are some examples of example!

Brief example: Your claim is that the United Nations does not adequately reflect the current balance of power in the world. You cite as countries that contribute significantly to the world economy, Germany and India, both current leaders in economic power. Neither have permanent or even temporary seats on the Security Council.

Hypothetical Example: Ask your listeners to imagine themselves in a particular situation. Have them assume that they constantly spend more money than they make. What would their ultimate fate be? Bankruptcy? Poverty? Hunger? Losing their home or car? You could then use this example to understand the quandary Congress faces as they create the federal budget.

Anecdote: A short story that can develop details and analogies to your point. You could describe the maze of telephone inquiries and form letter replies and your trek to the seat of power to solve a personal problem. You are constantly given the wrong office, direction, or help. Finally reaching the appropriate official, you are patronized by a clerk who says, "According to our records, you are dead."

Case Study: You can support a general claim by supplying one true case and discussing it in detail. If your topic were about whether or not campus codes to regulate offensive speech can be effective, you might describe one or two campuses that have tried this approach and then argue that their experiences illustrate whether such codes are workable in general. If you believe that making Election Day a national holiday would increase voter turnout, you might support your claim by drawing on cases of nations where Election Day is a holiday.

Note: Examples work by relating a part of something to the whole. You are implying that if one or two examples describe reality, then whatever is being discussed will have the same results. Keep in mind the strength of your claim is an inference based on limited examples.

Documents

Documents are used as a source of evidence and supporting material to establish the claim and verify the inference advocated. Documents can become definitive rules or guidelines accepted by society and final evidence that certain behaviors are approved. The Declaration of Independence is often quoted to support the belief that there are natural rights. For many people the Bible is the document most often quoted.

Handbooks, club constitutions, or bylaws of your club or organization can be considered the final say in policy and governance of the organization. By consensus of the members, what is written in its organizational paperwork is considered the final truth about governance and procedure. Members have agreed to abide by its content; therefore that becomes the final word of truth about the said organization.

Statistics

Supporting material presented in quantitative form, as statistics, is very useful when items of interest can be counted, added, or averaged. Numbers are excellent symbols of communication when any type of quantitative explanation is necessary. It should be made very clear, however, that numbers themselves carry no meaning. Only when numbers represent some tangible item do they convey meaning. Their key to communication rests in their ability to describe.

Statistics are numbers recording the extent of something or the frequency with which something occurs; they take such forms as medians, averages, ratios, indices, and standardized scores. Numbers become meaningful when they are compared with some base line or other groups to permit an inference about the relationship based on size, accumulation of numbers, or comparisons of items. For example, you might support a claim by comparing the median family income for different professions or different ethnic groups or different nations. Whenever statistics are used, it should be remembered that they provide a means of comparing groups of items with a standardized comparison. The following three types of analysis illustrate the point:

Surveys and Polls. People are questioned about physical and social issues and placed in categories. Whenever one category surpasses another in an agreed number of items measured, conclusions or inferences of description and comparison are considered valid. Political races are predicted, or even diet preferences are ranked to show what "the majority" would do. Individuals can then relate, either favorably, or unfavorably, with their individual preferences.

Rates of Change. Statistics not only count numbers in groups, but can also project percentage of change. For instance, it may be more important to know that the national debt doubled during the 1980's than to know the total dollar amount. Knowing that medical costs have increased at a much faster rate than has personal income may be more useful than knowing either of the exact amounts. Knowing how fast the population is increasing may be significantly more important than knowing the final total. Rate of change shows what is happening and can help an audience compare the situation to some known benchmark. By themselves, however, statistics may not tell much and can be misleading. Numbers themselves carry no meaning; interpretation of what numbers say by others is critical.[2]

Experiments. Experiments are controlled tests of the effect of one thing on another. They are conducted by comparing situations that are essentially similar except for the factor being tested. For instance, the claim that African-American drivers are stopped by police officers in a particular neighborhood more often than are Caucasian drivers could be tested by sending the same model car through the same neighborhood at the same time of day at the same speed with drivers who differ only in the color of their skin.

Testimony

Testimony is information or a statement expressed by someone other than the speaker. When using testimony, you rely on another person's judgment and statement to support your claim. To strengthen the quotation and build credibility for the speech, you need to describe that person's competence. By giving the person's credentials to the audience before quoting the statement, you convince the audience that your source is knowledgeable and trustworthy.

Factual testimony are pieces of information proven either true or false. Data attributed to others implies that you cannot verify the information yourself, but are willing to accept it because the source is credible.

Opinion Testimony is formed from experience and judgment. When you offer another person's opinion to support a claim, you are indicating that you accept another person's witness to a fact, and they are in a better position than you to make a valued judgment of opinion. You are asking the audience to accept their conclusion because of the person's expertise, judgment, or knowledge, not because you can verify the statement. Make sure the audience accepts the credibility of your chosen authority. You may have to report their credentials before quoting their opinion to show what they say is valuable.

Before including supporting material in your presentation, be sure the information is accurate, within context, and representative of the source cited. The following chart assists you in judging the value of your supporting materials:

Checklist

Testing the Strength of Supporting Material

1. **Personal Experience** *Are you sure your memory is reliable?*
   Is your experience generalizable?
   Will others interpret it the same way?
2. **Common knowledge** *Are you sure the audience shares it?*
   Are you sure it is correct?
3. **Direct observation** *Are you sure of what you saw?*
   Might you have any bias?
4. **Examples** *Are they representative?*
   Are there enough of them?
5. **Documents** Can they be trusted?
   Are they properly interpreted?
   Is the context made clear?
6. **Statistics** *Are appropriate measures used?*
   Are they reliable and valid?
   Have they been interpreted properly?
7. **Testimony** *Does the person have access to the data?*
   Is the person expert on the subject?
   Is the person reasonably objective?

Finding Supporting Material in Print

The search for supporting materials is usually not complete without consulting a library. Even with the advent of the electronic age, print material is still reliable, valid support for your claims. If your topic is of public significance, you will want material of broader scope than your personal experience or even what confidants have passed on. The library is the best source of printed material, and often audiovisual material as well. Library research will prove to be a treasure of valuable information. Consider the following guides for developing reliable supporting materials.

Books

Books fall into many categories and are all classified by a systematic method of numbers and letters to locate them by topic, author, and name.

Reference Works

Reference works are a special category of printed sources. They are not intended to be read from cover to cover; they do not develop a sustained argument or claim; and they usually are not written in narrative. They are convenient collections of facts and information. These collections are shelved in a special section of the library, where a reference librarian can help you find and use several types of collections.

Dictionaries not only tell you how to spell a word and give its definition, but also trace its origin and usage. There are specialized dictionaries that identify terms and usage within particular fields. Extensions of this work include words that are synonyms, anonyms, and foreign words.

Encyclopedias are still found in most libraries. But with the advent of the electronic information age, most references are found either in electronic databases, or online. Specialized encyclopedias focus on particular subjects, (such as *The Encyclopedia of Philosophy* and the *International Encyclopedia of Communications.)* Encyclopedias contain brief essays that will give you an overview of a subject. Information is generally summary and "in-depth" materials can be found other places. It should be noted that this reference material is rapidly becoming dated by the Internet because of the time delay between discovery and printing of information. References such as *Wikipedia* and *Encarta* provide a rapid, inexpensive database that has challenged the general reference books of yesteryear, but libraries still carry many of the print varieties.

Abstracts are short summaries of articles or books related to a particular discipline. Many academic and professional groups publish abstracts of the articles appearing in their current journals. By reading abstracts instead of entire journals, you can discover which articles include material that may be useful. Like encyclopedias, the internet provides many links to the abstracts of most periodic publications through reference sites such as EBSCOhost. Many other reference sites will site journal abstracts on specialized sites listed by subject title and topic. Such references can save research time by allowing you to preview published periodicals instead of reading entire articles.

Fact books are compilations of statistical information you can consult when you need specific data to support a point in your speech. Almanacs, World Records, and Fact Books on specific agencies such as the CIA can also be found on the Internet. Many helpful fact books on everything from construction to investing are often found at the library and over the Internet.

Biographical references identify particular individuals and outline their backgrounds and achievements. *Who's Who* is the best-known biographical reference, but a vast number of sources can tell you about both contemporary and historical figures. An Internet database entitled *Who's Who* contains thousands of references. Another database called *refdesk.com* can also trace many newsworthy people, both living and dead, and give vital information about them. As much or as little information as you wish can be located.

Compilations and yearbooks are edited collections of material of a given type. For example, *Editorials on File* is a digest of selected newspaper editorials arranged by topic; it is published regularly and then compiled into a yearbook each year. Other widely used compilations are *Facts on File* and *Congressional Quarterly Almanac,* an especially useful guide to the status of issues currently before the U.S. Congress. *Congressional Quarterly* publishes a pamphlet called *CQ Researcher,* which examines a different issue of public interest each week. This compilation of facts and opinions includes background information, editorials about each side of the issue, and a bibliography of important books and articles to help you start researching the issue.

Atlases provide geographical information, including the exact location and physical characteristics of specific sites, cities, and regions. Again the Internet comes to the forefront with the Google's *Earth* website. By knowing the coordinates of any spot on Earth, the patient researcher can view it directly on a computer monitor. This includes your family home, or your local shopping mall.

Collections of quotations are useful both for tracking down the origin of popular sayings and for finding maximums or brief quotations related to a particular topic. Several different types can be found, including humor, philosophy, and political quotations.

Periodical indexes, found in the reference section of the library, are described in the next section.

Reference Librarian. Most libraries have a special assistant to help the researcher if other searches fail: the reference librarian. These library experts are trained to help locate information. But their ability to assist depends on the preparation of the researcher. If only general questions and requests are made, only general results will happen. For example, if someone asks for something on World War II, the researcher will be overwhelmed by the volumes that have been written on the subject. But if the question were, "Where can I find information on the Crystal Night during World War II?" the librarian could locate through the library indexes that the event occurred when over a thousand church buildings and synagogues were pelted with rocks, breaking windows and causing destruction. The Time: November 9 & 10, 1938. The more specific and prepared the researcher, the better the results for finding vital, interesting, and meaningful information.

Periodicals

Periodicals (sometimes called "serials") are published at regular intervals–weekly, monthly, or quarterly–and have the advantage of being more up to date than books.

General-Interest Periodicals. These are sold at newsstands or by subscription, circulated widely. Examples include *Time, Newsweek, U.S. News & World Report,* and *People.* These are useful for current events, but their coverage of issues is fairly brief and not deep, with the exception of feature articles. These periodicals are an excellent source for ideas on topics, but often require further investigation for sufficient information for the speech.

Special-Interest Periodicals. These are intended for readers who have particular interests, which may be as broadly defined as business (*Fortune* and *Business Week)* or rock music (*Rolling Stone* and *Spin*) or may be as narrowly focused as snowmobiles, digital imaging, or coin collecting. Whatever your topic, you probably can find a periodical devoted to it. Some are aimed at specific demographic groups–based on age, gender, ethnicity, and so on–and even cities are the focus of magazines named after them.

Technical Periodicals. These are written primarily for specialists in a given field. Scholarly journals are the obvious example, with one or more publications dedicated to most academic disciplines: *American Political Science Review, Journal of the American Medical Association, Journal of American History, American Bar Association Journal, Quarterly Journal of Speech,* and so on. Although journals like these are intended mainly for subject-matter specialists, they sometimes include material that can be very helpful for a speech, such as the results of surveys, experiments, and historical and critical analyses conducted by experts in various fields.

Indexes to Periodicals. A few years ago the library used to be the source of magazine and periodical articles through their Reader's Guide to Periodical Literature.

That work is still available through electronic databases, and even available on CD for the dedicated researcher.

It contains over 270 popular publications, and has them indexed back to 1983. Many libraries have the CD available, or it can be purchased through the *Wilson's Reader's Guide* website.

Many libraries provide access to scholarly publications by providing access to websites that house databases of both abstracts and many complete articles in many scholarly publications. The database *jstor* indexes 47 disciplines containing over 1,850,000 articles in scholarly journals. The earliest entry is the year 1665. EBSCOhost also provides both abstracts and complete articles for hundreds of scholarly works. For current magazine articles reminiscent of the old reader's guides, try the *linxnet magazine index,* a database reproducing almost 300 popular magazines each month.

To locate articles in special-interest and technical periodicals, consult the large number of specialized indexes that are available. The *Bulletin of the Public Affairs Information Service* is useful for many topics dealing with public policy issues. The *Social Sciences Index* and the *Humanities Index* can point you to journals and periodicals relating to those many disciplines. The *Business Periodicals Index* can help you research topics about the economy and business conditions, and the *Index to Legal Periodicals* covers law reviews and journals. EBCSOhost databases are available through your public or campus library to access these materials. Finally, the *International Index to Periodicals* can guide you through journals published in other countries. If the subject of your speech falls outside these categories, check again with the reference librarian, or check the title for a database on the Internet.

Newspapers

Newspapers are the most important source of ongoing current information. Besides reporting the latest news, many newspapers analyze and interpret it and publish related feature articles. Your local newspaper will be a valuable source of information for speeches. If you do not already do so, develop the habit of reading the paper regularly and clipping material that you think may be useful in developing a speech. The database providing access to almost 700 daily newspapers nationwide is *proquest newspapers.* They contain not only current news, but also back issues if needed. Another vital source of news items can be found on the data base referenced as NewsBank.

Through partnerships with leading content providers worldwide, NewsBank provides a variety of libraries with Web-based access to current and archived content from more than 2,000 newspapers, as well as newswires, transcripts, business journals, periodicals, government documents and other publications. Through its databases, intuitive interfaces and powerful search technology, NewsBank enables users to easily explore tens of millions of articles, obituaries, notices, announcements and other news content in order to pinpoint information from primary sources at the local, state, regional, national and international levels.

Both of these databases can be accessed through the Internet, or the local library.

Government Publications

An often overlooked source of supporting material is the vast range of publications by state and national governments. Many college and university libraries are government depositories, which means they regularly receive copies of most federal (and sometimes state) government publications. Some also include the publications of foreign governments and the United Nations.

Covering virtually every public issue, government publications include bulletins, reports, pamphlets, research studies, congressional deliberations, judicial opinions, and agency publications. Often, however, these are not indexed in the card index or general periodical indexes. If your speech topic is of concern to government bodies, you are well advised to visit the government publications section of your library and to consult with the librarian in charge. Although government documents may seem intimidating at first, you can learn to use them effectively by following their few printed directions and seeking the help of the librarian.

Finding Supporting Material Electronically

The development of the World Wide Web (Internet) has changed the way the world collects, stores, indexes, and recalls information. Much of the material is useful, such as online library catalog indexes, databases, information from organizations, and subject-specific information unavailable anywhere else. Properly used, the Web can be a valuable supplement and often a key to finding library materials. Keep in mind anyone can publish on the Web; with no assurance of quality control, you also will find information that is inaccurate, useless, tasteless, or even willfully misleading, For this reason, no matter how critically you assess information on the Web, you should not rely entirely on it for your research.

The Web got its name because each site on it usually contains links to other related sites, thus forming a kind of web. Having found a site that contains useful information, you can follow its links to other sites that seem interesting. This is like using the bibliography of one book to find other books, only much faster.

Search Engines. There is not one overall organization for Websites that is similar to a library card index. Thus, when you are researching a speech, it is difficult to know where to look for useful information. You have to roam the Web until you happen to find what you are looking for. Your search might be immediately productive, or it might take a lot of time and still you might miss key sites altogether.

Assistance can be found using *search engines,* gigantic indexes created by robot programs that roam the Web collecting and indexing its pages. Earlier, such search engines as Alta Vista ruled the electronic world. Now Yahoo!, Google, and Ask are popular locations. Other search engines include Excite, Info Seek, Lycos, Web Crawler, and many others.

Alta Vista uses "words" as the key to indexing, whereas Yahoo! Is based on categories, and it shows links to Websites that cover the topics you specify. Google emphasizes symbols or visual images as a reference point. The end product is that competing search engines produce almost unlimited information sources. As a result, the researcher must be prepared with specific key words, objects, names, or incidents to locate the information desired.

To narrow the search as much as possible, use more than one search word, separated by words such as AND or NOT in capital letters between selected words. This can cut the search in half, but when there are several million hits, even that does not eliminate the information overload available to the researcher. Be as specific and descriptive as possible in describing what you wish to locate.

Finding Useful Information

Since anyone can construct a Website for any reason, the Web includes information that is biased, out of date, or simply inaccurate. But it also contains the most recent information about topics of current interest. You have to be careful in selecting what you choose.

Note the kinds of information databases collect. Recognize that most databases are dedicated to a specific topic genre but do try to collect both positive and negative support for the topic.

Pay special attention to the home pages of government agencies and think tanks. These organizations conduct extensive research and release policy papers on a range of issues. One of the most comprehensive is the Electronic Policy Net, <htp;//www.epn.-org/>, which includes an easily navigated image map. Clicking a location on this map brings you to the home page for a particular subject, such as

"Health Policy." When you click on one of these, you will enter a hypertext analysis of the issue.

Think tanks are often not neutral but are supported by organizations with a particular ideological perspective. The Electronic Policy Net, for instance, labels itself a progressive organization.

Evaluating Internet Evidence

Because the presence of information on the Internet is almost completely unregulated, we need to note some special precautions about supporting materials from electronic sources. The following questions are especially pertinent.[3]

- Who set up the Website? If you cannot tell who sponsors the site, be suspicious of its contents. People or organizations with an agenda can disguise their motive or identity, leading you to regard biased information as though it were neutral. One clue to a site's reliability is its *domain name*–the last portion of its URL. As a general rule, URL's that end in <gov> (government agency) or <edu> (educational institution) may be more reliable sites than those ending in <.org> (organization) or <com.> (commercial source).
- When was the site last updated? The value of the World Wide Web is that it can supply up-to-the-minute information about current topics. Often, however, sites are not updated regularly, and the information becomes obsolete. If you cannot tell when a site was last updated, that may be a reason to be wary of its content.
- Can you confirm the information? If something seems too good to be true, it probably is. And if you find information on the Web that seems to make your case air-tight or to refute someone's ideas conclusively, be careful. A good general rule is to check electronic information against other sources. Even if you can't find the exact same facts or ideas, what you obtain from the Web should be copatible with what you learn from people or in print.

Chapter 33: Analysis and Application Exercises

1. Throughout the text and the video lesson a wide variety of informational resources were shown or discussed. Which sources have you never used when doing research? Why?

2. The text says that you should use library sources as well as the internet rather than the internet exclusively. Explain why.

References

1. T. B. Farrell, "Knowledge, Consensus, and Rhetorical Theory," *Quarterly Journal of Speech*, 62 (February, 1976), 1-14.
2. For more on the misuse of statistics, see John Allen Paulos, *Innumeracy: Mathematical Illiteracy and Its Consequences* (New York: Hill and Wang, 1988).
3. Some of the problems with doing electronic research are explained in Steven B. Knowlton, "How Students Get Lost in Cyberspace," *The New York Times*, "Education Life," (Nov. 2, 1997) 128-21.

CHAPTER 34 Preparing Your Speech

LEARNING OBJECTIVES

When students have completed this chapter and lesson they should be able to:

1. Identify and clearly state in a simple sentence the topic of the assigned speech.
2. Complete an audience and occasion analysis for the speech.
3. Identify and justify the method of persuasion that will be used in the speech.
4. Carefully select the supporting information used in the speech.
5. Using Toulmin's rhetorical model, evaluate the materials to be presented.
6. Through audience analysis, identify the motivational appeals to be used in the speech.
7. Identify the organizational pattern to be used in the speech.
8. Prepare a full-sentence outline for the speech.

CHAPTER 34: Overview

This chapter helps the speaker establish and write a thesis or specific purpose for the speech. The number and statement of main ideas intended to develop the thesis will then be selected from the information gathered in Chapter 33. The process of ordering these main ideas, choosing from the possibilities of supporting evidence, and concluding with the outline structure for the speech prepares the speaker for a presentation.

The situation facing the United States was almost impossible. A struggling, young nation had been torn apart by civil war, and half the country was facing poverty and ruin because the feudal system of plantations and slave owners had been vanquished; some word of reconstruction and reconciliation was desperately needed. The ultra-conservative New England Society of New York invited a series of speakers to address the issues. Among the speakers were DeWitt Talmage, whose glorified description of the union soldiers returning in triumph and victory was followed by General William Sherman relating anecdotes belittling the south. "Marching Through Georgia" was lustily sung, then Henry Grady, editor of the Atlanta Constitution rose to speak. "When I found myself on my feet, every nerve in my body was strung as tight as a fiddle-string, and all tingling. I knew that I had a message for that assemblage, and as soon as I opened my mouth, it came rushing out!" The New York Times reported that Grady's address on the New South was declared a rousing success: "No oration of any recent occasion has aroused such enthusiasm in this city."[1]

The thesis statement is the critical element of your speech, the statement you want listeners to accept. The successful speech by Grady was as critical to binding up the nation's wounds as was Martin Luther King's "I have A Dream" speech to healing racial unrest and discrimination.

A clear, concise, vivid thesis dictates the pattern and development of any speech. When you ask questions about your thesis statement, you identify the issues you must address in order to establish the thesis. **Main ideas** are the claims that address the issues in your thesis statement, and they are the major divisions of the speech.

You identify the main ideas in your speech from your thesis or specific purpose. This also becomes evident in idea patterns that emerge from your research.

Thesis or specific purpose. Stuart Kim used this approach to identify his main ideas in a persuasive speech urging contributions to the United Way. Like many college students, Kim was a community service volunteer. He also tutored reading and math at an after-school center for children of low-income families. Stuart enjoyed the work and felt he was really helping children. As the year drew to a close, he was startled to learn that the center where he volunteered was going to be shut down. It had been funded by the United Way, and their resources were running low. Appalled that "his" children would have nowhere to go, Stuart decided to speak to community groups and urge them to support the United Way. His public speaking classmates were his test audience to create the speech.

Because Stuart's purpose was to persuade his audience to contribute to the United way, he immediately developed several ideas that he needed to address. He would have to tell listeners what the United Way was, that the agencies it supported such as Stuart's after-school tutoring center, were important and valuable. The United Way needed Stuart's classmates to give financial support. If the speech failed to address any of these elements, the audience was unlikely to be persuaded to donate money. Thus, Stuart divided the speech into three corresponding divisions:

I. The United Way is a federation of health, recreational, and social service agencies.
II. The activities of these agencies are important and valuable to our community.
III. These activities cannot be continued unless we support the United Way.

Stuart was able to immediately see the main ideas that developed from his thesis and purpose. But sometimes the connection is not so obvious. If Stuart had not identified his main ideas at once, he might have worked them out by quizzing his thesis statement:

TOPIC: The United Way
GENERAL PURPOSE: Inducing a specific action
SPECIFIC PURPOSE: Convincing listeners to give money to the United Way.
THESIS: Everyone should contribute to the United Way.

Issues:

1. Everyone	Why me?
2. Should contribute	Why? What does it do?
3. The United Way	What is it?

Main Ideas:

1. The United Way needs and merits *your* support.
2. The United Way supports important and valuable programs.
3. The United Way is an umbrella organization raising money for social service programs.

Looking over this list, Stuart decided to put main idea 3 first in the speech and to end with main idea 1. Why? Because listeners need to know what the United Way is before they can decide whether to support it and because the direct appeal in main idea 1 provides a strong conclusion. Applying these analytical steps, Stuart would derive the same main ideas that he was able to recognize instinctively.

Checklist 34.1 contains some of the standard questions to ask about a thesis statement in order to identify your main ideas.

Checklist 34.1

Questions to Help Identify Main Ideas

1. What does it mean?
2. How to describe it?
3. What are the facts?
4. What are the reasons?
5. How often does it occur?
6. What is my view?
7. What are the parts?
8. What is the reasoning?
9. What is the cause?
10. Which ones?
11. How will it happen?
12. Who is involved?
13. What are some examples?
14. Why is it strange?
15. What are the objections?
16. Compared with what?
17. What is the effect of this?
18. Any stories to tell?
19. How often?
20. What is preventing it?

Patterns in Your Research. Another approach to identifying main ideas is to observe patterns in the information you have discovered in your collection of materials. If the information received from the people you interview and the literature you read repeatedly mention two to five subjects, those would be the main ideas about your topic.

For example, suppose almost everything Stuart read about the United Way mentioned its low administrative costs and suggested that its reliance on volunteers meant that most of the money raised would be spent directly on providing services. This idea may not have emerged from Stuart's initial conception of a strategy to meet his purpose, and yet it may be very important to include the idea in the speech. It suggests that it is better for people to contribute to the United Way than to support a host of individual charities that might not use their funds as efficiently.

Choosing among Main Ideas

The thesis and purpose of the speech as well as the research material obtained are sources of main ideas. Often, however, you will have more ideas than you have time or energy to pursue–and more than your audience will be willing and able to consider. Suppose Stuart's research suggested all the following points:

The administrative costs of the United Way are low.

Organizations in the United Way must be nondiscriminatory.

The United Way had its origins in charitable organizations of the late nineteenth century.

Some groups within the public object to the programs of certain United Way organizations.

The United Way is staffed largely by volunteers.

It is not clear whether someone who lives in one community but works in another should support the United Way at home or at work.

The United Way substitutes a single annual campaign for what otherwise would be continuous solicitation for each of the member agencies.

The alternative to supporting the United Way is to expand the government's social welfare programs.

Each of the above topics could be discussed at length, and each might be supported by a variety of materials. Yet no speech of reasonable length could address them all. Therefore, like most speakers, Stuart will need to select from among the possible main ideas which ones to use in the speech.

Criteria for Selecting the Main Ideas

Most speeches cover between two and five main ideas. Although there is no magic number for main ideas, they do generally represent what an audience expects and can likely follow and remember.

If you have derived more than five main ideas from your research, you can reduce their number and select which ideas to include by asking two questions:

Is this idea really essential to the speech?

Can a more general statement combine several ideas?

Is this idea essential? In researching your topic, you may discover many interesting items about your subject that are sidelights to your main idea. Although they are fascinating, they distract from your specific purpose. For example, knowing that the United Way developed from nineteenth-century charitable organizations may reveal much information about American attitudes toward charity, or even how organizations evolve. But Stuart's purpose is to persuade audience members to donate money. Most people do not need to know the United Way's history to decide on making a donation. Likewise, if Stuart's goal is to convince people to give, it may not matter whether they do so at work or at home.

The first criterion is difficult to apply. Speakers are reluctant to omit ideas that interest them, and valuable research time seems wasted if the results do not find their way into the speech. But including nonessential material may distract the audience and prevent achieving the ultimate purpose. You must be hard-nosed and subject all potential main ideas to this rigorous test:

If an idea is not essential to your specific purpose, it does not qualify as a main idea and should be excluded!

Can several ideas be Combined? When considering a large number of main ideas, some may not be main ideas at all but illustrations of, or support for a more general statement. You might combine what you thought were distinct main ideas into one general statement. Your thesis could be a more general, inclusive statement.

In the United Way example, the low administrative costs, the nondiscriminatory policies, and the convenience of a single annual campaign might not turn out to be separate ideas, but just examples supporting a single statement like "The United way is the best way to contribute to charity." The three statements all answer the question "Once I have decided that it is important to make a charitable contribution, why should I do so through the United Way?" That question is a longer form of "Why me?" which came from the thesis statement. These examples could support the main idea, "The United Way merits *your* support." By using this thesis statement, we reduce three statements of main ideas into one.

Characteristics of Main Ideas

Cutting the number of main ideas may result in a speech that does not seem complete, coherent, or persuasive. It is also important that the selected main ideas have the following characteristics:

Checklist 34.2

Characteristics of Main Ideas

Taken together, the main ideas of the speech should be characterized by:

1. Simplicity
2. Discreteness
3. Parallel Structure
4. Balance
5. Coherence
6. Completeness

Simplicity. Because main ideas are memory aids for both speaker and audience, they should be stated simply and succinctly so they can be remembered. "The United Way is efficient" is a better statement of a main idea than is "The United Way has low administrative costs, economies of scale from combining campaigns, and simple distribution mechanisms." As a general rule, a main idea should be stated in a single, simple, short sentence.

Directness. Each main idea should be separate from the others. When main ideas overlap, the structure of the speech becomes confusing and difficult to remember. For example, if one main idea is "The United Way supports agencies that meet social needs" and another main idea is "The United Way supports health and recreational agencies," the two ideas overlap; they are not mutually exclusive. Health and recreation are also social needs. Such a structure will not be clear to listeners, and the speaker will not know where to put supporting material.

Parallel Structure. Main ideas should be stated in similar fashion. Sentences should have the same grammatical structure and should be of similar length. The principle known as **parallel structure** makes the pattern easy to follow and remember. For example, Stuart might use this pattern:

> The United Way is effective.
>
> The United Way is efficient.
>
> The United Way is humane.

In this example, "effective," "efficient," and "humane" are the key terms that listeners remember. Each of these value judgments can be supported with different forms of support, but the basic structure of the speech is parallel.

Balance. No one main idea should be loaded toward one particular aspect of the subject.

Each idea should receive an equal portion of emphasis. There should be a balanced perspective. In the preceding list, each of the three key terms refers to a different aspect of the United Way: what it accomplishes, what it costs, and what values it represents. These are three different factors affecting the decision to contribute, and together they offer a balanced perspective. If three or four main ideas related to the United Way's finances are presented, and only one dealt with its underlying values, the organization of the speech would appear unbalanced. Finances would be covered in detail, but other important aspects of the topic would be treated superficially or ignored. This would leave the audience feeling like they had heard only part of the story, and would be hesitant to contribute.

Coherence means that the main ideas have a clear relationship and hang together; listeners can see why they appear in the same speech. If Stuart wished to persuade listeners to contribute to the United Way but offered one main idea about the origins of charitable organizations, another about efforts to extend the United Way to Eastern Europe, another about controversial agencies that the United Way supports, and another about accounting procedures, it is hard to imagine how the speech could be coherent. These topics are clearly not related to each other (except they all involve the United Way), and they do not support any conclusion–certainly not the ultimate claim that "you should contribute to the United Way."

Completeness. The main ideas taken together should present a complete view of the subject. Everything of major importance should be included. If any one of the main ideas is omitted, the speech will project the feeling of lacking something. If Stuart wants to convince the audience to contribute to the United Way but fails to explain what the organization does with the money it receives, the pattern of main ideas would not be complete and the contributor would be left wondering what would happen to their contribution. Most people who make charitable gifts want to know how their contributions are used.

Chapter 34: Analysis and Application Exercises

1. Explain briefly how an analysis of audience and occasion might affect choice of (a) method of persuasion, (b) evidence, (c) reasoning, (d) motivation, and (e) organization for a speech.
2. You are required to use complete sentences for each element of your speech outline. What is a "complete sentence?"Why are you required to use them in your outlines–in other words, what benefit accrues from the use of complete sentences in an outline?

References

1. R.T. Oliver, *History of Public Speaking in America* (Boston: Allyn and Bacon, Inc, 1965), 349-50.

CHAPTER 35

Organizing and Outlining

LEARNING OBJECTIVES

When students have completed this chapter and lesson they should be able to:

1. Know why outlining and organization are important aids to understanding and listening.
2. Divide the major ideas of the speech into appropriate statements, forming a skeleton of the speech.
3. List four ways to connect major and subordinate statements in a speech.
4. Explain two types of outlining for a speech.

CHAPTER 35: Overview

The importance of outlining and organization is discussed, emphasizing its critical value in improving comprehension and acceptance of the speaker's ideas. The parts and construction of a preparation outline are identified, with particular attention to complete sentences, subordination, coordination, and citing supporting materials.

A proper speech could be compared to eating a chocolate cake. Its outward appearance looks good, but can only be appreciated if it is carefully sliced, and you are provided portions of it on a platter with an appropriate eating utensil. This is service that brings a smile. But if the presenter picks it up and throws it in your face without taking the proper steps of presentation, the effect is much different.

Using this as an analogy, too many times the speaker throws the message at you without proper preparation. Human nature prefers structure and order. If things are arranged properly, and we receive the information structured well, the message has increased credibility, is accepted with greater ease, and is comprehended to a greater degree.

Identifying and locating material for the speech is not enough. It is not enough to have the material shoved at you in disarray. As a listener you need an organized, well-planned message. **Organization** is the selection of ideas and materials and their arrangement into a discernible and effective pattern.

Why is organization important?

During freshman orientation, the College Counseling office provides a program where seniors deliver speeches about developing good study habits. The first speaker, Burt, maintained that "good habits depend on several important factors. For one thing, you have to avoid procrastination. Good reading skills are also helpful to college students. Oh yes, and by the way, you also need to be self-motivated." The incoming students looked puzzled and unconvinced; they stopped taking notes, and no one asked questions. The very next speaker, Laura, covered the same ground, but said, "Good study habits depend on a balance of skills plus motivation. On the one hand, you have to develop good reading skills; on the other hand, you need to overcome procrastination. You can do both if you focus on the priorities that motivate you to study." The audience responded very differently to Laura's speech; they took notes and asked a number of questions when she finished.

Laura knew that audiences understand, remember, and are influenced by an organized message more than by a disorganized one. Listening is difficult under any circumstances, and it is even more difficult when they cannot tell where the speaker is going, or how one idea relates to another. Ideas or examples that are not associated or connected are quickly forgotten.[1] The mental energy that listeners use in reconstructing a confused or disorganized speech is not available for absorbing and reflecting on its main points.[2] Listeners may also resent this additional work and may express their resentment by resisting the message.[3]

Beyond basic considerations about the audience, a speaker should recognize that organizational patterns or forms can be a method of persuasion. If listeners can identify a clear pattern in the speech, they can anticipate what idea is coming next. If a speaker describes the development of intercollegiate athletics by talking first about the past and then about the present, listeners reasonably can expect to focus next on the future. As the speaker develops the main ideas aloud, listeners follow along and develop the ideas in their minds.

The ability to follow a speaker's organizational pattern is important for several reasons:

- Sequence of ideas is best remembered in a designated pattern. Categories like past-present-future give a link to items remembered: Game 1: past; Game 2: today, Game 3 will be tomorrow.
- Strong organization encourages active rather than passive listening. Audiences can filter out irrelevant or distracting noise when there is structure.
- Anticipation makes listeners believe they are "in the know!"If point one is winning football, and point two is large revenues coming from televised winning football teams, the audience anticipates their winning football team will be televised in the future. If that is indeed the next main idea, satisfaction at having "called it right"' assists both comprehension and acceptance.[4]

Structure or form of the message is persuasive because listeners are more likely to be disposed positively toward ideas that they have helped shape, that they can remember well, and about which they feel personally satisfied.

Organization is important for the speaker as well. In any rhetorical situation, the goal is to anticipate a given response from your audience, and take advantage of building a message to achieve your purpose. Organization is a major strategic resource that directly affects the outcome of a speech. You need to bring critical thinking and reflection to such organizational decisions, considering the number and order of ideas, how you group them, what you call them, and how you relate them to the audience. In devising your strategic plan, you should question what your options are, how each option relates to your purpose, and how different choices are likely to be perceived by listeners.

Analytic planning and careful ordering of your ideas or main claims can be a guide to check that you have not accidentallly left anything out. For example, noticing that your speech covers both the past and the present of your topic, you recognize that the audience will likely think: "What about the future?" This prompts you to find the materials needed to discuss the future as well. During your presentation, keeping the organization in mind can prevent the embarrassment of suddenly forgetting what the next point should be.[5]

A speech **outline** is a display of the organizational pattern of the speech. Its purposes:

- The outline helps clarify the best organizational strategy for your claims.
- The outline helps you check to see that it is logically correct and complete. It quickly reveals how the main ideas support the thesis statement, it reveals the consistency of the logic linking two ideas together; it shows if there is enough supporting evidence to validate the claims; and shows whether the overall de-

sign of the speech logically describes your purpose. In other words, does it make sense?

- The outline is a written memory aid that helps you become familiar with the claims you want to make, the order you make them, and assists the memory in presenting them in the proper sequence.

Speakers depend on outlines at two stages: when they put the speech together and when they deliver it. Each stage requires a different kind of outline. The **preparation outline** is used in composing the speech and is developed in enough detail to show how each idea and piece of evidence fits into the overall structure. The **presentation outline,** or speaking outline, is simpler and briefer and is used as a memory aid while you deliver the speech. Although the character and use of these outlines are different, the preparation outline should lead naturally into the presentation outline.

The Preparation Outline

In preparing the preparation outline, the speaker calls on many of the skills discussed in previous chapters. You decide on your purpose and thesis statement; you identify the main ideas or claims and review the supporting material; and you develop the introduction, body, and conclusion. As you list your ideas, you plan a strategy for your speech, thinking about what to put where and why. You map out this plan by testing your thesis against the material that supports it. You think critically, inspecting the outline to ask which sections of the speech are complete and which need further development. Outlining a speech is like exercising; it is a "rhetorical workout" that helps you get in shape.

If you are required to submit an outline for the speech you are to give, the preparation outline should be submitted. It is written in complete, simple sentences so that anyone reading the outline can make reasonable guesses about what is included. For the beginning speaker, the full sentence outline causes the speaker to be better prepared for several reasons:

1. The Speaker is more confident that preparation is complete and the ideas are more sound.
2. The speaker is more confident that claims are clearly stated, and that he has supporting material shows they are correct.
3. The speaker is confident that lapses of memory will not occur, for the outline serves as an excellent memory aid.
4. The outline helps the speaker's critical thinking in creating the relationship between claims, and validating the solution to the claims that have been established.

What does a good outline look like?

The outline shows the hierarchy of importance of ideas within a speech. Typically, the main ideas are signed by Roman numerals, and each successive level of less important ideas is designated first by capital letters, then by Arabic numerals, and finally by lower case letters.[6] In short, you present the main ideas with Roman numerals; the divisions or sub categories of the major ideas with capital letters; the forms or support for the major idea (or claim) with Arabic numerals, and an explanation of the relationship or interpretation of evidence to the claim with small letters. The overall structure of your outline would look something like this:

I. Main idea or claim
  A. A sub category of the main idea
    1. Evidence or support material for the sub point
      a. Explanation of the relationship between evidence and claim

B. A second sub category of the main idea
   1. Evidence or support
      a. Explanation
   2. Evidence
      a. Explanation

C. A summation of evidence validating the first claim

II. Main idea or claim
   A. A sub category of the second main claim
      1. Evidence of the sub category
         a. Explanation
      2. Evidence of the sub category
         a. Explanation
   B. A summation of evidence validating the second claim

The above structure may extend to additional detail with deeper indentations for each level of sub points and evidence of minor claims that support the major claim. But if the structure of a speech is that complex, the audience probably will not be able to follow it carefully. If your preparation outline needs more than four levels of importance, your thesis is probably too broad and unfocused. This suggests you should narrow or condense your topic.

There are variations and different labeling nomenclature that can be used for the outline pattern. As long as the style designates descending importance of categories, and the relationship in validating the claim, another style would be acceptable. The critical factor to remember is that the outline is to strengthen the validation and importance of the claim, present it in a logical sequence, and assist the speaker in presenting it in a logical, flowing dialogue. These elements become the basis for understanding and accepting the message.

Constructing the Preparation Outline

The preparation outline should include three basic divisions and a heading. The completed outline would then include the Heading, which includes **statement of topic, general purpose, specific purpose, and thesis.** For example, a speech about Campus Food Service would look something like this:

TOPIC: Campus food service
GENERAL PURPOSE: Conversion
SPECIFIC PURPOSE: To convince listeners that the often-criticized Campus Food Service is really quite good.
THESIS: Campus Food Service is vastly underrated.

Following the above caption or heading, the **Introduction** should follow. A more detailed analysis of introductions and conclusions will be presented in Chapter 37. But for continuity, the rest of the outline would appear as follows. Please note that the introduction is where the speaker would begin presenting to the audience. Three specific objectives should govern the introduction:

1. Attention-getting device. This could be any one of a number of items of information. The objective is to get the audience's attention, to reveal the general topic being discussed, and acquaint the audience with the speaker. Its major purpose is to announce to the audience they should begin listening.
2. The introduction should also include a statement of thesis or purpose. It should be made very clear to the audience what the topic should be, and why this subject is being discussed.
3. A brief preview or announcement of what will be discussed.

Here is how you might outline the introduction of the speech about food service:

INTRODUCTION

I. *(Take on persona of student going through food service line.)* "Oh, Great! Another meal at Campus Food Service. Let's See. . .what do I want? What is that? Uh. . . no mystery meat tonight, thanks. What? Chicken again. There's some pasta. Ugh, it looks like three noodles and a gallon of water. That's it. I'm ordering in tonight."
II. Thesis: The Campus food service, however, is vastly underrated.
III. Preview: By showing how Campus Food service keeps costs to a minimum, keeps offering a good variety, keeps a democratic system sensitive to the needs of the consumer, and keeps maintaining high quality standards, I am going to prove that Campus Food Service is the best meal program for students.

Following the introduction is obviously the major portion of the speech. This is referred to as the **body** of the speech. For the Preparation Outline, the following characteristics should be followed.

Complete Sentences. One function of the preparation outline is to test the clarity and precision of your claims. Sometimes you may have a general idea of what you want to say but are unsure of the exact idea and way you want to say it. By writing the outline in complete sentences rather than just highlighting general topics, you will force yourself to specify exactly what claims you want to make. This avoids "talking around" the subject when you can see the claim stated exactly as you want it to be accepted.

For example, if your outline simply says "Voting bad," you would have little idea what you really want to say—other than there is something negative about voting patterns. In contrast, the complete sentence "Voting in presidential elections has declined over time" is much more precise and focuses your attention on your essential message.

Subordination. A primary purpose of the preparation outline is to map out the relationships between claims and supporting materials. The outline should clearly show **subordination;** supporting materials for a given idea should be outlined as indented under that idea. If you designate the main idea with Roman numerals, then you should identify its parts or sub-points with capital letters. It is easy to mistake sub-points for main ideas or for supporting points when your outline does not show their subordinate structure.

Look at this fragment of an outline:

I. Voter apathy has become a growing concern.
   A. During the years before World War I, voter turnout was high.
      1. Give examples of presidential elections in the late 1800's
         a. Explain the widespread excitement of elections
   B. In the modern age, the height of voter participation came in 1960.
      1. Review the Kennedy-Nixon election
         a. Explain the widespread controversy and how it impacted voter response
   C. Since 1960, there has been a slow but steady decline in political participation.
      1. Show difference in results of the Bush-Kerry election and the controversy and change in the 2008 campaign.
         a. Explain that interest in presidential campaigns has changed since 1960

II. Voter apathy is widespread.
   A. It can be found in the East.
      1. Cite election statistics in New York.
   B. It can be found in the Midwest.
      1. Cite election statistics in Illinois.
   C. It can be found in the South
      1. Cite election statistics in Florida.
   D. It can be found in the west.
      1. Cite election statistics in California.
   E. Data from all areas support the inference that voter apathy is widespread.

Details about the voting in different eras would be subordinate to a claim that voter apathy has increased over time. Likewise, information about voting rates in different regions of the ocuntry would be subordinate to a main idea about the geographic spread of the problem. Each subordinate point supports the idea under which it is indented. The distinction between main ideas and supporting points helps to make the subordinate structure clear and easy for an audience to follow. The evidence given for each supporting idea validates the claim. The explanation of the results under each point reinforces the support for the evidence validating the claim.

Coordination is closely related to the principle of subordination. Ideas with the same level of importance should be designated with the same symbol series–all with Roman numerals, or all with capital letters. Items so designated are not subordinate statements; they are parallel, or coordinate statements.

Above, the two statements "Voter apathy has become a growing concern" and "Voter apathy is widespread" are main headings. These are equally important ideas, and they are both parts of an overall topical organization that correlates the two aspects of the topic: chronology and geography. It would be a mistake to label as main headings "Voter apathy has become a growing concern" and "It can be found in the South." These statements are not united by a topical plan and might even be said to conflict since the first statement implies a national problem and the second focuses on a single region. In the same way it would be a mistake to label "Voter apathy has become a growing concern" as a main idea and "Voter apathy is widespread" as a supporting point, because the second point is on equal footing with the first, not subordinate to it.

It is easy to see in the abstract that these patterns are in error. But it is also easy to make these types of errors when you are not consciously thinking about outlining and organizational schemes–especially if you happen to find compelling supporting material about voting rates in the South. As you compose your preparation outline, ask whether the ideas that you have designed with the same symbol series are really *coordinate*—are they of the same importance and often parallel in structure?[7]

The **Conclusion** finishes the outline structure, and includes the ending of the oral presentation. To end a speech successfully, two things must be accomplished: bring vividly to the mind of the listener the specific purpose of the speech, and end! This can be gracefully done by considering three strategies:

Conclusion

I. **Summary:** This can be done by restating the main ideas, or using a graphic statement or quotation that summarizes the idea. In our speech on campus food service, an appropriate closing statement might say: "I have shown that the Campus Food Service.

II. **Action step:** The next time you hear people making ill-founded complaints about Campus Food Service, don't hesitate to set them straight.

III. **Closure:** We are just left with one problem. Now that we know all the benefits of eating at Campus Food Service, what are we going to complain about at dinner?

The preparation outline will help you check the flow of reasoning and the structural "joints" of your message. Check to see if the sections naturally link to one another. Is it clear that B is the next logical step after A? Can you envision how you will wrap up the discussion of idea I and then move to idea II.

If you need to make the transitions of your reasoning explicit, incorporate them into your outline. The easiest way is to insert items in the outline, such as including a statement about voter apathy between I and II to link the ideas together.

Citing Supporting Materials

You can physically add supporting materials such as statistics or quotations by inserting notes in the outline detailing the forms of support. By doing so, this easily shows which ideas still lack evidence or additional research to establish its validity.

Chapter 35: Analysis and Application Exercises

1. Write two sets of three-sentence ideas on a speech topic that would show sequence of major points of the speech. The first set would be ideas that produce an informative approach. The second set would produce a persuasive presentation.
2. Distinguish between transitions, internal previews, and internal reviews. In doing so, provide an example of each.

After the supporting materials have been added, the following three alternatives show benefits and drawbacks of your ideas:

a In the outline, reproduce the supporting material immediately below the idea being supported. This approach most closely resembles what you will do in the speech makes the flow of presentation easier for the speaker. The drawback is that the outline is longer and may disrupt the clarity of the structure.

b. Use footnotes in the outline and reproduce the supporting materials at the end. This preserves the clarity of the structure, but forces the speaker to flip the outline back and forth during the presentation.

c. Attach a bibliography at the end of the outline indicating supporting sources. This keeps the structure clear and will let the speaker know, in general, where supporting materials came from. The drawback is that sources and supporting materials are not specifically tied together.

References

1. Research shows that an audience retains more of an organized message than one that is not. See E.C. Thompson, "An Experimental Investigation of the Relative Effectiveness of Organizational Structure in Oral Communication," *Southern Speech Communication Journal*, 16 (Fall, 1960), 59-69.
2. Organized speeches are comprehended more fully than unorganized speeches. A. Johnson, "A Preliminary Investigation of the Relationship between Message Organization and Listener Comprehension," *Communication Studies*, 21 (Summer, 1970), 104-107.

3. An unorganized persuasive message may actually produce an opposite effect to what the speaker intended. R.G. Smith, "An Experimental Study of the Effects of Speech Organization upon Attitudes of College Students," Communication Monographs, 18 (November, 1951), 292-301. Another study simply concludes that an extremely unorganized speech is not very persuasive. J.C. McCrosky and R.S. Mehrley, "The effects of Disorganization and Nonfluendy on Attitude Change and Source Credibility," *Communication Monographs*, 36 (March, 1969), 13-21.
4. Rhetorical theorist Kenneth Berke envisions form as "the creation of an appetite in the mind of the auditor, and the adequate satisfying of that appetite," "Psychology and Form," *Counter-Statement* (Berkeley: Univ. Of California Press), 1931.
5. Speakers who have a plan and practice it have fewer pauses in their speeches. J.O. Greene, "Speech Preparation and Verbal Fluency," *Human Communication Research*, 11 (Fall, 1984), 61-84.
6. For variations in this numerology see Collin rae, "Before Outline–The Writing Wheel," *Social Studies*, 81 (July-August, 1990), 178.
7. Additional assistance in understanding mechanics of outlining, see J. Gibson, *Speech Organization: A Programmed Approach* (San Francisco: Rinehart Press, 1971; M.R. Cox, *Interactive Speechwriter* (Boston: Allyn & Bacon, 1995).

CHAPTER 36 Critical Thinking in Communication

LEARNING OBJECTIVES

When students have completed this chapter and lesson, they should be able to:

1. Understand and explain the differences between description, opinion, and analysis.
2. Know and explain the elements of analysis as explained in this chapter.
3. Know and explain the additional elements of critical thinking listed in this chapter.
4. Know and explain the elements of critical listening.

CHAPTER 36: Overview

For purposes of our discussion, and in the communication discipline in general, *critical thinking* can be thought of as synonymous with constructive problem solving. It is the ability to question meaningfully the claims of others, identifying the crucial elements and the pitfalls or benefits that might follow that line of thinking. It is to pay attention carefully and think deeply about the subject at hand. It is to apply what we know to the question or problem, using a proven system of analysis to explain the need and construct the answer.

This is the primary benefit we derive from an education. As we become educated, we acquire a systematic way of observing and understanding things. Then, we are able to apply that system to new questions or problems. We may or may not remember much of the content we read or received. But if we've been taught to think critically, then we are prepared to make a solid contribution to the social discourse and to problem solving at home and at work.

Critical Thinking

As previously stated, critical thinking is a systematic way of making reasoned judgments about arguments that are all around us–those we read, hear, write and speak. Critical thinking helps us avoid and solve problems. The methods and criteria advanced for accomplishing critical thinking are many and varied. All have value. Vidlak and West[1] (1997) list five principles of critical thinking:

1. The critical thinker should explore issues and ideas.
2. The critical thinker is open-minded.
3. The critical thinker is skeptical.
4. The critical thinker is intellectually honest.
5. The critical thinker respects other viewpoints.

How Critical Thinking Affects Learning

- **Writing:** This is the method by which your critical thinking skills will be measured. To succeed. . . you must move beyond mere description and opinion. . . and get to *analysis.*

- **Theory:** The study of theory must not be merely an exercise in mental self-gratification. Theory provides usable *systems of analysis* for real world problems.
- **History:** The study of history must not be merely an exercise of memorizing events, names and dates. A critical approach to history will identify important, relevant, and repeating *trends*, and explore the *implications* of those trends for those who lived that history and for all of us who have followed..
- **Practice:** The ability to do something is not the only consideration in life. If we act without understanding we are merely getting by. If we understand why we do something, and the implications for doing or not doing it, we are a thinking practitioner—one who can tackle and solve important practical problems.
- **Technology:** Technology is simply a tool; it has no intelligence and is useful only in the hands of a skilled and intelligent practitioner. Thus, it is not the device which matters most, but how, when, and why we use it. The human interface with technology should be the primary focus.

Critical Thinking in Speaking and Writing

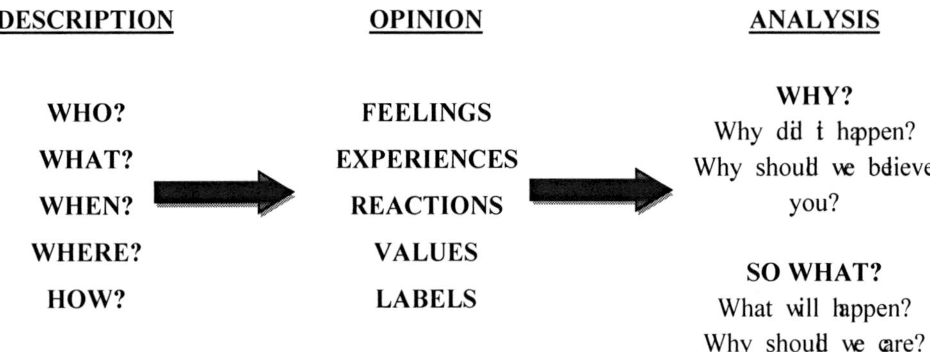

Figure 36.1 Moving from Description to Opinion to Analysis

Description and Opinion

Description. Every high school speaker or writer can do description. Telling the who, what, when, where, and how of things is a staple of high school essays. Description is important— painting the scene of the action, sharing the sensations of the moment, providing vivid details that give life to the essay or story. Creative writing is particularly dependent on accurate and vibrant description and on the dialogue of what the participants said and did. There's nothing wrong with description. But it does not require critical thinking, and critical thinking is much more important to an informed and thinking public

Opinion. Opinion is the next step toward critical thinking. When a writer or speaker reacts to what he or she has seen or heard or read, then we are getting closer to an evaluation of our world that might lead to positive change. The problem is, most high school writers have been forbidden to offer their opinions. "Do not use the word 'I,'" is a common rule. And why not? Because it's not "objective." Our discussion of objective and subjective thinking at the beginning of this text should provide ample support to the notion that *nothing* that is ever written or said is objective. When we strip the word 'I' from our writing and speaking, we start to use "passive voice" in an effort to sound scholarly and objective. But what we really become is passive and passionless writers and speakers. For example, which of the following is more vivid?

Active voice:	"I kicked the dog."	Subject-verb-object with a strong vivid verb.
Passive voice:	"The dog was kicked."	Object first (dog); No subject; weak verb (was).

Mature and thinking individuals are not afraid to place subjects in their sentences. These make the writing clearer and more vivid, and they demonstrate a reaction to circumstances, not just a description of them. In doing this, the writer or speaker adds an element of opinion to their work which, if well supported, is convincing to an audience. Passive voice does not do this.

The Elements of Analysis

Analysis. Opinion is not enough. We have not achieved critical thinking until we have reached the level of analysis. Analysis involves explaining the "why?" of things and the "so what?" It requires a higher level of thinking called synthesis which combines the present problem with known or theoretical solutions. It is at the heart of problem solving and conflict resolution. It is absolutely essential to academic success, and it is very highly prized in the working world.

—Explaining the "Why?" The discussions earlier in this text concerning rhetorical analysis and the use of rhetoric in writing and public speaking are useful in knowing how to fully analyze and explain something. But fundamentally, explaining the "why?" requires the following:

- *A System of Analysis.* To think critically, you need a set of predictions of what should happen under the circumstances. These may come from a text, from lectures, or from some other authoritative source. The challenge is to pick the most appropriate model by which to evaluate what you see.
- *Reasoned Explanations.* One by one, you must take each of the aspects of your analytical system—each element of the model—and show how the present circumstances do (or do not) match the model. As you do so, you must explain why, in light of the predictions of your model.
- *Based on Evidence.* You must provide supporting facts and examples, not just opinion. Describe how your evidence and examples illustrate your claims, and/or how they do (or do not) support the predictions of your chosen model.

—Explaining the "So What?" Critical thinkers concern themselves with the outcomes of things. What does or will this mean in people's lives? Why should we care about this subject? How can we make things better? Critical thinkers pay attention to things such as these:

- *An Uninformed Audience's Self-Interest.* A critical thinker assumes the reader or listener knows nothing about the subject—at least, nothing about the perspective that is being presented. In that context, he or she explains carefully why the audience should also care. In other words, what difference(s) do your observations make in your reader or listener's life?
- *Future Implications.* As part of problem solving, a critical thinker also considers and attempts to explain the likely outcome if conditions do (or do not) change. Using the system of analysis, the communicator can reason from current conditions to the likely outcomes. This is the part of critical thinking that industries value the most. Your ability to do it is essential to your employability and/or your success in a business of your own. It is also essential to your value as a citizen in the community and to your ability to deal with problems at home.

Additional Elements of Critical Thinking

In addition to these elements of analysis, Inch and Warnick[2] (1998) say critical thinking involves elements such as the following:

- Refining generalizations and avoiding oversimplification.
- Generating and assessing solutions to problems.
- Comparing perspectives, interpretations, or theories.
- Reading critically, seeking out information that disagrees with one's perspective.
- Listening critically, seriously considering views with which one disagrees.

Un-critical thinkers do not do these things. They will offer an opinion that seems obvious to them, with careful research and sometimes without careful thought. They will read and cite only sources that agree with their views, without considering possible objections and difficulties. They are unable to explain how their proposal fits in with known principles and procedures (the system of analysis). And if their proposal does not work, they rarely have thought of alternative approaches to the problem. It's the quick and easy and lazy way to approach problems.

Cognitive Complexity. Critical thinkers are able to do multi-level thinking—understanding a problem from a variety of perspectives and at various levels. They are not one-dimensional thinkers. We refer to people who show this ability as being "cognitively complex." For example, the oil crisis must be understood from multiple and simultaneous perspectives: the needs of consumers, the needs of industry, the relationship to and effect on global politics, the implications for domestic politics, the environmental impact, the economic impact, and a whole host of other related issues. Addressing such problems requires people (both speakers and audience members) who are comfortable thinking across all these perspectives and who can correctly compare, contrast, and evaluate their competing interests.

The Importance of Critical Thinking to Your Success. Critical thinking requires the ability to analyze and assess information.[3] This skill is important in college, but also throughout life. Becoming a critical thinker is one of the most valuable things you will learn in college. If you graduate without learning how to do it properly, you will not appear to be well-educated to those who work with you. It involves a number of attitudes and mental habits like being intellectually curious, flexible, objective, persistent, systematic, honest, and decisive. Critical thinkers love to explore issues and ideas. They are also skeptical, but open-minded. And they respect the viewpoints of others.

Critical Listening

Not only speakers, but also listeners, must do critical thinking. This involves carefully hearing what is claimed, judging the accuracy of it, and determining the reasonableness of its conclusions. Critical listeners also evaluate the presenter for credibility, motivation, soundness of thought, and persuasiveness. According to Inch and Warnick[4] Critical listening involves two phases: (1) assessing the speaker's values and intent, and (2) judging the accuracy of the speaker's conclusions.

Assessing the Speaker's Motivation. This involves at least three aspects of judgment: (1) judging the speaker's values and beliefs, (2) comparing our values to those of the speaker, and (3) evaluating the worth (to us and others) of the message.

(1) The speaker's values are the first consideration in assessing his or her motivations. Values are strongly held beliefs based in the individual's experience and perceptions of life. They greatly affect the perception and interpretation of messages. Then (2) we critically analyze how what the speaker is saying compares to our own values. Does the message ask us to conform or to go against our own values?. Finally, (3) we consider how valuable we consider the message to be, and how to respond (if at all) to it.

Judging the Accuracy of the Speaker's Conclusions. Inch and Warnick[5] suggest that we need to ask the following questions in order to critically think about the message its conclusions:

- Is the speaker qualified to draw the conclusion?
- Has the speaker actually observed what he or she is talking about?
- Does the speaker have a vested interest in his or her message?
- Is there adequate evidence presented to support the conclusion?
- Is the evidence relevant to the conclusion?
- Does contrary evidence exist that refutes what has been presented?
- Does the message contain invalid or inadequate reasoning?

Summary

The ability to think, speak, and listen critically is far more important to your future than your grades—or possibly even what you know. Employers want people who know how to apply what they know. Critical thinkers know how to analyze a problem correctly, and then solve it. If you graduate without learning to think critically, you've wasted your time and money. Your future success literally depends upon it, as does your success in college.

Chapter 36: Analysis and Application Exercises

1. Comment on a presidential candidate's response to a question asked of him during the 2008 Presidential campaign, considering both what he said and how he said it. Assess his/her motivation and judge the accuracy of the speaker's conclusions using the criteria listed under "Judging the Accuracy of the Speaker's Conclusions" above.
2. Watch an evening's newscast. Keep a tally of whenever a source is or is not cited for the information reported. How does this impact your opinions of the news? Should journalists always be required to cite their sources? When would this be undesirable?

References

1. West, R., & Vidlak, L.M. (1997). *Student Study Guide for Speaking with Confidence Telecourse.* Madison, WI: McGraw-Hill Companies, Inc.
2. Inch, Edward S. and Warnick, Barbara (1998). *Critical Thinking and Communication: The Use of Reason in Argument,* 3rd ed., Boston, MA: Allyn & Bacon. Quoted in Chase, R.S., and Jones, S.G., *Elements of Effective Communication,* 2nd ed., Boston, MA: Allyn & Bacon, 1999, p. 394.
3. Ennis, E.H. (1962). "A concept of critical thinking," in *Harvard Educational Review* 32, pp. 83–84.
4. Inch, Edward S. and Warnick, Barbara (1998). *Critical Thinking and Communication: The Use of Reason in Argument,* 3rd ed., Boston, MA: Allyn & Bacon. Quoted in Chase, R.S., and Jones, S.G., *Elements of Effective Communication,* 2nd ed., Boston, MA: Allyn & Bacon, 1999, p. 395.
5. Inch, Edward S. and Warnick, Barbara (1998). *Critical Thinking and Communication: The Use of Reason in Argument,* 3rd ed., Boston, MA: Allyn & Bacon. Quoted in Chase, R.S., and Jones, S.G., *Elements of Effective Communication,* 2nd ed., Boston, MA: Allyn & Bacon, 1999, p. 396.

CHAPTER 37
Introductions and Conclusions

LEARNING OBJECTIVES

When students have completed this chapter and lesson, they should be able to:

1. Understand and be able to perform the four purposes of an introduction.
2. List and explain the ten types of introductions.
3. Understand and be able to perform a successful conclusion.

CHAPTER 37: Overview

The speaker focuses on the beginning and ending of the speech–the introduction and the conclusion. The purposes of each are identified. Types of introductions and examples are provided. How to construct both introductions and conclusions is explained.

The occasion was the finals competition in an Intercollegiate Forensics Tournament. At stake was the championship of the Extemporaneous Public Speaking contest. Filling the room were several college students, some public observers, and five forensic judges. The first speaker stepped quickly into the room, and with a kind of smirk on his face, quickly faced the judges and audience. He was slightly over five feet in height, but conveyed an attitude of a giant. He held a white sheet of paper with writing hidden from the audience.

Silently standing before the audience for several seconds, he smiled broadly, then suddenly flashed his paper to the audience for everyone to see. Boldly written in dark letters was: SEX! Then he began to speak: "Now I have your attention, I would like to discuss with you the problem of terrorism in the Middle East!"

As noted in the first 36 chapters of this text, the critical part of a public message is getting the attention of the audience. But if the speaker is unsuccessful in attracting the audience to the message, or fails to prepare a proper atmosphere or climate for communication, the speaker will surely fail. Without a proper introduction or conclusion, the message would appear as a book without the first and last chapter, or a movie you join to just see the middle of the story.

Without providing the proper climate, or atmosphere, listeners will automatically turn the listening switch off and take a journey into fantasy, leaving the speaker alone with the message undelivered.

Audiences wish to be ushered into a complete event that starts, provides a critical message, and ends, leaving the receiver as satisfied as if they had been given a special treat. They expect to be guided into a topic, not dropped in its midst, and they expect the discussion to conclude naturally. Obviously, our public speaking contestant violated many rules for good communication. He did not win the contest, even though his speech, once started, was excellent. A good public speaker must have continuity between how the subject is introduced, the subject itself, and how the speaker asks to be remembered as he ends.

Introductions: Beginning the Speech

Both daily life and studies in the psychology of persuasion tell us that first impressions are extremely important. When you meet someone new, you quickly form impressions about that person, often based on personal dress, hairstyle, or even their way of speaking. Many first impressions become permanent, even influencing your interpretation of what they say[1].

Purposes of an Introduction

An introduction attempts to accomplish four major goals:

- Produce interest and attention in the audience.
- Produce a favorable climate or listening attention of the audience.
- State clearly the purpose or thesis of the speech.
- Introduce the structure or development of the topic.

Gaining the Attention and Interest of Your Audience. The introduction should make the audience want to hear what will follow. As we learned when studying listening, the audience very easily switches off a speaker and either day dreams of something more pleasant, or develops counter arguments as a reply to the speaker. They may even take a nap, or review an experience much more pleasant than the dull message being presented.

The primary way to make listeners pay attention is to convince them that what follows will be interesting. Like a menu at a restaurant, what follows must be appealing or everyone's attention will leave. *The climate, or topic must be attractive and favorable.* You can easily demand attention, as did our forensics speaker. Everyone in the room read and received the sex sign. But the disjointed topic of world terrorism did not fit and the listeners felt tricked! Trickery or hostility in an introduction is counterproductive. How much energy would you invest in following a speaker who is overbearing, deceptive, pompous, or dogmatic? That climate is quickly determined in the first few seconds of the speech.

The introduction aims to not only get attention, but to make the audience favorably disposed toward the speaker, topic, and presentation. Attention becomes the first, and critical element to start the listening process. But it must quickly be followed with the promise that what follows will be acceptable, interesting, and of value to the listener. Regardless of the topic and its message, the speaker must understand the audience is calling for material that will be judged, then either accepted or rejected. So the first portion of the introduction is an invitation to present a platform for the speaker's ideas.

The third step in the introduction requires a *clarification or basic thesis of the speech.* Listeners are more likely influenced by your presentation if you clearly identify what you want them to believe or to do. Many introductions will make a direct statement of purpose to assist the audience in determining the goals of the speech. For example, the speaker might include in the introduction something like: "The United States workforce cannot compete economically in the world market without strengthening public education." Or "After reviewing medical facts, I hope you will call the Red Cross and volunteer to donate blood."

One should never assume the audience can guess what you intend to achieve in the speech. By stating the specific purpose, and by clarifying the topic, the audience's interests are favorably disposed to accept the proposals of the speaker.

The audience can be helped even more in the listening process if the speaker will *preview the development or structure of the topic.* As we learned in the listening chapter, if the audience can be guided through the information you wish them to accept, their comprehension will be significantly improved. A simple presentation of the structure of your ideas can clarify not only your purpose, but also explain why your ideas are vital, and being presented in a logical sequence, ideas become more easily recalled. Classical theorists of public speaking refer to this step as the **partition;** the speaker divides the body of the speech into selected categories, or main ideas for discussion.[2] The speaker then reviews the main ideas created for the speech, as discussed in the chapter on organization. The speaker has now developed the structure for the listener to describe the entire speech in a logical, organized fashion. This becomes the road map leading to the speaker's conclusion, and ultimate acceptance. The more clearly the speech is structured, the more effective its impact.

An Example of an Introduction

Only your own imagination and creativity limits your ability to achieve the four goals of the introduction. Care should be taken that sensationalism and over reaction to creativity do not destroy the intent of the speaker. For example, one student went to the front of the room and passed out decorative foliage to each audience member, then quietly said, "My topic today is poison ivy!" The mass exodus to the washing facilities distracted from any further communication! Another creative student approached the podium with a large manila envelope. The speech began: "What if, on some dark night, someone in a dark ally suddenly jumped at you with this!" She then whipped out a sixteen inch butcher knife! With a soft moan, someone in the back fell over backwards, hitting the floor with a loud moan. The speaker was so overwhelmed with the disruption her introduction created that she could not go on with the speech.

Several standard successful introductions show up regularly in the classroom. Before examining them, consider this example of a successful introduction. Michelle was giving an informative speech in her public speaking class. As she walked to the podium, she turned, looked at her audience, and then suddenly dropped a large book on the floor. The resounding thud brought all eyes to Michelle as she began to speak: "Just as easily as that book fell to the floor, the innocence of a child can crash." Then retrieving the book, she continued:

However, unlike this book, a child's innocence cannot be picked up and placed back on the shelf. Children today encounter many experiences that lower the level of innocence. Along with gangs, guns, and drugs, they also face another monster that is not so well publicized. This monster is sexual abuse. Approximately one child out of four is sexually abused by the age of 18.

Michelle's book-dropping trick could have turned into a resounding flop or a major disaster if she had not connected it to her speech. She quickly and effectively gained her listeners' attention by saying that some of them might be victims themselves, emphasizing the personal relevance of her topic. It was obvious Michelle was going to talk about the horrors of child abuse. She took a serious tone of outrage and disposed the audience favorably toward her speech. Her final statement in the introduction then clearly previewed which main topics the audience could expect: the causes, effects, prevention, and treatment of childhood sexual abuse.

Types of Introductions

The speech itself should be a unified presentation of thoughts, ideas and information. A successful presentation, as noted earlier, requires a good introduction that gets the audience's attention, introduces the speaker, and brings the audience to accept the message. Michelle presented a startling event to begin her speech, but successfully tied the event with her ideas. Here are some other ideas to consider for introductions:

Identifying with your audience. Begin the speech by presenting evidence of something you share with your listeners–a common experience, common acquaintances, common values, or common goals. Present information that includes them. Here is an example:

> As students, we are well aware of a nightmare we call registration. Almost always, we cannot find an advisor, or all your desired classes are full or not of-

fered. Let me present a few ideas about how such a traumatic event can become a pleasant one with proper planning.

By identifying problems we all share, and suggesting a solution to remove negative events, you gain the attention of your audience.

Use the speech event as a starting point. Many speeches are delivered on a ceremonial occasion.

Using the event of the day as a starting point easily gains the attention and sympathy of the audience. Refer to why the audience is gathered, and begin with a story or personal example you have about that special day. Or you can refer to situational factors that preceded the events of the day. Relate a short, colorful explanation of why we are gathered, and what we can anticipate for the future. Such was Martin Luther King's speech, "I Have a Dream." The speech was planned prior to marching for freedom. What better occasion than an event designed for obtaining equality for all people, which was held at the Lincoln Memorial. King's selection of location as well as his introduction guaranteed success. Relating to the event can immediately develop credibility and interest for the audience.

If someone has spoken just before you, refer to their topic and build on it as a way of introducing your topic. Or point out issues of the day or previous speakers you feel were inaccurate. The tie-in provides an excellent introduction.

Stating the importance of your topic. Beginning a speech by alerting your audience to a vital topic is common. For example, a speech about preventing AIDS might begin with the statement "I have information that can literally save your life." A speech about purchasing a home might begin with "Today I want to discuss the most important and expensive financial decision most of us will ever make."

If you show your audience that your topic is important, most audiences will take notice. Obviously, both statements introduce an element of mystery, leading the audience to wonder just what it is that is so critical. Be aware however, that this type of introduction is very common, and sometimes the audience reacts by being skeptical. A speaker who opens with "This speech could change the course of your life" may actually prompt listeners to think, "Oh, sure; I've heard this before." Such a reaction can alienate the audience and you will never get their attention.

If your speech has a formal title, be sure that its specific wording is accurate and complete. Whenever a speaker is announced with a specific topic, it can be assumed that the people attending will be interested in the topic area advertised; that is the major objective of their attendance. By following through with the announced topic, the audience is satisfied, but if the speaker does not follow through as advertised, the audience can be turned off or even hostile.

Citing Statistics and Making Claims. Listeners sit up in interest when a speaker cites startling statistics or makes a surprising claim. Their astonishment on hearing information causes them to pay attention. For example, child abuse and sexuality was a hot topic when over 400 female children were seized in Texas in a child abuse case involving a religious group. Attention and controversy were immediately sparked with the newspaper headline:

> Almost two thirds of the female children age 14 to 18 were found to be either pregnant or mothers of children themselves.

This type of introduction works best when the statistics are accurate but not well known—when there is a gap between what listeners think they know and what is actually the case. Statistics can support the idea that our common assumptions are not accurate, that a problem is greater than we know, that a condition we viewed as worsening is actually improving, or that we are misinformed. The risk of using statistics is being questioned. Numbers themselves carry meaning only when they are related to people, issues, or things they describe. Numbers intensify meaning. One thirteen year old pregnant girl is sensational. Fifty three in one group is mind boggling.

However, too many times headlines like the one cited above are exaggerated, distorted, or purposefully created for a sensational effect. Listeners often reject the message because they believe numbers are being manipulated. You certainly want to encourage your listeners to think critically; but if their first response to your introduction is doubt, it will be difficult to build goodwill and regain their interest. Keep your primary purpose in mind when developing your introduction and make sure your statistics are accurate and representative of the issue being discussed.

Telling a story. Many speakers begin with an anecdote–an extended illustration, example or short story. It may be either truth or fiction. One of the most popular speeches in history started with a story. The speech, Acres of Diamonds, by Russell Conwall begins with the story of a farmer who wanted riches so badly he sold his farm to go in search of wealth. The new owners of the farm found a large diamond deposit on the property he left to seek his fortune. Conwell delivered this same speech over 6000 times[3].

The power of an anecdotal introduction lies in its narrative form. The story is engaging, and the chronological sequence is easy to follow. A narrative is concrete—it involves specific characters in a particular situation—and therefore listeners can more easily follow the logic. A narrative encourages the audience to sympathize and identify with its characters. Conwell's appeal was to teach that wealth and prosperity are found, not searching in a foreign land, but in your own back yard with your own personal talents and skills. In this case, the introduction almost dictated the structure of the speech.

The advantage of this structure is that the story helps the listener recall your message. The disadvantage is that the story may be so engaging that the point of discussion is forgotten and only the story is remembered. Try to create unity between the anecdote and the main points so that each reminds the audience of the other. If you can achieve unity, the anecdote alone will remind listeners later of what you said.

Using an Analogy. Closely related to the anecdote is the analogy, which is a comparison. An analogy draws attention to the similarities or differences between two objects, events or situations. A speaker can clarify an unfamiliar subject by comparing it with something the audience already understands.

Like anecdotes, analogies help make abstract concepts concrete. They are especially helpful for introducing technical material to novice listeners. For example, to inform his audience that the presence of human immunodeficiency virus (HIV) in a person's blood does not necessarily mean that he or she has AIDS, a student began with the following analogy:

> At the university, many students carry backpacks. So if you entered a building filled with people wearing backpacks, you probably would assume that it was a college building. However, the building could just as well be a restaurant where students hang out. Just as finding backpacks in a building does not always mean that you are on campus, HIV in a person's blood does not always mean that the person has AIDS. I am going to explore with you some of the causes and consequences of mistakenly assuming otherwise.

During World War II President Franklin D. Roosevelt used analogies to carry his messages. Discussing why the United States should lend rather than sell war materials to Great Britain and its allies, he offered the analogy of a man whose neighbor's house was on fire. When the neighbor ran up to ask for a garden hose, the man did not first demand payment; instead, he gave the hose to the neighbor on the promise that it would be returned when the threat was past. In just this way, Roosevelt reasoned, the United States should approach lending supplies to each cash-strapped ally.

Analogies are persuasive as well as effective in clarifying a concept because the speaker uses examples and language understood by the listener, yet presented in the new idea of the speaker. Like the old analogy of the West, we understand someone else's problem if we walk in their moccasins for a day. People understand us more easily if they think in our language, use our examples, and follow our logic for a speech.

Care must be taken that analogies are simple, directly mirroring the point the speaker wishes to make, and not too complex, requiring too much concentration to recognize the similarities of both thoughts. A long, extended analogy can cause the audience to forget what the point of persuasion was in the beginning. Always keep your point of persuasion foremost in the speech. If the analogy does not advance your purpose, look for some other way to begin your speech.

Asking a rhetorical question. Do you think you know what a rhetorical question is? Like the sentence you just read, a **rhetorical question** is one for which no answer is really expected. Instead, asking the question causes an audience or person to think about the answer.

Such a question raises the issues and involves the listener in focusing on his or her role in the issue.

The pitfall in asking rhetorical questions is that speakers have overused or misused this device. Some may ask an introductory question merely to ask it, rather than to induce listeners to start thinking about the subject of the speech. An even greater risk is that listeners will answer the question in their minds—with an answer that is different from what the speaker wants to discuss. In the worst case of all, someone in the audience may offer a response that undermines the entire introduction. One student began a speech about a popular movie hero appearing in many films over the years: "What do you think of when you hear the name "James Bond?" From the back of the room someone responded: "A third-rate movie!" As lawyers will tell you, you should never ask a question unless you already know the answer. It can be fatal if answered incorrectly as an introduction!

Beginning with a quotation. This is a very common introduction, especially in religious sermons or directive messages. When a religious scripture or a philosophical saying is used as the beginning of a speech, it can successfully introduce the topic, and involve the audience at the same time. Using a quotation from religious scripture immediately establishes a bond between the believer and the speaker in a positive way.

Quoting an opposing viewpoint is a variation of this type of introduction. Abraham Lincoln did this superbly in a famous speech he made at Cooper Union in 1860. He began by quoting what his political rival, Stephen A. Douglas, had said about the intentions of the country's founders; then Lincoln used the Douglas quotation to highlight and advance his own thesis and main points.

Beginning a speech with a quotation is such a common introductory device that whole books of quotations are published for this purpose. But the audience must see the connection between the clever, attractive quotation and the subject. Will your quotation lead naturally to the subject matter under discussion, or will it just get audience attention and reaction? A good test is to ask yourself if the quotation will naturally introduce your thesis statement, and then the subject matter in the body of the speech.

Using humor. Many speakers believe that a joke is the key to introductions. Humor does relax the audience, disposes listeners favorably toward the speaker, and disarms skeptics. It also places the speech in perspective, not taking the topic or speaker too seriously.

Despite all these advantages of humor, the worst advice for preparing the introduction to a speech is "every speech should start with a joke." Humor is not always appropriate for either the audience or the occasion. Sometimes the joke is just for attention, and has nothing to do with the topic. Unless the connection is clear to the audience, at best a joke delays the "real" speech, and at worst it distracts from both the speech and the occasion[4]. A classic example of attempted humor not associating with the topic was illustrated with the SEX sign introducing unrest in the Middle East.

This survey of introductions was not meant to be complete[5]. Anything can be used to begin a speech if it will achieve the four purposes of an introduction: it gets the attention of the audience, asks them to think well of the speaker and topic, clarifies the purpose and theme, and previews the topic's development. Remember that audiences are easily distracted, and without a sound introduction, the speech may never be heard.

Strategies for Preparing an Introduction

Prepare the body of the speech first. Some experts suggest you then select the most interesting, stimulating information in the speech, and preview that material for an introduction. Having already prepared the body, you know what your main ideas are and how you will develop them. The information will help you craft an appropriate introduction that will involve the audience.

As mentioned in several introductions above, the speaker **must relate the introduction to the body** or main ideas of the speech. The connection between the introduction and the body should be clear and direct. A particular anecdote, joke, or quotation might well arouse your audience's interest, but if it is unrelated to the ideas in the speech, it may not lead listeners in the desired thought process. Some introductions, as we have seen, can disrupt or undercut your purposes, weaken your speech, and alienate your audience. Remember: your goal is to convey a satisfying sense of idea development to the audience. The introduction starts this process. The following axioms state clearly what the speaker's objective should be with introductions:

1. **Keep the introduction brief.** Make sure it is just an introduction, and not a separate speech in itself.
2. **Make the introduction complete.** It must accomplish the following objectives: gets the attention of the audience, creates an interest in the topic, sets forth your purposes, and establishes you as the person in charge.
3. **Be guided by the examples given above.** Use the suggestions above as guidelines for creating the desired climate, focus on your ideas, and motivation to accept them.
4. **Plan the introduction word for word.** For the beginning speaker, this avoids introductions too long or not introductory of the subject. Prepare and practice your opening words carefully so you can begin with confidence, gain listener attention, and introduce interest in your subject matter. This gives the you greater confidence, reduces anxiety, and builds a secure feeling of speaking with success.

As you prepare the speech, **make a file of potential introductions.** This includes quotations, examples, stories, and other ideas that do not necessarily fit this speech, but can be useful for additional events. Arrange these helps in some order, such as alphabetizing them by subject for later speech activities. Then, when you start preparing your next speech, you already have resources and will not have to depend entirely on either memory or inspiration.

Conclusions: Ending the Speech

Conclusions to speeches are as critical as introductions. A speech should neither end abruptly nor trail off into oblivion. Three principles govern conclusions.

The Purposes of a Conclusion

Conclusions need to accomplish the following goals:

1. Conclusions must convey the feeling of ending.
2. Rather than introduce main ideas, conclusions end or summarize them.
3. When ending, the final statement must make an appeal to the audience.

Anticipating the end. The most significant function of the conclusion is to signal that the speech is ending. There are speakers who do this several times, frustrating the audience because the promise is never fulfilled. The polished speaker will deliver major ideas, then alert listeners that the end is near. If you do not end quickly after such a signal, the audience will leave anyway–either physically or mentally. If words such as "in conclusion" or "finally," are used, audiences shut down the listening functions and begin to relax. If the speaker continues, the audience will be confused, or become impatient when the speech does not end as expected.

On the other hand, the speaker can suddenly stop after presenting the major ideas of the speech. This leaves the audience with a feeling of incompleteness.

In both incidents, the speaker failed to provide a satisfying sense of form. Listeners notice when a speaker departs from customary form, and they resent it. They have either received messages of a "false conclusion," when premature messages of ending are sent, or they are surprised and confused by the lack of form if no sense of stopping is signaled. The speaker must coordinate the ending signal at the appropriate time.

The second purpose of a conclusion is to **summarize the main ideas.** This process helps the listener draw together the main points of the speech in a way that prepares the listeners to remember them. A critical aid to listening is to package all the critical ideas of your speech and present them to the audience as a **summary** statement. This summary does not entirely repeat the main ideas, and it certainly does not redevelop them. Rather, it reminds the listeners what was said, often by highlighted words or phrases stated in parallel form. This summary, or conclusion, increases the chances that listeners will recall the main ideas correctly.

The conclusion is a golden opportunity to **make a final appeal to the audience.** This should be an exact statement of what behavior or belief the audience should accept. It is the last chance to remind listeners about whatever they should think or do as a result of the speech.

Sometimes a speaker wants listeners to take a very specific action, such as signing a petition, donating money, writing to their legislators, purchasing a particular product, or accepting a belief. Other times the response you sought may be even more general:

> "In fast food restaurants, think twice about the effects of their food on your health."
>
> "If you ever consider an abortion, think about what I have said!"
>
> "At your next sunrise, remember the beauties, wonders and miracles of nature!"

None of these concluding statements call for action, yet each asks listeners to "do" something: to become more aware of something they had not recognized or thought critically about.

Virtually any speech–whether or not it is billed as a "persuasive" speech–asks for some response from the audience. In developing the conclusion of a speech, the goal is to make the audience understand exactly what response is sought.

An Example of a Conclusion

Here's how Michelle ended her classroom speech about the sexual abuse of children:

> Remember that children are our future generation and should be safe from plagues like sexual abuse. Committed by psychologically damaged men and women of all ages, sexual abuse is a crime that leaves a lasting scar on its childhood victims. Through education and knowledge we can help these children and prevent them from having to encounter experiences which will affect them forever after. I hope that the information I've shared with you today will be passed on to a younger audience and will help to stop sexual abuse in the future. Remember, prevention is always better than cure!

Michelle's first concluding sentence, keyed by words like "remember" and "future" signaled her audience that the speech was coming to an end. The next two sentences summarized the points she made in the speech: 1. Psychological damage, remedied by 2. education and knowledge. Finally, she asked the audience to "pass on" information that children need in order to prevent abuse from occurring. A conclusion of four sentences accomplished her goal of ending a successful speech.

Types of Conclusions

Conclusions fall into five categories:

1. Summaries
2. Quotations
3. Personal reference
4. A direct challenge
5. A utopian vision

Methods of stating conclusions mirror strategies for forming introductions, but their intent is to end. Conclusions should bring to the mind of the listener everything the speaker has presented in a very short restatement. It can be done several ways, depending on the response desired. The easiest and most common conclusion is a *summary.* Just a restatement of the major ideas accomplishes the purpose. Sometimes a succinct, bare-bones repeat of key phrases makes the most rousing finish. President Franklin D. Roosevelt warned the nation about the evils of isolation in 1937 with this conclusion:

> America hates war. America hopes for peace. Therefore, America actively engages in the search for peace.

These three simple parallel statements are a brief but highly memorable recapitulation of the main ideas of his "Quarantine"Speech, delivered in Chicago Oct 5, 1937.

Just as many speeches begin with a *quotation,* many end with one. The rules are the same for its use: tie in the quotation with the meaning of the speech. At times, the conclusion can actually forecast the impact of the speech. History remembers Douglas MacArthur returning as a hero from his role in the Korean war, and as a candidate for president of the United States. But his welcome home speech predicted his future. He quoted an old bunkhouse ballad[6]:

> Old Soldiers never die; they just fade away!

Politically, he did! But it was a dramatic ending to a great military career.

Personal reference can be a vivid, emotional conclusion. If the speaker can look into the eyes of the listeners and express personal beliefs in simple, vivid language, the conclusion can make a greater impact than the speech itself. A classic example occurred in Massachusetts following the trial of Nicola Sacco and Bartolomeo Vanzetti. Labor disputes, racial prejudice, and class struggles were critical and highlighted in Vanzetti's strong personal conclusion at his execution[7]:

> If I could be reborn two other times, I would live again to do what I have done already!

Nicola Sacco's conclusion:

> I am never be guilty, never—not yesterday nor today nor forever.

When your speech asks the audience to do something, concluding with a *direct challenge* may be effective. History is filled with great speeches that used this technique to alter history. A classic example was provided by Winston Churchill in the midst of World War II. France had fallen to the German assault, and it was obvious England was Hitler's next objective. On June 18, 1940, Churchill went on national radio with this challenge to not only Britain, but to all the free world[8]:

> Let us therefore brace ourselves to our duties, and so bear ourselves that, if the British Empire and its Commonwealth last for a thousand years, men will say, "This was their finest hour."

Closely related to challenging the audience is a conclusion referred to as a *Utopian Vision*. This conclusion offers an idealized, positive vision of what can be achieved if only the audience will work together with the speaker. Rather than focusing on the challenge, however, this approach emphasizes the results of meeting the challenge successfully. The vision is called "utopian" not to dismiss it but to emphasize that it usually transcends the immediate, practical world.

The most famous example of a utopian conclusion is Martin Luther King's "I Have a Dream" address, delivered in 1963 at the March on Washington:

> . . .When we allow freedom to ring–when we let it ring from every village and every hamlet, from every state and every city–we will be able to speed up that day when all of God's children, black men and white men, Jews and Gentiles, Protestants and Catholics, will be able to join hands and sing in the words of the old Negro spiritual, "Free at last! Free at last! Thank God Almighty, we are free at last!"

The utopian vision conclusion is most effective when the speaker is calling on the audience to make sacrifices or take risks to achieve a distant goal. By predicting ultimate success, the utopian vision assures listeners that the perceived goal is worth the effort to achieve it.

Besides these specific types of conclusions, notice that many of the introductory approaches discussed can also be used for the conclusion, including narratives, anecdotes, and rhetorical questions.[9]

Strategies for Preparing A Conclusion

1. Work on the conclusion after developing the body of the speech. Know first what you are concluding.
2. Connect the conclusion clearly to the body of the speech so that listeners understand its link to the main ideas.
3. Keep the conclusion brief so that it does not distract from the speech itself.
4. Aim for a complete conclusion, including both a wrap-up of the main ideas and a clear statement of action expected by the listeners. This means summarize your arguments memorably as well as suggest a belief or action carried out by the audience.

Chapter 37: Analysis and Application Exercises

1. Prepare an index or collection of materials that can be used for introductions and conclusions. Make sure you have examples of at least four kinds of introductions and conclusions.
2. Write 3 conclusions to a persuasive speech. The topic can be of your choice. Have one be a quotation, one be a utopian vision, and one be a summary.

References

1. N.H. Anderson & A.A. Barrios, "Primacy Effects in Personality Impression Formation," *Journal of Abnormal and Social Psychology*, 63 (September, 1961), 346-350.
2. Classical theorists kuse the language of architecture to describe the organization of speeches. See L.M. Griffin, "The Edifice Metaphor in Rhetorical Theory," *Communication Monographs*, 27 (November, 1960), 279-292.
3. Russell Conwell, Wikipedia encyclopedia.
4. C.R. Gruner, "Advice to the Beginning Speaker on Using Humor–What the Research Tells Us," *Communication Education*, 34 (April 1985), 142-147.
5. For additional discussion on introductions, see, Richard Whately, *Elements of Rhetoric*, Carbondale: Southern Illinois Univ. press, 1963, originally published in 1828, pp. 170-172.
6. Douglas MacArthur, "Old Soldiers Never Die," *Treasures of the Library of Congress*, April 19, 1951. Internet.
7. Houston Peterson, "Sacco and Vanzetti Proclaim Their Innocence," *Treasury of the World's Great Speeches*, (New York: Simon and Schuster, 1954), 741-744.
8. Peterson, "Churchill Anticipates the Battle of Britain," p. 781-782.
9. John W. Bowers and Michael M. Osborn, "Attitudinal Effects of Selected Types of Concluding Metaphors in Persuasive Speeches," *Communication*

CHAPTER 38 Language Use and Style

LEARNING OBJECTIVES

When students have completed this chapter and lesson, they should be able to:

1. Understand and explain the connection between language and style.
2. Know and explain Zarefsky's principles of effective style.
3. Know and explain stylistic patterns that are ineffective and should be avoided.
4. Know and explain how clarity, rhythm, and vividness are manifest in a speaker's style, and what techniques might be used to enhance all of these.

CHAPTER 38: Overview

When we move the discussion of language to the personal level, we begin to talk about personal style. Style can be defined as a pattern of language choices made by a speaker or writer which tend to distinguish him or her from others. Style can be manifested in a number of ways.

David Zarefsky (1999) identifies two common problems when we talk about a speaker's style. "First, style is not always a positive attribute. If a politician has a bullying manner or a preacher is known for mumbling, style will hurt rather than help their effectiveness. Recognize that the distinctive style of a speech can sometimes be negative, as when a speaker keeps saying 'uh,' or peppers the speech with 'like,' or repeats 'you know' so often that listeners start counting the repetitions. These are stylistic patterns, to be sure, but they are also nervous mannerisms; they detract from the message rather than helping it. For some speakers the goal is to remove negative characteristics from a speech. In removing them, however, the speaker is not removing style but is changing it from a nervous, unsure style to a smooth, confident one.

"The other problem is that we often think of style in a speech as ornamentation that is added to the content rather than as part and parcel of the content. In this view, it is enough just to speak plainly and clearly without concern for style. Abraham Lincoln's Gettysburg Address is often cited as an example of a plain speech that is remembered far better than the highly stylistic two-hour address delivered on the same day by Edward Everett. The mistake is to think that Lincoln's speech was pure, distilled content while Everett's had a great deal of added style. In fact, it simply is not possible for a speech to be 'without style.' Every speaker makes choices. In Lincoln's case, obvious stylistic features include plainness of structure, simplicity of wording, abstraction, and even brevity."[1]

Language and Style

Style is accomplished through careful planning of how you will present your speech. Your selection of resources and how you use them to achieve your purpose will both contribute to the resulting style of your speech. So, too, will your choice of the language you will use. Ineffective speakers might take language for granted, giving little thought to what words they choose or how they will use them. If they do, they will be ignoring the most powerful tool they have in making their speech effective and convincing.

Language choice (and therefore style) should vary according to the context and the audience. There is a clear difference in style between a comedy club performance and a political convention speech. In fact, if either speech were given in the other context, it would likely be a dud—completely inappropriate and ineffective.

The same is true of style when comparing a written essay with a public speech. Written communication generally conforms to official rules of grammar and structure called "langue." Speaking informally with your friends conforms to the rules of spoken language, which are much less formal and are called "parole." If someone used the formal rules of the former in his language on the street with his buddies, they would think there was something wrong with him. And the reverse is also true. Public speeches can fall anywhere in between these two extremes, depending on the situation and the audience. But it is absolutely true that a speaker must adopt an appropriate style for the particular subject, setting, and audience where the speech will be given. Otherwise, all credibility could be lost because of inappropriate style.

Written communication allows the readers to proceed at their own pace, to skim over some parts and to re-read others if something is unclear. This is not true of public speeches, which tend to be transient—here one moment and gone the next. The message must be understood in the moment of performance. If either the speaker or the listener are not careful, the message will be missed or misunderstood. If it is not delivered in an interesting and compelling and memorable style, it will be forgotten.

Principles of Effective Style

The following list of principles of effective style is adapted from Zarefsky's[2] excellent work on public speaking:

Simplicity. Oral messages must generally be simpler than written ones. Use shorter and more common words. Make descriptions more brief. Use shorter and less complex sentences. Avoid jargon and technical language. Organize the speech with clearly identified previews, transitions, and summaries. All of these will enhance immediate understanding. If listeners have to guess at the speaker's meaning or intention, they will tire from the mental energy required to understand the message. Their minds will wander and they will be more easily distracted. And because of this, the speech will be ineffective.

Repetition. Unless overdone, repetition serves a number of important purposes. It can highlight your main ideas and provide emphasis, much like italic or boldface type in print. Parallelism (repetition of a particular sentence structure) can help listeners "see" the pattern of your speech, allowing them to follow and anticipate its organization. Repetition is a memory aid for both speaker and listeners. And repetition has been shown by research to be the most powerful tool available in obtaining audience agreement with your claims. For all these reasons, oral style is usually more repetitive than written style. A speaker might repeat key ideas for emphasis or to ensure that listeners did not ignore them. A catchy phrase or refrain might recur throughout the speech. Even the structure of the speech might follow a repetitive pattern. A classic example is Dr. Martin Luther King's "I have a dream" speech in which he repeated that phrase over and over again to give emphasis to a whole series of memorable hopes for the future of race relations in the United States.

Informality. As mentioned earlier, oral style is generally more informal than written style. Few public speakers always speak in complete sentences. Run-on sentences are common in public speeches. And language use is not always grammatically correct. In fact, if a typical public speech were transcribed it would be full of these things. They would be completely inappropriate in written communication, but actually can be of benefit when speaking. The errors aren't noticed. They become part of the informal style of the speech and can add to the speaker's credibility among his or her peers. Of course, there are exceptions to this when speaking at a formal occasion. But generally, informality is preferred by audiences.

Reflexivity. Oral style is more reflexive than written style, meaning that speakers often refer to themselves and to the audience and situation. This is rarely done, and is usually discouraged, in written communication like essays or reports. In writing, the message and its supporting arguments and evidence are what matters. Everything else seems superfluous. But in public speaking, the message will be missed or easily forgotten unless it is delivered in a compelling and reflexive style.

Explicit Organizational Structure. Another form of reflexivity is making your organizational structure explicit be referring to it in your speech. Saying things like "I will present three reasons why I think this is important," "Let me begin by . . .," or "Let me summarize my points as we close." This kind of "signposting" along the way helps listeners to organize what they are hearing and keep track of where they are in the process. Otherwise, they might get lost and their concentration will suffer.

Eliminating Clutter. One dangerous style element in any public speech is clutter. Writers can re-write their messages to eliminate annoying or irrelevant diversions from the main point. Speakers have no such luxury. They cannot revise their remarks after they have come out of their mouths. Any effort to correct themselves adds to the feeling of clutter and reduces the credibility of the speaker. Irrelevant side points or anecdotes can clutter up and unnecessarily extend a speech. And vocalized pauses ("um," "er," "ah"), digressions, pointless repetition, and distracting words like "right," "you know," and "okay" can also be annoying and feel like clutter to an audience. The way to avoid this last problem is to prepare better. Clutter usually occurs when the speaker is trying to buy time to think about something they hadn't thought of before. While thinking, they fill up the void with noises.

Accuracy. If the things you say are incorrect (partially or fully), your listeners will consider your speech to be ineffective and consider you to be incompetent. Be sure to check your facts as well as your language to make sure that you are accurately describing things.

Appropriateness. Your language must be appropriate to the audience and situation. You want to show listeners that you understand and respect them. If your language is critical or patronizing then they will feel insulted, and your style will undercut your message. Also, be sure to match your overall tone to the situation in which the speech is given. Vulgar language, for example, would be jarring and inappropriate in a formal setting. And what you might consider to be dry wit could be interpreted by others as sarcasm.

This can be especially challenging when your listeners have different cultural backgrounds. If you are uninformed or insensitive to how a culture uses particular language, you may easily offend someone. On one occasion an exchange student from Asia came to my public speaking class in the United States. He had been in the country only a few days, and even though his English language skills were very good, he was basically clueless as to cultural language norms. He had spent the weekend watching late night television and movies to try to get a feeling for how people acted and spoke in public. Then, on Monday (the first day of classes) he showed up in my class and struck up conversations with fellow students. As he did so, he used the f-word in just about every sentence, and I could see the students wincing with every utterance. I pulled him aside after class and told him that it was not appropriate to use such language so freely in public places among people he didn't know. He was very apologetic and embarrassed. He had no idea what was, and what was not, appropriate.

Inappropriate Style—Things to Avoid

Self-important or pretentious language. Sometimes, in an effort to sound informed and intelligent, speakers come across as being arrogant. One example is the use of highly-technical language in front of an audience that does not understand such terms. Another would be to sound condescending while telling an audience that they are not intelligent or educated enough to understand or appreciate your views. The speaker's goal is to obtain a favorable response from the audience. This can be done more effectively if the audience feels understood and appreciated. Talking down to them will never achieve that purpose.

Disrespectful language. Racial slurs, sexist references, and ethnic jokes degrade other people and are inappropriate even if not directed at the audience in front of you. Avoid any comments that could be construed as disrespectful, even if they are aimed at your own race, gender, or ethnicity.

Inappropriate emotion. Your emotional tone should match the occasion. Generally, you would not offer criticism of a person at his funeral. Neither would you be negative and gloomy at a rally. While the rules regarding emotional tone tend to differ according to culture, and no rule regarding tone is absolute, you must ensure that your tone will be perceived as appropriate by your audience. Carefully assess the nature and context of the speaking situation, and match your tone to your audience's expectations.

Jargon. Jargon is specialized language. This may occur within a given field of knowledge, but can also be manifest in special language developed and used by social groups ("street language"). The legal profession, science, athletics, religion, medicine, music, accounting, and many other professional fields have specialized languages that people within the profession may understand clearly, but those outside of the group will not. Generally, you should not use jargon in a speech. If it is absolutely necessary you are obligated to define these terms in language that your audience will understand. When speaking with such groups, the use of jargon can actually be a positive thing. It establishes your credibility within the group and tends to bond you with your audience. But if you use such terms in front of such an audience, make sure you use them correctly so that you don't appear to be incompetent and phony.

Clarity, Rhythm, and Vividness

Clarity

Because your speech is transient—listeners cannot rewind and re-play it—you first make your speech as easy as possible to understand. The following stylistic resources can increase the clarity of your message.

Definitions. Offering definitions is one way to clarify technical language or to establish the meaning you intend when your meaning might be mis-construed. Such definitions might be denotative—the "official" definition found in a current dictionary. Or they might be connotative— the meaning generally associated with a term and/or the specialized meaning it might have to a particular individual. Remember that in most cases, audiences will interpret your language connotatively, according to their own meanings for your words and not according to any official meaning from a dictionary. If your terms might be misunderstood by your audience, you should always carefully define what you mean.

Concrete Words and Images. Highly abstract ideas are hard for an audience to follow. More specific, concrete examples are better. To say, "This will cost more than the combined cost of our current military and domestic spending overseas" is an abstract idea that may or may not be easily comprehended by your audience. To say, "This will cost 80 billion dollars" is more concrete. You can add to the concreteness of your idea by using images that are easily imagined by your audience. "That's enough dollars, if laid end-to-end, to stretch to Mars and back three times." Concrete, clear facts and images help an audience understand and remember a message.

Maxims. "Maxims, or aphorisms, are short, pithy statements—often in the form of proverbs —that are familiar to most people and can be used to describe a situation or idea. The speaker who explains scandals in government by saying, "We've put the fox out to guard the chicken coop," succinctly expresses an idea that most listeners will grasp instinctively: Those with a motive to cause trouble should not be put in a situation that permits them to do so. Maxims contribute to clarity by offering listeners a memorable phrase that encompasses a larger argument or theme."[3]

Word Economy. When speaking, you must use words efficiently and avoid unnecessary words. "Audiences find it difficult and tiresome to follow a speech that beats around the bush, that is cluttered with digressions, extraneous ideas, inexact wording, and nervous asides such as 'like,' 'okay,' 'now,' or 'right' in nearly every sentence. If you tape and listen to one of your speeches, you may be surprised to discover the amount of such clutter and to hear how it obscures the clarity of your message. Try to identify the things you do that create clutter; then make a conscious effort to reduce it. Especially avoid overly complex sentences, excessive use of adjectives and adverbs, and needless hedging terms or qualifiers."[4]

Active Voice. In the quest for "objectivity," scholars often resort to passive language—a pattern of expression that describes what happens but eliminates who did it. The examples below were discussed in chapter 36 of this text.

Active voice: "I kicked the dog."	Subject-verb-object with a strong vivid verb.
Passive voice: "The dog was kicked."	Object first (dog); No subject; weak verb (was).

Passive language uses "to be" verbs rather than strong, active, vivid ones. The "to be" verbs include "is," "are," "was," "were," "will be," and "has been" for example. A quick way to spot passive language is to look for these words. Wherever they are found, you can make the sentence more active by reorganizing it and make sure that there is a subject (the agent performing the action) and a strong active verb. Active voice makes statements more clear because they tend to be organized in a subject-verb-object fashion which listeners can easily follow. Passive sentences literally have to be reorganized in the listener's mind before they can make sense of them. And after a while, listeners tire of having to put forth that much mental energy to listen to a speech.

Irony. Irony is to say the opposite of what is meant. For example, if in exasperation I say, "Oh, great!" I am not really saying that something is good; I'm saying that it is bad. This usually involves the use of vocal tones or other nonverbal clues that make it clear that you should not take the words literally. Irony can add a bit of humor or color to a speech that audiences might appreciate. But be careful with irony. If listeners do not recognize that your statement is ironic, you may confuse them or even convince them in a way you did not intend.

Ambiguity. Ambiguity is a lack of clarity. It may seem odd to suggest that the use of ambiguity can be positive, when we have emphasized so much the need for clarity. But sometimes ambiguity can be helpful, particularly when you are trying to unify a group of people around a general idea who disagree with each other on the details. For example, the term "family values" can have more than one meaning to various individuals. But they could unite under the banner of "family values" nevertheless. Again, as with irony, you must use ambiguity sparingly and wisely, making sure you do not appear deceitful or contradictory in your claims.

Rhythm

Rhythm is the sense of pacing within a speech. Speeches are heard and therefore the "sound" of the speech becomes an issue. You might sound hurried, for example. Generally speaking, a varied rhythm is preferable because it does not become predictable and therefore maintains a sense of freshness. You can vary the pace of a speech, slowing down in places and speeding up in others to convey a different mood. You can deliberately repeat words or phrases as a way of connecting ideas under a common theme. Following are some of the ideas you might consider for the rhythm of your speech.

Repetition. When you repeat an idea, argument, phrase, or theme you add to its significance. Martin Luther King's "I Have a Dream" speech is probably the best known example of repetition as a method of persuasion.

Parallel Wording. One form of repetition that is particularly important in helping your listeners follow along is parallel wording. Consider the following examples.

Not parallel: My favorite hobbies are singing, to read books, and a hike in the woods.
Parallel: My favorite hobbies are singing, reading, and hiking.

In the second (parallel) example, each part of the series is stated similarly, with an "ing" on the end of it. Its rhythm flows easily. The non-parallel example is more jarring and harder to understand.

Antithesis. Antithesis is the pairing of opposites in order to compare them and suggest that a choice should be made between them. "Shall we spend our national treasure making war overseas or keep the money at home and help the poor?" pairs up two choices and suggests that it has to be one or the other. The technique provides a quick summary statement of ideas that the audience can weigh in their minds. Another example of antithesis is the one used by President John F. Kennedy in his inaugural address: "Ask not what your country can do for you—ask what you can do for your country." This lays out the choice between being dependent on the government and the spirit of voluntarism.

Inversions of Word Order. Kennedy's "ask not" phrase also illustrates how normal word patterns can be reversed for emphasis. Instead of the expected "do not ask," he reverses the words into "ask not." This can make the phrase more memorable because of its unusual rhythm, which draws more attention to it from the audience.

Vivid. Graphic; easy to picture. A speech is vivid if its language enables listeners to develop mental pictures of what is being said.

Description. A cumulation of details that suggest a mental picture of a person, event, or situation.

Vividness

To make something vivid is to make it easy to picture in our minds. Humans are uniquely visual creatures who remember best that which they see. Even a common phrase like, "Oh, I see" when telling somebody you understand them reveals the importance we give to visual images. Visual models help us understand abstract principles. A map helps us find our way through strange territory. And vividness in a speech helps the listener to "see" what you are saying. It also adds color and interest. Here are some ways to make your speech more vivid.

Description. You can help your audience picture what you are saying by providing careful description. I once read a student paper wherein the student painted the picture of a run-down apartment in New York City where she had gone to become a dancer. Her details of wallpaper hanging down, dimly lit corners, and the musty smell of mold painted a memorable picture in the reader's mind of the scene. Description can be used to paint images of people, places, or things. But to be effective it requires careful choice of words that evoke the mental images desired. You can't use general terms to paint a vivid mental picture.

Stories. It seems like everybody loves a good story, not only because it permits us to "see" characters and events, but because we love human connections. We can relate to the persons in the story as fellow human beings. A story has power not only because of its familiar narrative form but also because it permits listeners to "see" what is going on and to identify with it. We can try to understand the need for organ donation, for example, as an abstract principle. But it is much more powerful to tell the story of a young woman who is with us today because somebody donated a kidney.

Similes and Metaphors. Socrates once said that we cannot teach somebody something that they do not already know. What he meant was that unless a person can compare a concept to something they have already learned or experienced, they cannot comprehend it.

A simile is an explicit statement that one thing is like another. I might say, for example, that "paying taxes is like having your tooth pulled." Since most people have had the experience of having a tooth pulled, it enhances understanding of how I feel about paying taxes.

A metaphor names something as if it actually were the other. I might say that paying taxes is "a thorn in my side." Or I might say that my attorney's home is "a palace." In both of these examples, I'm not using the word "like" but assuming that if I call something by a different name you'll understand my point. But be careful, because metaphors tend to be culturally specific. If I say, "I'm bushed" in the United States you would probably understand that this figure of speech means I'm tired. It might not mean that at all in another culture.

Vivid Sounds: Alliteration and Onomatopoeia. You also can create vividness in a speech through patterns of word sounds. Alliteration is a repetitive consonant sound, as in "Big Bang" or "Long Lost" These examples repeat the hard consonant sound of the "b" or the "l" to give emphasis to the phrase. Onomatopoeia is the use of sounds that resemble what they describe. The "buzzing" of a bee or the "hissing" of a snake are words that sound like the very thing they are describing. These can certainly make an idea more vivid.

Personification. People prefer to hear about people, not abstract concepts. Therefore, we can sometimes personify a concept as a way of making it more vivid and memorable. Speaking of a specific starving young child, whose picture I display, would be more powerful than just talking about world hunger in general. The idea becomes more concrete in people's minds when they have a human example of it in front of them, with which they can relate and for whom they might be willing to take specific action.

Rhetorical questions. When a speaker asks a question for which no answer is expected; the audience still thinks about it and answers it in their minds. "Is this the kind of community we want to leave for our children to inherit?" is an example of a rhetorical question.

Dialogue. Dialogue is the reproduction of a conversation by including what both interactants said in a series of consecutive responses. The audience becomes like a fly on the wall listening to two people talk, and the "overheard" conversation gets them more involved in the speech. Sometimes dialogue is manufactured as way of presenting ideas. For example, the speaker might say, "Well, some of you might say, 'Why were you there in the first place?' And my answer would be 'because I was looking for friends.'"

Chapter 38: Analysis and Application Exercises

1. Experts study and discuss cultural differences in how language is used and interpreted. In the context of your culture and experiences, what kinds of words do you find unacceptable, and why? Would they be inappropriate in a different cultural setting? Why or why not?
2. Review the basic requirements for effective style discussed above. Within these guidelines, list at least five ways advertisers use language effectively to make certain products more appealing to consumers. For at least one of them, offer a specific example of a commercial that used effective style and explain why you think it is effective according to the principles discussed in this chapter.
3. Study evening television programs and/or commercials for an evening and note any inappropriate uses of language style. What made them inappropriate in the context within which they were used? For example, comedies often feature people being embarrassed by saying inappropriate things or by saying things in the wrong situation or context.

References

1. Zarefsky, D. (1999). *Public speaking: Strategies for Success*, 2nd ed., quoted in Chase, R.S., and Jones, S.G., *Elements of Effective Communication*, 2nd ed., Boston, MA: Allyn & Bacon, 1999, p. 283.
2. Zarefsky, pp. 421–422.
3. Zarefsky, p. 425.
4. Zarefsky, p. 426.

CHAPTER 39 Delivery

LEARNING OBJECTIVES

When students have completed this chapter and lesson, they should be able to:

1. Define effective oral delivery.
2. Define and identify circumstances where the speaker's method of delivery was:
   - **A.** Manuscript
   - **B.** From memory
   - **C.** Impromptu
   - **D.** Extemporaneous
3. Explain why nonverbal communication techniques are often as important as language.
4. List and demonstrate four vocal aspects of oral delivery.
5. Develop three suggestions for improving oral delivery.

CHAPTER 39: Overview

Delivery methods of impromptu, manuscript, memorized, and extemporaneous presentation are reviewed. The vocal and physical aspects of delivery are identified and discussed. Methods of improving vocal delivery are reviewed.

Public speaking in history is really the description of accomplished speakers who have learned the power of the human voice. Colonial history describes the Virginian Patrick Henry who was a giant in advocating and developing policy and law. As he spoke for separation from English domination, he was legend. Remembering his call for breaking with England, a Baptist clergyman described it vividly:

> The tendons of his neck stood out white and rigid, like whipcords. His voice rose louder and louder, until the walls of the building and all within them seemed to shake and rock in its tremendous vibrations. Finally his pale face and glaring eyes became terrible to look upon. Men leaned forward in their seats with their heads strained forward, their faces pale and their eyes glaring like the speaker's. When he sat down, the listener felt sick with excitement. Every eye was glued on Henry. It seemed as if a word from him would have led to any wild explosion of violence. Men looked beside themselves. There was no applause; only silence. No reply; just the vote, as the resolution was adopted viva voce. The Revolution was launched.[1]

The message delivered by a speaker is vital. The method of delivery is irreplaceable. An effective delivery conveys the speaker's purpose in a way that the audience either accepts and retains, or rejects. The effectiveness of a speech, therefore, depends on two vital characteristics: Its content and the way it is delivered. Both are necessary for success.

Few if any speakers could have been as effective in delivering the message to the world in August 28, 1963 as Martin Luther King did. Contemporary historians judge his presentation as one of the greatest of the century.

This speech, widely regarded as a masterpiece, was delivered to over 200,000 people gathered in Washington, D.C., to participate in a peaceful demonstration furthering the cause of equal rights for Americans. Historians are still applauding his rich baritone voice modulated by the cadences of a Southern Baptist preacher, and the fervor of the crusader. Overlooked are the repetitive hand movements, and the perspiration in the face. Remembered is the setting, the timing, and circumstances for change so critically needed. Under the shadow of Abraham Lincoln, King appealed for justice and equal rights for every person, especially the blacks that looked to him as a leader.

Beginning with these two examples, this chapter is dedicated to exploring how the speaker can deliver a message in a successful way. A poorly written speech can be improved by effective delivery, and a well-written speech can be ruined by ineffective delivery. No set of rules will guarantee an effective delivery in every situation. The only consistent rule is that you must be yourself. Questions immediately arise. What kind and now many notes should I have? Will I need a microphone? Where and how should I stand? Where or at whom should I look? How many and what kinds of gestures should I use? How and when should I use my visual aids? How loudly should I speak? How fast or slow should my speaking be?

These and many other questions are valid, but answers will vary from person to person and from situation to situation. Basically, effectively delivery comes from practice under the direction of a competent instructor. An awareness of self and knowledge of effective delivery also help improve the effects of the speech. The four most common ways of delivering a speech are impromptu, memorized, manuscript, and extemporaneous.

Impromptu delivery

This type of speech is given without any formal or specific planning. The speaker has no chance for research or organization. It often comes as a surprise or without warning to the speaker. You have used this method many times without even knowing it. Whenever you speak without prior preparation, whether in response to a question in class, to a sudden request at a business meeting, or to a comment make by a friend, you are using the impromptu method of delivery. Speakers generally avoid this method simply because there is no chance of preparing the speech. At times, however, you have no choice. In such cases, muster your self-control, relax, and concentrate on what you wish to say. Consider three major concepts we have previously mentioned, and utilize your training to sound prepared even in these conditions: Be organized, be informed, and be gone! Some guidelines.

1. *Stay calm,* and consider the situation or topic. If none is given, select one immediately.
2. *Think of a story,* a personal experience, or an incident that relates to the topic.
3. *Make a declarative statement* about the experience, forming a personal opinion about your stand on the topic. If you cannot think of one, change the topic to an experience you can remember.
4. State your position in terms of a ***single idea.*** Remember that disorganization is unattractive, but one can stay organized on one idea. Illustrate that idea by telling your memorable experience.
5. *Conclude by taking a positive, definite stand on the issue* in terms of an informed lesson learned from your experience.
6. After making a brief, pleasant concluding statement, ***stop***. Short impromptu speeches are best!

By thinking quickly on your feet, by telling an interesting experience, and by drawing a sharp conclusion from your experience, you sound informed, organized, and certainly not embarrassed.

Manuscript Delivery

Reading a speech word for word is known as **manuscript delivery.** This is totally opposite from the impromptu, beginning with the fact that the speaker is never at a loss for words. Sometimes the situation demands exact wording, where every word, phrase, and sentence must be stated precisely. Manuscript speeches are the rule rather than an exception for politicians, clergy, and even teachers when precision by words and precise meaning is necessary, especially if those words might be quoted.

Manuscript speeches are usually discouraged by professional communicators because delivery brings with it a host of problems: First: most people are not skilled in reading orally, and sound that way. The speaker buries their head in the manuscript, never looking at the audience. This greatly inhibits feedback, eye contact, and ability to respond to audience reaction. Speaking from manuscript limits adaptation to audience response, and it sounds mechanical. Any kind of audience interaction is greatly inhibited. Should question-answer situations arise, the speaker usually drops the manuscript and moves to impromptu or extemporaneous speaking style.

Successful manuscript speaking is more likely achieved when following the five rules for manuscript speaking:

1. *Write your manuscript for the ear.* Remember that a reader can go back and reread a sentence, but one cannot go back and rehear something read to them. Make sure the sentences are clear, concise, and easily understood.
2. *Prepare your manuscript in an easy-to-read format.* Use large font in a common print format. Triple space the lines. Use special marks and comments to note words and phrases you wish to give special emphasis.
3. *Think about what you are saying.* Concentrate on reading thoughts and not words. Try to make your voice sound spontaneous and meaningful. Try to *sound like you are talking.*
4. *Read with expression and vocal emphasis.* Novice readers are usually monotone, without expression, speaking too quietly and too rapidly. Your voice can add meaning to the words with proper inflection, and emphasis.
5. *Practice reading out loud,* preferably with a recorder. The key to success is to sound as if the thoughts you are reading are fresh. The manuscript should be presented with enthusiasm, vigor, and interest.[2]

Memorized delivery

A speech committed to memory, word for word, and delivered without notes is called memorized , or oratory style. This kind of delivery is used for short presentations, such as toasts, acceptance speeches, and introductions. It is also commonly used by speakers in contests and on lecture circuits. Speakers frequently memorize certain parts of their speeches, including examples, short stories, statistics, and quotations. Politicians, salesmen, tour guides, and entertainers often have a memorized speech to fit their needs.

Memorized speeches permit the speaker to focus on vocal emphasis and delivery, and less on what is said. This, however, tends to make the speaker want to be more dramatic and mechanical. The speaker should concentrate on precise language that produces the desired understanding and emotion as they practice for their "performance" intended in the speech.

The disadvantages of this delivery is that it takes time to commit the speech to memory, accompanied by the risk of memory loss and embarrassment. Even though the speaker can watch the audience carefully, flexibility in adapting, adding new information, or changing information is not possible. Effective presentation of a memorized speech requires a great deal of practice and confidence. The guidelines about manuscript speeches apply equally to memorized delivery. It is usually more effective, less work, and more satisfying to present an extemporaneous speech.

Extemporaneous Delivery

A speaker who uses carefully prepared notes delivered in a conversational, spontaneous delivery is an extemporaneous speaker. This method is most commonly used in speech classrooms and other communication situations. When you give a report at work or school, you are probably expected to do so extemporaneously. If you are a member of a problem solving group and are asked to present your findings, it is expected extemporaneously. This is the best style of speaking for most experiences because it suggests personal, honest response from a credible source.

Extemporaneous delivery is situated somewhere between memorized or manuscript delivery and impromptu delivery. Speakers depend on a brief presentational outline or notes and choose the actual wording of the speech at the time of delivery. Sometimes key word outlines or simple sentence outlines are used. Others use a more detailed format, but the idea is to put ideas in writing, and use spontaneous words, convincing the audience the speaker is more sincere and personal with the message.

It is much easier to listen to speakers who are conversational, lively, and spontaneous. Audiences value such presentations as more genuine and sincere than either memorized or manuscript speeches. This type of speaking gives the speaker better control over the presentation than does impromptu. It allows more spontaneity and directness than the memorized and manuscript method. It permits the speaker more flexibility to adapt and change ideas to better respond to the feedback audiences give the speaker. Most teachers and professional speakers use this method because it allows them to adjust to the situation moment by moment. Extemporaneous delivery also allows audience members to become more involved in listening to the message.

Table 39.1

Methods of Delivery: Advantages and Disadvantages

	Advantages	**Disadvantages**
Impromptu	Spontaneous Flexible Conversational	No preparation time Can be inaccurate Difficult to organize Stressful
Memorized	Good for short speeches Speaker can concentrate on delivery Easier to maintain eye contact Prepared	Inflexible Requires practice and repetition Speaker can forget Difficult to adapt to audience response May sound mechanical
Manuscript	Good for technical or detailed Material Provides preciseness Can be timed to the second Prepared	No flexibility Large preparation time Difficult to adapt to audience response, May sound mechanical Lack of eye contact Poor audience feedback
Extemporaneous	Organized Flexible Conversational Prepared Great amount of eye contact	May be intimidating to inexperienced speakers

Vocal and Physical Aspects of Delivery

Without solid content and valid sources, nothing is worth communicating; but without effective delivery, even the most compelling information cannot be clearly and vividly presented. The ultimate factor in communication, as we learned in the chapter on listening, is the audience. Without their acceptance, no communication occurs. People do not communicate in isolation. Following is a review of vocal and physical aspects and their critical importance in the communication process.

Vocal aspects

Vocal aspects of communication can be most easily understood with three axioms.

The accomplished speaker must speak
A. *Loudly enough to be heard!*
B. *Clearly enough to be understood!*
C. *Pleasantly enough to be endured!*

Vocal Quality

Combined with these axioms is the inference that the more natural, spontaneous, and effortless the speaker appears to be, the more listeners focus on **what** is said rather than **how** it is said. The first factor controlling our ability to communicate is to make the audience aware we are communicating. The key word is **intelligibility**, or the degree to which an audience can hear and understand the words spoken. To determine the proper volume, you must consider the size of the room and observe listener's reactions. Do listeners look as if they're straining to hear you?

Listeners are a lazy lot. If they have to strain to get the message, they will simply tune out the speaker and mentally visit some other domain. The speaker must carefully monitor the attention level of his audience to be sure they are getting the message in the first place.

Once the sound waves record a response from the audience, the speaker is responsible for monitoring that reaction to see how well the message is received. Voices may be harsh, nasal, thin, mellow, resonant, or even irritating. Through nuances of sound, the speaker can convey happiness, excitement, tiredness, or anger. Immediately our listeners record a reaction, placing a stamp of approval or rejection on the speaker. As listeners, if we have heard the sound, then recorded it as unpleasant, again we join that magic carpet of imagination and quickly leave the scene for more pleasant memories. Vocal quality is a highly accurate indicator of the presenter's sincerity. Also listeners tend to find speakers whose vocal delivery is interesting and easy to listen to more credible. People will listen to good articulation.

The most common "filler" is the word "ugh." Someone once said that speakers use "ugh" every few words to make sure the vocal system is still operating. The speaker is suspected of having a fear of silence, so fills every open space with "ugh." Others use an automatic test pattern to check the listeners by filling every vacant space with "you know" or "like."

A story is told of John Doe, who had a problem saying "ugh" too often in his reports in an English course. The class was taught by having students tell their short stories being studied by the class, then discussing their attributes after hearing the story. A schedule was posted as to when each student presented their story. When John spoke, the "ughs," which came about every fifth word, were vocalized and nasalized, but it did not really matter. None of the students showed up for his report!

Another story is told of a science teacher, who attempted to clarify the scientific principles he taught with constant redefinition, introduced by the phrase "or in other words."

The students in his class had a policy that any one sitting on the back row had to buy a "lottery ticket." The ticket bought a number, guessing how many times those fateful words were spoken. The student telling the story had won $21 the day before on the number 412. One of the more scientific students in the class determined that the professor said "or in other words" almost twenty percent of the time. Chances were that few students could remember the scientific principle for that day's lecture but for years they remembered the "other words" lottery!

One student in a public speaking class had a bad habit of saying "ugh." To remedy the problem, everyone decided to would raise their hand to alert the student to how bad the problem was. She started the first phrase with "ugh." All hands went up. Again she started, with the same result. Finally, in frustration she just sat down because "ugh" was her starter for talking, and without it she could not begin.

In these incidents, the problem with the delivery was the speaker was not aware of the problem. Habits are difficult to break. It requires constant listening to your own voice to correct these problems.

Unfortunately, many people do not realize their articulation or vocal production, or the way they speak can be a major roadblock to what is presented to an audience. Listen to what you say and how you sound. Concentrate on identifying and eliminating your most common articulation errors. Correcting your vocal errors can be well worth the effort; you will sound more intelligent and more professional, and you will further establish your credibility as an educated person.

Vocal variety

The combination of rate, force and pitch variations that add to a speaker's overall vocal quality are called **vocal variety.** Variety gives feeling to your delivery and adds emphasis to what you say. Your voice allows listeners to perceive subtle differences in the intent of your messages by altering rate, force and pitch, promoting a genuine understanding between you and your audience.

Rate is the speed at which a speaker speaks–usually between 120 and 150 words per minute. Speaking at the appropriate rate requires self-awareness. A rate that is too fast, too slow, or that never changes can detract from the impact of your message. Anxiety directly affects our speaking by causing us to accelerate, sometimes to the point where no one can understand. Such problems are usually known to the speaker, and drawing attention to the problem can remedy it.

The first approach should be to purposefully inject a pause at the end of each sentence, and everywhere a comma goes. Focus on emphasizing the meaning rather than racing toward a conclusion. Listen carefully to accomplished speakers. Notice how an effective speaker varies rate and uses pauses to set off ideas, to prepare for moving to the next point, and to provide silent emphasis to ideas. Practice using breaks of silence for emphasis. Accomplished speakers tend to do this within the context of a conversational style.

Force is the intensity and volume level of the voice. You must choose a volume level that is comfortable for your audience. However, you can use force to communicate your ideas with confidence, to emphasize an important point, and to regain lagging interest. By learning how to use force, you can greatly increase your effectiveness as a speaker.

Pitch refers to how low or high the voice is on a tonal scale. Variety in pitch can eliminate monotony and add emphasis to key words. Variety in pitch contributes to greater attention and listening, and thus makes it easy for the audience to maintain interest in and attention to the speaker and message.

A husband and wife minister team used to go on the revival circuit, drawing large numbers of teens. However, the response to the motivational messages seemed to be lacking. People attended not to hear the religious message, but to listen to the voices of the two speakers. The woman usually spoke first, challenging the audience to change their religious fervor in a very deep, contralto voice. After a rest song, the husband, in a very high pitched almost-soprano voice picked up the challenge even further. Few could report the message, but could go into vivid detail about the uniqueness and almost oxymoron message given by the pitch of the speakers' voices.

Obviously, any change in the rate, force, or pitch makes a word, phrase, or sentence stand out. The greater the amount of change or the more sudden the change, the more emphatic the word or statement will be. You can use vocal variety to make selected ideas seem more important than the material delivered without such variations.

Physical Aspects

Chapter 6 reviewed the concept of nonverbal communication in depth. Nonverbal communication makes a significant contribution to communication of a message, just by the appearance, actions and sounds produced by the speaker.

These variables include personal appearance, body movement, gestures, facial expressions, paralingual sounds, and eye contact. Each of these must be well coordinated and relevant to the purpose of the speech

Personal Appearance–what a speaker looks like and the way a speaker dresses, grooms, and presents himself or herself is an important consideration. Typical "student attire" or "publically acceptable" appearance is not speaker acceptable. As a general rule, appropriate dress should reflect the situation, the topic, and the physical conditions. Large, dangling earrings, crude t-shirts, and baseball caps worn backwards may distract your audience from what you are saying (both verbally and nonverbally). First impressions, followed by acceptance of your verbal message, are often based on appearance. First impressions form quickly and form hard-to-change opinions about your attitude toward them and yourself. In this way, appearance can affect your credibility. The old saying "What I see rings so loudly in my ears I cannot hear what you say" is more than a wise saying. It is almost a prediction of the results of your message.

Personal appearance in communication directly influences interpersonal responses to our communication messages. In some situations, appearance can have a profound impact on a speaker's self-image and therefore affect how he or she communicates with others.[3] Looking your best does help convey your message. Credibility alone is often established in the first few minutes of employment interviews. Audiences make evaluations about speakers on the same basis. In addition, looking good makes you feel good, which ultimately has a positive effect on performance.

Body Movement is closely related to personal appearance. It includes posture, which should be relaxed and natural; avoid slouching. An audience's attention instinctively follows moving objects. Therefore your movements should be easy and purposeful. Stepping to the side, forward, or backward, can aid in holding attention and communicating ideas more clearly. Movement can serve as a nonverbal transition between two points in the speech. Purposeful movement and posture can indicate confidence and a positive self-image. Random movement, nervous stepping or shifting weight conveys nervousness and translates into reduced credibility.

You can use *gestures*–movements of the head, arms and hands, to help illustrate, emphasize, or clarify a point. Gestures should be coordinated but spontaneous, not forced. Strong feelings usually include larger gestures. Sadness, anger, or happiness can be interpreted by hand movement, facial expression, and body movement. Audiences look for such cues to determine attitude and strength of belief. Gestures should be spontaneous and natural. Planned gestures generally come across as artificial, and sometimes even humorous if they are out of coordination.

Facial Expressions are configurations of the face that can reflect, augment, contradict, or be unrelated to a speaker's vocal delivery. You cannot control your face completely, which is why facial expressions become critical in such areas as assessing lying or other types of emotional responses. A speaker can be even more communicative if they attempt to coordinate facial expression with verbal messages. Such examples are anger, happiness, satisfaction, displeasure. If the speaker looks angry, and their vocal expression repeats the feeling, valid communication is increased. The audience will be able to "read" your face. Because your audience will infer a great deal from your facial expression, it is important to look warm and friendly. Such an expression will inform your listeners that you are interested in them and in what you are saying. Facial signals of emotion that an audience perceives when scanning your face to see how you feel about yourself have been identified as *affect displays*.[4]

Researcher Albert Mehrabian has devised a formula to account for the emotional impact of the different components of a speaker's message. Words contribute only 7 percent; vocal elements, 38 percent, and facial expressions, 55 percent.[5] Obviously these data are estimates. But even if they are off by a large margin, it is true that the face and eyes communicate volumes to an audience.

Your topic, your purpose, the situation, and your audience will all determine exactly which facial expressions are appropriate as you progress through your speech.

Eye Contact may be the most critical nonverbal message that can be sent. The extent to which a speaker looks directly at audience members seems more related to a speaker's feelings about the listeners. Eye contact is the most important physical aspect of delivery, as it indicates interest and concern for others, and implies self-confidence. Eye to eye contact often suggests direct link communication between communicators. Behaviorists have suggested the eyes are one of the more reliable sources of communication, for most individuals communicate most honestly, and even subconsciously through the eyes. Police departments have accepted as routine the "Reid Technique" for interviewing suspects to determine the truthfulness of their testimony. Many believe that is one source of communication that conveys messages honestly. It has become a major tool in police investigations.[6]

Communication teachers recommend you look your audience in their eyes while you are speaking, not over their heads, nor at a spot on the wall.

Eyes are the link that establishes a communicative bond between speaker and listener. Failure to make eye contact is the quickest way to lose listeners. Speakers who ignore their audiences are often perceived as tentative, ill at ease, insincere, or dishonest.

Eye contact with your audience should be pleasant and personal. Give your listeners the feeling you are talking to them individually. Try to look at each individual for a few seconds at a time. To avoid looking shifty, move your eyes gradually and smoothly from one person to another. Try to scan the whole audience if possible. Do not avoid some, or concentrate just on a few. Staring at one person can give the impression you are angry or hostile.

Your eyes should convey that you are confident and sincere and are speaking with conviction. The message your audience should get from your eyes is you care about them and about what you are saying. For the novice, eye contact is a bit uncomfortable, but as you gain experience, you will begin to feel more at ease. You will soon find that making eye contact puts you in control of the situation and helps you answer such questions as: Can they hear me? Do they understand? Are they listening?

As an aid to communication delivery, Table 39.2 lists several behaviors that distract from speech effectiveness. Ask a friend to listen to your speech, then comment on these distracting behaviors to help you avoid such problems.

Table 32.2 **Behaviors that Detract from Effective Delivery**

General Delivery	Speaking too fast, Speaking too slowly, Sighing, Nervous smiling or laughing, Choppy pacing, Awkward pausing
Face	Deadpan or serious look, Facial contortions (scowling), Listless or apathetic look
Hands	Fidgeting, Waving or meaningless motions, Hand in pocket or locked in a set position, Playing with hair
Eyes	ShiftygGlances, Rolling movements, Looking at the floor, Looking at one side of room, Looking at the ceiling, Staring, Lack of sustained eye contact
Voice	Sing-song speech pattern, Monotone voice, Nasal twang, Mumbling, Speaking too softly or too fast, Speaking too loudly, High pitch, Shrillness, Stridency, Lack of variety in pace, volume, or pitch
Body	Tense, stiff posture, Sloppy posture, Hunched shoulders, Wiggling, Leaning on lectern
Feet	Shuffling, Shifting weight, Swaying side to side, Crossing legs

Polishing Your Delivery

The best way to polish your deliver is to practice, practice, practice. Practice early and often until you feel comfortable with your speech content. Exactly how much practice you will need depends on a number of considerations, including how much experience you have had in speaking before audiences, how familiar you are with your subject, and how long your speech is.

If your speech is not to be memorized, make sure to use slightly different wording in each run-through. When you memorize a speech, it is possible to master the words without mastering the content. Your goal should be to learn your speech, which will mean that you have mastered its ideas.

Make a recording of the speech and critique it yourself. Have a friend or acquaintance watch you and also give a critique. Someone else can often spot ways to make your presentation more effective.

In practicing your delivery, it is important to start with small segments. For example, practice the introduction, then one main point at a time, and then the conclusion. After you have rehearsed each small segment several times in isolation, practice the entire speech until believe that you have mastered the content and the ideas flow smoothly.

If possible, practice in the same room where you will speak or under similar conditions. This helps you see how things look from the front of the room and to plan where you should place your visual aids. Your last practice session should leave you with a sense of confidence and a desire to present your speech.

Finally, concentrate on your audience, and what you wish them to hear. Above all, be yourself.

Chapter 39: Analysis and Application Exercises

I. Articulation exercise.
Read the following tongue twisters several times. Start slowly, then continue increasing your rate of speed until you are going faster than you usually speak.
A. Rubber Buggy Bumper Wheels

B. The sixth sick Sheik's sheep is sick.
C. She sells seashells by the seashore.
At your next class session, discuss these questions in small groups.
1. What problems did you first encounter?
2. What, if anything, made it easier to complete the exercise?

II. Using pauses:
Read aloud the first sentence without any pauses and then read the second sentence with pauses.
A. The little boy and his dog having tired of fishing wandered slowly along the dusty path in the late afternoon.
B. The little boy and his dog, having tired of fishing, wandered slowly along the dusty path in the late afternoon.
Discuss the following:
1. The difference in emphasis caused by the pauses.
2. The importance of the use of pauses as a means of making a message more meaningful.
3. The difference in the speaker's delivery of the two sentences.

III. Using your voice effectively:
Read the following excerpt from Lewis Carroll's "The Walrus and the Carpenter" with no vocal variety–that is, do not vary your rate, force, or pitch. Then read it using vocal variety–vary your rate, force, and pitch in order to put more meaning into the reading of the poem.

The sun was shining on the sea,
Shining with all his might.

He did his very best to make
The billows smooth and bright–

And this was odd, because it was
The middle of the night.

1. What difference between the two versions did you hear?
2. What is the message behind the exercise?
3. Practice reading this exercise in pairs–take turns reading.

IV. Nonverbal Behavior and Effective Presentation of Information.
Physical and vocal factors can play an important role in the effect of your presentation on your listeners. Your messages and your delivery can be enhanced or damaged by the way you present ideas. In an effort to analyze the behaviors of others in presenting information, take the next few days to observe professors, classmates, and others as they present information. Look at the messages and the manner of presentation. Focus on physical and vocal factors of their oral delivery. Take notes about the presenter and the presentation, answering these questions:
1. What ways did the speakers use "voice" to communicate ideas?
2. How did the speakers vary the rate? What was the effect?
3. How were pauses used? When? To what effect?
4. What positive factors of physical and vocal delivery did you observe?
5. What effect did these positive aspects have on you, the listener?
6. What negative factors of physical and vocal delivery did you observe?
7. What effect did these negatives have on you, the listener?
8. What can you learn from this activity?

References

1. Robert T. Oliver, *History of Public Speaking in America*, (Boston: Allyn and Bacon, 1965), 61-62.
2. J.C. Humes, "Read a Speech Like a Pro," Talking your way to the top (New York:

McGraw Hill, 1980), 125-135; J. Venlenti, *Speak Up with Confidence: How to Prepare, Learn, and Deliver Effective Speeches* (New York: Morrow, 1982)23-26.

3. S. Chaiken, "Communicator Physical Attractiveness and Persuasion," *Journal of Personality and Social Psychology*, 37 (1979), 1387-97.
4. P. Ekman, *Emotions Revealed: Recognizing Faces and Feelings to Improve Communication and Emotional Life* (New York: Henry Holt, 2003).
5. See R. Rivlin & K. Gravlle, *Deciphering the Senses: The Expanding World of Human Perception,* New York: Simon and Schuster, 1984), p98.
6. J. Layton, "How Police Interrogation Works," howstuffworks.com, 2008.

CHAPTER 40

Presentational Aids

LEARNING OBJECTIVES

When students have completed this chapter and lesson, they should be able to:

1. Know and be able to explain the advantages and disadvantages of each of the visual aids for speeches and presentations.
2. Know and be able to explain the advantages and disadvantages of each of the non-projected methods of displaying these aids.
3. Know and be able to explain the advantages and disadvantages of each of the projected methods of displaying these aids.
4. Know and be able to explain how computer-generated and computer-displayed presentational aids can and should be used.

CHAPTER 40: Overview

Humans are visual creatures, relying heavily on seeing things in order to understand them. In addition, we live in a visual age where the majority of people have grown up with media such as television and movies as their primary source of information and entertainment. Thus, they respond better and believe more readily that which they see.

For this reason and others, speeches and presentations are strengthened by the use of visual materials, and modern speakers frequently use presentational aids such as diagrams, models, photographs, tables, charts, graphs, and computer-generated materials to make their speech or presentation more vivid. In fact, many presentations depend on them. Coaches diagram plays. Architects show their plans and renderings. Business people display profits and losses using colorful graphs. And weather forecasters use high technology to display their maps and other data. It is, for sure, a visual world.

This chapter summarizes the various kinds of aids that you may use with your speeches or presentations, including a brief summary for each one of its advantages and disadvantages.

Visual Aids for Speeches and Presentations

Real Objects. A real object is the physical object itself about which you are speaking. So, for example, if you are speaking on how violins are made you might use a real violin as a visual aid. You might even have several such aids, showing the violin in its various stages of completion. Using real objects makes your presentation more immediate, visually stimulating, and memorable. But it can also create problems if the object is too large, too small, or too impractical (e.g., a restless pet) to show.

Aid:	Advantages:	Disadvantages:
Real Objects	• Makes topic more immediate	• Can sometimes be impractical or too difficult to set up (e.g., how to change oil in a car)
	• Makes topic more visually stimulating and memorable	

Models. When displaying the actual object is not practical, a model of the object can allow the speaker to enlarge or shrink the object to a convenient size for display. For example, to talk about changes to a college's landscape a presenter might bring a scale model of the campus that shows the planned changes. Or if a speaker is talking about the solar system, a scale model of the planets is helpful to show their relative sizes and distances from the sun. If the original object is very small, such as a strand of DNA, then a model makes it possible for the audience to visualize its structure. And, of course, models can also be life-size.

Aid:	Advantages:	Disadvantages:
Models	• Reduces size of actual object • Enlarges size of actual object	• Expensive and time consuming to prepare • Difficult to see if audience is large

Photographs and Prints. When models are not available nor practical, photographs or prints may be used. These are often helpful to show an object or a person in context, such as when showing a person visiting a site or an object as it appears in its present location. Photos can be difficult to see if the audience is large and may need enlarging to be useful. Whether they are small or large, they can sometimes be hard to handle in front of an audience. Also, once displayed photos and prints have a tendency to draw so much attention that they actually distract the audience for the content of the speech. For this reason, it may be best to show them for a sufficient length of time and then take them down.

Aid:	Advantages:	Disadvantages:
Pictures	• Inexpensive • Show people/objects in context	• Difficult to see if audience is large • Difficult to handle • Can be distracting from the message

Drawings, Sketches, and Diagrams. As an alternative to photographs or prints, drawings, sketches and diagrams can sometimes be used. These may be highly detailed and professional but they are not necessarily required to be so. Simple line drawings on the chalk or dry erase board can sometimes suffice. More professional renderings are required for architects blueprints, company charts, or instruction manuals. Once produced, drawings, sketches, and diagrams have basically the same advantages and disadvantages as photographs and prints.

Aid:	Advantages:	Disadvantages:
Drawings	• Inexpensive • Show people/objects in context	• Difficult to see if audience is large • Difficult to handle • Can be distracting from the message

Tables and Spreadsheets. Tables and spreadsheets are used mainly to display statistical data. They can make complex data more visual and therefore more easily understandable. Tables arrange data in a series of columns and rows. We often refer to tables today as "spreadsheets," especially if they have the capability of calculating values in one cell of the table by virtue of information in other cells. Tables can display large amounts of data in a finite space, making it convenient to look up specific information in an orderly way. However, a complex or lengthy table may need substantial explanation before it will make sense to those who use it. Also, because they are programmable, spreadsheets require special skills in order to properly use them. It is best to keep your tables and spreadsheets concise, simple, and clear. If your data is very complex, you may be better off to use a graph.

Aid:	Advantages:	Disadvantages:
Tables and Spreadsheets	• Make complex data visual explanations. • Make data understandable	• If too complex, requires lengthy explanation • Spreadsheets require special skills in order to properly use them

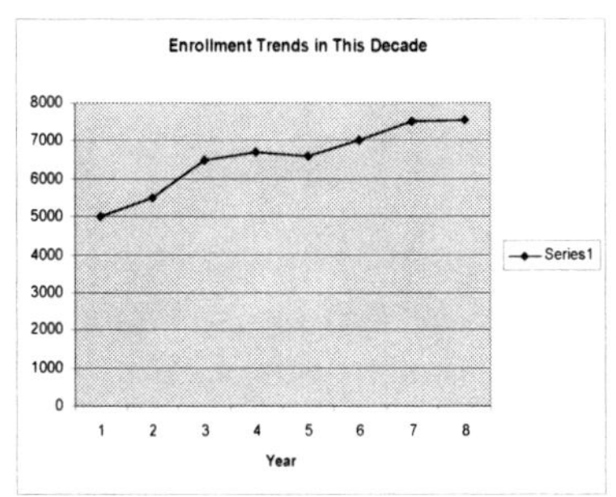

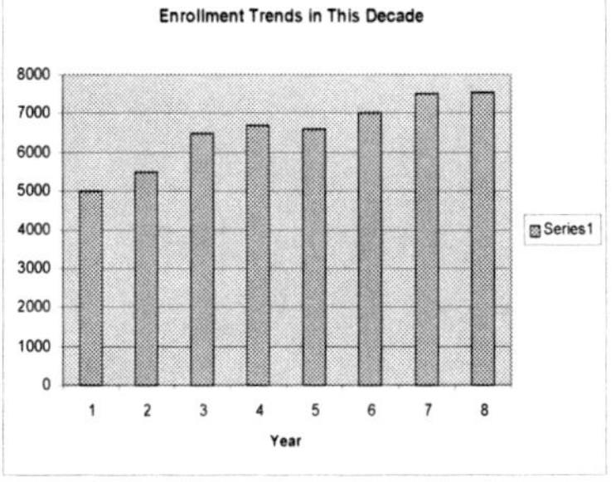

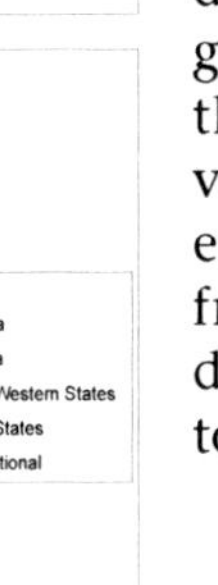

Graphs make statistical data vivid by visually illustrating relationships between the various rows and columns. They are particularly helpful in showing trends over time. It is possible to show multiple sets of data on the same graph, but normally you should present only one or two basic relationships on each graph so your audience does not get confused by which line represents which set of data.

Line graphs illustrate *trends* from one column to the next. So, for example, if we wanted to show college enrollment over the past ten years we could create a line graph that showed the up and down trends from year to year to year.

Bar graphs show *comparisons* between columns of data, though they can also be used for trends. Note how much easier it is to visually compare the data in the bar graph than it is to compare the same data in the line graph.

Pie graphs are used to show *proportional divisions* of a whole set of data. Each wedge of the pie represents a percentage of the whole. Pie graphs are often used to show distribution patterns, as in the case of the example to the left which shows the percentage of students from various geographical areas enrolled in a college. Normally, as in the example shown at left, a pie graph starts with a radius drawn vertically from the center to the twelve o'clock position. Each segment is then drawn in clockwise, beginning with the largest and continuing down to the smallest.

Aid:	Advantages:	Disadvantages:
Graphs	• Visually showing trends • Visually showing comparisons • Visually showing proportions	• If too complex, hard to understand • Can be tricky to create with accuracy

Methods of Presenting Aids

All of the above visual aids can be presented in a variety of ways—some projected and some not. The next section of our chapter deals with the advantages and disadvantages of each of these methods.

Non-Projected Methods

Handouts. Handouts can be a simple yet useful means of presenting information to your audience. They are relatively inexpensive and can usually be easily prepared in advance. Usually, each audience member can have his or her own copy. However, they can become a distraction as audience members tend to read them when you would rather have them listening to your speech. For this reason, you may be well advised to hand them out at the end of your speech rather than during it, unless you intend to have them follow along with it while you are speaking.

Method:	Advantages:	Disadvantages:
Handouts	• Inexpensive & easy to prepare • Can be saved by the audience • Complements presentation if used properly.	• Distracts the audience's attention from your speech

Chalkboard or Dry Erase Board. Chalkboards and dry erase boards are the most readily available methods of presenting visual aids in most classrooms. They are also generally present in most business board rooms. They are easy to use and suffice for the simplest of lists and line illustrations. But they can also be messy, and if not used properly, can become a distraction as you spend time writing while speaking. Generally, you should do your writing on the board before your speech so that it does not distract your audience and so that you can accurately gauge the amount of space you'll need for your lists and/or illustrations.

Seiler and Beall[1] offer the following list of suggestions whenever you choose to use a chalkboard or dry erase board during a speech.

1. When should you put information on the board? Preferences vary from speaker to speaker and from instructor to instructor. Some speakers write on the board before they speak. If putting the information on the board before you speak will not interfere with other presentations, and if you can cover what you have written (so as not to distract from other presentations), preparing the board in advance can simplify your delivery. To be safe, ask your instructor which way he or she prefers you to do it.
2. How should you write on the board? This, of course, depends on the size of the room and your writing skills. Your writing should always be large enough and neat enough for everyone in the room to read. The appearance of your writing on the board communicates a message about you and your speech. Thus, you want what you write to create a positive impression.
3. How should you use the board when delivering your speech? Even when reading from the board, you should always try to face your audience. Use a pointer, a ruler, or your outstretched arm to help guide your listeners to the information you want them to focus on. Whether writing on the board or reading from it, avoid talking to the chalkboard rather than your audience.

Method:	Advantages:	Disadvantages:
Chalkboard or Dry Erase Board	• Readily available • Easy to use • Suffices for simple lists and line illustrations	• Can be messy • Can be a distraction while writing on them • You may run out of space if you don't plan carefully in advance

Posters. Posters are a very common way of presenting visual information. They are prepared in advance, eliminating the distraction that writing on the chalkboard can bring. If well done, they make you look professional and prepared. Seiler and Beale[2] say that the guidelines for writing on the chalkboard also apply to posters, but add these three additional suggestions for using posters:

1. If an easel is not available, check to see if there are clips on the board for hanging posters or if you will need to use masking tape. If you must use masking tape, make large loops of tape and place them on the back of the poster in advance.

Then, when you are ready to display the poster, merely place it on the board, pressing firmly on the tape loops to secure it. If you have more than one poster, you can place several of them on the board at once, or you can display each individually as you need it.

2. Make sure the poster is made of firm cardboard so that it will support itself if you have to stand it on a chalk tray or a table.
3. Posters should be displayed only when they are referred to in the speech. The rest of the time they should be turned over or covered so they don't distract the audience.

Method:	**Advantages:**	**Disadvantages:**
Posters	• Can be prepared in advance • If well done, they make you look professional & prepared	• Can fall off of eraser trays on chalkboards • Can tend to curl or fold down forward • Requires an easel to stop these problems

Flip Charts. Flip charts are like a combination of a chalkboard or dry erase board and a poster. Typically, they come in the form of a large tablet of paper whose pages can be torn off or folded backward as you proceed. Thus, they bring all of the advantages of a chalkboard or dry erase board, but also all of the disadvantages. And, because they are poster-size, they can have some of the same problems as posters unless you have an easel on which to place them. They also have the following advantages and disadvantages that are all their own.

Method:	**Advantages:**	**Disadvantages:**
Flip Chart	• Easy to use • Easy to refer back to • Allows contact with audience	• Not useful with large groups • Lacks pictorial realism • Difficult to transport

Audio Tape/CD/DVD Players. Sometimes sound is important to a presentation, either in combination with any of the above visual aids or all by itself. When this is the case, an audio tape/CD/DVD player is required.

Method:	**Advantages:**	**Disadvantages:**
Audio Tape / CD / DVD Player	• Ideal complement to other aids when sound is important	• Time consuming preparation • Difficult to coordinate (needs some rehearsal time to coordinate the effects)

Projected Methods

When a whole series of visuals is needed, the most common solution is a projected aid of some kind—slides, transparencies, and videotapes. These have the same disadvantage as audio players in that they require planning, familiarity with the mechanical equipment, and in the case of videotapes some time for rehearsal. Each form has advantages and disadvantages, so knowing what each can and cannot do is vital. For example, showing slides and movies requires a totally darkened room, and the projectors maybe noisy. Yet both enable you to show places and things that you could not show any other way. Films and videos add motion, color, and sound.

But they can be costly and often tend to dominate a presentation by replacing the speaker for a period of time.

Overhead Projectors. The most common projected visual aid in classrooms is transparencies shown on an overhead projector. Transparencies can be easily and inexpensively prepared in advance or even created during a presentation by writing on them with a marker. They are also very easy to use without advanced technical skills and do not require a darkened room. The only concerns are that the projector is in focus and the transparencies remain covered until they are needed.

Method:	Advantages:	Disadvantages:
Overhead Projector	• Can face audience while using • Room can be lit • Transparencies are inexpensive • They can be used spontaneously (drawing on a transparency)	• Lacks three-dimensionality • Does not convert pictures directly (they must be made into transparencies)

Opaque Projectors. Opaque projectors work very much like overhead projectors except they do not require transparencies. Rather than requiring a light source that shines through the transparency to project it, opaque projectors reflect images from non-transparent sources like sheets of paper or magazines or books. Prior to the invention of cheap video cameras that could achieve the same thing, opaque projectors were very bulky and heavy and expensive. Now, the same opaque projection is achieved using small cameras with very high resolution.

Method:	Advantages:	Disadvantages:
Opaque Projectors	• Projects pictures directly from source onto screen • No special preparation needed	• Darkened room may be needed • Can be expensive

Slide Projectors. Because of computer-based PowerPoint® technology, slide projectors are becoming less and less common. Nevertheless, they may still be used when wanting to show a series of images. The advantages and disadvantages of slides are as follows.

Method:	Advantages:	Disadvantages:
Slide Projectors	• Useful to show series of photos • Operates easily • Can face audience while using	• Advance time needed to develop slides • Darkened room needed • Can be remote-controlled

Videotape Players. Because of the invention of DVDs and DVD players, videotapes are not as frequently used as they used to be. Videotapes lack the ability to instantaneously select a portion of the video; they have to be fast forwarded or rewound. Still, when showing an entire video of some kind they can be very effective. Of course, as with all electronic devices, you will need to prepare carefully in advance and rehearse to insure that things will work as planned.

Method:	Advantages:	Disadvantages:
Videotape Players	• Useful when motion needed • Fairly inexpensive today	• Cannot be easily fast forwarded or rewound • Can be bulky to handle • Advance preparation often needed • Can be difficult to see, if audience is large

DVD Players. These are the more common method for showing videos today because of their ease of use. Driven by menus and broken down into "chapters," DVDs can be easily manipulated to show a particular segment of a video without having to fast forward or rewind. They are also easy to handle—as small and lightweight as a CD. Because of their more recent entrance into the marketplace than videos, not all content is available on DVDs and you may have to copy content from other sources onto a DVD before you can use it.

Method:	Advantages:	Disadvantages:
DVD Players	• More lightweight than videos • Relatively inexpensive today • Can select specific segments without rewinding	• Not all content available on DVDs • Room may need to be darkened • Advance preparation may be needed

Computer-Generated Presentational Aids

Increasingly, computers are replacing all of the above as the preferred method of displaying presentational aids. It has become the norm for business and in many classrooms. Entire suites of software programs have been developed with presentational software as part of them. The first and most popular of these is Microsoft's PowerPoint®, which allows presenters to design each "slide" with a colorful background, various formats and layouts, and use a wide array of colors and effects. Both audio and video can be inserted into the presentation with ease. In fact, the possibilities of things that can be done with presentational software today are nearly endless. But a word of caution: don't overdo it. Seiler and Beal[3] make the following recommendations for computer-generated presentations.

Using Computer-Generated Aids

1. Do not overdo it! Just as you can have too many points in a speech and too many materials for traditional visual aids, you can present too much material on the computer. As a general rule, use a visual to support only 25 percent of your presentation. Select the materials carefully. Too many pictures, graphs, images, and animations can result in overload.
2. Make sure that the size of the font you use in your presentation is appropriate. Use nothing less than a 48-point font for a regular classroom. In a large lecture hall, use 60 to 72 points for headings and topics, and no less than 48 points for subpoints, quotations, and explanations.
3. Don't put too much on any given screen. It's easy to overdo it. If you put too many words or images on the "slides," people will not listen to what you have to say.
4. Remember that the computer visual is like any other visual: It is there to enhance the presentation, not to take the place of the speaker's words and ideas.
5. Practice using your computer visuals in the room in which you will present the speech, if possible, because what you see on the screen of your monitor and what people see on the screen in the presentation room may not be the same. Colors do not always enhance the material as well as they appear to on the small monitor screen. Sometimes the lighting can make a tremendous difference, and if you cannot dim the lights, you may want to change the background so that the materials are visible, clear, and easy to read anywhere in the audience. Check to see if lighting and reflections will cause problems and whether there are decreased sight lines at certain angles in the room. Also, practice to make sure you do not lose eye contact with your audience while presenting these aids. Using the computer should not distract you from staying in touch with your audience."

Chapter 40: Analysis and Application Exercises

1. This chapter has reviewed the advantages and disadvantages of some popular types of aids. Which of them would you rather use as a presenter, and why? Which would you rather see as a listener, and why? Which, if any of them, have you actually used in the past, and with what results?
2. Lists of suggestions from Seiler and Beall were included in this chapter. As you look at these lists, pick one of the items within them that you have had to deal with in the past when making a speech or presentation. Did you deal with it in the way they suggested? Do their suggestions make sense to you based on your experience? Why or why not?

References

1. Seiler, W.J. & Beall, M.L. (1999). *Communication: Making Connections*, 4th ed. Needham Heights, MA: Allyn & Bacon. In Chase, R.S., and Jones, S.G., *Elements of Effective Communication*, 2nd ed., Boston, MA: Allyn & Bacon, 1999, p. 455.
2. Seiler, W.J. & Beall, p. 456.
3. Seiler, W.J. & Beall, p. 458.

CHAPTER 41

Informative Speaking Strategies

LEARNING OBJECTIVES

When students have completed this chapter and lesson, they should be able to:

1. Identify three goals of informative speaking.
2. Name the informative strategies used in informative speaking.
3. Choose the appropriate strategy for presenting an informative speech.

CHAPTER 41: Overview

Novice speakers will learn how to match a strategy to their purpose in delivering an informative speech. The types of informative strategies are identified along with examples of their use. The chapter ends with a brief discussion of how to increase retention of information presented by the speaker.

Information speaking is teaching information.

The great naturalist, Agassiz, strongly believed that teaching was a system of gaining knowledge. Gathering knowledge and learning are not two separate processes–they are a single act of informative learning. His student best illustrated the process:

> I had assigned to me a small pine table with a rusty tin pan upon it. When I sat me down before my tin pan, Agassiz brought me a small fish, placing it before me with the rather stern requirement that I should study it, but should on no account talk to anyone concerning it, nor read anything relating to fishes, until I had his permission so to do. To my inquiry "What shall I do?" he said in effect: "Find out what you can without damaging the specimen; then when I think that you have done the work I will question you." In the course of an hour I thought I had compassed the fish; it was rather an unsavory object, giving forth the stench of old alcohol. Many of the scales were loosened so that they fell off. It appeared to me to be a case of a summary report, which I was anxious to make and get on to the next stage of the business. But Agassiz, though always within call, concerned himself no further with me that day, nor the next, nor for a week.
>
> At first, this neglect was distressing; but I saw that it was a game, for he was covertly watching me. So I set my wits to work upon the thing, and in the course of a hundred hours or so thought I had done much–a hundred times as much as seemed possible at the start. I got interested in finding out how the scales went in their series, their shape, the form and placement of the teeth, etc. Finally, I felt full of the subject and probably expressed it in my bearing; as for words about it then, there were none from my master except his cheery "Good Morning." At length, on the seventh day, came the question "Well?" and my disgorge of learning to him as he sat on the edge of my table. . . At the end of the hour's telling he swung off and away, saying "That's not right."
>
> It was clear that he was playing a game with me to find if I were capable of doing hard, continuous work without the support of a teacher, and this stimulated me to labor. I went at the task anew, discarded my first notes, and in another week of ten hours a day labor I had results which astonished myself and satisfied him[1].

The lesson in learning continued with a gallon tank full of fish skeletons. After two months of analysis, the second lesson finally finished, and a more difficult task was added. The point of the story is that informative speaking is not just a minor task before the serious stuff begins. The study of audience analysis, selecting a topic, gathering information through research and study, then reasoning, organizing, developing proper language, and practicing delivery becomes the tank of skeletons. After we have learned the preliminary concepts of communication we can begin preparation for accomplishing a specific purpose.

Matching Strategy to Purpose

Before this serious preparation begins, the speaker must have a purpose for speaking. Previously we examined the following purposes for presenting messages:

- Setting the agenda
- Providing new information or sharing a perspective
- Strengthening commitment to a position
- Weakening commitment to a position
- Converting the audience away from one belief and toward another
- Intensifying or weakening a feeling
- Inducing a specific action.

The next step is to determine what strategies are most appropriate for achieving these purposes. Broadly speaking, speech goals are generally achieved through strategies of informing, persuading, and entertaining. Careful thinking reveals, however, that successful sharing of information affects people's attitudes, so informing and persuading occur together. The speaker cannot "inform" without persuading the audience the topic is of interest or value. Unless the audience enjoys listening to the message, they are neither informed nor persuaded, because as we learned in the listening chapter, their attention has left the scene and they are entertaining themselves.

However, there are strategies that primarily attempt to teach information. Audience analysis can suggest how your listeners can be reached, based on your study of who is listening to your presentation.

For example, suppose many of your listeners believe that the Internet should be regulated to protect children from indecent material. Your own opinion is exactly the opposite, and you would like to change their minds. You believe that most of your listeners do not really understand exactly what the Internet is. You will be speaking to an educational conference that is exploring how the Internet can be used in the home. All these factors lead you not to try to convert your audience to be an information policeman, but to seek the more realistic goal of showing how the Internet is an exciting land of discovery, a goldmine of exciting knowledge and ideas. Thus giving information weakens a commitment to the view that it should be strongly regulated. To accomplish this, you will rely more on strategies to inform rather than strategies to persuade.

Sometimes an audience must be persuaded before it can be informed. Consider another example. During the Cold War years, most Americans approached foreign policy issues from the premise that the world was locked in moral struggle between freedom and communism. For a speaker to even discuss nationalism in Eastern Europe, it first was necessary to challenge the prevailing view that all of Eastern Europe was a monolith dominated by the Soviet Union. In order to share information effectively, it first was necessary to change listener's attitudes.

To separate purposes from strategies, consider the following structural organization of the purpose-strategy working model:

Speech Purposes and Strategies

I. Purposes achieved through primarily **Informative** strategies:
- A. Agenda Setting
- B. Providing new information or Sharing a Perspective

II. Purposes achieved through a balance of **Informative** and **Persuasive** Strategies
- A. Intensifying or weakening a feeling

III. Purposes achieved through primarily **Persuasive** Strategies
- A. Strengthening commitment to a position
- B. Weakening commitment to a position
- C. Converting the audience away from one belief and toward another.
- D. Inducing the audience to perform a specific action

Informing Your Audience

Here we are concerned with informing. **Information Strategies** presume that the overall goal of the speech is to share information and ideas with the audience. They rely on the metaphor of speaker as a teacher and the speech as a lesson. Listeners are asked to be attentive, to understand what is being said, and to modify their knowledge and belief systems to take this new information into account.

In a speech about the microscopic world around us, Kimo made his classmates think about something they had previously ignored:

> There are millions of living creatures in your house right now. They crawl through your carpet, reproduce under your bed, and snack in your closet. When examined under a microscope, they look like creatures from your worst nightmares. They are dust mites and we live with them every day.

In her speech about the Beat Generation, Elizabeth introduced her audience to an era that was unfamiliar to them:

> During the late 1940's and early 1950's, the Beat Generation began to explore the country in search of something to believe in. People like Jack Kerouac, Allen Ginsberg, and Gary Snyder listened to jazz, wrote "stream of consciousness" poetry, and celebrated freedom. Let's take a closer look at these people and their ideas.

Informative strategies do not explicitly ask listeners to believe or do any particular thing. Learning something new might stimulate them to take action, but attitude change is not requested. For example, imagine you heard a speech about the depletion of the ozone layer, knowing nothing previously about this scientific and ecological issue. The speaker's purpose was to share information about the thinning of the ozone layer so far, the role of the ozone layer in shielding us from the sun's ultraviolet rays, and projections for the future rate of ozone depletion. The speaker did not actually call on you to do anything; the goal was only to make you aware of a previously neglected issue. But it would not be surprising if, after hearing such a speech, you chose to stop using aerosol spray cans and began urging legislators to ban their use. In the next chapter we will contrast informative strategies with strategies of persuasion, which seek to influence and alter listeners' beliefs, values, or actions.

Clarifying Your Informative Goal

The two speech purposes primarily relying on informative strategies are agenda setting and providing new information or perspective. Information is essential if you are to induce listeners to think about something new, to view it from a unique perspective, or to take into account something they had previously ignored. Intensifying positive or negative feelings is dependent on both informative and persuasive strategies that are attractive to listeners.

Agenda setting creates awareness of a subject that listeners do not know about or think about. Until fairly recently, most of us simply did not think about the disposal of waste paper, glass, plastic, and aluminum. We tossed these materials in the trash can, counting on garbage collectors to get rid of them. Because solid-waste landfills are being exhausted, the subject now warrants our attention, and most people are aware of recycling. Communicators focused on a topic that had been ignored, and at some point it was put on the agenda.

Providing new Information or Perspective. Common knowledge about a subject is often quite general, and as a result misunderstood. For example, now the majority of eligible voters in the United States do not vote. But few people know what that means. Has the number of ineligible voters been increasing or has the number of actual eligible voters been decreasing? Or have fewer and fewer eligible voters voted? Little is commonly known about voting behavior. How has participation varied among different groups, what factors tend to increase or limit participation; what is the relationship between registration and voting, and so on. One informational goal for a speech would be to enrich the audience's common knowledge about voting rates, moving listeners from a broad understanding to a more detailed awareness of the issue.

Sometimes the speaker's objective is to update and revise the common knowledge of listeners. Audience belief may be distorted or mistaken, and social knowledge changes over time. For example what do people know about "Russia?" From 1945 to 1990, people "knew" that the Soviet Union, which included Russia, was engaged in a deadly economic and political struggle with the United States. But in the years since 1990, people have come to "know" that this is no longer the case. Listener perspective may not be dramatically changeable on all topics, but if your informative speech gives listeners information that leads to a new way of thinking about something like "terrorism" or "indecency" or "freedom," you will have accomplished the same purpose.

Intensifying or Weakening a feeling. Everyone knows the saying "Knowledge is Power!" The reason is the more information we have, the more competently we make informed decisions, giving confidence to people about their ability to control their lives. Ellen, for example did not think she was good at managing her time. There was never enough time to do her work, her skills were compromised, and she often forgot vital tasks. She attended a speech about time management skills and gained an understanding about her problems. Techniques were applied to managing responsibilities better. After the speech she told a friend, "I feel like this speech has given me a new way to take power over my own life!"

Ellen learned that making intelligent choices is a source of power. When faced with buying a home, a car, or even choosing a school to learn a life-skill, intelligent choices becomes a power move. You will be frustrated if you do not know how to decide which alternative is better. Informative speeches do not tell the audience which option to choose. But if they lay out the costs and benefits of alternatives, they help listeners form criteria for making decisions. By resolving a difficult question, people feel better both about the subject and about themselves.

Agenda setting, providing new knowledge, and creating a positive feeling are speech goals that rely heavily on informative strategies.

Informative Strategies

Informative strategies are seldom found in pure form. Speakers often combine a number of strategies, or tie them directly to purposes, but examining a few will assist the speaker in strengthening the acceptance of the informative speech.

Definition is a strategy used to clarify a term or concept. Definition permits the speaker to label a term in such a way that the audience understands exactly what is being discussed. Definitions also may be used to introduce a new or unexpected way of viewing the subject, so that the speech can develop the details and implications of a new approach. If a group can agree on a definition or interpretation of a difficult issue within their sphere of influence, much misunderstanding can be avoided and productivity of the group can be significantly improved.

Definition is required when a concept is not clear, and terminology influences behavior and satisfaction of the group. Nothing is a better example than the technology age where even the common laborer now is required to understand computer skills. In the early 1980's, when personal computers came into use most people suddenly needed to learn a whole new vocabulary. Words such as floppy disk, booting up, bytes, download, modem, were all new. Even words like google and iPod® have recently been added to the dictionary. A speech entitled "Deciphering the Personal Computer" defining its impact on modern vocabulary would have been and still could be well received.

Definition is also used to identify different or conflicting meanings of a common term and to establish the speaker's preferred meaning. Sonia believed that many of the unfortunate racial incidents and cases of "hate speech" on college campuses during the 1990's arose partly because the key concept "affirmative action" was misunderstood. She used the strategy of definition to clarify the concept:

> Mention the term "affirmative action," and some people will tell you that it means special recruiting efforts to attract minorities and women. Others say it means identifying a specific goal for the number of minorities and women to be hired. Still others think it means reserving a specific number of places for minorities and women. And people speak so often of the mechanics of affirmative action that they lose sight of the goal: We all benefit from the perspectives offered by a culturally diverse student body. If we keep track of that goal, then the best way to think of affirmative action is as special efforts to seek out qualified students who will enable us to achieve the goal.

Misunderstandings, conflict, and bad feelings result when participants have different ideas of what constitutes such issues as employment practices, productivity, or even fair labor practices. Different interpretations by participants can translate into major communication problems. For that reason Sonia's goals were to identify different possible meanings, to explain the implications of accepting one meaning or another, and to describe a preferred point of view. She organized the body of her speech like this:

I. Affirmative action has multiple meanings.
   A. It may mean aggressive recruiting
   B. It may mean numerical goals.
   C. It may mean tie-breaking preferences.
   D. It may mean quotas.

II. Selecting a meaning makes a difference.
   A. It will influence how actively the government takes an interest in the question.
   B. It will clarify whom affirmative action seeks to help.
   C. It will determine whether it is fair to place at a disadvantage people who have not themselves caused previous discrimination.
   D. It will influence how actively committed we should be to the goal.

III. Affirmative action really means aggressive recruiting
   A. This meaning is consistent with our belief that people should be evaluated as individuals, not as groups.
   B. It is consistent with our belief that decisions should ultimately be made on the basis of merit.
   C. It recognizes the historical under representation of minorities and the fact

that qualified minority candidates may not be identified through normal means.

In these examples the speaker uses definition to label and explain a preferred meaning. Such definitions are not neutral; they shape how we view or think about a subject. In educating listeners about a definition, the speaker is also influencing them to think about the topic in a particular way. Although the strategy of definition is intended mainly to be informative, definitions also are persuasive.

Reporting is journalism in the oral mode. It answers the question "What happened?" and usually does so in strict chronological order with little overt analysis or interpretation. Select this strategy if your analysis of audience, occasion, and purpose suggests that you need to explain a complex event by identifying each of its components.

If you were to give a speech about the recent visit to the campus of a world-famous artist and your goal was to share what happened, the body of the speech would report the major events of the visit:

I. Arrival at the airport
  A. Time and place
  B. Reception party
  C. Welcoming remarks

II. Visiting with classes
  A. Which classes were visited
  B. What topics were discussed in class.

III. Delivering a public lecture
  A. What the audience was like
  B. What the speaker's main topics were
  C. How long the speech lasted
  D. What the students thought of the speech

IV. Evaluating student work
  A.Which artworks were judged
  B. The results

V. The departure ceremony
  A. The gift given to the artist
  B. The final words from the artist

Even though the report is purely factual, usually far more has occurred than can be conveyed in a relatively short speech. Selecting which items to include and which to leave out therefore involves the speaker in making subjective judgments; in turn, these can influence what listeners think about the topic. Even reporting is not a purely informative strategy.

Oral description is a speaker's way of painting a verbal picture of a scene or event. The object is to place the listener verbally, in the midst of the action. The results produce more direct involvement, thus more likelihood of acceptance by the listener.[2] In a speech about travel to the French Riviera, we are unlikely to hear a set of arguments about why we should go. Rather the speaker will develop such a vivid image of beauty and comfort that we will want to go. Similarly, a speech about the San Francisco earthquake of 1906 might use description to convey a sense of what it was like rather than just reporting what happened.

A mental picture becomes vivid through its detail. Focus is on specific details, color of the eyes or hair, whether the person was standing erect or leaning against a post, facial expressions, and so on. But a steady stream of details becomes tedious.

The speaker selects a larger picture. Facial features may convey an attitude. In a speech about her favorite professor, Janet described many vivid details:

> I walked into Professor Alvarez's office and immediately noticed her desk. Or, rather, I noticed that I couldn't see her desk. One corner was piled high with new books. The telephone was covered with reminder notes. Students' papers and memos were strewn across the desk. There was yesterday's newspaper opened to the crossword puzzle. A napkin with crumbs from a leftover bagel was on top. Somewhere nearby was a coffee cup. Class notes were piled on top of the computer. A grade book was buried underneath a stack of paper.
>
> "What a desk," I thought. Yet I soon would discover that behind that desk was the most organized woman I ever met.

Description is a useful strategy when listeners share your appraisal of detail and will regard it as signs of a characteristic you could not report directly, such as the generalization that first appearances can be deceptive. Details are generally interesting and help audiences accept generalizations more easily.

Explanations or expansion of descriptions and generalizations make an idea more precise. This permits audiences a deeper understanding of events, people, policies, or processes. By expanding beyond reporting of basic detail, deeper understanding and feeling can be communicated. Consider different views of what happened, ask how or why it happened, or even speculate about what it means.

For example, the 1962 Cuban missile crisis. People who did not live through it or do not understand the implications can assume it was rather insignificant. Much more than facts took place from October 16 to October 28, 1962. You would discuss topics such as how and why Soviet missiles were placed in Cuba; why Americans regarded them as so threatening, and how President Kennedy and his advisors resolved a very serious political crisis; avoiding a devastating war could be explored. Confrontational rhetoric could be explained as Adlai Stevenson confronted Ambassador Valerian Zorin on the floor of the United Nations. Explanations could be explored on how the President of the United States confronted the Premier of the USSR over a direct attack on the United States when a U-2 aircraft was shot down over Cuba. Finally, an explanation of how such an inflammable international incident could be diffused by having the Soviet Union remove missiles from Cuba and in return U.S. missiles aimed at Russia were removed from Turkey.

If your explanation is successful, listeners not only will know more of the facts but also will grasp the significance of avoiding a potential nuclear war between two major military powers, and will appreciate why the issues you raised have fascinated people for nearly four decades. You might even supply option for world peace.

Speeches that explain events or people often begin simply and then build toward greater richness or complexity. In contrast, speeches that explain policies or processes generally proceed in the opposite direction. For most of the years between 1945 and 1990, for example, the chief military policy of the United States toward the Soviet Union was deterrence. A speaker who wants to explain this abstract concept would have to break it down into its components: what weapons were developed and maintained, which diplomatic channels were important, how the United States tried to reassure the Soviet Union that it would not begin a war–while also inducing the belief that if war started, the United States might use nuclear weapons–and so on. Only by understanding these components well could listeners really know what deterrence was and how it worked.

Speeches that explain complex operations can be broken down into a simple sequence of steps. Such a speech enables listeners to understand how a complicated world works even if they cannot explain it themselves. The process of public opinion polls is a classic example. You would explain all the steps in the process: framing questions, identifying the population to be sampled, the procedure for obtaining a valid sample, recording and coding responses, performing statistical analyses, and interpreting significant results. Listeners may not be able to conduct a valid poll, but they will at least recognize and understand the process as national news reports such events.

Demonstrating

Sometimes it is not enough to just explain a process; it becomes necessary for the audience to also see the process, or even do it themselves. These presentations are described as demonstrations, describing a seemingly mysterious or complex procedure as a series of fairly simple steps performed in a particular order. The message **tells how** to cook something, how to wallpaper a room, how to prepare a tax return, or any one of hundreds of topics that can inform the audience of a subject or act they could not do for themselves before. Here are the critical steps in the process:

Checklist for Demonstrations

- Do listeners really need to see the process to understand it? If not, it may seem boring or irrelevant; or it could be strategically essential.
- Is the subject precise enough that it can be demonstrated in the time available?
  Complicated operations, such as rebuilding an automobile engine cannot be covered in the time limit. Care should be taken to insure the demonstration is vital, yet not so complex that a short speech can never cover even essentials.
- Are the steps of the process clear, distinct, and in proper sequence?
  Listeners will not understand what they are supposed to do if your instructions are vague or difficult to follow. The speech will also fail if critical steps are skipped, or avoided. Be precise, exact, and complete.
- Are your actions and your verbal instructions coordinated?
  Avoid any long gaps in the speech while you are doing something or waiting for something to happen. You will lose both continuity of the speech and audience attention if you must wait for results. This problem often weakens a demonstration of how to cook something. If time sequences are necessary, plan "filler" material that can occupy the time while the process works. But filler material should be relevant to the topic, and not just jokes, wasting time, or irrelevant information.
- Visual aids are critical. See Chapter 40 for help in this area.

Comparing

A speech designed to explain similarities and differences between two objects, events, or philosophies is a common informative message. Comparing items can be used to make things seem more similar or different than anyone had imagined. The speaker can compare everything from automobiles to national dictators. These similarities to using analogy exist, but the point or purpose of the speech is to illustrate differences or similarities of like subjects. Topics comparing two different word-processing computer programs can be examined, or two presidents of the United States could be compared when faced with a given problem such as war, economic upheaval, colonization or some other event that would interest the audience.

It is generally wise to consider the **subject** under consideration and the characteristics you wish to emphasize. If you are comparing the taste difference between Coke and Pepsi, the method of analysis would be much different than comparing how President Franklin Roosevelt managed government during World War II, and how President George Bush managed the War in Iraq.

Comparing can provide listeners with a basis for making a choice. The speaker does not tell them what to do or urge them to accept one perspective over another, but does urge the audience to weigh the advantages of one event over another.

The public debate about health care during the early 1990's provides a good example. The skyrocketing cost of health insurance, and an observation that over thirty million Americans have none, prompted a variety of competing proposals for health care reform. President George Bush favored modest changes in the system, combined with cost controls on two federal health programs: Medicare and Medicaid. President Bill Clinton offered a detailed program based on managed competition among health-care providers. Some Democratic members of Congress championed a "pay or play" system in which employers would either provide health insurance for all workers or else contribute to a national fund that would do so. Still other advocates supported a system of national health insurance. Few citizens, however, fully understood the details of these various proposals, none of which ultimately was adopted. When the health care issue resurfaced in the late 1990's, understanding these earlier proposals became important. A speech of comparison might have increased public understanding by identifying the problem, describing the proposed options, and determining the strengths and weaknesses of each. The purpose of the speech would not be to urge any particular choice, but to make the alternatives clear so that listeners could apply their own criteria in deciding. The various reform proposals remained complex and were misunderstood. Along with political considerations, this helps to explain why none of the proposals was adopted, even given the widespread public support for some kind of change.

The body of the speech comparing the financing options for health care could be like this:

I. Modification of the current system is a possible solution.
   A. It offers certain benefits.
   B. It poses certain drawbacks.

II. Managed competition is a possible solution.
   A. It offers certain benefits.
   B. It poses certain drawbacks.

III. A "pay or play" plan is a possible solution.
   A. It offers certain benefits.
   B. It poses certain drawbacks.

IV. National health insurance is a possible solution.
   A. It offers certain benefits.
   B. It poses certain drawbacks.

V. Summary: The choices we must consider are modification of the current system, managed competition, a "pay or play" plan, and a national health insurance.

Many informative strategies have been examined as though they were completely separate and distinct. But often speakers mix and combine them. A speech may both report what happened, and attempt to interpret what it means, or maybe both explain and compare, or perhaps define and describe. The speaker can both demonstrate and explain. Always, however, the goal is to have understanding and insight in order to enhance listeners' awareness and their ability to make intelligent choices.

Applying Strategies

Excerpts from Carrie's Informative Speech on Body Piercing

How many of you are curious about body piercing when you see a pierced ear, nose, or navel? (Show navel ring) I contemplated getting my navel pierced a few years ago and decided to do research on this topic before I did it.

Perhaps you, too, are curious about this popular trend and would appreciate learning more about it. Today, I'll be discussing the history of body piercing, the most common piercing points, and the actual procedures involved.

I loved your attention getter of showing your navel. . . It was definitely a good thing that you employed the "conceal, reveal, conceal" rule because if your navel ring was visible throughout the speech, no one would have listened to you!
I like the three main points of this speech–history, common piercing points, and actual procedures. You develop these points sufficiently for a 3- to 4-minute speech assignment.

Speech Instructor's Comments

People in every culture throughout history have enhanced their appearances by either injecting dye under their skin or piercing odd parts of their body. I wasn't sure whether some of them would be appropriate to talk about in class, so I won't. Archaeologists have found evidence of Egyptian and Macedonian jewelry for pierced earrings dated back to 2,000 B.C.

Many contemporary cultures reserve piercing parts of the body for a rite of passage from child to adult. In the 1960's few women in the U.S. had their ears pierced and almost no men did.

Says whom? Don't forget to cite a source for this claim. Also, because this is such a visual topic, the speech could benefit from more visual aids. How about showing us some large photographs of body-pierced characters (close-ups) throughout history? Or a video tape from a recent movie where body-pierced characters are shown? The visual influence would help tell your story and keep the audience's attention throughout your speech.

And now in the '90's it's become an everyday thing for the ladies and very many of the guys. Piercing was reintroduced to this generation by "bikers, punks, and skinheads," and then became a trend for contemporary fashion.

How "every day" is this trend? How extensive is the practice? How many people elect to do it? How big a business is it now in the U.S.

A common question is, does it hurt? It hurts. The body responds to acute pain by releasing endorphins, which are a natural pain killer. It only hurts for a moment or two, and it doesn't hurt after it heals. For me it took about a month to heal. I went to Lake Bower right after I had it done, and that didn't help things too much. It depends on how you get it pierced. The most common but the worst way of piercing is, a friend does it for a friend. We didn't do that. A bunch of my friends and I had gone and got it done by a technician, and she used the right pair of tools and a stainless steel ring, which is supposed to keep it from being infected.

A personal story could be useful and powerful during your speech, especially when discussing how friends should not perform body-piercing acts on other friends. You would not have to include gruesome details but rather use a poignant example where the message is clear–go to a body-piercing professional for this procedure, not a friend.

Guns are only used on the earlobes, although some people have piercing guns available. Piercing guns on belly buttons can cause a lot of problems and disfigurement.

This is a generalization that has little follow through. You might explain, especially "disfigurement" with more detail and perhaps a visual aid.

Needles are never to be reused, even on the same person. It took them twice to get through mine. And the patient is carefully instructed in aftercare, after the piercing. We were supposed to use Bactine on ours. A lot of people use different things that worked for me.

A better conclusion needs to be given that sums up the topic and leaves the listener with enough information to draw his own conclusion about the positives and negatives of the topic.

Chapter 41: Analysis and Application Exercises

1. Today, take note of a situation where you gave information. How did you know if and when the information had been learned? What did you do to try to make the information you gave clear and memorable?
2. Write a description of a car designed for someone who has never seen one. Do you agree that pictures can be valuable when describing many concepts? Why or why not?
3. If you tried a joke in your speech and it fell flat, what would you do next and why?
4. Watch a 30-minute news broadcast. Try to identify at least two types of "informative" reports and label them. Describe how "information" reports differ from political news, weather, and sports events? What kind of techniques are used as described in this chapter?
5. Most of your teachers who lecture give "informative" presentations. Select one of your instructors and identify several "informative techniques" described in this chapter.

References

1. G. Highet, *The Art of Teaching* (New York: Alfred A. Knopf, Inc., 1950) pp. 242-244.
2. G. A. Hauser, "Empiricism, Description, and New Rhetoric," *Philosophy and Rhetoric*, 5 (Winter 1972), 24-44.

CHAPTER 42

Informative Speaking: Organization

LEARNING OBJECTIVES

When students have completed this chapter and lesson, they should be able to:

1. Explain the role organization plays in informative speaking.
2. Distinguish between the common patterns for organizing informative speeches
3. Know whether their strongest ideas should be first or last.

CHAPTER 42: Overview

This chapter focuses on the importance of organization. Factors affecting arrangement are discussed and the most common patterns for arranging ideas are identified and illustrated.

A review of the cartoon vividly illustrates that many of us have questions, and perhaps at times too many answers. But even more explicitly, the order or organization of the message certainly missed something. Obviously the structure was to span a river, but there seems to be some question as to exactly what should be placed there. Listeners almost uniformly agree that the critical part of a message is organization. The first axiom of Communication is always:

In this world of confusion, organization is key.

William V. Haney, in his work on Communication and Organizational Behavior, published in 1967,[1] begins by stating that for better or worse, society is becoming progressively organized. Fewer and fewer people are self-employed. Virtually everyone is temporarily or permanently involved in organizations. In the nearly half century since Haney's book, the electronic age has significantly intensified our dependence on organization, and the religious commitment to its structure, influence, and thought processes has accelerated at lightening speed.

Social psychologists, business executives, and even communicators infer that if our communication is organized, and the groups we affiliate with are organized, we will be more productive, persuasive, and satisfied individuals.

In preparing a message, the first step is to structure it for presentation. What should be said first? When do you present your strongest argument? If you are sending a message to a group, as were the military officers above, the structure should be vividly clear.

Factors affecting the topic under discussion should be organized properly. Are the main ideas dependent? Ideas can be arranged in a variety of patterns, making them either dependent or independent. Logically, dependent ideas are like links in a chain, because the strength of each depends on all the others. One weak link in a chain changes it from a very strong bond holding something together into a pile of scrap iron. If each idea is based on the acceptance of the idea before it, each must be accepted before the next can be presented.

If the ideas presented are independent, each idea is accepted on its own merit. With an independent pattern you do not have to present the main ideas in any particular order. In that case, additional questions will arise.

Are some main ideas relatively unfamiliar? Because most people comprehend unfamiliar ideas by linking them to familiar ideas, you might begin your speech with a main idea that is already acceptable to listeners. This will attract their interest and get them thinking about your topic. Then you can move to the less familiar ideas, knowing that the audience is working with you.

For example, your audience analysis suggests that most people realize there is generally a low dress standard among teenage students. But the audience may not realize this may not be just a teen problem. You might suggest that some parents are reliving their own teen fantasies by permitting their children to dress that way, or they may not understand that buying used clothing saves money many teens need.

There is another reason to begin with the familiar. If your first main idea were completely unfamiliar to the audience, it would be much more difficult for listeners to grasp. You might distract them by making them stop to think about what you mean by "teen dress codes," and they might miss your next point. On the other hand, discussion of a familiar main idea can be used to explain a less familiar idea. For example, knowing that listeners might quickly recognize that teen dress standards cause controversy, you might ask why the publicity is so strong against teen dress. This question would provide a natural transition into your second and third less familiar ideas.

Should the strongest idea come first or last? This raises the question: do you want to shock them first, or work into the major information gradually? What is remembered best, the ideas sent first (primacy) or the ideas you wish to leave with the audience at conclusion (recency)? Some argue that strong ideas that motivate an audience should hit them first before resistance can be created. Others believe that you should leave the audience remembering your best idea.

Discussions of learning curves, dissonance theory, impact of humor, threat, and reinforcement all suggest that order of presentation is a variable that interacts with other elements, not dictating a definite conclusion[2]. Too many other factors also influence the impact of arrangement. However, if one idea seems weaker than the others, you should present it in a middle position rather than either toward the beginning or the end.

The strength of an idea depends not on any inherent feature of the idea itself, but on how well the idea is accepted by the audience. This involves such factors as whether the idea relates to listeners' experience, whether it strikes most people as being consistent with common sense, and the amount of impact or contribution toward the overall goal of the speech. Because the strength of an idea depends on listeners' perceptions, your audience analysis is not finished when you first select a topic, purpose, thesis, and strategy; the audience affects all major decisions about speech preparation and delivery.

Patterns for Arranging Main Ideas

Speakers can arrange the order of main ideas in a variety of ways. There are several patterns easily followed. Consider these common patterns, and if you need a different approach, consider it. But keep in mind, the audience needs to perceive a logical progression of ideas. Here are the more common ones.

Chronological. The simple passing of time, presenting each event as it happened in its unfolding sequence. A typical three point approach is the past, the present and the future. Take the topic; Computers:

I. Personal computers could do only a few things in the early 1980s.
II. Personal computers are far more powerful today.
III. Personal computers will be even more versatile in the future.

Any set of conditions or statements that fit a logical time sequence can keep ideas organized.

Spatial order arranges ideas according to placement or position. Consideration is given to distance, location and space. Consider everything in position to you as a speaker: Your home, your city, your state, and your country. Consider a topic like inflation:

I. Inflation affects an individual's spending power.
II. Inflation affects state and local funded projects.
III. Inflation affects the federal budget.

Categorical (Topical). In the categorical pattern, each idea becomes a major division of the speech. For example, in considering schooling abroad, you may have decided that major elements include another culture, different historical interests, and associating with people of different lifestyles. Each topic becomes a major heading in your speech. Especially because a topical pattern has no required order it is important that main ideas be stated in parallel fashion and that they be easily recognized and remembered. Here is how the main ideas would appear:

I. You can experience another culture.
II. You can visit interesting places.
III. You can meet people with different experiences.

A simple category structure for this speech might be just key words: "People, places, events."

Cause-effect. In Chapter 6 you learned how to infer causes and effects. Cause-effect is also an organizational pattern, and it can proceed in either direction. You can focus on causes and identify their effects, or you can first identify effects and then try to determine their causes. For example, a speech about the depletion of the ozone layer might proceed like this:

I. Society has increased the use of aerosol spray cans.
II. These release fluorocarbons into the atmosphere.
III. Fluorocarbons erode the ozone layer surrounding the Earth.
IV. Depletion of the ozone layer exposes people to additional ultraviolet radiation.

Or, rather than moving from cause to effect, you might proceed from effect to cause:

I. We are becoming more vulnerable to ultraviolet radiation.
II. This effect results from the release of fluorocarbons into the atmosphere.
III. Widespread use of aerosol cans is one source of the problem.

The choice between these two arrangements would be governed by which topics you wanted to present first and last, not by anything intrinsic to the cause-effect organizational pattern.

Problem-solution pattern is a variation of the cause-effect approach focusing on problems and their answers. A speech using this pattern first lays out the dimensions of the problem and shows why it is serious; then it considers one or more potential solutions and explains why a particular solution is best. For example, a speech about the difficulties of the college registration system might be structured something like this:

I. The current registration system is both inefficient and unfair.
II. Registration by on-line Internet access would solve these problems.

The development of the first major heading might claim that the current registration system does not match students with their preferred courses as well as possible. It also gives confusion to students when classes fill. Perhaps after considering some other solutions, the speaker would then claim these problems can be overcome by using on-line and up-to-date technology.

Often problems are not self-evident to an audience. A speaker has to motivate listeners to feel that some important need is not being met before they will regard a situation as a problem. A variation on the problem-solution pattern is to emphasize *psychological order.* The speaker first motivates listeners to perceive a problem and then provides the solution. If Stuart had chosen this approach in speaking about the United Way, his speech might have been organized as follows:

I. We all have a responsibility to others.
II. This responsibility includes financial support for the social service organizations.
III. Giving to the United Way helps us meet our responsibilities.

The first step arouses an attitude, motive or desire among the audience members. Following steps refine the motivation and show how it can be satisfied by a given action. In Chapter 44 we will examine an elaborated version of this organizational pattern, called the "motivated sequence."

Comparison and Contrast. Sometimes it is easier to demonstrate similarities to and differences from other topics when the audience is already familiar with the topic.

From your studies of American history, you know that women and racial and ethnic minorities have sometimes been subjected to prejudice and discrimination in the workplace. Your speech might contrast the experiences among these groups:

I. Women often are not promoted to senior positions because executives believe women should be home raising children.
II. Many Mexican-Americans are hired mainly for menial jobs.
III. During the Second World War German-Americans and Japanese-Americans were fired from their jobs because they were considered unpatriotic.
IV. Today, immigrants of Spanish origin are at risk because they are seen as competing for existing jobs.
V. African-Americans have limited work opportunities because many white employers consider them lazy or unmotivated.

Now the question is whether you want to highlight the differences or the similarities among these groups. You might select either of the following as your last main idea:

VI. Although laws have been enacted to remove many of these discriminatory activities, a tight job market still shows some discrimination.

Or

VI. Although much has been done to curb these discriminatory practices, statistics still show artificial ceilings on their actual earnings.

In either case, the earlier main ideas are brought together in the last one, which shows either how differences outweigh similarities or the reverse.

Residues. A final organizational pattern is to arrange the speech by process of elimination. This pattern works well when there are a finite number of possibilities, none particularly desirable, and you want to argue that one of them represents "the least among the evils." For example, in a political campaign in which you find no candidate particularly appealing, you could use this pattern to rule out all but one candidate, whom you then support as being the least objectionable.

Jennifer used organization by residues to convince her classmates that tuition increases, although certainly unpopular, were necessary. She arranged her main ideas to rule out the other options available to the school:

> No one wants to pay more money. But let's look at the other options, Does anyone want larger classes? . . . How about fewer discussion sections? . . . Can we afford to make cuts in campus security? . . . What about student health care?

By talking about each of these other options, Jennifer was able to convince most of her audience that a moderate tuition increase was warranted and would be better than any alternative.

Chapter 42: Analysis and Application Exercises

Listen to a public speech given to an audience. This can be a broadcast, or an actual public event. (Church, Civic or Political.)

1. Write an outline of the speech, focusing on the Main points.
2. Identify the type of organization produced. (Chronological, Spatial, etc)
3. Determine the dependent, or independent style of the main ideas.
4. Evaluate whether "order" of materials played a role in its effectiveness (Primacy-recency, familiar-unfamiliar, or strongest-weakest ideas)

References

1. W.V. Haney, *Communication and Organizational Behavior,* (Homewood, Illinois: Richard D. Irwin, Inc), 1967.
2. See H. Gilkinson, S.F. Paulson, and D.E.Sikkink, "Effects of Order and Authority in an Argumentative Speech," *Quarterly Journal of Speech*, 40 (April, 1954), pp183-192; H.E. Gulley and D.K.Berlo "Effect of Intercellular and Intracellular Speech Structure on Attitude Change and Learning," *Communication Monographs*, 23 (November, 1956), pp 288-297; "Primacy-Recency," http://www.ciadvertising.org/student.account/fall-01.

CHAPTER 43

Persuasive Speaking Strategies

LEARNING OBJECTIVES

When students have completed this chapter and lesson, they should be able to:

1. Know the difference between informative and persuasive strategies.
2. Identify and list the goals of persuasive speaking.
3. Know and explain the terms Ethos, Logos, and Pathos as they relate to persuasion.
4. Describe and use the five requirements of effective persuasion.

CHAPTER 43: Overview

In the early 1950s, Ford Motor Company launched a project to produce the perfect automobile. By interviewing a number of potential customers, and by a little pressure from management, the Car built by the Customer was launched. Named after a president, the proud Edsel was introduced to the waiting world. Due to poor workmanship, design, and performance, the project was declared the biggest automobile mistake in history.

Vance Packard, in his book *Hidden Persuaders,* a book about the impact of advertising, described Ford's three major mistakes: 1. Consumers really do not know what they want; 2. If they do know, they will not tell you, and 3. Even if they do tell you, it does not mean they will act on what they say.

Considering the mistake, and looking at the auto industry, Ford launched a second auto, based on what they saw consumers buying: The Ford Mustang. Fifty years later it is still being produced.

Persuasion makes society move. For an overwhelming example, try visiting a major shopping mall. You can walk for hours observing thousands of items for sale, and less than ten percent of what is selling is not vital to the comfort or well-being of the customers. A massive consumer industry is based on one term: persuasion.

Being one of only two African-American students in a public speaking class, Nicole Wesley was not surprised to discover that her classmates knew little about the history of African-Americans. She decided to develop a speech that would inform them about soldiers of African descent who fought in the Revolutionary and Civil wars, former slaves who settled the West, the Tuskegee Airmen, the Harlem Renaissance, and the civil rights movement.

On reflection, Nicole realized that her speech would not really address the underlying issue. The real need was for an educational system that taught these basic historical and cultural lessons to students before they reached college. What Nicole had begun as a speech with an informative strategy soon evolved into a persuasive message to change the local high school curriculum.

As Nicole discovered, informative goals are sometimes insufficient. A speaker wants to have listeners think about something as well as influence what they think about it; speakers want listeners to do more than have a belief. Speakers want listeners to take action; or change their minds; or abandon one belief and accept another. In all these cases the speaker's goal is to persuade the audience, to prompt listeners to feel, act, or believe in a particular way. Consumer research has demonstrated that persuasion is a major factor in the modern world. Products, policies, politics, and even learning have become dominated by persuasion. This chapter focuses on use of persuasion in the public speaking venue.

Comparing Informative and Persuasive Strategies

Earlier we introduced seven specific speech purposes, and we saw that both agenda setting and providing new information or perspective are achieved mainly through informative strategies. The goals of strengthening commitment, weakening commitment, conversion, and inducing specific action all depend primarily on persuasive strategies.

As you know, informing and persuading are not entirely separate goals, and both create positive or negative feelings in the audience. If you want listeners to remember new information, you need to persuade them the new information is important. Persuading listeners to take action requires developing knowledge about what the action should be. Nevertheless, there are differences between informative and persuasive strategies.

Asking for Commitment

One difference between informative and persuasive strategies is in the degree of commitment the speaker requests from the audience. Informative strategies do not require listeners to commit themselves to any belief or action; the speaker mainly wants the audience to understand, think about, and remember the information in the speech. In contrast, persuasive strategies ask listeners to make a particular choice about believing or doing something—which to some degree eliminates another potential choice. In this sense, persuasive strategies ask listeners to put their beliefs or values on the line.

For this reason, speakers who seek to persuade must be sensitive to their ethical responsibility not to manipulate listeners. A speaker can so "load the deck" that the audience has an illusion of choice even though the speech predetermines what that choice will be. If a speaker moves listeners to action by persuasive but unsound appeals, or withholds crucial information or arguments because they might lead to an unwanted conclusion, or rushes listeners to judgment by pronouncing an issue more urgent than it actually is, then the audience has been manipulated.

Changing Degrees of Commitment

A speaker applies persuasive strategies because he or she assumes listeners can be either more committed or less committed to a position. By reasoning with audience members, the speaker seeks to move listeners from one point to another along a scale reflecting degrees of commitment. As shown in Figure 43.1, the speaker might want to strengthen commitment to a belief, moving listeners farther along the scale in the direction they are already headed. The speaker might want to weaken commitment to a belief, moving listeners closer to the other end of the scale. Or the speaker might even want to try to change listeners' minds, moving them from one end of the scale to the other—a process of conversion that seldom results from a single speech. Finally, the speaker might try to shift the entire scale, aiming to move listeners from a strong belief to approval of a specific action.

Both informative strategies and persuasive strategies seek to change the audience's perspective. But an informative speech seeks change by enlarging the audience's scope of concerns, whereas a persuasive speech seeks it by redirecting the audience's position.

Figure 43.1

Belief Intensity Scales

Before

After
Strengthening commitment

Before

After
Weakening commitment

Before

After
Conversion

Before

After
Inducing a specific action

Plan Your Strategy

Speechmaking has been expounded as strategic planning. Being able to analyze the audience, to size up the situation, and to determine its constraints and opportunities—the basic skills you learned in Chapters 3 and 4—will enable you to make the best use of persuasive strategies.

Earlier we reviewed the steps in strategic planning. Because persuasive strategies seek an increased commitment from listeners, you need to perform a more detailed audience analysis aimed at identifying your target audience and at assessing that audience's motivation. Essentially, your audience acts, moves, and makes decisions on the basis of trying to be rational people operating intelligently, or at least make others think they are rational, as they cope with four fundamental persuasive needs:

1. The first need is to survive. We are concerned about life itself, and whether we have the energy and well-being to meet its requirements.
2. The second need is a biological desire to improve our well-being by acting in what we consider our best interest—we condition ourselves to respond to signs and signals, because that is how we get things done. If we respond to expectations, we gain acceptance of others!
3. The third need is to meet dilemmas and difficulties, and take action to become more comfortable. We have a problem—we need a solution.
4. The forth need is to make rational choices when we have options that have similar rewards. The behavior here becomes complex, because we not only try to satisfy all our needs, but at the same time try to appear to be rational, intelligent decision makers.

Other needs affect us, but can be justifiably forced into the above choices: being popular, satisfying our creative wants, being accepted as an achiever are some examples. As a speaker, we try to capitalize on these needs in order to motivate people to accept our persuasive appeals.

Determine Your Target Audience

If your audience is diverse and you are not seeking unanimity, the first step is to determine as precisely as possible which members are your target audience. For example, suppose you are speaking at a corporate meeting attended by upper management and by the heads of all departments that might be affected by your presentation—even though any decisions ultimately will be made by only the president and the chair of the board. It would be nice to influence the department heads by your speech, but your real target audience is the president and the board chair. They are the decision makers, and it is they whom you want to persuade. You want their acceptance.

Assess Your Audience's Motivation

Listeners will be motivated to let your speech influence them if they perceive that your appeal is linked to their own motives and needs. Listeners want to appear to be rational, clear-thinking people, but they also want satisfaction--or biological rewards.

Psychologists have offered many different accounts of the nature of human motivation. At the most general level, people seek to attain pleasure and to avoid pain. They want acceptance and not rejection. They want respect. These motives are the basis for persuasive speeches about everything from the dangers of air pollution to the benefits of good nutrition—as student speaker Michael Masdea demonstrated in urging his audience to stop drinking so much caffeine:

> Caffeine can help us stay up during those frequent student all-nighters. But it can also cause severe headaches, stomachaches, and insomnia. The psychological and behavioral effects of caffeine are frightening. It is a highly addictive drug, and it may be the cause of many problems you are experiencing right now.

Another general account of human motivation was offered by psychologist Abraham Maslow, who theorized that human beings have a hierarchy of needs; we first seek to satisfy biological and safety needs, which include food, clothing, shelter, and protection from harm, and then proceed to higher-order needs, such as identity, meaningful relationships, and self-actualization.[1] Maslow argued that a person's higher-order motives become important only after lower-order needs are satisfied. It is useless, for instance, to discuss abstract ideals with someone who doesn't know where the next meal is coming from. On the other hand, people who have been able to satisfy their lower-order needs often find that they are not truly fulfilled; then higher-order needs and motives become important. According to this view of motivation, the persuasive speaker's task is to determine approximately where the listening audience is on Maslow's hierarchy of needs. Then the speaker must arouse the appropriate motive and show how needs can be satisfied by adopting the recommended action or belief.

Student speaker Kevin Krebs appealed to motives on different levels of Maslow's hierarchy in a speech favoring the new NCAA policy of enforcing stricter rules about athletes' minimum grade-point averages and test scores. Kevin first appealed to the athletes' basic need to make a living:

> How many of you really think you're going to get a job playing professional sports? If you do, the odds are stacked against you. Only a small percentage will actually make a living playing the game. Chances are, when you get out of college, you're going to need the education being forced upon you by the new NCAA rules.

Then, for athletes and sports fans alike, Kevin appealed to the higher need to enjoy winning:

> The policy at this university is already stricter than the new NCAA rules. By accepting these new guidelines, some of our competitors with lower standards will be eliminated from the field. Our school will finally get a chance to win a game or two!

The successful persuasive public speaker will consider all the elements of public speaking that have been discussed previously: everything from audience perception of meaning to understanding of logical argument. The following is an attempt to integrate these concepts into a meaningful, organized presentation that will achieve the speaker's objective.

Requirements for Effective Persuasive Speaking

Just as when you inform, to persuade you need a clear organizational structure and positive ethos. Listeners must have faith in your message. Likewise, successful persuasion requires that listeners remember what they heard. In addition, to persuade you must offer sound reasoning, and you must identify with your audience. Critical to the process is a positive emotional response to the message by the listener.

Follow Appropriate Organizational Patterns

Not only does being organized enhance persuasiveness, but the choice of one organizational pattern over another is significant. When seeking to influence others, the problem-solution pattern is often the structure of choice: Make the audience aware of a problem, and then provide a specific means to address that problem. Within this overall framework you can inject a number of other helpful patterns; narrative sequence lets you tell the story of how the problem developed, topical structure allows you to examine various dimensions of the problem, and biographical structure enables you to focus on key individuals in the evolution of the problem.

Also be astute in selecting supporting materials for a problem-solution speech.[2] A startling statistic, for example, might move listeners to take notice of an issue that is far larger than they might think. Describing interest on the national debt as the largest single government expenditure—larger than national defense, larger than social welfare—might cause listeners to regard the debt as a more serious problem than they had realized. If you then divide the national debt into a $1,600 bill to be paid by every man, woman, and child in America, you might translate its vast size into meaningful terms and personalize the problem for listeners. Then to expand the emphasis, add that the federal debt is expected to be expanded at least another $300 billion; this intensifies the data even more.

A personal narrative can be a potent form of supporting material, making an abstract problem concrete and showing its effects on the lives of real people. If you discuss how "taxpayer resistance has squeezed the public sector of the economy," the problem may seem distant, removed, and impersonal. Instead, you can make the issue more vivid and immediate by telling listeners, "the local elementary school has been forced to close its library, depriving children of books and the librarian of a job."

An effective speaker regards structure as an opportunity to sequence and highlight facts, leading his or her audience to a reasonable conclusion.

Establish Positive Ethos

Your ethos, or credibility, is a powerful resource in persuasive speeches. If listeners trust you, they will be more inclined to give your ideas a fair hearing. Particularly important among the many factors that engender trust are a speaker's previous record, association with trustworthy sources, and reluctant testimony. Impressive knowledge and quotation from authority can expand ethos even more.

Previous Record. A speaker who has established a record of being trustworthy is likely to be trusted in the specific situation at hand. If in earlier speeches you've convinced the audience that you are careful, faithful to the evidence, critical in reasoning, and don't make claims beyond what the evidence supports, you have created a strong presumption that what you say in this speech will be trustworthy as well.

Association with Trustworthy Sources. Particularly when your topic is something about which you are not an expert, you need to draw on the statements of people who do have expertise in the subject. If your sources have a reputation for trustworthiness, your association with them will suggest that you are trustworthy, too.

Reluctant Testimony Your statements will be weakened if listeners think you have something to gain by stating them. If your audience believes you have a vested interest—whether economic, political, or ideological—in a particular outcome of the speech, listeners will tend to discount what you say.

On the other hand, if you make a statement that is at odds with your own interest, that statement is considered to be reluctant testimony. Because you are working against your own interests by making this statement, listeners presume that you would not make it unless it were true.

Consider how reluctant testimony has worked in the political world. Ronald Reagan, for example—a Cold Warrior who had called the Soviet Union an "evil empire"—really began to dismantle the Cold War apparatus and seek arms reduction agreements with the Soviet Union. If someone else had attempted this, it might have seemed like a cave-in to Soviet demands. President Reagan was trustworthy because people believed that he would not betray conservative interests. Similarly, Lyndon Johnson, although he came from the region that most resisted civil rights, convinced Congress to enact the most sweeping civil rights legislation in history.

Since reluctant testimony generally is more credible than is evidence reflecting the source's self-interest, you should look for it when conducting your research. Reluctant testimony is the opposite of biased evidence, which you should try particularly hard to avoid.

Reluctant testimony enhances the credibility of classroom speakers too. Western State University had a tradition of strong social fraternities, a system that had come under fire because several recent initiation rituals clearly had been excessive. A vocal group of faculty members charged that all fraternities were anti-intellectual, and the campus newspaper called frats "social clubs for the privileged rich." Two students of public speaking addressed this issue, arguing that major changes were needed if fraternities were to survive on campus. Ben Peters was an independent who was known to dislike fraternities. Although his speech was well prepared, it had little impact on his classmates; it said exactly what everyone expected Ben to say. But when Charles Thompson, a fraternity president, acknowledged that the system had serious problems, listeners noticed. If a prominent fraternity man criticized the system, his views had to be taken seriously.

Just as the insider was more persuasive in this example, so will a dorm resident who is a smoker be more credible than one who is a nonsmoker in urging a smoke-free dormitory environment. Similarly, a biology student who argues that animal experiments on campus need to be monitored and reduced will be more believable than an English major who makes the same argument. As a speaker, you can enhance your credibility by pointing out when you are offering reluctant testimony.

Encourage Retention through Reinforcement

The slope of the forgetting curve is steep, particularly when the message involves new, unfamiliar, or uncomfortable ideas. Unless your persuasive goal is very specific and can be achieved through the speech itself, you should think creatively about how to reinforce what you want listeners to believe or to do. Your strategies might range from the simple act of thanking the audience for hearing your proposal to the extreme of asking listeners to participate actively in encouraging others to accept the view you propose.

Student Margaret Orsinger used an interesting metaphor to reinforce her message that bicyclists and motorcyclists should wear helmets:

> We do more to protect the melons in our grocery stores than we do to protect our own heads! Every time you see a cyclist without a helmet, take a good hard look at these "melon-heads." They are people in need of a good, solid crate around their ears.

There is no magic recipe for reinforcing a persuasive message. In general, though, you are more likely to succeed if you give listeners opportunities to remind themselves of your conclusion and how you arrived at it. If acceptance of your position enhances the listeners' self-worth and improves their comfort, well-being, or acceptance, persuasion can take place. The critical factor, however, is to present material that offers a reward for the listener who accepts your message. Earlier we mentioned the rewards that are most effective in benefiting the listener. Theory teaches that listeners are persuaded if they are convinced that: 1. Acceptance means the listener will survive, or live better; 2. Acceptance means they will receive a reward for being persuaded; 3. Acceptance means they will be more comfortable, enjoy life better, and be more respected; and 4. They will be rewarded for making a wise choice, and recognizing the folly of the alternative.

To create a speech based on persuasive strategies, you need to understand the ways by which people often resist efforts to persuade them. This will enable you to determine where your audience is positioned on the belief intensity scale (Figure 43.1). You also need to know what resources speakers have to overcome resistance.

Use Sound Reasoning

Because in a persuasive speech you are asking the audience to believe or to do something, it is particularly important that you use sound reasoning. If listeners think that your reasoning is shoddy, they will be far less likely to conclude that you have made a good case for what you want them to believe or do. If your case is weak, it is easy for them to disregard your request for their response. You may wish to review the discussion of reasoning in Chapter 4. Remember that we have focused on reasoning with the audience in mind, not on reasoning as an abstract exercise in logic.

Achieve Identification

Establishing common bonds between speaker and audience is referred to as identification.[3] The more listeners believe themselves to be basically like the speaker and share the same values or experiences, the more willing they are to be influenced by what the speaker says. Speakers can develop common bonds explicitly, by stating the features they share with the audience. Or bonds can be developed implicitly, when the speaker relates a personal experience any listeners also have had. Common bonds can even be developed with no mention at all. For example, the fact that a college student speaks to an audience of college students about concerns of college students is itself a source of common bonds. Not surprisingly, listeners are more likely to be persuaded by a peer than by a more distant figure with whom it is difficult to identify.

To keep identification from being perceived as pandering to the audience or telling listeners whatever they want to hear, apply the test you learned earlier: Use appeals that will satisfy not only the specific audience that is immediately present but also the broader audience of unseen critical listeners whom you might imagine as your court of appeal.

Other Goals for Persuasive Speeches

Persuasive strategies sometimes are used to achieve more specific goals. Some speeches seek mainly to strengthen the audience's conviction. Others seek conversion (to weaken commitment to one belief and to lead listeners to another). Still others are speeches of refutation that dispute the ideas someone else has advanced or that respond to someone else's criticism of your ideas. These variations on the problem-solution speech are described next.

Strengthening Conviction

Speakers often address audiences that already agree with them. Why, then, do listeners need to be persuaded? Suppose you believe your school should hire more faculty instructors to teach undergraduate courses, even if that means an increase in tuition. Since most students dislike tuition increases, objections from your classmates could outweigh support for more teachers. A speaker who favors hiring more faculty would know that convincing people like you is essential for academic improvement, and would improve your educational climate as well as insulate you from the possibility of being poorly educated. The body of this speaker's outline might look like this:

I. A tuition increase would benefit undergraduate education.
   A. It would make it possible to hire more faculty.
   B. It would enable the university to offer more small classes and seminars.
   C. These, in turn, would enrich faculty-student interaction and additional instruction.

II. The risks of a tuition increase are slight.
   A. The size of the increase would be modest.
   B. Financial aid would be increased along with tuition.
   C. After a slight initial decline, applications for admission would increase in response to the improved faculty.

You may have been vaguely familiar with these arguments, but you had not considered them carefully. Therefore, the speaker succeeds in strengthening your conviction that the benefits of additional faculty are worth the cost of tuition increases.

Is this really a form of persuasion? Yes, because your attitude about the subject differs after the speech as a direct result of the speech. The speaker has influenced you to believe more strongly about the subject than you did before. Strengthening conviction is a very common approach to persuasion because it takes advantage of people's tendency to seek out and accept messages with which they already agree.

Following are several common ways by which speakers try to strengthen listeners' convictions.

Consciousness-Raising. You undoubtedly have beliefs or values that you are barely aware of because you take them for granted. Only when you deliberately focus attention on those values will you acknowledge and reaffirm support for them. For example, people often don't realize how important families and loved ones are until they are separated from them or someone becomes ill.

In the 1970s the emerging women's movement used the term consciousness-raising to refer to the process of making people aware of values and commitments they had taken for granted.[4] This process recently has become popular with the acknowledgment of sexual harassment in the workplace. Prior to this movement toward public awareness, many people believed that sexual harassment was wrong, but they were not aware of how this conviction applied to everyday occurrences at work. By bringing such values to the surface and applying them to a specific situation, a speaker can cause listeners to identify with them consciously, thereby strengthening their convictions.

Moving from Education to Commitment. Informative strategies might provide listeners the background they need to understand an issue. For example, listeners need to be informed of the workings of the Electoral College to recognize the risk of selecting a president of the United States not favored by the popular vote. A persuasive speech would go further, building on listeners' new intellectual awareness of that risk and seeking to convince them that the issue is serious and should be addressed. The speaker's goal might be to convince listeners to support a Constitutional amendment that abolishes the Electoral College and selects the new President by popular vote.

Increasing the Sense of Urgency. Political campaign managers face the difficult problem of convincing a candidate's supporters that their ongoing support really matters. Tracy Baxter saw the need to fire up supporters when she was managing a political campaign for her neighbor, Martha Scott, who was running for the city council. Martha was well known in the neighborhood for such projects as increasing crime patrols, beautifying parks, and encouraging parents to volunteer at their child's school. She seemed certain to win the election—and that's what troubled Tracy. She was worried that Martha's supporters might think their efforts weren't needed and they wouldn't bother to contribute to the campaign or even to vote. If enough people felt that way, Martha could lose the election. So Tracy addressed a rally of Martha's supporters, stressing that the race was still in doubt, and their efforts, money, and votes were essential to victory.

Self-fulfilling prophecy is a prediction that comes true because of actions people take on hearing the prediction.

Tracy was worried that a self-fulfilling prophecy might derail Martha's campaign. If supporters believed that their efforts weren't needed and thus didn't contribute, the campaign wouldn't have the resources to advertise and mobilize voters; then, if Martha were defeated, supporters would conclude that they were right not to waste their money and time. To break this circular, self-fulfilling reasoning, Tracy needed to establish a sense of urgency among listeners. At the same time, she didn't want to overstate the situation because that might produce a boomerang effect. Instead, she convinced listeners that each person's action would make a real difference in averting defeat and ensuring victory. Her speech carefully balanced how serious the problem was and how easily listeners could be effective in solving it.

In such situations, speakers typically argue that (1) the issue is important, (2) it could be decided either way, (3) it will be decided soon, and (4) the listener's action could tip the scales. Properly crafted, such a message will jolt listeners out of complacency and intensify their commitment to the cause.

Conversion

Far more difficult than strengthening a conviction is changing it. Speakers who attempt conversion aim to alter listeners' beliefs, either by convincing them to accept something they had previously rejected or to reject something they had previously accepted.

Because people defend themselves against persuasion, no speaker is likely to achieve conversion through a single speech, unless listeners' opinions about the subject are not deeply held. Few if any speaking situations are like the old-time religious revivals in which the emotion of the situation and the magic of the preacher's words caused listeners to feel in a flash the seriousness of their situation and the need for reform.

Checklist 43.1

Steps in Conversion

1. Chip away at the edges of beliefs.
2. Identify a pattern of anomalies.
3. Employ consciousness raising.
4. See incremental changes.

How, then, can conversion ever take place? People do change their minds, do abandon positions they have held and replace them with others. Typically, a speaker attempts conversion through the following steps:

1. **Chip away at the edges of beliefs.** Rather than attacking beliefs head-on, where they are most strongly defended, work first on the periphery. During the civil rights movement of the 1950s and early 1960s, for example, many resistant Southerners who did not abandon racial prejudice were nonetheless convinced by marches and demonstrations that inhumane treatment of blacks was wrong. Sympathy was aroused for the demonstrators and led listeners to examine whether other aspects of the treatment of blacks were also wrong. Gradually attitudes, then policies and actions were changed.

   One effective way to chip away at the edges of beliefs is to defend a value that initially coexists with the value you want to challenge. Undermine the conflicting attitude. Again the civil rights movement furnishes an example. Many who believed in racial segregation also revered the Constitution. These two values could coexist as long as the Constitution was not seen as prohibiting segregation. Segregation was quietly challenged by implying the Constitution was for *all Americans*. This gradually challenged segregation by suggesting it violated the Constitution. When laws and court rulings indicated that segregation was unconstitutional, President Lyndon Johnson appealed to many Southerners not so much by discrediting racial prejudice (although he attempted that as well) but by appealing instead to reverence for the Constitution. Suddenly, the two values were in opposition, and one was used to undermine the other.

2. **Identify a pattern of anomalies.** People change beliefs when their old beliefs no longer explain things adequately. Anomalies are puzzling situations that an explanation does not fit. When we first discover them, we tend to dismiss them as freak coincidences or point to them as exceptions to the rule. But if anomalies continue, and especially if they intensify, they eventually call a position into question. Then the old view may collapse of its own weight, and the listener might convert to a new belief.

   Such a pattern has been used to explain why many Democrats during the 1980s converted to support Republican Ronald Reagan. Believing in the effectiveness of government programs, they watched through the 1960s and 1970s as those programs grew; yet, in their view, social problems worsened rather than improved. At first this was just a puzzle for them. But as evidence (and their taxes) continued to mount, they eventually came to believe that government was not a solution to social ills but was itself part of the problem. This, of course, was the position advocated by President Reagan.

3. **Consciousness-raising** is not only used as a means of strengthening convictions, it can also be used when a speaker wants the audience to change. Let's

look again at the example of the women's movement. Early advocates of consciousness-raising maintained that women had accepted their subordinate role because they had never regarded their role as being equal. By raising women's consciousness about the dominant/submissive pattern in many of their existing relationships with men, advocates were able not only to sensitize them to their situation but also to evoke a change in conditions. Such strategy has produced significant changes in women's role in the workplace. Drawing attention to a problem can often be the largest contributor to solving the problem.

In another example, student speaker Laura Davisson gave a speech to raise listeners' consciousness about discrimination against overweight people:

You might just laugh at them behind their backs. Perhaps you call them names like "whale" or "pig." Maybe they are the butt of your jokes. Or maybe it's something much more subtle than that. Maybe you just assume that fat people have no self-control, that they eat too much and too often, or that they get no exercise.

By pointing out the existence of listeners' discriminatory feelings and actions, Laura was able to begin altering them. Consciousness-raising made listeners sufficiently uncomfortable with their own actions and introduced a climate of change.

4. **Seek incremental changes** Conversion often comes about slowly, in a series of small and gradual steps. Persuasion more commonly comes about over time and with a series of small changes. People typically change their views incrementally rather than radically. By understanding this concept, successful persuaders keep their goals modest, and consider a long-range program. Don't ask for too much too soon. Plan a long-range program of change.

   Imagine, for example, that your goal is to defend public funding for the arts, even though you know the audience is hostile to it, considers most contemporary art unnecessary or even perverse, and sees public funding as a waste of tax money. Successful persuasion will probably require several steps, beginning with asking the audience to acknowledge the importance of art both in fostering self-expression and advancing culture. The persuader can then move to the position that one need not like or support all examples of art to believe strongly in the value of the arts. The persuader could explain why it is in the public interest to support art; then defend the overall administration of public funding programs and show that errors and mistaken judgments are few. The next question could consider whether the government should reduce funding for the arts. Getting to this point might require several speeches, over a long period of time. But a frontal assault on the audience's values is likely to fail, whereas a gradual, incremental approach has at least a chance of success or partial change. People often accept in small doses a belief that they would reject outright if it were presented all at once.

Refutation

In addition to persuasive speeches that seek either to strengthen or to change convictions, refutation is a type of speech that tries to disprove or dispute the arguments or appeals made by others. This strategy is defensive and seeks to prevent listeners from being persuaded by someone else.

The strategy is that if you convince them not to be persuaded by someone else, you have actually persuaded them yourself.[5]

Grounds for Refutation. Before you can refute an argument or appeal, you first need to understand what it says. Here tests of reasoning become critical. Once you have decided the other person's argument is weak and should be refuted, you can use either or both of the following strategies:

1. **Object to the claim itself, and develop a contrary claim.** This form of refutation does not target the internal workings of the argument; instead,

Checklist 43.2

Steps in Refutation

1. Decide on the grounds for refutation.
   - Object to the claim, and develop a contrary claim.
   - Object to the inferences, and thereby refuse to accept the conclusion.
2. Develop the refutation.
   - Identify the position to be attacked.
   - Explain the significance of the position you are attacking.
   - Present and develop the attack.
   - Explain the impact of the refutation.

it challenges the conclusion and offers an alternative proposal. For example, on hearing a speaker advocate abortion be restricted, you decide to refute the speaker, presenting evidence that restrictions force negative choices. Your arguments are independent of the other speaker's. You develop them not by analyzing the internal workings of the speaker's argument but through your own careful and independent thought, evidence, and reasoning. Refuting an opposing argument requires calling its claims into question and advancing your own.

2. **Object to the speaker's inferences, and thereby refuse to accept the conclusion.** In this case you analyze the internal workings of the other person's argument, applying the same tests of reasoning (see Chapter 4) that you used in developing your own speech. If the speaker employs hasty generalization, confuses cause with sign, develops a faulty analogy, or commits any other error in reasoning, the conclusion may well be faulty even if supporting evidence is true. You will want to point out these deficiencies in reasoning if your goal is refutation. This is especially effective when the opponent uses opinion and suggestion, or invalid or weak inferences rather than evidence and reasoning.

Developing the Message. Whether you want to refute a particular argument or an entire speech, the basic steps in developing your message are similar. You must specify what you are refuting, make your refutation convincing, and explain to listeners what the refutation has accomplished. To achieve these goals, the following steps are recommended.

1. **Identify the position to be attacked.** State the position as clearly and as fairly as you can. It is especially important to state the position in a way that its supporters would accept. Both speakers need to agree on definition of terms and correct wording of issues. Advocates who fail to do this usually end up speaking past each other rather than truly refuting each other's positions. Refutation requires a clash of ideas or facts. Failure to obtain definition of terms and issues only alienates audiences and causes frustration, confusion, and bad feelings. Nothing is accomplished.

   For example, if you opposed abortion and began to refute a pro-choice speech by stating, "Pro-choice speakers support the killing of innocent babies," you would not be stating the position fairly. You may regard the fetus as an innocent baby, but pro-choice supporters do not. In fact, that is the essential difference between those who support and those who oppose abortion. A fairer statement of the position might be, "Pro-choice supporters don't think the fetus is a human being, but I believe we must assume that it is."

Student speaker Bruno Campos very effectively identified the position he wanted to attack in a speech refuting President Bush's justification of the Persian Gulf War in 1990-1991. Taking the very words that Bush used to support his decision to send troops to Kuwait, Bruno created a visual aid: a chart listing the President's justifications for the war. Then, step by step, he responded to each item, crossing it off the list as he refuted it. When he finished the speech, nothing was left on the chart.

2. **Explain the significance of the position you are attacking**. This often-omitted step lets the audience know why your refutation is important. Most people dislike hearing disagreement for disagreement's sake. If your refutation can be granted and yet do no real damage to the opponent's position, then listeners will probably not take your speech seriously.

   Consider the abortion example again, but this time imagine the speaker is pro-choice and is refuting the statement that protesters stayed ten yards away from the entrance to an abortion clinic, instead insisting they were within five yards of it. In this case, the refutation is probably not very important; it is hard to imagine why the difference between five and ten yards would matter. But suppose the speaker were to say, "Pro-life supporters violated a local ordinance by entering the ten-yard radius and blocked the entrance to an abortion clinic," and then went on to explain, "This is important because the law was designed to balance the rights of protesters with the rights of women seeking abortions. If the ten-yard rule is too difficult to maintain, then it should be changed by the City Council, not by protesters." Now the speaker has both identified the argument to be refuted and explained why the refutation matters.

3. **Present and develop the attack.** State your position, and support it with appropriate materials. This step will probably take the most time. The process is basically the same as if you were developing a constructive position of your own. Pay special attention to the tests of evidence and reasoning.

4. **Explain the impact of the refutation.** Having presented and supported your own claim, do not assume that the significance of your achievement is self-evident. Include a sentence or two to explain exactly what your refutation has accomplished. If you are refuting the argument that all students should have parking privileges on campus, and you show first, that there are not enough parking spaces to go around; and second, the cost of building additional space is prohibitive, you may believe you have been very clear about what you've accomplished. But the audience often still needs help. It will not hurt to draw the argument together by saying, "So this proposal is not feasible because of parking space shortages, and creating more spaces is not financially practical. Even though the proposal appeals to your desire for parking privileges, you ought not to be swayed by it." Recognize that listeners will attend to the speech with different degrees of intensity, and you must provide a clear statement of what your refutation has accomplished.

Rebuilding Arguments ***Refutation*** is not solely a process of criticizing arguments; it is also a means of rebuilding an argument that has been attacked. You can rebuild an argument by responding to criticism against it—either by showing that the attack was flawed or by developing independent reasons for the audience to believe the original claim.

If your thesis were "Many people have argued that space limitations make it infeasible to guarantee parking to all students, but I wish to defend the guaranteed-parking proposal against these attacks," your analytical process would be exactly the same as if you were developing the refutation. Both attack and defense therefore come under the heading of refutation, and both should be seen as basically alike in analysis and composition.

Chapter 43: Analysis and Application Exercises

1. Look and listen to Herman Cain's words in the opening and closing of the video lesson. What characteristics of speaker credibility does he exhibit? What types of proofs does he use? Did you find him persuasive? Why or why not?

2. What makes the persuasive speech in lesson #26 effective? Memorable? For each answer, explain why

References

1. A. H. Maslow, "A Dynamic Theory of Personality," *Psychological Review,* 50 (July 1943): 370-396.
2. See John C. Reinard, "The Empirical Study of the Persuasive Effects of Evidence: The Status after Fifty Years of Research," *Human Communication Research,* 15 (Fall 1988): 3-59.
3. See Kenneth Burke, *A Rhetoric of Motives*, New York: Prentice-Hall, 1950. For a discussion of Burke's theory of identification, see Dennis G. Day, "Persuasion and the Concept of Identification," *Quarterly Journal of Speech,* 46 (October 1960): 270-273.
4. Consciousness-raising often occurred in group discussions but could also be the result of a more formal speech. See Anita Shreve, *Women Together, Women Alone: The Legacy of the Consciousness-Raising Movement* (New York: Viking Press, 1989).
5. Research has shown that messages which provide both arguments for a position and refutation of the opposition are more persuasive than messages that simply present arguments for a position. Mike Allen, Jerold Hale, Paul Mongeau, et al., "Testing a Model of Message Sidedness: Three Replications," *Communication Monographs*, 57 (December 1990): 275-291.

CHAPTER 44 Persuasive Speaking Organization

LEARNING OBJECTIVES

When students have completed this chapter and lesson, they should be able to:

1. Identify, explain, and demonstrate two persuasive speech patterns.
2. Understand the steps in the problem-solution organization and illustrate it with a contemporary problem suitable for a persuasive speech.
3. Understand and use the motivated sequence as a structure for a persuasive speech.

CHAPTER 44: Overview

Proper organizational structures for persuasive speeches include the Problem-solution organization, and the Motivated Sequence pattern of statements. Both successfully structure persuasive speeches.

Organizing for Persuasion

Some writers describe persuasion as a series of steps arranging statements in a specific sequence. William J. McGuire states that a person's attitudes can be changed by using a six-step process: receiving a communication, paying attention to it, comprehending it, yielding to it, retaining the new attitude, and performing the desired behavior[1]. Even if these steps are not always separate and do not always come in the same order, McGuire's scheme is useful for understanding what happens when someone is persuaded. An effective speaker regards structure as an opportunity to sequence and highlight facts, leading the audience to a reasonable conclusion. The problem-solution organization is a flexible pattern, allowing for variations that satisfy most persuasive purposes.

The Problem-solution Speech

Using the problem-solution speech, which establishes a serious problem and then identifies what should be an obvious solution is a successful persuasive strategy. The speaker uses persuasive strategies to create a positive feeling, to strengthen commitment, and to move the audience beyond concern, onto action[2]. Although problem-solution speeches can be organized in a variety of patterns, they typically follow the four-stage structure:

- Describe the situation.
- Evaluate the situation as a problem.
- Propose a solution.
- Argue for the solution.

Describe the Situation

This part of the speech is primarily informative. Your goal is to make listeners aware of the magnitude or importance of the problem. For example, in discussing how people are threatened by crime, report how often crimes are committed, the number of people who have been victimized by crime, how crime harmfully af-

The problem-solving speech requires you first to persuade the audience that there is a serious threat or problem, and then to persuade them that your solution is the best approach to the problem. This speaker is arguing that handgun-related deaths are excessive and that limitations must be placed on handgun ownership.

fects them psychologically, and what steps people have taken to deal with crime. The outline for this part of your speech is:

I. Crime is significant and growing.
   A. Rates of virtually all crimes are increasing.
   B. Loss of life and property because of crime are increasing.
   C. People in all segments of the community believe their neighborhoods to be unsafe.
   D. Crime is a growing problem even on this campus.

Evaluate the Situation as a Problem

The second stage is to convince listeners that the situation described at the first of the speech really does represent a problem—that it is cause for genuine concern. People often ignore inconveniences without taking action; but if you emphasize the amount of inconvenience, as explained in the first major point, they become concerned and acknowledge what they now regard as serious problems.

To establish that a situation is a problem, you need to show it violates a value important to your audience. In the case of crime, rising crime rates can lead people to feel insecure, undermine their sense of justice, and threaten the stability of the community. Because people care about these values, they will be disturbed by rising crime rates.

Values are rooted in emotions, and so persuasive strategies must be concerned with emotional appeals. Earlier you learned that an inappropriate appeal to emotions is an error in reasoning. The key word here is "inappropriate." Although emotional appeals can be misused, there is nothing irrational about responding to an appropriate appeal. When you decide not to go out alone at night because of safety concerns, when you try to mend fences with parents or siblings because family harmony is important, or when you strive to do your best in response to competition, your choices are perfectly reasonable and sensible.

The second part of the speech's body might be outlined like this:

II. Rising crime is a serious problem.
   A. It causes people to feel insecure and unsafe.
   B. It undermines a sense of justice.
   C. It threatens the stability and peace of the community.

Now the speaker is making the audience members aware of these emotions and internalizing them. When you evoke fear, pride, anxiety, or any other emotion, you also create a need to satisfy that emotion. Some emotions, such as fear and anxiety, can become highly disturbing. Your power as a speaker lies in the ability not only to arouse the emotion but also to satisfy it by providing a positive course of action. Arousing too much fear can cause a boomerang effect, causing the listener to avoid the topic entirely. But if you arouse an appropriate level of fear, then offer the means to relieve the fear—by taking advantage of a campus escort service, by learning the art of self-defense, or by deciding not to go out alone at night— the speech is likely to be persuasive. The speaker is trying to make sure the audience "identifies" with victims of crime, and takes some form of "ownership" in its happening. Such an attitude strengthens the emotional appeal and motivates the receiver to the persuaded solution.[3]

Propose a Solution

Having aroused an appropriate level of emotion, it is important to offer the audience a solution to the problem. Listeners will feel uncomfortable if you arouse fear, concern, or anxiety without also suggesting a solution that will restore their sense of harmony. Your solution might be simple (a single option) or complex (a range of options).

You might identify it at once, or you might first rule out alternatives. But your solution should be detailed enough to address the problem as you have described it. If you have presented three separate dimensions of the problem, for instance, each should be addressed by your solution.

In the crime example, few listeners would feel that a statement like "We have to have faith and hope that things will turn out for the best" is an appropriate solution. Once the need for a change has been established and accepted, you are more likely to be persuasive if a section of your speech details the solution, such as:

III. A successful solution to the problem has several components.
   A. It includes efforts to eliminate the root causes of crime.
   B. It includes more effective means to investigate crime.
   C. It includes making the justice system more efficient and more effective.
   D. It includes stiffer penalties for the most serious offenders.

Argue for the Solution

The final step in the problem-solution speech is to convince listeners that your solution really works—that it resolves the problem, is feasible, and produces benefits that outweigh its costs. Speakers too often neglect this final step, as though the value of the solution were self-evident. But if that were so, the solution would probably have been tried already!

Instead of taking the value of your solution for granted, give listeners reasons to believe that your solution is the best option. In the crime example this final section of your speech might be organized in the following way:

IV. The comprehensive solution I have proposed is the best way to deal with crime.
   A. It will stop crime at the source when possible.
   B. It will deter crime when possible.
   C. It will keep criminals off the streets.
   D. It will cause the public to feel safer and more secure.

From this example you can see that the basic problem-solution organizational pattern adapts easily to persuasive speeches. Although each step of the structure includes informative elements, the principal purpose of the speech is to affect the audience's beliefs, attitudes, values, or actions.

The Motivated Sequence

A sequential scheme for achieving persuasion in a speech was developed many years ago by Alan H. Monroe.[4] His motivated sequence is similar to the problem-solution speech, but instead of being organized with reference to the specific subject—health care or crime, for instance—it is organized in terms of the audience's motivation. The sequence has five steps, including the introduction and conclusion.

I. Attention step (Introduction)
II. Need step
III. Satisfaction step
IV. Visualization step
V. Action step (Conclusion)

Introduction. The *attention step*, as its name suggests, is intended to engage listeners' attention. It serves as the introduction to the speech and includes such appropriate devices as visual narratives, engaging anecdotes, and startling statistics.

Body. The *need step* is intended to convince the audience that something is amiss. The goal is to arouse listeners to believe that an important value is being lost, an opportunity is being wasted, or an objective is not being met. This belief will motivate them to take corrective action if they know what to do. The need step provides the same function as did the problem step in the problem-solution analysis.

The *satisfaction step* provides listeners with the means to fulfill the motivation that the need step aroused. People seldom respond to broad and abstract generalizations, however, and so slogans like "Stimulate the economy" or "Get tough on illegal immigration" are unlikely to satisfy listeners. To avoid this problem, the speaker goes on to explain how the solution will work and how it will affect listeners personally.

The *visualization step* gives the audience a mental picture of the solution. Instead of saying, "Stimulate the economy," the speaker shows what the solution will mean: "Putting an extra $1,000 saved from taxes into the hands of the average family will make it easier for them to buy the things they need. Increased demand for those products will create millions of new jobs, so that even more people will be better off."

Conclusion. The final step in the motivated sequence is the *action step*, in which the speaker asks the audience to do specific things to bring about the solution that they have visualized: change your personal behavior, sign a petition, patronize some stores but not others, write to senators and representatives, make a donation, and so on. The action step resembles the final plea that is one of the traditional functions of the conclusion of a speech. The action step is designed to give positive reinforcement to the audience as a "reward" for accepting the persuasive pitch.

Using the Motivated Sequence

The earlier outline for the problem-solution speech about crime might be organized into the motivated sequence as follows:

I. Attention step
   A. Description of recent crime on campus.
   B. Statistics suggesting a dramatic increase in crime in recent years.
   C. Translation of these statistics into the odds that someone you know will be the victim of crime.

II. Need step
   A. Crime undermines personal security and safety.
   B. Crime undermines your ability to control your life.
   C. Crime undermines your sense of justice.
   D. Crime weakens the fabric of society.

III. Satisfaction step
   A. Use technology to develop better databases about criminals.
   B. Increase the number of police officers on the street.
   C. Enact laws to compensate victims of crime.
   D. Increase penalties for the most serious offenders.

IV. Visualization step
   A. You will be able to walk safely at night on campus.
   B. You won't have to alter your schedule or routine because of fear of crime.
   C. You'll be able to trust other people more.
   D. You'll have support for your beliefs about what is right and wrong.

V. Action step
   A. Urge your public officials to support the crime legislation now before Congress.
   B. Urge five other people to write letters doing the same.

The criticisms raised against McGuire's theory of persuasion also apply to the motivated sequence. First, these steps are not always completely separate. It's possible, for example, that visualizing a solution is what alters the perception of a need. Second, not all listeners experience the steps in precisely the same order. Someone might be attracted to the satisfaction step, for example, without having grasped the full dimensions of the need. But even if the motivated sequence is not a universal account of human motivation, it still can provide a clear, coherent, and compelling way to organize speeches when the goal is persuasion.

Persuasive strategies aim not only to provide information but also to affect audience members' attitudes and behavior. They ask for a greater degree of commitment from listeners than informative strategies do, although no speaker can manipulate an unwilling audience. Listeners are often resistant to persuasion and may dispose of the message by denying it, by believing that it does not apply to them, or by belittling the source. They may compartmentalize the message in their minds so that it affects beliefs without affecting values or behavior. Or they may respond with a boomerang effect, becoming so upset by the persuasive message that they believe or do the opposite of what the speaker recommends.

Speakers, of course, have strategies to combat audience resistance. They need to understand that listeners must be motivated, must comprehend and agree with the message, and must incorporate the message into their overall system of beliefs and attitudes. To attain these results, speakers draw on their ability to analyze the audience and the situation, on their own credibility, and on the effective use of evidence, reasoning, and emotional appeals.

Chapter 44: Analysis and Application Exercises

1. In the video program, did you find Barbara Jordan persuasive? Why or why not? Was her topic appropriate for the audience and the occasion? Explain using examples.
2. In the video, Joel warned against making sweeping generalizations. What was his rationale? Use specific language from his discussion to provide your answer.

References

1. William J. McGuire, "Personality and Attitude Change: An Information-Processing Approach." In A. G. Greenwald, T. C. Brock, and T. M. Ostrom, ed., *Psychological Foundations of Attitudes* (Orlando: Atlantic Press, 1968)171-196.
2. See John C. Reinard, "The Empirical Study of the Persuasive Effects of Evidence: The Status after Fifty Years of Research," *Human Communication Research* 15 (Fall 1988): 3-59.
3. See Kenneth Burke, Rhetoric of Motives, New York: Prentice-Hall, 1950. For a discussion of Burke's theory of identification, see Dennis G. Day, "Persuasion and the Concept of Identification," *Quarterly Journal of Speech* 46 (October 1960): 270-273.
4. Alan H. Monroe, *Principles and Types of Speech*, Glenview, Ill.: Scott Foresman, 1935. The book has had multiple editions with various authors. In the most recent edition, the lead author is Bruce E. Gronbeck.

CHAPTER 45

Special Occasion Speeches

LEARNING OBJECTIVES

When students have completed this chapter and lesson, they should be able to:

1. Distinguish differences among special occasion speeches.
2. Identify the six guidelines for preparing a speech of introduction.
3. Explain the four major traits of a speech of welcome.
4. Describe the three major characteristics of a speech of presentation.
5. Describe and explain an acceptance speech, a speech of tribute, an after dinner speech, and a eulogy.
6. Identify the four suggestions for giving a successful special occasion speech.

CHAPTER 45: Overview

A general discussion of ceremonial and special occasion speeches is presented, including common elements and guidelines. Ceremonial speaking occasions are explained: speeches of greeting, tributes and marking awards. Goals of speeches posing challenges are discussed.

Jesse Owens

The broad jump preliminaries came before the finals of my other three events and everything, it seemed then, depended on this jump. Fear swept over me and then panic. I walked off alone, trying to gather myself. I dropped to one knee, closed my eyes, and prayed. I felt a hand on my shoulder. I opened my eyes and there stood my arch enemy, Luz Long, the prize athlete Hitler had kept under wraps while he trained for one purpose only: to beat me. Long had broken the Olympic mark in his very first try in the preliminaries.

"I know about you" he said. "You are like me. You must do it all the way, or you cannot do it. The same that has happened to you today happened to me last year in Cologne. I will tell you what I did then." Luz told me to measure my steps, place my towel 6 inches on back of the takeoff board and jump from there. That way I could give it all I had and be certain not to foul.

As soon as I had qualified, Luz smiling broadly, came to me and said, "Now we can make each other do our best in the finals."

And that's what we did in the finals. Luz jumped and broke his Olympic record. Then I jumped just a bit further and broke Luz's new record. We each had three leaps in all. On his final jump, Luz went almost 26 feet, 5 inches, a mark that seemed impossible to beat. I went just a bit over that and set an Olympic record that was to last for almost a quarter of a century.

I won that day, but I'm being straight when I say that even before I made that last jump, I knew I had won a victory of a far greater kind—over something inside myself, thanks to Luz.

The instant my record-breaking win was announced, Luz was there, throwing his arms around me and raising my arm to the sky. "Jazze Ownz!" he yelled as loud as he could. More than 100,000 Germans in the stadium joined in. "Jazze Owenz, Jazze Owenz, Jazze Owenz!"

Hitler was there, too, but he was not chanting. He had lost that day. Luz Long was killed in World War II and, although I don't cry often, I wept when I received his last letter–I knew it was his last. In it he asked me to someday find his son, Karl, and to tell him "of how we fought well together, and of the good times and that any two men can become brothers."

That is what the Olympics are all about. The road to the Olympics does not lead to Moscow, ancient Greece or Nazi Germany. The road to the Olympics leads, in the end, to the best within us[1].

Special occasion speeches are occasionally identified by ancient theorists as **epideictic** (ep-uh-DIKE-tik), or **ceremonial** speaking. These types of speeches of tribute at retirement dinners, speeches introducing distinguished guests, speeches upon receiving an award, and speeches commemorating a significant event are all examples of ceremonial speaking. The above speech was presented on the floor of the Senate protesting the United States withdrawal from the 1980 Summer Olympic Games. The speech contains all the critical elements of a successful "Special occasion" speech: fluent, enthralling story, filled with emotion, that delivered a bonding atmosphere with a sense of community with similar values and ideas. Ceremonial speeches bring to the forefront of consciousness some value or belief that a group holds but may not have thought much about. These values tend to guide an audience in decision making and superimpose values on the group to draw people closer together. Notice how the Owens speech rallied your feelings of community spirit about the Olympics.

Reexperiencing a Common Past

Recalling events or stories perceived as important to the group, the speaker permits the audience to relive the event vicariously. If the group faced or overcame a major obstacle, references to that obstacle strengthens a sense that the group has been tested and has met an important challenge. The common experience sustains the group's identity.

Invoking Common Values. Reminding listeners of principles or values shared, the speaker knits them together as a community. President Reagan frequently used this technique in his speeches. A classic example was his famous statement challenging Gorbachev at the Berlin Wall:
"General Secretary Gorbachev, if you seek peace, if you seek prosperity for the Soviet Union and eastern Europe, if you seek liberalization, come here to this gate. Mr. Gorbachev, open this gate. Mr. Gorbachev, tear down this wall!"

Reinterpreting Events. It is often said that events do not speak; they must be spoken for. By giving meaning to events, the speaker may interpret them within a frame of reference that draws the group together. If, for example, the group's membership has declined over the past year, is that a life-threatening crisis or a challenge to be met creatively? If the group has a history of rallying in the face of challenges, the speaker will want to interpret the event as a challenge. That interpretation will bring the event within the group's shared values and frame of reference.

Emphasizing people. In any community, some individuals play an especially important symbolic role. They may be the founders, or the football coach, or those who have been its leaders. Images of heroic times and overcoming odds help unify the community and add emotional force to the issue being discussed. For example, a civil rights group might invoke the memory of Martin Luther King, Jr, or again remember Ronald Reagan's campaign slogan: "Win one for the Gipper."

Guidelines for Ceremonial Speaking

The strength of a ceremonial speech does not depend on an informative or even persuasive strategy, but on the speaker's ability to craft words into images that build emotion and capture the occasion. The speaker's ability to articulate the audience's unexpressed feelings is called **resonance,** because the speaker's words echo the listeners' feelings.

By carefully selecting a mix of stories, images, arguments, and a descriptive vocabulary, the speaker enjoys great flexibility in crafting a specific purpose. But the tone must be appropriate for the occasion; the speech should build to an emotional climate; its length has to be controlled carefully; and humor must contribute to, rather than weaken the presentation. Such elements must not be left to chance, but carefully crafted.

Although successful ceremonial speeches seem natural, even effortless, they are actually difficult to prepare. The great variety of ceremonial occasions makes it impossible to explore them all, but a few will be considered.

Ceremonial Speaking Occasions

Ceremonial speaking can be grouped under three broad headings: Speeches of greeting, speeches of tribute, and speeches marking awards.

Speeches of Introduction are designed to announce a guest speaker. The goals of such a speech are to make the speaker feel welcome, to give listeners relevant information about the speaker, and to contribute to the speaker's credibility.

Guidelines for introduction include: mention only significant accomplishments that directly pertain to the occasion, carefully avoiding any incidents or information that might digress from the point. Avoid lavish praise, which either might be embarrassing or might raise the audience's expectations to an unattainable level. Promising "our guest is the most captivating speaker you will ever hear" may prime the audience for disappointment and reduce the guest speaker's impact.

A speech of introduction should not be read because a manuscript suggests that the introducer really does not know the speaker very well. Find out about the speaker, especially how to pronounce their name, and what topic they will be presenting. Finally, never anticipate or try to summarize what the speaker will say; besides stealing attention from the speaker, you might be mistaken. It can be embarrassing to the introducer to be corrected immediately by the guest speaker.

Speeches of welcome are often given for an individual or group upon their arrival. This aims not only to introduce the guest to the host but also to make the guest feel comfortable and at ease. Your tone should be upbeat and optimistic. You should explicitly express greetings to the guest, identify some common bond or interest between you and the guest, and honor the guest by saying how pleased you are by the visit.

Speeches of Tribute

Testimonials are one of the most common ceremonial speeches. Testimonials are designed to honor someone at a special occasion such as a wedding, a job promotion, an outstanding achievement, retirement from a career, and of course, death (eulogy).

The honoree's accomplishments are the organizing principle for a testimonial speech. Significant achievements and character traits are reviewed. You should discuss achievements that are significant in their own right as well as representative of the person's general character. Specific incidents, life experiences and significant life events are vividly described. If possible, select at least some incidents that might not be known to the audience. Be cautious about focusing on incidents or situations in which you played a part, since the point of the testimonial is to focus on the honoree and not you. Be careful not to exaggerate, for praise can be overdone. Doing so could be embarrassing to the honoree, cause listeners to doubt your sincerity, or suggest that you are so enthralled by the person that you cannot exercise independent judgement.

A *eulogy* is a special form of testimonial speech centered upon praising the dead. Eulogies are generally delivered at funerals or memorial services or on special occasions such as birthdays of the deceased. Eulogies typically celebrate the essential character of the person, so the organizing principle is the person's virtues rather than accomplishments. Cite specific examples and experiences that illustrate his or her virtues. A caring individual, for example, might have donated much time and money to various charity organizations. Someone who was "ahead of their time" might have recognized a cultural trend before it became popular.

A eulogy magnifies the persons strengths and minimizes weaknesses. Again praise can be overdone, but the objective is to help listeners recall the honoree's personality. A classic example is President Reagan's remarks about the astronauts killed in the 1986 *Challenger* disaster:

> We come together today to mourn the loss of seven brave Americans, to share the grief that we all feel and, perhaps in that sharing, to find the strength to bear our sorrow and the courage to look for the seeds of hope. . .
>
> Their truest testimony will not be in the words we speak but in the way they lived their lives and in the way they lost their lives–with dedication, honor, and an unquenchable desire to explore this mysterious and beautiful universe. The best we can do to remember our seven astronauts–our Challenger Seven–remember them as they lived, bringing life and love and joy to those who knew them and pride to a nation.[2]

A *toast* is a miniature version of the testimonial speech. It is usually delivered in the presence of the honoree and often concludes by raising a glass to salute the person.

Many people who give toasts–at wedding receptions or dinners honoring someone, or at the beginning of a new career or position–perform awkwardly. They are unsure of what to say, remarks are trite, and they do not do justice to the honoree because they do not prepare!

A toast is a variation of the one-point speech discussed in Chapter 1. It should celebrate one key characteristic of the honoree; supporting materials should include one or two incidents illustrating characteristics, talent, or virtue. A toast at a wedding reception might emphasize the devotion of the newlyweds by referring to an eight-year engagement that spanned three different states and two time zones. After stating the key characteristic and giving an example, the person giving the toast should recognize the honoree, wish for continued strength and success, and conclude.

A slightly different speech of tribute is the *roast,* which both honors and pokes fun at a person. When you roast someone, your deft handling of the humor is essential to the success of the roast. Humor can backfire if overdone. Humor is used to put listeners at ease and also to demystify the honoree, suggesting that he or she is "just one of us!" Remarks should avoid embarrassing the person and should not distract from the fact that you and the audience are engaged in a tribute.

A roast should focus on only one or two key themes or incidents in the honoree's life. Select incidents that poke fun in a good natured way and yet have an underlying positive message. Give examples that may have seemed strange at the time, but revealed a positive character trait. Avoid humor that could be misunderstood as prejudice. Although the roast may begin humorously, it should always end by pointing to the honoree's strengths. Like the toast, the roast should be relatively brief.

Speeches Marking Awards

Presentation speeches reward persons who have done an outstanding job of community or volunteer service. The award is presented at a dinner at the end of the year, and your job is to present a certificate or trophy. Avoid just handing out the award, suggesting either that you don't care much about the award, or that you think the wrong person won it. An award always calls for a speech.

The presentation speech typically has two basic elements: the importance of the award, and the winner's fitness to receive the award. The history and background of the award are given, relating the winner's conformance to those positive traits. Often this second step can be linked directly to the preceding part of the speech by citing examples of activity by the winner and illustrating the positive attributes the winner possesses.

Besides these two basic elements, presentation speeches may include other components. It may be appropriate to explain the selection process for choosing the recipient. If the choice reflects the subjective judgment of a committee, for instance, you might want to discuss some of the criteria the committee used. If a large number of eligible nominees were considered for the award, you might describe how they were screened, and the finalist chosen. There is no need to describe the selection process if the criteria for the award are purely mechanical, such as the highest grade point average, or the top salesman.

If the finalists who did not win the award are known to the audience, it may be appropriate to praise them as well. Everyone in the group could have been honored, and the choice of the selection committee was especially difficult, or that the judges wished they could have made multiple awards. Be sure such statements are sincere. Insincerity is easily detected. But if the competition was really keen, it takes nothing away from the winner to suggest that other candidates were also highly qualified. Such winning magnifies the recipient's achievement.

If your speech concludes with the physical presentation of the award, manage your gestures carefully to avoid any awkwardness. Present the award with your left hand into the recipient's left hand so that you can shake hands.

References

1. *Congressional Record,* April 1, 1980, p. 7248.
2. S. M. Mister, "Reagan's Challenger Tribute: Combining Generic Constraints and Situational Demands," *Central States Speech Journal,* 37 (Fall 1986), 158-165.

CHAPTER 46

Conclusions

Communication is the very essence of being human. The way that we conduct our lives is inseparably connected to our communication. Our relationships are our communication—they are one and the same thing. There is no other way to interact with another person, whether individually or in groups, organizations, or through many media that we use and encounter today. Thus, your ability to understand the elements of effective communication will largely determine your success in life.

We genuinely hope that this course has increased your sensitivity to and use of the practices and skills outlined in this text. You have been exposed to both theory and practice in a wide variety of settings, all of which should improve your ability to recognize and respond to communication needs and problems. Effective communication involves both understanding (theory) and practice (application of that knowledge in a skillful manner). As you conclude this course both of these should have been improved in your life.

Specifically, the course was designed to do the following. You can judge for yourself whether you have mastered all of these objectives:

Course Objectives:

1. A general knowledge of the basic theories of human communication in rhetorical, group, and interpersonal settings.
2. A basic understanding of the principles and techniques of persuasion in interpersonal, group, and public speaking contexts.
3. An ability to successfully apply the above knowledge in actual small group, interviewing, business, public speaking, and interpersonal situations. The ability to write well-worded and persuasive resumes and other business communication. Also, the ability to write a valid and well-supported analysis of communication problems encountered in real-world situations.
4. An understanding of how the perception of both verbal and non-verbal messages influences culture, behavior, and action of life itself.

Along the way to achieving these objectives you have participated in giving at least one speech that was fully and properly outlined, a group project, a written report, an interview assignment, and a resume' and cover letter . You have also explored all of the following:

- dyadic communication
- basic communication concepts and models
- negotiation and conflict management
- listening
- nonverbal communication
- culture and diversity
- written communication in the workplace

We believe by doing these things you have been well prepared to face your future with improved communication knowledge and skill. We wish you the best in all that you do.